Medical, Psychosocial and Vocational Aspects of Disability

Fifth Edition
2020

Edited by

Martin G. Brodwin, PhD, CRC
California State University, Los Angeles

Frances W. Siu, PhD, CRC
California State University, Los Angeles

John Howard, MD, MPH
George Washington University

Erin R. Brodwin, MA
Business Insider

Ashley T. Du, MS
Los Angeles Valley College, Los Angeles

Elliott & Fitzpatrick, Inc.
Athens, GA

Medical, Psychosocial and
Vocational Aspects of Disability (5th ed.)

Edited by
Martin G. Brodwin, PhD, CRC
Frances W. Siu, PhD, CRC
John Howard, MD, MPH
Erin R. Brodwin, MA
Ashley T. Du, MS

All rights reserved. No portion of this book, in whole or in part, may be reproduced, copied, recorded, duplicated, transmitted, or stored in any form or medium without the written permission of the authors or the publisher.

© 2020 Martin Brodwin, PhD

ISBN: 978-0-945019-07-7

Published and distributed by: **Elliott & Fitzpatrick, Inc**.
1135 Cedar Shoals Drive
Athens, GA 30605
800-843-4977
email: myorder@elliottfitzpatrick.com

Table of Contents

Preface	vii

Part I - Introduction to Rehabilitation Medicine

Chapter 1 - Case Study Approach, Rehabilitation Intervention, the ICF, and Medical Specialties — 1
Martin G. Brodwin, PhD, CRC and Sandra K. Brodwin, MEd, MS

Chapter 2 - Human Body Systems — 17
Frances W. Siu, PhD, CRC and Erin R. Brodwin, MA

Part II - Common Medical Conditions

Chapter 3 - Cancer — 37
Leo M. Orr, II, MD and Leo M. Orange, MS

Chapter 4 - Diabetes and Chronic Kidney Disease — 53
Martin G. Brodwin, PhD, CRC and Anne Haga, MS

Chapter 5 - Cardiovascular Disease — 65
Harvey L. Alpern, MD and Rose M. Gaw, MS

Chapter 6 - Chronic Obstructive Pulmonary Disease — 79
Hassan Bencheqroun, MD, FCCP

Chapter 7 - HIV/AIDS — 89
John J. Howard, MD, MPH

Part III - Sensory Organ Conditions

Chapter 8 - Hearing Loss, Deafness, and Related Vestibular Disorders — 103
Sandra Hansmann, PhD and Shawn P. Saladin, PhD, CRC

Chapter 9 - Visual Disabilities — 115
Bill Takeshita, OD, FAAO, FCOVD, Robin Langman, MS, CRC, and Rebekah Brod, MA, MFT

Chapter 10 - Chronic Pain Management — 129
Ashley T. Du, MS, John Lindberg, MD, and Brendon W. Bluestein, PhD

Chapter 11 - Complementary and Integrative Health — 139
Hua Gu, PhD, LAc and Sandra Brodwin, MEd, MS

Part IV - Brain and Spinal Cord Conditions

Chapter 12 - Traumatic Brain Injury — 151
Stacey Hunter Schwartz, PhD and Michelle Ranae Wild, MA

Chapter 13 - Stroke — 165
Andrew D. Barreto, MD, Frances Siu, PhD, CRC, and Cailine Kim, EdD, CRC

Chapter 14 - Epilepsy   177
Erica K. Johnson, PhD, CRC, FAES, Robert T. Fraser, PhD, CRC, and John W. Miller, MD, PhD

Chapter 15 - Neurological Diagnosis   189
David B. Peterson, PhD, CRC, NCC, LCP and Thomas VanVleet, PhD, LCP

Chapter 16 - Spinal Cord Injury   201
Gonzalo C. Centeno, MS, Nancy M. Crewe, PhD, and James S. Krause, PhD

Part V - Neuromuscular and Joint Conditions

Chapter 17 - Cerebral Palsy   215
Angie Juàrez, EdD and Sherwood J. Best, PhD

Chapter 18 - Muscular Dystrophy   229
Roy K. Chen, PhD, CRC

Chapter 19 - Multiple Sclerosis   241
Roxanna N. Pebdani, PhD, CRC

Chapter 20 - Rheumatic Diseases   249
Penny J. Chong, MD and Constance A. Richard, MFA, MS, CRC

Part VI - Psychosocial Conditions

Chapter 21 - Psychiatric Disabilities   263
David B. Peterson, PhD, CRC, NCC, LCP and Heidi Paul, PhD, CRC, CLCP, LPCC

Chapter 22 - Sexual Health and Disability   279
Leo M. Orange, MS

Chapter 23 - Substance-Use Disorders   287
Carol M. Calandra, MS

Part VII - Developmental Conditions

Chapter 24 - Learning Disabilities   299
Diane Haager, PhD, Martin G. Brodwin, PhD, CRC, and Leila Ansari Ricci, PhD

Chapter 25 - Intellectual Developmental Disorders   311
Julie Ton Fercho, PhD, Mary A. Falvey, PhD, Kathryn D. Bishop, PhD, and Susann Terry Gage, PhD

Chapter 26 - Autism Spectrum Disorder   325
Hung Jen Kuo, PhD, CRC, LPC MCSA, Frances W. Siu, PhD, CRC, and Jessica H. Franco, PhD, CCC-SLP, BCBA-D

Part VIII - Assistive Technology and Reconstructive Repair

Chapter 27 - Orthotics, Amputation, and Prosthetics   335
Lance R. Clawson, BS, CPO and Martin G. Brodwin, PhD, CRC

Chapter 28 - Societal Reintegration Following a Burn Injury   347
Cindy Rutter, RN, MS, Ann Malo, RN, and James Bosch, LMFT

Chapter 29 - Evaluating Upper Extremity Function and Impairment   359
George W. Balfour, MD, Martin G. Brodwin, PhD, CRC, and Ashley T. Du, MS

Chapter 30 - Assistive Technology and Universal Design   371
R. David Black, EdD, CRC and Martin G. Brodwin, PhD, CRC

Part IX - Genetics

Chapter 31 - Sickle Cell Disease and Hemophilia   381
John J. Howard, MD, MPH

Chapter 32 - Genetic Testing, Discrimination, and Counseling   391
John J. Howard, MD, MPH

Chapter 33 - Regenerative Medicine and Disability   397
John J. Howard, MD, MPH

Appendix - Mastering Medical Terminology   405

Index   413

PREFACE

Our appreciation and thanks to the more than 90 universities and colleges in the United States and beyond that have selected *Medical, Psychosocial, and Vocational Aspects of Disability* as a textbook for their rehabilitation counseling and rehabilitation services programs. It is also being used by continuing education programs, rehabilitation practitioners, as well as public and private rehabilitation agencies as a resource book. This fifth edition has combined the chapters on Addictions and Related Disorders and Alcohol-Related Disorders into "Substance-use Disorders." Chapter One has added a new section on the International Classification of Functioning, Disability, and Health (ICF) from the World Health Organization (WHO). There are eleven new authors since the fourth edition. This edition, like the second, third, and fourth editions, has major changes, modifications, additions, and updates.

Background

The enactment of the Americans with Disabilities Act (ADA) of 1990 signaled a new era for persons with disabilities. These individuals, often excluded from mainstream society, are participating in all phases of life to a far greater extent. Rehabilitation counselors, as well as educators, nurses, counselors in other settings, work evaluators, case managers, and family members participate in facilitating increasing progression into independent living, education, employment, and leisure activities with persons with disabilities. The ADA defined a person with a disability as someone who: "(1) has a physical or mental impairment that substantially limits one or more major life activities; (2) has a record of such an impairment; or (3) is regarded as having such an impairment."

Rehabilitation counseling involves assisting people with disabilities to acquire skills necessary for maximum functioning and independence. Professionals who have an understanding of medical and psychosocial aspects of disability and its relationship to employment are in demand within the counseling profession. Counselors need to read, comprehend, and interpret medical and psychological reports and other information regarding clients for whom they provide rehabilitation services. Knowledge of chronic illness and disability is crucial for counselors working with persons with disabilities. With comprehension of this information, counselors are better able to determine their consumers' functional capabilities and limitations, including potential to benefit from the provision of rehabilitation services.

Knowledge of functional capabilities and limitations allows the counselor and the individual with a disability to obtain information necessary for developing positive directions for rehabilitation. Rehabilitation services may include job modification, reasonable accommodation, educational pursuit, training or on-the-job training, supported employment, job placement, and independent living. The purpose of rehabilitation counseling is to empower the individual with a disability to successfully participate in all phases of life.

Overview

This is a textbook for students and a reference book for practicing counselors and other helping professionals. The intended audience includes rehabilitation counselors in public and private sectors, rehabilitation educators and students, vocational experts, work evaluators, counselors, and rehabilitation service providers. Allied health professionals in related disciplines also will benefit from the information within this textbook.

We encourage the readers to use a medical dictionary when reading this book. A glossary was not included, as the editors have found glossaries to be inadequate, both in providing sufficient explanations and in defining most of the required vocabulary. Various words throughout the text are provided with a short definition in parentheses.

The fifth edition of *Medical, Psychosocial, and Vocational Aspects of Disability* contains thirty-three chapters encompassing common disabilities encountered in the field of rehabilitation. Most chapters conclude with case studies to stimulate thinking and discussion about the topic. Case studies have a strong multicultural emphasis. We believe the richness of cultural diversity adds an important dimension to the text.

We suggest the reader begin with Chapter 1, "A Case Study Approach: Rehabilitation, Intervention, the ICF, and Medical Specialties," as this chapter describes the case study analysis approach used throughout the book. Subsequent chapters can be reviewed in the order that best suits the needs of the reader and the instructor.

Acknowledgments

The editors prepared the textbook to maintain the meaning and philosophy of each author, while conforming to a similar style within chapters. We sincerely appreciate each author's time and patience during the difficult writing and editing process. We believe that through their efforts, this text will provide readers with an excellent resource for medical and psychosocial aspects of chronic illness and disabling conditions, as well as the relationship to employment issues.

A special thanks and appreciation to our new authors: Anne Haga, Rose Gaw, Cailine Kim, Angie Juarez, Roxanna Pebdani, Constance Richard, Heidi Paul, Carol Calandra, Leila Ricci, Hung Jen Kuo, and James Bosch.

Martin G. Brodwin, PhD, CRC
Professor
Rehabilitation Education Programs
California State University, Los Angeles

Chapter 1

CASE STUDY APPROACH, REHABILITATION INTERVENTION, THE ICF, AND MEDICAL SPECIALTIES

Martin G. Brodwin, PhD, CRC
Sandra K. Brodwin, MEd, MS

Introduction

Rehabilitation professionals need expertise concerning medical aspects of disabling conditions to work effectively with persons who have disabilities. Increasingly, the profession expects counselors to have greater knowledge and skills and demonstrate case management expertise when working with employers to facilitate a return to work for individuals with chronic illnesses and disabilities. Counselors apply this expertise both when developing educational/vocational plans and determining functional limitations and rehabilitation potential. Knowledge of medical aspects of disability is a significant component when providing rehabilitation interventions.

Before delving into this chapter and the book, it is helpful to recognize two similar but different terms, impairment and disability. **Impairment** is an abnormality or a loss of a physiological structure or function. **Disability**, on the other hand, is the consequences of impairment – a restriction or lack of ability to perform some applicable activity.

The basic criterion for acceptance for vocational rehabilitation is the existence of a disability that causes functional limitations and results in an impediment to employment. One of the attributes differentiating rehabilitation counselors from other counselors and mental health professionals is specialized knowledge and expertise related to disability. As no two people are alike, there is a variety of characteristics affecting each person's potential to benefit from rehabilitation services. Similar medical diagnoses have different impacts, depending on a person's psychosocial circumstances, adaptation to functional limitations, vocational skills, education, and occupational history. Examples of components that affect rehabilitation potential for employment include (Brodwin, Parker, & DeLaGarza, 2010; Gilbride & Stensrud, 2012):

- Severity of disability (residual capacities and functional limitations)
- Age at onset of disability
- Current age
- Gender and ethnicity
- Psychological characteristics
- Pre-existing physical conditions
- Social functioning
- Educational and vocational training
- Employment
- Psychosocial adjustment to disability
- Use of assistive technology

A counselor must formulate a practical and realistic objective for a vocational or educational plan according to an individual's physical, intellectual, and emotional capacities. To establish a realistic and practical objective, the rehabilitation professional applies knowledge of the vocational profile, medical aspects of the disability, the individual's interaction with the environment, and the person's effort and persistence to accomplish goals.

This chapter addresses the functions of rehabilitation professionals when providing services in a variety of rehabilitation systems. The authors believe the use of the *vocational profile* approach will enhance a thorough case analysis and improve the opportunities for a client to become employed or reemployed. The chapter focuses on the importance of the holistic approach to enhance the potential for successful, meaningful, and satisfying rehabilitation. This chapter also discusses various aspects of functional limitations, rehabilitation potential, case intervention, a holistic approach, the International Classification of Functioning, Disability, and Health (ICF), and the medical specialties.

Vocational Profile

The *Vocational Profile* case study approach is one holistic method of evaluating a person's vocational potential using analysis of age, education, work history, occupationally significant characteristics of work, and transferable skills. Specifically, Vocational Experts (VEs) use the term, Vocational Profile, when testifying about disability-related issues for the Social Security Administration's (SSA) Office of Hearings Operations.

More broadly, the SSA vocational profile model is part of a nationally mandated program that is uniform throughout the country. Vocational profiles include age, education, and work history categories, as well as occupationally significant characteristics and transferability of work skills. The following categories - **age** (SSA Section # 404.1563), **education** (SSA Section # 404.1564), and **work experience** (SSA Section #s 404.1565, 404.1567, and 404.1568) - are taken from the guidelines of the Social Security Administration (Office of the Federal Register, 2001).

Age Category

The vocational expert considers age when evaluating the total person; as one ages, adaptation to new and unfamiliar situations becomes increasingly difficult. The magnitude of age as an evaluation factor varies with a person's work history. For example, if an individual has held only physically demanding jobs and developed few work skills, age can play a crucial role in rehabilitation.

Younger Person (Under Age 50) - An individual is within this category if under age 50. Generally, if in this category, the person's age will not impact the ability to adapt to new work.

Person Approaching Advanced Age (Age 50 to 54) - An individual between 50-54 years of age is a Person Approaching Advanced Age. A person in this age category who has a severe impairment and limited work experience may have major difficulty adjusting to many jobs within the labor market.

Person of Advanced Age (Age 55-59) - This category is appropriate if a person is between 55-59 years of age. With advancing age, it becomes more difficult to obtain employment, especially with an unskilled work background, a history of physically arduous work, and minimal education. Transferability of skills to similar jobs and work activity (often less physically demanding) become more relevant as the individual ages.

Close to Retirement Age (Age 60 to 64) - When individuals are 60 years of age or older, they are considered, by Social Security regulations, to be Close to Retirement Age. Skills at this age need to be highly transferable and are pivotal to success in the rehabilitation process.

Educational Level

Educational level is the amount of formal schooling a person has achieved. Grade level is only one means of assessment. When evaluating rehabilitation potential, the counselor considers how long ago a person attended school, quality of the educational experience, additional informal or formal education, and other training.

Illiteracy - an inability to read or write. People are within this category if they cannot read or write simple messages, such as basic instructions, inventory lists, and the like.

Marginal Education - Generally, this category involves a formal education at the 6th grade level or less. The person who has a Marginal Education is limited to basic reasoning, arithmetic, and language skills.

Limited Education - A person of Limited Education has been formally educated between the 7th and 11th grades, without having attained a high school diploma or its equivalence.

High School Education and Above - implies achieving a high school diploma or its equivalence. Attainment of a General Equivalency Diploma (GED) is within this level. Also classified within this category are individuals with education beyond high school. Persons classified as such have obtained reasoning, arithmetic, and language skills required for more complex and interpersonal work activity.

Work History

The following section of the vocational profile is subdivided into several categories. These include skill requirements, physical exertion, occupationally significant characteristics, vocational skills, and transferability of skills.

Skill Requirements

Unskilled Work

Unskilled work requires little or no judgment for the completion of simple duties; one learns the job in a short time. Unskilled jobs require 30 days or less to learn. While they are quickly learned, these jobs frequently require considerable physical strength. Primary work duties for an unskilled occupation could involve stock or material handling, machine feeding, sorting, simple assembling, or machine tending. Little specific vocational preparation or judgment are required. **A person does not gain work skills (transferable skills) by working in unskilled jobs**. When a worker develops skills, one considers that the work has changed from unskilled to semiskilled work.

Semiskilled Work

Semiskilled work requires some skills but not complex work activity. This category consists of activities that are less complex than skilled work but more complex than unskilled work. These jobs may involve alertness and close attention to observing machine processes or inspecting, testing, or quality control. Other aspects of semiskilled work include guarding equipment, materials, or persons against damage, loss, or injury. Typically, semiskilled work requires training from over 30 days to a maximum of two years.

Skilled Work

This category of work requires the use of judgment to determine fairly complex machine and manual operations performed to obtain the proper form, quality, and quantity of materials produced. Skilled work may require laying out work, estimating quality, determining suitability and needed quantities of material, making precise measurements, reading blueprints or other specifications, or making complex computations or mechanical adjustments to control or regulate the work. Other skilled jobs involve dealing with people, facts or figures, and abstract ideas at a high level of complexity. Skilled work typically requires two or more years of training.

Physical Exertion Requirements

When reviewing a client's past relevant work experience, the counselor evaluates the level of physical exertion required at work. The individual's residual functional capacity (RFC) in conjunction with age, education, and work experience determine whether the individual can engage in any other substantial gainful work that exists in the national economy.

The United States Department of Labor (DOL) (1991) defined each functional level by the extent of the activities of sitting, standing, walking, lifting, carrying, pushing, and pulling. *Occasionally* means occurring from very little up to one-third of the work time. Typically, one defines this as ranging from 5 minutes to 2½ hours per day. A *frequent* activity occurs one-third to two-thirds of the time (a total of 2½ to 5 hours). One defines c*ontinuously* as an activity that occurs for a total of more than 5 hours per day.

The following categories summarize the physical exertion requirements.

Sedentary Work

Sedentary work involves lifting no more than 10 pounds at a time and occasionally lifting or carrying items weighing 5 pounds or less, such as files and small tools. For some jobs, a certain amount of walking and standing may be necessary in carrying out job duties. Jobs are sedentary if walking and standing are required less than occasionally and it meets the other sedentary criteria. By its very nature, work performed primarily in a seated position requires no significant stooping, kneeling, or bending.

Light Work

The regulations define light work as lifting no more than 20 pounds at a time with frequent lifting or carrying of objects weighing up to 10 pounds. Even though the weight lifted in a particular light job may be very little, a job is in this category when it requires a significant amount of walking and standing. A job is also in this category when it involves sitting most of the time but with some pushing and pulling of arm-hand or leg-foot controls, which require greater exertion than in sedentary work. Examples of these are a sewing machine operator, motor-grader operator, and road-roller operator (skilled and semiskilled jobs in these particular instances).

Medium Work

Medium work involves lifting no more than 50 pounds at a time, with frequent lifting or carrying of objects weighing up to 25 pounds. A full range of medium work requires standing or walking, off and on, for a total of up to 6 hours in an 8-hour workday to meet the requirements of frequent lifting or carrying objects weighing up to 25 pounds. As in light work, sitting may occur intermittently during the remaining time. Use of the arms and hands is necessary to grasp, hold, and turn objects, as opposed to the finer activities in most sedentary work, which require precision use of the fingers as well as use of the hands and arms. The lifting required for the full range of medium work usually requires bending-stooping at the frequent level or less. Stooping is a type of bending in which a person bends his or her body downward and forward by bending the spine at the waist. Crouching is bending both the legs and spine to bend the body downward and forward. Most medium jobs require being on one's feet most of the time.

Heavy Work

Maximum of 100 pounds occasionally with frequent lifting or carrying up to 50 pounds defines heavy work.

Very Heavy Work

This category work involves lifting more than 100 pounds occasionally with frequent lifting or carrying of 50 pounds or more.

The following table summarizes the exertional categories of work.

TABLE 1
Exertional Categories of Work

Category	Lifting/Carrying	
	Frequent	Maximum (occasional)
Sedentary	2-5 pounds	10 pounds
Light	10 pounds	20 pounds
Medium	25 pounds	50 pounds
Heavy	50 pounds	100 pounds
Very Heavy	50 pounds or more	100 pounds or more

Occupationally Significant Characteristics

Occupationally significant characteristics are distinctive elements that contribute to the job, work environment, and work functions, but **do not involve skills or characteristics of a person**. Occupational characteristics exist independent of the worker. Examples of occupationally significant characteristics include eye-hand-foot coordination, visual perception, being around other people, exertional level of work, inside or outside work, routine and repetitive job functions, activities requiring occasional bending and stooping, work involving fumes and irritants, among others.

An individual who has worked as a secretary, for example, may have some or all of the following occupationally significant characteristics: indoor work, eye-hand coordination, sedentary work activity, work with other people, use of office equipment, clerical work, and work with information. In contrast, the work of a truck driver may include characteristics such as manual dexterity, eye-hand-foot coordination, work within the transportation industry, medium exertion, working alone, and being in a variety of environmental conditions. **As can be seen from these examples, occupationally significant characteristics do not involve the acquisition or use of skills.**

Vocational Skills and Transferability of Skills

Skills involve abilities that one learns during work, training, or educational programs. They require work experience and the acquisition of abilities. Skills involve expertise or knowledge specific to work functions, such as the ability to use personal judgment, work with specific tools and equipment, operate complex machinery, and/or work with people or ideas at a high level of complexity.

The skills of a rehabilitation counselor include capability to communicate and organize; ability to counsel individuals regarding personal concerns, career development, and vocational pursuits; skills involved in helping persons secure employment; management and supervision capabilities; knowledge of medical aspects of chronic illness and disability, medical terminology, and medical treatment; and ability to work with troubled individuals with serious problems. In comparison, the skills of a secretary include clerical skills, ability to operate various office machines, capability to use a computer and related equipment, compile/type/file letters, organize and maintain a record-keeping system, answer business telephones, communication capacities, and organizational skills required to maintain the clerical flow of an office.

Only skilled and semiskilled work provide transferable skills. One can transfer skills, abilities, and knowledge found in skilled and semiskilled work to an occupation requiring equal or lesser skills, but not to a position of greater skill requirements. An employer may promote a worker to a more skilled position before acquiring the skills of that position and then he or she can learn the skills of the new job. A counselor uses the *Dictionary of Occupational Titles (D.O.T.)* (U.S. Department of Labor, 1991) and related resources when evaluating the transfer of work skills from one job to another.

An example of transferability from a skilled position is illustrated by the occupation of rehabilitation counselor. Duties of this job can transfer to other skilled and semiskilled positions. Skilled positions include manager of a human resource department, college counselor, rehabilitation director, academic advisor, supervisor, teacher, mental health clinician, probation officer, and vocational evaluator. The skills of a rehabilitation counselor also transfer to semiskilled work activities such as personnel interviewer, job analyst, job placement specialist, research assistant, and work evaluator. A semiskilled occupation, such as secretary, has transferable skills to other semiskilled work such as office clerk, receptionist, file clerk, general office worker, and typist.

When analyzing rehabilitation potential, prior jobs need evaluation. Initial exploration includes determining the skill requirements of previous jobs to indicate potential transferable skills. The counselor can then identify other jobs within the same industry that use these skills. Next, the research process expands to jobs in related industries using transferability of skills. Finally, if no positions exist within the client's physical exertional (or emotional) restrictions using transferable skills, the counselor investigates alternative rehabilitation options. While determining transferability of skills, the counselor needs to assess how long ago the job was performed and whether the skills are outdated or forgotten, as well as length of time on the job.

If the client's skills are not immediately transferable to jobs within the current labor market (using direct job placement), the rehabilitation professional may consider recommending on-the-job training, vocational training, and educational programs. The counselor and client use various criteria when selecting the type of plan best suited for the client.

The rehabilitation professional in a provider system applies expertise in medical aspects of chronic illness and disability to develop vocational and educational plans with practical, realistic, and obtainable objectives. The basis for the rehabilitation objective includes analysis of the client's age, education, work history, occupationally significant characteristics, transferable skills, capacities, and functional limitations. Roessler and Rumrill (1995), in a discussion of reasonable accommodations and job retention, discussed the need for postemployment services. These services reduce or remove barriers to successful employment outcomes. Three factors are crucial to successful job retention: (a) identification of barriers to employment and job accommodation strategies, (b) initiation of requests for accommodation, and (c) implementation of accommodations with employer cooperation.

Functional Limitations

One defines a functional limitation as "the inability to perform an action or set of actions because of a physical, mental, or emotional restriction" (Martin et al., 2012, p. 7). A clearly specified limitation of function helps the counselor understand the performance limitation(s) of the client. The counselor can more readily analyze and understand the person's restrictions when the medical conditions are in functional terms.

Examples

Client 1: An individual has a below the knee (BK) amputation of the left lower extremity. In functional terms, this person may be limited to maximum ambulation of one hour during an eight-hour workday, no ambulation on rough or uneven surfaces, no stair climbing, and no continuous standing.

Client 2: A person has a low back injury and a problem with lifting and carrying. Functionally, the individual may be limited to lifting a maximum of 20 pounds on an occasional basis with repetitive lifting and carrying not to exceed 10 pounds (light work).

Client 3: This person has a psychiatric diagnosis involving moderate depression and anxiety. In functional terms, the individual may need low stress work with an understanding female supervisor (because of a problem with dominant male authority figures).

Client 4: The individual has a diagnosis of schizophrenia, chronic undifferentiated type. In functional terms, this person may need work that involves simple, routine, and repetitive activities with minimal personal interaction within a structured work environment.

A counselor assesses the client's vocational profile, then reviews the medical file, and assesses the functional limitations. The rehabilitation counselor determines the potential for vocational rehabilitation and employment.

Rehabilitation Potential

For individuals to maximize their potential for rehabilitation, four factors need assessment: (a) the attainment of increased functioning in the areas of physical and emotional growth and development, (b) a sense of well-being, (c) development of a personally satisfying level of independence, and (d) compatibility between the work and the person's capabilities and limitations. These four factors relate to employment and psychosocial adjustment. One's attitude and adaptation to disability also affect rehabilitation potential and success in a program.

Rehabilitation systems (e.g., disability management, long-term disability, Social Security, state vocational rehabilitation, independent living) define a client's rehabilitation potential differently. A person may have rehabilitation potential within an independent living program but not with the state department of rehabilitation. Another individual may have rehabilitation potential within a public agency but not in certain private agency settings (such as long-term disability).

Counselors need an understanding of the distinct requirements of the particular rehabilitation system that is providing services. Each system has its own advantages and limitations. Once the counselor determines the client's rehabilitation potential within the specific system, a rationale is developed and presented to support the decision to provide rehabilitation services. The counselor needs to clarify if the medical conditions are temporary or permanent, and expected to improve, remain the same, or deteriorate.

Additionally, one needs to assess whether the particular rehabilitation system providing services influenced this determination (e.g., eligibility criteria). The counselor should inform the client of the decision and the basis for that decision. If denying services, the counselor may be able to refer the client to another system where appropriate and applicable services or benefits can be provided. Each rehabilitation system evaluates rehabilitation potential, including length of time typically provided for rehabilitation services, medical expenses, rehabilitation costs, and the likelihood of return to employment. If a client does not qualify for vocational rehabilitation services, the counselor may refer the person for Social Security benefits (SSDI, SSI).

Rehabilitation Intervention

Through the provision of rehabilitation intervention, counselors may be able to modify environmental factors for clients with disabilities to empower them to succeed at productive activities. Modifications of the environment include accommodation, job modification, and restructuring of job sites.

Job Accommodation, Modification, and Restructuring

Reasonable accommodation is a logical adjustment made to a job or work environment that enables a qualified person with a disability to perform the duties of the position (Berkeley Planning Associates, 1982). Accommodation recommendations are considered on an individual basis for each employee and employer. Cooperation on the part of the employer is essential for success.

Section 503 of the Federal Rehabilitation Act of 1973 and the Americans with Disabilities Act (ADA) of 1990 mandated reasonable accommodation. Employers have an obligation to make reasonable accommodation for physical and mental limitations, unless the accommodation imposes an *undue hardship* on the employer. Undue hardship depends upon several factors including cost, financial resources of the company, overall size of the employer, employer's operation (including composition and structure of the workplace), and the nature of the proposed accommodation.

As indicated within the ADA, modifications necessary under the *reasonable accommodation* provisions include (Rubin, Roessler, & Rumrill, Jr., 2016):

- Restructuring a job to enable the person with a disability to perform the essential functions of the job.
- Establishing a part-time or modified work schedule for employees with disabilities who are not capable of working a typical workday or week.
- Reassigning a person with a disability to a vacant position.
- Acquiring or modifying equipment or devices (e.g., buying a hearing telephone amplifier for a person with a hearing impairment).
- Adjusting or modifying examinations, training materials, or policies (e.g., giving an application examination orally to a person with dyslexia, or modifying a policy against dogs in the workplace for a person with a service dog).
- Providing qualified readers or interpreters for people with vision or hearing impairments.
- Giving an employee with a psychiatric illness a private place to work to alleviate stress.
- Modifying the physical layout of a facility to make it accessible to employees who use wheelchairs or who have other impairments that make accessibility difficult.

Reasonable accommodation rarely involves considerable cost. Berkeley Planning Associates (1982) conducted a study for the DOL on accommodation in private sector employment and noted the following results:

- About 50% of the reasonable accommodations surveyed cost less than $50
- Thirty percent cost between $50-$500
- Ten percent cost between $500-$2,000
- Ten percent cost in excess of $2,000

The DOL study concluded that, based on the above figures, reasonable accommodation is *no big deal*. This study reported that the most expensive and extensive accommodations are usually provided to individuals with blindness and to persons who use wheelchairs. Frequently, reasonable accommodations that are expensive and extensive are provided by employers for current employees to maintain their ability to continue working. Assuming cooperation between employers and employees, most accommodations cost less than $100 (Muther, 1996).

Employers need to understand that accommodation efforts help persons with chronic illness and disabilities become employed or remain successful on the job. There appears to be no significant relationship between accommodation and upward mobility, either by providing an advantage to a specific employee or in limiting job potential. Highly skilled workers more often receive environmental adaptations of the workplace and special equipment, while lower skilled workers receive job redesign, retraining, and selective placement.

Types of Reasonable Accommodation

I. Physical access accommodation
   A. A change or modification of the physical structure
   B. Examples - Accessibility/ambulation solutions
      1. Situate job on first floor
      2. Situate job near employee parking lot
      3. Situate job near restroom

II. Resource accessibility accommodation
   A. Provide an assistive person to enable the individual to do the job duties
   B. Examples
      1. Hearing impairment - Provide note taker or sign language interpreter
      2. Impairment - Provide reader or note taker
      3. Developmental disability (e.g., intellectual disability) - Provide a job coach

III. Adaptive equipment accommodation
A. Provision of *low tech* and *high tech* assistive devices
B. Examples
1. Person with arthritis or carpal tunnel syndrome - Provide special pen/pencil holders
2. Orthopedic problems
   a. Provide desk or chair modifications
   b.. Provide speaker and earphone on telephone
3. Reaching problems
   a. Provide a turntable on a desk
   b. Provide a special desk that has easy accessibility
4. Neck problems - Provide a slant board on a desk
5. Visual impairment - Provide a talking calculator or talking computer
6. Hearing impairment – Provide a telephone amplifier or speaker telephone

IV. Job modification
A. Modify the performance of job duties while maintaining the same job duties
B. Examples
1. Energy or ambulation problems - Salesperson does more telephone sales and less field appointments
2. Energy problem - Design drafter can work part-time with an adjusted salary
3. Orthopedic problems
   a. Parking-lot attendant can use a chair for sitting instead of standing throughout the day
   b. Warehouse worker can lift and carry lesser weights by making more frequent trips with lighter weights

V. Job restructuring
A. Change some of the actual job duties performed (alter, eliminate, or replace job duties)
B. Examples
1. Ambulation problem - Rehabilitation counselor can be assigned more office work (labor market surveys, job development, job placement, initial interviews) and less field work (on-site job analysis, school visits, employer visits)
2. Emotional stress
   a. Social worker can be assigned more case file analysis and paperwork and less interviewing and field visits
   b. Attorney can be assigned more research, case preparation, and legal briefs and less time litigating in court
3. Lower extremity problems - Shipping and receiving clerk can be assigned more clerical work (typing reports, bills of lading, and expediting) and less lifting, carrying, standing, walking, and forklift driving

Job Accommodation Network (JAN) is a resource available for additional information about employer accommodations. They have a toll-free telephone number. JAN provides this telephone service at no cost and allows the counselor, employer, and consumer access to information on job restructuring possibilities and costs. Before calling JAN, one needs the specific medical restrictions of the client, job duties that are precluded because of the restrictions, and general information about the industry in which the job is located.

A Holistic Approach to Rehabilitation

Holistic rehabilitation stresses the importance of the person as a whole and the interdependence of the various facets of the individual. A person, with or without a disability, is not an isolated entity. There are continuous interactions between the person and the environment. Interventions in one area of the person's environment have an influence on other areas. Seven areas most pertinent to a holistic approach are the person's disability, psychological status, vocational experiences, educational background, social issues, spirituality/belief system, and culture (see Figure 1). One can express disability in functional limitations.

Psychological status involves emotional factors that impede rehabilitation planning. The more extensive the person's vocational experiences and education, the greater the opportunities for success. Social functioning of the person involving interaction with family, friends, and associates needs evaluation. Spirituality and one's belief system can enhance rehabilitation outcomes. The counselor needs an understanding, careful consideration, and acceptance of the client's culture and ethnicity. Viewing rehabilitation from a holistic perspective enhances the probability of a successful outcome.

FIGURE 1
A Holistic View of the Individual

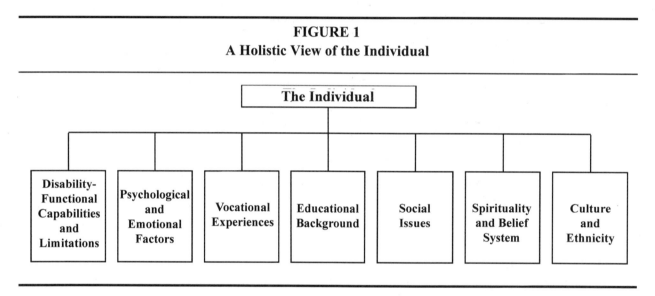

The International Classification of Functioning, Disability and Health (ICF)

The World Health Organization (WHO, 2001, 2015) developed the ICF as a universal system to interface with vocational rehabilitation, return to work, and inclusion and participation in community and society – emphasizing components of health rather than consequences of disability. The aim of the ICF is "to provide a unified and standard language and framework for the description of health and health-related states" (WHO, 2001, p. 3). There are three domains: the perspective of the body, the individual, and the environment (society). The ICF uses a comprehensive biopsychosocial model of disability encompassing a person's body functions and structures, activities and participation, as well as environmental and personal factors.

There are two prior approaches, which came before the biopsychosocial model: (a) the medical model and (b) the social model. The medical model sees disability as a problem of the person caused by disease, trauma, or other health conditions - emphasizing medical care (the physician and other medical professionals). A person's disability within this model is considered a deficiency or abnormality. Having a disability is seen as negative; therefore, one is seen as needing a cure to be able to fit into society as much as possible. Control is seen as belonging to the physician (the medical community), not the individual with the disability.

The social (or societal) model sees disability as neutral; disability is viewed primarily as a difference - it is society that disables individuals through designing everything to meet the needs of the majority of people who do not have disabilities. The remedy is to change the interactions between the individual and the environment which requires increasing social interaction, and placing the responsibility on society to modify the environment, allowing the person full access to and participation in all aspects of social functioning. Control is seen as belonging to social action to remedy the barriers, not the individual with the disability.

The ICF combines both the medical model and the social model and adds additional concepts. It defines disability as (a) impairments, (b) activity limitations, and (c) community restrictions. To minimize the effects of disability, one needs to evaluate the interaction between the individual with health conditions and personal and environmental factors (Parkin, Corcoran, & Stolfi, 2017). As indicated by these researchers, the ICF biopsychosocial model views disability and disease as an "intricate and variable interaction of three conditions: biological factors (genetic, physiological), psychological factors (attitudes, personality, behaviors), and environmental/social factors (culture, ethnicity, socioeconomic status, beliefs, spirituality)." Environmental factors include such aspects as architectural impediments, social barriers, and poor social support systems. Figure 2 illustrates the components and interactions of the ICF biopsychosocial model.

FIGURE 2

Interactions Among the Components of the ICF: A Biopsychosocial Model

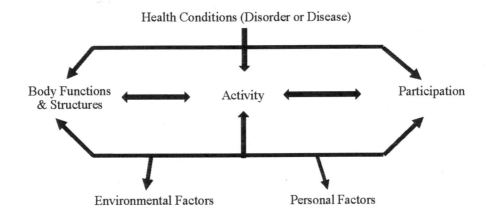

Source: WHO, 2001, 2015.

The focus of the ICF is on health and functions that relate to disability, rather than impairment and handicap" (p. 4). The ICF defines key terms in its conceptual framework as follows (WHO, 2001; Falvo & Holland, 2018):

Health - components of health (physical or psychological function) and components of well-being (capacity to function within the environment).

Function - all body functions, activities, and participation in society.

Disability - any impairment, activity limitations, or participation restrictions that result from the health condition or from personal, societal, or environmental factors in the person's life.

Impairment - a deviation from certain generally accepted population standards of function.

Individuals react quite differently to the same impairment and, hence, have a different degree of disability. Additionally, the workings of the body can affect the mind, and the workings of the mind can affect the body. An individual may not adjust well to a relatively minor physical impairment, whereas another person is able to excel despite the same or greater impairment. Someone with a major impairment, such as paraplegia, may overcome disability by returning to college and becoming a successful professional, whereas another person with paraplegia may stay at home developing overwhelming depression and anxiety. A person using a wheelchair will find less architectural barriers (eg., stairs) in a well-developed country, whereas in a less developed country, the person may not have accessibility because of a lack of ramps to access buildings. The stairs become the disabling barrier even with a positive attitude. Hence, the connection between disability and the environment.

The Medical Specialties

This section includes ideas, concepts, and the writings of Jean Spencer Felton, MD. He served as a physician and medical consultant to business and industry throughout southern California. Dr. Felton developed and taught medical aspects of disability courses within the rehabilitation counselor education program at California State University, Los Angeles for many years. This section also uses information from the American Board of Medical Specialties (ABMS, 2017).

Rehabilitation counselors have frequent and explicit need to involve the services of a variety of medical specialists, and they should be thoroughly conversant with the scope of each of the recognized specialties. In the interests of general orientation to the medical profession, counselors need an awareness of the role of the family physician (general practitioner) in modern medicine.

Role of the Family Practitioner

Many people in urban communities tend to assume that specialists practice all medicine today, but many families in this country receive all their medical care from family physicians (general practitioners), sometimes by choice and sometimes by necessity. In all probability, doctors in family practice will have seen most of the clients who come to rehabilitation counselors.

At their best, today's family practitioners are virtually as well rounded as internists (specialists in internal medicine). They are apt diagnosticians, and although of necessity they must be willing to assume an imposing amount of responsibility for independent action, they must decide for their patients if and when to involve a consultant in a specialized segment of medicine. Since there are many communities throughout the country where the specialties are undermanned, it is not unusual for a doctor in family practice to do obstetrics, anesthesiology, minor surgery, and even uncomplicated major surgery. Many family practitioners, without so labelling it, infuse their treatment of patients with supportive counseling.

Internal Medicine and Its Subspecialties

Internal Medicine is the specialty with the broadest scope, and the one whose jurisdiction is most difficult to define. The internist is sometimes identified as the physician who treats all disorders not requiring surgery. The range of the specialty of internal medicine can best be understood by identifying some of the major subspecialties which it includes:

Cardiology (heart) – The study of diseases of the heart. This usually includes disorders of the blood vessels, the two systems being termed jointly the cardiovascular system. It may also encompass evaluation of the lungs; often, the kidneys are involved.

Endocrinology (diabetes and other glandular disorders) – The study of the endocrine system, which secrete hormones. These glands include the pancreas, pituitary, pineal, thyroid, parathyroid, thymus, adrenals, ovaries, and testes.

Gastroenterology (colon and intestinal tract) – The digestive system and its disorders, including the esophagus, stomach, intestinal tract (gastrointestinal [GI] system), pancreas, and liver.

Hematology (blood) – The study of disorders of the blood, bone marrow, and lymphatic systems.

Pulmonary (lungs) – Diseases of the lungs and bronchial tubes, which often involve evaluation of the upper respiratory tract (nose, pharynx, and throat), as well as the heart.

Geriatrics (care of the elderly) – Concerned with the health and well-being of older adults.

Rheumatology (arthritis) – Treatment of diseases involving the joints, muscles, and bones.

Oncology (cancer) – Treatment of cancer. Two types of clinical oncologists are surgical oncologists and radiation oncologists.

Other Medical Specialties

Anesthesiology – Physicians who administer local and general anesthesia before and during surgical procedures; they participate in patient care before and after surgery. These physicians may be involved in the management of acute and chronic pain conditions.

Otolaryngology – The specialty that treats diseases of the ear, nose, and throat. The branch of medicine and surgery that specializes in diagnosis and treatment of diseases and disorders of the head and neck.

Ophthalmology – The specialty concerned with disorders of the eye; it is a surgical as well as a medical specialty.

Orthopedics – Involves conditions of the musculoskeletal system. Treats musculoskeletal trauma, sports injuries, degenerative diseases, infections, tumors, and congenital disorders.

Physical Medicine and Rehabilitation – A branch of medicine that aims to enhance and restore functional ability and quality of life for patients with physical impairments and disabilities.

Pediatrics – Medical care of infants, children, and adolescents. Includes treatment for physical, psychologic, and social problems related to growth and development.

Neurology – The study of diseases and disorders of the nervous system.

Psychiatry – The medical specialty devoted to the study, diagnosis, treatment, and prevention of mental disorders, including affective, behavioral, cognitive, and perceptual abnormalities. It is closely linked to the social sciences in its inquiry into human behavior.

Pathology – The science which deals with the nature of disease based on the gross and microscopic examination of diseased tissue.

Preventive Medicine – The specialty concerned with measures taken to prevent diseases from occurring. The focus is on the environmental conditions conducive to good health and to diminish disease.

Occupational Medicine – The branch of clinical medicine most active in the field of Occupational Health. Specialists in occupational medicine strive to ensure that the highest standards of health and safety at work are achieved and maintained. Occupational Medicine serves as a link between medicine and the changing economic, social, and political trends.

Case Study - A Vocational Profile Approach

The following case study is an example of those found in the remaining chapters in this book. The case study describes a person with presenting disabilities. After the case study, there is a series of questions. This chapter provides answers to the questions to illustrate the analysis of case studies.

Case Study

Mr. Samuel Williams is 60 years of age, currently married with three grown children. He has a Bachelor of Arts Degree in fine arts, completed a real estate course, and holds a current real estate license. For the past seven years, Mr. Williams has been active and successful in residential real estate sales. Before this, he was both a salesperson and an assistant manager in a men's specialty clothing store. The sales position lasted for five years, at which time the employer promoted Sam to assistant manager.

This client has hypertension (high blood pressure) and a heart condition. Six months ago, he had a myocardial infarction (heart attack). The treating physician reported that Mr. Williams has coronary artery disease and restricted him to a maximum of light work not involving excessive emotional stress. His physician recommends Sam consider sedentary work, as it would be less physically demanding. The position of real estate sales agent, *Dictionary of Occupational Titles (D.O.T.)* #250.357-018 (U. S. Department of Labor, 1991), involves renting, buying, and selling real estate property for clients. An agent is paid on a commission basis and does not earn a salary. Real estate sales agents are familiar with all state and local regulations relating to the purchase and sale of property. They review trade journals and other publications to keep current in the field and for information about marketing conditions and property values. A real estate sales agent holds a current license issued by the state. Agents interview prospective clients to solicit listings. They accompany clients to property sites, show properties, quote purchase prices, and describe features and conditions of sale or terms of lease. Agents draw up real estate contracts, such as deeds, leases, and mortgages, and negotiate loans on properties. Real estate agents typically are paid on a commission-only basis.

In addition to these functions, Mr. Williams served as an office manager, supervising clerical personnel in the real estate office. Sam received a salary for this part of the job. The work was conducted at the same time as he was a real estate sales agent, as much of his work as a sales agent was during weekends.

Questions

1. Describe the client's vocational profile, including age, educational level, work history (skill and exertional levels), occupationally significant characteristics, and job skills.
2. How do the occupationally significant characteristics of the job impact Mr. Williams' disability?
3. What, if any, reasonable accommodations can you suggest for the client to return to his usual and customary occupation as a real estate sales agent and part-time real estate office manager?
4. What is this client's rehabilitation potential? Your rehabilitation supervisor is of the opinion this client may be too old for the provision of rehabilitation services. Discuss this issue.
5. What jobs can Mr. Williams perform using transferable skills?

Answers

The vocational profile for this client, Mr. Samuel Williams, is the following:

Age: 60 years old – Close to Retirement Age (60-64).

Education:
Bachelor of Arts degree and completion of real estate license training course – High School Education and Above.

Work History:
2008-2018: Real Estate Sales Agent and Real Estate Office Manager (part-time) – Skilled. Light exertion.
2000-2007: Real estate Sales Agent – Skilled. Light exertion.
1990-1999: Retail Salesperson and Assistant Department Manager (men's clothing store) – Semiskilled. Light exertion.
Prior to 1990, Mr. Williams had unskilled and very basic semiskilled jobs.

Occupationally Significant Characteristics: Manual dexterity, eye-hand-foot coordination, attention to detail, visual acuity, capacity to work with others, inside as well as outside work, varying work tasks, clerical functions, light exertion, frequent standing and walking, and activities involving emotional stress.

Transferable Skills: An ability to lease, purchase, and sell properties for clients on a commission basis; knowledge of property listings and ability to study real estate listings; capability to review trade journals to keep current on market conditions and property values; skills in interviewing clients; capacity to show property; capability to draw up real estate contracts; negotiation skills; current real estate license issued by the state; facility with calculating costs, taxes, discounts, and other charges; mathematical ability as applied to real estate leases and sales; capability to work with financing; capacity to present property in a positive manner; facility with persuading, convincing, and finalizing sales and rentals; aptitude with words to clearly describe advantages of a product; capacity to use business diplomacy and tact when working with people; communication skills and organizational ability.

The work of a real estate agent and manager involve physical exertion at the light level. This is within Mr. Williams' physical capacity and limitations, although his physician recommends he consider sedentary work, as it would be less physically demanding. The work of a real estate sales agent is emotionally stressful, although the work of a real estate office manager or salesperson (not in real estate) are less emotionally demanding. Real estate sales is on a commission basis, increasing the stress. The counselor needs to explore this client's perception of emotional stress as it relates to prior work activity.

This client has good rehabilitation potential. His medical condition is under control with clearly specified functional limitations. There is an 28-year consistent employment history at the skilled and semiskilled levels. During this time, he developed a variety of transferable work skills. Age, in and of itself, cannot be used to deny the provision of rehabilitation services.

The following jobs use Mr. Williams' transferable skills for light and sedentary exertional employment positions. The positions are skilled or semiskilled. Industries for each position are in parentheses.

Light:
- Real estate firm manager or assistant manager (real estate)
- Title searcher (real estate)
- Real estate appraiser (real estate)
- Leasing or rental agent (real estate)
- Public events facilities rental manager (business service)
- Property manager (real estate)
- Apartment house or condominium manager (real estate)
- Salesperson (furniture; appliances; other products)
- Insurance sales agent (insurance; real estate)
- Sales representative (retail trade; wholesale trade)
- File clerk (clerical; real estate)
- Office clerk (clerical; real estate)

Sedentary:
- Real estate clerk (clerical; real estate)
- Real estate assistant (real estate)
- Risk and insurance sales representative (insurance)
- Mortgage closing or escrow clerk (real estate; clerical)
- Housing project manager (real estate)
- Receptionist (real estate; clerical)
- Credit-reference clerk (clerical)
- redit clerk (clerical)
- Credit-card clerk (retail trade; business trade)
- Check cashier (business service)
- Information clerk/assistant (real estate)

References

American Board of Medical Specialties (ABMS). (2017). *Specialties and subspecialties.* Chicago, IL: Author.

Americans with Disabilities Act of 1990 (ADA), PL 101-336, 42 U.S.C. §12101 *et seq.*

Berkeley Planning Associates. (1982). *A study of recommendations provided to handicapped employees by federal contractors* (Contract No. J-9-E-1-009). Berkeley, CA: Author.

Brodwin, M. G., Parker, R. M., & DeLaGarza, D. (2010). Disability and reasonable accommodation. In E. M. Szymanski & R. M. Parker (Eds.), *Work and disability: Contexts, issues, and strategies for enhancing employment outcomes for people with disabilities* (3rd ed., pp. 281-323). Austin, TX: Pro-ed.

Falvo, D. R., & Holland, B. E. (2018). *Medical and psychosocial aspects of chronic illness and disability* (6th ed.). Burlington, MA: Jones and Bartlett Learning.

Gilbride, D., & Stensrud, R. (2012). People with disabilities in the workplace. In R. M. Parker & J. B. Patterson (Eds.), *Rehabilitation counseling: Basics and beyond* (3rd ed., pp. 259-284). Austin, TX: Pro-ed.

Martin, F. H., Walls, R. T., Brodwin, M. G., Parker, R. M., Siu, F. W., & Kurata, E. (2012). Competitive employment outcomes of vocational rehabilitation. *Journal of Applied Rehabilitation Counseling, 43*, 3-10.

Muther, T. J. (1996). "Qualified" and "reasonable accommodations" under Title I of the ADA: Employer compliance. *Law Reporter, 15*(1), 18-20.

Office of the Federal Register. (2001). *Code of federal regulations - 20 CFR*. Washington, DC: United States Government Printing Office.

Parkin, K., Corcoran, J. R., & Stolfi, A. (2017). Introduction. In A. Moroz, S. R. Flanagan, & H. Zaretsky (Eds.), *Medical aspects of disability for rehabilitation professionals* (5th ed., pp. 1-18). New York, NY: Springer.

Rehabilitation Act of 1973, PL 93-112, 29 U.S.C. §701 *et seq.*

Roessler, R. T., & Rumrill, P. D., Jr. (1995). Promoting reasonable accommodations: An essential postemployment service. *Journal of Applied Rehabilitation Counseling, 26*, 3-7.

Rubin, S. E., Roessler, R. T., & Rumrill, P. D., Jr. (2016). *Foundations of the vocational rehabilitation process* (7th ed.). Austin, TX: Pro-ed.

U.S. Department of Labor. (1991). *Dictionary of occupational titles* (4th ed., Rev.). Washington, DC: Author.

World Health Organization (WHO). (2001). *ICF: International Classification of Functioning, Disability, and Health*. Geneva, Switzerland: Author.

World Health Organization (WHO). (2015). *Disability and rehabilitation. WHO Global Action Plan 2014-2021*. Retrieved from http://www.who.int/disabilities/about/action plan/en

About the Authors

Martin G. Brodwin, PhD, CRC, is Professor Emeritus in the Rehabilitation Education Programs at California State University, Los Angeles. He is a vocational expert for the Office of Hearings Operations, Social Security Administration, providing testimony on disability-related issues. As a rehabilitation and vocational consultant, he provides assessment for long-term disability, case management, and reasonable accommodation. Dr. Brodwin has published over 115 refereed journal articles, book chapters, and books on the subjects of counseling, disability, rehabilitation, and medical aspects of chronic illness and disability.

Sandra K. Brodwin, MEd, MS, is a part-time lecturer in the Rehabilitation Education Programs at California State University, Los Angeles, and a grant writer in the areas of disability, rehabilitation, and domestic violence. As a vocational rehabilitation counselor, she has provided reasonable accommodation, job restructuring, employer consultation, and a full range of rehabilitation services for employees on short-term and long-term disability due to chronic illness and injuries. Ms. Brodwin has published book chapters and journal articles on the subjects of medical aspects of disabling conditions, counseling, disability, job analysis, and rehabilitation.

Chapter 2

HUMAN BODY SYSTEMS

Frances W. Siu, PhD, CRC
Erin R. Brodwin, MA

Introduction

The human body is a complex network of some 63 trillion cells (McDowell & Windelspecht, 2015; Tortora, Grabowski, & Derrickson, 2016). Cells are the body's building blocks – cells of the same origin comprise tissues; organs are composed of multiple tissue types. Organs that work together to carry out specific functions are known as body systems (VanPutte, Regan, & Russo, 2017). These systems work together to meet the body's needs. Body systems can be broken down into two components: body functions, which include the physiological and psychological functions of body systems, and body structures, the anatomical components of the organs and limbs. Knowledge of the structure and function of the human body builds the foundation for understanding illnesses and disabilities (Martini, Nath, & Bartholomew, 2017). Preceded by an introduction to the chemical and cellular levels of the human body, this chapter provides readers with an overview of the skeletal system, muscular system, nervous system, cardiovascular and lymphatic systems, integumentary system, respiratory system, sensory system, digestive system, genitourinary system, and endocrine system. The visual and hearing systems are described in chapters in later chapters.

Cellular and Chemical Levels

In the human body, building blocks of matter, called atoms, interact and combine to form molecules such as sugar, fat, water, and protein. These molecules in turn form organelles, such as the plasma membrane and nucleus, which make up cells (VanPutte et al., 2017). Cells are the basic units of the human body; they carry out the functions of protection and support while providing the body systems with a means of communication. Cells additionally metabolize and release energy, provide the basic materials for genetic inheritance, and make movement possible. Each cell is encased by an outer layer known as the plasma membrane, which regulates what enters or leaves the cell. The hereditary material of the cell, Deoxyribonucleic Acid (DNA), is found inside the nucleus. DNA helps direct cell activities by utilizing Ribonucleic Acid (RNA) (Martini et al., 2017).

While the cellular level describes the physical structures that make up cells, the chemical level describes the chemical components within the cell. Oxygen, carbon dioxide, and water comprise the chemical levels of the cell. Oxygen fuels the chemical reactions that enable the cell to extract energy from food (VanPutte et al., 2017). Carbon dioxide and energy are released during metabolism, the process by which organic molecules from an energy source are broken down. Water, another essential chemical, works in the cells to stabilize body temperature and protect against friction and trauma. Water directly participates in chemical reactions, such as dehydration and hydrolysis (Martini et al., 2017).

Tissue Level

Tissues are collections of similar cells and the substances surrounding them (Martini et al., 2017). There are four primary types of tissue:

- Epithelium forms the internal and external linings of various organs of the body. It is usually involved in activities such as diffusion, filtration, secretion, and absorption.
  - Connective tissue connects and binds cells and other tissues together. Among the connective tissues, there are three types of specialized connective tissue (VanPutte et al., 2017):
  - Cartilage is made up of collagen, proteoglycans, and water; its slightly elastic, gummy-like consistency allows body parts to spring back when compressed. Examples are the external parts of the ears and connecting tissues between the bones of the spine.
  - Bone is a hard, calcified connective tissue composed of 35% organic substance, 45% inorganic substance, and 20% water that forms the internal framework of the body.
- Blood contains cell fragments called platelets, which play a key role in blood clotting. The cells and platelets are suspended in plasma. There are two types of blood cells. *Red blood cells* transport oxygen through the arteries and waste through the veins, while *white blood cells* fight infections and cancer.
- Nervous tissue, which responds to stimuli and transmits impulses throughout the body, is composed of neurons (conductive cells) and neuralgia (support cells) (Moore, Agur, & Dailley, 2013). Neurons have cell processes called dendrites that receive electric impulses and axons that conduct them.
- Muscle tissue provides for bodily movement. Muscles are grouped according to the presence or absence of striations (microscopic bands) in the muscle cells (Adams, 2015). Types of muscle tissue include: skeletal, cardiac, and smooth muscle. Skeletal muscle is classified as striated voluntary (usually consciously controlled) while cardiac muscle is striated involuntary (not normally consciously controlled). Smooth muscle is characterized by nonstraited involuntary tissue (VanPutte et al., 2017).

Organ Level

A body system is a group of organs that operate together to carry out a bodily function (VanPutte et al., 2017). Some organs carry out a variety of functions. The hypothalamus, for example, interacts with the nervous system and endocrine system. Similarly, the kidneys act as the body's filtration system and secrete hormones.

The body systems which perform specific purposes in our daily lives also play a significant role in homeostasis, the process by which the body maintains its stability (Moore et al., 2013). Environmental factors that negatively affect the body systems can upset the body's internal constancy and state of homeostasis (Martini et al., 2017).

The Musculoskeletal System

As the name implies, the musculoskeletal system consists of the muscular system and skeletal system.

Skeletal Structure and Function

The human skeleton consists of 206 bones. Bones provide the body with its internal structural framework and protect its vital internal organs (Moore et al., 2013). For purposes of classification, bones are grouped into the axial and appendicular skeletons. The axial skeleton, formed by the bones of the head and trunk, is distinct from the appendicular skeleton, which includes the bones of the upper and lower limbs and the shoulder and hip bones.

The structure of the skeletal system permits movement, storage, and maintenance of chemical levels. Skeletal muscles attach at bone sites, allowing the body to move. Connective tissues in these areas house bone-forming cells responsible for repair. Bones also store important minerals like calcium and phosphate, and fats for cellular energy production (Martini et al., 2017).

Inside the compact outer shell of dense material encasing the bone marrow, a thriving environment exists. The inner mass, known as spongy bone, is less dense than compact bone and has numerous small cavities where red and white blood cells and platelets exist.

FIGURE 1
Human Skeleton

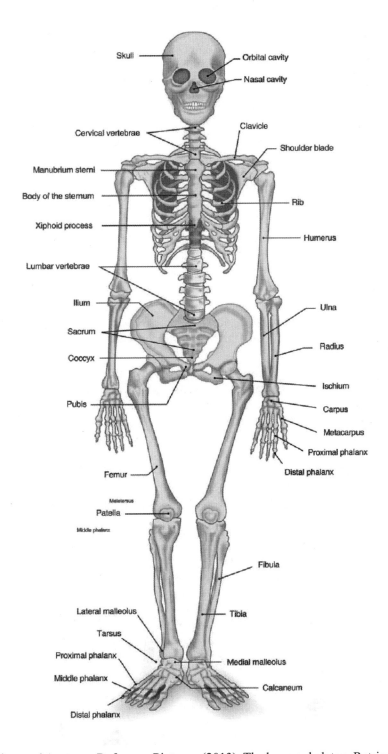

Source: Health, Medicine, and Anatomy Reference Pictures. (2013). The human skeleton. Retrieved from http://healthfavo.com/detailed-human-skeleton-diagrams.html

Human Body Systems

The skull is composed of two sets of bones: cranial bones and facial bones. Cranial bones, where the head muscles attach, protect and enclose the brain. Facial bones provide the framework for the face and mouth. Immovable joints connect all the bones in the skull—except for the mandible, which is attached to the skull via a freely movable joint. The cranium is made up of eight thin, eggshell-like bones that are self-bracing. The forehead is formed by the frontal bone, which also forms the upper half of the eye sockets. Two parietal bones make up the bulk of the cranium and comprise the sides of the skull. Temporal bones lie inferior to the parietal bones on both sides of the skull. The occipital bone, also named for the part of the brain it covers, shapes the posterior of the skull. The sphenoid bone encloses the cranial cavity (Tortora et al., 2016).

The spinal column, formed by 26 bones, connects the face and skull to the rest of the body. At the base of the flexible, curved spinal column is the sacrum, comprised of five fused vertebrae. Below the sacrum the coccyx is composed of four fused vertebrae. The entire spinal column is divided into three parts. Cervical vertebrae encompass the first seven vertebrae below the skull while thoracic vertebrae refer to the next 12, and lumbar to the last five vertebrae (Tortora et al., 2016).

Anterior to the spinal column is the sternum and rib cage. While 12 pairs of ribs exist, only the first seven are attached directly to the sternum. The rest are known as *false ribs*, meaning that they attach to the sternum indirectly or not at all. The seven attached ribs are connected to the sternum by cartilage. At the inferior end of the sternum, the xiphoid serves as an attachment point for the diaphragm.

On each side of the skeleton are the scapulae, posterior to the rib cage, connecting the upper arm to the rest of the skeleton by a bone called the clavicle which, together with the scapulae, comprises the shoulder girdles. The clavicle mainly acts as a brace holding the scapulae and the arms up and away from the ribs. It also enables people to raise their hands (Tortora et al., 2016).

The humerus is the only bone in the upper arm. At the end of the humerus are two bones: the radius and ulna. These long bones allow us to twist our hands from side to side. At the end of the radius and ulna lie the carpals, collectively referred to as the wrist. The palm of the hand is supported by the metacarpals, while the three phalanges make up the fingers.

The rest of the body could not be connected to the lower extremities without the existence of one structure, the pelvis. The pelvis works to provide support for the body's internal organs. Its flaring sides are called the ilium. The two ring-shaped portions located inferior to the hip sockets are called ischium while the femur refers to the bone in the thigh (Goldman & Schafer, 2015). The patella (kneecap) guards the knee joint against injury and improves leverage of thigh muscles responsible for raising the lower leg. The tibia and fibula form the lower leg.

The foot is much like the hand in the way the bones are grouped. The first group of bones, the tarsals, form half the foot. The calcaneus forms the heel, while the talus connects the foot with the tibia and fibula. The rest of the foot, excluding the toes, is composed of metatarsals (Tortora et al., 2016).

Cartilage

Along with bone, cartilage helps give the skeletal system its shape. Cartilage is a dense connective tissue composed of cells called chondrocytes that are dispersed in a firm gel-like ground substance called the matrix. It is avascular (contains no blood vessels) and can be found in the joints, rib cage, ear, nose, throat, and between intervertebral disks (Tortora et al., 2016).

The muscular system is the largest body system. The upper and lower extremities are almost entirely made up of muscles; over forty muscles are located in the skull alone. Muscles are distinct from all other tissues because of their unique ability to contract (Adams & Myers, 2015).

One motor unit contains anywhere from two to as many as 2,000 muscle fibers. Blood vessels provide muscles with nutrients and oxygen and remove waste. Nerves deliver signals that cause muscles to contract and relax, resulting in movements as delicate as a blink of the eyelid or as powerful as a punch of the fist.

The three types of muscles include skeletal, smooth, and cardiac (Adams, 2015; Goldman & Schafer, 2015).

FIGURE 2a
Muscular System– Front

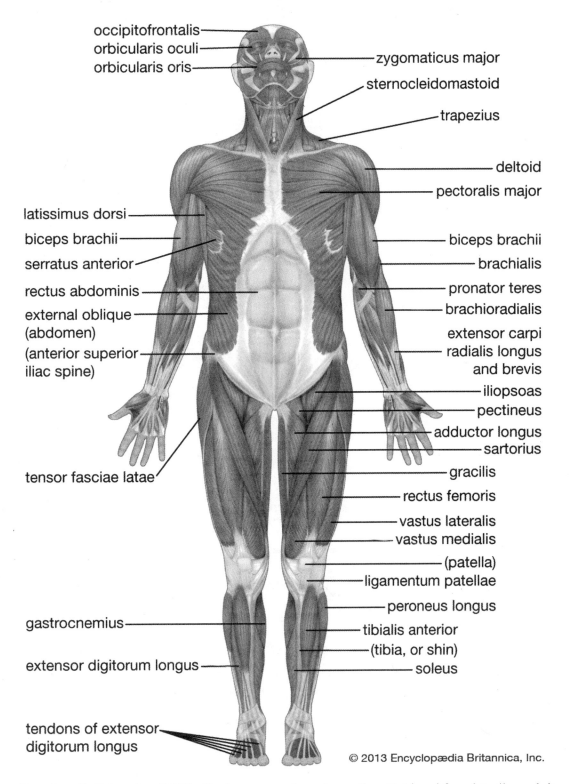

Source: Encyclopedia Britannica. (2010). *The human muscle system gallery*. Retrieved from http://www.britannica.com/EBchecked/media/147100/Posterior-view-of-human-muscular-system

FIGURE 2b
Muscular System – Back

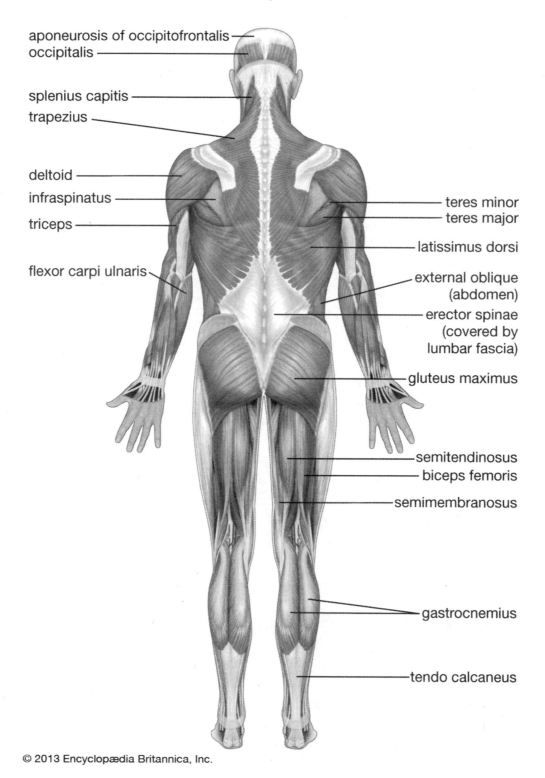

Source: Encyclopedia Britannica. (2010). *The human muscle system gallery*. Retrieved from http://www.britannica.com/EBchecked/media/147100/Posterior-view-of-human-muscular-system

- Skeletal muscle is the strongest, lengthiest, and hardest working tissue in the body. Known as striated muscle tissue because of the way it crisscrosses over each fiber, skeletal muscle tissue owes part of its strength to its protective sheath-like covering. Skeletal muscle is also the only type of tissue that is voluntary.
- Smooth muscle is involuntary and is commonly found in hollow organs such as the stomach, bladder, and respiratory passages. Its main function is to propel objects. These tissue are spindle-shaped and arranged in sheets or layers.
- Cardiac muscle tissue is found only in the heart; it is striated, involuntary, and responsible for pumping blood throughout the heart. Cardiac muscle tissue is protected by connective tissue.

Joints, Tendons, and Ligaments

Besides muscles and bones, joints play a pivotal role in body movement. These connecting structures of bones are classified either according to degree of movement or type of connective tissue that joins them. Fibrous joints are those ends of bones connected by fibrous tissue without a joint cavity; they are capable of little or no movement. Cartilaginous joints are attached by hyaline cartilage and are slightly moveable. Synovial joints have joint cavities where the fibrous connective tissue holds the bones together. These joints are highly moveable, depending on their location. Synovial joints allow for various types of common movement such as gliding, angulations, rotation, and the combination of two or more movements. Elevation and depression, protraction and retraction, excursion, opposition and reposition, and inversion and eversion are some special movements also made possible by synovial joints (Tortora et al., 2016).

Both tendons and ligaments are soft collagenous tissues. While tendons connect muscles to bone and carry the tension forces between them, ligaments connect bone to bone. Both tendons and ligaments play a significant role in musculoskeletal biomechanics.

As the foundation of the body, the skeleton functions alongside the muscular system, which together provide the body with range of movement. The nervous system, integral to both the skeletal and muscular systems, provides the means by which all body systems function.

FIGURE 3
Neuron

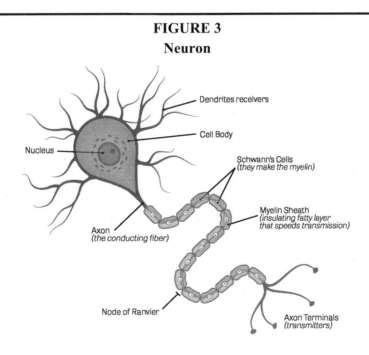

Source: US National Library of Medicine, Toxicology and Environmental Health Information Program, 2018. Retrieved from https://toxtutor.nlm.nih.gov/14-004.html

FIGURE 4
Human Brain

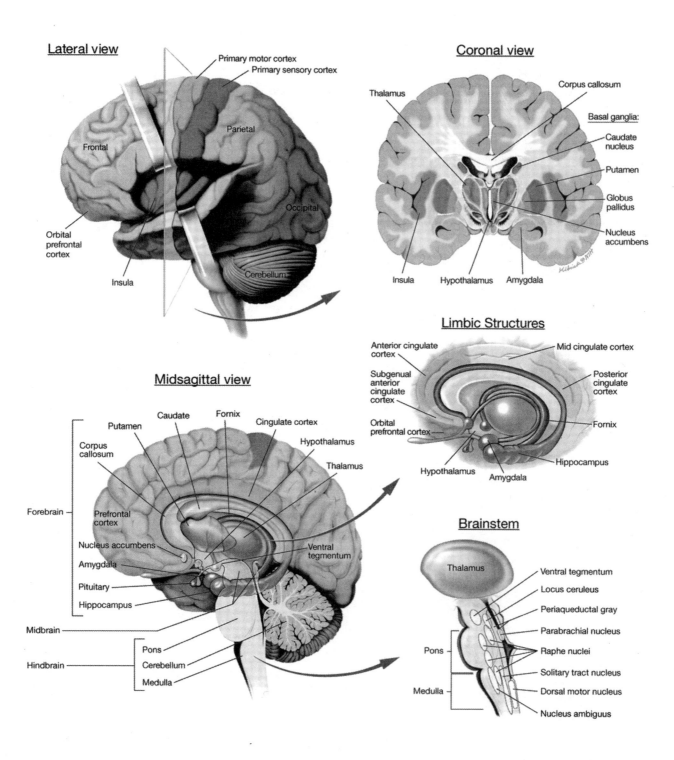

Source: National Heart Lung and Blood Institute. (2014). *Anatomy of the heart*. Retrieved from http://www.nhlbi.nih.gov/health//dci/Diseases/hhw/hhw_anatomy.html

The Nervous System

The nervous system is the master controlling and communicating system of the body; it directs human thoughts, actions, and emotions. It is the most rapid-acting and complex system of the body, and functions via intra-cellular communication through electrical signals. The nervous system is typically discussed in two parts: the central nervous system (CNS) and the peripheral nervous system (PNS).

Central Nervous System

The CNS consists of the brain and spinal cord. As the command center of the nervous system, the CNS interprets incoming signals and responds to these signals based on past experiences, reflexes, and current conditions.

Peripheral Nervous System

The PNS is distinguished from the CNS, consisting of the nerves extending from the brain and spinal cord. These nerves, respectively called cranial nerves and spinal nerves serve as the communications link from the body to the CNS. The PNS is further divided into the following functional subdivisions:

- Sensory contains nerve fibers that carry impulses to the CNS from sensory receptors located throughout the body. There are two types of sensory fibers.
- Somatic afferents convey information from the skin, skeletal muscles, and joints.
- Visceral afferents convey impulses from the visceral organs.
- Motor transports messages from the CNS to organs, muscles, and glands. The motor system is divided into two parts (Tortora et al., 2016).
  - *Somatic nervous system*, composed of motor nerve fibers that connect the CNS to the skeletal muscles, is often referred to as the *voluntary nervous system*. These motor neurons respond mainly to external stimuli. Reflexes, automatic reactions to a stimulus, are usually controlled by the spinal cord and brainstem.
  - *Autonomic nervous system*, consisting of nerve fibers that regulate the activity of smooth muscles, cardiac muscles, and glands, is not consciously controlled; therefore, it is generally referred to as the *involuntary nervous system*. The autonomic nervous system is subdivided into the sympathetic and parasympathetic nervous systems. These systems have opposing effects when they act upon the same organ. While the parasympathetic nervous system enhances activities and conserves energy, the sympathetic nervous system increases energy expenditures and prepares the body for action.

In the nervous system, there are two main types of cells – neurons and supporting cells. While neurons provide a pathway for messages traveling to and from the brain and spinal cord, supporting cells provide structural reinforcement, protection, insulation, and general assistance for neurons. As specialized cells, neurons provide for the transportation of signals. Although many different types of neurons exist, all neurons share common characteristics. For example, all neurons share large cell bodies and have fiber-like extensions called processes. Processes are further divided into dendrites and axons.

Dendrites convey signals toward the cell body. These short, numerous cells branch extensively around the nucleus. Perpendicular to the body of the neuron, the axon conducts signals away from the cell body. Along the length of the axon, the Schwann cells form an insulating layer called the myelin sheath. Branches of axons terminate in hundreds or thousands of telodendria branlets which, in turn, end in synaptic knobs. Synaptic knobs relay messages to other cells via neurotransmitters. Gaps in the synaptic knobs are called synapses.

The brain and body are linked by the spinal cord, a long bundle of white nerve matter residing in the middle of the spinal column. The spinal cord also serves as the center from which reflexes stem.

The brain has three divisions: brain stem, cerebellum, and cerebrum. The brainstem is the core for most life systems commands—vital functions that are not consciously controlled. The cerebellum, the next brain division, controls balance and muscle coordination. After the cerebellum, the most advanced part of the

FIGURE 5
Human Heart

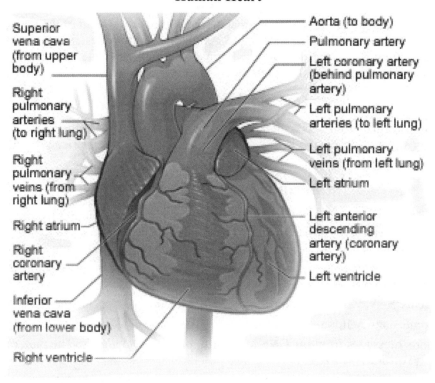

Source: National Heart Lung and Blood Institute. (2014). *Anatomy of the heart*. Retrieved from http://www.nhlbi.nih.gov/health//dci/Diseases/hhw/hhw_anatomy.html

FIGURE 6
Human Circulatory System

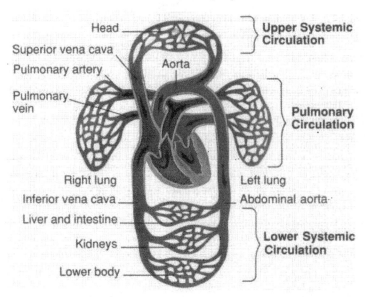

Source: Laas, M. (2009). *The circulatory system*. International School of Bremen. Retrieved from http://www.michael-laas.de/Circulatory%20System.htm

brain is the cerebral cortex—conscious thought takes place in this region. While the cerebellum can be divided into the left and right hemispheres, it can also be divided into functional parts. The right hemisphere, generally, is the artistic side of the brain. People who are *right brained* (the right hemisphere is dominant over the left) are thought to excel at activities involving abstract thinking, such as art and music. *Left brained* people are considered to be logical, allowing them to excel in math, physics, and other such logical thought processes. Although one sphere can be dominant, the two hemispheres are connected by the corpus callosum, which allows the two hemispheres to communicate (Mai, Majtakik, & Paxinas, 2015).

The Cardiovascular System (including the Lymphatic System)

The Cardiovascular System

The cardiovascular system controls a single vital function—blood circulation. Circulation is necessary for the growth and development of cells. The heart, the cardiovascular system's central organ, is responsible for moving blood throughout the body. Made of cardiac tissue, this vital fist-sized organ first pumps blood to the lungs, where it obtains oxygen. The heart then funnels the blood throughout the body via a series of arteries and veins. While the arteries carry oxygenated blood from the heart to the body, veins return the oxygen-depleted blood to the heart.

Centrally located in the upper body cavity, the heart can be divided into four chambers: left and right atria and left and right ventricle. The atria consist of the upper half of the heart, while the ventricles compose the lower portion. The left and right sides of the heart are divided by the septum. Four valves of the heart control circulation (Tortora et al., 2016).

Blood is composed of red and white blood cells, platelets, lymph, plasma, and water. Forty-five percent of blood consists of platelets (necessary for blood-clotting) and red and white blood cells. The remainder is liquid plasma, a mixture of glucose and water. Red blood cells, or erythrocytes, contain hemoglobin, the chemical compound that carries oxygen. White blood cells, or leukocytes, destroy and remove old cells and cellular debris and attack foreign or infectious agents (Collier, Longmore, & Amarkone, 2013).

Blood enters the heart through the left atrium from the superior and inferior vena cava. The superior vena cava collects blood returning from the upper body. The inferior vena cava returns blood from the lower body. During the systolic phase of the heartbeat, deoxygenated blood from the superior and inferior vena cava enters the heart through the right atrium. In this phase of the heartbeat, the atria begin to fill while the ventricles contract to pump the blood. Additionally, the pulmonary and aortic valves open allowing blood to exit the ventricles. During the diastole phase, the atria contract, pumping blood into the ventricles, and the tricuspid and mitral valves open, allowing blood to enter.

New blood entering the right atrium is pumped by the tricuspid valve to the right ventricle. Once the pulmonary valve opens to the pulmonary artery, blood is carried to the lungs where it is oxygenated. The pulmonary artery is the only artery in the body that carries deoxygenated blood.

The oxygen in the lungs, first diffused through the alveoli sacs, is next pushed through the wall of the lungs into the bloodstream where the blood distributes oxygen throughout the body. To enable direct oxygenation of the cells, the arteries are branched into smaller arterioles. These separate further into capillaries, the smallest blood vessels, whose walls are thin and elastic. When oxygen is released from the hemoglobin, it is diffused across the capillary wall, traveling to a nearby cell and entering through its membrane.

The carbon dioxide that returns to the blood travels back to the lungs via the capillaries. The capillaries fork into smaller venules, which divide further into veins. Carbon dioxide and blood are carried back to the heart by the veins, completing the circulatory cycle (Moore et al., 2013).

The Lymphatic System

A specialized component of the circulatory system is the lymphatic system, consisting of moving fluid (lymph/interstitial fluid), vessels (lymphatics), lymph nodes, and organs (adenoid, tonsils, thymus, thoracic duct, small intestine, appendix, liver, and spleen). By moving blood in and out of arteries and into veins and through the lymph nodes and into the lymph, the body is able to eliminate the products of cellular breakdown and bacterial invasion (McDowell & Windelspecht, 2015). The lymphatic system functions 1) to absorb excess fluid, thus preventing tissues from swelling; 2) to defend the body against microorganisms and harmful foreign particles; and 3) to facilitate the absorption of fat. The lymph system is made up of T cells, B cells, antibodies, and platelets.

The skin plays a major role in preventing disease by protecting organs, blood vessels, and the lymph system. To combat bacteria, viruses, and disease, the skin contains lymph nodes. These nodes transport white blood cells (phagocytes) throughout the body via a network of vessels.

FIGURE 7
Human Skin Diagram

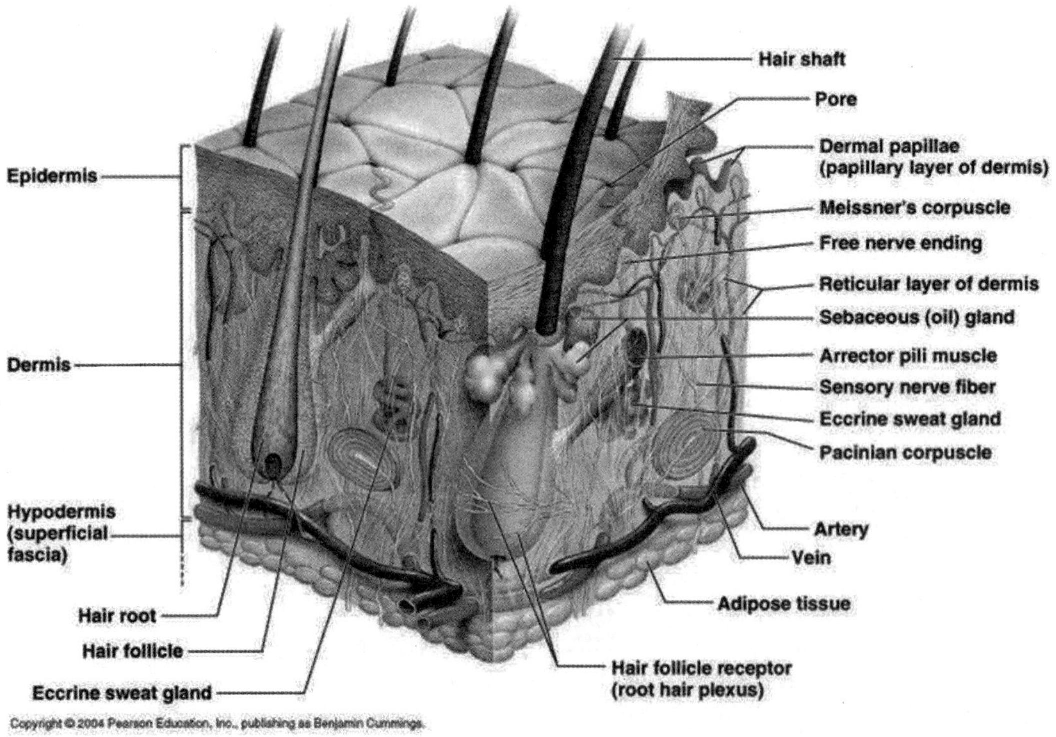

Source: Davis, F. A. (2017). *Taber's cyclopedia medical dictionary* (23rd ed.). Philadelphia, PA: F. A. Davis.

Mucous membranes, cells that line all openings of the body, provide a second line of defense against foreign bacteria. When dust particles enter the body, for example, they are trapped in the mucous membranes and then digested. Nose hair functions alongside the mucous membranes to protect the body; they act as an air filtration system.

Along with the lymph nodes, the lymphatic system includes lymph (interstitial fluid). Capillaries release excess water and plasma into intracellular spaces where they mix with lymph, a fluid containing proteins, fats, and a type of white blood cells called lymphocytes, the body's first-line defense in the immune system.

Lymph flows from small lymph capillaries into lymph vessels that are similar to veins in having valves that prevent backflow. The contraction of skeletal muscle propels lymph fluid through the valves. Lymph vessels connect to lymph nodes, lymph organs (bone marrow, liver, spleen, thymus), and the cardiovascular system.

Besides functioning as a line of defense for the body, the lymphatic system functions as a separate circulatory system working parallel to the cardiovascular system. The lymphatic system absorbs fats, returns approximately three liters of fluid from our body tissues to the circulatory system on a daily basis, and transports selected nutrients from the digestive system to the circulatory system (Collier et al., 2013). The next line of body defense includes the integumentary system.

The Integumentary System

The integumentary system, commonly called the skin, encases the body. It functions as a protective barrier against the environment, and is involved in maintaining proper body temperature. The skin gathers sensory information from the environment and helps protect the body from disease. The skin's functioning is divided into three parts, representing three layers of skin: epidermis, dermis, and subcutaneous tissue (Martini et al., 2017; Goldman & Schafer, 2015).

The epidermis, the outer layer of skin, varies in thickness. It is thinnest on the eyelids and thickest on the palms of the hands and soles of the feet. When cells divide or multiply, they push other cells into higher layers, where they flatten and eventually die. Humans shed this surface layer every two weeks.

Dermis, which connects the skin to the tissue underneath, includes collagen, elastic tissue, and reticular fibers. It contains many specialized cells and structures such as hair follicles, sebaceous (oil) glands, and apocrine (scent) glands. This layer also contains eccrine (sweat) glands. Blood vessels and nerves course through this layer, transmitting sensations of pain, itching, and temperature. Specialized nerve cells in the dermis transmit sensations of touch and pressure (Martini et al., 2017).

Subcutaneous tissue is a layer of fat and connective tissue that houses larger blood vessels and nerves. This layer is vital in regulation of skin and body temperature; its size varies throughout the body and from person to person.

The Respiratory System

The respiratory system supplies the body with oxygen. After air is inhaled through the nose or mouth, it travels into the pharynx, passes through the larynx, and makes its way down the trachea. When air reaches the lungs, it is diffused into the blood via the alveoli (Martini et al., 2017).

Nasal Cavity

As people breathe, air enters the body through the nostrils. Inside the nose, the nasal cavity is divided by the septum and lined by the respiratory mucosa. In the roof of the nasal cavity, the mucosa house the olfactory receptors. The mucosa help warm and moisten air entering the body while trapping invading pathogens.

Sinuses

The nasal cavity is surrounded by the paranasal sinuses located in the maxillary, ethmoid, sphenoid, and frontal bones. The sinus chambers lighten the weight of the skull, act as resonance chambers for vocalization, and secrete mucous for the nasal cavity.

Pharynx

The pharynx (throat) is the muscular passageway that provides a means of transportation for air and food. Air enters the pharynx through its superior portion, the nasopharynx, and descends to the oropharynx and laryngopharynx. From the laryngopharynx, air moves into the larynx. Food mirrors the passage of air from the nasopharynx to the laryngopharynx; however, instead of entering the larynx as air does, food enters the esophagus.

FIGURE 8
Respiratory System

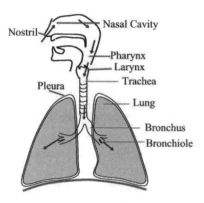

Source: Davis, F. A. (2017). *Taber's cyclopedia medical dictionary* (23rd ed.). Philadelphia, PA: F. A. Davis

Larynx

The larynx (voice box) routes food and air to the proper destination. The epiglottis prevents food from entering the superior opening of the larynx and traveling down the trachea, or windpipe. The epiglottis is opened by breathing, which allows air to pass freely to the lungs. Swallowing, conversely, causes the epiglottis to close. When the epiglottis is closed, food is forced down the esophagus. The mucous membranes of the larynx form the vocal folds. These folds are what give people the ability to speak; when expelled by air, the folds vibrate, resulting in vocal sound.

Trachea

The trachea, or windpipe, is a tube that connects the pharynx and larynx to the lungs, allowing for the passage of air. The trachea divides into the right and left bronchi, which enter the right and left lung. By the time air reaches the bronchi, it is warm, humidified, and cleansed of all pathogens. The tracheal walls, which beat constantly in the opposite direction of incoming air, are covered with ciliated mucous.

Lungs

Lungs are the primary organs of the respiratory system. Housed in the thoracic cavity, the lungs deliver oxygen to the bloodstream and release carbon dioxide. From the trachea, the bronchi enter the lungs, where they divide into smaller branches, or bronchioles, which divide further into respiratory zone structures. The respiratory zone is where the transfusion of air to blood takes place. These structures eventually divide into alveoli, which are responsible for the transfusion of oxygen into the blood.

The Sensory System

The sensory system is vital for survival, growth, development, and the experience of bodily pleasure. Sense perception depends on sensory receptors that respond to various stimuli. When a stimulus triggers an impulse in a receptor, the action potentials travel to the cerebral cortex where they are processed and interpreted as sensations. Some senses, such as pain, touch, pressure, and proprioception, are widely distributed in the body. These are called general senses. Other senses, such as taste, smell, hearing, and sight, are called special senses because their receptors are localized in particular areas (Tortora et al., 2016).

Sensory Components

The two components of sensory experience are reception and perception. Sensory reception is the process of receiving data from the internal and external environment through the senses and includes: visual (seeing); auditory (hearing); olfactory (smell); gustatory (taste); and tactile (touch).

Sensory perception is the conscious process of selecting, organizing, and interpreting data from the senses and transforming this data into meaningful information. This process is influenced by intensity, size, and shape, as well as by past experiences, knowledge, and attitudes. In some situations, the way in which a particular sensation is perceived depends on where it is interpreted in the brain. Nearly everyone is familiar with sensory adaptation in the sense of smell. A particular odor becomes unnoticed after a short time even though the odor molecules are still present in the air because the system quickly adapts to the continued stimulation (Moore et al., 2013).

General Senses

Visceral organs control general senses in the skin, muscles, and joints. General senses include touch, pressure, proprioception, temperature, and pain (Collier et al., 2013).

Touch and Pressure

As a group, the receptors for touch and pressure are widely distributed in the skin and are sensitive to forces that deform or displace tissues. Three of the receptors involved in touch and pressure are free nerve endings, Meissner's corpuscles, and Pacinian corpuscles. These receptors are important in sensing objects in continuous contact with the skin. While Meissner's corpuscles lie just beneath the epidermis and sense light touch stimuli, Pacinian corpuscles are deeper in the dermis and are sensitive to heavy pressure.

Temperature

Temperature receptors lie directly under the skin and are widely dispersed throughout the body. The sense of temperature is stimulated by cold receptors and heat receptors. Degree of stimulation depends on the number of each type of receptor stimulated. A person determines gradations in temperature by the degree of stimulation of each type of receptor. Extreme cold and extreme heat feel almost the same because the pain receptors are being stimulated.

The Digestive System

The digestive system, which prepares food for use, is one of the most complex systems of the body. When eaten, food cannot reach cells because it cannot pass through the intestinal walls to the bloodstream. The digestive system modifies food physically and chemically and disposes of unusable waste. Physical and chemical modification (digestion) depends on exocrine and endocrine secretions and the controlled movement of food through the digestive tract. It provides the body with the means of transforming food into energy. Food is transformed into enzymes, glucose, and other nutrients (Martini et al., 2017).

Mouth

Food enters the digestive system via the mucous membrane-lined oral cavity. The lips protect the mouth's outer opening, while the cheeks form its lateral walls. The hard and soft palates additionally form the anterior or posterior roof. The floor of the mouth is characterized by the muscular tongue. The breakdown of food requires mechanical and chemical processes. Taste buds, while making food enjoyable, also alert the body of potential hazards such as toxins.

Swallowing

Once food leaves the mouth, it crosses the respiratory tract. Swallowing empties the mouth and ensures that food does not enter the windpipe. This process involves coordinated activity of tongue, soft palate (pharynx), and esophagus. The first phase is voluntary, as food is moved from the pharynx by the tongue.

After this phase, reflex controls swallowing. Food moves into the pharynx and onwards by peristalsis aided by gravity. The esophagus, the first part of the digestive tract, runs from the pharynx to the diaphragm and stomach (Goldman & Schafer, 2015).

Stomach

The stomach stores and digests food. Two sphincters, circular valve-like muscles placed outside organs, surround the two openings. Cardioesophageal sphincter guards the entrance from the esophagus while the pyloric sphincter guards the outlet. The stomach secretes acid (to continue the digestive process) and mucus (for self-protection). Food in the stomach is churned by three muscular layers to form chyme, a creamy substance voided via pyloric sphincter to the duodenum.

Small Intestine

The small intestine is the primary organ of the digestive tract. The first part of the small intestine, duodenum, curves around the pancreas, forming the entry of the common bile duct. Most food digestion occurs in the small intestine. In addition to digesting chyme, the small intestine is responsible for absorbing the processed food into the bloodstream so that energy can be derived from food.

Large Intestine

The large intestine stretches from a valve resting between the bottom of the small intestine and the top of the large intestine to the anus. The main job of the large intestine is to digest any undigested chyme and rid the body of unneeded wastes. The large intestine has many subdivisions including the cecum, appendix, colon, rectum, and canal.

Accessory Organs

In addition to the main digestive organs, several accessory organs include the salivary glands, pancreas, liver, and gallbladder. Saliva, a mixture of mucus and serous fluids, is produced in various glands. The pancreas includes the endocrine and exocrine glands. Exocrine produces enzymes while endocrine produces insulin. Bile is produced by the liver and secreted via the hepatic duct and cystic duct to the gallbladder for storage. Bile salts and phospholipids emulsify fats. The liver is a multifunctional organ that receives fat and other nutrients from the small intestine via the hepatic portal system (Martini et al., 2017).

The Genitourinary System

The organs involved in production, formation, and release of urine and the sex organs make up the genitourinary system. This system includes the kidneys, ureters, bladder, urethra, and the reproductive organs – the ovaries, uterus, fallopian tubes, vagina and clitoris in women, and the testes, seminal vesicles, prostate, seminal ducts, and penis in men (Kasper et al., 2015).

Renal System

The kidneys are regulatory organs that maintain volume and composition of body fluid by filtering blood and secreting filtered solutes. Kidneys take blood from the aorta via the renal arteries and return it to the inferior vena cava via the renal veins. Urine, the filtered product containing waste materials and water, is excreted from the kidneys and passes down the ureters, collecting in the bladder. The bladder distends to accept urine, allowing large volumes to be collected without damaging the renal system. Urine is voided through the urethra (Martini et al., 2017).

Male Reproductive System

The organs of the male reproductive system are specialized for the following functions: production, maintenance, and transportation of sperm, protective fluid (semen), and male sex hormones. To best carry out these functions, the male reproductive anatomy includes internal and external structures. Most of the male reproductive system is located outside the body. These include the penis, scrotum, and testicles.

The penis, the male sex organ, is comprised of three parts: the root, which attaches to the wall of the abdomen; the body or shaft; and the glans, the cone-shaped end of the penis. The glans, which also is called the head, is covered with a loose layer of foreskin, sometimes removed through circumcision. The opening of the urethra, the tube that transports semen and urine, is at the tip of the glans penis. The body of the penis is cylindrical in shape and consists of three internal chambers made up of sponge-like erectile tissue. This tissue contains thousands of spaces that fill with blood during sexual arousal. As this process occurs, the penis becomes rigid and erect, allowing for penetration during sexual intercourse. Semen, which contains sperm, is expelled (ejaculated) through the end of the penis when the man reaches sexual climax (orgasm). When the penis is erect, the flow of urine is blocked from the urethra (Kasper et al., 2015).

Scrotum is the loose pouch-like sac located behind the penis. It contains the testicles (also called testes), as well as many nerves and blood vessels. The scrotum functions as a climate control system to protect the testes; normal sperm development requires the testes to maintain a temperature slightly cooler than that of the body.

Testes, oval organs about the size of large olives, lie in the scrotum. The two testes are responsible for making testosterone (the primary male sex hormone) and for generating sperm. Within the testes, coiled masses of seminiferous tubules are responsible for producing sperm cells.

The internal organs of the male reproductive system, also called accessory organs, include the vas deferens, ejaculatory ducts, urethra, seminal vesicles, prostate, and Bulbourethral glands. The vas deferens, a long, muscular tube that travels from the epididymis into the pelvic cavity to just behind the bladder, transports mature sperm to the urethra in preparation for ejaculation. Ejaculatory ducts are formed by the fusion of the vas deferens and the seminal vesicles and empty into the urethra. Urethra, a tube that carries urine from the bladder to outside the body also controls ejaculation of semen.

The male reproductive system could not function without hormones, chemicals that stimulate or regulate the activity of cells or organs. The primary hormones involved in the functioning of the male reproductive system include the follicle-stimulating hormone, the luteinizing hormone, and testosterone.

Female Reproductive System

The female reproductive system is designed to carry out the following functions: 1) production of female egg cells necessary for reproduction, called the ova or oocytes, 2) transportation of the ova to the site of fertilization, and 3) production of female sex hormones. Conception, the fertilization of an egg by a sperm, normally occurs in the fallopian tubes. After conception, the uterus provides a safe environment for fetal development. In the absence of fertilization, the system carries out menstruation (monthly shedding of the uterine lining).

The female reproductive anatomy includes internal and external structures. The function of the external female reproductive structures (the genitals) is twofold: to enable sperm to enter the body and to protect the internal genital organs from infectious organisms. The main external structures of the female reproductive system include the labia majora, labia minora, Bartholin's glands, and the clitoris. The labia majora enclose and protect the other external reproductive organs. Labia minora lie just inside the labia majora and surround the openings to the vagina (the canal that joins the lower part of the uterus to the outside of the body) and urethra (the tube that carries urine from the bladder to outside the body). Bartholin's glands, located next to the vaginal opening, produce a fluid secretion. The two labia minora meet at the clitoris, a small, sensitive protrusion comparable to the penis in males. The clitoris is covered by a fold of skin called the prepuce, which is similar to the foreskin at the end of the penis.

The internal reproductive organs include the vagina, uterus, ovaries, and Fallopian tubes. The vaginal canal joins the cervix (the lower part of uterus) to the outside of the body. The uterus (womb), a hollow pear-shaped organ, is home for a developing fetus. The uterus is divided into two parts: the cervix, which is the lower part that opens into the vagina, corpus, the main body of the uterus. The corpus easily expands to hold a developing baby. A channel through the cervix allows sperm to enter and menstrual blood to exit. The small, oval-shaped glands located on either side of the uterus are called ovaries which produce eggs and hormones. The Fallopian tubes are attached to the upper part of the uterus and allow the ova (egg cells) to travel from the ovaries to the uterus. Conception, the fertilization of an egg by a sperm, occurs in the fallopian tubes. The fertilized egg then moves to the uterus, where it implants in the uterine wall.

Females of reproductive age experience cycles of hormonal activity that repeat at about one-month intervals. *Menstru*, meaning *monthly*, provides us with the term, menstrual cycle. Each such cycle prepares a woman's body for a potential pregnancy. The average menstrual cycle takes about 28 days and occurs in phases: the follicular phase, ovulatory phase (ovulation), and luteal phase. The term *menstruation* refers to the periodic shedding of the uterine lining.

The Follicular phase starts on the first day of the cycle. During this phase, the follicle stimulating hormone and luteinizing hormone are released from the brain and travel in the blood to the ovaries. These hormones stimulate the growth of about 15-20 eggs in the ovaries, each in its own *shell*, called a follicle. As the follicular phase progresses, one follicle in one ovary becomes dominant and continues to mature. This dominant follicle suppresses other follicles, which then stop growing and die. The dominant follicle continues to produce estrogen.

The Ovulatory phase, which begins about 14 days after the start of the follicular phase, is the midpoint of the menstrual cycle. During this phase, a rise in estrogen from the dominant follicle triggers a surge in the amount of luteinizing hormone produced by the brain, causing the dominant follicle to release its egg from the ovary.

The Luteal phase begins immediately after ovulation. Once it releases its egg, an empty follicle develops into a new structure called the corpus luteum. Progesterone prepares the uterus for a fertilized egg to implant. If intercourse has taken place and a man's sperm has fertilized the egg (a process called conception), the fertilized egg (embryo) will travel through the fallopian tube to implant in the uterus, resulting in pregnancy. If the egg is not fertilized, it passes through the uterus, whose lining breaks down and sheds, starting the next menstrual period (Goldman & Schafer, 2015; Kasper et al., 2015).

The Endocrine System

The endocrine system is an integrated system of small organs that controls the release of hormones. This system is instrumental in the regulation of metabolism, growth, development and puberty, tissue function, and mood (Kasper et al., 2015; Martini et al., 2017).

The nervous system controls the sending of electrical messages that coordinate body movements. Conversely, the endocrine system uses chemicals, known as hormones, to communicate and coordinate functioning. Hormones, specific messenger molecules, are synthesized and secreted by a group of specialized cells called endocrine glands. These glands are ductless, meaning that their secretions (hormones) are released directly into the bloodstream to facilitate travel to target organs.

All hormones are characterized by a specific shape, which is recognized accordingly by the corresponding target cells. The binding sites on the target cells are called hormone receptors. Many hormones come in antagonistic pairs that have opposite effects on the target organs. For example, insulin and glucagon have opposite effects on the liver's control of blood sugar level. Insulin lowers the blood sugar level by instructing the liver to take glucose out of circulation and store it, while glucagon instructs the liver to release some of its stored supply to raise the blood sugar level (Kasper et al., 2015).

Hypothalamus and Pituitary

The major human endocrine glands include the hypothalamus and pituitary gland. The pituitary gland, called the *master gland*, is controlled by the hypothalamus. Together, these glands control many other endocrine functions and secrete a number of hormones, especially several important to female cycles (Moore et al., 2013).

A number of other hormones affect various target organs. One non-sex hormone secreted by the posterior pituitary is antidiuretic hormone or ADH. This hormone helps prevent excess water excretion by the kidneys. Another group of non-sex hormones include the endorphins which belong to a category of chemicals known as opiates and serve to deaden the pain receptors. Endorphins which are chemically related to morphine, are produced in response to pain.

Thyroid Gland

Thyroid hormones are responsible for the regulation of metabolism, body temperature, and weight. The thyroid gland requires iodine to manufacture hormones. If a person lacks dietary iodine, the thyroid cannot make its hormones, causing a deficiency.

Pancreas

The pancreas has two functions. First, it serves as a ducted gland, secreting digestive enzymes into the small intestine. Second, it functions using the islets of Langerhans to secrete insulin and glucagon to regulate blood sugar. By secreting glucagon, islets cells signal the liver to utilize carbohydrates and raise blood sugar level. These cells secrete insulin to command the liver to remove excess glucose from circulation.

Adrenal Glands

The adrenal glands sit on top of the kidneys and consist of the outer cortex and the inner medulla. While the medulla secretes epinephrine (adrenaline) and other similar hormones in response to stressors such as fright, anger, caffeine, or low blood sugar, the cortex secretes corticosteroids such as cortisone. Corticosteroids are anti-inflammatory regulators.

Gonads

In addition to producing gametes, the female ovaries and male testes secrete hormones. These hormones (sex hormones) are secreted by the gonads, which in turn are controlled by pituitary gland hormones. While both sexes make some of each hormone, male testes secrete primarily androgens, including testosterone. Female ovaries make estrogen and progesterone in varying amounts depending on menstrual timing.

Pineal Gland

The pineal gland is located near the center of the brain and is stimulated by nerves from the eyes. The pineal gland secretes melatonin at night when it is dark to promote sleep and depress activity of the gonads. Because melatonin production is affected by the amount of light to which a person is exposed, it additionally affects the circadian rhythm (having an activity cycle of about 24 hours), annual cycles, and biological clock functions (Martini et al., 2017).

Conclusion

By the time a human reaches adulthood, the body consists of approximately 100 trillion cells. Each is part of an organ system designed to perform essential life functions. The body's organ systems include: the skeletal system, muscular system, nervous system, cardiovascular and lymphatic systems, integumentary system, respiratory system, sensory system, digestive system, genitourinary system, and endocrine system. The human body is a fascinating and fantastic machine. No one understands all of its many mysteries, and no single source can do justice to its many parts. This chapter has provided an overview from the cellular level through ten body systems. The information learned in this chapter will be useful for the study of disabling conditions. As previously noted, the visual and hearing systems are discussed in chapters in this text specific to those areas.

References

Adams, A. (2015). The muscular system. In M. Windelspecht (Ed.), *Human body systems*. Westport, CT: Greenwood.

Collier, J. A. B., Longmore, M., & Amarakone, K. (2013). *Oxford handbook of clinical specialties* (9th ed). Oxford, England: Oxford University.

Davis, F. A. (2017). *Taber's cyclopedia medical dictionary* (23rd ed.). Philadelphia, PA: F. A. Davis.

Encyclopedia Britannica. (2010). *The human muscle system gallery.* Retrieved from http://www.britannica.com/EBchecked/media/147100/Posterior-view-of-human-muscular-system

Goldman, L., & Schafer, A. I. (Eds.). (2015). *Goldman's Cecil medicine* (25th ed.). Philadelphia, PA: Elsevier Saunders.

Health, Medicine, and Anatomy Reference Pictures. (2013). *The human skeleton.* Retrieved from http://healthfavo.com/detailed-human-skeleton-diagrams.html

Health, Medicine, and Anatomy Reference Pictures. (2013). *Simple brain diagram labeled.* Retrieved from http://healthfavo.com/simple-brain-diagram-labeled.html

Kasper, D. L., Fauci, A., Hauser, S., Longo, D., Jameson, J. L., & Loscalzo, G. J. (2015). *Harrison's principles of internal medicine* (19th ed.). New York, NY: McGraw Hill.

Laas, M. (2009). *The circulatory system.* International School of Bremen. Retrieved from http://www.michael-laass.de/Circulatory%20System.htm

Mai, J., Majtanik, M., & Paxinos, G. (2015). *Atlas of the human brain* (4th ed.). Cambridge, MA: Elsevier Academic Press.

Martini, F. H., Nath, J. L., & Bartholomew, E. F. (2017). *Fundamentals of anatomy and physiology* (11th ed.). Upper Saddle River, NJ: Pearson.

McDowell, J., & Windelspecht, M. (2015). The lymphatic system. In M. Windelspecht (Ed.), *Human body systems.* Westport, CT: Greenwood.

Moore, K. L., Agur, A. M. R., & Dailley, A. F. (2013). *Clinically oriented anatomy* (7th ed.). Philadelphia, PA: Wolters Kluwer Health.

National Heart Lung and Blood Institute. (2014). *Anatomy of the heart.* Retrieved from http://www.nhlbi.nih.gov/health//dci/Diseases/hhw/hhw_anatomy.html

Tortora, G. J., Grabowski, S. R., & Derrickson, B. H. (2016). *Principles of anatomy and physiology* (15th ed.). Hoboken, NJ: Wiley.

US National Library of Medicine, Toxicology and Environmental Health Information Program. (2018). Retrieved from https://toxtutor.nlm.nih.gov/14-004.html

VanPutte, C., Regan, J., & Russo, A. (2017). *Anatomy and physiology* (10th ed.). New York, NY: McGraw-Hill.

About the Authors

Frances W. Siu, PhD, CRC, is an Associate Professor at California State University, Los Angeles (CSULA). She received her PhD in Special Education and Counseling, option in Rehabilitation Counselor Education, from the University of Texas at Austin, her MS in Rehabilitation Counseling and BS in Psychology from CSULA. Research interests of Dr. Siu include psychosocial aspects of disability and violence against people with disabilities, and returning veterans entering higher education.

Erin R. Brodwin, MA, received her Master of Arts degree in journalism from City University of New York, and Bachelor of Arts degree in ethnic studies, with a minor in environmental science from the University of California, San Diego. Erin is a biotechnical reporter at *Business Insider* covering drugs, science, mental health, and the future of food. At *Business Insider*, she has worked as a writer, editor, and news correspondent, and been interviewed on several public radio stations including NPR and the BBC.

Chapter 3

CANCER

Leo E. Orr, II, MD
Leo M. Orange, MS

Introduction

According to the American Cancer Society (2017), cancer is a group of diseases characterized by the uncontrolled growth and spread of abnormal cells. If the spread is not controlled, it can result in death. The reasons for many cancers, particularly those that occur during childhood, remain unknown. Established cancer causes which are modifiable include lifestyle external factors, such as tobacco use and excessive body weight. Causes which are not modifiable include internal factors, such as inherited genetic mutations, hormones, and immune conditions. These risk factors may act simultaneously or in sequence to initiate and promote cancer growth. Cancer can be malignant (spread from their organ of origin) or benign (grow only at their site of origin). Oncology is the branch of medicine concerned with the study, diagnosis, treatment, and prevention of cancer.

The human body contains billions of cells; each of these cells in turn contains 46 chromosomes that house DNA, the genetic blueprint of life. Approximately 22,000 protein coding genes within the chromosomes instruct the growth and function of each body organ (Tannock, Hill, Bristol, & Harrington, 2013). Chromosomes reproduce themselves by cell division, ensuring that each daughter cell retains the same genetic information. However, cancer cells often show abnormally structured chromosomes and abnormal chromosome numbers. When these errors or mutations occur, genes send incorrect messages. When such an error is received, the cell begins to grow uncontrollably and rapidly, transmitting the new genetic characteristics to its progeny. If the growth proceeds to the point that a lump forms, it is called a malignant tumor or cancer.

The word *cancer* is derived from the Greek word *karkinos*, meaning crab. In the past, women who were found to have breast cancer often experienced large and highly visible veins surrounding the tumor with features resembling the claws of a crab. The earliest anthropological evidence of cancer was found in a million year-old skeleton of a man unearthed in Java, Indonesia. References to cancer are found in early Hindu and Egyptian writings; mummies from as early as the 3rd millennium BC showed signs of bone cancer. Though characterized by ancient roots, cancer has been interpreted with fear and stigma until recently (Raghavan et al., 2012).

For many years, the causes of transmission of cancer were unknown. At the beginning of the previous century, few methods existed to diagnose cancer at an early stage. The majority of individuals were diagnosed only after experiencing debilitation, pain, and oftentimes disfigurement. Surgery was the only treatment and was radical and only sporadically successful with patients who had advanced disease (Rossi, Cady, & Martin, 2000). The public thus learned to interpret the diagnosis of cancer as a severe and debilitating disability, ultimately causing death.

Cancer was often confused with findings of syphilis, another common but untreatable illness that often produced unsightly lesions. As a result of its common confusion with syphilis, individuals with cancer felt guilt and embarrassment of having a sexual connotation applied to the disease. Diagnosis of cancer came to be equated not only with physical effects such as severe pain, disfigurement, and disability, but with the emotional impact of dependence, isolation, and death. Even with modern methods of treatment and success rates, many fears and misconceptions continue to present challenges to physicians and counselors.

Incidence and Prevalence

Cancer currently affects one in four people in the United States. In 2017, over 1.68 million new cases were diagnosed; it is the second leading cause of death, following heart disease. Although cancer remains among the worst fears, it is becoming increasingly clear that cancer is no longer the death sentence which it had been called in the past. The most recent data on cancer incidence, mortality, and survival is based on incidence data from the National Cancer Institute and the SEER Cancer Statistics Review (Howlader et al., 2017). It is estimated by the American Cancer Society (2017) that there will be a total of 1,688,780 new cancer cases and 600,920 cancer deaths in the United States in 2017.

Cancer death rates declined 25% as of 2014. They continue to decline in four major cancer sites (lung, colorectal, breast, and prostate). Overall cancer death rates decreased by 1.5% per year from 2003 to 2012. Death rates decreased an average of 1.8% per year among men and 1.4% per year among women. Research noted that the reduction in deaths from these four major cancer sites were a key part in the overall decline. For example, lung cancer deaths in men decreased by 43% between 1990 and 2014, and in women by 17%

TABLE 1
Leading Sites of New Cancer Cases - 2017 Estimates

Male	Female
Prostrate-19%	Breast-30%
Lung & bronchus-14%	Lung & bronchus-12%
Colon & rectum-9%	Colon & rectum-8%
	Uterine corpus-7%
	Thyroid-5%
	Pancreas-3%
Melanoma of the skin-6%	Melanoma of the skin-4%
Non-Hodgkin lymphoma-5%	Non-Hodgkin lymphoma-4%
Kidney & renal pelvis-5%	Kidney & renal pelvis-3%
Leukemia-4%	Leukemia-3%
Urinary bladder-7%	
Oral cavity & pharynx-4%	
Liver & intrahepatic bile duct-3%	
All sites - 100%	All sites - 100%

Source: American Cancer Society. (2017). *Cancer facts and figures.* Atlanta, GA: Author.

between 2002 and 2014. The rates of death from colorectal cancer decreased by 51% between 1976 and 2012 (American Cancer Society, 2017; Smith, Brooks, Cokkinides, Salsow, & Brawley, 2013).

The leading sites of new cancer cases are shown in Table 1.

Although lung cancer incidence rates have recently stabilized and declined, it still remains the leading cause of cancer death. This highlights the need for reduced smoking and avoidance of environmental tobacco smoke.

Among major racial/ethnic groups, African-Americans have the highest rate of new cancers. Rates are relatively low among American Indians/Alaska Natives with regionally higher rates of some cancers. These disparities are not likely due to genetic differences; rather, they are more likely caused by social, cultural, behavioral, and environmental factors (National Cancer Institute, 2016).

Etiology

Gene Transformation

A landmark scientific discovery was that normal genes may be altered and become cancer genes via oncogenes. Oncogenes, normally held in check by tumor suppressor genes, usually remain dormant. However, when a stimulus or chemical agent turns off the tumor suppressor genes, these oncogenes can be initiated to transform normal cells into cancer cells. Cancer is currently viewed as a multi-step process, with changes to the gene accumulating over time, leading to malignancy. When triggers for such growth derive from chemical or foreign sources, they are termed carcinogens (El-Deiry, 2003).

Environmental Factors

Major carcinogens associated with an increased risk of cancer include tobacco (20-25%), diet (30-35%), and viruses and infections (10%). There are at least 45 known or suspected carcinogens present in tobacco and alcohol; these may be synergistic rather than additive in some cancer causation (Howlader et al., 2013). Tobacco use is linked to a number of malignancies, including those occurring in the lungs, larynx, pharynx, esophagus, bladder, pancreas, and cervix. Epidemiological studies have suggested that up to 37% of all cancers are due to the effects of smoking. Alcohol is associated with many cancers of the upper respiratory and digestive tracts; both alcohol and tobacco serve as initiators and promoters and are synergistic rather than additive in cancer causation (El-Deiry, 2003; Tannock et al., 2013). Other causes include gender factors (7%), unknown causes (5%), industrial occupations (4%), alcohol (3-4%), heredity (2%), environmental pollution (2%), radiation - environmental, medical, and diagnostic (1%), sunlight - ultraviolet (1%), and additives (1%).

Diet

Diet has a major effect on overall health, including the development of diseases, such as cancer. High fat intake is closely related to an increased risk of cancer (Kleinsmith, 2006). The evidence of the link between diet and cancer rates is undeniable. Migrant workers who take on the diet of a foreign country experience frequencies of cancer similar to those of natives of the country. Additionally, rates of cancer are correlated with changes in dietary practices. Striking examples include the decline in both fat consumption and cancer mortality in Europe during World Wars I and II, and the parallel increase in breast cancer rates and fat consumption in Japan.

Research has shown that poor diet and not being active are two key factors that increase a person's risk of cancer. Each year, more than 601,000 Americans die of cancer; about one-third of these deaths are linked to poor diet, physical inactivity, and obesity (American Cancer Society, 2017; Siegel, Miller, & Jemal, 2017; Smith et al., 2013). Research studies have established that obesity correlates with a higher incidence of cancer. Studies suggest that people with a diet high in fat are more at risk for cancer of the colon, uterus, and prostate (Lichtman, 2010; Rossen & Rossen, 2012).

Occupational Causes

A minority of cancers are connected with occupational exposures (Cohen & Markman, 2008). Exposure to ultraviolet light (e.g., the sun) is known to increase the risk of skin cancer, while exposure to ionizing radiation is a rare but long recognized cause of cancer. Development of malignancy following exposure to atomic bomb blasts and intense nuclear radiation have been quantified. Viruses cause several different malignancies including cervical cancer, Burkitt's lymphoma, a variety of lymphocytic leukemias, and AIDS-related neoplasms.

Genetics

Genetic factors are powerful but uncommon determinants of cancer. Many families demonstrate increased risk of breast, ovary, colon, lung, and malignant melanomas. When identifiable abnormal oncogenes are found in family clusters with breast and ovarian cancer, family members have up to a 50% higher risk of developing that type of tumor. Although controversial, the discovery of a genetic predisposition in an unaffected individual may allow for increased cancer surveillance, possible early destruction of a new neoplasm, and other preventive treatment modalities (Kleinsmith, 2006; Mendelsohn et al., 2015).

Symptoms of Cancer

Tumor presence can be found in several ways: (a) the tumor presses on nearby tissues producing pain; (b) the tumor becomes so large that it is seen or felt; (c) the malignancy grows into nearby blood vessels and produces bleeding; and (d) the tumor causes a change in the way some organs work, resulting in symptoms (Smith et al., 2013). For example, persistent dysphagia (trouble swallowing) may indicate a tumor involving the esophagus. The symptoms of pressure, bleeding, a mass, unusual appearance, or interference with function, are reflected in the American Cancer Society's (2017) list of Seven Early Warning Signs (noted by the letters C-A-U-T-I-O-N):

Change in bowel or bladder habits.

A sore that does not heal.

Unusual bleeding or discharge.

Thickening or lump in the breast or elsewhere.

Indigestion or difficulty swallowing.

Obvious change in mole or skin nodule.

Nagging cough or hoarseness.

Diagnosis

Physical Examination

If a person identifies any of the early signs of cancer, an appointment with a physician for cancer screening is warranted. During cancer screening, the physician examines the body, emphasizing the parts of the body most prone to malignancy. Salient regions include the nose and throat, breasts in women, and prostate in men. Pelvic examinations in women, including Pap smears, are essential to aid in detecting cancer of the cervix, uterus, and ovaries. The examination also includes questions about abnormal bodily functions and information about a family history of cancer.

Laboratory Testing

Nonspecific Tests

The physician analyzes blood tests that reveal abnormalities in the blood and indicate the presence of illness. These tests provide clues used to determine whether more definitive testing is needed. Anemia or abnormalities in white blood cells or platelets suggests the need for more specific tests. Likewise, screening of serum chemistries is standard; this laboratory test highlights function of the kidneys, liver, pancreas, and other internal organs. A chest x-ray may be conducted during screening.

Specific Tests

Specific tests are ordered if a physician suspects the presence of a malignancy. Serologic tumor markers are the most crucial blood tests indicating the presence of cancer. Blood serology confirms a physician's diagnosis, and is useful in monitoring a neoplasm following treatment to confirm that a remission has occurred.

Imaging Studies

Imaging studies include the use of x-ray, computerized tomography (CT) scans, magnetic resonance imaging (MRI), positron emissions tomography (PET) scans, radionucleide scans, and selective angiography (Cohen & Markman, 2008). These studies identify the tumor location, tumor size, and involvement of surrounding tissue. An ultrasound can detect cancer and be used to guide tissue biopsies.

Interventional Treatments

At times, physical examinations are insufficient and modern medical instruments are used for direct visualization inside body cavities. Thin, flexible telescopes are introduced into the lungs, bladder, rectum and colon, esophagus and stomach, and the nasopharynix. Instruments which allow for examination of the abdominal cavity are referred to as laparoscopic instruments. A thorascopy involves the introduction of a visualizing scope into the thoracic (Raghavan et al., 2012).

Biopsy

A definitive diagnosis of cancer depends on a microscopic evaluation of a small amount of tissue analyzed by a pathologist. Special histochemical stains or immunologic markers help identify a neoplasm. Biopsies are obtained with special needles used to sample tissue, fluid from body cavities (through aspiration), or from tissue removed during a surgical procedure. Pathologic examination is usually the final step in diagnosis prior to the formulation of a treatment plan. The pathologist's evaluation is crucial in determining the origin of the cancer. Four broad cancer classifications are as follows (American Cancer Society, 2017).

1. Sarcomas – cancer of the bones, muscles, and connective tissue.
2. Carcinomas – cancer of epithelial cells which line the lungs, colon, breasts, and prostate.
3. Leukemias – cancer of the blood and bone marrow.
4. Lymphomas – cancer of the infection-fighting organs.

Staging Classifications

Once cancer is diagnosed, the physician must determine the extent to which it has spread (metastasized). Staging is a method used to describe if the cancer is localized or has spread to other organs. The most modern staging classification includes the TNM system with subscript numbers 0 - 4 (0 = least; 4 = most) by the American Joint Commission on Cancer (American Cancer Society, 2017):

T = Tumor size, location, and adjacent tissue involvement (T_1 through T_4).

N = Regional lymph node involvement with tumor (N_O = no tumor involvement with lymph nodes; $N_1 - N_4$ = increasing degrees of tumor involvement with lymph nodes).

M = Absence (M_0) or degree of spread (metastases) to distant organs ($M_1 - M_4$).

Thus, a tumor staged $T_2N_1M_0$ is less extensive and potentially more curable than one staged $T_1N_1M_1$ (Rossi et al., 2000; Tannock et al., 2013).

An older staging system is still used to a limited extent. In this system, Stage I refers to a state in which the tumor is confined to a single area, usually the tissue of origin. With involvement of adjacent or regional lymph nodes, the cancer is considered to be in Stage II. Stage III involves the local spread of cancer beyond the confines of the tissue or organ initially involved. In Stage IV, cancer has metastasized to distant sites of the body.

Functional Capacity Categories

The patient's functional capacity is categorized using either the Eastern Cooperative Oncology Group (ECOG) or the Karnofsky scale. Because the ECOG is the most commonly used categorization method, the Karnofsy Scale is not described here.

ECOG performance scale:

- O   Normal activity without physical limitations.
- I   Symptomatic, but able to complete daily activities.
- II Assistance needed at times, but can be out of bed more than 50% of the time.
- III Needs skilled care; in bed more than 50% of the time.
- IV In bed 100% of the time.

When determining the modality and extent of treatment possibilities, the physician considers the patient's age, degree of tumor-associated weight loss, nutritional level, and presence of comorbid conditions (i.e., heart disease, lung disease) (Kleinsmith, 2006; Mendelsohn et al., 2015). These factors help in development of an individualized treatment plan.

Treatment

Once a definitive diagnosis is obtained, the physician develops and recommends a treatment plan. Major modalities for cancer treatment are surgery, radiation, chemotherapy, and biologic therapy. These methods are employed alone or in combination, depending on the nature of the malignancy and stage of the tumor. Bone marrow and stem cell transplantation are used in selected circumstances. The treatment modality chosen depends primarily on the stage of the neoplasm, the degree to which the neoplasm impacts the patient's health and ability to function, overall health of the patient, and feasibility for surgical intervention.

Surgery

Surgery is the oldest form and most effective cancer treatment. More cancers are cured with surgical interventions than with any other treatment modalities. Surgery is often curative and is the primary treatment approach for several types of cancer. These include breast, prostate, stomach, colon, head and neck, sarcoma, skin, thyroid, and certain lung cancers. Surgical procedures occur during the diagnosis, treatment, and post-treatment phases of cancer management to (Tannock et al., 2013):

- Diagnose or stage the disease, either with a biopsy or an open operation to remove non essential organ parts.
- Remove the primary tumor which may be curative or used to improve the effectiveness of other treatments by reducing tumor volume. It may also relieve pain and improve quality of life.
- Remove other tumors that escaped prior treatment or are due to recurrent disease.
- Relieve symptoms. Used when the tumor blocks or compresses vital organ structures and functions.
- Reconstruct or rehabilitate. Examples include reconstructive surgery following mastectomy, removal of cancer of the head and neck, and extensive limb surgery.
- Support radiation and chemotherapy. Catheters filled with radiation implants are surgically placed in body cavities or organs to access deep-seated cancers when curative treatment with external beam radiation alone is inadequate. Treatment includes implantation of a venous access port to facilitate delivery of concentrated chemotherapy.

Radiation Therapy

About half of all cancer patients require radiation during treatment. This modality is used alone or in combination with chemotherapy, surgery, or both. The main goal is cure or relief of major symptoms. Radiation therapy employs high-energy x-rays, electron beams, and radioactive isotopes to destroy cancer cells. Malignant cells are destroyed through a process called ionization, which damages the DNA in the nuclei of cells so that cell division is stopped. There are several methods of delivering radiation, including external beam radiation, internal radiation, and hyperthermia.

External Beam Radiation

This treatment involves delivery of electrons, x-rays, or gamma rays. Generally, the equipment emits either low energy (orthovoltage) or high energy (megavoltage) beams. The *gamma knife* is a high energy apparatus capable of brief, focused, and intense treatment to the target area using stereotactic techniques.

Internal Radiation

Internal radiation involves use of interstitial radiation, radiation implants, and brachytherapy. Radioactive seeds are placed temporarily or permanently into the cancer area. Intracavity radiation is used primarily for tumors of the cervix, uterus, and esophagus. Special hollow applicators are implanted within the body (where the applicator usually remains for two to three days), followed by insertion of a radioactive isotope.

Side Effects

Common side effects of radiation therapy include nausea, fatigue, skin inflammation, and temporary lowering of blood counts. Specific side effects characterize different cancer types. If radiation is given to the brain, for example, hair loss occurs. After treatment to the head and neck, the patient may experience dry mouth. Diarrhea is a side effect of rectal and bladder therapy, while frequent urination occurs after prostate radiation. Neoplasms that are treated by radiation with a curative intent include prostate, head and neck, rectum, Hodgkin's lymphoma, and certain lung cancers (Tannock et al., 2013).

Chemotherapy

Chemotherapy is another form of treatment that involves use of medications to interrupt cancer cell growth by attacking specific stages of cell division. These drugs are often administered in combination with other treatments. A major drawback of chemotherapy is the eventual development of drug resistance. Many cancers acquire the ability to overcome or evade the toxic effects of pharmaceuticals.

Delivery routes and methods for administration of chemotherapy include (a) oral administration; (b) intravenous (the most common route); (c) ambulatory infusion pump (employed for long-duration chemotherapy); (d) intra-arterial infusions (used for deep-seated localized tumors, e.g., found in liver cancer); and (e) intracavitary (used for some neoplasms of the chest cavity lining and ovaries). Since chemotherapeutic agents destroy rapid growing abnormal tissues, other rapid growing tissue such as hair follicles, gut mucosae, and bone marrow are often temporarily affected (Tannock et al., 2013). Common effects of chemotherapy include fatigue, nausea, diarrhea, hair loss, sore mouth, loss of sensation or tingling in fingers, diminished appetite or taste, and compromised blood count.

Chemotherapy is a curative treatment for some malignancies and is also used for palliative causes. Adjuvant treatment involves the use of drugs to eradicate microscopic or subclinical areas of cancer that may remain following surgery.

Immunotherapy

Biologic therapies are used to treat cancer by helping the functioning of the immune system. They are also referred to as biologic agents, biological response modifier therapy, and immunotherapy. Biologic therapy works with the immune system helping to fight cancer or control side effects of the disease or its treatments (Raghavan et al., 2012; Tannock et al., 2013).

Immunotherapy is a type of cancer treatment designed to boost the body's natural defenses to fight the cancer. Immunotherapy is a broad category of cancer therapies that use the body's immune system to fight cancer cells. Immunotherapies fall into three general categories: checkpoint inhibitors, which disrupt signals that allow cancer cells to hide from an immune attack; cytokines, protein molecules that help regulate and direct the immune system; and cancer vaccines, which are used to both treat and prevent cancer by targeting the immune system.

This therapy uses substances made by the body or in a laboratory to improve or restore immune system function. Immunotherapy works in these ways:
- Stopping or slowing the growth of cancer cells
- Preventing cancer from spreading to other parts of the body
- Helping the immune system work more effectively at destroying cancer cells

There are several types of immunotherapy, including:
- Monoclonal antibodies
- Non-specific immunotherapies
- Oncolytic virus therapy
- T-cell therapy
- Cancer vaccines

Transplantation

Bone marrow transplants are performed to treat illnesses in which the stem cells are defective or preclude the production of normal cells. Bone marrow contains immature (stem) cells capable of continuously producing blood cells. Bone marrow transplantation is recommended when bone marrow or the immune system is defective. Many cancers are combated with high doses of radiation which irreversibly damages bone marrow, the most sensitive of all tissues to chemotherapy and radiation.

Types of Transplants

Allogenic. Allogenic transplants involve the transfer of marrow from one individual to another. Donors are matched immunologically as close as possible using a process known as human leukocyte antigen typing. The closer the match of a transplant, the less likely of immune incompatibility and graft versus host disease.

Autologous. This technique harvests cryopreserves from the patient's own marrow and stem cells. Marrow or stem cells are then reintroduced after high-dose radiation or chemotherapy has ablated the old marrow. There is no risk of marrow rejection with this technique.

Syngeneic. Syngeneic transplantation is when bone marrow is obtained from a person's identical twin. There is no risk of rejection.

Complications

After receiving a bone marrow transplant, individuals are at high risk for infection (Kleinsmith, 2006; Mendelsohn et al., 2015). The greatest window of susceptibility occurs between marrow ablation and repopulation of the bone marrow spaces by the transplanted marrow. Some people experience excessive bleeding after a transplant, while others develop pneumonia, usually caused by cytomegalovirus infection. Complications associated with marrow grafts occur when new marrow recognizes the host as foreign and begins attacking various tissues including the liver, skin, and intestines. Heart damage is an additional potential obstacle (Rossi et al., 2000).

Targeted Therapy

Targeted therapies are drugs or other substances designed to block the growth and spread of cancer by preventing cancer cells from dividing or by destroying them directly. While standard chemotherapy affects all cells in the body, targeted therapy directs drugs or other specially created substances (e.g., immune system proteins developed in the lab) to attack cancer cells. The goal of targeted therapy is to block the spread of the disease by interfering with genes or proteins involved in tumor growth.

By targeting specific molecules that are responsible for the growth, progression, and spread of cancer, targeted therapy differs from standard chemotherapy, which attacks the disease systemically and, therefore, also damages healthy cells. Because targeted therapy specifically seeks out cancer cells, it is designed to reduce the harm to healthy cells, which may lead to fewer side effects than standard chemotherapy.

Hormone Therapy

Hormone therapy is a form of systemic therapy that works to add, block, or remove hormones from the body to slow or stop the growth of cancer cells. Hormones are known as the body's chemical messengers and are produced in the endocrine glands, which include glands such as the thyroid, pancreas, and ovaries in women and testicles in men. Some hormones encourage the growth of some cancers, such as breast and prostate. But, in some cases they may kill, slow, or stop cancer cells from growing.

Hormone therapy usually involves taking medications that prevent cancer cells from getting the hormones they need to grow. In some cases, a physician may surgically remove the gland responsible for hormone production. Physicians may use hormone therapy in combination with other cancer treatments, such as chemotherapy and radiation therapy.

Negative Effects of Cancer Treatment

Negative effects of cancer treatment vary for each individual; everyone experiences symptoms of varying intensity (El-Deiry, 2003). The most common physical changes and negative effects experienced from cancer treatment include: hair loss, weight loss or gain, appetite loss or increase, fatigue, disfigurement from surgery, difficulty concentrating, nausea and vomiting, diarrhea, pale skin and changes in skin tone, sleep disruption, and sexual dysfunction.

For many people diagnosed with cancer, the most prominent and challenging negative effect is fatigue, an effect of chemotherapy that can be overwhelming and persistent. "Fatigue has an impact on the quality of life and cognitive tasks, which adversely affects the patient and the caregiver" (Jajoo & Batra, 2017, p. 145). Chemotherapy can involve months of strong medications that cause fatigue and weakness as the body tries to negotiate the healing process and regenerate affected tissue. Family, friends, and co-workers of the individual may experience stress and emotional involvement as a result of the individual's concerns and emotional changes, which in turn further impacts the person experiencing these changes (Raghavan et al., 2012).

Psychosocial Implications – Stress and Adjustment Reactions

Diagnosis and treatment of cancer are stressful events, followed by a range of distressing symptoms, including anxiety and depression. While these symptoms are likely to be transient, the experience of cancer is not a single, undifferentiated event. Rather, people with cancer encounter a series of stressful events and challenges over time that poses different demands and difficulties. A person's distress may become heightened at particular times, such as at the time of diagnosis or disease recurrence, before surgery, at the commencement of adjuvant therapy, during the advanced disease stage, or when presenting for medical surveillance. Reactions to a diagnosis of cancer vary widely. These reactions are not necessarily related to the kind and severity of the cancer, but instead to the person's own preconceived perceptions and ability to cope and adjust. Advanced cancer and its treatment create chronic and severe stress situations in which the limits of patients' coping abilities are constantly challenged. This often leads to difficulties in coping with both treatment and its side effects (Civilotti et al., 2015).

Severe Emotional Distress

Stress and adjustment problems include negative feelings lasting for one or more weeks. If such problems are not acknowledged, they may develop into more serious emotional states. Major psychological disorders resulting from emotional distress include major depressive episodes, anxiety disorders, PTSD, and negative emotional, behavioral, and cognitive states that are overwhelming and persistent (lasting more than two weeks). As noted by Jajoo and Batra (2017), "You have cancer is one of the most difficult statements to say as a health care professional and to hear as a patient" (p. 133).

Anxiety

Anxiety in response to a stressful life event is normal; yet, severe anxiety interferes with relationships, social or occupational functioning, and disrupts personal health. Symptoms associated with anxiety include heightened physical arousal, sleep disturbance, impaired concentration and decision-making, agitation, and anger. Severe anxiety problems include panic attacks, pervasive and generalized worrying, treatment phobias, social anxiety, and post-traumatic stress reactions.

Depression and Fatigue

Depression undermines the capacity of the person to cope with illness, and is associated with increased medical symptoms and impairment in social, educational, and vocational functioning (Livneh, 2000). Patients with depression are three times more likely to be non-compliant with medical treatment recommendations. Depression is a major risk factor for potential suicide.

Diagnosis of a major depressive episode is best evaluated by the severity of the depressed mood, loss of interest and pleasure, the degree of feelings of hopelessness, guilt, and worthlessness, and the presence of suicidal thoughts. Recurrent tearfulness is often accompanied by social withdrawal and loss of motivation. Patients with depression may feel they are unable to control their negative feelings; as a result, these feelings begin to dominate one's life. Cancer fatigue is also a common occurrence. It is defined by the National Comprehensive Cancer Network (Jajoo & Batra, 2017) as a "distressing, persistent, subjective sense of physical, emotional, and/or cognitive tiredness or exhaustion related to cancer or cancer treatment that is not proportional to recent activity and interferes with usual functioning" (p. 145).

Suicide

Accurate figures of the incidence of suicide in patients with cancer are difficult to obtain. Studies undertaken in Sweden and Denmark suggested that the incidence of suicide is higher in people with cancer than in the general population, and that suicide is more likely to occur during the first year after diagnosis. Risk factors for suicide include severe depression, a family history of suicide, past history of self-harm, alcohol or other substance abuse issues, poor social support, and a negative outlook for the future. Assessment and exploration of an individual's suicidal thoughts is crucial to early recognition and treatment of psychological distress (Marini, 2018).

Post-Traumatic Stress Disorder (PTSD)

Classifications of mental disorders have been revised to include diagnosis of a potentially life-threatening illness as a sufficient stressor for the precipitation of PTSD. There is limited but increasing research on traumatic symptomatology in patients with cancer. Most of this research has focused on patients with breast cancer (Oeffinger & McCabe, 2006). The stressor criteria for PTSD have recently been modified to include life-threatening illnesses, such as cancer, as precipitating traumatic events (American Cancer Society, 2017; Smith et al., 2013). The use of the PTSD diagnostic spectrum is currently being debated to categorize psychological adjustment in cancer patients (Civilotti et al., 2015).

Sexuality Issues

Sexuality encompasses body image, self-esteem, mood, support, intimacy, and a sense of emotional connection. The role of body image in sexuality is illustrated by the number of patients reporting sexual problems whose cancers do not directly affect sexual organs (Livneh, 2000). This finding suggests the need to address patients' issues of sexuality regardless of the cancer site. Psychological factors such as emotional stress, depression, and grief may diminish interest in sex and create performance anxiety. Pressures of not working or feelings of being a burden influence one's sexuality (Orange, 2014).

As a topic in counseling, sexuality has received little scholarly attention. Professional training in sexual health is equally limited. Although literature demonstrates the integral role sexuality plays in the life of patients, physicians rarely introduce the subject during clinical encounters. Patients who have chronic diseases find that because of the complexity of their illnesses and medical treatments, concerns regarding sexuality are often ignored. Without prompting on the part of the counselor or physician, patients are reluctant to voice sexual concerns (Huddart et al., 2005).

Yet, it is often these patients with chronic illnesses who have difficulties with sexual functioning. By understanding the impact of chronic illness on sexual functioning, health care professionals can more readily screen for and help the person manage sexual dysfunction, thereby enhancing quality of life. "Regardless of whether cancer directly or indirectly affects individuals' ability to engage in sexual intercourse, the need for closeness and demonstration of affection, such as hugging, touching, or kissing, is usually unchanged" (Falvo & Holland, 2018, p. 368).

Emotional Adjustment

The psychosocial aspects of cancer including dependence, stigma, discrimination, and self-concept, can have negative effects equal to the physical components of the disease. To achieve physical, mental, and emotional health, individuals need time to adjust to the diagnosis. The acute stress of illness and treatment can result in distress and dysfunction in all areas of life. Due to the stigmatizing impact of disability in society, people with disabilities tend to develop negative feelings about their own and other types of disabilities and limitations.

Rehabilitation researchers and counselors have long recognized the benefits of identifying and addressing the psychosocial needs of the client who currently has or is recovering from cancer (Falvo & Holland, 2018). Cancer is unpredictable and symptoms can vary daily. To address and adapt to this unpredictability, individuals and healthcare professionals should focus on the following psychosocial issues during the rehabilitation process: (a) feelings of loss of control during treatment; (b) difficulty coping with physical changes; (c) need for social support within the family and community; (d) impact and consequences of role changes and need for internal and external resources to aid in adjustment; (e) interpersonal issues associated with stress; and (f) psychosocial factors related to both unemployment and potential return to work (Livneh, 2000).

Rehabilitation Potential and Employment Issues

Challenges

Work is a vital aspect of self-worth and identity. While many persons who have had cancer view return to work as the apex of achievement, those resuming employment face many challenges including discrimination, avoidance, financial concerns, reduced opportunities for advancement, and changes in physical and emotional capacity.

Many people return to employment during or after experiencing illness and medical treatment. Cancer survivors benefit from making contributions within the workplace and society, as well as financially contributing to their families. An essential component of rehabilitation is support and collaboration from the employer (McDonough, 1992). Unfortunately, cancer survivors face problems when employers have misconceptions about the consequences of cancer, medical treatment, and survival.

Together, survivors of cancer and vocational rehabilitation counselors can dispel the following societal *myths* about the disease: (a) health insurance rates for employee coverage increase when individuals who have cancer are hired; (b) attendance by these workers is substandard and job turnover is high; (c) employees who have cancer are less flexible; and (d) cancer survivors are less able to perform essential job functions, thereby imposing more duties on other employees and entailing added costs to employers (Slivon, Hicken, & Marini, 1994). These myths continue to have a negative impact (Brodwin & Orange, 2014).

To Disclose or Not to Disclose

Whether or not to disclose a disability or functional limitations to a potential employer is a difficult decision. Negative attitudes, stereotypes, and fears about people with cancer form major hurdles for cancer survivors who wish full participation in the work place. Even with federal legislation incorporated within the Americans with Disabilities Act (ADA) of 1990, it is not always clear if the individual should disclose the presence of a disability. The most appropriate response depends on personal choice and functional limitations. If a disability affects a worker's performance on the job, or if accommodation is necessary to perform the duties of the position, disclosure is potentially beneficial. The ADA states that an employer is not entitled to information about a disability unless it directly relates to (a) ability to perform the job, and (b) a request for reasonable accommodation.

Reasonable Accommodation and the Americans with Disabilities Act

The ADA provides protection for individuals with a history of cancer, regardless of whether the cancer is cured, in remission, or being treated. People with limitations due to past or current disabilities are to be given the same opportunities as everyone else. Reasonable accommodation for individuals with disabilities under the statute include: modifications or adjustments to a job or work to participate in the application process, perform essential job functions, and enjoy the rights and privileges available to other employees. An employer is not required to provide accommodation under ADA unless the employee discloses that a disability exists.

Empowerment and Employment

Employment is a significant component of building one's identity and conception of self-worth. Individuals who have been diagnosed with a disease like cancer may place increased emphasis on work because it focuses on capabilities, rather than on illness and limitations. Work thus becomes a haven away from medical intervention, providing routine as well as psychosocial stability. It also provides familiarity, potential for reward, and a source of companionship. Being around people who are supportive is not only a source of comfort, but acts as an alternative to the isolating effects of cancer, and helps the individual surviving cancer maintain a sense of autonomy and control (Simon, 1999).

Counselors facilitate empowerment by encouraging and supporting a person's efforts to take an active role in the rehabilitation process. Determining the client's knowledge and awareness with respect to the disease and prognosis helps clarify directions for inquiry. People who survive cancer and understand their disability and its implications are better able to actively participate in decision making during medical treatment and rehabilitation (Brodwin & Orange, 2014).

Multicultural Perspectives

Americans with disabilities face varying societal beliefs, feelings, and behaviors from society. As noted by McDonough (1992), "Americans in society have a negative attitude about the disabled in general and those in the workplace in particular" (p. 58). Persons who possess attributes that are viewed negatively by the prevailing group in a society tend to be devalued by that society; individuals with disabilities often are evaluated and judged by their disability. Rehabilitation literature emphasizes the maintenance of positive regard and advocacy for people with disabilities and chronic medical conditions.

Counselors must be aware and understand the complexities of the multicultural society in which they live. "Inequality is perhaps America's most egregious, embarrassing, and least desirable trait as an industrial nation" (Marini, 2018, p. 503). If quality counseling services are to be provided to ethnic minority persons with disabilities, rehabilitation counselors and other human service professionals must be sensitive and understanding in interactions with culturally diverse individuals.

To be effective, rehabilitation counselors must be able to address the issues, needs, and beliefs of a culturally diverse population, while maintaining respect and positive attitudes toward cultural and gender differences. Counselors rehabilitate the whole person and dedicate their efforts to increasing the quality of life for all individuals, including survivors of cancer.

Case Study

Steve McPherson is married, 22 years of age, and the father of one child. Although Steve dropped out of high school, he attended adult education and successfully completed his G.E.D. He is a partner in a small but highly successful company involved with telephone and communication systems installation. By trade, he is an electrician and a member of the local electricians' trade union.

The *Dictionary of Occupational Titles* (U.S. Department of Labor, 1991) classifies Mr. McPherson's job as telephone electrician (telephone and telegraph) (D.O.T. # 822.281-018). Steve and his business partner install, test, and repair telephone and communication systems. They update and expand old equipment, install new computerized systems, and wire burglar alarm devices and related equipment. The work involves the use of hand tools and testing devices, an ability to read schematics, and knowledge of electrical and electronic principles. Lifting and carrying on the job involves a maximum of 50 pounds, with repetitive lifting up to 25 pounds.

Mr. McPherson felt in good physical and emotional health when he noticed a non-tender lump on his right scrotum. Two months later, he was diagnosed with embryonic cell carcinoma of testicular origin, well-differentiated, stage $T_2N_0M_0$. Steve underwent a right orchiectomy (testicle removal) and lymph node dissection and received a complete course of chemotherapy. Three months postoperatively, he was assessed as being disease-free with an excellent prognosis. Steve returned to work, continued to have an active family life, and maintained sexual function.

Approximately one year later, a routine cancer follow-up visit (including a chest x-ray) revealed a solitary metastatic right lower lobe pulmonary lesion. His oncologist initiated chemotherapy using a combination of agents and the lesion disappeared. Again, the oncologist believed him disease-free or in remission. After completion of chemotherapy, Steve returned to work and was fully independent.

Two years hence, Mr. McPherson was diagnosed with lung cancer. Within one month of open chest surgery to remove the cancer, Steve developed left-sided brain seizures. After a new diagnosis which identified metastatic testicular disease of the brain, he underwent neurosurgery for removal of the brain tumor. After undergoing the craniotomy procedure, Steve again developed left-sided weakness in the form of significant loss of strength in his left arm and leg. He not only required crutches for ambulation, but had poor balance, and was required to be in bed or in a chair most of the day.

Following radiation therapy, Steve received physical and occupational therapy. He maintained a 25% residual deficit in his left, nondominant upper extremity and could walk for short distances with a cane. Symptoms gradually subsided and he was able to return to work part-time at a functional capacity of sedentary work. His major responsibilities became administrative, including work site analysis, writing bids, and service contract negotiations. Mr. McPherson remained asymptomatic and was able to gradually increase his work effort to full time at the sedentary level of exertion.

Questions

1. Discuss the various forms of cancer treatment.
2. Identify psychosocial implications of cancer.
3. Why was radiation therapy not given to his lung nodules?
4. Was the diagnosis of $T_2N_0M_0$ accurate? Please explain your reasoning.
5. Provide a vocational profile for Mr. McPherson including age, educational level, exertional and skill level of work activity, occupationally significant characteristics, and transferable skills (if any).
6. Was the return to modified work realistic? How were transferable skills used in this return to work?
7. Identify other vocational possibilities using transferable skills or additional training.

References

American Cancer Society. (2017). *Cancer facts and figures*. Atlanta, GA: Author.

Americans with Disabilities Act of 1990 (ADA), PL 101-336, 42 U.S.C. §12101 *et seq.*

Brodwin, M. G., & Orange, L. M. (2014). Attitudes toward disability. In J. D. Andrew & C. W. Faubion (Eds.), *Rehabilitation services: An introduction for the human services professional* (3rd ed., pp. 164-185). Linn Creek, MO: Aspen.

Civilotti, C., Castelli, L., Binaschi, L., Cussino, M., Tesio, V., Di Fini, G., & Torta, R. (2015). Dissociative symptomatology in cancer patients. *Frontiers in Psychology, 6,* Article ID 118.

Cohen, L., & Markman, M. (2008). *Integration oncology*. Totowa, NJ: Humana.

El-Deiry, W. S. (2003). *Tumor suppressor genes*. Totowa, NJ: Humana.

Falvo, D. R., & Holland, B. E. (2018). *Medical and psychosocial aspects of chronic illness and disability* (6th ed.). Burlington, MA: Jones and Bartlett Learning.

Howlader, N., Noone, A. M., Krapcho, M., Miller, D., Bishop, K., Kosary, C. L., . . . Cronin, K. A. (Eds.), (2017), *SEER Cancer Statistics Review, 1975-2014*. Bethesda, MD: National Cancer Institute.

Huddart, R., Norman, A., Moynihan, C., Horwich, A., Parker, C., Nicholls, E., & Dearnaley, D. (2005). Fertility, gonadal, and sexual function in survivors of testicular cancer. *British Journal of Cancer, 93*(2), 5-9.

Jajoo, P., & Batra, R. (2017). The role of rehabilitation in cancer patients. In A. Moroz, S. R. Flanagan, & H. Zaretsky (Eds.), *Medical aspects of disability for the rehabilitation professional* (5th ed., pp. 133-147). New York, NY; Springer.

Kleinsmith, L. J. (2006). *Principles of cancer biology* (2nd ed.). San Francisco, CA: Pearson Benjamin Cummings.

Lichtman, M. A. (2010). Obesity and the risk for a hematological malignancy: Leukemia, lymphoma, or myeloma. *Oncologist, 15*, 1083–1101.

Livneh, H. (2000). Psychosocial adaptation to cancer: The role of coping strategies. *Journal of Rehabilitation, 66*(2), 40-49.

Marini, I. (2018). Social justice, oppression, and disability: Counseling those most in need. In I. Marini & M. A. Stebnicki (Eds.), *The psychological and social impact of illness and disability* (7th ed., pp. 503-519). New York, NY: Springer.

Mendelsohn, J., Howley, P. M., Israel, M. A., Gray, J. W., & Thompson, C. B. (2015). *The molecular basis of cancer* (4th ed.). Atlanta, GA: Elsevier.

McDonough, H. (1992). You and the ADA. *Graduating Engineer*, 56-58.

National Cancer Institute. (2016). *Cancer trends progress report*. U.S. Department of Health and Human Services, National Institutes of Health (NIH Publication No. 05-5498). Retrieved from http://www.cancer.gov

Oeffinger, K. C., & McCabe, M. S. (2006). Models for delivering survivorship care. *Journal of Clinical Oncology, 24*, 5117-5124.

Orange, L. M. (2014). Sexual health and disability. In M. G. Brodwin, F. W. Siu, J. Howard, & E. R. Brodwin (Eds.), *Medical, psychosocial, and vocational aspects of disability* (4th ed., pp. 285-293). Athens, GA: Elliott and Fitzpatrick.

Raghavan, D., Ahluwalia, M. S., Blanke, C. D., Brown, J., Kim, E. S., Reaman, G. .H., & Sekeres, M. A. (Eds.). (2017). *Textbook of uncommon cancer* (5th ed.). Hoboken, NJ: Wiley.

Rossen L. M., & Rossen E. A. (2012). *Obesity 101*. New York, NY: Springer.

Rossi, R. L., Cady, B., & Martin, R. F. (Eds.). (2000). *Multidisciplinary approach to cancer*. Philadelphia, PA: W. B. Saunders.

Siegel, R. L., Miller, K. D, & Jemal, A. (2017). Cancer statistics. *A Cancer Journal for Clinicians, 67*(1), 7-30.

Simon, D. (1999). *Return to wholeness: Embracing body, mind, and spirit in the face of cancer*. New York, NY: Wiley.

Slivon, D., Hicken, N., & Marini, I. (1994). Employer attitudes towards hiring persons with visible disabilities. *Journal of Job Placement, 10*(2), 23-26.

Smith R. A., Brooks D., Cokkinides V., Salsow D., & Brawley, O. W. (2013). Cancer screening in the United States: A review of current American Cancer Society guidelines, current issues in cancer screening, and new guidance on cervical cancer screening and lung cancer screening. *Cancer Journal for Clinicians, 63*, 87-105.

Tannock, I. F., Hill, R. P., Bristow, R., & Harrington, L. (Eds). (2013). *The basic science of oncology* (5th ed.). New York, NY: McGraw-Hill.

U.S. Department of Labor. (1991). *Dictionary of occupational titles* (4th ed., Rev.). Washington, DC: Author.

About the Authors

Leo E. Orr, II, MD, is in private practice in Los Angeles, California. At the Don P. Loker Cancer Center and Good Samaritan Hospital, he is involved in clinical research with primary interests in the development of tumor markers for early detection of cancer and biopharmacology research. Dr. Orr is Co-founder and Co-director of the Transfusion-free Center at Good Samaritan Hospital, and Assistant Clinical Professor at the University of Southern California Medical School.

Leo M. Orange, MS, is Director of Disabled Students Programs and Services at Oxnard College in Oxnard, California, and a part-time adjunct professor in the rehabilitation education program at California State University, Los Angeles. Mr. Orange is a cancer survivor who was successfully treated by his co-author, Dr. Orr, in 1985. He has written many book chapters and articles in rehabilitation and counseling journals addressing reasonable accommodation, multicultural counseling, psychosocial aspects of disabilities, sexual abuse, and sexuality.

Chapter 4

DIABETES AND CHRONIC KIDNEY DISEASE

Martin G. Brodwin, PhD, CRC
Anne Haga, MS

Introduction

Diabetes mellitus (commonly called diabetes) is the leading cause of end-stage renal disease requiring renal dialysis. For this reason, the authors combined the material on diabetes and renal failure. The first part of the chapter discusses diabetes, while the second part describes chronic kidney disease and renal failure.

Diabetes Mellitus

Diabetes is a complex group of metabolic diseases that are characterized by elevated blood glucose (blood sugar) resulting from defects in insulin secretion, insulin action, or both (American Diabetes Association, 2015). Along with abnormal blood glucose, diabetes is associated with a set of physical abnormalities collectively referred to as chronic complications of diabetes. Diabetes is the leading cause of such conditions as blindness, end-stage kidney disease, and lower extremity amputation. It is these complications that are responsible for the mortality and morbidity associated with diabetes. Additionally, diabetes is also a risk factor for high blood pressure (hypertension), stroke, heart disease, and peripheral neuropathy (Benjamin, Griggs, Wing, & Fitz, 2016).

Prevalence

Diabetes, popularly referred to as sugar diabetes, is a health concern of worldwide proportion. An estimated 30.3 million children and adults (9.4% of the United States population) had diabetes in 2015 (Centers for Disease Control and Prevention, 2017a). If current trends continue, one in every three U.S. adults could have diagnosed or undiagnosed diabetes by 2050 (Polansky, 2012). It is estimated that 366 million people worldwide will be diagnosed with diabetes by the year 2030, with the largest number of cases occurring in India, China, and the United States. Prevalence of diabetes is higher among American Indians/Alaska Natives (15.1%), non-Hispanic Blacks (12.7%), and Hispanics (12.1%), than among Asians (8.0%), and non-Hispanic Whites (7.4%) (Centers for Disease Control and Prevention, 2017a).

Risk Factors

The four major risk factors for diabetes development are genetics, age, obesity, and race. A positive family history of the disease increases the potential risk of developing diabetes (American Diabetes Association, 2015, 2016). Aging also increases one's risk, as glucose tolerance and the ability of the body to metabolize sugar deteriorates with age. Obesity induces insulin resistance; therefore, overweight individuals are more likely to develop diabetes.

Costs

As noted by the American Diabetes Association (2015), the total cost of diagnosed diabetes in 2012 was $245 billion, an increase of 41% since 2007. Of this amount, $176 billion was spent for direct medical costs and $69 billion in reduced productivity.

Diagnosis

Blood glucose values are a vital determining factor in the current American Diabetes Association (2016) criteria for diagnosis of diabetes. A fasting blood glucose of 100 to 125 mg/dl (milligrams per deciliter) per deciliter is considered diabetes. The measurement of glycated hemoglobin, a form of hemoglobin that is measured primarily to identify the three-month average plasma glucose concentration, was adopted as an optimal test for diagnosing diabetes by the American Diabetes Association in 2010 and by the World Health Organization in 2011 (Inzucchi, 2012).

Type I, Type II, and Gestational Diabetes

There are two major forms of diabetes. Type I diabetes (T1DM) results from autoimmune destruction of the insulin-producing cells of the pancreas (â-cells). This type is characterized by absolute insulin insufficiency. This was formerly referred to as juvenile-onset diabetes, brittle diabetes, or ketosis-prone diabetes. TIDM accounts for 5% of the cases of diabetes, and most patients manifest severe symptoms resulting from little or no insulin secretion. Even though primarily a disease with onset in childhood or adolescence, it can occur at any age.

Type II diabetes (T2DM) is the most common form of the disease (90-95% of cases of diabetes), and is associated with defects in insulin secretion and/or insulin resistance at the tissue level. T2DM diabetes, formerly referred to as maturity-onset diabetes or non-ketosis prone diabetes, is found especially in overweight individuals as obesity itself causes some degree of insulin resistance. T2DM diabetes can remain undiagnosed over many years because insulin resistance and elevated blood sugar occur gradually. Over time, T2DM patients may require oral agents to lower their elevated blood sugar and ultimately insulin supplementation therapy.

Gestational diabetes (GDM) is when glucose intolerance occurs during pregnancy. This term is applied regardless of whether insulin or only dietary modification is used for treatment. In 2014, GDM complicated up to 9.2% of all pregnancies in the United States. Subsequent to delivery, in most cases blood glucose levels return to normal, although women with GDM have a much higher risk of developing T2DM later in life (American Diabetes Association, 2016).

Complications

Diabetes-related chronic complications are similar in both T1DM and T2DM. Risk factors for complications include smoking, obesity, physical inactivity, high blood pressure, high cholesterol, and high blood glucose (Centers for Disease Control and Prevention, 2017a). Even though the rates of those complications have decreased substantially in the past two decades, the continued increase in the prevalence of diabetes within the U.S. is indicative that these complications will continue to be seen (Gregg et al., 2014). These are discussed below.

Peripheral Neuropathy

About half of patients with diabetes develop abnormal nerve function, especially in the lower extremities. Common symptoms of this complication are painful sensations in the feet such as burning or tingling, known as paresthesia. The individual also may experience a loss of sensation. Because of decreased feeling in the lower extremities, these areas of the body are more susceptible to trauma. Such trauma may lead to foot ulcers, infection, and ultimately lower extremity amputation. The cause of diabetic neuropathy is unknown; theories include decreased blood supply and abnormal chemical metabolism of the involved nerves (Carbone, Tribuna, Wegner, Green, & Miano, 2017; Skyler, 2012).

Peripheral Vascular Insufficiency (PVI)

PVI involves narrowing and/or occlusions of arteries, especially in the lower extremities. When larger blood vessels are involved, the disorder is referred to as macro-vascular disease, while occlusion of the smaller blood vessels at the tissue level is called micro-vascular disease. In PVI, the patient experiences a significant decrease in blood flow, precluding the delivery of nutrients and oxygen beyond the areas of occlusion. PVI is a major contributing factor in development of foot ulcers, infection, gangrene, and subsequent amputation (Unger, 2012).

Combined Peripheral Vascular Insufficiency and Peripheral Neuropathy

In combined peripheral vascular insufficiency and peripheral neuropathy, the lower extremities of the individual with diabetes are affected by both conditions. This potentially lethal coexistence causes the involved lower extremity to be particularly vulnerable to further problems (Carbone et al., 2017). The loss of protective sensations in a limb leads to trauma, resulting in foot ulcers and subsequent infection. PVI slows healing of such lesions and makes therapy a difficult process. Frequently, the end result is amputation. Diabetes is the leading cause of lower extremity amputation.

Diabetic Retinopathy

Diabetic retinopathy is the major cause of new cases of blindness in adults annually (American Diabetes Association, 2015, 2016). In diabetic retinopathy, the small arteries in the retina of the eye develop lesions known as micro-aneurysms which become weak and are subject to bleeding. These lesions often lead to hemorrhaging, which can severely interfere with vision.

Diabetic Nephropathy/Renal Failure

This is the main cause of kidney disease, renal failure, and the need for dialysis. Diabetic nephropathy is a progressive kidney disease, usually occurring about 15 years after the onset of diabetes. It is caused by diabetes-induced abnormalities within the capillaries in the kidney glomeruli. This abnormality interferes with normal kidney function and causes abnormal loss of protein in the urine and buildup of metabolic waste products in the blood. Diabetic nephropathy is usually progressive and may ultimately result in end-stage kidney disease and renal failure. About 44% of new cases of renal disease are linked to diabetes (Rennke & Denker, 2014).

Cardiovascular Disease and Stroke

The heart and blood vessels are subject to many complications in patients with diabetes. Studies have shown the importance of therapies aimed at improving cardiovascular outcomes in individuals with diabetes (Rawshani et al., 2017). The risk of cerebral vascular accidents (stroke) also is much greater. Cardiovascular events, such as myocardial infarction (heart attack) and strokes, are recognized as the leading causes of death among patients with diabetes (Skyler, 2012).

Lower Extremity Amputation

Lower extremity amputation is a frequent occurrence. Approximately 60% of all nontraumatic amputations in this country occur to people who have diabetes (Centers for Disease Control and Prevention, 2017a). Risk of amputation is twice as likely in individuals with diabetes. The frequent co-existence of peripheral neuropathy and peripheral vascular insufficiency increase vulnerability to trauma, as numbness makes it difficult to feel pain. If the skin is broken during a trauma and not treated, severe infection may follow. PVI makes therapy of foot infections difficult to treat. Local spread of infection may occur in the soft tissue. Osteomyelitis, infection in the underlying bone, may be seen. Before serious infection develops, medical treatment is essential to prevent possible amputation (Skyler, 2012).

Therapy of Diabetes

Strategies to control blood glucose, and thus minimize chronic complications, are the mainstay of treatment of diabetes. Simple in theory but difficult in practice, diabetes requires four variables to be carefully balanced. These variables are diet, exercise, medication, and management of blood sugar levels through blood sugar testing (Standards of Medical Care in Diabetes, 2017). The patient with diabetes is committed to continuous involvement in daily management of the condition. Patient education and knowledge is crucial; aside from contact with a physician or other health care practitioner, health care of diabetes is primarily dependent on self-care (Carbone et al., 2017).

Diet

Adherence to a healthy food plan is mandatory for all patients with diabetes and is a cornerstone of therapy. Yet, diet is the single most difficult aspect of therapy to teach, learn, and apply. Dietary regulation is all that is required for some T2DM patients to control their diabetes, especially those who are significantly overweight. The total number of calories and the proportion of carbohydrate, protein, and fat that make up those calories are all crucial factors. Flexibility is a key to maintaining a prescribed diet. Emphasis needs to be on an individualized and flexible healthy diet which the person is more likely to follow and maintain, taking into account cultural factors.

Exercise

Exercise helps lower blood glucose levels and is beneficial in maintaining peripheral arterial circulation. Yet, variability of physical exercise when it is not maintained on a daily basis, contributes to development of labile blood glucose and hypoglycemic (low blood sugar) episodes, especially in patients using insulin. Patients with T2DM, who tend to be older, may be limited in their exercise tolerance due to cardiovascular disease, peripheral vascular problems, or other medical conditions. All patients with diabetes, despite age or physical shape, need to engage in regular physical activity.

Insulin

Insulin is the mainstay of therapy for T1DM and is also used in some cases of T2DM. Insulin is now manufactured by recombinant DNA technology, is identical to human insulin in chemical structure, and has completely replaced animal source insulin. Biochemists have been able to alter the structure of the basic insulin molecule and produce insulin analogs with differing properties, onset, and duration of action. The four types of insulin are rapid acting, short acting, intermediate acting, and long acting. Currently, the majority of insulin-dependent patients require mixtures of different insulin types. Most patients use rapid acting insulin in conjunction with an intermediate or longer acting insulin, administered in multiple daily injections. Continuous subcutaneous insulin infusion is available for use via an insulin pump.

A side effect of using insulin is the risk of insulin reaction, referred to as hypoglycemia. Such reactions can occur when the individual misses a meal, increases physical exercise, or inadvertently takes too much insulin. When appropriately recognized, treatment is relatively easy, and includes immediate ingestion of carbohydrate (sugar) in a readily available form, such as eating candy or fruit. This ingestion will usually raise the blood sugar level and relieve a hypoglycemic situation in a few minutes.

Non-Insulin Therapies

Multiple different classes of medication (in addition to insulin) are currently available to help control blood glucose levels in T2DM patients who are unable to maintain adequate blood glucose control using diet and exercise alone. These drug classes lower blood glucose through a number of different mechanisms including enhancing endogenous insulin release from the pancreas, increasing glucose uptake by muscles, reducing the rate of ingestion of sugars in the gut, causing excretion of glucose in the urine (Holt, Cockram, Flyvbjerg, & Goldstein, 2017).

Blood Sugar Testing

The introduction of small, inexpensive, and accurate blood glucose sensors for home use makes the self-monitoring of blood glucose easily accessible. This procedure is simple and fast; a drop of blood, obtained from a finger or forearm via a small lancing device, is placed on a test strip, which is read by a blood glucose meter in a few seconds. The result is displayed visually. Self-monitoring of blood glucose is an effective self-management technique to maintain blood glucose control.

Many individuals are on insulin pump therapy. This offers flexibility and improved blood glucose control. The insulin pump is a small device, about the size of a cell phone, which the person wears externally. It delivers precise doses of rapid-acting insulin to closely match the body's needs. Small amounts of insulin are delivered continuously for normal body functions. Additional insulin is delivered on demand by pushing a button on the meter before eating or to correct a high blood sugar level.

First made available in 2013, a continuous glucose monitoring system enables patients to check their blood glucose levels at any time, by simply pushing a button on a meter. A sensor is worn on the body which reads the blood glucose level and sends the reading continuously to the meter which is carried like a cell phone. The meter alerts the individual when blood glucose is abnormally high (hyperglycemia) or low (hypoglycemia), and indicates whether blood sugar is trending up, down, or remaining the same. In 2015, the "smart insulin patch" was introduced. This silicone patch, the size of a small coin, will be worn to constantly detect blood glucose levels, rapidly releasing insulin into the bloodstream when levels are high. The patch is still in development and not currently available to the public (Yu et al., 2015). As of 2018, research is continuing to test the smart insulin patch on laboratory mice.

Functional Limitations

A person who maintains good blood glucose control and lacks complications will have few, if any, work restrictions. Persons taking insulin or oral hypoglycemic agents should try to avoid working irregular hours or rotating work shifts. A work schedule that remains consistent helps the person control blood glucose, as fluctuations in exercise cause variations in blood glucose levels. An occupation that requires consistent amounts of physical activity throughout the workday is preferred to one in which physical demands vary greatly. Of course, jobs often require a variety of work duties with differing physical demands. A knowledgeable person with good fundamental diabetes control can adjust medication and diet to compensate for varying physical activity (Brodwin, Parker, & De La Garza, 2010).

People taking insulin need a readily available source of sugar to combat potential insulin reactions. All individuals who are insulin-dependent should carry candy or another source of sugar to alleviate insulin reactions immediately when they occur. Persons who are in good metabolic control manage occasional minor hypoglycemic episodes so that they go unnoticed by others at the workplace.

An individual with diminished vision requires job accommodation. Degree of visual loss and prognosis for further loss are vital factors. The greater the amount of visual loss, the more the counselor needs to evaluate occupations requiring less reliance on vision for primary work functions. Secondary job duties may be modified or eliminated through provision of reasonable accommodation (Brodwin et al., 2010).

Lower extremity complications require job modification involving less ambulating, lifting, carrying, and standing (Unger, 2012). The degree of lower extremity involvement determines the amount of work restrictions required. If a lower extremity amputation has occurred, sedentary work is realistic. The level of amputation and the individual's adaptation are considered before restricting someone to sedentary work. Above-the-knee amputations are rarely necessary for persons with diabetes.

Mild to moderate neuropathy of the lower extremities does not preclude heavier types of work, whereas moderately severe to severe neuropathy may preclude all but sedentary work activity (Falvo & Holland, 2018). The worker, treating physician, and counselor can offer advice on the appropriateness of certain physical activities at the workplace and at home. Additional limitations of function may occur when there are skin problems at an amputation site. Minor skin problems can quickly develop into ulcerations, which impede proper fit of a prosthesis, limit ambulation, and require medical care.

Complications involving the circulatory system significantly limit physical activity. The counselor is guided by the restriction of physical activity noted by the treating physician. Persons with renal failure usually have multiple complications. Depending on the multiplicity of complications and degree of renal failure, work activity may be restricted to part-time or home-based, at best. The counselor needs to evaluate the possibility of working at home for certain individuals.

Emotional factors play a role in control of diabetes from a physiological and psychological perspective; emotional instability complicates treatment. A stressful event may result in a temporary rise in blood glucose levels. If an occupation is stressful and affects good blood glucose control, intervention by a rehabilitation counselor is appropriate. When providing rehabilitation services, the counselor needs to assess the stressful components of work. Some people handle emotional stress well and almost *thrive on stress*. For some, occupational stress is not a significant factor.

The longer diabetes has been present, the greater the potential complications. Complications are at least partially dependent on the degree of control of blood glucose a person has maintained over the long term, how quickly a physician is consulted for treatment, and adherence to medical recommendations. Although some people remain relatively free of complications, rehabilitation professionals see those persons who have complications interfering with work functions.

Rehabilitation Potential

Attitude is important in this and other disabilities. The person with diabetes who has a positive attitude and outlook has much greater potential for successful rehabilitation.

Individuals with diabetes using insulin therapy appropriately and careful adaptation to medical recommendations increase their chances of successful rehabilitation planning. Poor control and failure to adhere to medical advice impedes chances for a successful outcome.

Visual loss impacts the ability to perform many job functions. This is dependent on the amount and type of visual acuity required to conduct various job duties. It may be possible to redefine work responsibilities through the provision of reasonable accommodation. Visual loss affects rehabilitation potential to a variable extent (Brodwin et al., 2010).

Many persons of working age with lower extremity amputation are appropriate candidates for fitting and use of prostheses. The purpose of a prosthesis is to restore mobility and increase independence. If the prosthesis fits well and is used properly and regularly, rehabilitation potential remains positive. In most cases, a person with a bilateral lower extremity amputation requires a wheelchair for mobility.

Rehabilitation potential must be evaluated on an individualized basis. Factors include physical limitations, control of daily blood sugar levels, motivation, attitude, psychosocial functioning, and coping strategies. Ninety-seven percent of 300 physicians surveyed by the Integrated Benefits Institute (2002) stated that "return-to-work is good medicine." The American College of Occupational and Environmental Medicine Guidelines (2006) noted that safe, early return-to-work programs are in patients' best interests and promote recovery. Prolonged absence makes adjustment to the job more challenging and lessens the probability of a successful return to work. Counselors knowledgeable in medical aspects of diabetes, ways to provide accommodation in business and industry, and a caring attitude can do much to assist clients with diabetes maximize work potential and independent functioning.

Chronic Kidney Disease and Renal Failure

Prevalence and Cost

Chronic kidney disease is any condition that reduces kidney function over a period of time; it can lead to end-stage renal (kidney) disease which is incompatible with life. The overall prevalence of chronic kidney disease in the U.S. is about 14% with more than 660,000 Americans having end-stage renal disease requiring dialysis or kidney transplantation to survive. Each year, about 90,000 people die of kidney failure; it is the 8th leading cause of death in this country. Approximately 2% of the population has kidney disease; African Americans and Hispanics are at increased risk. The annual Medicare cost for chronic kidney disease is over $50 billion, making this 20% of all Medicare spending (Centers for Disease Control and Prevention, 2017b).

Kidney Functioning

The role of the kidneys exemplifies the interdependence of various body systems. The urine excretory function of the kidneys plays a major role in maintaining a chemical balance within the body and comprises one of the most effective filtering systems known to humankind (Benjamin et al., 2016). The two kidneys function separately; to sustain life, a person needs only one functioning kidney.

When filtering the blood, the kidneys have a remarkable ability to retain blood cells and certain proteins while passing on unwanted waste products. As the filtrate continues by way of the tubules within the kidneys, the process of reabsorption takes place. In this process, the tubules take back certain substances that have been filtered out and return them to the bloodstream, while allowing other products to be eliminated through the urine. This helps maintain the chemical composition and balance of the blood (McAninch & Lue, 2013).

Kidney Malfunction

When the kidneys begin to fail, they lose their ability to perform the functions of absorption and excretion; this disruption leads to a chemical imbalance with abnormal clinical consequences. When this happens, the body retains water causing generalized edema (swelling). The person gains weight and appears to be bloated. As the severity of edema increases, the volume of fluid within the body increases. As a consequence, there is a rise in blood pressure; this places a strain on the heart as it must pump harder to circulate the blood.

During renal failure, unwanted by-products, such as urea and creatinine (byproducts of metabolism), are retained within the body. When toxic chemicals build up, they cause uremia, which can be life threatening. Failing kidneys not only retain but also excrete abnormal amounts of certain proteins, which are essential in maintaining the delicate fluid balance of the body (Bhusal, Neelakantappa, & Lowenstein, 2017).

Kidney Failure

The term *kidney failure* refers to the malfunctioning of both kidneys to such an extent that kidney function is below the level required to remain healthy and sustain life. The functional progress of chronic renal failure is most often monitored by repeated laboratory measurement of urea and creatinine blood levels over time. The two most common causes of kidney failure are diabetes and high blood pressure (McAninch & Lue, 2013).

Chronic renal failure begins as a slow, progressive decline in kidney function that results in the build-up of metabolic waste products within the body. Anemia and metabolic bone disease are the most common complications in patients with chronic kidney disease. Five stages have been recognized depending on the failing ability of the kidneys to filter the blood. Kidney failure is considered present when the filtration rate is less than 15 cubic centimeters of urine per hour (Lerma, Sparks, & Topf, 2018).

Human kidneys, like many other organs of the body, have a reserve capacity meaning that they are able to perform their normal work load with as little as 10% remaining function. Beyond this point, life is not sustainable. In cases where less than 10% of function remains, one must seek alternative or substitute kidney functioning. Two alternatives are dialysis and kidney transplantation.

Treatment Options

Dialysis

Dialysis serves to support and rehabilitate an increasing number of persons with end-stage irreversible renal failure. According to the United States Renal Data System (2016), about 400,000 people in this country are receiving dialysis. Most of these people are on hemodialysis rather than peritoneal dialysis.

The process of dialysis makes use of the physical properties of a semi-permeable membrane. When two solutions, one more concentrated with small particles or molecules than the other, are separated in a container by a semi-permeable membrane, the concentrated substances move across the membrane until the two solutions become equal in concentration. Microscopic holes in the semi-permeable membrane allow for diffusion of waste products but prevent the passage of proteins or cells, such as red and white blood cells, which would otherwise be lost (Lerma et al., 2018). Dialysis removes excess fluids and impurities from the body and serves as a substitute for functioning kidneys. Two principal forms of dialysis are (a) hemodialysis and (b) peritoneal dialysis.

Hemodialysis

This is a circular process wherein the person's arterial blood is transported outside the body to a dialysis machine where it is cleansed of waste products and returned to the circulatory system. In contrast to the transitory use of hemodialysis during acute kidney failure where the condition is temporary, hemodialysis for chronic renal failure is a lifetime requirement. As a consequence of repeated and life-long needle puncture of the involved blood vessels, thick scar tissue eventually develops which makes the procedure difficult and painful. To avoid this complication, a surgical procedure known as an arteriovenous fistula is performed. It produces a large vein that can be entered safely and easily with large needles for the three times a week procedure (Lerma et al., 2018).

While dialysis is a life-saving procedure, it is not as efficient as normal kidney functioning. The patient with end-stage renal disease undergoes dialysis for three to five hours a day three days per week. In contrast to human kidneys that function 24 hours a day, dialysis results in the gradual build-up of waste products between treatments. Depending on the extent of this accumulation, the person may experience fatigue, loss of appetite, and lapses in concentration.

There are newer regimens of hemodialysis. These include short daily hemodialysis, daily nocturnal hemodialysis, and long overnight hemodialysis three times weekly at home. These new techniques are intended to improve the efficiency of dialysis and thereby increase life expectancy, as 16% of people with end-stage renal disease die annually (United States Renal Data System, 2016).

Peritoneal Dialysis

Peritoneum is the lining of the abdominal cavity. This tissue has the properties of a semi-permeable membrane, allowing the process of diffusion to take place within the abdominal cavity. An incision is made through the anterior abdominal muscle wall; through this opening, a tube (catheter) is inserted into the abdominal space. Sterile dialysate (solution used to clear waste products) is introduced and allowed to remain in the cavity four to six hours, or overnight. During this time, through the process of diffusion, impurities pass through the peritoneum into the dialysate. The dialysate and its collected impurities are then eliminated from the body (Lerma et al., 2018).

Kidney Transplantation

Over 225,000 individuals in the United States have undergone kidney transplant. There are 100,000 on the waiting list; about 16,000 kidney transplants are done each year (Bhusal et al., 2017). When possible, kidney transplantation is the best alternative for end-stage renal disease. A major complication of this procedure, however, is the negative reaction of the immune system to a foreign organ. In this scenario, a new donor kidney is not recognized as the body's own, but rather is rejected as an invader threatening the body. To overcome this reaction to kidney transplantation, the recipient must undergo a medication regimen to suppress the immune system.

A national computerized kidney-harvesting program serves to locate donor kidneys and eligible recipients. Donor kidneys, however, are ideally obtained from living relatives to avoid the recipient's immune system rejection of a new kidney. Potential donors are carefully evaluated for compatibility (El Nahas & Levin, 2009). In recent years, donors who are not compatible with the recipient can participate in a paired kidney exchange program, or "kidney swap," where the donor's kidney can be matched with another recipient in exchange for that recipient's donor kidney.

Cadaveric donor kidneys come from individuals who have recently died as a result of fatal brain trauma. In these cases, the compatibility procedures undergone mirror those performed for transplants from living donors. Surgical procedures for kidney transplantation are usually successful. In these procedures, a donor kidney is implanted in the front groin area of the body and the recipient's non-functioning kidneys are left intact as long as they do not seriously impact the patient's overall health.

To suppress the immune system and avoid donor kidney rejection, medications are prescribed. Careful laboratory monitoring is essential as too low a concentration in the bloodstream exposes the kidney to rejection, and high doses inhibit the body's capability to protect itself against infection. People with transplants remain on immune suppressors throughout their lives (Rennke & Denker, 2014). As there are a great deal more people needing kidneys than those that become available, an individual may have to wait for several years before a donor kidney is obtainable.

In comparison with dialysis, kidney transplantation has advantages that positively affect the person's medical and vocational rehabilitation potential. The person with a kidney transplant does not spend three to five hours a day three times a week on a dialysis machine experiencing, in some cases, wide fluctuations in body chemistry. Furthermore, the individual is not exposed to the hazards of bleeding, clotting, and infection associated with constant use of needles and fluid exchanges.

Emotional Issues

Kidney failure causes severe emotional stress for both the individual undergoing treatment and family members. Uncertainty of the future is a major stressor in all chronic conditions, including end-stage renal failure. Even after a successful kidney transplant uncertainty remains as the new kidney may be rejected by the body's immune system at any time. People on dialysis experience a drastic shift in lifestyle, as the tri-weekly dialysis procedures take precedence over all other life activities. With effective treatment, however, improvements in quality of life occur. If a person receives a transplant, overall health and outlook on life improves substantially as one regains control over life. Some transplant recipients who are not employed return to work. A return to work is more feasible for those who have undergone successful kidney transplantation than when receiving dialysis. Sedentary and light work activities are recommended for both transplant and dialysis patients to facilitate a successful return to the vocational environment. Emotional counseling and support groups aid in the process of coping.

Complicating Factors Affecting Employment

Anemia

End-stage renal disease results in the kidney's failure to produce erythropoietin, resulting in anemia. To help prevent anemia from occurring, physicians prescribe human erythropoietin, available by means of recombinant DNA (Rennke & Denker, 2014).

Infection

For people on hemodialysis, the frequent introduction of needles into blood vessels and the repeated need to control blood leaks lowers resistance to infection. To avoid complications, individuals and paramedical team members must adhere rigidly to appropriate aseptic techniques.

Rigid Treatment Requirements

When undergoing hemodialysis, most people require three to five hours of treatment each day three days a week. As a result, individuals must plan their home and work activities around treatment times, giving dialysis precedence over work and other life activities (El Nahas & Levin, 2009). Many dialysis centers operate 24 hours a day, allowing recipients of dialysis to work regular daytime hours.

Rehabilitation Potential

Many persons who have left their jobs because of declining kidney function may be able to return to work once they are on a consistent treatment regimen, such as dialysis or kidney transplant. Dialysis and kidney transplant recipients should avoid jobs involving physically strenuous work activities. Maintenance of optimal health is essential for persons on dialysis since they are predisposed to anemia, have lowered resistance to infection, and experience fatigue.

To help maintain a life-long program of well being, including a well-balanced diet and an appropriate exercise program, hospitals employ a team of professionals consisting of the treating physician, dietician, social worker, psychologist, and vocational rehabilitation counselor to encourage, counsel, and assist the person (Lerma et al., 2018). Ideally, the counselor coordinates the services of all participants to bring about a successful return to independence, daily activities, and employment.

Despite passage of the Americans with Disabilities Act (ADA) (1990), job placement remains challenging for those who have undergone kidney transplantation or are currently undergoing dialysis. Employers have the perception that their overall medical insurance costs will increase, and the individual may have too many days off work due to illness. The rehabilitation counselor can help the person overcome obstacles like these by being persistent in following up with employers and medical insurance companies to assure the medical and employment stability of the client and, if needed, to explain the client's rights under the ADA (Brodwin et al., 2010).

Case Study

Mr. Jack Lin is 63 years old and immigrated to the United States from Taiwan in his early 30's. While in the United States, he received an Associate of Science degree in computer science and was employed as a computer programmer at a software development company close to his home. Previously, Mr. Lin worked as an electronics warehouse manager, computer hardware salesperson, and office coordinator. Jack enjoys gardening and thrives on having a regular daily schedule. He lives with his wife; they have three adult children who live on their own.

In his early 40's, Jack was diagnosed with Type II diabetes. At age 60, he developed kidney disease. As a result, he had to limit his work hours to part-time and is restricted to a maximum of light and sedentary work. In end-stage renal failure for the past year, he is on a list to receive a transplant. Mr. Lin requires dialysis three times a week for approximately four hours each time, which he receives early in the mornings. For the year he has been on dialysis, he has needed to take a leave from work requiring his wife to obtain part-time employment.

Recently, Jack sought vocational rehabilitation services because he would like to contribute to the family income. He has been feeling down because traditionally in his culture the man of the household supports the family; he is uncomfortable with the situation requiring his wife to work. In addition, receiving dialysis and not knowing whether he will be able to obtain a kidney transplant is emotionally challenging.

Questions

1. Does Mr. Lim have transferable skills he might use for alternative work? Describe possible skills and occupations using these skills.
2. Identify factors significant in assessing rehabilitation potential of this client.
3. Discuss Type I and II diabetes and complications that can occur. Relate this to the case study. What may have caused this client to have renal failure?
4. Describe the two types of dialysis and kidney transplantation. Identify advantages of a transplant over dialysis.
5. Considering that Mr. Lin is on dialysis and may be receiving a kidney transplant within the year, what kinds of rehabilitation services will you provide at the present time and in the future? Are there any considerations needed for his diabetes?
6. What concerns related to dialysis and kidney transplant need to be considered in vocational planning?
7. Describe issues of reasonable accommodation for clients on dialysis.
8. As his rehabilitation counselor, how would you handle Mr. Lin's current emotional state?

References

American College of Occupational and Environmental Medicine Guidelines. (2006). Preventing needless work disability by helping people stay employed. *Journal of Occupational and Environmental Medicine, 48*(9), 972-987.

American Diabetes Association. (2015). *Fast facts – Data and statistics about diabetes*. Retrieved from http://www.diabetes.org.

American Diabetes Association. (2016). *Diabetes basics*. Retrieved from http://www.diabetes.org

Americans with Disabilities Act. (1990). 42 U.S.C. § 12101 *et seq.*

Benjamin, I., Griggs, R. C., Wing, E. J., & Fitz, J. G. (2016). *Andreoli and Carpenter's Cecil essentials of medicine* (9th ed.). Philadelphia, PA: Elsevier Saunders.

Bhusal, S., Neelakantappa, K., & Lowenstein, J. (2017). Chronic kidney disease. In A. Moroz, A. S. Flanagan, & H. H. Zaretsky (Eds.), *Medical aspects of disability for the rehabilitation professional* (5th ed., pp. 507-532). New York, NY: Springer.

Brodwin, M. G., Parker, R. M., & DeLaGarza, D. (2010). Disability and reasonable accommodation. In E. M. Szymanski & R. M. Parker (Eds.), *Work and disability: Contexts, issues, and strategies for enhancing employment outcomes for people with disabilities* (3rd ed., pp. 281-323). Austin, TX: Pro-ed.

Carbone, A, M., Tribuna, J., Wegner, E., Green, S., & Miano, A. (2017). Diabetes mellitus. In A. Moroz, A. S. Flanagan, & H. H. Zaretsky (Eds.), *Medical aspects of disability for the rehabilitation professional* (5th ed., pp. 191-212). New York, NY: Springer.

Centers for Disease Control and Prevention. (2017a). *National diabetes statistics report: Estimates of diabetes and its burden in the United States.* Atlanta, GA: U.S. Department of Health and Human Services.

Centers for Disease Control and Prevention. (2017b). *National chronic kidney disease.* Atlanta, GA: U.S. Department of Health and Human Services.

El Nahas, M. E., & Levin, A. (Eds.). (2009). *Chronic kidney disease: A practical guide to understanding and management.* New York, NY: Oxford University.

Falvo, D. R., & Holland, B. E. (2018). *Medical and psychosocial aspects of chronic illness and disability* (6th ed.). Burlington, MA: Jones and Bartlett Learning.

Gregg, E. W., Li, Y., Wang, J., Burrows, N. R., Ali, M. K., Rolka, D., . . . Geiss, L. (2014). Changes in diabetes-related complications in the United States, 1990-2010. *New England Journal of Medicine 370*(16), 1514-1523.

Holt, R. I. G., Cockram, C., Flyvbjerg, A., & Goldstein, B. J. (2017). *Textbook of diabetes* (5th ed.). Hoboken, NJ: Wiley Blackwell.

Integrated Benefits Institute. (2002). *Physicians managing disability: Identifying opportunities and constraints.* Retrieved from http://www.ibiweb.org

Inzucchi, S. E. (2012). Diagnosis of diabetes. *New England Journal of Medicine, 367*(6), 542-550.

Lerma, E. V., Sparks, M., & Topf, J. (2018). *Nephrology secrets* (4th ed.). Philadelphia, PA: Elsevier.

McAninch, J. W., & Lue, T. F. (Eds.). (2013). *Smith and Tanagho's general urology* (18th ed.). New York, NY: Lange Medical Books/McGraw-Hill.

Polansky, K. S. (2012). The past 200 years of diabetes. *New England Journal of Medicine, 367*(14), 1332-1340.

Rawshani, A., Rawshani, A., Franzen, S. Eliasson, B., Svensson, A-M, Miftaraj, M., . . . Gudbjornsdottir, S. (2017). Mortality and cardiovascular disease in Type 1 and Type 2 diabetes. *New England Journal of Medicine, 376*(15), 1407-1418.

Rennke, H. G., & Denker, B. M. (2014). *Renal pathophysiology: The essentials* (4th ed.). Philadelphia, PA: Lippincott Williams & Wilkins.

Skyler, J. S. (Ed.). (2012). *Atlas of diabetes* (4th ed.). New York, NY: Springer.

Standards of Medical Care in Diabetes – 2017. (2017). *Diabetes Care 40*(Suppl 1), 54-55.

Unger, J. (Ed.). (2012). *Diabetes management in primary care* (2nd ed.). Philadelphia, PA: Lippincott Williams and Wilkins.

United States Renal Data System. (2016). *2016 USRDS annual report: Epidemiology of kidney disease in the United States.* Bethesda, MD: Author.

Yu, J., Zhang, Y., Ye, Y., DeSanto, R., Sun, W., Ranson, D., . . . Gu, Z. (2015). Microneedle-array patches loaded with hypoxia-sensitive vesicles provide fast glucose-responsive insulin delivery. *Proceedings of the National Academy of Sciences of the United States of America, 112*(27), 8260-8265.

About the Authors

Martin G. Brodwin, PhD, CRC, is Professor Emeritus in the Rehabilitation Education Programs at California State University, Los Angeles. He is a vocational expert for the Office of Hearings Operations, Social Security Administration, providing testimony on disability-related issues. As a rehabilitation and vocational consultant, he provides assessment for long-term disability, case management, and reasonable accommodation. Dr. Brodwin has published over 115 refereed journal articles, book chapters, and books on the subjects of counseling, disability, rehabilitation, and medical aspects of chronic illness and disability.

Anne Haga, MS, is Adjunct Professor within the Rehabilitation Services Program at California State University, Los Angeles. Previously, she served as Director of Counseling Services at Southwestern Law School in Los Angeles. In this position, she assisted law students with disabilities in obtaining special accommodations, as well as advising the law school on the Americans with Disabilities Act and reasonable accommodations. Ms. Haga has been a presenter at the annual conferences of the Association of Higher Education and the California Association for Postsecondary Education and Disability.

Chapter 5

CARDIOVASCULAR DISEASE

Harvey L. Alpern, MD
Rose M. Gaw, MS

Introduction

Heart disease is the leading cause of death in the United States in both men and women. About 610,000 people die of heart disease every year (Centers for Disease Control and Prevention [CDC], 2017). This accounts for one in every four deaths. Heart conditions are the third leading cause of incapacitation and often affect physical, emotional, and vocational functioning.

The purpose of this chapter is to help rehabilitation counselors comprehend medical evaluations that identify cardiovascular impairments so they can use this understanding to help individuals restore independent functionality in the workplace. This chapter describes the New York Heart Association's (NYHA) classification system of heart disease, the different kinds of heart disease, diagnosis and treatment, therapeutic and diagnostic procedures, disability rating, functional limitations, and rehabilitation potential for individuals with cardiovascular impairment. The authors describe the causes, symptoms, pathology, and evaluation of physical capabilities of persons with cardiovascular disease to give counselors a better understanding of each type of condition. The chapter concludes with a case study.

Increasingly, the direction of medical research and treatment is on determining the principle course of heart disease in the employed population. Modern research is directed toward preventing and decreasing the progression of this disease, with the goal of increasing longevity and improving quality of life and productivity. There is also an emphasis on less invasive procedures. The rehabilitation counselor's challenge is to assist this growing population to remain vocationally competitive and productive. The following seven major types of heart conditions are discussed within this chapter: (1) congenital heart disease in adult life; (2) valvular heart disease; (3) mitral valve prolapse; (4) cardiomyopathy; (5) hypertension and hypertensive heart disease; (6) coronary artery disease; and (7) congestive heart failure. Counselors encounter these major types of cardiovascular conditions.

In the first five categories, heart strain or progressive heart muscle failure may eventually develop into congestive heart failure. In all groups, employability is dependent on a timely diagnosis, the potential for correcting or improving the disease process, anatomical abnormalities, and provision of rehabilitation services. In coronary artery disease, which represents the largest category of heart conditions, there is progressive inability of the heart muscle to function properly, primarily as a result of decreased blood flow to the heart muscle due to occluded coronary arteries (Mayo Clinic, 2017). After a given quantity of muscle mass has been damaged or destroyed, pump failure or congestive heart failure, can result in the inability of the heart to pump sufficient blood to the rest of the body.

Functional and Therapeutic Classifications of Heart Disease

The following discussion refers to the functional capacity of the heart and is adapted from criteria of the NYHA. Physicians and researchers accept this protocol as a standard of classification for cardiac conditions. The two classifications are evaluated to derive a cardiac status determination (Criteria Committee of the New York Heart Association, 1994).

Functional Classification – NYHA

Functional Classification is an estimate of a person's symptoms. There are four classes, I through IV (see Figure 1). Class I represents a person with no symptoms, while Class IV is an individual who develops discomfort with any physical activity and has symptoms even at rest. Classes II and III describe symptoms between these extremes, and are individuals most likely to be seen by rehabilitation counselors.

Therapeutic Classification – NYHA

Therapeutic Classification reflects the amount of physical activity recommended by the treating cardiologist considering all factors. There are five classes from Class A representing those individuals with no physical activity restriction to those in Class E whose physical activity is almost totally restricted. Counselors will most likely see persons in Classes B through D.

The NYHA classification is dependent on the subjective reporting of the patient. Impairment ratings should preferably be done using objective guidelines, such as those described in the section Disability Rating of this chapter.

FIGURE 1
Classifications of Patients with Heart Disease

FUNCTIONAL CLASSES

Class I	Patients with heart disease who have no symptoms of any kind. Ordinary physical activity does not cause fatigue, palpitation, dyspnea, or angina pain.
Class II	Patients who are comfortable at rest but have symptoms with ordinary physical activity.
Class III	Patients who are comfortable at rest but have symptoms with less than ordinary effort.
Class IV	Patients who have symptoms at rest.

THERAPEUTIC CLASSES

Class A	Patients whose physical activity need not be restricted.
Class B	Patients whose ordinary activity need not be restricted, but who should be advised against severe activity.
Class C	Patients whose ordinary activity should be restricted.
Class D	Patients whose ordinary activity should be markedly restricted.
Class E	Patients who should be at complete rest in bed or a chair.

Source: Criteria Committee of the New York Heart Association. (1994). *The diseases of the heart and blood vessels: Nomenclature and criteria for diagnosis* (9th ed.). New York, NY: Little, Brown.

Congenital Heart Disease in Adult Life

Congenital heart disease (CHD) is caused by various malformations of the heart, which develop during gestation and become apparent in infancy or childhood. Many congenital heart problems require surgical or manipulative procedures early in life to improve cardiovascular function. Not all untreated individuals have residual problems; however, those who live into adulthood develop serious problems that require intervention to improve or correct abnormalities (Armstrong, 2016). Due to current progress in medical advances for the pediatric population, there are now an estimated 750,000 adults with congenital heart diseases in just the United States. The number of children with a type of congenital heart disease reaching adulthood in this country is projected to increase by 9,000 per year due to an 85% recovery rate in pediatric patients (Kasuski, 2010).

For the first time in history, the number of adults with congenital heart disease is comparable to the number of children with the same defects. There are a few categories of adults living with congenital heart disease that rehabilitation counselors should be aware of to properly assess each case: (a) people who are living with CHD without prior surgical intervention, (b) those enduring successful surgical or nonsurgical treatments, and (c) others dealing with surgical or nonsurgical ongoing or specialized medical care. A few common congenital heart defects seen in adults today include atrial septal defect, patent ductus arteriosus, aortic stenosis, and pulmonary stenosis (American Heart Association, 2017).

Atrial Septal Defect

Septal defects are shunts, holes, or lesions in the heart. Atrial Septal Defect (ASD) is one of the most common congenital heart diseases seen in adults, due to children born with the defect showing subtle or no symptoms until after age 30. Individuals with asymptomatic ASD may only exhibit minimal exercise tolerance. Small shunts close on their own, but medium to large ones are less likely to do so. Survival rates in adults with ASD are high. By the fifth and sixth decades of life, complications developing from ASD fully manifest and need medical treatment (Adler, 2017).

In a normal heart, blood flows from right to left. The right side of the heart pumps out to the lungs for oxygenation. The left side receives the oxygenated blood back from the lungs and pumps it into the body. ASD is a shunt in the wall, the septum that separates the two sides of the heart. When there is a shunt in the septum wall, the oxygen-rich blood from the left side leaks into the right side, and gets pumped back into the lungs where it had just been, causing the right side of the heart and lungs to work harder (see Figure 2) (National Heart, Lung and Blood Institute [NHLBI], 2011).

Medical therapy is not typically required due to the lack of symptoms in atrial septal defect. The most common treatment for the defect is primary surgical closure using autologous pericardium (a graft taken from another part of the patient's body to close the hole).

FIGURE 2
Normal Heart Versus Heart with Atrial Septal Defect

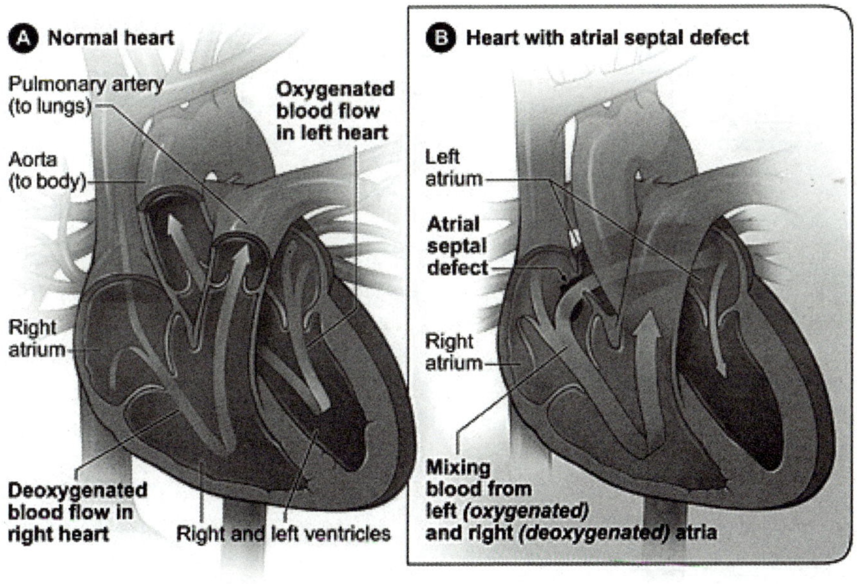

Source: National Heart, Lung, and Blood Institute. (2011). *Types of holes in the heart*. Retrieved from https://www.nhlbi.nih.gov/health/health-topics/topics/holes/types

Patent Ductus Arteriosus

Patent Ductus Arteriosus (PDA) is another common birth defect seen in adults. If untreated, it can cause various heart problems that drastically decrease an individual's lifespan. Ranging from 33% mortality rate at age 40 to 66% at age 60, the most common cause of death in individuals with PDA is congestive heart failure (Kim, 2016).

Ductus arteriosus is a blood vessel that connects the aorta and pulmonary artery to the unborn baby. The aorta is the artery that pumps fresh blood back to the body; the pulmonary artery pumps old blood out to the lungs for oxygenation. While the baby is still in the mother's womb, the ductus arteriosus vessel connects the aorta and pulmonary arteries during the developmental stages. During the first 15 to 18 hours of birth, ductus arteriosus begins to constrict, completely closing by two to three weeks, and the newborn's pulmonary arteries open up to allow blood flow to the lungs for oxygenation (NHLBI, 2011). PDA occurs when the ductus arteriosus does not close on its own and stays open leaking fresh blood from the aorta into the pulmonary arteries through the ductus arteriosus, reducing blood flow back to the rest of the body (see Figure 3) (Kim, 2016).

Valvular Heart Disease

Rheumatic Fever

Valvular heart disease is usually a result of childhood rheumatic fever. It is an inflammatory condition that damages the heart valves. Impairment of the heart valves can lead to dysfunction in the ventricles, heart failure, and possible death. Inadequate closure of the mitral valve occurs so that blood flows backward into

FIGURE 3
Normal Heart Versus Heart with Atrial Septal Defect

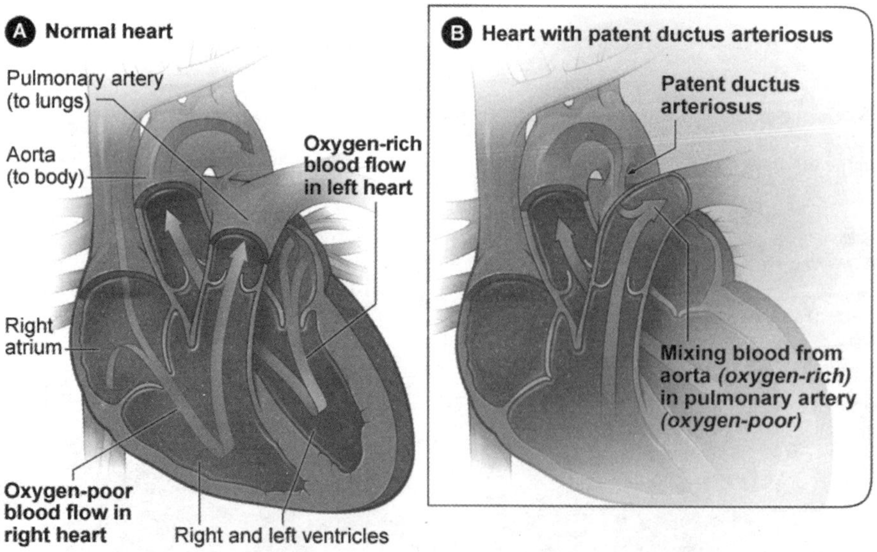

Source: National Heart, Lung, and Blood Institute. (2011). *Types of holes in the heart*. Retrieved from https://www.nhlbi.nih.gov/health/health-topics/topics/holes/types

the atria during ventricular contraction (Carabello, 2012). If the damage affects the performance of the heart, it is rheumatic heart disease. Improved understanding of prevention and antibiotic treatment has reduced not only the incidence and recurrence rate of rheumatic fever, but severity and frequency.

Rheumatic valvular disease, however, is still a major source of concern. One chief complication of this disease is that depending on the severity of the original acute process, a person may become symptomatic during the middle teens through the mid-30s. Acute rheumatic fever leads to acute cardiomyopathy (abnormal changes in the heart muscle). The disease causes damage to the heart valves, including the mitral valve, aortic valve, and tricuspid valve. The mitral and aortic valves may become stenotic (i.e., constricted or narrowed), insufficient (i.e., the valve leafs do not come together, thus allowing leakage), or both. Although not subject to stenosis, the tricuspid valve can become insufficient. The greater the number of valves affected, the sooner the person develops heart failure, and the more severe the failure. Severe damage of a valve requires surgical intervention with placement of an artificial valve to correct the damaged one (Carabello, 2012).

Benefiting from emerging technology of prosthetic heart valve replacement, a growing number of people with rheumatic valvular disease hold jobs that do not require heavy lifting or exposure to trauma. Individuals with valve replacement require medication to prevent abnormal blood clotting. People on this and similar medications bruise easily and should not work in areas where physical trauma could occur. Today, there are an increasing variety of valve prostheses available.

Pulmonary Stenosis

Pulmonary Stenosis (PS) is the second most common valvular disease seen in adults (Kasuski, 2010). This defect, although in most cases is mild and not requiring treatment, can have a higher likelihood of coexisting with other common congenital heart abnormalities (American Heart Association, 2017). In PS, the valves which control the blood flow from the heart to the lungs do not develop properly causing obstructed blood flow within the heart. Patients in the fourth or fifth decade of life are more likely to exhibit life-threatening symptoms, especially with severe PS (Armstrong, 2016).

Aortic Stenosis

Aortic stenosis (AS) is one of the most serious valvular diseases in adults. These individuals have a mortality rate of 25% at the first year and 50% at year two as it has a latent period of 10-20 years before gradually developing symptoms (Ren, 2017). AS involves a progressive narrowing or stiffening of the valves in the heart. The main artery, the aorta, carries blood from the heart to the rest of the body; aorta valves regulate this blood flow. When those valves do not open fully, it reduces the amount blood flow to the rest of the body (Chen, Zieve, & Ogilvie, 2016).

Surgical solutions may be needed in severe cases for replacement of the defective valve. Symptoms, when they develop, include heart murmurs/clicks, low blood pressure, chest discomfort or pain, bloody coughs, breathing problems, weakness, fainting, dizziness with activity, and fatigue (Chen et al., 2016). AS is detected with the use of an electrocardiography, chest radiography, echocardiography, or cardiac catheterization. Treatments differ according to severity of the disease.

Mitral Valve Prolapse

The most common cause of mitral valve prolapse (mitral stenosis) is childhood rheumatic fever. This involves a narrowing of the heart valve, or an incompetent valve which does not close completely. The exact cause of the condition is not known. Possible causes include an undetected congenital defect, viral infection, or most likely, a degeneration of the heart valve. The most common symptoms experienced are anxiety, fatigue, palpitations, and chest pain. MVP may be accompanied by a degeneration of the valve musculature. In some cases, this degeneration affects the tricuspid valve. When both mitral and tricuspid valves are diseased, the person develops valvular insufficiency (Carabello, 2012). This condition, if left untreated, may progress to heart failure.

Cardiomyopathy

Medical Implications

This group of diseases, also known as myocardiopathies (cardiac muscle weakness), involves inflammation, resulting in weakness and an inability of the heart muscle to function effectively. It may be secondary to infectious processes, usually viral or chemical toxic exposure, as well as part of the disease process of diabetes mellitus and alcohol abuse (American Heart Association, 2017). Virus cardiomyopathies are more frequently found in younger people. The virus causes inflammation and weakness of the heart muscle and sometimes interferes with normal nerve conduction throughout the heart.

People with cardiomyopathies may require short-term medication, or in more serious cases, a pacemaker for cardiac irregularities and life-long medication. In most cases, after the acute stage has passed, the person can continue in customary work requirements, with the exception of heavy lifting and arduous labor. A physician may recommend surgical correction of associated valve abnormalities (Whiteson & Sweeney, 2017).

Diabetes Mellitus

Individuals with diabetes are two to four times more likely to have circulatory problems, leading to heart disease and stroke (American Heart Association, 2017). When diabetes is not optimally controlled, it may lead to complications resulting in poor function of one or more organs or systems. Over time, high blood sugar levels can lead to increased plaque buildup in the arteries. Although an infrequent occurrence, poorly controlled diabetes may cause cardiac muscle disease and renal disease, resulting in progressive, congestive heart failure. The probability and severity of diabetic cardiomyopathy is diminished with proper medical care. Cardiomyopathy usually restricts a person to light or sedentary work.

Alcoholic Cardiomyopathy

Toxic effects of alcohol and poor nutrition bring about alcoholic cardiomyopathy. Proper medical care for the person with alcoholism and complete abstinence from alcohol (and tobacco) reduces the severity of the myocarditis (inflammation of the myocardium). General improvement in health and overall functioning are the goals of alcohol rehabilitation programs, requiring total abstinence from alcohol and illicit drugs, good nutrition, and treatment of complications. Every effort is made to provide and maintain an ongoing therapeutic prevention program, such as Alcoholics Anonymous (AA).

Hypertension and Hypertensive Heart Disease

Hypertension (high blood pressure) occurs when the pressure of the blood against the walls of the vessels exceeds normal limits for a sustained period of time (Whiteson & Sweeney, 2017). About 50 million people in this country have hypertension, many with no recognizable symptoms. An additional 45 million people have pre-hypertension and are more susceptible to develop hypertension. Although hypertension in and of itself is not incapacitating, if prolonged and untreated, it becomes a major risk for heart attack, heart failure, stroke, peripheral vascular disease, and kidney failure. The major goal of treatment is to lower a person's blood pressure, which will reduce possible complications. Once the pressure is lowered, it is essential that the patient do everything possible to maintain blood pressure control (Bashore, Granger, Hronitzky, & Patel, 2013).

During the normal heart cycle, action of the heart can be compared to a hydraulic pump. When the heart muscle contracts, it propels blood out of the heart chambers. This forceful action is called systole. Pressure is high during this expulsive phase. The phase immediately following, when the heart muscle is at rest, is called the diastole. Blood pressure, as expressed as a fraction, is written with the systolic pressure on top and diastolic pressure on the bottom (e.g., 120/80 = systolic/diastolic). Diastolic pressure thus represents blood pressure when the heart is at rest; elevated diastolic blood pressure is a serious condition. Systolic pressure greater than 140 mm Hg (mercury), and diastolic pressure greater than 90 mm Hg is considered hypertension.

Causes of Hypertension

Ninety-five percent of hypertension cases are of unknown causes. The remaining five percent are related to kidney disease, endocrine abnormalities, increased cardiac output, and vascular abnormalities (Zipes, Libby, Bonow, Mann, & Tomaselli, 2018). Heredity is a factor in hypertension; therefore, there is a genetic predisposition to heart disease.

Detection of Hypertension

Symptoms of hypertension may surface suddenly without warning. Commonly encountered nonspecific complaints such as fatigue, headache, nosebleed, changes in vision, or muscle weakness are typical. Complications include coronary artery disease, renal failure, stroke, and peripheral vascular disease. Since most individuals do not have symptoms, hypertension has been called the silent killer.

When hypertension is suspected, physical examination includes assessment for any abnormalities of the kidneys, heart, and cerebrovascular system. Additionally, the physician uses chest x-ray, electrocardiogram, and echocardiogram to assess cardiac status (Zipes et al., 2018).

Complications

Hypertension may cause significant renal damage possibly leading to kidney failure; this damage contributes to further perpetuation of hypertensive problems. Frequently associated with hypertension, peripheral vascular disease is a major cause of disability. Unlike hypertension, this complication causes pain within the lower extremities brought on by exercise, due to diminished blood flow in the legs. Physical limitations experienced with hypertension primarily result from coronary artery disease, heart failure, stroke, and renal failure. Each of these conditions has specific guidelines as to physical disability and resulting levels of activity (Alpern, 1996). Through consultation with the treating physician to identify functional limitations, the counselor is able to assist the individual through the vocational rehabilitation process.

Levels of disability for individuals with hypertension are related to occurrence and severity of complications and presence of end-organ damage (Whiteson & Sweeney, 2017). Persons responsive to treatment may be able to continue their customary work activities. Individuals with hypertension who do not have major systemic complications but are unable to perform their current jobs may need vocational retraining for support and future success. Despite a diagnosis of hypertension, most people continue leading productive lives without serious limitations in work activity, recreation, and lifestyle.

Coronary Artery Disease

Coronary artery disease, also known as coronary heart disease, is a broad term describing many heart-related conditions, all involving narrowed coronary arteries affecting blood flow to the heart. In this country, more than 12 million people have this condition (CDC, 2017). Symptoms usually occur only when the disease is advanced, making it a particularly dangerous condition. Individuals reporting symptoms generally have one or more of the following: discomfort; dull ache or sharp chest pain, especially with strenuous physical activities; discomfort in the shoulder, throat, or left arm; and shortness of breath (Bashore et al., 2013). Extreme narrowing of the coronary arteries (arteriosclerosis) can result in heart attack or heart failure.

Coronary artery disease is the leading cause of death in the United States; approximately 715,000 Americans have heart attacks each year. More than 385,000 of these people die. Of those who experience heart attacks each year, 525,000 are experiencing one for the first time; 190,000 occur in individuals who have already had at least one before. Overall, the disease costs $109 billion annually, including total payments for health care services, medications, and lost productivity (CDC, 2017). The various medical conditions associated with coronary artery disease can lead to major problems and disability (Bashore et al., 2013).

Etiology

Risk factors for coronary artery disease include high cholesterol levels, hypertension, diabetes, emotional stress, a poor diet (rich in fats), obesity, physical inactivity (e.g., lack of exercise), excessive alcohol use, and cigarette smoking. Of the risk factors mentioned, the most significant are high cholesterol, blood pressure elevation, and cigarette smoking, especially when these factors are combined. High cholesterol leads to accumulation of plaque in the coronary vessels, restricting blood flow. Nicotine from cigarette smoking diminishes blood flow by constricting vessel walls during smoking.

Manifestations of Coronary Artery Disease

Coronary artery disease leads to myocardial anoxia (insufficient oxygen to the heart muscle), due to diminished or absent blood flow. When this occurs, the person experiences chest pain (angina pectoris) and pressure that radiates from the left shoulder and arm, or sometimes from the heart to the abdomen. Other symptoms include a feeling of high anxiety or impending doom, sweating, pale (cyanotic) face, labored breathing, and rapid pulse (Bashore et al., 2013). This disease affects the myocardium and nerve conducting pathways, causing abnormal nerve conduction. Irregular heartbeats (arrhythmias) or ventricular fibrillation (rapid, ineffective pulsations of the heart) occur. During this time, the heart muscle receives insufficient oxygen; if this condition persists, the affected myocardium dies (myocardial infarction). Persistent arrhythmias result in an inefficient pumping action of the heart.

Four major clinical signs of coronary artery disease are angina pectoris, myocardial infarction, arrhythmias, and congestive heart failure. Angina pectoris is precipitated by physical exertion and relieved by rest or cessation of the specific physical activity. Discomfort lasts from a few seconds to several minutes, but can be a forerunner of a myocardial infarction. Shortness of breath, a feeling of the need to sit up in bed, and leg edema (swelling) are experienced during or as a precursor to congestive heart failure.

Myocardial Infarction

A heart attack occurs when a coronary artery becomes partially or completely occluded by plaque. This clot can develop suddenly at a narrow space in the artery. When the plaque ruptures, it cuts off the heart's oxygen supply, permanently damaging heart tissue. Warning signs and symptoms usually begin with chest discomfort, similar to angina pectoris. This pain is more severe and longer lasting than in the case of angina. Associated symptoms include upper body pain or discomfort in the arms, back, neck, jaw, or upper stomach; shortness of breath; nausea; and lightheadedness or cold sweats (CDC, 2017). In some cases, there are no warning signs and sudden death may occur.

Diagnosis and Treatment

Ideally, an individual with symptoms of myocardial infarction is immediately hospitalized. Paramedics initiate treatment by administering pain relievers and oxygen. In the emergency room, a physician may administer a clot-dissolving medication called a thrombolytic agent to improve blood flow in the affected artery. Alternatively, the patient may be referred to a catheterization laboratory for immediate evaluation and possible angioplasty and stent placement (American Heart Association, 2017).

After stabilization of the acute event and observation of the patient in a critical care hospital unit, symptoms and medical findings dictate ongoing treatment, which may involve a medical regimen and possible surgery. Medications are prescribed to control angina and arrhythmias. Nitroglycerine, for example, is a short-acting serum that dilates the coronary arteries to relieve angina (McMurray & Pfeffer, 2012).

For most individuals, the physician recommends a rehabilitation program involving gradual increases in physical activity. This program begins in the hospital and continues on an outpatient basis, often in a cardiac rehabilitation program. The program provides information on coronary artery disease including dietary and weight management, proper exercise programs, information on medications, assistance with stress reduction, and cessation of smoking. Cardiac rehabilitation involves a comprehensive and multidisciplinary program individualized for each person, with the goal of improving and maximizing both physical and psychosocial functioning.

If damage to the heart is severe, resulting in end-stage heart disease, the cardiologist may recommend a heart transplant. For a transplant, the patient must be in sufficiently adequate health to withstand this extensive medical procedure.

Diagnosis

Echocardiogram (EKG, ECG)

An echocardiogram is a non-invasive procedure using high frequency ultrasound to show a functioning heart and its moving parts. An EKG displays the muscle activity measured from various directions. This display indicates overall rhythm of the heart and weaknesses in different parts of the heart muscle to measure and diagnose abnormal heart rhythms. EKG identifies damaged heart muscle.

Holter Monitor

A Holter monitor is a small, battery-powered device carried like a cell phone which records a continuous electrocardiogram for up to 24 hours. The individual is asked to keep a written record of the time of any special symptoms and physical exertion. Results are compared with the corresponding time on the EKG to denote abnormalities.

Cardiac Radionuclide Imaging

Cardiac radionuclide imaging involves a procedure wherein a liquid radioactive substance (tracer) with an affinity to heart muscle is injected into a vein. A gamma camera scans the heart to detect that portion of heart muscle that has poor circulation and does not take up tracer material.

Treatment

Cardiac Catheterization

In cardiac catheterization, a thin catheter tube is inserted into an artery or vein and guided into the heart. Different types of catheters are designed to instill medications or dyes that appear on x-ray, allowing physicians to view abnormalities in heart structure, function, and circulation.

Surgical Procedures

Several surgical procedures correct the narrowing or blockage of coronary arteries associated with cardiovascular problems. Coronary angioplasty involves the surgical insertion of a balloon-type device (catheter) into a narrowed artery to flatten the occlusion and allow blood to flow more freely. Laser angioplasty uses lasers to clear plaque; catheters can be used to install stents, tube-shaped metal devices that remain in place at the problem site to hold the artery open (Mayo Clinic, 2017).

Evaluation of coronary artery disease includes radioactive tracers or coronary arteriogram. Using a catheter (introduced in another body area and guided into the heart), the cardiologist injects the substance by means of the catheter directly into coronary vessels. The cardiologist is able to visualize blood flow restrictions, called stenosis, brought about by an accumulation of cholesterol plaques within coronary vessel walls. This condition is treatable through angioplasty or coronary bypass surgery. While angioplasty is effective when the person has only one or two narrowed arteries, it is not practical when more arteries are obstructed. When this occurs or when angioplasty proves unsuccessful, the physician may recommend coronary artery bypass surgery. Instead of repairing the affected region, this procedure reroutes blood around that particular region (Bashore et al., 2013).

Congestive Heart Failure

Congestive heart failure is the end stage of deteriorated heart function. An impaired heart must work harder to deliver a sufficient supply of blood to the body. Eventually, it becomes unable to pump the amount of blood needed by the various body systems. The heart chambers gradually enlarge (cardiac hypertrophy); the muscle walls become thicker. Symptoms include dyspnea (shortness of breath), edema in the lower extremities, fatigue, weakness, and abdominal discomfort. This disorder occurs either suddenly (due to a heart attack) or over a period of years. If the underlying problem is treated, however, the condition can improve.

Cardiac Transplantation

When a person's heart is damaged to the point of end-stage heart disease, a heart transplant may be the only option. Over the years, the success of cardiac transplantation surgery has gradually improved (Jessup, 2012). To become eligible for a heart transplant, a patient needs to be in adequate general health, be able to withstand the surgical procedure, the prolonged recovery time, and follow a strict medical regimen. In addition to the operation, even being placed on a transplant list is emotionally stressful (McMurray & Pfeffer, 2012). The individual does not know when the surgery will occur or even if it will, and must respond immediately when a donor heart is ready. The person's health may deteriorate while on the waiting list for a donor heart. Similar to the patient, the family experiences emotional stress, anxiety, and possible depression.

When successful surgery is accomplished, the person is given immunosuppressants to prevent the body from rejecting the donor heart. Long-term exercise training after transplantation in a cardiac rehabilitation program increases exercise capacity. Three to six months is necessary to become sufficiently functional for work. However, emotional factors often impede a successful return to work (Jessup, 2012). Negative employer attitudes toward people with chronic, medical conditions make it more difficult to secure gainful employment.

Functional Limitations

Functional limitations of people with cardiovascular disorders depend on the severity of the condition and whether medical treatment alleviates the symptoms. Individuals with mild congestive heart failure controlled by medication may be able to continue their usual work with minimal modifications. Workers performing physically arduous jobs need changes in employment. People with moderate heart failure who are limited to light or sedentary work may seek rehabilitation counseling services. Those with severe conditions have extremely limited capacities for physical exertion and employment; some require cardiac transplantation, for which there is a lengthy waiting list.

Disability Rating

The treating physician determines the extent of disability resulting from coronary artery disease after carefully evaluating data obtained from a medical history, objective testing documentation, and response to treatment. Historical information is correlated with the NYHA classifications (see Figure 1) to determine symptomatic as well as therapeutic classification of the person's status, and in assessing ability to perform various activities (Alpern, 1996).

The NYHA classification system is one of the most helpful clinical determinants in establishing levels of cardiac disability. Physicians utilize these guidelines to classify patients on both functional and therapeutic levels. Factors relating to disability are compared with objective evaluations, which are then correlated with the results of exercise testing on a treadmill. The cardiologist performing an exercise test estimates the energy expenditure of physical activity in terms of oxygen consumption required to accomplish certain tasks.

The basic metabolic unit for this estimation is the MET (metabolic equivalent). Studies have established MET requirements for various activities, both occupational and recreational. Workload is expressed in

METs, which corresponds to the amount of oxygen required to perform a given activity. For example, a patient performs a Bruce Protocol exercise level of nine minutes (on a treadmill). This individual could be expected to perform up to ten METs activity, indicating ability to perform mid-heavy to heavy activity by the NYHA, Functional Class 1 and Therapeutic Class A. The Bruce and Naughton treadmill tests are used to determine functional classification of disabilities. Performance test levels have been correlated with levels of physical activity related to a variety of job activities (Alpern, 1996; Zipes et al., 2018).

Information obtained from the patient's history and objective data from stress treadmill testing and other laboratory and physical findings are used to establish a classification of impairment and determine an optimal level of physical activity (Alpern, 1996). Goals of treatment are to decrease existing impairment and improve functional capacity to help the person establish a meaningful and productive life.

Physical Limitations

Most individuals, depending on the extent of cardiovascular disease, can perform at least light work. Some can engage in medium level work activity. Heavy lifting and carrying are usually discouraged, while moderate activities, such as standing and walking, are beneficial. The physician recommends physical exercise as part of the recovery process. Exercise testing reveals the exertion limit in METs so that a decision may be made as to the possibility of employment and type of work. Undue emotional stress is contraindicated.

Chest pain (angina pectoris) occurs in some people with cardiac disease. This involves severe pain and a feeling of constriction around the heart area, including radiation of pain down the left arm. Angina is caused by an insufficient supply of blood to a portion of the heart and may occur with physical overexertion. Pain is usually transitory and relieved by oral medication (nitroglycerine), which dilates the arteries. After angina pectoris, the person may resume work activity, usually in a few minutes, but is cautioned to avoid the activity that precipitated the event (Alaeddini & Shirani, 2017). A rehabilitation counselor needs to provide vocational guidance in accordance with the person's physical capacity.

Some people experience arrhythmias and heart palpitations (throbbing sensations) in the chest area. These sensations may occur because of excessive physical activity. In all cases, the counselor needs to inquire about client compliance with prescribed medications. The cardiovascular system is affected by environmental extremes of temperature. Poor air quality must be avoided by many with cardiovascular disease. A counselor's awareness of this and other factors in the work environment helps promote successful rehabilitation.

Psychosocial Limitations

The experience of hospitalization and separation from home and family produces emotional stress. Early intervention can decrease this stress by helping the person cope in a more realistic manner. Fear, anxiety, and depression are common emotions felt by persons with any chronic condition, including cardiovascular disease (Livneh & Antonak, 2018). The impact these emotions produce on one's life can range from minimal to devastating. Emotional support and counseling helps individuals cope with anxiety and depression and adjust to daily life with a disability. Denial, a normal psychological defense, is often part of this adjustment to life with a disability. If denial causes a person to ignore symptoms, it may be dysfunctional and lead to selection of an inappropriate vocational rehabilitation plan.

Today, treatment emphasizes early ambulation and involvement in a cardiac rehabilitation program as preventive measures to help avoid immobilizing reactions (McMurray & Pfeffer, 2012). With modern advances in technology and medical treatment along with rehabilitation intervention, one minimizes symptoms of psychological distress. As a result of modern treatment, most people regain strength and functional capacity to return to being productive and gainfully employed.

Rehabilitation Potential

Multidisciplinary cardiac rehabilitation programs assist persons with cardiovascular problems in increasing performance during work, recreation, and leisure (Whiteson & Sweeney, 2017). Improved physical functioning and enhanced mental and social capacities aid in facilitating an active and productive life. A comprehensive and multidisciplinary treatment approach allows persons with cardiovascular problems to achieve increased awareness of their underlying conditions, and participate in exercise as a preventive and therapeutic measure. With cardiac rehabilitation programs, individuals are able to increase strength, endurance, and improve overall functioning and psychological outlook. By educating the patient in the various manifestations of cardiovascular disease, the counselor can improve rehabilitation potential. Many persons with cardiac problems do not understand their condition, its severity, or their functional limitations. Some refuse to regularly and consistently take prescribed medications. Denial may play a part in this, along with the misconception that a lack of symptoms means medications are no longer necessary.

Rehabilitation potential for persons with Functional Class I and Therapeutic Class A (see Figure 1) is excellent; these individuals have only slight restrictions in overall activities. Most do not require rehabilitation counseling services. Counselors see persons with Functional Classes II and III and Therapeutic Classes B through D, who need to modify their work activity to become reemployed. The amount of work adjustment necessary depends on extent of cardiovascular disease and the physical and emotional components of the person's work activity. Individuals with Functional Class IV and Therapeutic Class E display such severe symptoms that their potential for rehabilitation is minimal.

Factors that negatively influence return to work include: (a) duration of temporary disability, (b) perception of an inability to work, and (c) availability of disability income benefits. Rehabilitation potential is best for an individual who completes a cardiac rehabilitation program and feels positive about the results of therapy and the future. Development of appropriate educational and vocational goals consistent with physical and emotional restrictions is essential. Vocational rehabilitation ranges from returning to a former job with the same employer and minimal modifications, to establishing entirely new vocational objectives.

Investigation of job modification through reasonable accommodation helps both employee and employer maintain a productive work situation. One must consider both physical and emotional stress factors present in the employment environment; emotional components are more difficult to define. Each person perceives emotional stress differently. Negative attitudes of employers complicate and interfere with a successful return to work.

A final dimension in rehabilitation of persons with cardiovascular disease is employer discrimination (Brodwin, Parker, & DeLaGarza, 2010). Rehabilitation counselors can help educate employers and dispel negative stereotypes they may possess toward persons with chronic disease. As stated by Yuker (1992), "employers value employees who have job skills, social skills, and dependability" (p. 17). Employers who have had past experiences with employees who have disabilities usually develop positive attitudes toward them. As more people with disabilities return to or enter the labor force and prove to be motivated and productive employees, one can expect further positive attitude change. Counselors play a crucial role in initiating and continuing this process.

Case Study

Detective Jesus Rodriguez is a 60-year-old police detective who is married with two adult children, one starting college. He currently works for a police department and is approaching retirement in five years with full benefits. For him to reach retirement, he has to reduce the amount of stress he encounters in his daily life by exercising alcohol abstinence since he is a recovering alcoholic. Detective Rodriguez was recently diagnosed with alcoholic cardiomyopathy and hypertension. Over the duration of work, he has lost a few of his close friends as well as encountered many stressful life and death situations on the job. The way he has dealt with the psychological ramifications of these situations has been with excessive consumption of alcohol.

Detective Rodriguez was referred to a cardiologist by his family practitioner due to complaints about shortness of breath regardless of whether he was standing, sitting, or laying down, in combination with increased heart rate, dizziness, chest discomfort, and fatigue. The severity of the symptoms affected his work performance. Although he is a recovering alcoholic, he has not completely stopped his alcohol consumption. Due to his health issues, his superior at work no longer allows him to go into the field because of liability issues. Jesus would like to get back into the field and finish his career as a detective.

The current outlook of Detective Rodriguez's condition requires reconditioning of his destructive behavioral patterns for him to return and finish his career in the field. He is not able do the basic daily tasks without being short of breath or having dizzy spells. The first step is to address his desire for alcohol consumption. Seeing a psychologist or counselor on a regular basis could help him work through years of possible suppressed emotional stress encountered in the field. This could assist in his efforts to abstain from alcohol, in turn, reducing the symptoms that are preventing him from doing his job.

In conjunction with receiving psychological help, meditation, journaling, and quiet time for introspection, developing better eating habits and reducing sodium intake will help manage and control the hypertension. Adding physical activity or regular exercise to his routine, once his symptoms improve, would benefit his health condition, and better prepare him for a return to work in the field.

Questions

1. Provide a vocational profile for this client.
2. Detective Rodriguez' wife does not want him to go back in the field and this disagreement is causing tension at home. How can you assist with the situation?
3. Are there functional limitations preventing this detective from working in the field? Please discuss.
4. Specify some transferable skills Detective Rodriguez has to help him acquire another occupation in the same or a different field.
5. What can motivate Mr. Rodriguez to exercise alcohol abstinence?
6. Is going back into the field realistic in Mr. Rodriguez's condition, even if he is able to manage his alcoholic cardiomyopathy and hypertension?

References

Adler, D. H. (2017). *Atrial septal defect.* Retrieved from http://emedicine.medscape.com/article/162914-overview

Alaeddini, J., & Shirani, J. (2017). *Angina pectoris.* Retrieved from https://emedicine.medscape.com/article/150215-overview#showall

Alpern, H. L. (1996). Cardiac disability. In S. L. Demeter, G. B. J. Anderson, & G. M. Smith (Eds.), *Disability evaluation.* St. Louis, MO: Mosby.

American Heart Association. (2017). Retrieved from http://www.heart.org/HEARTORG/Conditions/Heart Attack/TreatmentofaHeartAttack/Treatment-of-a-Heart-Attack_UCM_002042_Article.jsp#.WezQ72hSw2w

Armstrong, G. P. (Ed.). (2016). *Overview of cardiac valve disorders.* Retrieved from http://www.merckmanuals.com/professional/cardiovascular-disorders/valvular-disorders/overview-of-cardiac-valvular-disorders

Bashore, T. M., Granger, C. B., Hronitzky, P., & Patel, M. R. (2013). Heart disease. In S. J. Papadakis, S. J. McPhee, & M. W. Rabow (Eds.), *Current medical diagnosis and treatment.* New York, NY: McGraw Hill-Lange.

Brodwin, M. G., Parker, R. M., & DeLaGarza, D. (2010). Disability and reasonable accommodation. In E. M. Szymanski & R. M. Parker (Eds.), *Work and disability: Contexts, issues, and strategies for enhancing employment for people with disabilities* (3rd ed., pp. 281-323). Austin, TX: Pro-ed.

Carabello, B. A. (2012). Valvular heart disease. In L. Goldman & A. I. Schafer (Eds.), *Goldman's Cecil medicine* (24th ed., pp. 334-337). Philadelphia, PA: Elsevier Saunders.

Centers for Disease Control and Prevention (CDC). (2017). *Heart disease facts.* Retrieved from https://www.cdc.gov/heartdisease/facts.htm

Chen, M. A., Zieve, D., & Ogilvie, I. (2016). *Aortic stenosis.* Retrieved from https;//medlineplus.gov/ency/article/000178.htm

Criteria Committee of the New York Heart Association. (1994). *The diseases of the heart and blood vessels: Nomenclature and criteria for diagnosis* (9th ed.). Boston, MA: Little, Brown.

Jessup, M. (2012). Cardiac transplantation. In L. Goldman & A. I. Schafer (Eds.), *Goldman's Cecil medicine* (24th ed., pp. 482-486). Philadelphia, PA: Elsevier Saunders.

Kim, L. K. (2016). *Patent ductus arteriosus (PDA) medication*. Retrieved from http://emedicine.medscape.com/article/891096-medication#3

Kasuski, R. A. (2010). *Congenital heart disease in the adult*. Retrieved from http://www.clevelandclinicmeded.com/medicalpubs/diseasemanagement/cardiology/congenital-heart-dease-in-the-adult/#bib2

Livneh, H., & Antonak, R. F. (2018). Psychosocial adaptation to chronic illness and disability: A primer for counselors. In I. Marini & M. A. Stebnicki (Eds.), *The psychological and social impact of illness and disability* (7th ed., pp. 77-90). New York, NY: Springer.

Mayo Clinic. (2017). *Coronary heart disease*. Retrieved from https://www.mayoclinic.org/diseases-conditions/coronary-artery-disease/symptoms-causes/syc-20350613

McMurray, J. J. V., & Pfeffer, M. A. (2012). Heart failure: Management and prognosis. In L. Goldman & A. I. Schafer (Eds.), *Goldman's Cecil medicine* (24th ed., pp. 303-318). Philadelphia, PA: Elsevier Saunders.

National Heart, Lung, and Blood Institute. (2011). *Types of holes in the heart*. Retrieved from https://www.nhlbi.nih.gov/health/health-topics/topics/holes/types

Ren, X. M. (2017). *Aortic stenosis treatment and management*. Retrieved from http://emedicine.medscape.com/article/150638-overview

Whiteson, J. H., & Sweeney, G. (2017). Cardiovascular disorders. In A. Moroz, S. R. Flanagan, H., & Zaretsky (Eds.), *Medical aspects of disability for the rehabilitation professional* (5th ed., pp. 149-173). New York, NY: Springer.

Yuker, H. E. (1992). Attitudes toward persons with disabilities: Conclusions from the data. *Rehabilitation Psychology News, 19*(2), 17-18.

Zipes, D. P., Libby, P., Bonow, R. O., Mann, D. L., & Tomaselli, G. F. (Eds.). (2018). *Braunwald's heart disease: A textbook of cardiovascular medicine* (11th ed.). Philadelphia, PA: Elsevier Saunders.

About the Authors

Harvey L. Alpern, MD, is in private practice with an emphasis on cardiac disability. Formerly, he was Clinical Chief of Cardiac Rehabilitation at Cedars-Sinai Medical Center in Los Angeles, California, and currently is Assistant Clinical Professor of Medicine at the University of California, Los Angeles. Dr. Alpern is a Fellow of the American College of Cardiology and Past-President of American College of Disability Evaluating Physicians. For many years, Dr. Alpern has been serving as a medical expert for the Office of Hearings Operations, Social Security Administration.

Rose M. Gaw, MS, has a Master of Science degree in Rehabilitation Counseling from California State University, Los Angeles (CSULA). Currently, she is a college academic and career counselor at Rio Hondo College in Whittier, California, and an Adjunct Professor at CSULA. Her specialties are chronic illness and disability, medical aspects of disabling conditions, and higher education counseling. Through Ms. Gaw's research, she hopes to educate future rehabilitation service providers and counselors on the needs of individuals with cardiovascular disease and other conditions.

Chapter 6

CHRONIC OBSTRUCTIVE PULMONARY DISEASE

Hassan Bencheqroun, MD, FCCP

Introduction

An obstructive lung disease is defined as a limitation of air flow into the lungs. Lung damage due to various factors can make patients take longer to exhale. This impairment is called obstruction or airflow limitation. The two major obstructive lung diseases encountered are asthma and chronic obstructive pulmonary disease (COPD). This chapter discusses COPD.

COPD is defined as a preventable and treatable disease state, in which the airflow limitation is not fully reversed when treated with inhaled medicines called bronchodilators (in contrast to asthma which is fully reversible). In addition, COPD is usually progressive, and associated with an abnormal inflammatory response of the lungs to noxious particles or gases, primarily caused by cigarette smoking. In the past decade, research has established that although COPD affects the lungs, it also produces significant physical consequences on the entire body due to the overall inflammation it generates (Decramer, Janssens, & Mirevitlles, 2012; Fabbri, Luppi, Beghé, & Rabe, 2008).

Incidence and Prevalence

Chronic lower respiratory disease, primarily COPD, is the third leading cause of death in the United States, with mortality rates still rising according to the National Center for Health Statistics (2016). It is also the fifth-leading cause of death worldwide and estimated to become the third-leading cause of death worldwide by 2030 (Jagana, Bartter, & Joshi, 2015). Although COPD has been traditionally associated with men, the numbers of men and women who died from COPD-related causes leveled around the year 2000, and even showed some decline in the age-adjusted COPD-related death rate primarily due to declines in the prevalence of smoking in the United States.

Globally, about 24% of people over the age of 40 with a history of smoking have airflow limitations, compared to 12% for individuals who have never smoked (Lamprecht et al., 2011). Prevalence of COPD rises with age. In addition, up to 60-85% of people with COPD (mostly mild/moderate severity) appear to be undiagnosed (Hoyert & Xu, 2012). Besides tobacco smoking, secondhand smoke, air pollution, biomass exposure, and work exposure to fumes and dust can cause COPD in susceptible individuals.

Pathology

At the lung tissue level, traditionally COPD is characterized both by destruction of the lung tissue with loss of its elasticity (called emphysema), and by infiltration of the walls of the small airways by inflammatory cells (causing chronic bronchitis). These two broad COPD types are usually presented as distinct entities, when in reality they coexist and overlap to varying degrees in virtually everyone with COPD.

Not everyone who smokes develops COPD. Several pathophysiological and pathobiological processes must interact for the disease to develop. These include a complex interplay of genetic determinants, lung growth, and environmental stimuli. The disease is further aggravated by exacerbations, particularly in patients with severe or untreated disease.

It is almost impossible nowadays to talk about lung disease without mentioning the Lung Microbiome. Historically, the lungs have been considered sterile, despite their continuity with the upper airways, proximity to the gastrointestinal tract, and continuous exposure to the environment. That is largely due to the fact that the studies used to identify any living organisms in the lungs relied on laboratory cultures that have a number of limitations. Novel techniques to identify microorganisms in the lungs demonstrate that most of the surfaces of the respiratory tract are colonized by bacteria that rarely cause disease in healthy individuals. This ecosystem is referred to as Lung Microbiome.

In contrast, in COPD patients with exacerbations, studies traditionally also struggled to isolate specific microorganisms in a predictable pattern using conventional culture methods, even as it has always been known that exacerbations treated with antibiotics have a better response than those not treated. Using novel methods such as real-time PCR (polymerase chain reaction) has been successful in demonstrating that infections are present in the majority of COPD exacerbation with near half being viral infections (Shimizu et al. 2015). Due to the nature of the disease and its direct link to cigarette smoking, it often coexists with other disease states, which are likewise related to smoking.

Symptoms

A patient with COPD often first experiences shortness of breath (dyspnea). This occurs primarily during physical exertion ranging from vigorous exercise, chores around the house, laundry, cleaning, pushing a cart at the supermarket, to more mundane activities such as taking a shower, making a bed, putting on shoes, or walking up stairs. In the advanced stages of COPD, dyspnea can become so distressing that it occurs during rest and is constantly present. Other symptoms of COPD include a persistent cough, mucus production, chest tightness, and weight loss.

Symptoms often become temporarily more pronounced and severe. These are *exacerbations*. They are usually preceded by a common cold, acute bronchitis, or both. Exacerbations are not random, but clustered around each other, often making the progression of the disease worse. During exacerbations, the patient may appear to be breathing faster and shallower, or through pursed lips. There is active use of the muscles in the neck to help with breathing, and longer exhalation time due to the airflow limitation (Calverly et al., 2017). These events contribute to the progression of the disease, and make patients feel worse.

In extreme circumstances, people with advanced COPD may develop respiratory failure. The body becomes unable to meet the demands for oxygen, and the person requires assistance of a ventilator until the precipitating factor is treated. Advanced COPD may overburden the heart, which is working against rising pressure in the chest to channel blood flow. This causes a complication of advanced COPD called *cor pulmonale*, a form of heart failure exerted mainly on the right side of the heart, with swelling of the ankles and shortness of breath.

Diagnosis

Obstruction or airflow limitation is diagnosed using *Pulmonary Function Testing*, a test which measures forced airflow exhaled in one second (called Forced Expiratory Volume or FEV1) and the total forced exhaled volume (called Forced Vital Capacity or FVC). A diagnosis of COPD occurs if the ratio of FEV1/FVC is less than 70%. The patient is then given a bronchodilator medicine (one that opens the airways if they are constricted) to inhale before a second test is given. If the FEV1 improves by 12% or more, it suggests the obstruction is reversible (i.e., asthma). If it shows less than 12% improvement, then the obstruction is only partially or not at all reversible (i.e., COPD). Once the diagnosis of COPD is made, the physician has to determine the severity of the disease. The Global Initiative for Chronic Obstructive Lung

Disease (GOLD) classification is the main method used to describe the different severities of COPD (Rabe et al., 2007).

GOLD is a collaboration between the National Institutes of Health (NIH) and the World Health Organization (WHO) for the advancement of knowledge, prevention, and treatment of COPD worldwide. In the GOLD classification, the worse a person's airflow limitation is, the lower their FEV1. As COPD progresses, FEV1 tends to decline.

Based on the value of FEV1, GOLD staging uses mild, moderate, severe, and very severe categories to classify COPD (Rabe et al., 2007). In addition, the severity of symptoms including dyspnea as well as the number of exacerbations classifies the patient into a GOLD category (GOLD, 2017). This has a direct impact on the choice of medications and management.

Associated Diseases

The most common comorbidities of COPD are ischemic heart disease, diabetes, sarcopenia (muscle wasting), cachexia (loss of weight), osteoporosis (decrease in bone mass), depression, and lung cancer (Cavaillès et al., 2013). These comorbidities influence the course of COPD, increasing the risk for admission to a hospital or causing death. Comorbidities of COPD are responsible for over 50% of expenditures for the disease (Fabbri et al., 2008).

The BODE Index was developed to include more meaningful clinical data with the FEV1 and enhance the predictability of prognosis and mortality. The BODE Index stands for: the body-mass index, airflow obstruction (FEV1), dyspnea, and exercise capacity index (Cote & Celli, 2005).

Management of COPD

Inhalers constitute the mainstay of treatment. They encompass bronchodilator and anti-inflammatory medications. Research has found several molecules called receptors embedded in the smooth muscle of the airways. Activation of these receptors leads to dilation and partial reversal of the airflow limitation, in turn alleviating some shortness of breath associated with the disease. Those receptors are called â2 receptors; they lead to bronchodilation when turned on (activated), hence the discovery of â2 agonist bronchodilators. Cholinergic receptors, in contrast, lead to bronchodilation when turned off (blocked). Therefore, anticholinergic inhalers lead to bronchodilation, helpful for people with COPD.

Physicians frequently prescribe both â2 agonists and anticholinergic agents. Development of fast acting and long acting inhalers has widened the types of medications used for treatment, with the fast-acting inhalers being the *rescue* medicine, and the long acting inhalers being the *maintenance* medicine.

Additionally, since a certain degree of inflammation accompanies the disease, anti-inflammatory inhalers (corticosteroids) are prescribed to combine with bronchodilators to treat symptoms, both during exacerbations and on a maintenance basis (Decramer et al., 2012). Besides improving symptoms, these treatments are thought to lead to some positive disease modifications. Recently, prevention of exacerbations has been found to be as important as managing the dyspnea.

Medical Limitations

Muscle Dysfunction

Patients with COPD often complain of shortness of breath during activity, reduced exercise capacity, and a progressive decline in lung function with increasing age. However, aside from decline of lung function, muscle weakness is a central component that contributes to reduced exercise capacity and poor quality of life, and is a separate predictor of morbidity and mortality.

Limb and respiratory skeletal muscle dysfunction in patients have been attributed to several factors. These include the presence of low grade inflammation throughout the body, poor nutrition, long term inactivity due to difficulty breathing, advancing age, intermittent or long term reduced oxygen, oxidative stresses along with protein degradation, and poor vascular circulation. Weakness in muscles is often generalized to all muscle groups tested, impacting mostly lower extremity function, and resulting in patients becoming less physically active.

Nutritional Status

The Obesity Paradox concept emerged in studying various COPD populations. COPD patients who are overweight or obese were found to survive longer than their counterparts with lower Body Mass Index. This suggests that nutritional status has an impact on the functional status of patients (Goto, Hiray, Faridi, Carmargo, & Hasegawa 2018).

Dynamic Hyperinflation

In COPD, pressure in the chest during exhalation compresses rather than expands the airways. In theory, breathing more forcefully increases airflow. However, in COPD, there is often a limit to how much this can actually increase airflow, a condition called expiratory flow limitation.

Consequently, the patient is unable to exhale completely before taking the next breath. This is particularly common during exercise, when breathing must be faster and exhalation is shorter. When the lungs do not deflate completely, some volume of air from the previous breath still remains in the lungs before the next breath is started. This result is a process called *dynamic hyperinflation*, characterized by stacking of breaths and trapping of air inside the lungs. The lungs become inflated to a point where patients feel they can no longer inhale and need to stop the activity because they are constantly out of breath.

Pulmonary Rehabilitation

Rehabilitation Potential and Methods

The benefits of pulmonary rehabilitation have been shown to be effective, long lasting, reproducible, and cost saving. These benefits translate into improved ventilatory efficiency, longer walking distances, enhanced ventilatory muscle function, and less breathlessness (Spruit, 2013).

Pulmonary rehabilitation does not directly improve lung mechanics or oxygen and carbon dioxide exchange. Instead, it improves the function of other body systems, minimizing the effects of lung dysfunction. High-intensity rehabilitative exercise programs improve function by reconditioning the muscles to tolerate higher work rates.

If lower limb muscle function is the primary limitation, delaying fatigue directly enhances exercise tolerance. More specifically, rehabilitation targets endurance capability of the leg muscles with walking, using a stationary bicycle, and exercising on a treadmill. If respiratory muscle function seems to be the primary limitation, increasing the efficiency of breathing and decreasing the level of hyperinflation will be the focus. This in turn decreases demand on respiratory muscles and breathlessness during physical exertion.

It is important to optimize the clinical status of each individual with regards to medical therapy while undergoing a rehabilitation program. Bronchodilation, oxygen supplementation, and antibiotic maintenance are treatments to reduce the potential for exacerbations and allow for completion of the prescribed rehabilitation program.

Composition of a Medical Rehabilitation Program

The most commonly encountered type of program for pulmonary rehabilitation in the United States is multidisciplinary, hospital-based, outpatient, with incorporated education classes. The education component may include smoking cessation advice, translation of the exercises performed in the home setting, demonstration of proper use of inhaled therapy and oxygen use, promotion of adherence to therapy, and development of an action plan for earlier detection and treatment of COPD exacerbations (Fuld et al., 2005). Other programs may be provided at home, in the community, or as an in-patient. Usually, each patient will undergo 6 to 12 weeks of rehabilitation. A specially trained coordinator (nurse, physical therapist, or respiratory therapist) is responsible for designing the day exercise plan and delivering the therapy, while a pulmonologist oversees the overall program.

Outcomes of Rehabilitation in COPD

For three outcomes, the benefit is unequivocal: exercise capacity (in increasing type of exertion, steady exertion, and walking tests), severity of shortness of breath, and health-related quality of life. For these three outcomes, the magnitude of benefit is generally superior to any other COPD therapy (Wedzicha et al., 2017).

Psychosocial outcomes can be achieved through classes that provide action plans on how to cope with exacerbations, while promoting self-sufficiency. Social interaction with individuals with the same disease helps build support systems and decreases depression related to the disability. This has been demonstrated to optimize the effectiveness of the rehabilitation program regarding quality of life.

Unfortunately, access to pulmonary rehabilitation is minimal, due to such factors as geographic considerations, socioeconomic situation, and so forth. Home-based rehabilitation programs have been presented as an alternative to expand the benefit to larger populations (Vieira, Maltais, & Bourbeau, 2010). Maintenance of benefits gained in a pulmonary rehabilitation program is essential to continued success.

Rehabilitation after a COPD Exacerbation

Pulmonary rehabilitation is recommended as part of long-term management of COPD. A push toward incorporating it following a recent exacerbation or hospitalization follows the rationale that patients may be more likely to adhere to the lifestyle change, smoking cessation, and other medical recommendations. A recent review suggested that pulmonary rehabilitation is effective in reducing the chance of hospitalization and mortality following an acute exacerbation. Additionally, pulmonary rehabilitation following acute COPD exacerbation also results in improvements in health-related quality of life, as well as exercise capacity. The timing of initiation of rehabilitation varied widely between studies, but, in general, the new American Thoracic Society/European Respiratory Society (ATS/ERS) guidelines show that pulmonary rehabilitation initiated within three weeks following discharge reduced hospital readmissions and improved quality of life; if it is initiated within eight weeks following discharge, it increased exercise capacity (Wedzicha et al., 2017).

Vocational Aspects

With respect to COPD, return to work can be considered the best measure of health outcomes. As such, it is aligned with the goals of pulmonary rehabilitation, aimed at helping individuals improve daily living and restoring the ability to function independently. In addition, proper evaluation of the patient's capacities is essential to vocational rehabilitation. After completion of pulmonary rehabilitation, the potential to return to work depends upon the degree of functional and respiratory impairment, as well as adherence to lifestyle modifications recommended to the patient.

Recommendations for Return to Work

Individuals should avoid inhaling irritants at the workplace (i.e. gases, fumes, dust), and sudden and wide changes in ambient temperatures. Work in high altitudes may be discouraged for patients with moderate or severe COPD. Tolerance for physical exertion may also be limited. This could be improved with supplemental oxygen and bronchodilation. Some patients may be advised for home employment, or work in facilities that can accommodate respiratory equipment and flexible rest schedules.

Pulmonary Disability

Disability is a broad term that encompasses impairment, limitations in activity, and restrictions in participation. The Americans with Disabilities Act (ADA) of 1990 has a three-part definition of disability. Under ADA, an individual with a disability is a person who: (1) has a physical or mental impairment that substantially limits one or more major life activities; or (2) has a record of such an impairment; or (3) is regarded as having such an impairment.

Many individuals with COPD are considered to have disabilities under the ADA. They can request reasonable accommodations from current or prospective employers under the ADA and can ask for assistance from the state department of rehabilitation.

A disability may be multifactorial, representing the interplay of a person's own hindrances, as well as adverse environmental factors. Individuals with COPD may have a respiratory impairment with such level of severity that they are unable to engage in substantial gainful activity. This can be due to advanced irreversible lung obstruction or various hospitalizations because of exacerbations. A COPD patient may qualify for Social Security disability if he or she is unable to work due to severe limitations in one or more of the following areas (Social Security Disability Representation, 2013):

- Walking, standing, sitting, lifting, pushing, pulling, reaching, carrying, or handling
- Seeing, hearing, and speaking
- Understanding, carrying out, and remembering simple instructions
- Responding appropriately to supervision, co-workers, and usual work situations
- Adjusting to changes in work routines

Role of the Rehabilitation Counselor

Employment provides individuals with COPD a sense of purpose and a role beyond that of being a patient. A daily routine and time spent away from home helps improve financial, emotional, and physical health. The counselor and healthcare professionals play pivotal roles in helping persons with COPD in recovery and return to work (Marini & Stebnicki, 2009). The patient's vocational potential should be assessed from various aspects including personal-social background, family support, financial resources, prior job satisfaction, recent life changes, psychological and social dysfunction, substance abuse, and transferable skills (Brodwin, Parker, & DeLaGarza, 2010).

Vocational and Rehabilitation Aspects of COPD

Team Approach

Successful vocational rehabilitation of patients is achieved through effective participation of all members of a rehabilitation team. The team includes the rehabilitation program physician whose primary goal is to optimize the activity level of the patient. Working alongside the medical team members are the occupational therapist, social worker, rehabilitation counselor, and job placement specialist. The ideal time to begin vocational counseling is during the psychosocial interview when the patient may still be able to return to prior employment, with or without reasonable accommodation.

Unfortunately, some patients are subject to severe respiratory infections frequently requiring hospitalization. This may result in a patient's inability to cope with regular employment, causing a disruption of socioeconomic status that imposes significant psychological impact on the individual and family, often leading to feelings of depression, despair, and uselessness.

Vocational Factors

Information is obtained from the patient regarding personal-social background and educational-vocational history. The history needs to include all prior work, job duties, dates of employment, salaries, job duties, job satisfaction, reasons for termination of employment, and a transferable skills analysis (if applicable). Information about present means of financial support, educational background, as well as social and psychological factors is taken into consideration in vocational counseling. Rehabilitation counselors, other multidisciplinary team professionals, and liaisons with community agencies make a significant impact on the psychosocial and vocational aspects of pulmonary rehabilitation (Baydur, 2009).

Persons with COPD may be classified into four clinical and vocational rehabilitation groups (Hodgkin, Celli, & Connors, 2008):

1. Individuals who can return to their previous work activities.
2. Individuals who should be retrained for more suitable work.
3. Individuals who are capable of work only in sheltered employment.
4. Individuals who can be trained for self-care only.

Proper evaluation and categorization of the patient's capacities are essential to successful educational and vocational rehabilitation. When selecting patients for vocational rehabilitation, counselors need to consider such factors as recent changes in lifestyle and evidence of rapid clinical deterioration, personality change, substance abuse, and psychological or social dysfunction (Brodwin et al., 2010). Counselors must additionally assess whether a person's cardiorespiratory reserve will enable a return to a previous job on a full or part-time basis. If the individual's tolerance to work requires job modification, the rehabilitation counselor can help facilitate this process. Once the patient is physically rehabilitated, training in new vocational areas commensurate with educational level and decreased respiratory capacity may be needed.

Sheltered or Home Employment

Some people who have COPD can only function in locations where special respiratory equipment is available, such as in sheltered employment or at home. Occupational therapists, rehabilitation counselors, and job placement specialists work together to help locate settings for employment. The occupational therapist provides training in energy-saving methods for those who have a difficult time with self-care. This helps the individual perform tasks including housekeeping, shopping, and other activities of daily living with less dependence on others. An occupational therapist may recommend the following to the person to help conserve needed energy (Baydur, 2009; Hodgkin et al., 2008):

1. Perform activities slowly.
2. Avoid noxious fumes.
3. Avoid areas of excessive heat, cold, and humidity.
4. Plan ahead to decrease ambulation and minimize body movement.
5. Change activities frequently.
6. Spread activities that promote fatigue or dyspnea throughout the day.
7. Transport heavy objects using carts or tables with wheels.
8. Perform most work activities while standing with the work surface (table) at hip level to minimize flexion and abduction.
9. Perform most work activities while standing with the work surface at a body level that minimizes trunk flexion and hyperextension.
10. Store utensils, tools, and similar devices in cabinets where height minimizes active trunk flexion, hyperextension, and active flexion of the shoulder girdle.
11. Use electric appliances (can opener, mixer, and electric knife) to eliminate or minimize manual performance of daily activities.
12. Use a handheld fan, which has shown to diminish the sensation of shortness of breath including during exertion (Luckett et al., 2017).

Several factors impede vocational rehabilitation. These include psychosocial problems, severity of respiratory impairment, progression of disease, advancing age, limitation in skills and capabilities, and poor labor markets in certain fields.

Conclusion

In the past, COPD was considered solely a pulmonary disease, but now it has taken its place among systemic diseases, which have consequences for more than one organ, and require interventions beyond medical therapy alone. Pulmonary rehabilitation coupled with adequate patient-centered education, optimization of therapy, and psychosocial support, results in significant improvement of health status, improves quality of life, enhances independence, and reduces the socioeconomic impact on society.

Case Study

Mr. Leroy Smith is a 57-year-old male, who completed high school but has no further education. He is divorced and takes care of his two teenage boys on his own. This client shared that it has been a struggle to spend time with his sons because of his work schedule. Furthermore, he often finds himself short tempered from stress at work and occasionally "blows up" at his boys. As stated by the client, he is increasingly becoming more concerned about his career in construction because of his aging body. Since graduating high school, Leroy has been in the construction industry. This work encompasses lifting and carrying up to 50 pounds. As a carpenter, his job includes working at construction sites, helping build and remodel residential homes.

Because of a persistent cough with phlegm production for over six months, Mr. Smith sought medical attention. Three months ago, he first visited a doctor, who prescribed antibiotics; this medication did not fully resolve the problem. Leroy smokes one pack of cigarettes a day, and has done so since he was 20 years old. On several occasions, he attempted to quit but was unsuccessful.

Mr. Smith noted that he was having trouble lifting heavy equipment, which was not a problem before. Symptoms include shortness of breath when walking upstairs, and he often has to stop to rest. The physical examination showed "rattling and wheezing" on auscultation of his lungs on both sides. He is able to speak comfortably when well rested. Pulmonary function testing noted a severe obstruction, which showed some response to the inhaler he was given for the test. Chest imaging indicated he has emphysema.

Questions

1. Provide a vocational profile for Leroy. Using a multidisciplinary approach, identify additional information you need to best help this client and discuss how you will obtain the information.
2. What is the patient's medical condition? Discuss.
3. Identify factors that can be modified in the patient's life (triggers and medical therapy).
4. What recommendations can be made for the patient to keep his job?
5. Describe rehabilitation potential for Mr. Smith based on his condition.

References

Americans with Disabilities Act (ADA) of 1990, P.L. 101-336, U.S.C. § 12101 et seq.

Baydur, A. (2009). Chronic obstructive pulmonary disease and neuromuscular disorders affecting the respiratory system. In M. G. Brodwin, F. W. Siu, J. Howard, & E. R. Brodwin (Eds.), *Medical, psychosocial, and vocational aspects of disability* (3rd ed., pp. 97-109). Athens, GA: Elliott & Fitzpatrick.

Brodwin, M. G., Parker, R. M., & DeLaGarza, D. (2010). Disability and reasonable accommodation. In E. M. Szymanski & R. M. Parker (Eds.), *Work and disability: Contexts, issues, and strategies for enhancing employment outcomes for people with disabilities* (3rd ed., pp. 281-323). Austin, TX: Pro-ed.

Calverly, P. M., Tetzlaff, K., Dussler, D., Wise, R., Mueller, A., Metdorf, M., & Anzueto, A. (2017). Determinants of exacerbation risk in patients with COPD in the TIOSPIR study. *International Journal of Chronic Obstructive Pulmonary Diseases, 12*, 3391–3405.

Cavaillès, A., Brinchault-Rabin, G., Dixmier, A., Goupil, F., Gut-Gobert, C., Marchand-Adam, S., ... Diot., P. (2013). Comorbidities of COPD. *European Respiratory Review, 22*, 454-475.

Cote, C. G., & Celli, B. R. (2005). Pulmonary rehabilitation and the BODE index in COPD. *European Respiratory Journal, 26*(4), 630-636.

Decramer, M., Janssens, M., & Miravitlles, M. (2012). Chronic obstructive pulmonary disease. *Lancet, 379* (9823), 1341-1351.

Fabbri, L., Luppi, F., Beghé, B., & Rabe, K. F. (2008). Complex chronic comorbidities of COPD. *European Respiratory Journal, 31*(1), 204-212.

Fuld, J. P., Kilduff, L. P., Neder, J. A., Pitsiladis, Y., Lean, M. E., Ward, S. A., & Cotton, M. M. (2005). Creatine supplementation during pulmonary rehabilitation in chronic obstructive pulmonary disease. *Thorax, 60*(7), 531-537.

GOLD. (2017). From the Global Strategy for the Diagnosis, Management, and Prevention of COPD, *Global Initiative for Chronic Obstructive Lung Disease (GOLD)*. Retrieved from http://goldcopd.org

Goto, T., Hirayama A., Faridi, M. K., Camargo C., & Hasegawa, K. (2018). Obesity and severity of acute exacerbation of chronic obstructive pulmonary disease. *Annual American Thoracic Society, 15*(2), 184–191.

Hodgkin, J. E., Celli, B. R., & Connors, G. L. (2008). *Pulmonary rehabilitation: Guidelines to success* (4th ed.). Philadelphia, PA: Mosby Elsevier.

Hoyert, D. L., & Xu, J. (2012). Deaths: Preliminary data for 2011. *National Vital Statistics Reports, 61*(6), 1-52.

Jagana, R., Bartter, T., & Joshi, M. (2015). Delay in diagnosis of chronic obstructive pulmonary disease: Reasons and solutions. *Current Opinion in Pulmonary Medicine, 21*(2), 121-126.

Lamprecht, B., McBurnie, M. A., Vollmer, W. M., Gudmundsson, G., Welte, T., Nizankowska-Mogilnicka, E., & Buist, S. A. (2011). COPD in never smokers: Results from the population-based burden of obstructive lung disease study. *Chest, 139*(4), 752-763.

Luckett, T., Phillips, J., Johnson, M. J., Farquhar, M., Swan, F., Assen, I., . . . Booth, S. (2017). Contributions of a hand-held fan to self-management of chronic breathlessness. *European Respiratory Journal, 50*(2), 1700262.

Marini, I., & Stebnicki, M. (2009). *The professional counselor's desk reference*. New York, NY: Springer.

National Center for Health Statistics. (2016). *Health, United States: 2015 with Special Feature on Racial and Ethnic Health Disparities*. Hyattsville, MD: U.S. Department of Health and Human Services. Retrieved from http://www.cdc.gov/nchs/hus/

Rabe, K. F., Hurd, S., Anzueto, A., Barnes, P. J., Buist, S. A., Calverley, P., . . . Zielinski, J. (2007). Global strategy for the diagnosis, management, and prevention of chronic obstructive pulmonary disease: GOLD executive summary. *American Journal of Respiratory Critical Care Medicine, 176*(6), 532-555.

Shimizu K., Yoshii, Y., Morozumi, M., Chiba, N., Ubukata, K., . . . Kuwano, K. (2015). Pathogens in COPD exacerbations identified by comprehensive real-time PCR plus older methods. *International Journal of Chronic Obstructive Pulmonary Disease, 10*, 2009–2016.

Social Security Disability Representation. (2013*). Chronic obstructive pulmonary disease (COPD) and Social Security Disability Insurance.* Retrieved from http://www.allsup.com/about-ssdi/ssdi-guidelines-by-disability/chronic-obstructive-pulmonary-disease-(copd).aspx

Spruit, M. A., Singh, S. J., Garvey, C., Zuwallack, R., Nici, L., Rochester, C., . . . Wouters, E. F. M. (2013). An official American Thoracic Society/European Respiratory Society Statement: Key concepts and advances in pulmonary rehabilitation. *American Journal of Respiratory and Critical Care Medicine, 188*, e13–e64.

Vieira, D. S., Maltais, F., & Bourbeau, J. (2010). Home-based pulmonary rehabilitation in chronic obstructive pulmonary disease patients. *Current Opinion in Pulmonary Medicine, 16*(2), 134-143.

Wedzicha, J. A., Miravitlles, M., Hurst, J. R., Calverley, P. M. A., Albert, R. K., Anzueto, A., . . . Krishnan, J. A. (2017). Management of COPD exacerbations: A European Respiratory Society/American Thoracic Society guideline. *European Respiratory Journal, 17*(49), 1600791.

About the Author

Hassan Bencheqroun, MD, is a Pulmonary and Critical Care Specialist serving as faculty at the University of California, Riverside, School of Medicine, with a medical practice at Desert Regional Medical Center in Palm Springs and Alvarado Hospital in San Diego. Board certified in Internal Medicine, Critical Care, and Pulmonary Disease, he serves in the leadership of the American College of Chest Physicians, chairing several committees including the Pulmonary Physiology, Function, and Rehabilitation Steering Committee. He was presented with the Patients' Choice Award for seven consecutive years, and is on the 2017 list of Top Physicians of America. Additionally, he received several awards including a Compassionate Doctor Recognition Award in 2011-2012. Dr. Bencheqroun's areas of expertise include COPD, interstitial lung disease, lung cancer, pulmonary arterial hypertension, and chest infections.

Chapter 7

HIV/AIDS

John J. Howard, MD, MPH

Introduction

In 1981, the first four cases of a new immunodeficiency syndrome in young gay men were reported in the United States (Gottlieb et al., 1981). Since then, the causative agent - the human immunodeficiency virus (HIV) - has infected tens of millions of people worldwide. By the end of 2016, an estimated 36.7 million people worldwide were living with HIV, and 1 million died from diseases and cancers associated with the acquired immunodeficiency syndrome (AIDS) (United Nations Joint Programme on HIV/AIDS, 2017). HIV/AIDS has not only had a profound impact on the medical world, but problems caused by HIV/AIDS have touched families, schools, communities, business, industry, courts, religious institutions, and government throughout the world (Piot & Quinn, 2013).

When HIV/AIDS was first recognized in 1981, few thought that persons with HIV/AIDS would ever have rehabilitation potential. At that time, AIDS was medically diagnosed only after HIV had completely destroyed the immune system. Medical progress has transformed HIV/AIDS from a severely activity-limiting condition with a very short survival time into a chronic medical condition with normal life expectancy. Many HIV-affected persons can now benefit from early recognition of rehabilitation potential, establishment of therapeutic goals, and prompt referral to a rehabilitation counselor.

Modes of HIV Transmission

HIV infection occurs through the introduction of HIV-containing blood cells or bodily fluids from an infected individual into the bloodstream of an uninfected person. This occurs either through sexual or blood-related contact.

Sexual Contact

Sexual transmission is the most common mode of HIV transmission. Penetrative sexual intercourse involving the passage of HIV-containing blood cells and bodily fluids, such as semen or vaginal secretions, can result in HIV transmission. The efficiency with which sexual contact transmits HIV varies with the particular type of sexual practice and gender of the sexual partners involved. Epidemiologic data points to anal intercourse between two males, especially for the receptive partner, as the most efficient means of sexual transmission.

Blood Contact

HIV transmission can occur through blood-related contact in different ways. Whole blood from an HIV-infected blood donor can be transfused to an uninfected person, or a blood-clotting factor isolated from the blood of an HIV-infected blood donor can be transfused into an uninfected person with a blood-clotting disorder. HIV transmission through blood contact has markedly decreased in the United States due to mandatory screening of all blood donations and heat inactivation of blood-clotting products.

Shared needle behavior through intravenous drug use accounts for most blood-related HIV transmissions. Intravenous drug users often share their equipment (e.g., needles or syringes) with other drug users. This equipment can contain minute amounts of HIV-infected blood, and when shared with an uninfected person, HIV transmission may occur.

HIV is also transmitted from an infected pregnant woman to her fetus. This route of HIV transmission, called maternal-fetal transmission or vertical transmission, accounts for most of the cases of pediatric HIV/AIDS globally. Before the advent of anti-HIV therapies, approximately half the infants born to HIV-infected mothers developed clinical HIV/AIDS. The use of medications has dramatically decreased the proportion of babies infected from HIV-infected mothers.

HIV is also transmitted inadvertently in a health care setting (occupational exposure). The routes of transmission that occur in these occupational settings are needlestick (sharp object injuries) and direct skin or mucous membrane contact with blood or other potentially infectious materials. For example, HIV can be transmitted when an uninfected health care worker is stuck with a needle or cut with a scalpel which contains blood from an HIV-infected patient (Marcus & Centers for Disease Control [CDC], 1988).

Natural History of HIV Infection

Acute Retroviral Syndrome

Most people infected with HIV are initially unaware of the infection, although a few people experience symptoms of a condition called acute retroviral syndrome. Acute HIV infection is called retroviral syndrome because HIV is a member of the family of viruses called retrovirus.

The natural history of acute HIV infection is characterized by a very high level of HIV viremia (the presence of virus in the blood) and a vigorous immune response (Rosenberg, 1997). During the peak of HIV viremia, the CD4+ helper T-lymphocyte cell count (a white blood cell that is the major target of HIV) declines precipitously. Within 5 to 30 days of initial HIV infection, during the peak of HIV viremia, some individuals become acutely ill with symptoms of acute retroviral syndrome (Cohen, Shaw, McMichael, & Haynes, 2011a). Acute retroviral syndrome manifests itself as a flu-like illness characterized by fever, swollen lymph nodes, sore throat, rash, fatigue, weight loss, and myalgias (muscle aches) and lasts about 14 days.

HIV Antibody Formation

A prolonged period of well-being follows recovery from acute retroviral syndrome, during which time the HIV viral load in the blood decreases, the number of CD4+ T-lymphocytes increases, and HIV antibodies become detectable. Most people do not realize they are infected with HIV until they undergo a blood test for the presence of HIV antibodies and are told they are HIV positive (CDC, 1992). HIV antibody testing is usually performed in an outpatient clinic setting, but home test collection systems are available. The individual collects the blood at home, sends the sample to a laboratory, and then telephones an information line for the result. In 2006, the CDC issued a recommendation urging physicians to include HIV testing as a routine part of their patients' healthcare. In this way, more people can learn whether they are HIV-infected, allowing them to benefit from earlier access to treatment and reducing the risk of infecting their partners (CDC, 2006b).

Progressive Immunodeficiency

HIV begins to destroy the body's immune system almost immediately after infection even though a person remains without symptoms. The immunological destructive process begins when HIV invades the CD4+ T-lymphocyte (Stebbing, Gazzard, & Douek, 2004). Once inside, HIV replicates thousands of times, a process which eventually kills the CD4+ T-lymphocyte. Since this cell is responsible for coordinating the body's immune response to certain invading microorganisms, its destruction is the major cause of progressive immunodeficiency, the hallmark of HIV/AIDS.

Clinical Manifestations

Early HIV Disease

When the AIDS epidemic was initially identified, the CDC defined AIDS to facilitate tracking the number of persons who manifested the syndrome. In 1981 when the cause of AIDS was unknown, an AIDS diagnosis could be made when an individual had one of several qualifying types of infections or tumors, and lacked a medical reason to have such an infection or tumor, such as receiving chemotherapy for cancer or receiving medications associated with the development of immunodeficiency (CDC, 1981, 2016). In 1986, the AIDS surveillance case definition was refined to take into account the development in 1984 of the HIV antibody test (CDC, 1987).

In 1992, the CDC recognized that HIV infection resulted in a spectrum of levels of HIV-generated disease: asymptomatic, early, and late/advanced disease or AIDS. In the 1992 revision, the CDC emphasized the importance of measuring the number or percentage of CD4+ T-lymphocytes and provided three categories based on such measurements: (1) Category 1 (a count of greater or equal to 500 CD4+ lymphocytes per microliter); (2) Category 2 (200 to 499 CD4+ cells per microliter); and (3) Category 3 (less than 200 CD4+ cells per microliter). For disability evaluations, an individual has AIDS when they have laboratory confirmation of HIV infection (e.g., a positive HIV antibody test) and a CD4+ T-lymphocyte count of less than 200 CD4+ T-lymphocytes or a CD4+ T-lymphocyte percentage of total lymphocytes less than 14% (CDC, 1992; Social Security Administration [SSA], 2005).

In addition to laboratory testing, CDC has defined three clinical categories of HIV infection (CDC, 1992). Category A consists of asymptomatic HIV infection, persistent generalized swelling of the lymph nodes, or acute retroviral infection. Category B consists of a variety of symptomatic conditions that meet at least one of the following criteria: (a) the condition is attributed to HIV infection or is indicative of a defect in cell-mediated immunity; or (b) the condition is considered by a physician to have a clinical course, or to require management that is complicated by HIV infection. Examples of Category B conditions include: oral candidiasis (thrush), persistent vulvovaginal candidiasis, oral hairy leukoplakia, herpes zoster (shingles), and peripheral neuropathy.

In general, early symptomatic HIV disease (Category B) is characterized by relatively non-specific signs (what the physician notices) and symptoms (what the patient notices). These include swollen glands or lymph nodes, mild intermittent fever, and fatigue or low energy. In people with early symptomatic HIV disease, these signs and symptoms worsen while new symptoms appear. Left untreated, HIV-infected individuals begin to manifest daily fever, night sweats, fatigue and weakness, weight loss, intermittent diarrhea, oral thrush or candidiasis (yeast growing on the tongue and along the sides of the mouth), and experience various immunodeficiency-related skin conditions or rashes.

Advanced HIV Disease

The CDC's Clinical Category C includes certain infections and types of cancer. When present, any of these conditions result in a diagnosis of AIDS. Category C infections are caused by different bacterial, viral, fungal, or protozoal organisms. Since these microorganisms rarely cause disease in immunocompetent individuals, they are called opportunistic infections. Opportunistic infections take advantage of the opportunity of the body's defenseless posture caused by HIV destruction of CD4+ T-lymphocytes to produce infection. Early in the HIV/AIDS epidemic, the most common opportunistic infectious disease seen in advanced HIV disease was Pneumocystis carinii pneumonia or PCP (Thomas & Limper, 2004), but the number of patients with PCP has declined significantly. The most frequent complications of advanced HIV/AIDS involving the lungs are acute bronchitis, bacterial pneumonia, and increasingly, hospitalizations for cardiac conditions (CDC, 2016; Grubb et al., 2006).

Treatment Strategies

Due to medical advances in the treatment of HIV/AIDS, deaths from HIV/AIDS decreased 75%, and the occurrence of AIDS-defining diseases decreased by 73% between 1994 and 1997 (Palella et al., 1998). Persons with HIV/AIDS now function at higher levels for longer periods of time (Dybul et al., 2002) due to advances in antiretroviral therapy (primary treatment) and advances in treating the infections and tumors that make up AIDS (secondary treatment). In fact, the life expectancy of HIV-positive individuals on anti-retroviral therapy with an undetectable amount of HIV in their blood have no increased mortality compared to the general population.

Primary Treatment

Primary treatment is directed either at interrupting the life cycle of the virus itself (antiretroviral therapy), or aimed at positively modulating the body's immune response to the virus (immunomodulatory therapy). Several classes of antiretroviral medications have been discovered to be effective against HIV. The first class of antiretroviral medications developed were nucleoside analogs that inhibited a vital enzyme HIV used to reproduce itself called reverse-transcriptase. This class of anti-HIV drugs are called nucleoside reverse transcriptase inhibitors (NNTIs). In 1986, a nucleoside analog called zidovudine (AZT) was the first antiretroviral medication shown to prolong the lives of persons with AIDS.

In the 1990s, significant knowledge about the life cycle of HIV was discovered, making it possible to design drugs that interrupt different phases of HIV's life cycle. Two additional classes of antiretroviral drugs - non-nucleoside reverse transcriptase inhibitors (NNRTIs) and protease inhibitors (PIs) - were introduced in the 1990s. Protease inhibitors block HIV replication in the late phase by binding to HIV protease which stops maturation of newly formed HIV virus, and as a result the capsid of the virus does not form properly (Stix, 2006). By 1996, the widespread use of these newer medications - especially protease inhibitors - markedly reduced the mortality rate associated with HIV/AIDS.

Antiretroviral medications of these major classes are now used together. Simultaneous administration of three to four or more antiretroviral medications has become standard practice, often referred to as highly active "anti-retroviral therapy" or ART (Barbaro, Scozzafava, Mostrolorenzo, & Supuran, 2005). The therapeutic aim of combination therapy is complete suppression of HIV growth as measured by the viral load (Friedland, 1990). An undetectable viral load serves as laboratory confirmation that HIV growth has been suppressed. Three newer classes of antiretroviral drugs include: (1) fusion or entry inhibitors, which interfere with HIV's ability to fuse with the cellular membrane, thereby blocking entry of HIV into the CD4+ T-lymphocyte and interfering with an essential early step in viral replication (Poveda, Briz, Quinones-Mateu, & Soriano, 2006); (2) integrase inhibitors, which inhibit the complex, multi-step process of integration of HIV provirus into the host genome (Havlir, 2008; Walmsley et al., 2013); and (3) maturation inhibitors, which block HIV from forming a protective outer coat or from emerging from human cells (Nguyen et al., 2011).

Drug Resistance

HIV's inherent mutability can make it resistant to even the newest anti-retroviral medication or an entire class of medications. The phenomenon of viral resistance was demonstrated shortly after the introduction of the first antiretroviral, AZT (Larder, Darby, & Richman, 1989). As many as half of HIV- infected persons under treatment have been found to be infected with viruses that are resistant to at least one drug in their current combination therapy regime (AIDS.gov, 2016; Richman et al., 2004). When resistance is identified, patients must have their drug regimen changed to continue viral suppression (CDC, 2016).

Side Effects

Even when viral suppression is achieved, antiretroviral medications can produce serious side effects which often necessitate discontinuation of a medication. The most common side effects include lowered red cell count (anemia), fatigue, headaches, sore tongue, nausea, vomiting, muscle aches, hepatitis and pancreatitis, numbness and pain in the arms and legs (peripheral neuropathy), elevated blood sugar (diabetes mellitus), elevated fats in the blood (hypertriglyceridemia), and fat wasting of face and limbs with central obesity (peripheral lipodystrophy) (Dube & Sattler, 1998; Lenhard et al. 2000). As each new antiretroviral medication is introduced into practice, new side effects emerge. Even for people living with HIV/AIDS and employed, management of side effects can pose a challenge for them and their rehabilitation counselor (AIDS info, 2016).

HIV Eradication

Success in the treatment of HIV/AIDS has given rise to the hope that HIV can be completely eradicated after the administration of a sufficiently lengthy period of antiretroviral suppressive therapy. Achieving complete HIV eradication, though, is difficult. There are various HIV-infected tissue compartments, such as the germinal centers of lymph nodes, which cannot be reached by antiretroviral drugs. Unless HIV can be destroyed in these so-called sanctuary sites, complete eradication of the disease is difficult. Also, even after an undetectable level of HIV is attained following a lengthy period of antiretroviral suppressive therapy, HIV is still capable of regrowth. This is possible because of the prolonged life span of some latently infected cells, which after undergoing cell division, can serve as a source of infectious HIV (Wong et al., 1997a, 1997b). However, there has been one well documented case of an HIV-infected adult who experienced complete eradication of replication-competent HIV-1 after a hematopoietic stem cell transplant (Hutter et al., 2009). Even though the goal of complete viral eradication of HIV remains elusive, it has become the subject of considerable research (Hammer, 2013). Innovative approaches, including the use of genetic engineering techniques (Yin et al., 2017), are being tried to purge HIV from latent viral reservoirs (Marsden & Zack, 2009).

Antiretroviral Treatment as Prevention

Public health efforts are directed in identifying HIV-infected individuals and treating them early in the course of infection with antiretroviral therapy (Hammer, 2011). During the past 20 years, the use of antiretroviral therapy for the prevention of HIV has been carefully studied. Strong evidence now exists that (1) antiretroviral treatment of a HIV-infected partner reduces the rate of infection in the HIV negative partner (Rodger et al., 2016); and (2) immediate therapy slows progression in a newly-infected person (Cohen et al., 2011b). These findings have led to the test and treat approach to prevent the spread of HIV. The premise of test and treat is that HIV/AIDS can be eliminated from society if all adults are tested for the presence of HIV and treated with antiretroviral medications regardless of their level of immunodeficiency (Health Resources and Services Administration [HRSA], 2012).

Secondary Treatment

Secondary treatment is directed not against HIV itself. Rather, it is directed against the specific infections and tumors that are indirectly caused by HIV infection.

Prevention of HIV Transmission

Public health education is directed at interrupting the sexual transmission of HIV among high risk individuals by encouraging people to engage in safe sex practices (using condoms during sexual intercourse), and by avoiding shared needle behaviors through intravenous drug use. Ideally, a vaccine against HIV would reduce new infections significantly; however, vaccine development faces several challenges (Baden & Dolin, 2012; Yin et al., 2017). HIV quickly integrates itself into the DNA of the host cell where it can hide, remain latent, and essentially be invisible to the immune system. The ability of HIV to mutate makes it substantially more complex than any other human virus, potentially making any vaccine quickly obsolete (Johnston & Fauci, 2008). Despite these formidable obstacles, numerous HIV/AIDS vaccine formulations have been tested since 1988, but none have, as yet, proven successful.

Functional Limitations

Energy-restricting disorders are the most common functional impairments resulting from HIV/AIDS infection. Fatigue often occurs, especially in individuals who have a low CD4+ T-lymphocyte cell count. As HIV-related immunodeficiency progresses, persons infected with HIV begin to experience decreased states of energy that restrict activities of daily living (Patel, Hyppolite, Shatzer, & Epstein, 2017). Employed individuals with HIV not well controlled on medications experience frequent exhaustion, and often require midday rest periods.

Respiratory and Cardiac Disorders

A major contributor to energy restriction in advanced HIV disease is the presence of a respiratory infection. Respiratory infections cause shortness of breath and fatigue during an acute episode and persist for weeks after recovery. HIV can also affect the heart, causing an inflammation of the heart muscle itself (myocarditis) or the thin lining around the heart (pericarditis). Both conditions restrict energy by causing shortness of breath, chest pain, and fatigue.

Gastrointestinal Disorders

Individuals infected with HIV often have functional impairments caused by gastrointestinal disorders. Chief among these are infectious and non-infectious diarrheal diseases that cause prolonged bouts of profuse diarrhea, impairing a person's ability to absorb vital nutrients from food. This malabsorption causes progressive weight loss, profound fatigue, and an aversion to food out of fear of triggering diarrhea. In addition, painful oral lesions are common in HIV infection and include recurrent and painful aphthous ulcers ("canker sores") and fungal and viral conditions like candidiasis and herpes simplex, which may impair the ability to chew.

Liver Disorders

Hepatitis C virus (HCV) and hepatitis B virus (HBV) infections are common in HIV-infected individuals because of shared routes of viral transmission. Liver disease due to chronic HBV and HCV infection is becoming a leading cause of death among persons with HIV infection worldwide; risk of death related to liver disease is inversely related to the CD4+ cell count (Koziel & Peters, 2007). An increase in the incidence of hepatocellular carcinoma and hepatotoxic effects associated with antiretroviral drugs in patients with HCV and HBV co-infection has been observed (Weber & the Data Collection on Adverse Events of Anti-HIV Drugs Study Group, 2006). Drug interactions and the high cost of new, curative treatments for HCV may complicate use in persons with AIDS.

Musculoskeletal Disorders

HIV affects joint, muscle, and bone tissues. Prevalence of musculoskeletal disorders in individuals is high (up to 50%) and increases with disease progression. Arthralgias ("painful joints") and frank arthritis (inflammation of the joints) are the most common forms of musculoskeletal disorders. The following three conditions involve the muscles: (1) AZT myopathy (found in patients on AZT and manifested by proximal muscle weakness, myalgias, and muscle wasting); (b) HIV-related polymyositis (muscle weakness in patients not on AZT); and (c) infectious myositis (tenderness and swelling of a muscle caused by staphylococcal bacteria) (Rodriguez, 1998). Management of musculoskeletal pain includes the use of analgesic medications, some of which produce drowsiness and impaired judgment. The physician may prescribe physiotherapy, hypnosis, acupressure, or acupuncture. Musculoskeletal disorders associated with HIV can partially or totally impair ambulation because of pain or muscle weakness in one or both legs.

Neurological and Sensory Disorders

Nearly 20% of patients with HIV/AIDS experience some neurological dysfunction. Neurological disorders related to HIV include: those that affect the peripheral nervous system (nerves to the arms and legs); the central nervous system (brain and spinal cord); and those affecting sensory organs, such as the eyes.

Disorders affecting the peripheral nervous system include painful sensory neuropathies of the arms and legs that result in pain and weakness, both of which restrict an individual's activities. Impairment of the brain causes limitations ranging from serious (such as recurrent seizures due to an opportunistic infection or a tumor) to mild (such as mild dementia or mental slowness due to an HIV-related cognitive impairment).

Opportunistic infections and tumors, which can affect the central nervous system, include toxoplasmosis (a protozoan infection causing seizures), cryptococcal meningitis (a fungal infection causing inflammation of the lining of the brain), and various types of brain tumors, such as lymphoma. In addition, sub-acute encephalitis (AIDS encephalopathy or AIDS dementia complex) is the most insidious neurological problem. Symptoms such as poor memory, inability to concentrate, verbal and motor slowing, affective and behavioral changes, and social apathy are the chief manifestations of AIDS dementia (CDC, 2006a). Individuals with AIDS dementia complex manifest a myriad of cognitive impairments, such as short-term memory deficits and a decrease in concentration ability, as well as affective and behavioral disorders ranging from impatience, irritability and mania, to apathy, social withdrawal, and even psychosis.

Sensory organs like the eye can be affected. Most commonly, visual loss due to infection of the retina either by HIV itself or by cytomegalovirus (CMV) can occur. A person who loses any degree of vision faces physical challenges, such as loss of reading and writing, mobility impairments, and other daily living limitations.

Metabolic Disorders

Hypothyroidism may lower energy levels. Globally, the most debilitating metabolic complication of HIV disease is wasting syndrome. The wasting syndrome is manifested by weight loss (in excess of 10% from baseline), weakness, chronic diarrhea, and fever. Successful treatment depends on anti-retroviral therapy, treatment of secondary infections and tumors, adequate nutrition, and measures to correct underlying androgen deficiency (Reiter, 1996).

Emotional Disorders

The psychological reaction to impairments caused by HIV depends chiefly on the severity and rate of progression of the particular impairment, the underlying personality of the affected individual, including self-image and coping style, any neuropsychiatric changes caused by HIV itself, and the reaction of those around the patient to the condition. The extent of the patient's social support network and quality of psychological care available are crucial factors. Emotional disturbances are common, the most common of which are depression and anxiety (Basu, Chwastiak, & Bruce, 2005).

Disturbances of sleep, appetite, and weight are only a few of the physical effects that can be a direct result of the emotional manifestations associated with HIV disease. Undiagnosed and untreated mental illnesses already present in an individual are compounded by the knowledge of having to face a life with HIV/AIDS (Basu et al., 2005).

Social Factors

Social factors exert significant effects on health and rehabilitation. A person's ethnic and cultural background, marital status, family support system, educational level, financial capability, and vocational background have an effect on the provision of rehabilitation services. Understanding the social aspects that influence the daily life of a person with HIV/AIDS is essential since the disease is transmitted mostly through sexual contact and shared needle behaviors, both of which are fundamentally social phenomena (Friedman, Kippax, Phaswana-Mafuya, Rossi, & Newman, 2006).

A great challenge facing rehabilitation for a person with HIV infection or disease is that of overcoming the social limitations associated with HIV/AIDS. The HIV epidemic elicits strong responses from society as HIV transmission involves forms of behavior that are either illegal or socially taboo. The groups at greatest risk for becoming infected with HIV and developing AIDS, men who have sex with men and intravenous drug users, have traditionally been the subject of legal sanctions and social stigma. Further, HIV/AIDS affects a disproportionate number of African-Americans and Latinos, racial and ethnic groups already the subject of various social limitations and prejudices (Darbes, Crepaz, Lyles, Kennedy, & Rutherford, 2008; An et al., 2012).

Vocational Limitations

Vocational rehabilitation services for persons with HIV/AIDS makes an individualized approach to rehabilitation crucial. Although no single method of evaluation can be applied universally, three questions should be stressed: (1) is the individual able to return to his or her previous job or occupation? (2) are the skills or abilities of the person transferable to a new job? (3) in conjunction with the medical and emotional factors, what type of rehabilitation training needs, if any, to be conducted to facilitate reemployment? (Matheson, 1984).

Young adults are most commonly affected by HIV/AIDS, ranging from 20 to 40 years of age. Although they may later seek disability benefits, they can remain in the workforce. Prior to the advent of effective antiretroviral therapies, many persons could not continue working at their prior levels of activity. They had to quit their jobs because of functional impairments (Patel et al., 2017). Now, more individuals with HIV/AIDS are maintained on effective antiretroviral medications and continue to work, but may need vocational assessment and rehabilitation.

During vocational evaluation, physical, emotional, and social factors associated with HIV/AIDS need to be kept in mind. Individuals have different levels of medical stability given the different side effects from antiretroviral medications they are taking. Unlike impairments that reach a level of permanence before the process of vocational rehabilitation begins, impairments associated with HIV/AIDS may be progressive. A challenging factor in the vocational environment may be the lack of physical endurance to work a full day. A rehabilitation counselor can assess physical tolerance for work by ascertaining daily energy patterns and energy requirements expended in the home. Assistance in home management activities may save energy that can be used for work.

Individuals can develop various cognitive impairments. Moderate to severe degrees of AIDS dementia complex manifested by memory deficits, lack of coordination, and poor concentration ability create challenges in the work environment. Cognitive impairments may exist in any infected person; neuropsychological testing should be part of rehabilitation evaluation. Changes in facial appearance due to fat redistribution secondary to antiretroviral medications (especially protease inhibitors) can lead to reluctance to participate in the work environment (Patel et al., 2017).

Two social factors are particularly disabling for someone attempting to re-enter the workforce after being diagnosed. The most important factor relates to the false belief that individuals infected with HIV pose a communicable disease risk in the workplace. The only possible risk of transmission in the workplace is if an accident occurs resulting in blood from the individual infected with HIV coming into direct contact with the non-intact skin of an uninfected co-worker. Another social factor is the prejudicial treatment persons with HIV infection face based on judgments and misconceptions of others about their sexual behavior or drug use. This prejudice may severely limit vocational rehabilitation.

Rehabilitation Potential

Rehabilitation potential for persons affected by HIV depends in large part on the level of their underlying immunodeficiency, the presence of any physical limitations arising from specific disorders, and complications from multi-drug treatments. Individuals with greater degrees of immunodeficiency, as measured by increases in their HIV viral load, or in reductions in their level of CD4+ T-lymphocytes, have less residual capacity for rehabilitation. Severity of physical impairments frequently worsens with increased immunodeficiency. Many persons with HIV disease and severe immunodeficiency, however, manifest significant capabilities for rehabilitation (Patel, 2017). The development of effective antiretroviral therapies in the mid-1990s greatly enhanced rehabilitation potential.

Since HIV/AIDS primarily affects previously healthy young adults, these individuals maintain fairly high rehabilitation potential. A minority are in the category of limited rehabilitation potential, usually those who remain untreated or who have had the condition for many years. The vast majority of persons have sufficient physical, mental, emotional, and educational capabilities to respond favorably to vocational rehabilitation. Rehabilitation counselors should note, that by 2012, half of the U.S. population living with HIV/AIDS was older than 50 years of age (Mills, Barnighausen, & Negin, 2012).

An additional positive factor contributing to rehabilitation potential is the absence of severely disabling neuromuscular impairments such as spinal cord damage, loss of appendages, and reduction in arm or leg mobility. Most ambulatory individuals with HIV/AIDS have adequate residual neuromuscular capacity to engage in sedentary or higher exertional levels of work, and those with energy-restricting disorders usually maintain sufficient capacity to engage in sedentary to light work levels.

The rehabilitation counselor needs to conduct a comprehensive assessment of a person's strengths, capacities, and skills. As medical science improves the quality and length of life for those with HIV/AIDS, rehabilitation professionals are being called upon more frequently to help restore the individual's ability to live and work successfully, and to the fullest extent.

Case Study

Mr. James Dexter is 29 years of age and works in an oil refinery. Mr. Dexter did not finish high school, completing most of the 12th grade. His job of equipment mechanic (petroleum production), Dictionary of Occupational Titles (D.O.T.) # 629.381-014 (United States Department of Labor, 1991), puts him in charge of the installation, maintenance, and repair of oil well drilling machinery and equipment. He uses hand tools and power tools, and reads diagrams and schematics to repair equipment such as pumps, transmissions, and diesel engines. All oil refinery mechanics run tests to make sure that the equipment is fully functional. One to two years are required for proficiency in this field, which requires occasional lifting of 50 pounds and repetitive lifting and carrying of 25 pounds. Mr. Dexter worked as an oil-field equipment mechanic for six years.

Before this job, Mr. Dexter worked in the construction field as a Construction Worker II (construction), D.O.T# 869.687-026, a position which did not involve any skills but required lifting up to 120 pounds occasionally and 50 to 75 pounds frequently. The job responsibilities included loading and unloading of building materials, tools, and supplies. Also involved were digging, spreading, and leveling dirt and gravel using a pick and shovel. He held this job for four years.

James developed a painful tingling sensation on the left side of his chest, followed the next day by water blisters in the same area. He was diagnosed with shingles (herpes zoster). His physician advised him that herpes zoster was a sign of an impaired immune system. James thought no more about it; after a month, the shingles disappeared.

Later that year, James began to develop feelings of fatigue at work, especially when climbing the cracking towers at the oil refinery. Gradually, his fatigue worsened and his work performance began to decline. James never felt rested. His boss told him to "shape up" or he would be fired. His fatigue became severe and he lost 11 pounds. When he developed shortness of breath, a dry cough, and a fever, Mr. Dexter saw a physician, who diagnosed him with pneumonia. He was admitted to the hospital.

A thorough medical and social history revealed that, except for a broken leg a few years previous, Mr. Dexter had been in good health all his life. James has been married for several years and has three young children but he and his wife have had marital difficulties. During a period of about two years, when he and his wife were separated, Mr. Dexter had sexual contacts with other women.

Mr. Dexter's pneumonia turned out to be caused by Pneumocystis jiroveci, a fungal infection of the lungs common to persons with AIDS. His doctors became suspicious that he was infected with HIV and ordered an HIV antibody test which was positive. He was found to be severely immunodeficient with a CD4+ T-lymphocyte count of 127 (CDC CD4+ T-Lymphocyte Category C) and an HIV viral load of 250,000 copies (normal is undetectable). His wife tested negative for the HIV antibody.

During hospitalization, James experienced intermittent diarrhea with no diagnosed cause. He lost about 30 pounds and developed cytomegalovirus retinitis in the left eye which left him with a 50% visual loss in that eye, even after treatment with medication; he was hospitalized for a total of six weeks. Upon hospital discharge, James was sent home on three antiretroviral medications. After a tumultuous three weeks, his wife moved out with the children and filed for divorce. James considered suicide. His physician recommended emotional counseling, but Mr. Dexter turned it down.

After six months of convalescence, James began to feel better. His CD4+ T-lymphocyte count rose from 127 to 487, and his HIV viral load became undetectable. James decided to return to work. He has been experiencing pain in the muscles of his upper legs, which his physician thinks may be a side effect (myopathy) due to his medications. Mr. Dexter believes he can work an eight-hour shift. The physician restricted him light work activity.

Mr. Dexter wants to return to his previous job because he feels confident and physically fit enough to do the work. Concerned about his ability to support himself and his family, he desires to return to work as soon as possible. Recently, the oil company terminated his employment.

Questions

1. What is the nature of James Dexter's HIV-related disease and what are the possible physical limitations associated with his medical condition that may influence his rehabilitation potential?
2. What emotional limitations does Mr. Dexter have that need to be addressed during the process of rehabilitation?
3. Discuss the social limitations of James' medical condition.
4. What is this client's rehabilitation potential? Discuss the possibility of him returning to his previous job.
5. Provide a vocational profile including age category, educational level, exertional level of previous work, occupationally significant characteristics, and work skills. Note if any of Mr. Dexter's skills are transferable and, if so, to what jobs.
6. Identify types of rehabilitation training that will facilitate this client's reemployment.

References

AIDS.gov. (2016). *Drug resistance*. Retrieved from https://www.aids.gov/hiv-aids-basics/just-diagnosed-with-hiv-aids/treatment-options/drug-resistance/index.html

AIDS.info. (2016). *Side effects of HIV medications*. Retrieved from https://aidsinfo.nih.gov/education-materials/fact-sheets/22/63/hiv-medicines-and-side-effects

An, Q., Hernandez, A., Prejean, J., German, E. J., Thompson, H., & Hall, H. I. (2012). Geographical differences in HIV infection among Hispanics or Latinos – 46 states and Puerto Rico. *Morbidity and Mortality Weekly Report, 61*(40), 805-810.

Baden L. R., & Dolin, R. (2012). The road to an effective HIV vaccine. *New England Journal of Medicine, 366*(14), 1343-1344.

Barbaro, G., Scozzafava, A., Mastrolorenzo, A., & Supuran, C. T. (2005). Highly active antiretrovira therapy: Current state of the art, new agents and their pharmacological interactions useful for improving therapeutic outcome. *Current Pharmacy Descriptions, 11*, 1805–1843.

Basu, S., Chwastiak, L. A., & Bruce, R. D. (2005). Clinical management of depression and anxiety in HIV-infected adults. *AIDS, 19*, 2057-2067.

Centers for Disease Control and Prevention. (1981). Surveillance case definition for the acquired immunodeficiency syndrome. *Morbidity and Mortality Weekly Report, 30*, 305.

Centers for Disease Control and Prevention. (1987). Revision of the CDC surveillance case definition for acquired immunodeficiency syndrome. *Morbidity and Mortality Weekly Report, 36*, 1S-15S.

Centers for Disease Control and Prevention. (1992). 1993 revised classification system for HIV infection and expanded surveillance case definition for AIDS among adolescents and adults. *Morbidity and Mortality Weekly Report, 41*(RR-17), 1-19.

Centers for Disease Control and Prevention. (2006a). Twenty-five years of HIV/AIDS - United States, 1981-2006. *Morbidity and Mortality Weekly Report, 55*(21), 585-589.

Centers for Disease Control and Prevention. (2006b). Revised recommendations for HIV testing of adults, adolescents, and pregnant women in health-care settings. *Morbidity and Mortality Weekly Report, 55* (NoRR-14).

Centers for Disease Control and Prevention (2016). *Living with AIDS*. Retrieved from http://cdc.gov/hiv/basics/living with hiv/index.html

Cohen, M. S., Shaw, G. M., McMichael, A. J., & Haynes, B. F. (2011a). Acute HIV-1 infection. *New England Journal of Medicine, 364*, 1943-1954.

Cohen, M. S., Chen, X. Q., McCauley, M., Gamble, T., Hosseinipour, M. C., Kumarasamy, N., . . . Celentano, D. (2011b). Prevention of HIV-1 infection with early antiretroviral therapy. *New England Journal of Medicine, 365*, 493-505.

Darbes, L., Crepaz, N., Lyles, C., Kennedy, G., & Rutherford, G. (2008). The efficacy of behavioral interventions in reducing HIV risk behaviors and incidence in sexually transmitted diseases in heterosexual African Americans. *AIDS, 22*, 1177-1194.

Dube, M. P., & Sattler, F. R. (1998). Metabolic complications of antiretroviral therapies. *AIDS Clinical Care, 10*(6), 41-44.

Dybul, M., Fauci, A. S., Bartlett, J. G., Kaplan, J. E., Pau, A. K., & Panel on Clinical Practices for Treatment of HIV. (2002). *Annals of Internal Medicine, 137*, 381-433.

Friedland, G. H. (1990). Early treatment for HIV: The time has come. *New England Journal of Medicine, 322*, 1000-1002.

Friedman, S. R., Kippax, S. C., Phaswana-Mafuya, N., Rossi, D., & Newman, C. E. (2006). Emerging future issues in HIV/AIDS social research. *AIDS, 20*, 959-965.

Gottlieb, M. S., Schroff, R., Schanker, H. M., Weisman, J. O., Fan, P. T., Wolf, R. A., & Saxon, A. (1981). Pneumocystis carinii pneumonia and mucosal candidiasis in previously healthy homosexual men: Evidence of a new acquired cellular immunodeficiency. *New England Journal of Medicine, 305*, 1425-1431.

Grubb, J. R., Moorman A. C., Baker, R. K., Masur, H., & the HOPS Investigators. (2006). The changing spectrum of pulmonary disease in patients with HIV infection on anti-retroviral therapy. *AIDS, 20*, 1095-1107.

Hammer, S. M. (2011). Antiretroviral treatment as prevention. *New England Journal of Medicine, 365*(6), 561-562.

Hammer, S. M. (2013). Baby steps on the road to HIV eradication. *New England Journal of Medicine, 369*, 1855-1856.

Havlir, D. V. (2008). HIV integrase inhibitors – Out of the pipeline and into the clinic. *New England Journal of Medicine, 359*, 416-418.

Health Resources and Services Administration (HRSA). (2012). *HRSA care action*. Retrieved from http://hab.hrsa.gov/newspublications/careactionnewsletter/hab_test_and_treat_january_careaction_pdf.pdf

Hutter, G., Nowak, D., Mossner, M., Ganepola, S., Müßig, A., Allers, K., . . . Thiel, E. (2009). Long-term control of HIV by CCR5 Delta32/Delta32 stem-cell transplantation. *New England Journal of Medicine, 360*, 692-698.

Johnston, M. I., & Fauci, A. S. (2008). An HIV vaccine – Challenges and prospects. *New England Journal of Medicine, 359*, 888-890.

Koziel, M. J., & Peters, M. G. (2007). Viral hepatitis in HIV infection. *New England Journal of Medicine, 356*, 1445-1454.

Larder, B. A., Darby, G., & Richman, D. D. (1989). HIV with reduced sensitivity to zidovudine (AZT) isolated during prolonged therapy. *Science, 243*, 1731-1734.

Lenhard, J. M., Furfine, E. S., Jain, R. G., Ittoop, O., Orband-Miller, L. A., Blanchard, S. G., . . . Weiel, J. E. (2000). HIV protease inhibitors block angiogenesis and increase lipolysis in vitro. *Antiviral Research, 47*(2), 121-129.

Marcus, R., & Centers for Disease Control (CDC) Cooperative Needlestick Surveillance Group (1988). Surveillance of healthcare workers exposed to blood from patients infected with the human immunodeficiency virus. *New England Journal of Medicine, 319,* 1118-1122.

Marsden, M. D., & Zack, J. A. (2009). Eradication of HIV: Current challenges and new directions. *Journal of Antimicrobial Chemotherapy, 63,* 7-10.

Matheson, L. (1984). *Work capacity evaluation: Interdisciplinary approach to industrial rehabilitation.* Anaheim, CA: Employment and Rehabilitation Institute of California.

Mills, E. J., Barnighausen, T., & Negin, J. (2012). HIV and aging - Preparing for the challenges ahead. *New England Journal of Medicine, 366,* 1270-1273.

Nguyen, A. T., Feasley, C. L., Jackson, K.W., Nitz, T. J., Salzwedd, K., Air, G. M., & Sakalian, M. (2011). The prototype HIV-1 maturation inhibitor, bevirimat, binds to the CA-SP1 cleavage site in immature Gag particles. *Retrovirology, 8*(11), 101-114.

Palella, F. J., Delaney, K. M., Moorman, A. C., & the HIV Outpatient Study Investigators. (1998). Declining morbidity and mortality among patients with advanced human immunodeficiency virus infection. *New England Journal of Medicine, 338,* 853-860.

Patel, K. G., Hyppolite, N. Shatzer, M., & Epstein, M. (2017). Disabling conditions seen in AIDS and HIV infection. In A. Moroz, S. R. Flanagan, & H. H. Zaretsky (Eds.), *Medical aspects of disability for the rehabilitation professional* (5th ed., pp. 19-29). New York, NY: Springer.

Piot, P., & Quinn, T. C. (2013). Response to the AIDS pandemic - A global health model. *New England Journal of Medicine, 368,* 2210-2218.

Poveda, E., Briz, V., Quinones-Mateu, M., & Soriano, V. (2006). HIV tropism: Diagnostic tools and implications for disease progression and treatment with entry inhibitors. *AIDS, 20,* 1359-1367.

Reiter, G. S. (1996). The HIV wasting syndrome. *AIDS Clinical Care, 8*(11), 89-96.

Richman, D. D., Morton, S. C., Wrin, T., Hellman, N., Berry, S., Shapiro, M. F., & Bozzette, S. A. (2004). The prevalence of antiretroviral drug resistance in the United States. *AIDS, 18,* 1393-1401.

Rodger, A. J., Cambiano, V., Bruun, T., Vernazza, P., Collins, S., van Lunzen, J., . . . PARTNER Study Group. (2016). Sexual activity without condoms and risk of HIV transmission in serodifferent couples when the HIV-positive partner is using suppressive antiretroviral therapy. *Journal of the American Medical Association, 316*(2), 171-181.

Rodriguez, W. (1998). Musculoskeletal manifestations of HIV disease. *AIDS Clinical Care, 10*(7), 49-52.

Rosenberg, E. (1997). Primary HIV infection and the acute retroviral syndrome. *AIDS Clinical Care, 9*(3), 19-25.

Social Security Administration (SSA). (February, 2005). *Social Security for people living with AIDS.* SSA Publication No. 05-10019. ICN 454510. Retrieved from http://www.socialsecurity.gov/pubs/10019.html

Stebbing J., Gazzard, B., & Douek, D. C. (2004). Where does HIV live? *New England Journal of Medicine, 350,* 1872-1880.

Stix, G. (June, 2006). A new assault on HIV. *Scientific American,* 77-79.

Thomas, C. F., & Limper, A. H. (2004). Pneumocystis pneumonia. *New England Journal of Medicine, 350,* 2487-2498.

United Nations Joint Programme on HIV/AIDS (UNAIDS). (2017, July). *Global HIV statistics.* Retrieved from http://www.unaids.org/en/resources/documents/2017/UNAIDS_FactSheet

United States Department of Labor. (1991). *Dictionary of occupational titles* (4th ed., Rev.). Washington, D.C.: Author.

Walensky, R. P., Paltiel, A. D., Losina, E., Mercincavage, L. M., Schackman, B. R., Sax, P. E., . . . Freedberg, K. A. (2006). The survival benefits of AIDS treatment in the United States. *Journal of Infectious Diseases, 194,* 11-19.

Walmsley, S. L., Antela A., Clumeck, N., Duiculescu, D., Eberhard, A., Gutierrez F., . . . Nichols, G. for the SINGLE Investigators (2013). Dolutegravir plus Abacavir - Lamivudine for the treatment of HIV-1 Infection. *New England Journal of Medicine, 369,* 1807-1818.

Weber, R., & the Data Collection on Adverse Events of Anti-HIV Drugs Study Group. (2006). Liver-related deaths in persons infected with the human immunodeficiency virus. *Archives of Internal Medicine, 166,* 1632-1641.

Wong, J. K., Ignacio, C. C., Torriani, F., Havlir, D., Fitch, N. J. S., & Richman, D. D. (1997a). In vivo compartmentalization of HIV: Evidence from the examination of pol sequences from autopsy tissues. *Journal of Virology, 71,* 2059-2071.

Wong, J. K., Hezareh, M., Gunthard, H. F., Havlir, D., Ignacio, C. A., Spina, C. A., & Richman, D. D. (1997b). Recovery of replication-competent HIV despite prolonged suppression of plasma viremia. *Science, 278,* 1291-1295.

Yin, C., Zhang, T., Qu, X., Zhang, Y., Putatunda R., Xiao, X., . . . Hu, W. (2017). In vivo excision of HIV-1 provirus by saCas9 and multiplex single-guide RNAs in animal models. *Molecular Therapy, 25*(5), 1168-1186.

s*Online References*. The Internet hosts thousands of Web pages devoted to HIV infection and AIDS. Typically, these pages are more current than other sources of AIDS-related information. The United Nations (UNAIDS) Website at http://www.unaids.org/en/ provides a current global perspective on HIV/AIDS. The U. S. Centers for Disease Control and Prevention offer the latest statistics about HIV/AIDS in the U. S. at http://www.cdc.gov/hiv/topics/surveillance/basic.htm. Current information about AIDS clinical drug trials is available at http://aidsinfo.nih.gov/.

About the Author

John J. Howard, MD, MPH, is Professorial Lecturer in Environmental and Occupational Health, Milken Institute School of Public Health and Health Services, The George Washington University, Washington, D.C. Dr. Howard is board-certified in internal medicine and occupational medicine. He is admitted to the practice of medicine in California and the District of Columbia.

Chapter 8

HEARING LOSS, DEAFNESS, AND RELATED VESTIBULAR DISORDERS

Sandra Hansmann, PhD
Shawn P. Saladin, PhD, CRC

Introduction

The inability to hear has far reaching social, rehabilitative, and health-related consequences and may negatively impact speech, language, academic, social, and vocational development (Luft, 2013). This chapter reviews selected medical, psychosocial, and vocational aspects of major disorders of the auditory and vestibular systems that impact hearing and communication, specifically focusing on Deafness, hearing loss, and disorders associated with hearing loss.

This chapter provides a brief overview of the anatomy of the ear, followed by a discussion of basic hearing evaluation and classification techniques. Next, the chapter describes common disorders of the auditory system, followed by a discussion of several related conditions of the vestibular system. Also reviewed are treatment, management, and aural rehabilitation options. The authors conclude with functional limitations and related psychosocial, vocational, and rehabilitative implications of hearing loss for individuals who are Deaf or hard of hearing.

Anatomy of the Ear

To understand hearing disorders, it is helpful to have a basic understanding of anatomy of the human ear and the process through which sound waves are perceived as sound by the brain. The human ear includes two distinct but interrelated systems that provide important sensory functions - the auditory system (pertaining to hearing sound) and the vestibular system (pertaining to balance, proprioception, and the detection of movement and acceleration).

The auditory system of the ear consists of three principle sections: the outer ear, middle ear, and inner ear (as shown in Figure 1). Sounds may consequently be conducted through the air into the outer, middle, and inner ear structures, or through the bones around the ear. Dysfunction in any one of the primary areas of the ear can result in difficulty hearing or the inability to hear.

The outer ear consists of the pinna, the externally visible part of the ear which is also called the auricle, and the ear canal up to the tympanic membrane, also known as the eardrum. Sound energy is collected by the pinna and then directed into the outer ear canal and onward to the tympanic membrane. The elastic cartilage of the pinna has an intricate funnel-like shape that facilitates the effective collection and transmission of sound energy into and through the ear canal (Kaiser Permanente, 2012; Ross, 2016). Audition, or hearing, begins when sound waves of various frequencies travel through the atmosphere and reach the pinna.

The middle ear functions to transfer and amplify vibratory energy deeper into the inner ear, where it can be perceived as sound. It is an air-containing space that includes the inside of the tympanic membrane and the ossicular chain, made up of three very small bones known collectively as ossicles and individually as the malleus, incus, and stapes. The tympanic membrane seals the middle ear. In hearing, sound waves vibrate the tympanic membrane which then presses against and vibrates the ossicles. The incus lies between the

FIGURE 1
The Auditory System

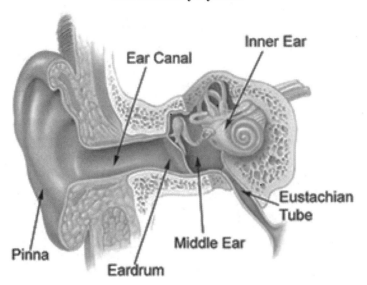

Source: Kaiser Permanente. (2012). *The basics of how we hear*. Retrieved from http://kphearingservices.com/hearing health/understandinghearingloss.html

malleus (attached to the middle ear) and the stapes. The middle ear also connects to the back of the nose and throat through the eustachian tube, which functions to maintain equal pressure between the middle ear and the external environment (Kaiser Permanente, 2012).

The inner ear is a complex fluid-filled structure involved in both hearing and balance. The major structures include the labyrinth and the vestibule, which contains the saccule, utricle, three semicircular canals, and cochlea. The saccule and utricle are beds of cells that detect vertical and horizontal movement. The semicircular canals detect rotational movement. The stapes footplate in the middle ear is attached to the base of the cochlea, a small, spiral structure crucial to hearing that includes the organ of Corti to convert sound vibrations into electrical signals through transduction. This is performed by specialized inner and outer hair cells, so called because they include stereocilia, cellular projections that look like fine hairs (Ross, 2016). In hearing, the movement of the stapes vibrates the stereocilia, which when connected to an intact and functional cranial nerve VIII or auditory nerve root pass signals to the brain for identification, localization, and understanding of sound (Martin & Clark, 2014).

Hearing Assessment

The assessment of hearing ability may encompass a variety of subjective, objective, and alternative methodologies, beginning with a standard otolaryngological examination. Many of these are increasingly automated and utilize smart phone and tablet technologies (Swanepoel, Mngemane, Molemong, Mkwanazi, & Tutshini, 2010). Standard otolaryngological examinations based on best professional practices include a thorough physical review of systems that describes the nature and chronology of symptoms. Any environmental or other factors that support or limit hearing are noted along with any patterns of fluctuation in hearing ability. Severity of hearing loss is quantified using commercial audiometers for pure tone audiometry, speech audiometry, and tympanometry (Kamrava & Roehm, 2017). Audiometric testing results are documented on an audiogram to provide a visual representation of severity of hearing loss in each ear.

Pure Tone Audiometry

Pure tone audiometry is a behavioral test that measures a person's sensitivity to sound. It is the preferred standardized method for evaluating hearing loss (American National Standards Institute [ANSI], 2009). Audiometers are used to assess hearing and measure in decibels and hertz. Decibels (dB) measure the intensity or loudness of a sound, while the tone or pitch of a sound is expressed as hertz (Hz). Using pure tone audiometry, an audiologist uses an audiometer to establish a pure tone threshold (PTT), defined as the softest sound a person can hear at least half the time. During a test, the individual responds to high and low pure tones delivered over a wide range of frequencies. The audiologist repeats each sound at increasing lower volume until the person cannot detect the sound. Bone conduction audiometry is an alternative procedure that uses a sound vibrator fitted to the bone behind each ear to present sound frequencies at decreasing volumes (ANSI/ASA S3.21-2004 R2009, American National Standards Institute, 2009; ANSI S3.6-2010, American National Standards Institute, 2010). Both variants of the test depend on the cooperation of the person tested to accurately report the tones the person can and cannot hear.

Speech Audiometry and Tympanometry

Speech audiometry is conceptually similar to pure tone audiometry, and is also considered a behavioral test dependent upon the individual's cooperation. It is used to determine the softest speech sounds a person can hear in each ear at approximately 50% accuracy, known as the speech awareness threshold (SAT) or speech reception threshold (SRT). This test also provides important information about a person's ability to recognize specific words and to comfortably tolerate more general speech stimuli. Tympanometry is a measure of the stiffness of the eardrum and is used to evaluate middle ear function. Unlike pure tone audiometry and speech audiometry, it is an objective rather than behavioral test. It is helpful in detecting fluid in the middle ear, negative middle ear pressure, tympanic membrane perforations, and disruption of the ossicles. An important aspect of both audiograms and tympanograms is the combination of subjective and objective information they provide about the configuration of an individual's hearing loss.

Configuration of Hearing Loss

Hearing configuration refers to the specific location, consistency, and quality of an individual's hearing difficulties. Determining the configuration of a person's hearing loss provides a more holistic view of hearing ability. Initially, a person may be described as having hearing loss in either one ear, termed a unilateral hearing loss, or a bilateral hearing loss, affecting both ears. If the degree or severity of hearing loss is the same in both ears, the person has a symmetrical loss; if the degree differs in each ear, the loss is asymmetrical. Configuration also includes the amount of hearing loss present at low, mid, and high frequencies (Arndt, Hassepass, Wesarg, Aschendorff, & Laszig, 2016). For example, a person who only has difficulty hearing low frequencies has a low-frequency hearing loss.

Medical Standards of Hearing Impairment

Most medical definitions of hearing impairment in the United States rely on the average of audiometric test results at three specific frequencies, most often at 500, 1000, and 2000 Hz. However, although some standards, such as those published by the Centers for Disease Control and Prevention National Institute for Occupational Safety and Health (NIOSH), base definitions of hearing loss on test results at frequencies of 1000, 2000, 3000, and 4000 Hz. Known as the pure tone average (PTA), this number is a basic indicator of how much hearing a person has in each ear independently without any type of amplification device. Diagnostic weight is given to the better ear (Margolis et al., 2015).

In general, unimpeded hearing ability is typified by PTA thresholds of 0 dB to 25 dB. Mild hearing loss is usually diagnosed when PTA results demonstrate a 26 dB to 40 dB threshold, while mild-to-moderate hearing loss is diagnosed in individuals around thresholds of 41 dB to 55 dB. An individual with 56 dB to 70 dB PTA has a moderate hearing loss. Threshold ranges from 71 to 90 dB indicate a person with a severe hearing loss. Persons with a 90 decibel threshold or greater have a profound hearing loss. Those with hearing in the mild to moderate categories are considered hard of hearing, while people assessed in the severe and profound categories are considered Deaf (Tye-Murray, 2008).

Onset and Progression of Hearing Loss

Onset and progression are important dimensions of hearing loss classification. Onset encompasses both the rapidity of hearing loss and the life stage at which it occurs. Progression refers to the course of the hearing loss. If a person's hearing loss occurs quickly and unexpectedly, it is considered a sudden hearing loss. If hearing status worsens slowly over time, an individual has a progressive loss. A person may also have a fluctuating hearing loss, one that alternates in severity or a loss that does not change and thus is considered stable (Martin & Clark, 2014).

In terms of life stage, when a child is Deaf or hard of hearing from birth, the loss is termed congenital; about 80% of these cases are due to genetic heredity. If hearing problems develop later, the person has an acquired loss. Congenital hearing loss and some acquired hearing losses are pre-lingual, or occurring before the development of speech. If hearing loss occurs after the development of effective speech, the loss is post-lingual (Smith, Shearer, Hildebrand, & Van Camp, 2014). Late-deafened is a term describing people whose acquired hearing loss occurs well into adulthood. In children, most acquired hearing loss is due to infections, such as rubella, herpes, and cytomegalovirus. For adults, most acquired loss is due to environmental causes, such as noise or injury (Yamasoba et al., 2013).

Cultural Definitions of Deafness

The cultural definition of Deafness represents a life and worldview manifested by beliefs, values, and traditions unique to Deaf people and grounded in personal choices about self-identification and language use. The term Deaf is capitalized when referring to people with hearing loss who identify themselves as part of the Deaf cultural group, and when referring to Deaf Culture. Historically, the use of American Sign Language (ASL) and attendance at a residential School for the Deaf have been important signifiers of membership in Deaf culture (Jassal, 2017). However, as other manual languages, such as Signed Exact English (SEE), have become more prevalent and attendance at residential schools has declined, more inclusive conceptualizations of Deaf cultural identity are emerging.

Within Deaf culture, social and socio-cultural models of identity remain preferred over impairment-oriented definitions common to medical models of disability. Thus, Deafness as an identity may be completely independent of audiometric and medical definitions of severity (Jassal, 2017; Leigh, Andrews, & Harris, 2016). An individual may identify as culturally Deaf, despite medically having a mild hearing loss. The converse may also be true; a person may have a medically profound hearing loss but not identify with Deaf culture.

Types of Hearing Loss

Deafness and hearing loss occur due to a wide variety of genetic, obstructive, neural, age-related, and environmental factors, several of which are discussed later in this chapter. Regardless of exact etiology, hearing loss is described as sensorineural, conductive, or mixed. Hearing loss stemming from conditions of the inner ear or auditory nerve is sensorineural. Most often, sensorineural hearing loss is due to damage from the hair cells of the inner ear to the auditory nerve and the brain. Conductive hearing loss most often originates in the outer and middle portions of the ear from some form of interference that results in the inability of sound waves to conduct from the pinna into the ear, such as wax blockage, a punctured eardrum, scarring from infections, and congenital or acquired irregularities. Mixed hearing loss results from a combination of both conductive and sensorineural losses (Smith et al., 2014).

Specific Etiologies

The population of people with hearing loss and other auditory disorders is very diverse. Two accepted etiological categories of hearing loss are acquired and genetic. Acquired hearing loss is sometimes labeled non-genetic hearing loss and may be sensorineural, conductive, or mixed. Acquired hearing loss is related to a number of causes such as acoustical injury, chronic infections, inner ear disorders, and exposure to toxins (Martin & Clark, 2014). Genetic hearing loss is caused by differences or changes in genes; it may be inherited or occur as the result of an isolated gene mutation, and may be conductive, sensorineural, or mixed.

Acquired Hearing Loss

Injuries to either the external or internal structures of the ear as well as infections of the middle and inner ear can result in significant hearing-related problems. If the external ear cannot adequately gather sound energy, hearing ability is significantly impacted. Internally, penetrating objects such as cotton swabs, pencils, or other small sharp objects can injure the tympanic membrane. Sudden severe pressure changes can perforate the eardrum. Ear pain may be present and range from mild to severe; hearing loss often accompanies these injuries as well. Internal ear damage may occur due to otitis media (OM), an infection of the middle ear and middle ear structures. Causes of OM include bacterial infections, infections following injuries, and presence of fluid in the ear. Symptoms include ear pressure or pain, dizziness, and discharge. Chronically occurring OM can result in permanent damage to the tympanic membrane, with or without permanent changes to the middle ear (Jaber, 2017).

Noise-induced hearing loss (NIHL) occurs when excessive sound exposure seriously and permanently injures the inner ear. It is a common but mostly preventable health concern with serious negative economic impact. Occupational, recreational, and accidental causes of noise-related hearing loss includes sound exposure through either continuous or impulse noise exposure. Continuous exposure occurs when an individual is frequently in environments that include noisy on-going sounds, such as industrial machinery or loud music. Various sources suggest 10% to 25% of adults in the United States have some level of NIHL; this type of loss is a major public health issue (Neitzel, Swinburn, Hammer, & Eisenberg, 2017). While NIHL has been closely linked to the volume, duration, and type of noise exposure, it is often due to a more complex interaction of factors, including age, psychological well-being, and lifestyle.

Presbycusis is a progressive age-related disorder that may be conductive, sensorineural, or mixed. Symptoms include decreased auditory sensitivity and loudness perception, and reduced speech intelligibility. Due to aging, the external ear may become less firm and elastic, middle ear structures become more rigid which decreases vibratory response, while the hair cells and cochlea of the inner ear may also deteriorate. These changes act simultaneously to impact the effectiveness of the ear. Presbycusis is a common and critical health concern for older adults, affecting about 25% of individuals 65 to 74 years old, and about half of all individuals 75 years old and older (Garrison-Diehn, 2017; National Institute on Deafness and Other Communication Disorders, 2011). Males tend to have more high-frequency hearing loss, while females tend to have a more generalized hearing loss typified by a flatter audiometric pattern (Ozmeral, Eddins, Frisina, & Eddins, 2016).

Ototoxicity refers to the negative effects some medications, solvents, and other substances have on the nerves and organs of the ear. A number of industrial chemicals are classified as ototoxic, including mercury and styrene. Most individuals do not come into contact with these substances unless they work in occupations where they are in direct contact with industrial chemicals. More typically, people are exposed through prescription medications used to treat infections and those used in cancer treatments and following organ transplants, especially with prolonged use or at high dosages (Sheth, Mukherjea, Rybak, & Ramkumar, 2017). These agents, including the common chemotherapeutic drug Cisplatin, may result in sudden deafness or permanent high frequency hearing loss (Brooks & Knight, 2017).

Genetic Hearing Loss

One in every 500 people in the United States is born with hearing loss largely due to inherited genetic causes (Sloan-Heggen et al., 2016). Genetically-linked hearing losses may be classified broadly as either nonsyndromic or syndromic in nature. About 80% of hereditary hearing loss is nonsyndromic, meaning that is not associated with any specific medical problems and has no visible physiological differences. Conversely, syndromic hearing loss is associated with well-identified clinical features involving one or multiple body systems; more than 400 genetic syndromes have been identified. Most syndromic hearing loss is mild, and rarely additional serious complications occur.

Hereditary hearing loss is further classified by the pattern of inheritance. Autosomal recessive loss occurs when both parents carry a recessive gene for hearing loss and the trait is inherited by the child. Autosomal dominant hearing loss, which accounts for about 80% of genetic hearing loss, occurs when at least one parent carries a dominant gene for hearing loss. Otosclerosis is a relatively common autosomal dominant conductive hearing loss that occurs due to the ossicles in the inner ear growing and hardening into a mass, usually between ages 10 to 30 (Bagger-Sjöbäck et al., 2015). Otosclerosis can be treated surgically by replacing the hardened bone with a prosthetic implant, a procedure that is generally effective and low-risk (Plichta, Skarzynski, Krol, & Skarzynski, 2017).

Vestibular Disorders

The vestibular system of the inner ear is responsible for orientation of sound location and balance. The system works in conjunction with visual images and head movement to send information to the brain regarding the physical orientation of the individual. Disturbances to this system, even when minor, may result in hearing loss as well as a variety of nonspecific sensations of varying severity.

Tinnitus is estimated to affect about 15% of the population. It is a condition characterized by the perception of sounds such as ringing, buzzing, or whining that originate in the head or ears not in the environment. Tinnitus is caused by damage to the nerve endings in the inner ear and may be associated with hearing loss. It may be symptomatic of other health concerns such as hypertension, diabetes, thyroid problems, injuries, or infections. Recent research suggests a genetic component to the disorder (Bogo et al., 2017). Usually, symptoms are not troublesome, but occasionally severe symptoms are physically debilitating and/or have significant mental health consequences, such as depression (Henry et al., 2016).

Vertigo is a sensation of disorientation or movement, usually rotational, when no actual movement is occurring. It is a vestibular dysfunction itself, as well as a common symptom of other dysfunctions, including inner ear problems, tumors, brain hemorrhages, migraines, hypertension, and other concerns. Hearing loss in one ear, abnormal eye movements, nausea, tinnitus, and gait disturbances, all of which may range from mild to severe, are typical. Generally, there are two types of vertigo, central and peripheral. Peripheral vertigo is caused by issues in the inner ear, while central vertigo is caused by changes in the brain or brainstem. Benign paroxysmal positional vertigo (BPPV) is the most common form of peripheral vertigo, and generally produces short but frequent sensations of motion or dizziness (Tan, Deng, Zhang, & Wang, 2017).

More severe disruptions of the vestibular system may result in **Ménière's Syndrome**, a disorder related to volume and pressure changes in inner ear blood flow and fluids. It is a complex and frequently debilitating disorder that combines symptoms of tinnitus, vertigo, and progressive hearing loss. In its early stages, symptoms may be mild and episodic, but over time progress with worsening vertigo and tinnitus and more severe unilateral sensorineural hearing loss. A number of treatments are available, including low sodium dietary changes, prescription medications, including oral diuretics and aural drops or injections, positive pressure therapy, and surgery. Yet, while these interventions provide relief from vertigo and tinnitus, they may further damage hearing (van Sonsbeek, Pullens, & van Benthem, 2015).

Treatment Strategies for Hearing Loss

Treatment and management strategies for hearing loss share the goal of achieving the best possible auditory functioning and speech recognition. Options depend on the type, severity, and etiology of the condition (Luft, 2013). The most common hearing management method involves use of assistive listening devices including hearing aids, cochlear implants, and assistive listening devices designed to work in conjunction with aids and implants. This section reviews common devices and strategies.

Hearing Aids

Hearing aids are usually prescribed for people whose hearing thresholds are 25 dB or greater in the better ear, but are often not sought until the person experiences noticeable difficulties at about 40 dB threshold, or the point at which background noise markedly affects hearing ability. Rapid technological development has radically improved modern hearing aids; most are now digital. Digital hearing aids convert sound waves into binary code to represent the frequency, intensity, and patterns of the signal, a function termed digitized sound processing (DSP). With extreme speed, digital aides discriminate between useful sound or unwanted noise, providing an undistorted signal and improved filtering of background sounds. The most sophisticated devices incorporate wireless and Bluetooth technologies, frequency lowering, highly sensitive directional microphones, and digital noise reduction algorithms (Arsinte, Lupu, & Sumalan, 2017). Models are tailored to different functional and aesthetic needs, and range from behind-the-ear devices to aids that fit completely and almost invisibly inside the ear canal in one or both ears.

Cochlear Implants

Cochlear implants are prosthetic devices surgically placed in the inner ear to bypass the external, middle, and inner ear hair cells to stimulate the auditory nerve directly through electrical impulses. Recent research indicates cochlear implants may have an added benefit of possibly preventing or slowing further hearing and speech deterioration. As a result, cochlear devices are now the preferred restorative treatment for children and adults with severe to profound hearing loss. Use has more recently expanded from profoundly deaf individuals to individuals with moderate diagnoses, including those with single-sided hearing loss. Surgical implantation criteria include personal traits, educational background, age, and communication skills. Post-surgically, the length and severity of deafness prior to implantation and existence of useful speech reading skills are among many critical factors that influence implant outcomes. In general, individuals who are younger with shorter-term hearing loss and good speech reading abilities have more successful outcomes than people with more adverse profiles, individuals who are pre-lingually Deaf, and those who have exclusively used manual communication (Eng & Learner, 2011).

Assistive Listening Devices (ALD)

Assistive listening devices (ALD) as a term encompasses a wide variety of digital and wireless sound-boosting devices that helps a person hear or communicate without distracting noise in the environment (NIDCD, 2011). Hearing induction loops, also termed audio loops, are a common assistive option that allows the sound system in a room to connect wirelessly directly to an individual's hearing aid via the telecoil, a technical feature present in many hearing aids and cochlear implants. This eliminates background noise and improves the clarity of sound. FM systems are somewhat similar to audio loops, but sound is transmitted wirelessly directly to the receiver. Usually portable, FM systems can be carried from location to location by the user (American Speech-Language-Hearing Association [ASHA], 2016). Infrared systems are another type of ALD that uses a combination of light and electromagnetic signals. They do not transmit through walls, making them useful when confidentiality is necessary. Despite the usefulness of all these systems, many hearing aid users are unaware their device includes a telecoil, so adoption of these tools is limited.

Aural Rehabilitation

Aural rehabilitation plays a significant role in the treatment and management of Deafness and hearing loss. For adults, aural rehabilitation focuses on improving effectiveness of communication, primarily through maximization of residual functional hearing and reinforced visual cueing for auditory awareness and speech. Auditory methods use residual hearing abilities, with or without assistive devices, to hone listening skills. Kinesthetic methods focus on awareness of eye contact, motions of speech, facial expressions, body movements, and proximity. Oral methods combine assistive listening devices, kinesthesis, and speech reading to develop verbal speech. Speech reading (inaccurately termed lip reading) allows a person to understand speech by observing mouth, facial, and body movements to determine words and contexts. Manual communication exists in contrast to oral strategies, embracing rather than discouraging non-verbal signed communication. Common techniques include American Sign Language (ASL) and Signed Exact English (SEE). Total communication is the most inclusive approach, using the most effective and appropriate strategies in combination to maximize communication. Increasingly, sophisticated internet-based systems are being used to deliver all of these approaches (Mayer, 2016).

Health Disparities

A growing body of research indicates significant health disparities and health literacy challenges exist for people who are hard of hearing or Deaf, although precise data is difficult to obtain due to the exclusion of these groups from health-related research. For individuals who are profoundly Deaf, the disparities are especially pronounced and may affect rehabilitation and related services.

Most differences in health-related behaviors and health outcomes among individuals who are Deaf are due to communication barriers. Many of these differences begin very early in life, as Deaf and hard of hearing children miss the incidental learning other children access by overhearing family history and health issue discussions. Similarly, individuals who are Deaf or hard of hearing are often unaware of media-based public health messages, such as anti-smoking television campaigns (McKee, Moreland, Atcherson, & Zazove, 2015). Lower socioeconomic status and less educational attainment are factors that may further complicate health literacy and access to health-related information. Taken in combination, these issues contribute to the higher rates of smoking, obesity, and mental health concerns reported among people who are Deaf.

In addition to more generalized concerns, Deaf and hard of hearing patients are more likely to be dissatisfied with their interactions with doctors and other healthcare providers than their hearing counterparts, especially when few to no options for sign language interpretation are available. Often, this dissatisfaction leads to lower levels of medication compliance and adherence to physician orders, as well as lower levels of seeking healthcare (Barnett et al., 2011). Healthcare providers are typically unaware of the preferred information networks that exist among many culturally Deaf people, which generally include highly esteemed Deaf community peers, counselors for the Deaf, and clergy members at predominately Deaf churches. These networks are critical in addressing health disparities among individuals with hearing loss. Also, they contribute to key protective factors, such as individual ability to cope with adversity and community capacity for linguistically and culturally relevant support.

Psychosocial and Vocational Implications

The psychosocial impact of communication barriers for people who are Deaf and hard of hearing can begin at a very early age and may result in social isolation, familial alienation, lower self-esteem, and poorer educational outcomes. Nearly a third of Deaf and hard of hearing children have difficulties with social interactions and behavior, as do many Deaf adults, who may present with a variety of emotional and behavioral problems (Heffernan, Coulson, Henshaw, Barry, & Ferguson, 2016; Zöller & Archer, 2015). In addition, recent research suggests auditory and cognitive processing are closely interrelated, with potentially negative effects on comprehension, memory, perception, and other higher-order functions due to the higher cognitive efforts required. Regarding late-acquired and age-related hearing loss, declines in social participation, communication, and higher-order cognition can occur, leading to increased risk of isolation and depression (Danielsson et al., 2017).

Broad vocational implications exist for people who are hard of hearing or Deaf, but the most significant are trends in underemployment and unemployment. Functional communication limitations in the areas of social development and educational achievement, in addition to limited abilities in detecting environmental sounds, difficulties in communicating with others, and specific occupational hearing requirements negatively affect employability (Perkins-Dock, Battle, Edgerton, & McNeill, 2015). In particular, functional limitations in detecting environmental stimuli may result in significant work safety concerns. Abilities to locate the source of sounds and to discriminate between sounds such as warning bells, alarms, and door chimes are especially crucial if an individual is working with or near machinery. Other problems with balance, dizziness, and tinnitus impact a person's ability to function effectively in work and social settings (Punch, 2016).

Conclusion

Understanding the unique needs of individuals with hearing loss is a complex and sometimes challenging rehabilitation task. To serve the needs of people with hearing loss, rehabilitation professionals need an understanding of the critical dimensions of hearing, listening, and communication, as well as the effects these factors have on service provision. Many people who are Deaf or hard of hearing have useful residual hearing abilities, and successfully use devices such as hearing aids and cochlear implants; some individuals are skilled in speech reading, while others are fluent in sign language. Each person has unique strengths on which to build. Assistive listening devices, communication technologies, environmental modifications, and reasonable accommodations may effectively address limitations. These and many other options need to be explored as part of comprehensive rehabilitation planning and service provision.

Case Study

Alan Parchman is a 42 year-old college educated married man with three children, ages 12, 15, and 16. He has been working at a chemical plant as a kettle operator and tender for several years. Mr. Parchman's job has required frequent exposure to both noise and ototoxic chemicals. Before this job position, he was employed by a local school district as a special education reading specialist. Alan felt this was an emotionally rewarding job, but the position in the chemical plant paid a higher salary.

Three years ago, Alan began to notice a decrease in hearing ability and developed intermittent severe tinnitus. Due to concerns about losing his position or being placed on unpaid medical leave, he did not report these symptoms to his employer. About six months ago, Mr. Parchman's symptoms worsened significantly, and at his wife's urging, he sought evaluation by his general practitioner.

His physician noted that Mr. Parchman had difficulty understanding speech in the office environment. She referred him to an audiologist for further evaluation. The audiological results demonstrated a pure tone average (PTA) in the right ear of 60 dB, and a PTA in the left ear of 55 dB. Alan further demonstrated 82% word understanding in the right ear, and 78% word understanding in the left ear. The tympanogram was within normal limits. He was diagnosed with sensorineural hearing loss due to noise and ototoxic chemical exposure at work and was scheduled for fitting of hearing aids.

Questions

1. Classify the level of hearing loss of this consumer. Identify other characteristics of the hearing loss.
2. Outline Alan's vocational profile.
3. What transferable skills does this individual have? Identify occupations using these skills.
4. If the consumer decided to remain in his current job, how would you as the rehabilitation counselor approach this decision? Provide supporting arguments.
5. Identify Mr. Parchman's likely functional limitations and recommend accommodations.
6. What are the implications of this type of hearing loss in regard to possible future functional limitations?

References

American National Standards Institute. (2009). *Methods for manual pure-tone threshold audiometry* (ANSI/ASA S3.21-2004 (R2009). New York, NY: Author.

American National Standards Institute. (2010). *Specification for audiometers* (ANSI S3.6-2010). New York, NY: Author.

American Speech-Language-Hearing Association (ASHA). (2016). *FM systems*. Retrieved from http://asha?.org/public?/hearing/fm-systems

Arndt, S., Hassepass, F., Wesarg, T., Aschendorff, A., & Laszig, R. (2016). Treatment of single-sided deafness and asymmetric hearing loss in adults. *Journal of Laryngology and Otology, 130,* S111.

Arsinte, R., Lupu, E., & Sumalan, T. (2017, June). A rapid prototyping model concept for a DSP-based hearing aid. *E-Health and Bioengineering Conference (EHB) Proceedings* (pp. 337-340). Institute of Electrical and Electronics Engineers (IEEE).

Bagger-Sjöbäck, D., Strömbäck, K., Hultcrantz, M., Papatziamos, G., Smeds, H., Danckwardt-Lilliestrōm, N., . . . Fridberger, A. (2015). High-frequency hearing, tinnitus, and patient satisfaction with stapedotomy: A randomized prospective study. *Scientific Reports, 5,* 13341.

Barnett, S., Klein, J. D., Pollard Jr, R. Q., Samar, V., Schlehofer, D., Starr, M., . . . Pearson, T. A. (2011). Community participatory research with deaf sign language users to identify health inequities. *American Journal of Public Health, 101*(12), 2235-2238.

Bogo, R., Farah, A., Karlson, K. K., Pedersen, N. L., Svartengren, M., & Skjonsberg, A. (2017). Prevalence, incidence proportion, and heritability for tinnitus: A longitudinal twin study. *Ear and Hearing, 38*(3), 292-300.

Brooks, B., & Knight, K. (2017). Ototoxicity monitoring in children treated with platinum chemotherapy. *International Journal of Audiology, 24,* 1-7.

Danielsson, H., Pichora-Fuller, M. K., Dupuis, K., Rönnberg, J., Chasteen, A. L., & Nilsson, L. G. (2017*). The effect of early age-related hearing loss on memory and participation in social leisure activities.* Retrieved from https://doi.org/10.31219//osf.io/4X3jv

Eng, N., & Learner, P. K. (2011). Speech, language, and swallowing disorders. In S. R. Flanagan, H. H. Zaretsky, & A. Moroz (Eds.), *Medical aspects of disability: A handbook for the rehabilitation professional* (4th ed., pp. 195-222). New York, NY: Springer.

Garrison-Diehn, C. (2017). Age-related hearing loss. In N. A. Pachana (Ed.), *Encyclopedia of geropsychology* (pp. 145-150). Singapore: Springer.

Heffernan, E., Coulson, N. S., Henshaw, H., Barry, J. G., & Ferguson, M. A. (2016). Understanding the psychosocial experiences of adults with mild-moderate hearing loss: An application of Leventhal's self-regulatory model. *International Journal of Audiology, 55*(Suppl. 3), S3-S12.

Henry, J. A., Griest, S., Thielman, E., McMillan, G., Kaelin, C., & Carlson, K. F. (2016). Tinnitus Functional Index: Development, validation, outcomes research, and clinical application. *Hearing Research, 334,* 58-64.

Jaber, M. R. (2017). Sensorineural hearing loss in patients with chronic suppurative otitis media. *Al-Qadisiyah Medical Journal, 11*(20), 159-163.

Jassal, Y. R. (2017). Learning about Deaf Culture: More accessible than previously thought. *American Annals of the Deaf, 161*(5), 583-584.

Kaiser Permanente. (2012). *The basics of how we hear.* Retrieved from http://kphearingservices.com/hearing health/understandinghearingloss.html

Kamrava, B., & Roehm, P. C. (2017). Systematic review of ossicular chain anatomy: Strategic planning for development of novel middle ear prostheses. *Otolaryngology-Head and Neck Surgery*, 0194599817701717.

Leigh, I. W., Andrews, J. F., & Harris, R. (2016). *Deaf Culture: Exploring Deaf communities in the United States.* San Diego, CA: Plural Publishing.

Luft, P. (2013). Independent living services for Deaf and hard of hearing students: Results of a national survey of school programs. *Journal of Applied Rehabilitation Counseling, 44,* 18-27.

Mayer, C. (2016). Rethinking total communication: Looking back, moving forward. *The Oxford Handbook of Deaf Studies in Language*, Oxford, United Kingdom: Oxford University.

Margolis, R. H., Wilson, R. H., Popelka, G. R., Eikelboom, R. H., Swanepoel, D. W., & Saly, G. L. (2015). Distribution characteristics of normal pure-tone thresholds. *International Journal of Audiology, 54*(11), 796–805.

Martin, F. N., & Clark, J. G. (2014). *Introduction to audiology* (12th ed.). Boston, MA: Allyn and Bacon Communication Sciences and Disorders.

McKee, M. M., Moreland, C., Atcherson, S. R., & Zazove, P. (2015). Hearing loss: Communicating with the patient who is deaf or hard of hearing. *FP Essentials, 434*, 24-28.

National Institute on Deafness and other Communication Disorders (NIDCD). (2011). *NIDCD fact sheet: Assistive devices for people with hearing, voice, speech, or language disorders.* Retrieved from http://www.nidcd.nih.gov/staticresources/health/hearing/NIDCD-Assistive-Devices-FS.pdf

Neitzel, R. L., Swinburn, T. K., Hammer, M. S., & Eisenberg, D. (2017). Economic impact of hearing loss and reduction of noise-induced hearing loss in the United States. *Journal of Speech, Language, and Hearing Research, 60*(1), 182-189.

Ozmeral, E. J., Eddins, A. C., Frisina, D. R., & Eddins, D. A. (2016). Large cross-sectional study of presbycusis reveals rapid progressive decline in auditory temporal acuity. *Neurobiology of Aging, 43*, 72-78.

Perkins-Dock, R. E., Battle, T. R., Edgerton, J. M., & McNeill, J. N. (2015). A survey of barriers to employment for individuals who are Deaf. *JADARA, 49*(2-3), 1-20. Retrieved from http://repository.wcsu.edu/jadara/vol49/iss2/3

Plichta, L., Skarzynski, P. H., Krol, B., & Skarzynski, H. (2017). Revision surgery after unsuccessful surgical treatment of hearing loss and tinnitus in otosclerosis. *Journal of Hearing Science, 7*(2), 121.

Punch, R. (2016). Employment and adults who are Deaf or hard of hearing: Current status and experiences of barriers, accommodations, and stress in the workplace. *American Annals of the Deaf, 161*(3), 384-397.

Ross, L. M. (2016). *Atlas of anatomy* (Vol. 3). New York, NY: Thieme.

Sheth, S., Mukherjea, D., Rybak, L., & Ramkumar, V. (2017). Mechanisms of cisplatin-induced ototoxicity and otoprotection. *Frontiers in Cellular Neuroscience, 11*, 338.

Sloan-Heggen, C. M., Bierer, A. O., Shearer, A. E., Kolbe, D. L., Nishimura, C. J., Frees, K. L., . . . Ranum, P. T. (2016). Comprehensive genetic testing in the clinical evaluation of 1119 patients with hearing loss. *Human Genetics, 135*(4), 441-450.

Smith, R. J., Shearer, A. E., Hildebrand, M. S., & Van Camp, G. (2014). Deafness and hereditary hearing loss overview. *Gene Reviews* (Internet).

Swanepoel, D. W., Mngemane, S., Molemong, S., Mkwanazi, H., & Tutshini, S. (2010). Hearing assessment - Reliability, accuracy, and efficiency of automated audiometry. *Telemedicine and e-Health, 16*(5), 557-563.

Tan, J., Deng, Y., Zhang, T., & Wang, M. (2017). Clinical characteristics and treatment outcomes for benign paroxysmal positional vertigo comorbid with hypertension. *Acta Oto-Laryngologica, 137*(5), 482-484.

Tye-Murray, N. (2008). *Foundations of aural rehabilitation: Children, adults, and their family members* (3rd ed.). Clifton Park, NY: Cengage Learning.

van Sonsbeek, S., Pullens, B., & van Benthem, P. P. (2015). *Positive pressure therapy for Ménière's disease or syndrome.* Cochrane Library Database (internet).

Yamasoba, T., Lin, F. R., Someya, S., Kashio, A., Sakamoto, T., & Kondo, K. (2013). Current concepts in age-related hearing loss – Epidemiology and mechanistic pathways. *Hearing Research, 303*, 30-38.

Zöller, M. E. T., & Archer, T. (2015). Emotional disturbances expressed by Deaf patients: Affective Deaf syndrome. *Clinical and Experimental Psychology, 2*(1), 1-8.

About the Authors

Sandra Hansmann, PhD, is Associate Professor, School of Rehabilitation Services and Counseling at the University of Texas Rio Grande Valley. Dr. Hansmann has conversational skills in ASL and Signed English. Her research agenda is focused on Deaf rehabilitation, technology, gender-based violence, and online and distance counselor education.

Shawn P. Saladin, PhD, CRC, is Professor, School of Rehabilitation Services and Counseling and Associate Dean, College of Health Affairs at the University of Texas Rio Grande Valley. As a person who is Deaf and communicates through both oral and signed modalities, he is skilled in American Sign Language

(ASL), total communication, and Signed English. His research interests include assistive technology, Deaf-hearing relationships, and employment of people who are deaf or hard of hearing.

Chapter 9

VISUAL DISABILITIES

Bill Takeshita, OD, FAAO, FCOVD
Robin Langman, MS, CRC
Rebekah Brod, MA, MFT

Introduction

Vision is a complex and fascinating process of the human body. Although vision can be described as being analogous to a camera, it involves much more. The eyes are a matrix of millions of cells that convert light information into electrical signals. Two-thirds of the brain is involved in the complex process of vision (Kanski & Bowling, 2015). The visual centers of the brain communicate with the motor, auditory, language, speech, and executive processing areas of the brain to impact reading, facial recognition, spatial awareness, and problem solving.

In a matter of milliseconds, vision allows us to gather information about the surrounding environment at distances well beyond the reach of the arms and fingers. The central visual system allows us to identify details and enables us to read, identify faces, and perform fine motor tasks. The peripheral visual system provides the brain with continuous information to assist with independent mobility in familiar and unfamiliar areas. Integration of both central and peripheral visual information allows adults with normal vision to perform tasks efficiently and independently (Kanski & Bowling, 2015).

Blindness and loss of vision are frightening and emotionally stressful events. Vision impairment causes functional difficulties with reading, driving, walking, and working independently and may result in emotional, psychological, social, and financial difficulties (Corn & Erin, 2010). In the United States, over 70% of adults between the ages of 20 and 65 who have significant visual impairments are unemployed (Erickson, Lee, & von Schrader, 2017). The absence of employment can exacerbate emotional, psychological, and financial difficulties of patients with vision impairment and contribute to the development of other problems. To provide training and promote maximum productivity and independence at home and in the workplace, rehabilitation counselors play a pivotal role in developing treatment plans that may involve ophthalmologists, optometrists, psychologists, orientation and mobility specialists, and teachers for the visually impaired. In this chapter, the many different aspects of vision are described, along with diseases and disorders that impact the functional abilities of individuals.

Vision Impairment and Disability

The rehabilitation counselor must have a thorough understanding of the degree of vision impairment and functional vision of a client before developing a vocational plan. This can be challenging because the counselor must rely on medical reports, chart notes, and information provided by the client. Unfortunately, medical reports and chart records may describe the diagnosis without reflecting the client's visual strengths and limitations.

In the United States, eye care professionals, the Social Security Administration, and other government agencies have adopted the definitions set forth by the World Health Organization (2001) to provide a uniform definition of vision impairment and set standards to determine qualifications for government services and benefits. This definition follows below:

Definitions of Visual Impairment

- Functionally blind describes individuals who are not able to perceive light.
- Legal blindness is visual ability with a best-corrected acuity of 20/200 or worse in the better eye, or the widest diameter of peripheral vision measuring 20 degrees or less in the better eye.
- Visually impaired or partially sighted describes individuals with a best-corrected visual acuity of 20/70 to 20/180 in the better eye, or a peripheral field of vision between 21 degrees and 140 degrees.
- Fully *sighted* describes people with a best-corrected visual acuity of 20/40 or better in the best eye.

Although the definitions of functionally blind, legal blindness, and visually impaired or partially sighted are often used in medical reports, they do not completely describe a client's functional vision. These definitions only consider visual acuity and peripheral vision. Clarity of sight, depth perception, eye-hand-foot coordination, color vision, day and night vision, and visual processing skills are some of the visual sub-skills that affect visual functions (Corn & Erin, 2010). Deficits in a specific skill can have significant ramifications regarding the client's ability to perform one task but may not have an impact on another. It is crucial to define vision impairment as it relates to specific occupations or job tasks (Brodwin, Parker, & DeLaGarza, 2010).

Prevalence of Visual Loss

According to the American Community Survey (Erickson et al., 2017), the number of non-institutionalized males and females, ages four through age 20 in the United States who were reported to have a visual disability in 2015 was the following:

- Total = 678,000
- Girls = 324,000
- Boys = 354,000

The number of non-institutionalized males and females of all ages in the United States reported to have a visual disability in 2015 was as follows:

- Total = 6,833,000
- Women = 3,738,400
- Men = 2,971,600
- Age 16-64 = 3,847,100
- Age 65 and older = 2,985,900

Eye Care Professionals

A counselor works with eye care professionals to obtain information regarding the client's functional vision. In the United States, optometrists and ophthalmologists are licensed to diagnose and treat diseases and disorders of the visual system. Optometrists are considered to be the primary eye care professional in health systems. If the patient requires surgery or additional medical treatment, the optometrist refers the patient to an ophthalmologist (Kanski & Bowling, 2015).

The Eye Examination

The general eye examination involves a case history, measurement of the distant and near clarity of sight, screening of neurological function, inspection of the health of the eyes, and refraction to determine the need for corrective lenses (Corn & Erin, 2010). This section describes information obtained with the eye examination and specific tests performed to quantify various visual skills and functional implications.

Case History

The case history is one of the most informative components of the eye examination. A medical history and results from prior eye examinations provide clues to explain the patient's symptoms and complaints. Questions regarding vision problems of family members help the examiner gain insight into the possible patterns of genetic eye conditions and prognosis.

Visual Acuity Testing

A Snellen eye chart is the most common test used to measure clarity of sight. It is typically placed 20 feet from the patient, who is then directed to identify letters of varying sizes with each eye. Each letter on the Snellen chart, called an optotype, has a specific size. The physician records the distance from the chart to the patient. A patient who identifies the 20-size letter from 20 feet has 20/20 visual acuity, whereas a person who can only read the 200-size letter from 20 feet has 20/200 acuity. If the individual is not able to read the 200-size letter from 20 feet with either eye with the best corrected vision, he or she is considered to be legally blind. The patient with 20/200 acuity has difficulty identifying faces, and reading street signs and chalkboards (Kanski & Bowling, 2015; Rosenthal, Cole, & Escalera, 2017).

Visual Field Testing

Visual field testing measures the width or area of vision a person can see. Glaucoma, retinitis pigmentosa, and cerebral vascular accidents (stroke) can cause loss of peripheral vision and affect a person's mobility, night vision, balance, and spatial orientation. Macular degeneration and diabetic retinopathy affect central field of vision and may cause blurred sight, blind spots in the central vision, reduced contrast vision, and diminished color vision. Visual field defects in the central vision affect one's ability to read, identify faces, drive, and carry out other activities needed at school and work (Sheth et al., 2012).

Visual field defects are not always noticed by the patient. If the location of a visual field defect is different in both eyes, one eye compensates for the other. The visual field defect may be mild and not cause an absolute blind spot but rather, vision appears faded.

The most sophisticated method of testing peripheral vision is through the use of computerized perimetry. In this test, the patient is positioned in front of a large dome in which lights of varying sizes and intensities flash in different parts of the central and peripheral fields. Low vision specialists use this information to map out regions of the eye that have the highest sensitivity and use lenses and prisms to deflect images onto functional fields of vision.

Refraction

Refraction is a test that determines the optimal prescription to sharpen a person's sight. Myopia (nearsightedness) is a condition where light rays focus in front of the macula, causing blurred distance sight. Hyperopia (farsightedness) is when the light rays focus behind the macula, causing blurred near vision. Astigmatism is another refractive error where the shape of the eye is distorted, causing distorted vision. Eye doctors prescribe glasses with prescription lenses that focus the light rays on the central retina (macula) to produce clarity of sight. Contact lenses and refractive surgery also correct myopia, hyperopia, and astigmatism.

Color Vision Testing

Color vision is generally tested with pseudo isochromatic plates, which display numbers of different colors on backgrounds of varying colors. Color vision deficiencies are more common among males than females and affect a person's ability to differentiate between similar colors. For instance, someone with a color vision deficiency may confuse red and burgundy. Individuals with complete color blindness are unable to identify any colors and their vision can be thought of as similar to watching a black and white television. People with complete color blindness also may have blurred sight and sensitivity to bright light.

Eye Teaming and Binocular Vision Testing

Binocular vision involves the ability to coordinate the eyes. Eye coordination testing is administered to patients who complain of double vision, frequent loss of place when reading, and eye strain. Each eye has six extra-ocular muscles that control the movement of the eyes along with one internal muscle, which changes the shape of the internal crystalline lens to focus on near and distant objects. Abnormal coordination of these muscles results in a crossed or turned eye (strabismus), double vision (diplopia), poor depth perception, blurred sight, headaches, and eye strain. Trauma, tumors, amyotrophic lateral sclerosis (ALS), Parkinson's disease, diabetes, multiple sclerosis, and myasthenia gravis can affect eye movement and hinder a person's ability to perform daily activities (Falvo & Holland, 2018).

Parts of the Eye

Orbit

The orbit, often called the eye socket, houses and protects the eyeball from direct trauma. It consists of several bones that are susceptible to fracture during trauma. The orbit provides the foundation which allows for eye movement. Brain tumors, thyroid disease, and trauma to the orbit itself can restrict the movement of the eyes, and cause diplopia (double vision), affecting the positioning of the eyes.

Eyelids

The eyelids lubricate and protect the cornea and the anterior portion of the eye. Whenever an individual blinks, various glands produce tears to lubricate the eyes. Trauma, tumors, and neurological disorders can affect the function of the eyelids. Incomplete closure of the eyelids causes dry eyes, blurred vision, sensitivity to light and glare, and eye pain.

Cornea, Sclera, and Conjunctiva

The cornea is the transparent structure in the front of the eye. The vision of patients with a corneal scar is similar to looking through frosted glass; patients with corneal scars have blurred sight and extreme sensitivity to light. A patient with corneal disease may benefit from laser treatment, as well as corneal transplantation surgery. Some patients with myopia and astigmatism benefit from refractive surgery, a procedure that alters the shape of the cornea to eliminate the need for glasses (Kanski & Bowling, 2015; Rosenthal et al., 2017).

Iris, Pupil, and Anterior Chamber

The iris is the colored muscular tissue of the eye. A round opening called the pupil in the center of the eye regulates the amount of light entering the eyes. The pupils dilate in dim illumination and constrict in bright illumination. Trauma to the iris, aniridia, and iritis (inflammation of the iris) cause sensitivity to light (photophobia) and moderate to severe eye pain. Chronic inflammation of the iris (iritis) produces severe sensitivity to light, blurred vision, and disabling eye pain (Kanski & Bowling, 2015).

Crystalline Lens

Behind the iris is a transparent focusable lens called the crystalline lens. The crystalline lens changes its shape when the ciliary muscle contracts and relaxes, enabling the eye to focus at varying distances. With aging, the lens loses the ability to change shape and patients may require glasses for reading. Cataracts involve the clouding of the transparent lens leading to blurred sight.

Vitreous

The vitreous, located behind the lens and iris, is filled with a gel-like substance called vitreous humor. Light must pass through the pupil, crystalline lens, and vitreous humor before it can focus on the retina. Scar tissue and blood interfere with the manner that light focuses on the retina, causing blurred sight, reduced peripheral vision, poor color vision, and distorted vision (Kanski & Bowling, 2015).

Retina

The retina is the light-sensing tissue that consists of millions of rod and cone cells that absorb light and send electrical signals through the optic nerve to the brain. Cone cells are located in the centermost region of the retina. The macula is the area of the retina that consists entirely of cone cells and is responsible for clarity of sight, color vision, spatial contrast sensitivity, and ability to adapt to different lighting conditions. Macular degeneration, diabetic retinopathy, and Stargardt's disease negatively affect the macula and one's ability to read. These conditions cause blurred central vision. Rod cells are located on the periphery of the retina and provide peripheral vision, perception of movement, night vision, and low spatial contrast sensitivity used for mobility. Retinitis pigmentosa, Leber's congenital amaurosis, and retinopathy of prematurity affect peripheral vision and cause problems with walking and seeing at night (Bagheri, Wadia, Calvo, & Durrani, 2017).

Optic Nerve

The optic nerve is a bundle of nerve fibers that send information from the rod and cone cells to the visual cortex of the brain. Abnormalities of the optic nerve are diagnostic of eye diseases such as glaucoma, optic nerve hypoplasia, optic nerve atrophy, as well as systemic illnesses, such as multiple sclerosis, brain tumors, and increased intra-cranial pressure. Eye injuries and trauma to the head also cause optic nerve damage. Optic nerve disorders lead to varying degrees of blurred sight, color blindness, peripheral and central visual field defects, and total blindness (Sheth et al., 2012).

Low Vision Rehabilitation

Low vision rehabilitation is beneficial for adults with sub-normal vision (Crandell, Jr. & Robinson, 2007). Low vision specialists are doctors who design, customize, and prescribe visual aids, and provide training to help patients with low vision perform their desired goals independently. Individuals are generally referred to low vision specialists by ophthalmologists when medical and surgical treatments no longer correct vision.

The low vision examination identifies visual strengths and limitations and offers possible solutions. Specialized glasses, filters, prisms, and technology are used to help a person read, write, use a computer, cross the street independently, and perform other activities.

Customized Low Vision Aids

Low vision specialists develop glasses and visual aids to maximize the individual's visual strengths and compensate for weaknesses (Corn & Erin, 2010). Telescopes and high-powered lenses magnify images to allow a person to see small print, while prisms are used to reduce eyestrain, headaches, and double vision caused by binocular vision disorders. Filters and colored lenses reduce glare, maximize the perception of colors, increase contrast, and simulate lighting conditions that provide the best acuity. Prisms and eccentric viewing training can be incorporated to deflect the image onto the most usable areas of the retina, maximizing overall visual function.

Bioptic Spectacles

Bioptic spectacles are glasses that contain a small telescope to improve visual acuity, helping individuals see traffic signals and street signs, and read a computer screen. These glasses are one of the most useful low vision aids enabling people to read small print and perform specialized work tasks, such as reading the labels of items on store shelves and the numbers on a cash register. For students at school who are not able to clearly see print on the front board, bioptic glasses are beneficial.

High-powered Reading and Writing Glasses

Glasses with specialized lenses magnify reading materials up to six times (Crandell, Jr. & Robinson, 2007). They may be customized to reduce glare, increase contrast, and are available in bifocal forms to allow a person to focus on both far and near vision.

Visual Field Expanding Glasses

Prisms, reverse telescopes, and amorphic lenses can be incorporated into the design of glasses to help individuals with reduced peripheral vision due to glaucoma, retinitis pigmentosa, and traumatic head injury or stroke. Reverse telescopic glasses shrink the peripheral vision into the usable field of vision to help individuals see better. Orientation and mobility training is recommended for patients with reduced peripheral vision.

Telescopes

Hand held telescopes are helpful when a person has blurred distance sight. Monocular telescopes focus on both distant and near objects. To assist with independent mobility, adults with low vision use telescopes to read bus numbers, street signs, and traffic signals. They are helpful for students and employees who have to read text from the board or see PowerPoint presentations.

Magnifiers

Magnifiers are available with their own light source and are useful in helping people read mail and text on grocery items or other small objects. Magnifiers are affordable and come in magnification powers up to 14 times. The latest magnifiers come with a L.E.D. bulb which is brighter and lasts longer than incandescent bulbs.

Electronic Video Magnifiers

Electronic video magnifiers are useful for people with low vision. They are available in desktop and portable forms to allow individuals to have access to books, newspapers, documents, photographs, and medications. Video magnifiers offer more magnification, a brighter image, and a wider field of view than optical hand magnifiers. Additionally, video magnifiers are capable of changing the colors of text and background to reduce glare, and magnify up to 85 times. Some video magnifiers will focus on distant objects such as overhead projections, whiteboard displays, and PowerPoint presentations. Many video magnifiers scan and read text aloud.

Head Mounted Video Magnifiers. The advances in computer and photographic technology have resulted in the development of hi-tech glasses that contain a small camera that produces a high-resolution image on the organic light-emitting diode (OLED) screen of the glasses. These video glasses allow people to move anywhere they need to go and see objects clearly. The head mounted video glasses magnify up to 24 times, customize the colors of background and text, scan and read text aloud, and access the Internet. Some models of video glasses help the totally blind in that the user simply wears the glasses and the image is sent to a staff member of the company who then describes to the person what is seen on the screen. These glasses are effective for people who have low vision and those with total blindness.

Computers and Software. Computers, smart phones, and adaptive software are helpful for people with low vision and for the totally blind. Software programs magnify the text and images on the computer screen, while text-to-speech software reads the text aloud. Optical character recognition software allows users to scan text and have it read aloud instantly on their computer as well as on smart phones, while global positioning software allow users to travel independently. Voice recognition software is effective at typing documents, e-mail, and text messages, allowing users to write quickly.

Common Causes of Vision Impairment

Diabetic Retinopathy

Diabetic retinopathy is the leading cause of blindness among adults between the ages of 20 to 74; there are 5.5 million Americans who have this condition (Erickson et al., 2013). Diabetic retinopathy is a progressive disease in which the retina is damaged due to prolonged lack of oxygen. The onset of vision problems among those with diabetes is usually during adulthood.

The prevalence of diabetic retinopathy is directly related to the duration and control of the disease. For those with Type I (insulin dependent diabetes mellitus), more than 90% demonstrate evidence of diabetic retinopathy within 15 years. Sixty to 80% of individuals with Type II (non-insulin dependent diabetes) show signs of diabetic retinopathy after the same time period (American Diabetes Association, 2013).

Diabetic retinopathy slowly causes damage to the cells of the retina and initially causes the loss of peripheral vision and night vision. In the later stages, it affects the macula, causing blurred sight, sensitivity to glare, and fluctuating vision. Individuals with diabetes can help stabilize their vision with proper control of blood sugar. Low vision aids are helpful for these individuals (Rosenthal et al., 2017).

Optic Atrophy

Optic atrophy is a rare condition in which some or all of the optic nerve fibers have been damaged, resulting in mild to severe loss of vision. This can be present at birth or develop from various conditions. Optic atrophy is caused by lack of oxygen (anoxia, hypoxia), trauma, inflammation, vitamin deficiency, drug toxicity, demyelinating diseases such as multiple sclerosis, and increased intra-cranial pressure (Sheth et al., 2012). Persons could experience blurred sight, red-green color blindness, reduced contrast sensitivity, limited depth perception, poor eye-hand-foot coordination, and large blind spots in the visual field. Visual loss related to optic atrophy causes difficulties with reading, walking, driving, and performing a wide variety of tasks. Low vision aids and assistive technology are helpful for those with this condition.

Glaucoma

Glaucoma affects 2.3 million people in the United States (Erickson et al., 2013). Intra-ocular pressure is elevated, causing damage to optic nerve fibers. In a normal eye, aqueous humor is continually produced and drained through a structure called the trabecular meshwork, located in the angle of the anterior chamber. In open angle glaucoma, the trabecular meshwork does not drain aqueous fluid normally, resulting in an increase in intra-ocular pressure. Elevation of pressure is slow and generally not noticeable in vision until significant loss has occurred. Small blind spots in the mid-peripheral field of vision initially develop and later progress to cause severe peripheral vision loss, reduced night vision, tunnel vision, and blindness. Advanced glaucoma creates difficulties with walking, reading, writing, and performing activities under dim illumination.

Glaucoma is common among adults of specific sub-groups. It is more prevalent among adults over age 40, African-Americans, Hispanics, and those with a family history of glaucoma (Kanski & Bowling, 2015).

Daily medication is required to sustain a healthy level of intraocular pressure. Compliance with therapy is frequently a problem because symptoms often are not immediate when medications are discontinued (Kanski & Bowling, 2015). An individual with glaucoma needs a consultation with a low vision specialist to prescribe visual aids, including visual field expanders, high powered reading glasses, night vision aids, computer and assistive technology, and specific lighting for the workplace and home.

Retinitis Pigmentosa

Retinitis pigmentosa (RP) is a variety of degenerative eye conditions that affect the cells of the retina causing night blindness, reduced peripheral vision, sensitivity to glare, and blurred sight. Symptoms generally develop between the first and second decade of life. In severe forms of RP, individuals lose nearly all peripheral vision and are left with a small central island of vision. They are considered legally blind due to the absence of peripheral vision. Some people maintain 20/20 visual acuity, while others have blurred sight and a blue-yellow color vision deficiency.

Patients with RP tend to have many functional problems. Night blindness is the most common occurrence. Adults with night blindness may have trouble finding their chairs in dimly lit restaurants or movie theatres, and may avoid going out at night. As peripheral vision deteriorates, driving and walking become increasingly difficult. Low vision aids are helpful for individuals with RP. Visual field expanding glasses help compensate for the reduced peripheral vision, while night vision glasses enhance mobility at night. Low vision spectacles improve visual acuity for distance and reading, while specialized filters enhance contrast vision and allow patients to adapt more readily to different lighting conditions. Desk lamps, track lighting, and full spectrum fluorescent light fixtures enhance illumination level. Orientation and mobility training is essential for independent mobility (Kamski & Bowling, 2015).

One of the more recent advances in surgical and electronic technology involves the surgical implantation of an electrical chip in the retinas of people with retinitis pigmentosa. The patient wears a special pair of glasses that contains a high definition camera which sends signals to the chip. The chip then sends electrical signals to the brain via the optic nerve; many people who were totally blind regain some vision with this device.

Macular Degeneration and Stargardt's Disease

Macular degeneration, a disease of the central retina, is a leading cause of vision impairment. Two million Americans are affected by this condition (Erickson et al., 2013). The macula (central retina) is a small region of the retina responsible for detailed clarity of sight, color, depth perception, and adaptation to light and glare. There are two main forms of macular degeneration. Dry (atrophic) macular degeneration is the most common and occurs when the cells of the macula atrophy due to age. When it occurs in teenagers and young adults, it is called Stargardt's disease.

The second form is called wet (disciform) macular degeneration. In this form, abnormal blood vessels develop under the retina forming a sub-retinal neovascular membrane that result in sub-retinal hemorrhages. Leakage of blood under the macula can result in a sudden loss of central vision (Sheth et al., 2012). Symptoms of macular degeneration include blurred distant and near sight, sensitivity to glare and bright light, poor contrast vision, reduced stereoscopic depth perception, and color vision problems. People with this disability experience difficulty driving, reading, and performing tasks requiring fine dexterity.

Research studies are investigating the use of gene therapy and stem cells to treat dry macular degeneration and Stargardt's disease. Anti-oxidant vitamins and protection from harmful rays of the sun have been reported to be beneficial for people with both types of macular degeneration. Low vision aids and video magnifiers are particularly helpful. Laser photocoagulation, photodynamic therapy, and intra-ocular injections of anti-angiogenic medications help with wet macular degeneration (Sheth et al., 2012).

Head Injury, Neurological Vision Impairment, and Traumatic Eye Injuries

Head injury, blunt trauma, sports, and employment-related injuries are common causes of vision loss among adults. There are approximately 2.5 million eye injuries in the United States annually; 50,000 of these injuries result in permanent loss of partial or total vision (Erickson et al., 2013). Penetrating injuries to the cornea and globe of the eye can result in total blindness due to retinal detachment, glaucoma, optic nerve damage, and ocular inflammation. In other cases, symptoms include blurred sight, distorted vision, severe sensitivity to glare, blind spots in the central and peripheral fields of vision, eye movement problems, and double vision. These eye problems interfere with reading, depth perception, eye-hand-foot coordination, balance, and mobility.

Traumatic brain injuries (TBI) cause significant vision problems, including double vision, poor depth perception, severe sensitivity to light, and profound visual processing difficulties. Patients have difficulty perceiving size, shape, depth, and have problems performing basic tasks. Some people with TBI have visual neglect, where they ignore all objects on one side of their midline, including their own body; they may not comb half their hair, as well as leave food untouched on one side of the plate.

Cerebrovascular accidents (stroke) cause symptoms similar to traumatic head injury. When the stroke or injury affects the right side of the brain, there may be no peripheral vision on the left side with either eye and weakness on the left side of the body. Neurological involvement to the right occipital and parietal lobes of the brain often significantly impact visual perception. As a result, the individual has poor depth perception, difficulty recognizing faces, and impaired visual-spatial perception skills. Conversely, strokes and injuries to the left occipital and parietal lobes of the brain cause a loss of peripheral vision on the right side of each eye, reduced motor function on the right side of the body, as well as affecting language, reading, speech, word recognition, and ability to remember sequences of information (Sheth et al., 2012).

Cataracts

Cataracts affect nearly 22 million Americans (Erickson et al., 2013). A cataract occurs when the internal lens of the eye becomes clouded or opaque. Cataracts may be present at birth or develop at any age as a result of trauma, diabetes, steroid use, and aging (Kanski & Bowling, 2015; Rosenthal et al., 2017). They cause a wide variety of vision problems ranging from blurred sight, reduced color vision, glare sensitivity, reduced peripheral vision, double vision, and sometimes total blindness. Dense cataracts that significantly impair vision may be surgically removed and an artificial lens implanted in the eye to restore focusing power.

Children who are born with congenital cataracts may continue to have sub-normal vision even after cataract extraction surgery. Limitations include blurred vision, nystagmus (uncontrollable shaking of the eyes), strabismus (mis-aligned eyes), and severe sensitivity to glare. Visual acuity can range from 20/40 to 20/200. Low vision aids and assistive technology help enhance remaining vision.

Congenital Causes of Vision Impairment

Albinism

Albinism is a congenital, inherited condition that affects the pigmentation and color of the eyes (Sheth et al., 2012). Individuals with albinism have a high degree of functional vision because they have generally learned to adapt to their vision impairments. These persons usually have visual acuity ranging from 20/70 to 20/200, and have normal peripheral and color vision. People with albinism tend to have better vision at night and respond well to tinted contact lenses, specialized filters, and low vision aids to improve both their distance and near clarity of sight. Computer and assistive technology, orientation and mobility training, and independent living skills training are helpful for those with albinism who have severe sensitivity to light (Brodwin, Siu, & Cardoso, 2018).

Retinopathy of Prematurity

Retinopathy of Prematurity (ROP) is a congenital condition that develops as a response to premature birth. It primarily affects the retina of newborn children born before 32 weeks of gestation and those weighing under two pounds. Children with ROP may develop abnormal blood vessels in the retina which form scar tissue and can pull or detach the retina, causing blindness. The scar tissue in the eye often alters the shape of the eye causing it to be elongated, resulting in high myopia. ROP is related to exposure of a newborn to concentrated oxygen.

Functional Limitations

Emotional Adjustment

While discovering new ways to accomplish tasks which formerly required sight, some clients experience a conflicting desire to deny that any change in method or lifestyle need occur. There are feelings of loss, sadness, and anger after learning of permanent visual impairment. Adjusting to vision loss is an emotional process; clients need ways to express their feelings and adapt to this radical change. Losing one's sight involves creating a new identity. Life can return to normal once the client begins to use other senses and finds alternative ways of performing activities (Guide Dogs for the Blind, 1999).

Family and friends often find it difficult to accept a loved one's vision loss. They may become overprotective, thus limiting an individual's ability to function independently. The period of greatest emotional stress usually occurs at the onset of visual loss. While sudden loss of vision is extremely traumatic, it may be easier to cope with than the uncertain, slow visual loss seen in many chronic ocular diseases.

Age plays an important part in the way the person reacts emotionally to loss of sight. Younger people are more resilient from the severe emotional sequelae generated by loss of sight. Middle-aged individuals are at greater risk of having severe psychological difficulties, perhaps because of other stresses associated with changes occurring during mid-life. Another variable is the overall degree of visual loss; the more profound the visual loss, the slower and more challenging the adjustment (Crandell, Jr. & Robinson, 2007).

The stages of grieving outlined by Dr. Elizabeth Kubler-Ross apply to vision loss, as with most disabling conditions. Denial, anger, bargaining, depression, and acceptance are the major steps of reaction to visual loss. Not everyone goes through all the stages or in this order (Kubler-Ross & Kessler, 2005).

Carroll (1961) outlined secondary losses that occur with loss of sight, including diminished physical integrity, decreased visual contact with the environment, loss of a means of communication, and reduced mobility. With some loss of physical integrity, the individual may no longer feel like a whole person, resulting in feelings of isolation and withdrawal from one's social network. The sighted person easily recognizes characteristics of distant objects including size, shape, position, speed, and direction; persons with visual impairment lose part or all of this recognition ability (Crandell, Jr. & Robinson, 2007). This limitation evokes fear and anxiety.

Visual disability refers to one's inability to perform tasks visually. Both physical and psychological factors define functional status of individuals with visual impairment. A person with total visual loss but with newly acquired competencies may still achieve physical, emotional, and financial independence, as well as social integration.

Physical Adjustment

Loss of sight is a major disruptive factor in daily living. Inability to perform essential tasks such as reading, driving, and recognizing faces poses barriers to successful employment, along with fatigue, depression, and anxiety. Visual loss negatively impacts most activities and places stress on daily living. Use of one's other senses compensates for loss of visual acuity. Orientation and mobility specialists train clients to navigate with the assistance of white canes or guide dogs. Orientation and mobility play a vital role in perception of personal freedom and independence. Factors that contribute to the degree of orientation and mobility include residual vision, age at onset of visual loss, posture and balance, intelligence, body image, space orientation, auditory tactile abilities, and personality. Substantial loss of peripheral field of vision is more debilitating than loss of central vision.

A white cane is the primary mobility aid used by persons who are blind or visually impaired. It is recommended that training begin following diagnosis; yet, clients with some progressive eye disorders may decide to wait until vision loss impacts mobility. Those in need of aid must first acknowledge loss of vision to be comfortable using a white cane, a clear identifier of a person with vision impairment both to the individual and to others. Clients are taught to walk safely down the street by rhythmically touching the tip of the cane side-to-side in front of them to obtain advanced knowledge of what is ahead.

While many people prefer to use a red-tipped white cane for ambulation, some feel more comfortable relying on a guide dog (Guide Dogs for the Blind, 1999). Traveling with a guide dog differs from using a cane in that the dog navigates around obstacles, stops for stairs and other changes in elevation, and avoids overhead obstructions. The guide dog and owner work together as a team.

Vocational Adjustment

Vocational skills are a major component of successful independent functioning. The capability to perform job tasks well and provide for one's self and family greatly enhances self-esteem, reduces financial concerns, and diminishes family conflict. In addition to remaining visual capabilities, those with visual impairment can function independently by using physical dexterity, non-visual job skills, natural talents, and refinement of the senses.

Advances in assistive technology enable persons with vision impairment to perform essential job tasks. The rehabilitation counselor plays a significant role in assessing assistive technology needs and potential accommodations that enable clients to succeed in the workforce (Brodwin et al., 2018). Counselors can help dispel employer misconceptions about the capabilities of people with visual impairment.

Rehabilitation Potential

The goals of rehabilitation are optimal physical functioning, economic independence, and social integration. Potential for rehabilitation depends on the physiology of the impairment (amount, type, and progression), conditions in the immediate environment, attitude and motivation, and use of residual vision. The auditory system is the mainstay of mobility for clients with severe visual impairment. The counselor can contact the person's physician to determine the status of his or her auditory system. Duration and severity of disability, degree of personal adjustment, and positive or negative attributes of the family and the environment influence vocational rehabilitation of people with visual impairment (Carroll, 1961; Falvo & Holland, 2018).

Rehabilitation efforts focus on providing the best possible use of residual vision (vision enhancement), and assisting with development of non-visual skills that can substitute for lost visual function (vision substitution). Vision enhancement involves the use of magnifiers, telescopic aids, colored filters, and computer and video-generated magnification screens. These devices generally present an enlarged image that is more readily seen. Braille, an example of vision substitution, is a tactile system. Braille typewriters make it easier for people to take class notes, write, and read. Software is available that converts computerized text into Braille which can then be embossed on a Braille printer.

Computers and assistive technology help enhance residual vision. Advances in technology allow patients with vision impairment to read, write, and perform job tasks and daily living activities independently (Brodwin et al., 2018). Thorough assessment of the client's need for assistive technology is beneficial. A vocational evaluator can assess the worksite to determine which aids promote optimum performance of essential job functions.

An effective technology for clients with low vision is video magnifiers, also known as closed-circuit televisions (CCTVs). This equipment provides significant magnification and offers a brighter, sharper, and wider field of view than magnifiers and glasses. Other models can be interfaced with a computer and allow the user to share the same screen to see text both on the computer and on paper. Video magnifiers can scan the reading material and read the text out loud for the person.

Hand-held video magnifiers are useful for people with low vision to read print when they do not have access to a desktop magnifier. These video magnifiers produce a bright and sharp image on LCD screens. Distance and near focusing video magnifiers allow the user to see distant objects and reading material in a magnified view at work, school, and home (Crandell, Jr. & Robinson, 2007; Rosenthal et al., 2017). This equipment is portable and useful for clients who are attending conferences, lectures, and presentations.

Many clients with low vision who are re-entering the workplace need assistance in seeing print on a computer screen. Specialized glasses maximize sight at the distance of a computer screen, while a larger computer monitor facilitates seeing. Users can magnify the text on the computer screen or use the speech output to hear what is presented on the screen. There are software programs that are designed specifically to magnify computer screens, read text aloud, and scan documents.

Working age adults who require additional help to see a computer screen may benefit from special computer software for the visually impaired (Brodwin et al., 2010; Falvo & Holland, 2018). Software magnification programs enlarge all images on the computer screen and can change the color of the background and text to help people with poor contrast vision and those with sensitivity to glare.

Screen reading programs help people who are functionally blind, as well as those who experience eye strain after reading for short periods of time. These programs read text aloud from the screen thus allowing clients to access information from the Internet, type documents, and perform other software applications. Scanning software programs are available that allow users to scan books, letters, and other documents. The text is displayed in a magnified view on the computer screen and read aloud. Other technological advances include software programs that convert printed text into Braille, voice recognition software, telephone voice-controlled Internet access, and talking personal data assistants (PDAs) (Crandell, Jr. & Robinson, 2007; Kanski & Bowling, 2015).

Smart-phones enable people with low vision to be more independent. These telephones incorporate global positioning systems that help people travel independently. There are applications for cell phones that can identify currency, colors, bar codes, and even geographical landmarks. With accessible cell phones, individuals who are blind access text messages, e-mail, and the Internet.

Working age adults who have visual impairments face greater underemployment and unemployment (Brodwin et al., 2010). Through careful interviewing and assessment, counselors can enhance their rehabilitation potential. Vocational rehabilitation counselors can enable clients to choose realistic, practical, and attainable goals through the provision of rehabilitation services in a holistic manner. A variety of resources are available within the community. These include Braille foundations, low vision centers, service organizations (e.g., Lions' Clubs), centers for the partially sighted, college programs and services, and public school programs with specialists who have knowledge of available community services.

Case Study

Ms. Alexa Bitari is a 51-year old female diagnosed with (dry) macular degeneration. She is not married and lives alone. Ms. Bitari's best corrected vision is reported as 20/40 (right eye) and 20/100 (left eye). Her central vision is somewhat compromised in both eyes due to macular degeneration. The client reports that her vision loss interferes with personal grooming and managing her finances, causing difficulties performing essential functions of her job. To be able to read effectively, Alexa needs bright light and large print with two times magnification. She reports no hospitalizations or medications, and no major emotional problems.

Alexa earned a bachelor's degree in communications. Subsequently, she obtained clerical skills training at a local business college and took classes related to advancement in the entertainment field. For the past 25 years, Alexa has worked for a large entertainment firm as an administrative secretary. This position was in the corporate graphics design department which was recently eliminated due to downsizing. Ms. Bitari is currently working within the clerical pool, and will have to interview for a new position to remain with the employer. Attitudes prevail throughout the entertainment industry that few jobs can be performed by someone who is visually impaired. Alexa recognizes that the entertainment industry is populated primarily by young workers; she is concerned that she will be viewed as "washed up," especially if she discloses that she is coping with vision loss due to macular degeneration.

Despite her long tenure with the employer and excellent clerical skills, Ms. Bitari believes she will not be retained by the company in a permanent position because of her disability. She enjoys working in the entertainment industry, especially the challenging, fast-paced, and at times, glamorous working environment. Because she has trouble using the computer and reading file labels, Alexa fears that her request for accommodation will be denied. Alexa is worried that she will begin making errors on the job if her eye condition worsens.

In her most recent position as an administrative secretary, Ms. Bitari was responsible for typing purchase orders and correspondence, answering telephones and making appointments, coordinating meetings, and performing other staff responsibilities. An administrative secretary lifts and carries a maximum of ten pounds, with frequent lifting of less than five pounds. Most of the work is conducted while sitting. It takes approximately one year to acquire the skills for this position and two years to learn it proficiently. Alexa has consulted with a rehabilitation counselor regarding the requirements and potential reasonable accommodations that will be needed for retaining a position with her employer.

Questions

1. Discuss possible limitations, both physical and psychosocial, for individuals with low vision or blindness.
2. Describe Ms. Bitari's job as an administrative secretary in terms of physical exertion and skill levels. Provide a vocational profile.
3. As Alexa's rehabilitation counselor, describe the steps you would take to identify appropriate rehabilitation technology services.
4. Given the size of Ms. Bitari's employer, discuss how you would propose she be accommodated through assistive technology.
5. If she is unable to continue working for her present employer, identify the alternatives you will recommend. Include short-term goals, as well as long-term goals.

References

American Diabetes Association. (2013). Clinical practice recommendations 2013: Standards of medical care in diabetes. *Diabetes Care* (Supplement 1), S5.

Bagheri, N., Wadja, B., Calvo, C., Durrani, A. (2017). *Wills eye manual: Office and emergency room diagnosis and treatment of eye disease* (7th ed.). New York, NY: Lippincott Williams and Wilkins.

Brodwin, M., Parker, R. M., & DeLaGarza, D. (2010). Disability and reasonable accommodation. In E. M. Szymanski & R. M. Parker (Eds.), *Work and disability: Contexts, issues, and strategies for enhancing outcomes for people with disabilities* (3rd ed., pp. 281-323). Austin, TX: Pro-ed.

Brodwin, M. G., Siu, F. W., & Cardoso, E. (2018). Users of assistive technology: The human component. In I. Marini & M. Stebnicki (Eds.), *The psychological and social impact of illness and disability* (7th ed., pp. 345-353). New York, NY: Springer.

Carroll, T. J. (1961). Blindness. *What is it, what it does, and how to live with it*. Boston, MA: Little, Brown.

Corn, A. L., & Erin, J. N. (Eds.). (2010). *Foundations of low vision: Clinical and functional perspectives* (2nd ed.). New York, NY: AFB Press.

Crandell, Jr., J. M., & Robinson, L. W. (2007). *Living with low vision and blindness: Guidelines that help professionals and individuals understand vision impairment*. Springfield, IL: Charles C Thomas.

Erickson, W., Lee, C., & von Schrader, S. (2017). *Disability statistics from the 2011 American Community Survey (ACS)*. Ithaca, NY: Cornell University Yang-Tan Institute. Retrieved from www.disabilitystatistics.org

Falvo, D., & Holland, B. E. (2018). *Medical and psychosocial aspects of chronic illness and disability* (6th ed.). Burlington, MA: Jones and Bartlett Learning.

Guide Dogs for the Blind. (1999). *At a glance: An educational resource guide*. San Rafael, CA: Author.

Kanski, J. & Bowling, B. (2015). *Clinical ophthalmology: A systematic approach* (8th ed.). London, England: Butterworth-Heinemann.

Kubler-Ross, E., & Kessler, D. (2005). *On grief and grieving: Finding the meaning of grief through the five stages of loss*. New York, NY: Scribner.

Rosenthal, B. P., Cole, R. G., & Escalera, E. (2017). In A. Moroz, S. R. Flanagan, & H. Zaretsky (Eds.). Visual impairments. *Medical aspects of disability for the rehabilitation professional* (5th ed., pp. 597-620). New York, NY: Springer.

Sheth, V. S., Marcet, M. M., Chiranand, P., Bhatt, H. K., Lamkin, J. C., & Jager, R. D. (Eds.). (2012). *The Massachusetts eye and ear infirmary illustrated manual of ophthalmology* (4th ed.). Philadelphia, PA: Lippincott Williams & Wilkins.

World Health Organization (WHO). (2001). *ICF: International Classification of Functioning, Disability, and Health* (2nd ed.). Geneva, Switzerland: Author.

About the Authors

Bill Takeshita, OD, FAAO, FCVD is a low vision optometrist who received his doctorate from the Southern California College of Optometry. He is a fellow of the American Academy of Optometry and the College of Optometrists in Vision Development. Dr. Takeshita lectures throughout the country on low vision and vision development. Currently, he is the director of Low Vision Services at the Braille Institute of America, Los Angeles, California.

Robin Langman, MS, received her Master of Science degree in rehabilitation counseling from California State University, Los Angeles. She completed a Certificate in Assistive Technology through California State University, Northridge. Ms. Langman was employed by the State of California, Department of Rehabilitation, as a vocational rehabilitation counselor.

Rebekah Ketover Brod, MA, MFT is a licensed marriage and family therapist with a private practice in Santa Monica, California. Ms. Brod received her Master's Degree in Counseling from Antioch University in Santa Monica.

Acknowledgements

Special thanks for assistance to Jaymie Takeshita, June Takeshita, Garry Brod, and Marissa Langman.

Chapter 10

CHRONIC PAIN MANAGEMENT

Ashley T. Du, MS
John Lindberg, MD
Brendon W. Bluestein, PhD

Introduction

Pain is one of the most common reasons for physician visits, use of medication, and cause of work disability. Pain management represents one of the most difficult healthcare issues facing the medical profession and general population. Chronic pain is described as persistent pain which lasts more than three to six months and sometimes for years (American Chronic Pain Association [ACPA], 2013, 2016). In 2012, approximately 100 million adults in the United States were affected by chronic pain; about 50 million Americans today are either partially or totally disabled by it. The annual national economic cost associated with chronic pain is $560-635 billion (ACPA, 2013). Chronic pain has been ranked as the third greatest healthcare problem in this country, following heart disease and cancer. Annual costs related to pain management are higher than those for heart disease, cancer, and diabetes combined (Pizzo & Clark, 2012).

Though advances have been made in pain management, chronic pain is still an overlooked problem in the United States (Pizzo & Clark, 2012). Students in medical schools receive minimal training or education regarding pain and how to treat patients who have chronic pain. Prevention strategies need to include approaches such as workplace changes to minimize or prevent repetitive tasks which may lead to injury. This strategy advocates providing a "biopsychosocial approach to chronic pain, including coordinated care at all levels. Chronic pain is a significant public health problem which affects millions of Americans and incurs substantial economic costs to society" (Anderson, 2016, p. 2). Pain as a primary disease has only been a focus in research for the past 50 years and was previously viewed only as a secondary response to an illness (Flor & Turk, 2011). This chapter summarizes the theoretical and practical aspects of treating chronic pain. Emphasis is placed on the multifactorial nature of pain and the need to treat each patient as an individual within a biopsychosocial environment.

The following topics are discussed in this chapter: definition of pain, medical evaluation of chronic pain disorders, psychosocial assessment, medical management of chronic pain, patient involvement in treatment, and vocational aspects/rehabilitation. The chapter concludes with a case study of an individual with chronic pain after a workplace accident.

Definition of Pain

Pain is a universal experience that is unique and subjective for each individual. A widely accepted definition given by the International Association for the Study of Pain (IASP) (1986) is the following: "Pain is an unpleasant sensory and emotional experience associated with actual or potential tissue damage, or described in terms of such damage. Pain is always subjective" (p. S217). It is classified by nociceptive, neuropathic, and sometimes undetermined causes. Common origins of chronic pain are motor vehicle accidents, sports injuries, migraines, diabetes, arthritis, and illnesses such as shingles (Davis, 2010). Less understood pain disorders include phantom-limb pain, central pain, atypical facial neuralgias, fibromyalgia, and enthesopathies. The IASP definition of pain includes those experienced in mental disorders that have no known noxious somatic source of the pain. Examples are pain as a symptom of mood disorders (depression and unresolved grief reactions), conversion disorders (e.g., hysterical neurosis), and delusional states.

Due to the subjectivity of pain and lack of objective diagnoses and treatments, healthcare providers and insurance companies encounter difficulties serving individuals with chronic pain. A subjective experience, the sensation of pain is an interaction between pain signals from the nervous system and a host of psychosocial factors such as past pain experiences and emotional responses (Pizzo & Clark, 2012).

Other than diagnosis, distinguishing between acute and chronic pain may be the most important factor influencing a treating clinician's options. Most researchers define acute pain as pain that lasts for less than six months (short-term pain). "Acute pain is characterized as being of recent origin, transient, and usually from an identifiable source." On the other hand, "chronic or persistent pain can be described as ongoing or recurrent pain, lasting beyond the usual course of acute illness or injury healing, more than 3 to 6 months, and which adversely affects the individual's well-being. Another definition for chronic or persistent pain is pain that continues when it should not" (ACPA, 2016, p. 9). The terms, acute and chronic, refer to the period of time the pain has lasted, not the severity of the problem or intensity of the pain (ACPA, 2013).

Impacting all aspects of life, chronic pain is complex, debilitating, and influenced by a variety of psychosocial factors. Rehabilitation often includes a team of healthcare providers and a carefully developed and implemented plan. Focus of care differs for patients experiencing acute versus chronic pain. Acute pain is typically managed with rest, immobilization of the particular joint(s), medication to reduce inflammation or provide analgesia, physical therapy, massage, pain control medications, surgery, exercise, and other health strategies. Interventions for acute pain are oriented towards resolution or return to baseline health and functioning.

While acute pain treatment strives for a cure, chronic pain treatment focuses on a longer-term solution aimed at managing pain by teaching the patient techniques to actively manage symptoms. Interventions such as injections, adjunctive medications, implanted devices, cognitive and behavioral techniques, relaxation strategies, and exercise are common methods used. The healthcare provider reorients the individual to achieve quality of life despite pain, while pursuing long-term strategies for pain reduction.

Medical Evaluation of Chronic Pain Disorders

Assessment/Evaluation

Due to the subjective nature of chronic pain, it is widely known that both patients and physicians report discontent regarding pain management. Assessment of chronic pain requires a comprehensive and multidisciplinary approach. The medical history of an illness may be pertinent to the cause of the pain. Specifying the location, frequency, intensity, and radiation of pain forms the foundation of most medical assessments. Just as important are how the pain began, what aggravates it, and what helps alleviate it. These are crucial questions prior to making a definitive diagnosis. The treating physician should investigate coexisting diseases or symptoms that appear unrelated but, on further evaluation, may point to previously undiscovered pathology (Clark & Treisman, 2004).

Examples of Common Chronic Pain Disorders

Headaches

Migraines and other severe headaches are common presenting pain complaints with a multitude of causes. Chronic headache is characterized as occurring more than 50% of days in the last three months (Treede et al., 2015). Treatments include medications, biofeedback, stress reduction, and dietary changes (National Institute of Neurological Disorders and Stroke, 2016).

Lumbar Spine Disorders

According to the Centers for Disease Control and Prevention (CDC) and the National Center for Health Statistics, lower back pain is the most reported cause of chronic pain and most common cause of job-related disability (Institute of Medicine, 2011). About 80% of adults will experience lower back pain, of which 20%

will develop chronic back pain (National Institute of Neurological Disorders and Stroke, 2016). Spinal stenosis, failed back syndrome, and chronic musculoligamentous strain are examples. Successful formulation of a treatment plan and education of the patient with chronic low back pain necessitates a specific diagnosis.

Fibromyalgia Syndrome

This disorder is marked by a presentation of chronic widespread muscular pain. Diagnosis is confirmed by findings of specific, localized tender points. Insomnia, headaches, and irritable bowel syndrome are common associated problems. Fibromyalgia is resistant to treatment and is a chronic condition in which minimal improvement is typical. People who have this condition need to remain as active as possible, while avoiding activities that exacerbate symptoms.

Arthropathies

Arthritic conditions, such as osteoarthritis and rheumatic arthritis, are common chronic pain conditions. Other arthropathies include systemic lupus erthymatosus and ankylosing spondylitis. Multiple joint involvements are typical, although only one joint may be involved with a chronic, progressive course. Diagnostic tests are beneficial for categorizing the arthritis and enhancing treatment options. With social support and encouragement, as well as effective coping strategies, adjustment issues such as anxiety and depression tend to decrease and outlook improves.

Neuropathies

These disorders often lead to chronic pain. Polyneuropathies, such as diabetic peripheral neuropathy, cause severe distal lower extremity pain that is resistant to treatment. A single traumatic nerve injury can be disabling if high intensity chronic pain becomes resistant to treatment. Carpal tunnel syndrome and cubital tunnel syndrome are neuropathies that are common and the result of cumulative traumas.

Complex Regional Pain Syndrome

This syndrome has had many names including causalgia, shoulder-hand syndrome, and most often, reflexive sympathetic dystrophy. Sensitivity to touch, tissue swelling, burning pain, excessive sweating, and changes in bone and skin are common symptoms of the syndrome (Reflex Sympathetic Dystrophy Syndrome Association, 2013). Trauma to an extremity usually precedes the onset of symptoms. Treatment outcome improves with early recognition, along with aggressive treatment of the sympathetic nervous system abnormality.

Phantom Limb Pain

Phantom limb sensation typically follows an amputation. The individual feels sensations that the amputated limb is still present. An adjustment period after an amputation is normal and phantom limb typically diminishes over time (Falvo & Holland, 2018). Some people, however, experience phantom limb pain, described as moderate to severe chronic pain in the amputated area which can reach a point where it becomes disabling. Medical treatment includes nerve blocks, surgical removal of neuromas, and chronic pain management (Clark & Treisman, 2004).

Psychosocial Assessment

In preparation for treatment of acute and chronic pain, the clinician assesses the complete physical and psychological status of the individual (Davis, 2010; Smith, 2007). The intake should focus on the individual's current and historical reports of pain. A three-part evaluation process begins with classification of the pain experience, followed by patient feedback and development of treatment goals.

Adequate understanding of the pain complaints includes an assessment of the duration (acute vs. chronic), location, cause, frequency, and intensity of pain. The McGill Pain Questionnaire (Melzack, 1975) is still the most widely used instrument addressing these factors. However, the resulting data will lack coherence without a detailed psychosocial history that places the pain complaints in the appropriate context.

The following should be addressed during chronic pain evaluations (Institute of Medicine, 2011; Melzack, 1975):

1. Orientation and neurocognitive status
2. Depression and the potential for suicide
3. Anxiety and post-traumatic stress disorder
4. Substance abuse
5. Pain behaviors (assess systemic reinforcers and punishers)
6. Status of litigation
7. Beliefs about pain
8. Consequences of pain reduction
9. Expectations of treatment

Regardless of the specific syndrome, chronic pain is recognized as a *biopsychosocial* disorder. Biopsychosocial assessment is used to identify the individual's attitudes, emotions about pain, environmental circumstances, and knowledge and beliefs about treatments (Institute of Medicine, 2011). According to Block, Kremer, and Kremer (2005), "there is now fairly strong literature demonstrating that, at least for some medical interventions, psychosocial variables are more potent indicators of treatment outcome than medical variables" (p. 219). As patients continue to experience chronic pain, they develop a constellation of beliefs. These attitudes become the psychological modulators of pain. Cognition and perceptions interact with affective, behavioral, and environmental factors in the interpretation of pain. As depicted in Figure 1, pain, stress, and their cognitive interpretations create affective, social, occupational, and physical disruption.

FIGURE 1
The Cycle of Pain and Influences

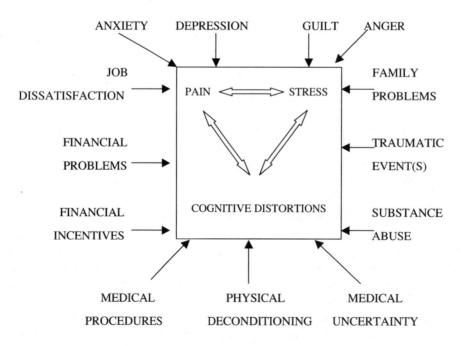

Source: Gatchel, R. J., & Turk, D. C. (1996). Psychological approaches to pain management: A practitioner's guide. New York, NY: Guilford.

Medical Management of Chronic Pain

Treatment of chronic pain can be a complicated process because many attempts often have to be made to find a treatment that is effective. Furthermore, many people with chronic pain do not know where to go for help, and when they do, they become discouraged and frustrated at the trial and error process of finding effective treatment or because of a practitioner's perceived insensitivity (Pizzo & Clark, 2012). Throughout this section, emphasis is placed on the need for a multidisciplinary team approach that blends a variety of treatments for each patient.

Treatment Modalities

Physical Therapy

Therapists utilize a variety of physical therapy modalities as adjuncts to overall treatment plans. Application of heat and cold, electrical stimulation, and ultrasound relax underlying tissues; this assists injured tissues to become more amenable to other treatments. Physical therapy is considered the first approach during the acute phase of pain. If pain persists despite several weeks of physical therapy, other modalities are prescribed for the person to administer at home. Individuals experiencing chronic pain commonly use the application of heat and/or cold to alleviate symptoms of pain. Transcutaneous electrical nerve stimulation (TENS) is helpful for short-term pain relief. By carrying a small battery-operated unit attached to a belt, this portable device can provide effective pain relief at the job site and at home.

Manual Techniques

Massage, manipulation, manual adjustments, and physical therapy may relieve common ailments that cause both acute and chronic pain. These techniques are applied to increase function, control pain, or help speed recovery (Institute of Medicine, 2011). Research shows that spinal manipulation is often more effective than bed rest, topical gels, traction, or no treatment (ACPA, 2013, 2016). Myofascial pain syndrome benefits from specific massage techniques which can be curative. During the acute phase of pain, these techniques attempt to correct the underlying problem.

Medications

For many clinicians, medication is the primary treatment of choice for chronic pain. Medications are used to treat the underlying condition and alleviate pain. Principles of pain management include strategic use of medications, conservative dosages, and frequent review of the necessity for continuing medications (Gharibo, Patel, & Aydin, 2017; Smith, 2007). The following is a review of the major medication categories used for chronic pain management.

Anti-inflammatory Medication. Reducing inflammation is a goal of chronic pain treatment. When an injury occurs, inflammatory cells respond, causing pain. Medications to treat inflammation allow tissues to heal while concurrently alleviating pain. Nonsteroidal anti-inflammatory medications (NSAIDs) comprise the majority of pain relieving medications. They serve two roles: as a pain reliever and an anti-inflammatory agent (Davis, 2010).

Narcotic Analgesic Medications. Narcotics are one of the most prescribed medications for chronic pain (ACPA, 2016; Davis, 2010). Narcotic analgesics are divided into two categories: opiates (alkaloids found in opium-like morphine) and opioids (fully synthetic and semi-synthetic derivatives of opiates like oxycodone and hydrocodone). They are used for acute pain, post-surgical pain, and pain related to malignancy. Controversy exists concerning the use of long-term narcotic analgesics due to addiction concerns. However, studies show that when used appropriately, often along with a combination of other medications, narcotic analgesic medications can be a beneficial component of pain management (Falvo & Holland, 2018).

Non-narcotic Analgesic Medications. To prevent drug dependence on narcotic medications, non-narcotic analgesic medications are used for chronic pain. The most commonly used non-narcotic analgesic is acetaminophen, which is sold without a prescription (more commonly known as Tylenol)

(ACPA, 2013). The daily maximum dose of acetaminophen is 4000 milligrams; taking more than the maximum suggested dose or long-term use increases the risk of liver damage.

Muscle Relaxants. These medications are used during acute pain when muscle contractions are the predominant symptom. Muscle relaxants are sedating and are a concern when driving or when performing other high-risk activities. Careful caution should be taken when this category of drugs is used along with opioids (ACPA, 2013, 2016). Side-effects make long term use difficult, especially when a person experiences cognitive deficits. Muscle relaxants are frequently avoided for long term management of chronic pain.

Antidepressant Medications. Neurotransmitters, such as serotonin and norepinephrine, play a key role in depression and are also used for chronic pain (ACPA, 2013, 2016). Antidepressants neurochemically alleviate depression, directly relieve pain, and improve sleep by adjusting brain chemical levels (Clark & Treisman, 2004; Davis, 2010). This class of medication is helpful for fibromyalgia, headache, and pain due to nerve damage, but is less helpful for musculoskeletal injuries.

Injections

A multitude of injected medications exist for short-term pain relief. Injections are considered invasive and are not recommended until less invasive treatments are exhausted. Repetitive injections over an extensive time are contraindicated due to possible side-effects (ACPA, 2013, 2016). Chronic pain programs use injections strategically as an adjunct within a comprehensive program.

Implanted Devices

Morphine pumps and intraspinal drug infusion therapy are used for chronic spine pain that has been resistant to other treatment modalities (Banks & Mackrodt, 2005). An implanted catheter releases small amounts of morphine or other medications into the spine, allowing pain relief with small timed doses (ACPA, 2013). Spinal cord stimulators are used for chronic pain, including pain in the extremities, secondary to radiculopathy. Spinal cord stimulators are only considered when all other methods have been unsuccessful (Davis, 2010).

Exercise

There is strong evidence that exercise is beneficial for individuals with chronic pain and should be a part of any pain management program. Building and maintaining strength, flexibility, and endurance, while increasing function and range of motion helps alleviate discomfort and pain (ACPA, 2013, 2016). The chronic pain cycle commonly deconditions a person, secondary to the sedentary lifestyle of bed rest and medications for the treatment of minor exacerbations. Exercise is a method used to prevent this unnecessary slide into a deconditioned state of health (Smith, 2007). The act of exercise, however, is often difficult for the individual with chronic pain, and health care professionals need knowledge about designing an appropriate exercise program. Tai chi, yoga, and aquatics are possible exercise modalities that may be included in a comprehensive rehabilitation program for people with chronic pain (ACPA, 2013, 2016).

Biopsychosocial Treatment Management

As noted previously, treatment choice is dependent upon diagnosis, biopsychosocial background, and treatment goals. Pain interventions should be multidisciplinary and begin as soon as possible from the time of injury. The most effective chronic pain management programs provide medical intervention, physical therapy, occupational therapy, psychological treatment, and vocational therapy (McCarberg & Passik, 2005). Biopsychosocial treatment of chronic pain syndromes relies on cognitive-behavioral techniques and self-regulation.

Operant Conditioning

Current psychological interventions in pain management are based on the conceptual understanding of operant pain. As respondent pain leads to altered accommodative behavior, expression of pain is shaped by behavioral reinforcement. Operant intervention occurs on two levels. Behavior is extinguished by withholding reinforcement, including switching to fixed medication intervals and eliminating social attention for pain. Concurrently, well behaviors are reinforced and attention is given for behaviors that are incompatible with pain. As with other psychological methods of pain management, self-regulation strategies (e.g., relaxation and biofeedback) are based upon operant conditioning theory.

Cognitive-Behavioral Techniques

Cognitive-behavioral techniques are based on the assumption that a person's thoughts and beliefs influence pain. For instance, negative feelings about pain can increase sensitivity to pain and decrease activities that may alleviate pain (ACPA, 2013, 2016). Patients with chronic pain often fear that steps toward progress will lead to reinjury, worsening pain, failure, and loss of financial support. Thoughts, behaviors, emotions, and physiology affect one another. Four goals of cognitive-behavioral techniques follow (Smith, 2007; Turk, Meichenbaum, & Genest, 1983):

1. **Act rather than react.** Assist patients to perceive problems as manageable by developing problem-solving skills instead of being consumed by emotional reactions.
2. **Monitor.** Increase self-monitoring of thoughts, emotions, and behaviors in response to changes in physiology or the environment.
3. **Just do it.** Change behaviors regardless of feelings or belief in the response.
4. **Develop flexibility.** Maintain and develop effective coping strategies and continually adapt them.

Cognitive restructuring and self-regulation techniques are part of a comprehensive treatment plan for individuals who have chronic pain. Strategies of cognitive-behavioral techniques enhance coping skills and confidence, as well as self-efficacy for managing pain (Institute of Medicine, 2011).

Self-Regulation Strategies

Current developments of self-regulation strategies are diverse and multimodal, and include regulating physiological states and autonomic responses to the environment. Active strategies for regulation include relaxation, biofeedback, hypnosis, and guided imagery.

Relaxation. Relaxation exercises include techniques such as diaphragmatic breathing, progressive muscle relaxation, guided imagery, and cue-controlled relaxation (ACPA, 2013, 2016). These techniques, along with biofeedback or hypnotic induction, often form the foundation of treatment. Progressive muscle relaxation increases awareness of the level of tension or relaxation.

Biofeedback. Biofeedback focuses on training the mind to control body functions to help reduce anxiety and stress reactions by controlling muscle tension, breathing, and heart rate (Davis, 2010). Equipment is used to measure muscle tension, hand temperature, and skin conductance to help teach patients about the responses of their bodies and how to relax (ACPA, 2013, 2016).

Hypnosis. When considering hypnosis, it is meaningful to assess the person's attitudes and expectations concerning the nature and practice of this therapy. Direct induction procedures include (a) eliciting the patient's full cooperation, (b) focusing attention on the clinician's voice, (c) turning attention inward, and (d) suggesting dissociation. Once dissociation has been established, therapeutic suggestions are made to alleviate pain symptoms.

Guided imagery. Guided imagery incorporates relaxation techniques with clinician-directed or self-directed suggestions. It is an internally mediated sensory (typically visual) experience of focused attention. Association of pain and relaxation to positive images promotes control over an abstract concept, along with dissociation from the experience of pain.

Patient Involvement in Treatment

One of the most challenging aspects of pain management is *patient compliance and involvement in treatment*. Faced with the perceived simplicity of psychological techniques, the patient is often skeptical about the efficacy of treatment (Falvo & Holland, 2018). They may believe that therapists are discounting medical procedures, suggesting that the pain is not real, but rather "all in their head." Aligning patient expectations with the treatment plan enhances patient compliance and treatment outcomes.

While enhancing the person's motivation for treatment is difficult, there is a great imperative for patient involvement in medication, physical rehabilitation, and psychological treatment. Responsibility for treatment is shifted from the professional to the patient; the patient is given the lead in treatment and management of his or her pain. Individuals need to be encouraged to develop realistic and practical goals to meet their specific needs and interests (Pizzo & Clark, 2012).

Vocational Aspects and Rehabilitation

Early intervention in vocational rehabilitation increases motivation of injured workers. Employer interest and involvement, as well as an understanding of chronic pain, helps facilitate return to work. Reasonable accommodations for workers with chronic pain are variable and depend upon individualized assessments. Key factors to success include a motivated worker, an involved employer, and a successful pain management treatment program. Williams et al. (1998) found that job satisfaction is a strong predictor of pain management success and eventual return to work. Employees who had reported high levels of dissatisfaction were two and a half times more likely to incur job-related back injuries than employees who reported work satisfaction. Individuals who blame their employers for the accident had poorer treatment outcomes (Gharibo et al., 2017). The rehabilitation counselor can best improve employment opportunities for those who have chronic pain by implementing a comprehensive evaluation of a person's capabilities and limitations, analysis of the types of worksite accommodations needed, and assessment of potential assistive devices.

Early intervention enhances the motivation of an employee to remain on the job if currently working or to return to work if on disability. Through participation in a chronic pain management program, identifying the causes of pain, understanding the side-effects of medication, and assessing pain factors at work, the client can more effectively work with a counselor toward successful rehabilitation. Side-effects of medication may require modification of certain work duties and in some cases, a change in medication regimen may alleviate problematic side-effects that affect work functions. Employers who comprehend the dynamics of chronic pain are more willing to consider reasonable accommodation and job modification. Accommodations and job modifications are as variable as chronic pain itself.

Conclusion

The factors and wide-ranging effects of chronic pain give healthcare practitioners no simple solutions. Rather, a comprehensive rehabilitation team needs to take into account all aspects of the individual and how pain uniquely affects that person. Multi-disciplinary treatment programs with a *biopsychosocial* emphasis are approaches that have the greatest chance for success.

Understanding the psychosocial aspects of chronic pain is often more important than the diagnosis or degree of pathology when predicting success. Though at times professionals would like to view pain as a purely mechanical problem that needs to be *fixed*, the more successful approach involves widening one's scope to include the multifactorial nature of pain. Through proactive rehabilitation, the counselor can assist the employee to remain on the job, minimize consequences of impairment, and effectively work with the employer to understand the significance of accommodation in diminishing disability and increasing job productivity.

Case Study

Bryant Beckon is 40 years of age, married, and has a nine-year-old daughter. He and his family live a very active lifestyle, where Bryant coaches his daughter's soccer team and on the weekends the family goes on hikes. Recently, Bryant and his wife have been talking about having a second child.

Mr. Beckon has been working as a postal service mail carrier for the past seven years. Nine months ago, Bryant was delivering a large package when he slipped on loose gravel. Bryant injured his back and since then has been receiving comprehensive multidisciplinary treatment first for acute, and then for chronic low back pain. Presently, Bryant's chronic pain has diminished from moderately severe to moderate pain. His treating physician restricts him to a maximum of light work activities. Mr. Beckon has been on workers' compensation but has been feeling down about not being able to maintain his active lifestyle, including employment. He also feels that his daughter and he are not as close as they were because of his injury.

Questions

1. Discuss the differences between acute and chronic pain. Relate this to the case study.
2. Describe a comprehensive, multidisciplinary treatment program for chronic pain.
3. Explore the psychosocial factors involved in chronic pain and its relevance to this case.
4. Assess the various treatment modalities used for chronic pain.
5. Develop several vocational rehabilitation plans for Bryant Beckon.

References

American Chronic Pain Association. (ACPA). (2013). *ACPA resource guide to chronic pain medicine and treatment*. Rocklin, CA: Author.

American Chronic Pain Association. (ACPA). (2016). *ACPA resource guide to chronic pain treatment and an integrated guide to physical, behavioral, and pharmacologic therapy*. Rocklin, CA: Author.

Anderson, J. (2016). HHS releases national pain strategy. *Medscape*. Retrieved from http://www.medscape.com/viewarticle/861626#vp 1

Banks, C., & Mackrodt, K. (Eds.). (2005). *Chronic pain management. Part 1*. Philadelphia, PA: Whurr.

Block, A. R., Kremer, E. F., & Kremer, A. M. (2005). Chronic pain syndromes. In H. H. Zaretsky, E. F. Richter, & M. G. Eisenberg (Eds.), *Medical aspects of disability: A handbook for the rehabilitation professional* (3rd ed., pp. 213-239). New York, NY: Springer.

Clark, M. R., & Treisman, G. J. (2004). *Pain and depression: An interdisciplinary patient-centered approach*. New York, NY: Basel.

Davis, J. L. (2010). *Chronic pain relief: New treatments*. Retrieved from http://www.webmd.com/pain-management/features/chronic-pain-relief-new-treatments

Falvo, D., & Holland, B. E. (2018). *Medical and psychosocial aspects of chronic illness and disability* (6th ed.). Burlington, MA: Jones and Bartlett Learning.

Flor, H., & Kurk, D. C. (2011). *Chronic pain: An integrated biobehavioral approach*. Seattle, WA: Lippincott Williams and Wilkins.

Gharibo, C. G., Patel, H., & Aydin, S. M. (2017). Chronic pain syndromes. In A. Moroz, S. R. Flanagan, & H. H. Zaretsky (Eds.), *Medical aspects of disability for the rehabilitation professional* (5th ed., pp. 175-190). New York, NY: Springer.

Gatchel, R. J., & Turk, D. C. (1996). *Psychological approaches to pain management: A practitioner's guide*. New York, NY: Guilford

Institute of Medicine. (2011). *Relieving pain in America: A bluebook for transforming prevention, care, education, and research*. Washington, DC: National Academies.

International Association for the Study of Pain. (1986). Classification of chronic pain: Descriptions of chronic pain syndromes and definitions of pain terms. *Pain, 13*, S1-S225.

McCarberg, B., & Passik, S. D. (Eds.). (2005). *Expert guide to pain management*. Philadelphia, PA: American College of Physicians.

Melzack, R. (1975). The McGill Pain Questionnaire: Major properties and scoring methods. *Pain, 1*, 277-299.

National Institute of Neurological Disorders and Stroke. (2016). *Headache: Hope through research*. Bethesda, MD: Author.

Pizzo, P. A., & Clark, N. M. (2012). Alleviating suffering 101 - Pain relief in the United States. *New England Journal of Medicine, 366*(3), 197-199.

Reflex Sympathetic Dystrophy Syndrome Association. (2013). *About CRPS*. Retrieved from http://www.rsds.org/2/what_is_rsd_crps/

Smith, H. S. (2007). *Pain management. Part 1*. Philadelphia, PA: Saunders.

Treede, R. D., Rief, W., Barke, A., Aziz, W., Bennet, M. I., Beneoliel, R., . . . Wang, S. J. (2015). A classification of chronic pain for ICD-11. *Journal of Pain, 156*(6), 1003-1007.

Turk, D. C., Meichenbaum, D., & Genest, J. (1983). *Pain and behavioral medicine: A cognitive-behavioral perspective*. New York, NY: Guilford.

Williams, R. A., Pruitt, S. D., Doctor, J. N., Epping-Jordan, J. E., Wahlgren, D. R., Grant, I., . . . Atkinson, J. B. (1998). The contribution of job satisfaction to the transition from acute to chronic low back pain. *Archives of Physical Medicine and Rehabilitation, 79*(4), 366-374.

About the Authors

Ashley T. Du, MS, received her Master of Science degree in counseling, with options in rehabilitation and school counseling leadership. Her interests are in the areas of chronic pain management, and in providing the most effective counseling and rehabilitation services for students. Ms. Du specializes in transitional counseling with an emphasis in college and career. As a counselor at Los Angeles Valley College in Valley Glen, California, she assists community college students with academic advisement, career counseling, and transition to a four-year college or university. Additionally, Ashley provides career assessment.

John Lindberg, MD, specializes in treatment and management of chronic pain patients. He is a board certified physiatrist by the American Board of Physical Medicine and Rehabilitation. Dr. Lindberg is Medical Director of the Chronic Pain Management Program at Casa Colina Center for Rehabilitative Medicine in Pomona, California. Additionally, Dr. Lindberg is Medical Director of Rehabilitation Medicine at Citrus Valley Medical Center in Covina, California.

Brendon W. Bluestein, PhD, is a clinical psychologist with a specialty in behavioral analysis and chronic pain management. He practices in Fort Meade, Maryland. Dr. Bluestein was the Coordinator of the Chronic Pain Program at Casa Colina Center for Rehabilitative Medicine. While a Captain in the United States Army, he served as a psychologist at Walter Reed Hospital and worked in pain management with paratroopers and pilots in Alabama and Georgia.

Chapter 11

COMPLEMENTARY AND INTEGRATIVE HEALTH

Hua Gu, PhD, LAc
Sandra K. Brodwin, MS

Introduction

Alternative and complementary medicines, together with East Asian and other forms of traditional medicines, have attracted the attention of people worldwide. In 2002, the National Library of Medicine classified alternative medicine under the term complementary and alternative medicine (CAM): therapeutic practices which are not currently considered an integral part of conventional medical practice. These treatments are typically not available in physician offices, hospitals, or medical school training curricula in the United States.

It is accepted that a number of diseases remain incurable by Western medicine. With all its successes, Western medicine has its limitations, such as alleviating symptoms, the side effects of medications, high costs of treatment, and the inaccessibility of facilities and treatment. A Kaiser Family Foundation/New York Times survey found that one in five people who are of working age reported that paying for medical care caused serious financial challenges that lead to lifestyle changes (Kaiser Family Foundation, 2016). CAM is part of a solution to some of these inadequacies (Bishop, Yeardley, Cooper, Little, & Lewith, 2017).

In 2016, the National Institutes of Health (NIH) adopted the terminology of complementary integrative health (CIH) rather than complementary alternative medicine (CAM), noting that when a "non-mainstream practice is used together with conventional medicine, it is considered complementary and when a non-mainstream practice is used in place of conventional medicine, it is considered alternative." In that most often non-mainstream treatment is used with conventional treatments, the NIH chose to identify the practice as complementary integrative health (CIH). Integration of CAM with conventional medicine is occurring throughout the U.S. More than 30% of adults and perhaps as many as 12% of children use healthcare techniques based on practices not within the confines of conventional medicine (U.S. Department of Health and Human Services, 2016ab).

When Western medicine began to address this growing trend toward CIH treatment, the NIH formed a policy panel that defined complementary, alternative medicine as "a broad domain of healing resources that encompasses all health systems, modalities, and practices, and their accompanying theories and beliefs, other than those intrinsic to the politically dominant health system of a particular society or culture in a given historical period." Most CIH practices are guided by four common principles: prevention, natural healing, active learning, and holistic approaches. Physicians who are embracing CIH therapies, combining them with conventional medical therapies, often use the term integrative medicine to refer to their practices (Mayo Clinic, 2010).

In its 2016 strategic plan, the National Center for Complementary and Integrative Health (NCCIH) Director, Josephine P. Briggs, MD, stated that NCCIH carefully examined how recent developments in science, medicine, and health care have affected the NCCIH's strategic approaches in the diverse arena of complementary and integrative health. This leads to a plan that takes into account "scientific gaps and opportunities under three scientific and two cross-cutting objectives: Advancing Fundamental Science and

Methods Development, Improving Care for Hard-to-Manage Symptoms, Fostering Health Promotion and Disease Prevention, Enhancing the Complementary and Integrative Health Research Workforce, and Disseminating Objective Evidence-Based Information on Complementary and Integrative Health Interventions."

What we now define as alternative or integrative medicine was first discussed by Chinese philosophers over 3,000 years ago (Pham, Yoo, Tran, & Ta, 2013). Foundational differences between Western and Eastern medical models has made it difficult for medical providers in the U.S. to embrace the idea of health as a state of balance between the physical, mental, social, and super-natural environment. Western medicine tends to approach disease by assuming it is due to an external force, such as a virus or bacteria, or a slow degeneration of the functional ability of the body. Disease, in the eyes of Western medicine, is either physical or mental. The Eastern approach, on the other hand, adopts that each part of the body is intimately connected. Each organ is viewed as having a mental as well as a physical function (Carteret, 2011).

The goal of CIH treatment practices is to promote health and prevent or manage conditions. There is a growing trend toward integrated health in the U.S. The Anderson Cancer Center at the University of Texas offers more than 75 complementary therapy program options. The Mayo Clinic founded "The Complementary and Integrative Medicine Program" in 2001. Johns Hopkins Medicine has included on its webpage a section for Community Physicians, Specialty Areas, and "Acupuncture." Columbia University Medical Center, and New York-Presbyterian/Morgan Stanley Children's Hospital, have established the Center for Comprehensive Wellness in the Division of Pediatric Hematology, Oncology and Stem Cell Transplantation.

A greater number of physicians are including CIH therapies in their practices. Education of professionals and consumers becomes essential to ensure safe and effective medical practice and that "the potential benefits of various CIH are fully recognized (Bodeker & Burford, 2008). To meet these goals and to address the increased interest by people in the U.S., a study was undertaken by the National Academies of Sciences to:

1. Describe the use of CAM therapies by the public in the U.S. and provide a comprehensive overview, to the extent that data are available, of the therapies in widespread use, the populations that use them, and what is known about how they are provided.

2. Identify the major scientific, policy, and practice issues related to CAM research and to the translation of validated therapies into conventional medical practice.

3. Develop conceptual models or frameworks to guide public- and private-sector decision making as research and practice communities confront the challenges of conducting research on CAM, translating research findings into practice, and addressing the distinct policy and practice barriers inherent in that transition (Institute of Medicine, 2005).

The National Academies' 2005 Report recommended that "the same principles and standards of evidence of treatment effectiveness apply to all treatments, with the understanding that certain characteristics of some CAMs and some conventional medical interventions make it difficult or impossible to conduct standard randomized controlled trials. For these therapies, innovative methods of evaluation are needed as are measures and standards for the generation and interpretation of evidence" (Institute of Medicine, 2005, p. 278).

Between 1990 and 2015, more adults turned to CIH to treat conditions including back pain, neck pain, joint pain, stiffness, anxiety, and depression (the latter two are commonly associated with chronic pain) via acupuncture, deep breathing exercises, massage therapy, meditation, naturopathy, and yoga (Kim, 2017). Lifestyle, diet, obesity, lack of exercise, and stress are contributing factors in the causation of non-communicable diseases; therefore, complementary and conventional approaches to these factors in particular will be increasingly important for the development of future health care strategies.

CIH therapies are classified into the following categories: Whole Medical Systems, Mind-body Medicine, Biologically-based Practices, Manipulative and Body-based Practices, and Energy Therapy. Whole Medical Systems is based on the idea that a system is not just a single practice or remedy but many practices that center on a philosophy, such as the power of nature or the presence of energy in one's body.

Homeopathy uses minute doses of a substance that causes symptoms to stimulate the body's self-healing response. Naturopathy focuses on noninvasive treatments to help the body do its own healing and uses a variety of practices, such as massage, acupuncture, herbal remedies, exercise, and lifestyle counseling. Mind-body techniques target strengthening the paths of communication between the mental and physical states of being, enabling them to function in harmony. Examples of mind-body connection techniques include meditation, prayer, and relaxation and art therapies (Mayo Clinic, 2010).

Biologically-based practices include dietary supplements and herbal remedies using ingredients found in nature. Examples of herbs are ginseng, ginkgo, and Echinacea. Other dietary supplements include selenium, glucosamine sulfate, and self-assembled monolayers (SAMs). Herbs and supplements can be taken as teas, oils, syrups, powders, and tablets or capsules. The methods of Manipulative and Body-based practices use human touch to move or manipulate a specific part of the body. They include chiropractic and osteopathic manipulation and massage. Energy Therapy is based on balancing the body's flowing energy force. When this energy flow is blocked or unbalanced, the individual can become sick. This energy is referred to as chi, prana, or life force. Energy Therapies include qi gong, therapeutic touch, reiki, and magnet therapy (Kim, 2017).

It is not possible in one chapter to capture all the pertinent information on the total spectrum of CAM. Therefore, the authors have chosen the most commonly used of these therapies in the U.S. Whole Medical Systems (i.e., Traditional Chinese Medicine-Acupuncture and Homeopathy), Manipulative and Body-based (i.e., Chiropractic Medicine), and Biologically-based (i.e., Biofeedback/Neurofeedback).

Whole Medical Systems

Traditional Chinese Medicine - Acupuncture

Traditional Chinese Medicine (TCM) is one of the most ancient forms of medicine and embodies achievements accumulated over millennia (Tan et al., 2007). Practice of this ancient form of medicine began in earnest in the U.S. in the early 1970s after President Richard Nixon visited China in 1972. TCM is based on a personalized and holistic approach to health and disease. Herbal remedies and acupuncture are the treatments most commonly used by TCM practitioners. Other TCM practices include moxibustion, cupping, massage, mind-body therapy, and dietary therapy. This chapter focuses on the practice of acupuncture.

Overview and History

The Yellow Emperor's Internal Classic, the oldest known work of Chinese medical theory, was compiled around the first century BCE (Before the Common Era) on the basis of shorter texts from different medical lineages. Written in the form of dialogues between the legendary Yellow Emperor and his ministers, it offers explanations on the relation between humans, their environment, and the cosmos; on the contents of the body; on human vitality and pathology; on the symptoms of illness; and on how to make diagnostic and therapeutic decisions in light of all these factors. Unlike earlier texts, such as Recipes for Fifty-Two Ailments, excavated in the 1970s from a tomb that had been sealed in 168 BCE, the Yellow Emperor's internal classic rejected the influence of spirits and the use of magic. It was one of the first books in which the cosmological doctrines of Yingyang and the Five Phases were brought to a mature synthesis (Gu, 1989).

Traces of therapeutic activities in China date from the Shang Dynasty ($14^{th} - 11^{th}$ centuries BCE). Though the Shang did not have a concept of medicine as distinct from other fields, their oracular inscriptions on bones and tortoise shells refer to illnesses that affected the Shang royal family. These included eye disorders, toothaches, bloated abdomen, and so forth, which Shang elites usually attributed to curses sent by their ancestors.

In 600 BCE, TCM doctors began practicing bone-setting along with palpation, observation, and measurement. Hua Tou of the Eastern Han Dynasty, performed orthopedic surgery and used herbs for anesthesia. Between 341 and 265 BCE, TCM practitioners used wood splints to stabilize fractures and avoid surgery. Splints enabled doctors to treat and rehabilitate their patients simultaneously. From 206 to 112 BCE, functional exercises and rehabilitation were widely used in the therapy of trauma and bone/joint diseases. Physicians asked patients to do exercises similar to other animals, such as the monkey, bear, bird, and rhino called the five animal exercises. These exercises are used today after surgery to assist in the healing process (Wax & White, 2000).

TCM practices a complete system between treatment and rehabilitation based on the theory of Qi (Ch'i) and blood, Yin and Yang, internal organs, and the five elements and meridians within the body. The concept of Qi was first introduced in TCM in the 5th Century BCE. Body movement is key to maintaining Qi circulation. If the body is injured and not able to move, the Qi will stagnate and cause problems. In 475 to 221 BCE, the first TCM book was written describing Qi as consisting of blood, brain, spinal cord, joints, and muscles (Beijing College of Traditional Chinese Medicine, 2011).

When Qi or blood circulation is interrupted, injury or disease occurs. To protect the body with proper Qi and blood movement, TCM emphasizes prevention with acupuncture, herbs, and exercises. Generally speaking, the word Qi connotes both substance and function, two different but closely related concepts that cannot be entirely separated. Each function must be based on a certain substance and vice versa (Beijing College of Traditional Chinese Medicine, 2011).

Patterns of Use

As noted by Gu (1989), the theory of yin-yang is that every object or phenomenon in the universe consists of two opposite aspects: yin and yang, which are at once in conflict and act interdependently. This relationship is the universal law of the material world, the principle and source of existence, and the root cause for the flourishing and perishing of living things. These relationships between yin and yang are extensively used in TCM to explain the physiology and pathology of the human body, and serve as a guide for diagnosis and treatment in clinical work.

The theory of the five elements indicates that wood, fire, earth, metal, and water are basic materials constituting the material world. There exists among them an interdependence and inter-restraint that determines their state of constant motion and change. The theory of the five elements explains the symbiotic and counter active relationship of yin-yang. Using the theory of the five elements and yin-yang, TCM is classified into different categories: natural phenomena, tissues and organs of the human body, and human emotions (Gu, 1989, 2010).

The internal organs connect in the body through channels and collaterals with the various tissues and organs of the superficial portion of the body to create organic integrity (Teppone & Avakyan, 2007). In the network of channels and collaterals, the channels pertain to the respective organs; the collaterals are their minor branches which are distributed throughout the body. Along each channel are points for applying acupuncture. The efficacy of acupuncture in prevention and treatment of disease is due to regulating and strengthening the defensive function and helping restore relative balance within the human body, as well as that between the body and its environment. Points are the specific sites through which the Qi of the organs and channels is transported to the body surface. When the body is affected by a disease, treatment will center on puncturing the corresponding points on the body surface.

Seven emotional factors are classified in TCM: joy, anger, melancholy, meditation, grief, fear, and fright. These factors are reflections of the human mental state as induced by various stimulations in the environment. They are physiological phenomena that do not cause disease under normal conditions. However, if the emotions are very intense and persistent or the individual is hypersensitive to the stimulations, they may result in drastic and long-standing changes in emotion, which can lead to chronic physical problems or disease. Traumatic injuries, for example, can cause stagnant blood or phlegm and induce pain or deformity (Xinnong & Deng, 2010).

The four diagnostic methods in TCM include: inquiring about the patient's condition; inspection or examining the expression, color, and appearance of the tongue; auscultation or listening; and palpation (feeling the patient's pulse). The palpation of pulse means not only the speed, but also the quality (thready, wiry, or slippery) (Gu, 1989).

Identifying a syndrome entails further analysis and synthesis of the clinical data obtained using the four diagnostic methods. The differentiation of diseases can be derived from eight principles: exterior and interior, cold and heat, deficiency and excess, and yin and yang (Maciocia, 2015). Disorders of channels may affect the corresponding organs, and disorders of the organs are reflected at the corresponding channels. Channels connect with organs and exteriorly with the body surface where points are distributed.

Herbal medicine is a part of TCM; there are roughly 13,000 medicinals used in China and over 100,000 medicinal recipes recorded in the ancient literature. Plant elements and extracts are by far the most common elements used. In the classic Handbook of Traditional Drugs from 1941, 517 drugs were listed. Out of these, only 45 were derived from animal parts, and 30 were based on minerals.

There are many differences between Chinese medicine and conventional medicine (Gu, 1989). Conventional medicine tries to locate where the problem specifically originates, such as organ level (heart, liver, kidney), cell level, or even molecular level. Rather, Chinese medicine focuses on the whole body and tries to balance the body with acupuncture and herbs. Sometimes TCM concentrates on the result and may not seek to understand what happened inside the body. Acupuncture helps induce the body's own healing power to regain balance (Beijing College of Traditional Chinese Medicine, 2011). As an example, a recent successful trial study using acupuncture with 504 women was conducted by Liu et al. (2017). Researchers found that electro acupuncture in the lumbar-sacral region resulted in a significant decrease in urinary leakage after six weeks of treatment than a control group given sham electro acupuncture.

Professionals working in the area of acupuncture attend formal training. The intensity and length of training varies, including certificate or diploma programs and degree programs – bachelor's, master's, and doctorate degrees.

Homeopathy

Homeopathy ("home-ee-AH-pah-thy") is derived from the Greek words homios (similar) and pathos (suffering) and focuses on stimulating the body's natural healing properties to cure or alleviate illness or disease. A practitioner of homeopathy treats a patient by introducing a substance into the body that induces symptoms identical to those caused by the disease to stimulate healing energy. Homeopathy is based on Hippocrates' Law of Similars, otherwise known as the philosophy that like cures like (Yuan, Bieber, & Bauer, 2006). Homeopathic remedies are dilutions of natural substances from plants, minerals, and animals. Once the patient's initial symptoms are resolved, the practitioner treats underlying symptoms.

Overview and History

In the late 1700s, Samuel Hahnemann, a physician, chemist, and linguist in Germany, developed homeopathy as an approach to treating illness (Haller, 2005). This was at a time when the most common medical treatments included bloodletting, purging, and blistering, using harsh substances such as sulfur and mercury. Few effective medications existed to treat patients, and knowledge about the effects of existing treatments was limited.

Hahnemann was interested in developing a less-threatening approach to medicine. It is alleged that Hahnemann stumbled upon his first major discovery while translating an herbal text about the use of cinchona bark to cure malaria. Curious, an otherwise healthy Hahnemann ingested some cinchona bark. He developed symptoms very similar to those experienced by sufferers of malaria. This led Hahnemann to consider that a substance may create symptoms that it can also relieve. He began experimenting with other single, pure substances on himself and, in more dilute forms, on healthy volunteers. As a researcher, Hahnemann kept meticulous records of his experiments and participants' responses, and combined these observations with information from clinical practice, the known uses of herbs and other medicinal substances, and toxicology, eventually treating the sick and developing a homeopathic clinical practice (Yuan et al., 2006).

Homeopaths evaluate not only a person's physical symptoms but emotions, mental states, lifestyle, nutrition, and other aspects. In homeopathy, different people with the same symptoms may receive different homeopathic remedies (Yuan et al., 2006).

Boston-born physician Hans Burch Gram introduced homeopathy into the U.S. in 1825. European immigrants trained in homeopathy made the treatment increasingly available in America. In 1835, the first homeopathic medical college was established in Allentown, Pennsylvania. By the turn of the 20th Century, 8% of all American medical practitioners were homeopaths; there were 20 homeopathic medical colleges and more than 100 homeopathic hospitals in this country (Andrasik & Lords, 2009).

In the 1960s, the popularity of homeopathy increased in North America. In 1999, over six million Americans reported using homeopathy. In 1994, the World Health Organization reported that homeopathy had been integrated into the national health care systems of numerous countries (Jonas, Kaptchuk, & Linde, 2003).

Patterns of Use

Many who seek homeopathic care use it to alleviate chronic medical conditions; most treat themselves with homeopathic products and do not consult professional care. Those who do seek professional help experience a lengthy first visit during which the provider takes an in-depth assessment which guides the selection of one or more homeopathic remedies. During follow-up visits, patients report how they are responding to the remedy or remedies to help the practitioner make decisions about further treatment (Jonas et al., 2003).

A homeopathic remedy is prepared by diluting a substance through a series of steps. Providers refer to the Homeopathic Pharmacopoeia of the United States to match symptom profiles of patients with the appropriate remedy. Homeopathy asserts that this process can maintain the healing properties of a substance regardless of how many times it has been diluted. Many homeopathic remedies are so highly diluted that none of the original natural substance remains. The U.S. Food and Drug Administration recognizes homeopathic dilutions as official drugs and regulates the manufacturing, labeling, and dispensing of homeopathic medications.

Researchers have found that homeopathic remedies give off electromagnetic signals; each homeopathic substance has a specific dominant frequency (del Giudici & Preparata, 1990). It is theorized that homeopathic remedies convey the electromagnetic message to the body that matches the frequency of the illness, stimulating the healing properties of the body: one subtle energy (remedy) affects another subtle energy (human energy field). As in other CIHs, this subtle energy field in the body is called the vital force.

Manipulative and Body-Based

Chiropractic

As with acupuncture practitioners, the goal of chiropractic is to support the natural ability of the body to heal itself. The Greek word chiropractor means done by hand. Chiropractic is a health care approach that focuses on the relationship between the body structure, primarily the musculoskeletal system and its functioning. Although practitioners may use a variety of treatment approaches, they mainly perform manipulation (an ancient healing art) with the goal of correcting body alignment (World Federation of Chiropractic, 2012).

Overview and History

The word chiropractor combines the Greek words cheir (hand) and praxis (action) to describe a treatment done by hand. Hands-on therapy, especially adjustment of the spine, is central in chiropractic care. No one culture has been identified as the originator of chiropractic. It has been found in the ancient cultures of China, Japan, Polynesia, India, Egypt, Tibet, and in the Aztec, Inca, Maya, Sioux, and Winnebago cultures of the Americas. Through the 17th Century, there are medical records throughout the cultures of Europe detailing the use of traction applied to parts of the body while pressure was applied on a specific area of the spine (Bergman & Peterson, 2011).

Therapeutic manipulation practice was founded in the late 19th century. While Andrew Still watched his wife and their three children die, he became convinced that the body needed to heal itself, but had to be structurally sound to accomplish the healing. He decided that healing would take place when the life force could be accessed. The life force could be released when the spine was manipulated to relieve mechanical pressure on blood vessels and nerves. If the nerves were impinged in any way, blood flow was reduced resulting in pain, necrosis, and impingement of the healing life force (Still, 2009).

While some procedures associated with chiropractic care can be traced back to ancient times, the modern profession of chiropractic was founded by Dr. Daniel Palmer in 1895 in Davenport, Iowa. Palmer, a self-taught healer, believed the body has a natural healing ability. Misalignments of the spine interfere with the flow of energy needed to support health. Palmer theorized that the key to health is to normalize the function of the nervous system, especially the spinal cord. As with acupuncture providers, chiropractors perform diagnosis by visual inspection and palpation, in addition to x-ray and other diagnostic methods. Chiropractic is the leading complementary and alternative medicine model (Singer, 2013).

Patterns of Use

According to the 2014 National Health Interview Survey, which includes a comprehensive survey of the use of complementary health practices by Americans, about 8% of adults and nearly 3% of children had received chiropractic care within the past year. There has been a growing trend of chiropractic use among U.S. adults from 2002 to 2012. Back and neck pain (63.0% and 30.2% respectively), were the most prevalent health problems for chiropractic consultations. People seek chiropractic care primarily for pain conditions such as back and neck pain, headache, musculoskeletal conditions, menstrual pain, and asthma. Adults (older than 30 years) and those who are diagnosed with spinal stenosis were more likely to have consulted a chiropractor in the past year. Positive outcomes were reported for general health and for specific issues where they had also received conventional care (Adams et al., 2017).

Chiropractic is based on these key concepts: (a) the body has a powerful self-healing ability; (b) the body's structure (primarily the spine) and its function are closely related; and (c) this relationship affects health. Therapy aims to normalize this relationship between structure and function and assist the body as it heals. The theory of chiropractic is that misaligned spinal vertebrae interfere with nerve function, resulting in altered physiologic conditions which contribute to pain and disease. A common diagnosis to support this theory is subluxation, an impinged nerve as a result of misalignment in the spine, causing pain. Chiropractic belief is that this misalignment also prevents body defenses from performing appropriately. By adjusting the spinal joints, subluxation is resolved, restoring normal nerve function and optimal health. Chiropractic has expanded to include improving joint mobility and alleviating restricted movement as a result of spinal fixation (Gatterman, 2011).

During the initial visit, chiropractors take a health history and perform a physical examination, with a special emphasis on the spine. The chiropractor may perform other examinations or tests, such as x-rays. If chiropractic treatment is considered appropriate, the practitioner develops a treatment plan. During follow-up visits, practitioners may perform one or more of the many different types of adjustments used in chiropractic care. Centered mainly in the spine, a chiropractic adjustment (sometimes referred to as a manipulation) involves using the hands or a device to apply a controlled, sudden force to a joint, moving it beyond its passive range of motion. The goal is to increase range and quality of motion in the area being treated, and to aid in restoring health (Ernst, Pittler, & Wider, 2006).

Adjustment procedures, including adjustments, manipulations, and mobilization, are the defining technique of chiropractic treatment. Terms associated with chiropractic include: adjustment, manipulation, and zhiyaand mobilization. These terms relate to joint movement, which can be divided into active end range (how far the patient can, with muscular effort, move a joint in a particular direction), passive end range (at the end of the active end range, a clinician can safely move the joint further), anatomic end range, and paraphysiologic joint space which exceeds the passive end range but not the anatomic end range (Andrasik & Lords, 2009). Manipulation is passive movement of the joint past the passive end range but not the anatomic end range. Mobilization is the clinician-assisted passive movement within the anatomic end range resulting in an increased overall range-of-joint motion (Cox, 2011).

Chiropractors combine the application of spinal adjustments with several other treatments, such as application of alternating temperatures, electrical stimulation, and rehabilitative exercise. They also prescribe lifestyle changes including adjustments to the patient's diet.

To practice within the U.S., a chiropractor must earn a Doctor of Chiropractic (D.C.) degree from a college accredited by the Council on Chiropractic Education (CCE, 2017). CCE is the agency certified by the U.S. Department of Education to accredit chiropractic colleges. Admission to a chiropractic college requires a minimum of 90 semester credits (approximately three years) of undergraduate study, primarily in the sciences. Chiropractic training is a four-year academic program that includes both classroom work and direct experience caring for patients. Coursework typically includes instruction in the biomedical sciences, as well as in public health and research methods.

Biologically-Based Practices

Biofeedback/Neurofeedback

Biofeedback/neurofeedback is a treatment technique in which patients are trained to improve their health by using signals from their own bodies (Collura, 2014). While physical therapists may use biofeedback, for example, to help stroke survivors regain movement in paralyzed muscles, psychologists use it to help clients reduce tension and anxiety. Specialists in different fields sometimes administer biofeedback to help patients cope with pain. Using biofeedback machines, clinicians detect a patient's internal bodily functions, which they then use to gauge and direct the progress of treatment. A biofeedback therapist acts as a coach, helping the patient set goals and limits on what to expect and how to improve performance.

Overview and History

In the early part of the 20th century in Germany, J. H. Schultz developed a technique called autogenic training in which verbal instructions are used to guide a person to a different, more relaxed and controlled physiological state. Years later, an American, Edmund Jacobson, developed the technique of progressive relaxation training, a series of muscle activities designed to teach people how to control tension and relaxation through awareness of reducing muscle tension and stress. During the 1960s and 1970s, gradual awareness of Eastern yogic traditions involving voluntary physiologic adjustments began to emerge in the Western world attracting the attention of a few key researchers. Gurus taught these researchers that by using relaxation and control, they could change a number of variables previously thought to be autonomously regulated, including blood pressure, heart rate, and body temperature. These functions are managed by the autonomic nervous system (ANS), so named precisely because it was thought that such functions could not be voluntarily altered (Collura, 2014).

The ANS has two divisions—the sympathetic and the parasympathetic. The sympathetic nervous system regulates the flight/fight response. The parasympathetic nervous system calms and relaxes and manages body functions. The two work in tandem in a reciprocal relationship. Canon and Selye, two researchers who focused on the body's response to stress, brought an increase in the general awareness of the role of stress in physical diseases and mental disorders (Robertson, Biaggioni, Burnstock, Low, & Paton, 2011).

Yogic practices, such as hatha yoga, became established in the U.S. as techniques for physical relaxation and enhancement of conscious control over physiology. Additionally, meditation techniques stimulated the elaboration of the relaxation and attention training techniques, influencing and controlling the body with the conscious mind to promote relaxation and manage pain and stress. A number of these techniques, combined with biofeedback/neurofeedback, enhance learning physiological self-regulation (mind-body control).

Patterns of Use

The word biofeedback was coined in the late 1960s to describe laboratory procedures then being used to train experimental research subjects to alter brain activity, blood pressure, heart rate, and other bodily functions that normally are not controlled voluntarily. Research has demonstrated that biofeedback/neurofeedback help in the treatment of many diseases and painful conditions. It has shown that people have more control over so-called involuntary bodily function than researchers once thought possible (Rajeswaran, 2012).

At the highest level of organization, each life form may possess an innate biologic field (biofield), a complex, dynamic field of energy involved in maintaining an organism's integrity regulating its physiologic and biochemical responses, and allowing it to develop, heal, and regenerate (Rubik, 2015). Both life force and biofield proponents agree that a form of life-giving energy flows through the body, and illness arises as a result of blockages, excesses, or irregularities in this flow.

Samples of commonly used measures of the biofield include electrocardiogram (ECG) and electroencephalogram (EEG) to assess the function of the heart and brain. Corresponding magnetic field measurements of the heart and brain have been discovered: magnetocardiogram (MCG) and magnetoencephalogram (MEG). The MEG allows for localizing the activity of a region of the brain the size of a pea. Lie detectors and biofeedback use galvanic skin response (GSR) to measure the electrical conductance between electrodes on the skin. Thermography, an accepted diagnostic procedure in conventional Western medicine, measures the emission of infrared radiation from the body (Rajeswaran, 2012).

Biofeedback patients are taught a form of relaxation exercise which allows them to identify the circumstances that trigger their symptoms. While some may be taught how to avoid or cope with stressful events, most are encouraged to change their habits. The majority of patients who choose to use biofeedback are trained in special techniques aimed at giving them self-control. Biofeedback is a tool that reminds physicians that behavior, thoughts, and feelings profoundly influence physical health.

A biofeedback therapist is required when the problems that are experienced become greater than a person can handle. Biofeedback can be seen as a journey toward increased self-awareness. Despite a strong self-help component, it is prudent that biofeedback be conducted under the care of a trained mental health professional, and only after medical evaluation has determined that a more serious condition will not be neglected by the training. Initially, the biofeedback/neurofeedback therapist does a history of past health and current symptoms. The biofeedback practitioner guides the trainee by designing an individualized program for improved health, encouraging regular practice, monitoring results, and supporting the training process in various ways, including advice regarding complementary interventions (Yucha & Montegomery, 2008).

References

Adams, J., Peng, W., Cramer, H., Sundberg, T., Moore, C., Amorin-Woods, L., . . . Lauche, R. (2017). *The prevalence, patterns, and predictors of chiropractic use among U.S. adults: Results from the 2012 National Health Interview Survey*. Bethesda, MD: National Center for Biotechnology Information, U.S. National Library of Medicine

Andrasik, F., & Lords, A. O. (2009). Biofeedback. In L. Freeman (Ed.), *Mosby's complementary and alternative medicine: A research-based approach* (3rd ed., pp. 189-214). St Louis, MO: Mosby Elsevier.

Beijing College of Traditional Chinese Medicine. (2011). *Essentials of Chinese acupuncture* (3rd ed.). Beijing, China: Foreign Languages.

Bergman, T., & Peterson, D. (2011). *Chiropractic technique: Principles and procedures* (3rd ed.). St. Louis, MO: Elsevier.

Bishop, F. L., Yeardley, L., Cooper, C., Little, P., & Lewith, G. T. (2017). Predicting adherence to acupuncture appointments for low back pain: A prospective observational study. *BMC Complementary and Alternative Medicine, 17*(1), 1-12.

Bodeker, G., & Burford, G. (2008). Traditional, complementary, and alternative medicine: Policy and public health perspectives. *Bulletin of the World Health Organization, 86*(1), 77-78.

Carteret, M. (2011). Traditional Asian health beliefs and healing practice. *Dimensions of culture: Cross-cultural communications for healthcare professionals*. Retrieved from http://www.dimensionsofculture.com

Collura, T. F. (2014). *Technical foundations of neurofeedback*. New York, NY: Taylor and Francis.

Council on Chiropractic Education Accreditation Standards: Principles, processes, and requirements for accreditation (CCE). (2017). Scottsdale, AZ: Council on Chiropractic Medicine.

Cox, J. M. (2011). *Low back pain: Mechanism, diagnosis, and treatment* (7th ed.). Philadelphia, PA: Lippincott Williams & Wilkins.

del Giudici, E., & Preparata, G. (1990). Superradiance: A new approach to coherent dynamical behaviors of condenses matter, frontier perspectives. *Medical Hypotheses, 44*(6), 527-535.

Ernst, E., Pittler, M. H., & Wider, B. (Eds.). (2006). *The desktop guide to complementary and alternative medicine: An evidence-based approach* (2nd ed.). St. Louis, MO: Mosby Elsevier.

Gatterman, M. I. (Ed.). (2011). *Foundations of chiropractic: Subluxation* (3rd ed.) St. Louis, MO: Mosby Elsevier.

Gu, H. (1989). *Clinical traditional Chinese medicine: Orthopedic Volume*. Guangxi, China: Chinese Medical Science.

Gu, H. (2010). Acupuncture treatment for piriformis syndrome following lumbar diskectomy. *Journal of Medical Acupuncture, 22*(3), 203-206.

Haller, J. S. (2005). *The history of American homeopathy: The academic years*. London, England: Haworth.

Institute of Medicine. (2005). Board on Health Promotion and Disease Prevention, Committee on the Use of Complementary and Alternative Medicine by the American Public. *Complementary and alternative medicine in the United States*. Washington, DC: National Academies.

Jonas, W. B., Kaptchuk, T. J., & Linde, K. (2003). A critical overview of homeopathy. *Annals of Internal Medicine, 138*(5), 393-399.

Kaiser Family Foundation. (2016). *New Kaiser/New York Times survey finds one in five working-age Americans with health insurance report problems paying medical bills*. Retrieved from http://www.kff.org/health-costs/press-release/new-kaisernew-york-times-survey-finds-one-in-five-working-age-americans-with-health-insurance-report-problems-paying-medical-bills/

Kim, C. (2017). Integrative medicine. In A. Moroz, S. Flanagan, & H. H. Zaretsky (Eds.), *Medical aspects of disability for the rehabilitation professional* (5th ed., pp. 621-630). New York, NY: Springer.

Liu, Z., Liu, H., Xu, H., He, L., Chen, Y., Fu, L., . . . Liu, B. (2017). Effect of electroacupuncture on urinary leakage among women with stress urinary incontinence. *Journal of the American Medical Association, 317*(24), 2493-2501.

Maciocia, G. (2015). *The foundations of Chinese medicine: A comprehensive text for acupuncturists and herbalists* (3rd ed.). New York, NY: Elsevier.

Mayo Clinic. (2010). *Mayo Clinic book of alternative medicine: Integrating the best of natural therapies with conventional medicine* (2nd ed.). New York, NY: Oxmoor.

Pham, D. D., Yoo, J. H, Tran, B. Q., & Ta, T. T. (2013). Complementary and alternative medicine use among physicians in Oriental medicine hospitals in Vietnam: A hospital-based survey. *Evidence-Based Complementary and Alternative Medicine,* 392191.

Rajeswaran, J. (2012). *Neuropsychological rehabilitation: Principles and applications*. New York, NY: Elsevier.

Robertson, D., Biaggioni, I. Burnstock, G., Low, P. A., & Paton, J. F. R. (2011). *Primer on the autonomic nervous system* (3rd ed.). Salt Lake City, UT: Academic.

Rubik, B. (2015). The biofield: Bridge between mind and body. *Cosmos and History: Journal of Natural and Social Philosophy, 11*(2), 83-96.

Singer, D. C. (2013). *Equal rights for all chiropractors*. Arlington, VA: American Chiropractic Association.

Still, A. T. (2009). *Philosophy of osteopathy* (Classic Reprint). Charleston, SC: BiblioBazaar.

Tan, G., Craine, M. H., Bair, M. J., Garcia, M. K., Giordano, J., Jensen, M. P., . . . Tsao, J. C. (2007). Efficacy of selected complementary and alternative medicine interventions for chronic pain. *Journal of Rehabilitation Research and Development, 44*(2), 195-222.

Teppone, M., & Avakyan, R. (2007). Modern view on the theory of channels, collaterals, and organs. *Medical Acupuncture, 19*(1), 43-48.

U.S. Department of Health and Human Services, National Institutes of Health, National Center for Complementary and Integrative Health. (2016a). *Complementary, alternative, or integrative health: What's in a name?* (NIH Publication No. D347). Retrieved from https://nccih.nih.gov/health/ integrative-health

U.S. Department of Health and Human Services, National Institutes of Health, National Center for Complementary and Integrative Health. (2016b). *2016 Strategic Plan: Exploring the science of complementary and integrative health* (NIH Publication No. 16-AT-7643). Retrieved from https://nccih.nih.gov/sites/nccam.nih.gov/files/NCCIH_2016_Strategic_Plan.pdf

Wax, W. A., & White, K. R. (2000). A short history of a long tradition. *American Journal of Nursing, 100*(9), 40-45.

World Federation of Chiropractic (2012). *The current status of the chiropractic profession: Report to the World Health Organization.* Toronto, Canada: Author.

Xinnong, C., & Deng, A. (2010). *Chinese acupuncture and moxibustion* (3rd ed.). Beijing, China: Foreign Languages.

Yuan, C. S., Bieber, E. J., & Bauer, B. (Eds.). (2006). *Textbook of complementary and alternative medicine.* (2nd ed.). London, England: Taylor and Francis.

Yucha, C., & Montgomery, D. (2008.) *Evidence-based practice in biofeedback and neurofeedback.* Wheat Ridge, CO: Association for Applied Psychophysiology and Biofeedback.

About the Authors

Dr. Hua Gu, PhD, LAc, is an integrative medical practitioner with a practice in Woodland Hills and Agoura Hills, California. He received his Master's and Doctoral Degrees in Integrative Medicine from China Academy of Traditional Chinese Medicine, Beijing, China. After receiving his medical degree, Dr. Gu practiced as a surgeon in integrated Chinese and conventional medicine. Dr. Gu published three books and over a dozen papers in medical journals, including the *New England Journal of Medicine.* He is the founder of the American Acupuncture Academy, Los Angeles, which specializes in education, integrating biomedicine and traditional Chinese medicine. Dr. Gu served as the Chief Research Scientist with West Coast Spine Institute, where he operated research programs of spine disc herniation, stenosis, and biomechanics; created databases for research; evaluated patients with orthopedic neurological disorders; and reviewed, abstracted, and summarized personal injury and workers' compensation cases.

Sandra K. Brodwin, MEd, MS, is a part-time lecturer in the Rehabilitation Education Programs at California State University, Los Angeles, and a grant writer in the areas of disability, rehabilitation, and domestic violence. As a vocational rehabilitation counselor, she has provided reasonable accommodation, job restructuring, employer consultation, and a full range of rehabilitation services for employees on short-term and long-term disability due to chronic illness and injuries. Ms. Brodwin has published book chapters and journal articles on the subjects of medical aspects of disabling conditions, counseling, disability, job analysis, and rehabilitation.

Chapter 12

TRAUMATIC BRAIN INJURY

Stacey Hunter Schwartz, PhD
Michelle Ranae Wild, MA

Introduction

Traumatic brain injury (TBI) involves sudden physical damage to the brain. "Each type of traumatic brain injury has its own consequences, from acute to chronic, from mild to severe" (Rao & Vaishnavi, 2015). Males ages 14 to 24 years are at the highest risk of TBI, followed by infants and the elderly. Men are twice as likely as females to sustain TBI because of differences in risk exposure and lifestyle. Each year, an estimated 2.8 million people in the U.S. sustain TBI. Annually, about 282,000 Americans are hospitalized and 56,000 die because of TBI (Centers for Disease Control and Prevention [CDC], 2018). Emergency rooms typically treat 2.5 million Americans for brain injuries; of these, up to 15% of those diagnosed with a mild TBI have long-term problems.

About 75% of TBIs are concussions or other forms of mild injury. After one traumatic brain injury, the risk for a second injury is three times greater; after a second TBI, the risk for a third injury is eight times greater (Kraus & McArthur, 1999). CDC (2018) estimated that at least 5.3 million Americans currently have long-term or lifelong need for help to perform activities of daily living because of having sustained a TBI.

A traumatic brain injury produces an injury to one's core sense of self. Persons with TBI undergo such dramatic cognitive and personality changes that they seem, to both themselves and those closest to them, to be different people than they were pre-injury. Many persons with TBI regard their post-injury experiences as their second lives. At the same time, some have called TBI an *invisible disability* because the physical appearances of many persons with TBI do not change because of their head injury. While persons with other disabilities may feel frustrated because they are treated as different, individuals with TBI often feel frustrated because others treat them as if they were the same as before the injury. This disjunction between appearance and functionality complicates adjustment.

Rehabilitation is particularly challenging for other reasons as well. Counselors usually rely on their clients for information regarding their skills, abilities, and limitations. Like other individuals with new disabilities, people with TBI may experience a state of psychological denial about the extent and ramifications of their deficits; additionally, they may have a neurologically induced failure to recognize the deficiencies. They may have become cognitively incapable of knowing their limitations. Others with TBI do not remember what they were like before their injuries, or have an idealized memory of their pre-injury capabilities. Consequently, some people with TBI insist on unrealistic goals for rehabilitation.

Other people with TBI are able to set realistic goals, but implementing those goals presents challenges. Deficits in attention or auditory processing interfere with successful educational and vocational planning (Rios, Periàñez, & Munoz-Céspedes, 2004). Counseling may be unproductive because the client is unable to distinguish relevant from irrelevant information. Other clients show great insight and understanding while in counseling sessions, but forget the content of the sessions soon after each session ends. For these reasons and others, rehabilitation presents unique challenges to rehabilitation counselors.

Etiology

Brain injuries result from a variety of causes, including vehicle collisions, falls, stabbings, gunshots, explosions, infections, tumors, and strokes. Although a survivor of an automobile accident and a survivor of an aneurysm may experience similar symptoms, benefit from the same cognitive strategies, and face the same vocational outcomes, the two may qualify for different assistance programs. The labels used by those who study or work with persons with TBI relate to the causes of injury; outcomes tend to be similar across causal groups, based on severity of injury and location within the brain (Reilly & Bullock, 2005).

Professionals divide brain injury into two categories. Traumatic injuries are those caused by something outside the body, such as by the impact of an automobile accident or penetration of a bullet. Atraumatic injuries are those that occur because of internal causes, such as a cerebrovascular accident (stroke) or infection. Consequences of brain injury detailed in this chapter apply to survivors of traumatic as well as atraumatic brain injury.

The Brain Injury Association, formerly the National Head Injury Foundation, defines traumatic brain injury as "an insult to the brain, not of degenerative or congenital nature, but caused by an external physical force that may produce a diminished or altered state of consciousness, resulting in an impairment of cognitive abilities or physical functioning." Vehicle accidents are the leading cause of TBI, accounting for 50% of all injuries. Falls are the second leading cause, accounting for more than 20%. Alcohol is a significant risk factor, with more than 50% of persons intoxicated at the time of traumatic brain injury (Kraus & McArthur, 1999; Kreutzer, Witol, & Marwitz, 1996). TBIs include both open and closed head injuries.

Traumatic Injuries

Open Head Injury

In an open head injury, verification of TBI is not difficult. The patient's brain matter has been penetrated, such as by stabbing or gunshot. Skull fractures, visible brain matter, and obvious bleeding indicate the trauma. Often, the patient goes into a coma or a physician pharmacologically induces a coma immediately following the trauma. This type of head injury is more likely to damage a specific area of the brain. Additional risks exist as well; some patients develop infections or need to have their lost skull material replaced with artificial plates (Zink & McQuillan, 2005).

Closed Head Injury

In a closed head injury, the skull is not penetrated. Damage usually occurs when the brain experiences rapid acceleration and deceleration because of a blow to the head, such as in a motor vehicle accident or a fall. The brain hits against the skull in an initial impact called the coup. Next, the brain stem turns and twists on its axis causing localized or widespread damage to the brain. The brain then rebounds and hits the opposite side of the skull (the contre coup). Consequently, in a closed head injury, damage often occurs to diffuse areas of the brain. Swelling and bleeding, problems that frequently occur with open head injuries also cause injury to various areas of the brain.

Loss of consciousness may result, but in other instances, the survivor remains conscious and there are no outer signs of brain injury. The medical team typically concentrates on and provides treatment for more obvious wounds. Later on, the person with TBI and those who attempt to offer help may have a difficult time identifying and documenting that an injury occurred.

Severity of injury is a good predictor of eventual outcome, but many people who sustain what appear to be mild injuries nonetheless suffer life-altering deficits. Consequences of mild TBIs are particularly pronounced among persons whose careers involve high-level cognitive demands. The American College of Rehabilitation (ACR) has developed a definition of such injuries. Although the definition adopts the somewhat understated term *mild* traumatic brain injury, it clearly communicates the idea that these non-coma type injuries are serious with permanent consequences. According to the ACR definition of mild traumatic brain injury, a permanent brain injury can occur under four conditions. These are any period of loss of consciousness, a loss of memory for events immediately before or after the accident (amnesia), an alteration in mental state at the time of the accident (e.g., feeling dazed, disoriented, or confused), or focal neurological deficit(s) (Mild Traumatic Brain Injury Committee, 1993).

For some, the symptoms of a mild brain injury will subside, but for those with post-concussion syndrome, the symptoms will be permanent. Recently, the phenomenon of chronic traumatic encephalopathy (CTE), in which repeated concussions sustained in contact sports like football lead to behavioral or mood symptoms, cognitive symptoms, and signs of dementia, has received attention in the scientific literature (Mez et al., 2017) and in the media.

Blast Injuries

The signature injury of veterans of the wars in Afghanistan and Iraq are traumatic brain injuries caused by explosions (blast injuries). According to brainlinemilitary.org (2012), over 244,000 service members sustained TBIs between 2000 and the first quarter of 2012. The impact of improvised explosive devices (IEDs) typically cause blast-related TBIs. The impact of a blast can produce unique multi-system injuries that may be life threatening.

According to the CDC (2012), the four basic mechanisms of blast injury are primary, secondary, tertiary, and quaternary. The primary mechanism is associated with the high over-pressurization of the blast wave as it affects body structures and causes multi-system injuries as described above, including injuries to the brain, such as concussion, hemorrhage, and diffuse axonal injury. The secondary mechanism is associated with flying debris and shrapnel from the explosion, resulting in a variety of possible penetrating wounds. Effects of individuals being thrown by the wind generated by the blast are part of the tertiary mechanism, which causes a variety of brain injuries. Quaternary are injuries not caused by the first three mechanisms.

Atraumatic Brain Injury

A category of brain injury which receives less attention in the literature, but which some experts say is growing, is atraumatic causes of brain injury. Atraumatic injuries are those that occur due to internal causes. Examples include arterial-venous malformations (blood vessels with weaknesses present at birth) and infections in the brain, both of which can result in cerebrovascular accident. In recent years, more people are benefiting from new surgical procedures, which help increase survival of people with vascular injuries. Similarly, persons who have brain tumors survive more often today because of advances in oncology. Meningitis (inflammation of the brain and spinal cord) and cardiac arrest leading to anoxia (where the brain has been completely deprived of oxygen for a period) or hypoxia (where the brain has been partially deprived of oxygen) also cause serious diffuse brain damage. Recently, oncologists have begun to study "chemobrain," in which chemotherapy and other factors lead to a decline in cognitive functioning in as many as 45% of patients during and after cancer treatment (Janelsins et al., 2017).

Functional Limitations

Because the brain is such a critical organ that performs a wide variety of necessary functions, injury to the brain causes a host of deficits. No one survivor is likely to exhibit all the functional limitations described below. Severity and location of injury vary as do resulting cognitive deficits. Even the number of locations of injury and severity at those locations are not necessarily determinative of functional outcome. Impairment of life processes related to deficits also depends on the client's personal lifestyle and career demands (Nielson, Im, Hibbard, Grunwald, & Swift, 2017; Rios et al., 2004). The description of deficits is helpful in understanding the potential consequences of TBI; each client must be assessed for the particular injuries and resulting deficits. Table 1 summarizes the types of sequelae and deficits that commonly follow TBI.

TABLE 1
Various Categories of Deficits

Physical	Balance difficulties, fatigue, pain, hemiparesis, uneven gait, ataxia, apraxia, decreased motor speed, seizure disorders, sensory deficits
Cognitive	Impairments in attention/concentration, memory, visual or auditory perceptual processing, verbal reasoning, critical thinking/logic, language, awareness
Psychosocial	Personality changes, emotional lability, flat affect, depression, substance abuse, frustration intolerance, impulsivity/disinhibition, lack of initiative

Physical

Traumatic events like automotive accidents and falls may result in physical impairments (such as immobility caused by bone fractures), which are unrelated to the brain. There also may be physical consequences resulting directly from the brain injury, as described below.

Balance

Many people have difficulty with balance and coordination immediately following injury. In some, dizziness and unsteadiness are permanent conditions. Special retraining programs exist for these problems.

Fatigue

For several reasons, extreme mental and physical fatigue are common after TBI, as are sleep disorders. Ouellet, Beaulieu-Bonneau, and Morin (2006) found that over half of patients with mild to severe brain injuries reported symptoms of insomnia. Tasks, which were formerly easy, become far more mentally challenging and, consequently, physically exhausting. For example, four hours of concentrated activity may necessitate several hours of rest.

Pain

Individuals with TBI frequently report persistent headaches. Those with concussions often have neck and back pain and require ergonomically correct workstations to reduce pain complaints. There may be increased sensitivity to pain.

Hemiparesis

The opposite side of the brain controls each side of the body. Therefore, injury to the motor strip of one hemisphere affects movements on the opposite side. For example, a person may have paralysis on the left side of the body because of injury to the right hemisphere. Although a leg or arm may not itself be injured, the brain may not be able to control that leg or arm properly, resulting in dysfunctions of movement (Kraus & McArthur, 1999).

Other Disorders of Movement

Many persons have permanent impairment of movement caused by an inability of the brain to control the extremities. The individual experiences impaired gait, ataxia (jerky movements), apraxia (uncontrolled movements), muscle spasticity, tremors, and impaired fine motor control.

Decreased Motor Speed

Many people feel as though they are moving in slow motion. Their brain signals travel at a slower pace and tasks take longer. These individuals appear to have a few seconds delay between when they decide to move and when they carry out the planned action.

Seizure Activity (traumatic epilepsy)

Following TBI, recurrent seizures are possible (17% of all cases) (Reilly & Bullock, 2005). Most of those who experience seizures have their first seizure within 24 hours of injury. Usually, seizures are controllable with anti-convulsive medication. For the rare individual, however, continuing seizures may provide the greatest obstacle to rehabilitation.

Cognitive

Repeated mild TBIs occurring over an extended period (i.e., months and even years) can result in cumulative neurological and cognitive deficits while repeated mild TBIs occurring within a short period (i.e., hours, days, or weeks) can be catastrophic or fatal. People with TBI are likely to need assistance to perform activities of daily living. TBI can cause epilepsy and increases the risk for conditions such as Alzheimer's disease, Parkinson's disease, and other disorders affecting the brain. Professionals divide cognitive deficits into some common classification areas, although the distinction is somewhat artificial. In real-world experiences, it is difficult to find a task that draws exclusively upon a single, distinct skill. Almost every activity involves two or more of the cognitive skills described below.

Attention/Concentration and Arousal

Some persons with TBI find it difficult to focus and maintain attention on a task (Rios et al., 2004). Persons may have difficulty becoming sufficiently aroused (i.e., alert) to focus on a specific activity, and they may have a shortened attention span. Executive functioning impairment refers to difficulty in the self-regulation skills, which are required for decision making and staying on task.

Some are unable to shift mental tasks (alternating attention) or follow multi-step directions. As an illustration, assume that Sam has TBI but is able, with effort, to focus on a particular work task. If the telephone rings, interrupting his attention for even a minute or two, Sam might be unable to return to the prior task on which he had been working. Many tasks involve divided attention, such as driving which requires that a person is able to concentrate on steering while also obeying speed limits, monitoring other drivers, and perhaps navigating a new route, all while listening to the radio and having a conversation. Driving is often impossible after TBI.

Memory

Television shows and movies about persons with TBI usually depict memory loss as the chief cognitive deficit of TBI. These media depictions are misleading in both the narrow focus on memory loss and the dramatization of the type of memory loss that occurs. While memory loss is common, the type of loss depicted in the media (where the person awakens from a coma and needs to be informed about events that have occurred) is uncommon. Retrospective amnesia (long-term memory loss), the inability to remember all that happened before the injury, seldom occurs.

Far more common is anterograde amnesia (short-term memory loss). For example, many persons cannot remember new information, such as what they had for breakfast that same morning. Individuals may have prospective amnesia (inability to remember plans). Some persons cannot keep track of their appointments, and even struggle to use memory aids, such as day and week planning tools (e.g., Day Timer). Such tools, while helpful for persons with TBI, assume the user will remember to write down appointments, remember where to write the appointments, and remember to look at the planning guide with regular frequency.

Intensive training may be necessary to establish what will become vital organizational habits. Hellgren, Lundqvist, and Borsbo (2015) showed that computerized working memory training improves cognitive and daily performance for individuals who have undergone brain injury. The earlier the professional introduces this following injury, the greater the chances of success. New technologies, discussed next, have emerged which make memory compensation easier and more consistent (Gillespie, Best, & O'Neill, 2012).

Perception/Visual Processing

Some persons have problems with spatial orientation. They get lost in a parking lot, going home or to work, or even in their own home environment. These individuals can lose the ability to deal with smaller-scale spatial relations, as well. For example, they may find themselves unable to figure out which container is an appropriate size for storing leftovers or may have difficulty wrapping gifts. They struggle with visual field cuts, in which a large portion of their visual field is missing.

Sensory Deficits

Other sensory deficits include visual processing difficulties (e.g., neglect of one side of the visual field), sensitivity to light, loss of hearing, and loss of the senses of smell or taste.

Verbal Reasoning

Many persons have problems understanding conversations. They cannot identify the main idea of written or spoken communication, distinguish relevant from irrelevant details, detect similarities and differences, or understand analogies. They struggle to organize ideas, important papers, and their lives. Many have difficulty paying bills, even if sufficient funds are available, because of organizational or comprehension difficulties.

Critical Thinking/Logic

One individual with TBI might declare an inability to return to work despite having received a medical clearance. On the contrary, another person may attempt to return to work without recognizing the presence of severe cognitive deficits. Judgment and the ability to process information accurately with consistency and speed can be impaired, as well as an inability to make decisions (Rios et al., 2004).

Language

Persons with TBI often have communicative disturbances (aphasia). Individuals may have difficulty expressing thoughts (i.e., expressive aphasia), such as having word-finding problems. For example, one might say, "that thing you write with" to communicate the word "pen." Other speech problems stem from physical impairments, including speech that is unclear when the person has decreased control of the muscles in the lips, tongue, and jaw, or because of poor breathing patterns. Dysarthria, where motor function interferes with correct formation of sounds, produces slurred speech that is extremely difficult to understand. In addition, some persons have problems understanding others (i.e., receptive aphasia).

Unawareness

Anosognosia is a failure to recognize one's own impairment. It can be difficult to distinguish anosognosia from psychological denial, a normal defense mechanism. Giacino and Cicerone (1998) found evidence that three factors underlie lack of awareness of deficits following TBI: (a) diminished awareness of deficits secondary to impaired cognition, especially memory and reasoning deficits; (b) psychological reaction and denial of deficits; and (c) a relatively pure inability to recognize areas of impaired functioning as a direct consequence of brain injury.

Psychosocial

Various psychological, behavioral, and emotional changes are common following TBI, especially major depression and anxiety disorders. Major depression and substance abuse disorders are more likely to remit than anxiety disorder (Nielson et al., 2017). Discussed next are these conditions and others of a psychosocial nature.

Personality Changes

TBI frequently exacerbates negative pre-injury personality traits. For example, someone who had a short temper now has angry, emotional outbursts. An adult daughter said of her father after his TBI, "He's Dad, just more Dad." A man who was formerly self-confident is now annoyingly arrogant and critical of others. Conversely, family members often report that the shy have become outgoing, and vice versa. A common complaint of family members is that the survivor has become intensely egocentric.

Emotional Lability

Heightened emotional responses or reactions are common. Some feel unable to control mood swings from moment to moment. They laugh or cry for no apparent reason and at inappropriate times.

Flat Affect

Some survivors show a complete lack of emotions. For example, they report a sense of puzzlement that they neither feel elation at happy times, nor anxiety in stressful times.

Depression

Major depression is present in about 40% of individuals who have been hospitalized for TBI. TBI may be accompanied by loss of defining personality traits, career, status, income, relationships, or feelings of competency. Persons with TBI have a high divorce rate, lose many of their friends, and suffer family estrangements. They discover that, after the initial burst of rapid gains from rehabilitation, progress levels off. Some deficits are temporary, while others are permanent. Consequences of TBI have emotional costs not only for the person who is injured, but also for their families.

Substance Abuse

Hibbard, Uysal, Kepler, Bogdany, and Silver (1998) investigated TBI survivors eight years post-injury and found that a significant percent had substance abuse disorders prior to injury. Kreutzer et al. (1996) found that young persons with TBI had pre-injury drinking patterns similar to the general population. There was evidence of a decline in alcohol use at initial follow-up, but pre-injury and secondary follow-up show similar alcohol use patterns. Post-injury illicit drug use rates remained relatively low, falling below 10% at follow-up intervals. Men with moderate to heavy pre-injury alcohol use and those taking prescribed medications are at greatest risk for long-term alcohol use.

Decreased Frustration Tolerance

After TBI, people may become frustrated more easily. For example, they may realize that particular tasks on which they are working seem elementary. They could competently perform the activities before injury, yet post-injury may be unable to perform them with ease or at all.

Impulsivity/Disinhibition

People have many thoughts each day that they do not express, or urges on which they do not act. The frontal lobes within the brain keep individuals from acting on these ideas. Without this check system, people with TBI may ask inappropriate personal questions of co-workers, make sexual advances, touch others inappropriately, act in an aggressive manner, or make prejudicial remarks.

Lack of Initiative

Some individuals with brain injury, especially those with frontal lobe injuries, lack initiative. If not presented with prompts or structure, such persons may be content to watch television all day.

Treatment

An individual with signs or symptoms of moderate to severe TBI needs immediate medical attention. Priorities of treatment are to maintain passages to the airway, breathing, and circulation. Medical professionals attempt to stabilize the person and focus on preventing further injury; concerns include ensuring the brain has sufficient blood supply, maintaining blood flow, and monitoring blood pressure.

Imaging Tests

Neuroradiological tests using computer-assisted scans can help assess the areas and extent of damage to the brain. Computed axial tomography (CT or CAT) scan is the most common imaging test. It uses a computer to combine X-rays of thin slices of the brain into one unified three-dimensional image. Magnetic resonance imaging (MRI) tests rely on a magnet and radio waves to produce computerized images of the brain. Unfortunately, many mild brain injuries involve such subtle damage that tests may not detect the injury (Belanger, Vanderploeg, Curtiss, & Warder, 2007),

New forms of imaging continue to develop. Single-photon emission computed tomography (SPECT) scans are used to form cross-sectional images of the brain using images from a camera, which detects the presence of radioactive particles that have been injected into the blood. Positron emission tomography (PET) scans similarly use radioactive particles, but PET scans produce data regarding metabolic activity, not anatomic data. Diffusion tensor imaging (DTI) holds promise as a technique which may detect more subtle damage. DTI is a type of MRI that measures fluid movement in the brain, and can show where normal fluid flow is not occurring.

Depending on type and severity of injury, rehabilitation typically includes physical therapy, speech therapy, occupational therapy, and cognitive therapy. Described next are these therapies.

Physical Therapy (PT)

After a coma, many patients need to learn to walk again. It may take weeks, months, or years for a patient to progress from using a wheelchair to a walker, to a cane, and finally to ambulate unassisted. Some persons never progress past wheelchair use. Nevertheless, because the physical impairments are most visible, survivors frequently put the bulk of their energy into PT, sometimes to the detriment of other therapies.

Speech Therapy

Beginning with relearning how to swallow (while in the hospital), TBI patients frequently receive a wide spectrum of therapy from speech and language pathologists. Depending on location of injury, a speech therapist helps the person learn to speak again, and may assist with developing word-finding skills or forming sounds. Many speech therapists teach cognitive remediation skills.

Occupational Therapy (OT)

Occupational therapists help with such skills as learning to button a shirt with one hand to compensate for hemiplegia, or increasing independence by structuring an environment using memory cues. OT addresses learning to drive post-injury by teaching compensatory strategies for coping with physical and visual deficits.

Cognitive Therapy/Retraining/Remediation

Cognitive retraining principally occurs in five settings: hospitals (especially immediately after injury), neuropsychologists' offices, speech therapy clinics, therapeutic milieu settings such as the New York University Rusk Institute, and in educational settings such as the Coastline Community College Acquired Brain Injury Program in Orange County, California.

The cognitive retrainer begins by assessing cognitive functioning and prescribing cognitive remediation. Such treatment includes tasks designed to help individuals utilize their cognitive strengths to compensate for limitations. This involves teaching new strategies for common tasks. The cognitive retrainer seeks to stimulate progress for those activities with which the person is having difficulties. By stimulating these activities, the cognitive retrainer attempts to build new neural pathways to replace damaged areas, although most researchers currently believe that after childhood, no new brain cells develop. The dendrites or fibers on each neuron, however, can grow and be functional. From this, neuropsychologists have developed the theory of neural plasticity, which posits that a new neural pathway can be developed to take over a brain function that has been lost because of damage to the area (Reilly & Bullock, 2005).

Assistive Technology for Cognition

"Cognitive assistive technology is a subclass of AT that is designed to increase, maintain, or improve capabilities for individuals whose cognitive abilities limit their effective participation in daily activities" (Jette, Spicer, & Flaubert, 2017, p. 384). ATC devices vary from low-tech (e.g., watch alarms) to high-tech ҫ., smart phone apps). High-tech ATC devices range from specialized augmentative and alternative ⁓unication devices (AAC) that can cost several thousand dollars to commonly used smart devices (e.g., ⁓h, iPhone, tablets) that may cost several hundred dollars.

⁓t al. (2012) found that ATC devices effectively support many common cognitive functions ⁓in injury, including those related to memory, attention, organization, planning, and time management. The CDC recommended to Congress that the rehabilitation field should "increase widespread dissemination of emerging practices, such as the use of smartphones to aid with cognitive rehabilitation" (CDC, 2015, p. 47). The common use of such devices among the general population serves to destigmatize their use as a compensation tool for people with brain injuries.

The popularity of smart devices, the vast number of applications (apps) available, and their relatively low cost (as compared to specialized ATC devices) all work together to increase their viability as ATC devices. Smart devices are used as ATC devices at this time include the iPod Touch, smartphones (Apple, Android, and Windows), tablets, Kindle Fire, and Nook. As of 2017, over 77% of Americans owned a smartphone (Pew Research Center, 2017). In addition, over 22 million tablets have been sold in the U.S. in the first half of 2012. Smart devices have become commonplace.

Although smart devices vary in size, storage capacity, number of available add-on apps, and price, they all provide a number of similar features and come with several native apps that can be used to assist with cognitive issues resulting from brain injury. These include a calendar, contacts (address book), camera, maps, task lists, email, browser, and notes. These apps play a role in assisting with a variety of daily activities such as scheduling appointments, storing contact information (including pictures of the contact), and creating to-do lists. All smart devices have add-on apps available from their respective app stores. The Apple App Store and the Android Google Play Store have the largest collection of free and for-pay apps, quickly nearing a million. Add-on apps are available in many categories that help with brain-injury related issues.

Memory compensation is one of the primary advantages of using ATC after brain injury. People with brain injury who use traditional paper notebooks do not perform as well as those who use hand-held computers programmed to prompt the performance of various common tasks. Additionally, they found that personal data assistant (PDA) use not only improved survivors' functioning, but also improved their sociability, self-esteem, and independence (Gilette & DePompei, 2008). The systematic training of brain injury survivors, caregivers, and rehabilitation professionals is essential to successful implementation of smart device technology.

Although there are any number of books and manuals related to using the various smart devices, there are limited resources currently available for training individuals with brain injury to use smart devices as cognitive prosthetics. Brain Education Strategies and Technology provides training resources specifically structured as learning tools for those with brain injury. The training resources emphasize the Making Cognitive Connections® approach that teaches the fundamental technical skills necessary to operate a smart device while drawing attention to the cognitive skills. The Making Cognitive Connections® approach integrated into the various training resources allows users to focus on the cognitive skills required to operate the device and how those same cognitive skills apply to daily living.

Rehabilitation Features and Rehabilitation Outcomes

Rehabilitation Features

Cognitive rehabilitation is a relatively new field, having first gained prominence in the 1980s. Chestnut et al. (1999) conducted a systematic review of over 3,000 studies to evaluate evidence for the effectiveness of rehabilitation methods throughout the phases of recovery. They found significant practice variations occur across clinics and professionals. While some studies have demonstrated highly individualized treatment and assessment, others have shown that standardization of treatment is possible and results in positive outcomes. The CDC (2015) concluded that cognitive rehabilitation is effective during the post-acute period (even more than a year after injury), and that the empirical support for cognitive rehabilitation is growing.

It is difficult to know when an individual has reached maximum recovery and improvement (O'Keeffe, Dockree, Moloney, Carton, & Robertson, 2007). Many physicians believe that the outer limits of functional improvement are between six months and one to two years following TBI; yet, cognitive retraining has produced successes as long as 20 years post-injury.

Factors Affecting Outcome

A variety of factors affect outcome. Severity of injury is the strongest predictor of recovery. Professionals working with TBI survivors measure severity of injury using several methods. First, TBI experts use length of coma to predict outcomes. Studies indicated that the longer the coma, the more likely the outcome will be worse. Second, duration of post-traumatic amnesia helps predict outcomes. The longer it takes to start remembering daily events, the more negative the outcome. Some people never regain ability to remember daily events (Zink & McQuillan, 2005).

Age correlates negatively with outcomes. The older a person is at time of injury, the more negative the outcome. Research has established a relationship between age and increased psychosocial limitations, especially in persons over the age of 60. Consequences of TBI worsen with age.

Researchers (Faul, Wald, & Coronado, 2010; Nielsen et al., 2017) have determined that higher pre-injury educational level correlates with improved outcomes. Most persons with TBI have difficulty learning new information, but a good portion of pre-injury knowledge and skills can be left intact. Persons who were well educated before injury frequently need to learn new ways to organize and access their previous knowledge and cognitive skills.

A final predictor of positive outcome is pre-injury work history. Those who have poor employment histories before their injuries are likely to have even greater problems post-injury.

Vocational Rehabilitation and Placement

There is wide variance in outcomes after injury. Some people with TBI recover fully and return to their former routines. Others are able to learn compensatory strategies and perform modified versions of their former routines; still others retrain for new occupations. Some require structured work settings or find volunteer positions. Unfortunately, some return home to nonproductive lives.

It seems clear for some persons with severe brain injuries that a reasonable rehabilitation long-term goal is supported employment or volunteer work designed to increase life activities (Brodwin, Parker, & DeLaGarza, 2010). Other persons with TBI are able to return to some form of work. Briel (1996) and Sherer et al. (1998) addressed supported employment programs. Briel described an approach for promoting the effective use of compensatory strategies at the job site through supported employment programs. Self-awareness is essential for succeeding at work. Characteristics of supported employment that can promote successful return to work include: community placement and integration, competitive hiring and wages, zero exclusion policy, holistic assessment, emphasis on choice and job matching, intervention after placement, co-worker and employer education, long-term follow along, job completion guarantee (through job coaching), and intensive ongoing analysis of program outcomes.

Because the disability is not visible and often misunderstood, the employer and the TBI survivor must cooperate to work out appropriate accommodations. For example, the employee may require written instructions from the employer or may need to be assigned only one or a few tasks at a time. The employer must have knowledge of the employee's strengths and limitations (Brodwin et al., 2010). For example, a mechanic may still be able to diagnose what is wrong with an automotive engine by listening to it and observing its functioning, even though the person is no longer able to reassemble the engine. An attorney might be able to assist with legal strategizing, but be unable to remember what steps have been taken or which forms have been filed with the court. Persons who process information slowly take longer to perform assigned tasks. Some employers can work around this deficit, but not if impulsivity makes accuracy poor. Therefore, persons with TBI need to be trained to work more slowly when accuracy is essential.

Individuals whose TBI has caused them to lose their inhibitions often struggle to successfully return to work (Brodwin et al., 2010; O'Keeffe et al., 2007). Most jobs require working with others. Impulsive sexual remarks, racial slurs, and low frustration tolerance are not the characteristics of those who succeed in most employment contexts. Job coaching may help in these situations.

Conclusion

Each year, TBI changes the lives of over a million people (Nielsen et al., 2017; Rao & Vaishnavi, 2015). Those at highest risk are young males. Physicians classify these injuries as closed head injury and open head injury. One finds a variety of deficits, such as physical impairments, pain, fatigue, mobility disorders, seizures, cognitive dysfunctions, speech impairments, and changes in personality. These can be devastating and challenging to the injured persons, family members, physicians, and helping professionals. Individuals may experience not only trauma to the brain but also alterations in body image, changes in personality, age-related and role-related problems, and financial difficulties. Immediate attention to their physical and psychosocial needs, in addition to maintaining the focus on early rehabilitation and prevention of recurring injury or complications, are imperative to the recoveries of people with TBI.

Case Study

Mr. Randall Owens is 47 years of age, African-American, with an Associate of Science degree in the Building and Construction Trades from a trade college. While on a construction site, he fell 25 feet from the roof of a house, landing on his right side. He was unable to speak for approximately five minutes and was moving in and out of a comatose state. Paramedics transported Mr. Owens to a local trauma center where a CT scan revealed cerebral contusions, intracranial air in the subarachnoid space of the frontal lobe, punctate hemorrhages in the frontal lobe, a right orbital fracture, a fracture at the base of the skull, right frontal skull fracture, right temporal skull fracture, and temporal bone fracture.

Discharged home after eight days of hospitalization, Mr. Owens received outpatient physical therapy and speech therapy. Eight months later, he initiated outpatient full-time day treatment at a comprehensive post-acute rehabilitation center where an evaluation indicated the following problems: minimally decreased visual processing speed, reduced binocular vision, diminished convergence skills, impaired depth perception, decreased strength in both upper extremities, word finding errors, decreased verbal fluency, diminished auditory and visual recall, and decreased abstract reasoning. Through participation in a full-time day-treatment program for two weeks, Randall was able to transition to a part-time program at a rehabilitation center. The center discharged him after two weeks.

Six months later (1½ years after injury), Randall was struggling to operate his own construction company, started years before the injury. The physical demand of working 12-hour days was difficult; there were problems remembering details of jobs, sequencing the steps of the jobs, and communicating effectively with customers, vendors, and his two employees. He reported, "I want to get my life back. I want the motivation and the desires I used to have to work and enjoy life. I feel like I have lost control of my life."

Mr. Owens recognized that he might need to work for someone else instead of operating his own business. He enrolled in a community college-based cognitive retraining program, which taught him compensatory strategies to use for memory, sequencing, and communication deficits. He learned to use smartphone apps to keep him on task and to monitor his energy levels to avoid exhaustion and maximize productivity. With help, he learned to identify and accept his limitations, emphasize his strengths, and set realistic expectations.

While enrolled in the program, a large home-improvement store hired him. Randall found he could utilize his experience as a contractor by working in the window and door department helping customers and writing orders. He used smartphone apps to record his supervisor's instructions and to keep track of his responsibilities on each shift. Able to concentrate on a rather isolated portion of the building process, he was less overwhelmed, receiving a promotion to department assistant manager. Randall was successful and satisfied with his position.

Questions

1. Identify possible functional limitations of traumatic brain injury, including physical, cognitive, andpsychosocial.
2. Define emotional lability and its potential impact on job performance.
3. Some individuals with brain injury have problems with impulsivity and make inappropriate remarks (including sexual remarks and racial slurs). Discuss implications of this for vocational rehabilitation.
4. Evaluate cognitive retraining and assistive technology from the standpoint of this case.
5. Describe other possible vocational rehabilitation plans for this client.
6. Discuss supported employment for clients with severe head trauma and its applicability to this case. For further information on intellectual disabilities and supported employment, please refer to the chapter on intellectual disabilities.

References

Belanger, H. G., Vanderploeg, R. D., Curtiss, G., & Warder, D. L. (2007). Recent neuroimaging techniques in mild traumatic brain injury. *Journal of Neuropsychiatry and Clinical Neuroscience, 19*(1), 5-20.

Brainline Military. (2012). *About traumatic brain injury*. Retrieved from http://www.brainlinemilitary.org/categories/abouttbi.php

Briel, L. W. (1996). Promoting the effective use of compensatory strategies on the job for individuals with traumatic brain injury. *Journal of Vocational Rehabilitation, 7*(3), 151-158.

Brodwin, M. G., Parker, R. M., & DeLaGarza, D. (2010). Disability and reasonable accommodation. In E. M. Szymanski & R. M. Parker (Eds.), *Work and disability: Contexts, issues, and strategies for enhancing outcomes for people with disabilities* (3nd ed., pp. 281-323). Austin, TX: Pro-ed.

Centers for Disease Control and Prevention (CDC). (2012). *Explosions and blast injuries: A primer for clinicians*. Retrieved from http://www.bt.cdc.gov/masscasualties/explosions.asp

Centers for Disease Control and Prevention (CDC). (2015). *Report to Congress on traumatic brain injury in the United States: Epidemiology and rehabilitation*. National Center for Injury Prevention and Control; Division of Unintentional Injury Prevention. Atlanta, GA. Retrieved from https://www.cdc.gov/ traumaticbrain injury/pdf/tbi_report_to_congress_epi_and_rehab-a.pdf

Centers for Disease Control and Prevention (CDC). (2018). *Statistics on traumatic brain injury in the United States*. Retrieved from http://www.cdc.gov/traumaticbraininjury

Chestnut, R. M., Carney, N., Maynard, H., Mann, N. C., Patterson, P., & Helfand, M. (1999). Summary report: Evidence for the effectiveness of rehabilitation for persons with traumatic brain injury. *Journal of Head Trauma Rehabilitation, 14*(2), 176-188.

Faul, M., Xu, L., Wald, M. M., & Coronado, V. G. (2010). *Traumatic brain injury in the United States: Emergency department visits, hospitalizations, and deaths*. Atlanta, GA: Centers for Disease Control and Prevention, National Center for Injury Prevention and Control.

Giacino, J. T., & Cicerone, K. D. (1998). Varieties of deficit unawareness after brain injury. *Journal of Head Trauma Rehabilitation, 13*(5), 1-15.

Gilette, Y., & DePompei, R. (2008). Do PDAs enhance the organization and memory skills of students with cognitive disabilities? *Psychology in the Schools, 45*(7), 665-677.

Gillespie, A., Best, C., & O'Neill, B. (2012). Cognitive function and assistive technology for cognition: A systematic review. *Journal of the International Neuropsychological Society, 18*, 1-19.

Hibbard, M. R., Uysal, S., Kepler, K., Bogdany, J., & Silver, J. (1998). Axis I psychopathology in individuals with traumatic brain injury. *Journal of Head Trauma Rehabilitation, 13*(4), 24-39.

Janelsins, M. C., Heckler, C. E., Peppone, L. J., Kamen, C., Mustian, K. M., Mohile, S. G., . . . Morrow, G. R. (2017). Cognitive complaints in survivors of breast cancer after chemotherapy compared with age-matched controls: An analysis from a nationwide, multicenter, prospective longitudinal study. *Journal of Clinical Oncology, 35*(5), 506-514.

Hellgren, L., Lundqvist, A., & Borsbo, B. (2015). Computerized training of working memory for patients with acquired brain injury. *Open Journal of Therapy and Rehabilitation, 3*, 46-55.

Jette, A. M., Spicer, C. M., & Flaubert, J. L. (2017). *The premise of assistive technology to enhance activity and work participation*. Washington, DC: National Academies Press.

Kraus, J. F., & McArthur, D. L. (1999). Incidence and prevalence of and costs associated with traumatic brain injury. In M. Rosenthal, J. S. Kreutzer, E. R. Griffith, & L. B. Pentland (Eds.), *Rehabilitation of the adult and child with traumatic brain injury* (3rd ed., p. 3-18). Philadelphia, PA: F. A. Davis.

Kreutzer, J. S., Witol, A. D., & Marwitz, J. H. (1996). Alcohol and drug use among young persons with traumatic brain injury. *Journal of Learning Disabilities, 29*(6), 643-651.

Mez, J., Daneshvar, D. H., Kiernan, P. T., Abdolmohammadi, B., Alvarez, V. E., Huber, B. R., . . . McKee, A. C. (2017). Clinicopathological evaluation of chronic traumatic encephalopathy in players of American football. *Journal of the American Medical Association, 318*(4), 360-370.

Mild Traumatic Brain Injury Committee of the Head Injury Interdisciplinary Special Interest Group of the American Congress of Rehabilitation Medicine. (1993). Definition of mild traumatic brain injury. *Journal of Head Trauma Rehabilitation, 8*(3), 86-87.

Nielsen, A., Im, B., Hibbard, M. R., Grunwald, I., & Swift, P. T. (2017). Traumatic brain injury. In A. Moroz, S. R. Flanagan, & H. H. Zaretsky (Eds.), *Medical aspects of disability for the rehabilitation professional* (5th ed., pp. 91-111). New York, NY: Springer.

O'Keeffe, F., Dockree, P., Moloney, P., Carton, S. & Robertson, I. H. (2007). Awareness of deficits in traumatic brain injury: A multidimensional approach to assessing metacognitive knowledge and online awareness. *Journal of the International Neuropsychological Society, 13*(1), 38-49.

Ouellet, M. C., Beaulieu-Bonneau, S., & Morin, C. M. (2006). Insomnia in patients with traumatic brain injury: Frequency, characteristics, and risk factors. *Journal of Head Trauma Rehabilitation, 21*(3), 199-212.

Pew Research Center. (2017). *Mobile fact sheet*. Washington, DC: Author.

Rao, V., & Vaishnavi, S. (2015). *The traumatized brain: A family guide to understanding mood, memory, and behavior after brain injury*. Baltimore, MD: Johns Hopkins Press Health Book.

Reilly, P. L., & Bullock, R. (Eds.). (2005). *Head injury: Pathophysiology and management* (2nd ed.). London, England: Arnold.

Rios, M., Periàñez, J. A., & Munoz-Céspedes, J. M. (2004). Attentional control and slowness of information processing after severe traumatic brain injury. *Brain Injury, 18*(3), 257-272.

Sherer, M., Bergloff, P., Levin, E., High, W. M., Oden, K. E., & Nick, T. G. (1998). Impaired awareness and employment outcome after traumatic brain injury. *Journal of Head Trauma Rehabilitation, 13*(5), 2-61.

Zink, E. K., & McQuillan, K. (2005). Managing traumatic brain injury. *Nursing, 35*(9), 36-43.

About the Authors

Stacey Hunter Schwartz, PhD, is Vice President and Chief Operating Officer of Brain Education Strategies and Technology (BEST), a non-profit organization that develops apps and provides app training for people with brain conditions. Dr. Schwartz was Dean of Instruction for Special Programs at Coastline Community College in Costa Mesa, California. She served as instructor, counselor, and director of the Acquired Brain Injury Program, which provides cognitive retraining.

Michelle Ranae Wild, MA, is professor at Coastline Community College and has taught in Coastline's Acquired Brain Injury Program for over 25 years. Her experience teaching cognitive retraining techniques led her to design apps for people with brain injury and other conditions and to become the founding President and CEO of BEST. Ms. Wild has authored workbooks on the use of Apple-based, Android-based, and Windows-based smart devices as cognitive prosthetics. Her apps and materials are in use in schools, rehabilitation facilities, and VA hospitals around the country, and are also available for active duty military personnel.

Chapter 13

STROKE

Andrew D. Barreto, MD
Frances W. Siu, PhD, CRC
Cailine Kim, EdD, CRC

Introduction

About 140,000 Americans die from stroke each year, and one in every 20 deaths in this country is due to stroke (Centers for Disease Control and Prevention [CDC], 2017). It is the 2nd leading cause of death and the 3rd leading cause of serious disability in the world. In the United States, stroke is the 5th leading cause of death (Fusco, Ishida, Levine, & Torres, 2017). Unfortunately, about one-third of all people who have stroke are under age 65 (Benjamin et al., 2018). Stroke is a leading cause of incapacitation and long term disability.

Stroke (also known as cerebral vascular accident [CVA]) is a medical emergency characterized by rapid loss of brain function due either to interruption of its blood supply (ischemic stroke) or bleeding into the brain from rupture of a blood vessel (hemorrhagic stroke). Ischemic strokes account for approximately 87%, and hemorrhagic strokes are about 13%. Both types result in reduction of oxygen and nutrition to the brain which leads to the symptoms of stroke and resultant brain damage (Barreto et al., 2017). Many of these are recurrent strokes in patients who have already had a prior CVA. A stroke can result in temporary or permanent neurological dysfunction (Benjamin et al., 2018). Stroke occurs in people of all ages, but predominantly among those over 60 years of age.

Approximately 12% of all cerebral vascular events are transient ischemic attacks (TIA), a condition of temporary neurological deficit usually lasting less than five minutes without permanent brain damage and full recovery of all functions (American Stroke Association [ASA], 2016). Importantly, TIA symptoms mimic those of stroke and should be treated as emergencies. Symptoms which persist longer than 24 hours or result in permanent brain damage are always defined as stroke. This brain damage can be imaged using either computed tomography (CT) or magnetic resonance imaging (MRI) scans.

Since 1995, the Federal Drug Administration (FDA) approved medication which has improved treatment for ischemic stroke and reduced resulting disability (George et al., 2017; CDC, 2017). After the turn of the millennium, novel treatments and cutting-edge technology continue to be discovered and tested in clinical trials. Specialized emergency care and stroke centers have proven to be effective in further improving care (Anderson et al., 2013). This chapter provides an overview of stroke as a disability. It begins with etiology, followed by anatomy of the brain, categories of stroke, diagnosis, complications and limitations, and concludes with treatment, prevention, and rehabilitation potential of stroke survivors.

Etiology and Statistics

Risk Factors and Costs

The two major categories of stroke risk factors are labeled modifiable and non-modifiable. Modifiable risk factors are under control of the patient, while non-modifiable are beyond one's control. Modifiable risk factors for stroke include the following: hypertension, cigarette smoking, heart disease, Type II diabetes mellitus, excessive alcohol intake, high LDL cholesterol, drug abuse (especially cocaine and amphetamines), and carotid artery atherosclerosis (cholesterol build-up causing blockage of an artery). The most important modifiable risk factor which contributes to the highest rate of stroke is hypertension; many clinical studies have proven that blood pressure reduction results in lower rates of stroke (ASA, 2016; CDC, 2017).

Non-modifiable stroke risk factors include age, a history of prior stroke or TIA, male gender, race, certain genetic disorders of blood clotting, and a family medical history of stroke or cardiovascular disease. About half of Americans have one of the three following risk factors for stroke: high blood pressure, high LDL cholesterol, and smoking (Grysiewicz, Thomas, & Pandey, 2008).

Patients who have a history of TIAs are nine times more likely to have subsequent strokes than those without (ASA, 2016). Each year, there are 795,000 strokes in the United States; of these, 185,000 are recurrent and 610,000 are first strokes. African-Americans have higher rates of stroke, partly because higher rates of diabetes and high blood pressure are found within this population. This is especially true of African-Americans who live in the stroke-belt, an area in the southeastern United States where stroke incidence leads the nation (Benjamin et al., 2018).

In this country, stroke costs an estimated $34 billion a year. This figure includes health care services, medications, and missed work days (CDC, 2017). These costs will, of necessity, continue to rise.

Signs and Symptoms

Stroke is defined by the sudden onset of neurological deficits. Although some patients may have warning signs (TIAs) that appear before an actual stroke, many strokes occur without warning. Some of these symptoms include sudden (a) numbness or weakness in the face, arm, or leg, which usually occurs on one side of the body, (b) severe headache with unknown cause, (c) vision impairment in one or both eyes, (d) confusion, such as having trouble understanding or speaking, and (e) trouble walking and a problem with motor coordination. As discussed above, when these symptoms dissipate rapidly, the patient may have had a TIA (CDC, 2017; George et al., 2017). The diagnosis is stroke if the symptoms persist for at least 24 hours from onset or when neuroimaging demonstrates brain damage.

Anatomy of the Brain

Stroke occurs within the brain, the control center for the majority of body functions. The cerebral cortex, the largest part of the brain, is responsible for language abilities and personality. The brainstem and cerebellum control automatic functions such as heartbeat, breathing, and coordination. A wide range of symptoms and deficits results from damage to various areas of the brain. Blood is transported to the brain from the heart via arteries, and is returned to the heart through veins.

Stroke is primarily caused by interruptions in either the arterial circulation of the brain or, less commonly, abnormalities in the venous circulation. The four major arteries that supply the brain include two carotid arteries in the front of the neck and two vertebral arteries in the back of the neck. Each artery supplies a specific area of the brain. When an artery is occluded, lack of oxygen (ischemia) leads to abnormalities of brain function and, if persistent, results in death of brain cells supplied by the involved artery. The brain can tolerate only four minutes of anoxia (a lack of oxygen) before brain cells begin to die. It has been estimated that for every minute the brain lacks oxygen, 1.9 million brain cells (neurons) are lost (Saver, 2006).

Inside the skull, the internal carotid artery splits into the middle cerebral arteries and anterior cerebral arteries. These arteries supply the parietal lobe and portions of the frontal lobe and anterior portion of the temporal lobe. If the dominant hemisphere middle cerebral arteries are blocked (usually the left brain), language and speech are affected. Blood from the anterior cerebral artery supplies the anterior frontal lobe. Small perforating arteries provide the blood supply to areas deep within the brain (e.g., the thalamus and basal ganglia).

In the back of the brain, two vertebral arteries combine to form a basilar artery, which supplies blood to the brainstem and cerebellum. The terminal branches of the vertebrobasilar system supply the visual cortex. These small arteries are susceptible to rupture from long-standing hypertension. Collateral circulation generally does not occur in the blood supply of the central nervous system, even though it is present in most areas of the body. When collateral circulation does develop, arterial interconnections occur between major arterial systems – that is, when one artery is blocked, the area needing oxygen obtains blood from another major artery.

Categories of Stroke

The two main categories of stroke are (a) ischemic stroke due to blood vessel blockage, and (b) intracranial hemorrhage stroke caused by blood vessel rupture. Etiology, diagnosis, and treatment differ for these two types of stroke. The following section reviews the different types of stroke in both categories.

Ischemic Stroke

Ischemic stroke is the most common type of stroke, accounting for approximately 87% of all events (ASA, 2016). It results from blockage of an artery due to a blood clot. The origination of the blood clot can be multifactorial, but the two major categories are cerebral embolus and cerebral thrombus (Hemmen et al., 2010).

Cerebral Embolus

When a plaque or particle travels from the heart or a larger artery and lodges in a smaller artery, obstruction of blood flow causes an embolic stroke. If the obstruction persists for over a few minutes, brain cells (neurons) begin to die. The death of brain cells and tissue lead to functional limitations. Sources of emboli are typically the heart, ascending aorta or aortic arch, and carotid arteries. Cerebral emboli are usually caused by atherosclerotic vascular disease (hardening of the arteries) in which a small portion of atherosclerotic plaque breaks off and travels to the blood vessels within the brain. Embolic stroke may also be caused by a blood clot originating in the heart (Grysiewicz et al., 2008). In people over 60 years of age, atherosclerotic vascular disease and cardiac disease are the most common causes of ischemic stroke. Cerebral embolus is less common in younger people, but might be associated with blood clotting disorders known as coagulopathy.

Cerebral Thrombus

Another form of stroke, caused by a blood clot (thrombus), develops from atherosclerotic plaque in the wall of a vessel (Goldstein, 2016). Years of uncontrolled hypertension, tobacco abuse, and high cholesterol may cause atherosclerosis or hardening of the arteries. Build-up of cholesterol plaque can result in a localized clumping of platelets occluding a vessel. The resultant mix of platelets and fibrin, a thrombus, does not travel; rather, it causes an arterial obstruction at the site of origin. Depending on the length and severity of the obstruction, resulting disability varies from partial to full recovery (Hemmen et al., 2010).

Intracranial Hemorrhage Stroke

Intracranial hemorrhage, occurring in approximately 10-15% of strokes, is caused by a ruptured blood vessel (Mayer, 2016). The focus of this section includes the three main forms of intracerebral hemorrhage (ICH): (a) hypertensive hemorrhage due to uncontrolled high blood pressure, (b) subarachnoid hemorrhage due to aneurysm rupture (a congenital weakness and ballooning of the vessel wall), and (c) rupture of a vascular malformation (usually a congenital lesion).

Cerebral Hypertensive Hemorrhage

Long-standing uncontrolled hypertension can lead to damage in the arteries of the brain (as well as other organs, such as the kidneys and eyes). The resulting damage, called lipohyalinosis, affects the small blood vessels in the brain. Lipohyalinosis is a progressive process that weakens the wall of an artery, in turn increasing the risk of rupture. The most common sites of cerebral hypertensive hemorrhage occur in deep structures supplied by the small, penetrating arteries affected by lipohyalinosis. These structures include the basal ganglia and pons.

In addition, the cerebellum (the portion of the brain responsible for coordination) is subject to hemorrhage. Morbidity and mortality for hypertensive hemorrhage is extremely high; one-third of these individuals die within a month. Potential treatments for these strokes have focused on limiting the size and rate of bleeding, surgical removal of the hemorrhage, as well as rapidly lowering the blood pressure upon emergency room admission (Anderson et al., 2013). Since emergency treatment options for hypertensive hemorrhage are generally lacking, the focus of treatment is on preventative strategies, specifically control of a person's hypertension.

Aneurysmal Subarachnoid Hemorrhage

An aneurysm is an out-pouching of a blood vessel due to thinning of the arterial wall. It is usually located at the branching points of cerebral blood vessels. Approximately 85% of cerebral aneurysms develop in the middle cerebral artery, as well as the anterior and posterior communicating arteries. Roughly 15-20% of those who experience aneurysm have additional aneurysms in the future (ASA, 2016). Aneurysm formation is more likely to occur in individuals with long-standing high blood pressure. Weakened arterial walls can rupture, resulting in subarachnoid hemorrhage (SAH). Patients with aneurysmal SAH are typically younger than their ischemic stroke cohort (typically 40-60 years old) (Grysiewicz et al., 2008). Risk factors for aneurysmal rupture include: size of the aneurysm (larger aneurysms are higher risk), excessive alcohol intake, tobacco abuse, and congenital abnormalities.

Patients who undergo aneurysmal ruptures usually present with severe headache and focal neurological deficits. Aneurysmal SAH is a catastrophic condition affecting 30,000 people in the United States yearly. Sixty percent of these individuals either die or suffer permanent disability; fifty percent of the survivors with favorable outcomes experience considerable neuropsychological dysfunction. Cerebral vasospasm (i.e., narrowing of proximal arterial segments) complicates 20-50% of cases, and is the major cause of disability and death associated with aneurysmal SAH.

Cerebral Vascular Malformation

Cerebral vascular malformation, also known as arteriovenous malformation (AVM), is characterized by congenital abnormalities of blood vessels in the brain. AVM, tangled networks of blood vessels, consist of arteries that directly empty into veins without the normal intervening capillaries that support brain tissue. These lesions, usually present at birth, tend to become apparent later in life when they leak or bleed. AVM rupture typically occurs abruptly without symptoms and results in neurological deficits (Reddy et al., 2009).

Diagnosis

Physicians diagnose stroke by finding acute neurological symptoms, abnormalities seen during a clinical neurological examination, aided by imaging techniques. Upon arrival at the hospital, all patients who have had a stroke receive a CT scan or MRI of the brain, which evaluates for intracranial hemorrhage, establishes ischemic stroke from hemorrhagic stroke, and eliminates other possible causes of the neurological symptoms (e.g., brain tumors). Specialized centers for the treatment of stroke can rapidly evaluate the cerebral arteries using either ultrasound or arteriography (injection of intravenous contrast dye to visualize the anatomy of the cerebral circulation). These studies assist the clinician with diagnosis, cause, and treatment. Additional studies obtained during hospitalization include a cardiac evaluation, including electrocardiogram and echocardiogram (Barreto et al., 2017).

Complications and Limitations

Cerebrovascular diseases, such as stroke, follow a spectrum of severity. Frequently, small strokes occur resulting in mild or non-noticeable residual deficits. Contrastingly, a stroke classified as severe is a devastating occurrence. One-third of individuals with severe strokes die within two weeks. Mortality rates increase with advancing age and the presence of other comorbid diseases such as hypertension, heart disease, and diabetes. Approximately one-third of CVAs result in significant neurological deficit, while one-third of individuals have minor or no deficits.

A stroke can affect any part of the brain and symptoms vary depending on size and location of the damage. When brain tissue is damaged, far reaching deficits occur including paralysis, cognitive decline, language difficulty, behavioral and mood changes, and psychological effects, such as depression. Those surviving a severe stroke are at much higher risk for other medical complications, including pneumonia, blood clots in the legs, and aspiration or dehydration caused by dysfunction of swallowing. Other long-term complications of stroke include development of contractures, seizure disorders, bowel and bladder problems, and spasticity of muscles.

Neurological Deficits

In general, when the stroke occurs on one side of the brain, the opposite side of the body is affected. Brainstem strokes caused by abnormalities of the posterior circulation (i.e., vertebral or basilar arteries) are associated with crossed neurological findings. These patients display abnormalities both ipsilateral (affecting the same side) to the side of the stroke involving the face, and contralateral (affecting the opposite side) to the side of the stroke involving the body. After a stroke, typical neurological deficits range from paralysis, to hemiparesis, to minimal or unnoticeable deficits (Fusco et al., 2017). An overview of physiological effects and physical limitations related to post-stroke neurological deficits follows.

Typical clinical residual findings of middle cerebral artery (MCA) stroke include abnormalities of the motor and sensory cortex leading to spastic hemiparesis and sensory loss, respectively. If the stroke occurs in the right MCA territory, the patient may suffer from anosognosia (also known as neglect), a state in which the individual does not recognize the affected side of the body as belonging to himself or herself. In such cases, the person is unable to perceive objects on either the right or left side of the central field of vision and is unaware of the deficit.

When the stroke occurs in the right side of the brain, visual-spatial deficits result. Individuals with visual-spatial problems may incorrectly interpret visual information and have difficulty orienting to the surrounding environment. A stroke on the left side of the brain can result in paralysis to the right side of the face, arm, and leg. Lesions of the left MCA affect the language centers, causing speech or comprehension impairment. When the speech center is affected, the condition is known as aphasia. Patients with aphasia have difficulty sounding words, understanding words, or both; these different forms of aphasia are termed expressive, receptive, and global aphasia.

Posterior circulation strokes involving the vertebral and basilar arteries can be fatal. Basilar artery occlusion is known for its extreme mortality rates, as high as 80% (ASA, 2016). These patients initially present with declining mental status, coordination difficulties (ataxia), double vision (diplopia), severe dysarthria (slurred speech), dysphagia (difficulty swallowing), and trouble controlling saliva. Patients with posterior circulation strokes often require mechanical (artificial) ventilation with a breathing tube.

Paralysis

The complete loss of function of one or more muscle groups due to damage to the brain is referred to as paralysis. Depending on the area and size of damage, post-stroke survivors experience weakness, as well as loss of muscle function and sensation.

Paresis

Paresis refers to weakness of muscle strength. Paresis can be localized, and often follows a pattern. For example, localized paresis of one side of the face may result due to damage of the brain tissues that leads to inflammation of the facial nerve affecting that side of the face.

Hemiplegia

Hemiplegia is a common consequence of stroke, involving paralysis on one side of the body. A person is said to have right hemiplegia if the right side of the body is paralyzed. As mentioned earlier, the lesion causing paralysis is typically located in the opposite hemisphere of the brain. When the stroke occurs on the left side of the brain, paralysis limits functions of the arm and leg on the right side. This condition usually has more impact on the upper extremity than on the lower extremity. These individuals have deficits in ability to solve problems. Visual-spatial deficits occur when the stroke takes place in the right brain. An individual with visual-spatial problems may incorrectly interpret visual information and have difficulty with environmental orientation. A stroke on the left side of the brain results in paralysis to the right upper and lower extremities (Duncan et al., 2011).

Aphasia

When the dominant hemisphere of the brain (in the majority of people, this is the left side) is damaged, a communication disturbance can result (CDC, 2017; George et al., 2017). This problem with communication is called aphasia and takes several forms. First, the ability to understand might be affected (receptive aphasia). Patients appear confused since they will not understand the words or commands being spoken to them. Other patients might be able to understand, but not be able to get words out (expressive aphasia). Expressively aphasic (Broca's aphasia) patients typically appear frustrated since they know what they want to say, but are not able to form sentences. In some cases, both reception and expression are affected and these patients are mute and unable to comprehend (global aphasia).

Cognitive/Psychosocial Deficits

Strokes cause a wide variety of cognitive, as well as psychosocial deficits. It is common to find survivors of stroke having difficulties in memory retention, especially of newly acquired information. Results of such accidents include slowed retention and disorganized processing of information. Intellectual deficits, behavioral changes, and problem-solving difficulties, can result. Intellectual deficits are minimized and others circumvented with relearning and through job accommodations. For example, patients with memory difficulty can use a notepad or I-pad to record information. Specific intellectual tasks crucial to an individual vocation can be reassigned to other employees. If job modification cannot accommodate the extent of intellectual impairment, use of transferable skills or retraining needs assessment.

Depression

The most common psychological problem found among stroke survivors is depression. This may be related to the degree of functional disability and negatively impacts a person's ability for rehabilitation (Ahn, Lee, Jeong, Kim, & Park, 2015). Common symptoms of depression include (a) persistent sadness and anxiety, (b) feelings of hopelessness, (c) loss of interest, (d) fatigue and lack of energy, (e) insomnia or hypersomnia, (f) loss or increase of appetite and weight changes, and (g) difficulties in concentrating, remembering, and decision-making (ASA, 2016). Treating depression improves the stroke survivor's mood and physical recovery. Social support from family, friends, stroke support groups, and rehabilitation professionals remains a crucial part of recovery for stroke survivors dealing with depression.

Emotional Lability

Emotional lability (partial loss of emotional control) may be experienced and expressed clinically as various emotional states, such as crying, sudden laughter, depression, and anger. Such emotions change rapidly and for no apparent reason; the individual may additionally express emotions considered inappropriate for particular situations. Persons with stroke also have irritability, frustration, insecurity, hesitancy, anger, hostility, depression, flat affect, and generalized indifference.

Family Disruption

In addition to affecting the patient, stroke impacts family members and caregivers. The results of a stroke are physically, financially, and practically demanding, as well as emotionally distressing for all involved. Feelings of sadness, grief, exhaustion, fear, and anger are common reactions to increased dependence and vulnerability following a stroke. The disruption in family relationships resulting from a stroke, in addition to resulting heightened conflicts and loss of supportive ties, is decreased with help from support groups (Gittler & Davis, 2018).

Treatment

Emerging treatments for ischemic stroke and hemorrhagic stroke vary. Regardless of the type of stroke, timing is crucial. Emergency medical care must be provided at the onset of stroke symptoms. The sooner treatment is delivered, the less severe the resulting disability limitations. Brain damage and other negative results are significantly reduced through prompt emergency care.

Medications

With ischemic stroke, pharmacologic thrombolytic therapy can be administered (within three hours) which aims to dissolve the clot causing the obstruction and unblock the artery. Tissue plasminogen activator (tPA) is the most commonly administered thrombolytic. Delivered intravenously, tPA has been shown in a large clinical trial to improve functional outcomes by dissolving blood clots and restoring blood flow (National Institute of Neurological Disorders and Stroke rt-PA Stroke Study Group, 1995). Benefit was maintained at 3-12 months after stroke (Kwiatkowski et al., 1999). Patients who received tPA were 30% more likely to achieve minimal or no neurological symptoms when compared to those who received the placebo.

If a narrowed carotid artery in the neck proves to be the cause of an ischemic stroke, a patient can undergo surgery called carotid endarterectomy. This procedure removes plaque from the carotid artery, reopens the blocked artery, and improves blood flow. Carotid endarterectomy reduces subsequent risk of ischemic stroke. An alternative to traditional carotid endarterectomy surgery, carotid artery stenting has been proven effective (Brott et al., 2016). Treatments for hemorrhagic stroke are minimal. Researchers have failed to show that drugs which can reduce bleeding lead to improved outcomes (Mayer, 2016). Surgical decompression or blood removal has failed to prevent disability or death.

Physical and Occupational Therapy

For patients who have post-stroke hemiplegia or hemiparesis, physical therapy provides strengthening exercises for both the upper and lower extremities. Occupational therapy provides range-of-motion activities and splints which assist in preventing contractures and spasticity. Programs can be oriented toward recovery of occupational modalities and may utilize orthotic devices, such as leg braces, which help the person ambulate. Once the counselor and client have decided on a return to work objective, special orthotic devices can help the person perform specific job functions (Brodwin, Parker, & DeLaGarza, 2010).

Medical Advances

The brain was once thought to be a static, non-repairable organ. Although neurons do not regenerate, recent brain-imaging techniques have given researchers and physicians new understanding of the ability of the brain to adapt and regain function after stroke. Brain-plasticity, one such adaptation, is the ability of one area of the brain to take over the function of a damaged region. Brain cells surrounding the damaged area assume the functions of the damaged cells. Recent rehabilitation advances include (a) constraint-induced therapy; (b) focused-use therapy that includes thousands of passive movement repetitions to help the injured brain relearn how to use the impaired limb; (c) electrical stimulation; and (d) biofeedback. Although the science is currently in the preliminary phase, research on stem cell implants has been initiated. It is hypothesized that delivery of stem cells to a stroke patient could stimulate other cells to grow in the brain and form new connections to help restore motor function (Fusco et al., 2017).

Prevention

Preventing a first-time stroke (primary prevention) and recurrent stroke (secondary prevention) are the goals of neurologists specializing in stroke. Targets that provide protection include: blood pressure reduction, antiplatelet medications (e.g., aspirin), cholesterol reduction, diabetes control, smoking cessation, and blood thinners for heart arrhythmias. Because compliance with medication and resulting side effects is challenging for some individuals, vocational rehabilitation counselors are key in providing support and assistance (Brodwin et al., 2010; Gilbride & Stensrud, 2012). Familiarity with medications and their side effects, especially when considering return to work, is crucial to successful rehabilitation.

Blood Pressure Control

Blood pressure reduction remains the most critical means of avoiding stroke. Long-term damage to the arteries that results from unmanaged hypertension increases the risks of stroke. Numerous clinical studies have shown a reduction in stroke when blood pressure was reduced with antihypertensive medications (Dahlöf et al., 2002; Qureshi et al., 2016). Aspirin and the combination of aspirin plus extended-release dipyridamole help prevent recurrent stroke. Management of high cholesterol decreases the risk of stroke, as well as heart disease.

Diet and Exercise

The maintenance of a healthy diet low in saturated fats and high in complex grains, fruit, and vegetables reduces the risk of stroke. Many metabolic changes occur during dietary restriction including (a) lower blood pressure; (b) reduced arterial stiffness, cholesterol points, and triglyceride level; (c) slower age-related decline in functional and cognitive capacities; (d) enhanced resistance to stress; and (e) improved ability to adapt to stress at the cellular level (ASA, 2016; CDC, 2017). Along with a healthy diet, exercise is an important part of a healthy lifestyle. Recommendations include at least an hour of moderately intense daily exercise, which may be distributed throughout the day. Exercise is crucial for the individual's health and promotes proper functioning of blood vessels, improves delivery of oxygen to muscle tissues, and increases the good-to-bad cholesterol ratio.

Smoking and Drug Use

Tobacco and illicit drugs should be avoided since they are addictive and have deleterious effects on blood vessels. Damage to the arteries can lead to accelerated atherosclerosis. Along with the medical community, the American Heart and Stroke Associations have bolstered their opposition to smoking and illicit drugs, as both these are associated with the development of cerebrovascular and cardiovascular disease.

Rehabilitation Potential

Rehabilitation is a significant component of recovery, improving the outlook for survivors of stroke. Approximately half of stroke survivors experience some permanent disability; the success of rehabilitation depends on several key factors. Such factors include (a) timing of treatment, (b) extent and size of brain injury, (c) intensity and frequency of therapy, (d) availability of companionship and emotional support, and (e) the stroke survivor's personal outlook and attitude (ASA, 2016; CDC, 2017; George et al., 2017). Maximum return of function after a stroke can require a six-month recovery period; counselors must take this into account before determining an individual's rehabilitation potential. Early intervention helps encourage and maintain the individual's return to work, keeping in mind that maximum return of function does not occur immediately.

The goal of stroke rehabilitation is to help the individual maximize independence. The level of independence reached after rehabilitation is different for each individual, depending on the size and extent of the stroke and previous functioning. Physical, speech, and occupational therapy aid in recovery. Individuals can improve independence in many areas such as mobility, communication, swallowing, cognitive and behavior modifications, and self-care. Below, are a few characteristics of rehabilitation unique to stroke survivors.

Passive Exercise

Manually-assisted movement serves two primary purposes. First, the repetitive movements help prevent spasticity and contractures which are limiting and painful for stroke patients. Development of contractures lead to skin breakdown and infections. The inability to flex and extend muscles due to contractures inhibits caregivers from providing effective bowel and bladder care. Second, passive movement of the affected limbs may aid the brain in reorganization and recovery of function. This conventional forced-use therapy is performed in thousands of repetitions with the help of a physical therapist or caregiver (Falvo & Holland, 2018; Fusco et al., 2017).

Assistive Devices and Technology

Canes, walkers, and motorized carts increase mobility after stroke. Hoists used at home and some worksites assist lifting and care of the person. Mechanical devices aid pushing and pulling work activities. A variety of work-related equipment is adaptable for one-hand operations. Various types of orthotic devices improve hand function. Use of a computer minimizes writing. Rearranging desk and file cabinets diminish functional limitations. Often, simple accommodations provide for access by wheelchair users. Various accommodations can be recommended, depending on the particular work site and functional needs of the individual (Brodwin et al., 2010; Gilbride & Stensrud, 2012).

Technology has improved the range and availability of adaptive devices for post-stroke survivors. For individuals with limited strength or hand dexterity, low-tech devices are available such as doorknob-turners which slip over a doorknob to allow the door to be opened with lever action. Fine motor skill impairments cause changes in the individual's daily routine. Assistive devices, such as those that allow buttons to hook, make the resumption of independence easier. High-tech devices include computers with specialized programs that speak for people with severe aphasia or to enhance vision. Such programs allow survivors to express their needs and wants with greater ease. Computerized robotic gait trainers allow patients to be mobile at early stages (Brodwin et al., 2010). Funding for such technology can be assisted by programs, such as Medicaid, Medicare, Social Security Disability Insurance (SSDI and SSI), state rehabilitation work incentive programs, and private insurance (ASA, 2016).

Increased Dependency on Caregivers

As a result of physical and cognitive deficits, stroke survivors may need assistance from caregivers. These individuals are likely to be immediate family members. Because stroke is characterized by its sudden onset, change of roles and family dynamics occurs quickly and without preparation, causing emotional distress. Stroke survivors with high levels of emotional support demonstrate enhanced levels of recovery. Lack of perceived support is associated with the presence and severity of depression. Survivors and family members can experience positive effects after stroke, such as increased compassion and empathy for others, self-confidence, attention to relationships, spiritual growth, reassessment of personal values, and enhanced sense of meaning of life (Gittler et al., 2018; Winstein et al., 2016).

Psychosocial Factors

Studies of post-stroke outcomes focus on recovery of physical function and reduction of medical complications. Some studies cite psychosocial factors, such as motivation, as a key to successful vocational rehabilitation (Brodwin et al., 2010; Gilbride & Stensrud, 2012; Szymanski, Enright, & Hershenson, 2012). Socioeconomic issues also impacts return to gainful employment. Workers with higher education levels and professional, managerial, and technical jobs successfully return to work at a significantly higher rate than those with lower levels of education and unskilled manual job experience. Vocational programs that offer a multidisciplinary approach to stroke rehabilitation have had great success in rehabilitation and attaining successful employment. A key to success is careful coordination of comprehensive services by a multidisciplinary team made up of rehabilitation counselors, physicians, therapists, psychologists, and social workers.

Conclusion

As the most common cause of long-term disability, stroke impacts all aspects of a person's life, as well as the lives of family and friends. Disability adjustments range from attending to medical and financial needs to physical and psychological adaptations to addressing loss of interpersonal relationships and employment. Recovery from stroke is a challenging journey that can last the rest of the person's life. Rehabilitation counselors, working together with a multidisciplinary team of healthcare providers, can improve the individual's quality of life and aid the family in coping with the complications of stroke.

Case Study

Three years ago, Maurice Campbell (age 39), a formerly incarcerated Jamaican American, reintegrated into the workforce as a movie set worker. At work, he is known to be a man of few words, skillful with his "arts," and proficient with cartoon sketches and developing sets for the film industry. A year ago, he experienced a major fall at work, underwent brain surgery, and had a stroke during the operation. As a result of the cerebral hemorrhage, Maurice has hemiplegia on the dominant side of his body and face, resulting in slurred speech, hearing impairment, and neglect of one side of his body. The trauma caused physical limitations and concurrent emotional problems.

According to his file, upon graduation from high school, Mr. Campbell worked as a movie set worker, a movie extra, and a waiter. He met Tiki while working at a neighborhood diner and got married as soon as they found out she was pregnant with their son. Life was a struggle and the couple fought frequently over finances. Police were called twice and children's protective services (CPS) threatened to remove their son from the family. Within a week of the CPS's last visit, Tiki moved out, taking their child along with her, and filed a restraining order against Maurice. Since then, Mr. Campbell's life took a nosedive. He found comfort in alcohol and drugs, lost his jobs due to unacceptable behaviors, became homeless, and committed crimes. To date, Maurice has several felonies involving drug possession, and five years of incarceration due to robberies and drug dealing.

A multidisciplinary rehabilitative program began almost immediately after Mr. Campbell's medical condition stabilized. Rehabilitative therapy was started in the acute-care hospital within the first month following the stroke. After months of intensive care and physical therapy, Maurice regained 75% of his cognitive and physical functioning. His physician released him to work in an environment with minimal stress. The position must be sedentary, with time allowed for post-stroke care and rehabilitation.

Questions

1. Provide a vocational profile for Mr. Maurice Campbell. Identify additional information you need to help this client.
2. How does Maurice's incarceration history affect your provision of rehabilitation services? Discuss social discrimination and other stereotypical factors relevant to this client.
3. Would addiction history impact Maurice's vocational rehabilitation plan and why?
4. Outline the rehabilitation services you intend to provide, including when to begin and the time frame for each step in the process.
5. Identify any resources needed. How would you counsel Mr. Campbell if he has mixed feelings about returning to the film industry?

References

Ahn, D. H., Lee, Y. J., Jeong, J. H., Kim, Y. R., & Park, J. B. (2015). The effect of post-stroke depression on rehabilitation outcome and the impact of caregiver type as a factor of post-stroke depression. *Annals of Rehabilitation Medicine, 39*(1), 74–80.

American Stroke Association (ASA). (2016). *Impact of stroke: Stroke statistics*. Retrieved from http://www.strokeassociation.org

Anderson, C. S., Heeley, E., Huang, Y., Wang, J., Stapf, C., Delcourt, C., . . . Chalmers, J. (2013). Rapid blood-pressure lowering in patients with acute intracerebral hemorrhage. *New England Journal of Medicine, 368*(25), 2355-2365.

Barreto, A. D., Ford, G. A., Shen, L., Pedroza, C., Tyson, J., Cai, C., . . . Grotta, J. C. (2017). Randomized, Multicenter Trial of ARTSS-2 (Argatroban with recombinant tissue plasminogen activator for acute stroke). *Stroke, 48*(6), 1608-1616.

Benjamin, E. J., Virani, S. S., Callaway, C. W., Chamberlain, A. M., Chang, A. R., Cheng, S., . . . Muntner, P. (2018). Heart disease and stroke statistics – 2018 update: A report from the American Heart Association. *Circulation, 137*, e67-e492.

Brodwin, M. G., Parker, R. M., & DeLaGarza, D. (2010). Disability and reasonable accommodation. In E. M. Szymanski & R. M. Parker (Eds.), *Work and disability: Contexts, issues, and strategies for enhancing employment opportunities for people with disabilities* (3rd ed., pp. 281-323). Austin, TX: Pro-ed.

Brott, T. G., Howard, G., Roubin, G. S., Meschia, J. F., Mackey, A., Brooks, W., . . . Hobson, R. W. (2016). Long-term results of stenting versus endarterectomy for carotid-artery stenosis. *New England Journal of Medicine, 374*, 1021-1031.

Centers for Disease Control and Prevention (CDC). (2017). *Stroke facts*. Retrieved from http://www.cdc.gov/stroke/facts.htm

Dahlöf, B., Devereux, R. B., Kjeldsen, S. E., Julius, S., Beevers, G., de Faire, U., . . . Wedel, H. (2002). Cardiovascular morbidity and mortality in the Losartan Intervention for Endpoint Reduction in Hypertension Study (LIFE): A randomized trial against atenolol. *Lancet, 359*, 995–1003.

Duncan, P. W., Sullivan, K. T., Behrman, A. L., Azen, S. P., Wu, S. S., Nadeau, S. E., . . . Hayden, S. K. (2011). Body-weight-supported treadmill rehabilitation after stroke. *New England Journal of Medicine, 364*(21), 2026-2036.

Falvo, D. R., & Holland, B. E. (2018). *Medical and psychosocial aspects of chronic illness and disability* (6th ed.). Burlington, MA: Jones & Bartlett.

Fusco, H. N., Ishida, K., Levine, J. M., & Torres, J. (2017). Stroke. In A. Moroz, S. R. Flanagan, & H. H. Zaretsky (Eds.), *Medical aspects of disability for the rehabilitation professional* (5th ed., pp. 571-596). New York, NY: Springer.

George, M. G., Fischer, L., Koroshetz, W., Bushnell, C., Frankel, M., Foltz, J., & Thorpe, P. G. (2017). CDC grand rounds: Public health strategies to prevent and treat strokes. *Morbidity and Mortality Weekly Report, 66*, 479–481.

Gilbride, D., & Stensrud, R. (2012). People with disabilities in the workplace. In R. M. Parker & J. B. Patterson (Eds.). *Rehabilitation counseling: Basics and beyond* (5th ed., pp. 259- 284). Austin, TX: Pro-ed.

Gittler, M., & Davis, A. M. (2018). Guidelines for adult stroke rehabilitation and recovery. *Journal of the American Medical Association, 319*(8), 820–821.

Goldstein, L. B. (2016). Ischemic cerebrovascular disease. In L. Goldman & A. I. Schafer (Eds.), *Goldman's Cecil medicine* (25th ed., pp. 2434-2445). Philadelphia, PA: Elsevier Saunders.

Grysiewicz, R. A., Thomas, K., & Pandey, D. K. (2008). Epidemiology of ischemic and hemorrhage stroke: Incidence prevalence, and risk factors. *Neurologic Clinics, 26*, 871-895.

Hemmen, T. M., Raman, R., Guluma, K. Z., Meyer, B. C., Gomes, J. A., Cruz-Flores, S., . . . Lyden, P. D. (2010). Intravenous thrombolysis plus hypothermia for acute treatment of ischemic stroke (ICTuS-L): Final results. *Stroke, 41*(10), 2265-2270.

Kwiatkowski, T. G., Libman, R. B., Frankel, M., Tilley, B. C., Morgenstern, L. B., Lu, M., . . . Brott, T. (1999). Effects of tissue plasminogen activator for acute ischemic stroke at one year. *New England Journal of Medicine, 340*, 1781-1787.

Mayer, S. A. (2016). Hemorrhagic cerebrovascular disease. In L. Goldman & A. I. Schafer (Eds.), *Goldman's Cecil medicine* (25th ed., pp. 2445-2454). Philadelphia, PA: Elsevier Saunders.

National Institute of Neurological Disorders and Stroke rt-PA Stroke Study Group. (1995). Tissue plasminogen activator for acute ischemic stroke. *New England Journal of Medicine, 333*, 1581-1587.

Qureshi, A. I., Palesch, Y. Y., Barsan, W. G., Hanley, D. F., Hsu, C. Y., Martin, R. L., . . . Yoon, B. W. (2016). Intensive blood-pressure lowering in patients with acute cerebral hemorrhage. *New England Journal of Medicine, 375*(11), 1033-1043.

Reddy, C., Chae, J., Lew, H., Lombard, L., Edgley, S., & Moroz, A. (2009). Stroke and neurodegenerative disorders: 1. Stroke management in the acute care setting. *Physical Medicine and Rehabilitation: Journal of Injury, Function, and Rehabilitation, 1*, s4-s12.

Saver, J. L. (2006). Time is brain – Quantified. *Stroke, 37*(1), 263-266.

Szymanski, E. A., Enright, M. S., & Hershenson, D. B. (2012). An ecological approach to the vocational behavior and career development of people with disabilities. In R. M. Parker & J. B. Patterson (Eds.), *Rehabilitation counseling: Basics and beyond* (5th ed., pp. 199-258). Austin, Tx: Pro-ed.

Winstein, C. J., Stein, J., Arena, R., Bates, B., Cherney, L. R., Cramer, S. C., . . . Zorowitz, R. D. (2016). Guidelines for adult stroke rehabilitation and recovery: A guideline for healthcare professionals from the American Heart Association/American Stroke Association. *Stroke, 47*, e98-e169.

About the Authors

Andrew D. Barreto, MD, is a cerebrovascular neurologist who specializes in stroke at the University of Texas-Health Science Center in Houston. Dr. Barreto is an Associate Professor at the University of Texas-Houston Medical School and is involved with all aspects of management of stroke, including emergency treatment, hospital care, and clinic follow-up. Research interests of Dr. Barreto include the use of ultrasound technology and novel adjunctive medical treatments aimed at enhancing stroke treatment.

Frances W. Siu, PhD, CRC, is an Associate Professor and Undergraduate Coordinator of the Rehabilitation Services Program at California State University, Los Angeles (CSULA). She received her PhD in Special Education and Counseling, option in Rehabilitation Counselor Education, from the University of Texas at Austin, her MS in rehabilitation counseling, and B.S. in psychology, both from CSULA. Research interests of Dr. Siu include medical aspects of disability, multicultural issues, and violence against people with disabilities. She has published numerous articles and book chapters, and given state and national professional presentations on violence against people with disabilities, rehabilitation education, and rehabilitation services.

Dr. Cailine Y. Kim, EdD, CRC, received her doctoral degree in Counseling Psychology from Argosy University, Los Angeles, and her MS in rehabilitation counseling from CSULA. Dr. Kim is employed by the U.S. Department of Veterans Affairs (VA) in Long Beach, California, as a Case Manager in the Vocational Rehabilitation Therapy unit. For the past 20 years, she has been with various State and Federal agencies providing rehabilitation services to people with disabilities. For the past several years, Dr. Kim has been an Adjunct Professor with the Division of Special Education and Counseling at CSULA. Research interests include improving quality of life and developing effective service delivery systems for veterans and geriatric populations.

Chapter 14

EPILEPSY

Erica K. Johnson, PhD, CRC, FAES
Robert T. Fraser, PhD, CRC
John W. Miller, MD, PhD

Introduction

Several well-known individuals throughout history, including Socrates, Leonardo de Vinci, Charles Dickens, Thomas Edison, and Julius Caesar, had active seizure conditions. Today, approximately 65 million people worldwide have epilepsy, making it the most common neurological disorder after stroke (Schmidt & Schachter, 2014). The word epilepsy derives from the Greek word meaning to be seized and is an umbrella term that refers to a spectrum of seizure conditions. A seizure is a discrete event and is a symptom of brain dysfunction (Fisher et al., 2014; Wiebe, 2012). It is characterized by a transient disruption of the normal activity of the brain through neuronal instability or firing in an abnormally rapid manner. The excessive electrical discharge results in a seizure.

A seizure may be confined to one area of the brain (focal seizure) or may arise from both sides of the brain (generalized seizure). Epilepsy is defined as: (a) two unprovoked seizures more than 24 hours apart, (b) one unprovoked, or a reflex seizure where there is a greater than 60% probability of future seizures, or (c) diagnosis of an epilepsy syndrome. Individuals are considered resolved after ten years of seizure freedom, with at least the last five years including freedom from antiseizure medications (Fisher et al., 2014).

The extent to which seizure disorders affect brain functioning and behavior depends on the location, spread, and duration of seizures. Consequently, some seizures cause minimal overt impairment, while other seizures result in a complete disruption of normal brain activities. Risk factors are diverse but include perinatal pathology, traumatic brain injury, hypertension, substance abuse, depressive illness, and lower socioeconomic status. Direct causes of epilepsy include genetic disorders, malformations of the brain, traumatic brain injury, anoxia (insufficient oxygen), brain tumors, infectious diseases, parasitic infections, stroke and other vascular diseases, and malformations of blood vessels. Only 2-3% of people in the general population have a risk of developing epilepsy, but offspring of adults with epilepsy carry a four-fold elevated risk (Xu et al., 2017).

This chapter discusses seizure classification and terminology, diagnosis and treatment, functional and psychosocial aspects, and vocational rehabilitation, including job development and accommodations. The chapter concludes with a case study analysis of an individual who has focal unaware and generalized motor seizures.

Classification

Seizures are classified by review of clinical symptoms, electroencephalogram (EEG), and video EEG monitoring. Seizure classifications and terminology were revised in 2017 by the International League Against Epilepsy (ILAE), in an effort to clarify relevant seizure features such as semiology, impairment of awareness, and motor involvement (Fisher et al., 2017). The new classification is summarized in Table 1.

TABLE 1
Seizure Types Classification (ILAF, 2017)

Onset
    Activity Pattern
    Presentation
    Focal, Aware
    No change in the person's awareness, even if s/he is unable to talk or respond during the event.

Motor seizures
    Changes in muscle activity: clonus, tonus, hypotonia, or automatisms.

Non-Motor seizures
    Changes in autonomic arousal; behavioral arrest; cognitive changes; emotional state; sensory perception.
    Focal, Impaired Awareness
    If awareness is impaired at any time during a focal seizure, it is called a focal seizure with impaired awareness.

Motor seizures
    Changes in muscle activity: clonus, tonus, hypotonia, or automatisms.

Non-Motor seizures
    Changes in autonomic arousal; behavioral arrest; cognitive changes; emotional state; sensory perception.
    Focal to Bilateral Tonic-Clonic
    Seizure begins as focal (as described above) and progresses to a generalized seizure, as described below. Presentation will vary accordingly.
    Generalized
    Person's awareness or consciousness is always affected, so the terms 'aware' or 'impaired awareness' are not needed.

Motor seizures
    There are various presentations involving muscle stiffening and jerking. The most common type is the tonic-clonic seizure (aka, grand mal).

Non-Motor seizures
    These are absence seizures, which typically involve behavioral arrest and sometimes automatisms (eyelid flutter, staring, lip smacking, finger rubbing).

Source: Adapted from Fisher et al., 2017

The primary distinctions among seizure types are the same as prior classifications and is based on the EEG and semiology at the seizure onset. Generalized seizures refer to events that begin in both cerebral hemispheres; partial (focal) seizures refer to events that begin in one cerebral hemisphere, in a region of the neocortex or limbic system; unknown seizures are those whose origin has not been determined.

Generalized Epilepsy

These conditions involve both cerebral hemispheres, as well as deeper areas of the brain (i.e., thalamus and brain stem structures), with resulting impairment in consciousness. They are sub-categorized into two major types: (a) Motor (e.g., tonic-clonic convulsive seizures, or other motor seizures, such as myoclonic or tonic) seizures, and (b) Non-motor (absence) seizures.

Generalized Motor Seizures

One form of generalized seizure, sometimes called grand mal seizure, is the stereotypic seizure with which most people are familiar – approximately 25% of epilepsy cases (Fisher et al., 2017). Although most convulsions last just a few minutes, an individual may have a continuous prolonged seizure, or repeated seizures without regaining consciousness. This is called status epilepticus and requires emergency medical intervention when the seizure exceeds five minutes. First aid for all generalized tonic-clonic seizures involves turning a person's body on its side to prevent choking and protecting the head from hitting hard surfaces. People cannot swallow their tongue during seizures. Depending on the severity of the seizure, it may leave some individuals disoriented and fatigued afterwards. Some individuals may return to work immediately, while others may require a full day of rest or more before returning (Fraser, Miller, & Johnson, 2011b).

A second form of generalized epilepsy, juvenile myoclonic epilepsy, is the most common syndrome of generalized epilepsy in adults. It begins around puberty. The characteristic features of this syndrome are sudden single jerks of the hands, upper body, or infrequently the whole body. These jerks usually happen in the morning, more likely when the person is sleep deprived. Most often, this syndrome requires lifelong treatment with antiseizure medication.

Generalized Non-Motor Seizures

These seizures, also called absence, last only a few seconds and involve a brief disruption of activity and awareness. Epilepsy syndromes with absence seizures may begin in childhood (Childhood Absence Epilepsy) or at puberty (Juvenile Absence Epilepsy). Childhood Absence Epilepsy remits within 15 years of onset for up to 90% of individuals. This category involves less than 5% of all epilepsy cases and is not common in adults (i.e., < 1% of cases) (Wiebe, 2012). The disruption of awareness interferes with learning and makes it dangerous to drive a motor vehicle, so early treatment is essential. From a functional perspective, absence seizures may have minimal vocational impact. Exceptions occur when an individual is experiencing many seizures of this type throughout the day or has a physically high-risk occupation, where even brief losses of consciousness affect job performance.

Focal Seizures

Approximately 60% of people with epilepsy have seizures that are classified as focal seizures (Fraser et al., 2011b). These seizures are first categorized based on impairment of awareness and divided into three categories:

(a) Focal seizures with retained awareness: The individual retains awareness of self and environment during the event; seizures are linked specifically to the affected area of the brain. Often focal aware seizures last less than 30 seconds; because consciousness is not impaired, this is often not a significant problem in regard to simple job performance.

(b) Focal seizures with impaired awareness: The individual experiences impaired consciousness and possibly an associated aura or warning prior to a convulsion that can involve an odor, aphasia, dizziness, nausea, headache, unusual stomach sensation, or a déjà vu experience. These seizures affect the individual's daily activities due to the unpredictable loss of consciousness. It is fortunate when an individual has a brief aura or warning before a seizure, as it allows the person to take safety precautions or alert others of an impending seizure.

(c) Focal seizures evolving into generalized seizures: These events have a variable presentation, as they vary according to affected brain areas (Fisher et al., 2017).

Nonepileptic Episodes

These events mimic or may be mistaken for seizures but are not seizures; rather, they are a manifestation of a psychiatric disorder - panic attacks, conversion disorders, dissociative events, or other diverse psychological causes (e.g., depression, personality disorder, trauma), and do not involve abnormal brain electrical activity. About 20-35% of patients evaluated at epilepsy centers have nonepileptic seizures.

Diagnosis and Treatment

Diagnosis

When individuals initially experience seizures, they generally see an emergency room or primary care physician first. Typically, the individual is then referred to a general neurologist for a workup for the cause of seizures and optimization of treatment. If seizure control cannot be achieved after 12 months by the general neurologist, a referral should be made to an epilepsy specialist.

Neurological consultation includes a physical examination and patient history, metabolic studies, EEG testing, and other evaluations. When a patient starts having seizures, a magnetic resonance imaging (MRI) of the head is used to look for lesions that might be the cause of seizures (Wiebe, 2012).

As recommended by the National Association of Epilepsy Centers (2010), when the general neurologist does not achieve seizure control within 12 months, referral to an epilepsy center should be made. These centers are staffed with neurologists who specialize in epilepsy treatment and are located within a health center that has specialized teams devoted to the medical and psychosocial needs of persons with epilepsy.

Treatment Principles and Medications

Drug selection depends on the epilepsy syndrome, age, medical comorbidity, and gender. Today, there are various medications available to treat focal, generalized, and refractory (i.e., drug-resistant) seizures. It is desirable that individuals use one medication (monotherapy), if possible, to control symptoms, and start medication after the first seizure. When effective, one drug is easier to manage and has less potential for adverse effects. Schmidt and Schachter (2014) reported that 70-80% of adults with new onset epilepsy will become seizure free with current antiseizure medications, but that 50% of these will experience adverse effects.

A dosage should be established that maintains seizure control without unacceptable adverse effects. Not following prescribed medication is a major issue. This noncompliance is often attributed to the unpleasant side effects of some antiseizure medications, primarily somnolence, dizziness, and weight changes. Cognitive changes, organ and blood disorders, as well as depression and behavioral problems can occur (Bano & Numanb, 2016; Schmidt & Schachter, 2014).

Other treatment approaches are available if medications do not adequately resolve seizures. One option is the vagal nerve stimulator. This small device is implanted under the skin within the chest and stimulates the vagal nerve at a steady cycle or if activated by a magnet swiped externally over the device (Thomas & Jobst, 2015). Approximately 30-35% of those using the stimulator achieve greater than 50% seizure reduction, and another third have some benefit with seizure frequency reduced 20-50%; only 1% achieve complete control (Al Omari et al., 2017).

Implantation of a Responsive Neuostimulation System (RNS) is an option for adults with refractory focal seizures. The RNS is a pre-programmed device implanted within the skull, with leads connected to electrodes inserted over or into the seizure focus. If the device records the onset of a seizure, it delivers electrical pulses to interrupt the seizure. Outcomes for seizure control are similar to those reported with the Vagus Nerve Stimulator (VNS) (Carrette, Boon, Sprengers, Raedt, & Vonck, 2015).

Surgery

Brain surgery is considered when seizures (most commonly, focal) are not controlled after several trials of appropriate antiseizure medications, and either pose a significant safety hazard or substantially impair independent living, school performance, work capacities, or social activities. Some individuals and their families choose to accept the discomfort and risks of the surgical procedure and the possibility of minor memory and cognitive deficits for possible elimination or reduction in seizures. The outcome in temporal lobe surgery for those with hippocampal sclerosis is 60-70% seizure free, 20-25% with greater than 85% seizure reduction, and 10-15% with no worthwhile improvement, measured one year after the operation (Devinsky, 2008).

With laser ablation, outcome data are newer, so long-term results are lacking. However, a lower surgical risk is expected, and follow-up data at one year indicate about 50% of patients become seizure free (Prince, Hakimian, Ko, Ojemann, & Miller, 2017). A major benefit of laser ablation is that it is non-invasive, requires a short amount of time, and can be attempted again. Consequently, its use is increasing.

Functional and Psychosocial Aspects

Functional Issues

Unless seizures are due to stroke or other acquired brain impairment, individuals with epilepsy generally are fully independent in eating, walking, personal hygiene, and dressing. At times, adverse effects of antiseizure medication may impair the individual's physical and intellectual functioning. Even low-grade toxicity can produce awkwardness of gait, coordination problems, and eye-focusing difficulties. Other adverse effects include problems in physical functioning and cognitive issues, such as memory and attention span. These effects may improve with alteration in the drug regimen. While independent living is possible for most people with the condition, driving is prohibited for people with uncontrolled epilepsy (Fraser et al., 2011b; Wiebe, 2012).

Psychosocial Issues

The psychosocial issues that accompany epilepsy are considered a significant source of disease burden and co-morbidity (Schmidt & Schachter, 2014). Individuals with epilepsy may have specific emotional problems that occur from having a seizure disorder. There are three prominent features of adjustment that persons with epilepsy encounter:

1. Epileptic seizures are episodic, where the person is functioning normally one minute and not the next. The time, place, and circumstances are often unknown and unpredictable; the individual has to live with a great degree of ambiguity, fear, and anxiety.

2. The epileptic seizure itself is often an alien, unusual, and frightening spectacle to observers. Bystanders may not know how to safely respond to a person during a seizure.

3. Not only does the individual usually lose control during the seizure, but he or she also does not have control of the initiation of the seizure. All societies desire and respect predictability and regularity. This is particularly true in the United States, a society that stresses self-control and responsibility.

Psychological adjustment in epilepsy involves multi-etiological considerations (Fraser et al., 2011a). Neurological concerns include seizure severity and frequency, duration of epilepsy, and neuropsychological impairment. Psychosocial considerations involve parenting style, available social support, vocational/educational functioning, and perceived stigma. Adolescents with epilepsy are particularly at risk of poor mental health and associated suicidality.

Anxiety and particularly depression are common in adult epilepsy and significantly affect quality of life and mortality (suicide rates are three times that observed in the general population) (Johnson, Jones, Seidenberg, & Hermann, 2004; Mula, 2017). Research conducted by de Souza and Salgado (2006) indicated that depression was diagnosed in 41% of women with epilepsy and 22% of men with this disability. Depression has been found to strongly predict both early drop-out from epilepsy-specific vocational rehabilitation programming, as well as poor vocational rehabilitation outcomes (i.e., competitive job placement), more than seizure severity (Sung, Muller, Jones, & Chan, 2014).

The Centers for Disease Control and Prevention promotes a public health agenda related to epilepsy with an emphasis on self-management and self-determination in clinical and community care. Self-management programs are patient education programs that emphasize patients as active participants in treatment. Daily management of the illness is the responsibility of the patient, as opposed to medical providers. Wellness management skills become a focus of intervention.

The Managing Epilepsy Well Network, comprised of eight research centers across the United States has developed several evidence-based programs aimed at epilepsy self-management and depression (Helmers et al., 2017). Significant results were seen in epilepsy self-management, sleep quality, self-efficacy, and social support (DiIorio et al., 2009a, 2009b). Project UPLIFT is a mindfulness-based group telephone intervention and significant results have been reported in terms of both depression treatment and prevention of depression onset (Thompson et al., 2015). PACES is a consumer-driven group intervention that has been shown to improve depression, quality of life, self-efficacy, and self-management (Fraser et al., 2015). Self-management interventions appear to hold promise in their ability to improve social and emotional functioning, health maintenance, and quality of life. Involving the client in the identification of self-management needs should be emphasized (Johnson et al., 2012).

Vocational Limitations and Rehabilitation Potential

Seizure Status

A review of functional seizure-related considerations is necessary when determining employment potential. For those who do not achieve seizure control, employability is most affected by seizure type, related symptoms, duration, frequency, and pattern of occurrence. For example, a person can have generalized tonic-clonic seizures on a weekly basis, but have them nocturnally (at night) in a way that does not affect employment, as long as driving and other hazardous activities are avoided.

Neuropsychological and Psychosocial Assessment

Within epilepsy treatment centers, neuropsychological assessment is used to evaluate for vocational and rehabilitative purposes in addition to informing medical and surgical decisions. With regard to the former, test results can inform the job development and placement process. Most commonly, an evaluation includes measures of general intellectual ability and psychological functioning, language, auditory processing, visuospatial perception/reasoning/organization, attention, motor speed, problem-solving/fluency/cognitive flexibility, and learning and memory. Common cognitive concerns include attentional issues, speed of mental processing, cognitive flexibility, memory and learning, and executive functioning.

Although neuropsychological evaluation attracts criticism in terms of its ecological validity, older studies have shown a connection between scores and employment status. Batzel, Dodrill, and Fraser (1980) established that a 16-test battery, which included the Washington Psychosocial Seizure Inventory, differentiated well between the unemployed (64% of test scores outside normal limits), the underemployed (53% of the battery outside normal limits), and the employed (only 22% of scores outside normal limits). When possible, testing should be customized to specific job goal demands (e.g., aspects of memory, problem solving, speed of information processing, motor functioning language), in which case the rehabilitation counselor can effectively serve a client by providing advance referral questions as well as a job analysis and vocational information for the neuropsychologist to consider during evaluation.

Vocational Evaluation and Work History Assessment

The rehabilitation counselor carefully reviews employment history when available and determines reasons for any job changes or terminations. At times, the individual had adequate abilities, but lost employment due to discrimination because of seizure occurrences at work. Conversely, some clients identify seizures as the reason for job termination when difficulties at work were more related to lack of abilities or interpersonal functioning. For some clients with epilepsy and associated brain impairment, on-the-job training (OJT) and supported employment are more effective avenues to placement than formal academic or technical training. On-the-job training can be effective for people who have had negative experiences in the school environment, and can be a more efficient access route to placement.

Considerations for the Rehabilitation Counselor

The rehabilitation counselor carefully reviews prior job activities and determines any needed job accommodations or changes. It is important not only to address the client's strengths and limitations, but also suitable employment options that will provide a viable and safe work environment consistent with the client's interests. Each client must be evaluated individually, with job skills and experience carefully assessed. Assets and limitations of clients vary widely. Frequently occurring absence seizures can pose more problems than well-controlled tonic-clonic seizures. The counselor should consider these crucial questions concerning seizure status (Fraser et al., 2011a, 2011b):

- What type of seizures and specific symptoms does the client have? What is the seizure activity during and after the seizure? If there is a loss of consciousness, how much time is involved?
- How well controlled are the seizures? If the client has active seizures, how frequently and when do they occur?
- Does the client have a warning or aura before a seizure? How consistent are the warnings and how much time do they provide the client?
- Are there certain precipitants (e.g., flickering lights, stress, fatigue, substance use) to seizure events?
- Is the client on the correct type or level of medication for the seizure type? Is there consistent medication compliance, as 29-58% are not compliant (Bano & Numanb, 2016)? Does the client complain of side effects from medication? How specialized was the medical evaluation? Did a general practitioner, neurologist, or epileptologist (neurologist specializing in epilepsy) perform the evaluation?
- When was the last medical evaluation?
- What is involved in the recovery period following a seizure? What is a reasonable time in which a client can return to work?
- Does the client have any other physical, mental, or sensory disabilities? If so, have they been evaluated in the area of disability (e.g., cognitive concerns requiring neuropsychological evaluation)? These issues can be more impairing than the seizures.

The above information is helpful in establishing daily functional capacities. Motor performance can be slowed, primarily in cases involving repeated severe seizure activity over time, but also as a result of side effects or toxicity from medication and other acquired brain impairment. For people with epilepsy, ability to drive is often affected. In most states, a specific seizure-free period must occur. If driving is not possible, access to public transportation is crucial.

When beginning vocational rehabilitation services, the counselor should carefully evaluate the client's financial needs. Those on federal subsidy, such as Supplementary Security Income (SSI) or Social Security Disability Income (SSDI), may need to seek part-time work instead of full time work to avoid jeopardizing their benefits.

Job Development and Placement

Service Methodology

Interpretation of assessment data and individual counseling is helpful. The philosophy of the Epilepsy Foundation vocational programs is that of shared responsibility between employment services staff and clients. The philosophical emphasis is on personal empowerment and independence.

Most clients benefit from job-seeking skills training provided within a job club format. The job club setting provides emotional support and encouragement in addition to teaching basic skills and ongoing organization of job search activities. Reinforcing information from individual counseling sessions within the group setting helps assure that clients retain information (Miller & Rollnick, 2013).

Disclosure and Accommodation

The issue of whether to disclose epilepsy to a potential employer is a topic for discussion within the job club setting. Although an individual may have a seizure condition that does not affect job performance, many clients with epilepsy prefer to disclose their condition to prospective employers. Job seekers with seizure conditions have a responsibility to consider various work-related factors. These include type of seizure, frequency and times of occurrence, as well as risks associated with specific job duties. A related issue is whether the person experiences an aura or warning before a seizure occurs. For some with no significant seizure or safety issues in the workplace, disclosure may not be a concern (Bishop, 2004).

People with seizures that will occur during the workday need to discuss their epilepsy with prospective employers. Some individuals have decided not to disclose their seizure condition on the job application but discuss it during the interview process. This enables them to describe their skills and aptitudes in relation to the job before mentioning their seizure status. Others decide to disclose epilepsy immediately upon receipt of a job offer, or after being hired or being on the job. There is no one strategy that is appropriate for all (Fraser et al., 2011b). The ADA Amendments Act of 2012 indicates that employers cannot discriminate because of a person's epilepsy, and will need to consider reasonable accommodation. If the seizure disorder does not affect job performance, the job seeker can choose not to disclose.

Applicants should be capable of discussing their seizure conditions clearly, comfortably, and succinctly, in terms that are understood by the layperson, keeping the information brief and job-related. For example, people who have partial complex seizures may describe periods lasting a few seconds in which they may look distracted. Following the seizure, they are able to resume work quickly. A job seeker with a seizure condition needs to practice disclosure (using a disclosure script) to present information comfortably and clearly to prospective employers, including specific accommodations as needed. A successful placement program includes active job development and a job bank from interested companies with integration of employers on an advisory board.

Interacting with Employers

Information can be presented to the employer to affect positive hiring (Fraser et al., 2011a; Miller & Rollnick, 2013; Sung, Lin, Connor, & Chan, 2017). The most valued information for the employer is the client's suitability for a job. The following considerations can guide the vocational counselor and prospective job candidate.

Work and Job Performance

With today's safety standards, it is less common that machinery will require special modifications for people with epilepsy. Plastic guards on hazardous machinery or rubber matting on a concrete floor are examples of inexpensive jobsite modifications. In other cases, assigning driving tasks to a different worker produces simple job restructuring. Both jobsite modifications and job restructuring are examples of reasonable accommodations. Most studies suggest attendance and performance records for those with epilepsy are equal to or better than the general working population (McLellan, 1987; Sung et al., 2014).

Accident Rates

Although research in this realm has been sparse, Risch (1968) demonstrated the actual time lost due to seizures was approximately one hour for every 1,000 hours worked for individuals with active seizure conditions. According to research completed by Sands (1961), when comparing workers' compensation cases over a 13-year period in New York, accidents caused by sneezing or coughing on the job were twice as frequent as those related to seizure occurrences. More recently, with control groups or comparison groups, the concern for accidents and workplace safety issues for workers with epilepsy has been determined to be an insignificant issue (Cornaggio, Beghi, Moltrasio, & Beghi, 2006; Téllez-Zenteno, Hunter, & Wiebe, 2007).

Insurance Rates

Hiring a person with epilepsy does not increase industrial insurance rates. These rates are linked to hazards of specific occupational classifications. Health insurance providers generally link rates to age and gender in larger companies, while among smaller companies the providers usually pool claim experiences and no one employer is penalized. State second injury funds generally cover injury cost for individuals with pre-existing conditions. People with epilepsy generally refrain from drinking alcohol or using illegal drugs since these aggravate their conditions. Thus, they are often safer on the job than typical employees.

Predictors of Successful Placement

Factors that influence successful vocational rehabilitation can be considered across different categories: demographic, neuropsychological, and psychosocial. The Epilepsy Foundation has found that individuals with less than one seizure per month, 12 years of education, no additional disabilities, and the capacity to drive, are more successful. Other factors associated with employment outcome include the recency and extent of substantial employment (months employed pre-program) before program entry, previous salary earned, and compliance with an anticonvulsant medicine regimen.

Case Study

Rachelle is a 42-year-old female who was forced to leave her job as a retail sales representative due to focal unaware and generalized tonic-clonic seizures. Additionally, she has had two cases of continuing generalized tonic-clonic seizuring requiring hospitalization for stabilization. Her treatment is provided by a neurologist; she is taking two medications. Rachelle describes some difficulties with balance and appropriate word-finding. Presently, she is living with a roommate, but has no income subsidy other than food stamps and she needs financial assistance. Rachelle is a high school graduate with some college and semi-skilled to low level-skilled retail sales work activity. She wants to work, but is unsure as to a viable goal(s) or her functional capacity. She was referred by the hospital vocational rehabilitation unit to the local state vocational rehabilitation office (DVR) for establishing eligibility and service funding.

Questions

1. What would be helpful to know about Rachelle's seizure type? Is there a particular area of interest about her seizure descriptions and severity?
2. What would be helpful to know about the neurologist who is treating her?
3. What might be possible effective seizure treatment if medications continue to be non-effective?
4. What services would be initially requested from DVR, particularly in relation to the continued nature of her extended tonic-clonic seizures and issues with word-finding?
5. What might be the next likely step after the initial evaluations?
6. Given Rachelle's seizure status and income needs, what other financial resources might be pursued? How would receipt of these resources affect her planning a job goal?
7. In planning for her work return, what other supportive resources might be considered?

References

Al Omari, A. I., Alzoubi, F. Q., Alsalem, M. M., Aburahma, S. K., Mardini, D. T., & Castellanos, P. F. (2017). The vagal nerve stimulation outcome and laryngeal effect: Otolaryngologists roles and perspective. *American Journal of Otolaryngology, 38*, 408-413.

Bano, S., & Numanb, A. (2016). Factors influencing antiepileptic drug non-compliance in epileptic patients of Pakistan. *Pakistan Journal of Neurological Sciences, 11*(1), Article 5.

Batzel, L. W., Dodrill, C. B., & Fraser, R. T. (1980). Further validation of the WPSI Vocational Scale: Comparisons with other correlates of employment in epilepsy. *Epilepsia, 21*, 35-42.

Bishop, M. (2004). Determinants of employment status among a community-based sample of people with epilepsy: Implications for rehabilitation interventions. *Rehabilitation Counseling Bulletin, 47*(2), 112-122.

Carrette, S., Boon, P., Sprengers, M., Raedt, R., & Vonck, K. (2015). Responsive neurostimulation in epilepsy. *Expert Review of Neurotherapeutics, 15*, 1445-1454.

Cornaggia, C. M., Beghi, M., Moltrasio, L., & Beghi, E. (2006). Accidents at work among people with epilepsy. Results of a European prospective cohort study. *Seizure, 15*, 313-319.

de Souza, E. A. P., & Salgado, P. C. B. (2006). A psychosocial view of anxiety and depression in epilepsy. *Epilepsy & Behavior, 8,* 232-238.

Devinsky, O. (2008). *Epilepsy: Patient and family guide* (3rd ed.). Philadelphia, PA: F. A. Davis.

DiIorio, C., Escoffery, C., McCarty, F., Yeager, K. A., Henry, T. R., & Koganti, A. (2009a). Evaluation of WebEase: An epilepsy self-management Web site. *Health Education Research, 24*, 185-197.

DiIorio, C., Escoffery, C., Yeager, K. A., McCarty, F., Henry, T. R., & Koganti, A. (2009b). WebEase: Development of a web-based epilepsy self-management intervention. *Preventing Chronic Disease: Public Health Research, Practice, and Policy, 6*, 1-7.

Fisher, R. S., Acevedo, C., Arzimanoglou, A., Bogacz, A., Cross, J. H., Elger, C., . . . Wiebe, S. (2014). ILAE Official Report: A practical clinical definition of epilepsy. *Epilepsia, 55*, 475-482.

Fisher, R. S., Cross, J. H., D'Souza, C., French, J. A., Haut, S. R., Higurashi, N., . . . Zuberi, S. M. (2017). Instruction manual for the ILAE 2017 operational classification of seizure types. *Epilepsia, 58*, 531-542.

Fraser, R. T., Johnson, E. K., Lashley, S., Barber, J., Chaytor, N., Miller, J. W., & Caylor, L. (2015). PACES in epilepsy: Results of a self-management randomized controlled trial. *Epilepsia, 56*(8), 1264-1274.

Fraser, R. T., Johnson, E. K., Miller, J. W., Temkin, N., Barber, J., & Caylor, L. (2011a). Managing epilepsy well: Self-management needs assessment. *Epilepsy & Behavior, 20*, 291-298.

Fraser, R. T., Miller, J. W., & Johnson, E. K. (2011b). Epilepsy. In S. R. Flanagan, H. H. Zaretsky, & A. Moroz (Eds.), *Medical aspects of disability: A handbook for the rehabilitation professional* (4th ed., pp. 177-194). New York, NY: Springer.

Helmers, S., Kobau, R., Sajatovic, M., Jobst, B., Privitera, M., Devinsky, O., . . Hovath, K. J. (2017). Self-management in epilepsy - Why and how you should incorporate self-management into your practice. *Epilepsy & Behavior, 68*, 220-224.

Johnson, E. K., Fraser, R. T., Miller, J. W., Temkin, N., Barber, J., & Caylor, L. (2012). A comparison of self-management needs: Provider and patient perspectives. *Epilepsy and Behavior, 25*, 150-155.

Johnson, E. K., Jones, J. E., Seidenberg, M., & Hermann, B. P. (2004). The relative impact of anxiety, depression, and clinical seizure features on health-related quality of life in epilepsy. *Epilepsia, 45*, 544-550.

McLellan, D. L. (1987). Epilepsy and employment. *Journal of Social and Occupational Medicine, 3*, 94-99.

Miller, L., & Rollnick, S. (2013). *Motivational interviewing: Helping people change* (3rd ed.). New York, NY: Guilford.

Mula, M. (2017). Depression in epilepsy. *Current Opinion in Neurology, 30*, 180-186.

National Association of Epilepsy Centers. (2010). Guidelines for essential services, personnel, and facilities in epilepsy centers. Minneapolis, MN: Author.

Prince E., Hakimian S., Ko A. L., Ojemann J. G., & Miller J. W. (2017). Laser interstitial thermal therapy for epilepsy. *Current Neurology and Neuroscience Reports, 17*, 63-72.

Risch, F. (1968). We lost every game. . . but. *Rehabilitation Record, 9*, 16-18.

Sands, H. (1961). Report of a study undertaken for the Committee on Neurological Disorders in Industry. *Epilepsy News, 7*(abstract), 1.

Schmidt, D., & Schachter, S. C. (2014). Drug treatment of epilepsy in adults. *British Medical Journal, 348*, g254.

Sung, C., Lin, C. C., Connor, A., & Chan, F. (2017). Disclose or not? Effect of impression management tactics on hireability of persons with epilepsy. *Epilepsia, 58*, 128-136.

Sung, C., Muller, V., Jones, J. E., & Chan, F. (2014). Vocational rehabilitation service patterns and employment outcomes of people with epilepsy. *Epilepsy Research, 108*, 1469-1479.

Téllez-Zenteno, J., Hunter, G., & Wiebe, S. (2008). Injuries in people with self-reported epilepsy. *Epilepsia, 49*, 954-961.

Thomas, G. P., & Jobst, B. C. (2015). Critical review of the responsive neurostimulator system for epilepsy. *Medical Devices: Evidence and Research, 8*, 405-411.

Thompson, N. J., Patel, A., Selwa, L., Stoll, S., Begley, C. E., Johnson, E. K., . . . Fraser, R. T. (2015). The efficacy of Project UPLIFT for prevention: Distance delivery of mindfulness-based depression prevention. *Journal of Clinical and Consulting Psychology, 83*, 304-313.

Wiebe, S. (2012). The epilepsies. In L. Goldman & A. I. Schafer (Eds.), *Goldman's Cecil medicine* (24th ed., pp. 2283-2294). New York, NY: Elsevier Saunders.

Xu, T., Yu, X., Ou, S., Liu, X., Yuan, J., Huang, H., . . . Yang, J. (2017). Risk factors for post-traumatic epilepsy: A systematic review and meta-analysis. *Epilepsy & Behavior, 67*, 1-6.

About the Authors

Erica K. Johnson, PhD, CRC, FAES, is a rehabilitation psychologist and research consultant at the University of Washington Health Promotion Research Center in Seattle. Also, Dr. Johnson is a practitioner and researcher in the areas of vocational rehabilitation counseling, rehabilitation and neuropsychology, and neurological disabilities, and is a Fellow of the American Epilepsy Society.

Robert T. Fraser, PhD, CRC, is Professor within the University of Washington, Department of Neurology, a joint appointment with Neurological Surgery and Rehabilitation Medicine in Seattle. Dr. Fraser began the Vocational Services Unit of the University of Washington Regional Epilepsy Center in 1976, which has expanded to provide vocational services for the Department of Neurology.

John W. Miller, MD, PhD, is Professor of Neurology and Neurological Surgery at the University of Washington. He is Director of the University of Washington Regional Epilepsy Center at Harborview Medical Center in Seattle. Previously, Dr. Miller was Director of the Washington University Comprehensive Epilepsy Center in St. Louis, Missouri.

Chapter 15

NEUROLOGICAL DISABILITIES

David B. Peterson, PhD, CRC, NCC, LCP
Thomas VanVleet, PhD, LCP

Introduction

Neurology is a specialty of medicine concerned with the study and treatment of the nervous system and related disorders. The practice of neurology requires specialized knowledge of anatomy and physiology of the nervous system, and familiarity with many diseases encountered in general medicine. Neurologists may partner with other professionals, such as neuropsychologists, who are experts in evaluating brain-behavior relationships. Through a wide array of assessment techniques, neuropsychologists interpret the brain's myriad processes of thought, memory, judgment, decision-making or goal-directed behavior, and motor function (Lezak, Howieson, Bigler, & Tranel, 2012).

This chapter provides a general orientation and overview of a very complex topic. The complexities of the neurological system challenge the expertise of the most experienced health professionals. Thus, consultation with neurologists, neuropsychologists, or other related health professionals is recommended. While there are many aspects of brain functioning that are not well understood, considerable advances have occurred in recent years, and there is a growing confidence among neuroscientists that "a real understanding is beginning to emerge" (Beaumont, 2008, p. 3).

This chapter familiarizes rehabilitation counselors with basic aspects of the neurological examination and frequently diagnosed neurological illnesses and conditions. It is not intended to be an all-inclusive discussion of neurology. Standard textbooks are referenced for in-depth inquiry (Greenberg, Aminoff, & Simon, 2018; Beaumont, 2008; Brust, 2018; Hauser & Josephson, 2016; Lezak et al., 2012; Ropper, Samuels, Klein, & Prasad, 2015).

Neurological Examination

Individuals with complaints suggesting disease of a neurological origin (e.g., headaches, motor weakness, pain, sensory disturbance, vertigo, difficulties in cognition and speech) seek help from their treating physicians. After a preliminary evaluation, the family practitioner may refer the patient to a neurologist for further evaluation. The neurologist attempts to determine the source of the abnormality within the nervous system and assesses possible etiology. Causes or origins of the problem may include trauma, tumor, immunological response, stroke, inherited dysfunction, or any of a great number of other disease processes. Based on the evaluation, history of the illness, and specialized testing, the neurologist establishes a specific diagnosis (Biller, Gruener, & Brazis, 2017; Papadakis, McPhee, & Rabow, 2017).

The neurologist begins the examination by obtaining a thorough medical history. A neurological evaluation is made that includes a systematic examination of mental status, general cognitive abilities (e.g., orientation, memory), cranial nerves, gait and station, cerebellum, and motor and sensory function. Based upon the data, the neurologist may order laboratory tests, imaging procedures, or neuropsychological testing.

Mental Status

The mental status examination evaluates the patient's orientation (e.g., time, place), short-term memory, reasoning, comprehension and communication, and problem solving ability. It reveals gross abnormalities of mental functioning, including difficulties in speech. When dysfunction exists, return to typical functioning is dependent on the cause or course of the dysfunction and may improve, worsen, or remain unchanged over time. During acute, subacute, and post-acute recovery, neuropsychological testing is used to further monitor treatment progress; once the condition is stable, the physician uses additional testing to estimate the individual's functional capacity (Lezak et al., 2012).

Cranial Nerves

Examination of cranial nerves involves evaluation of the nerves that emerge directly from the brain, not the spinal cord, and largely attend the areas of the head and neck, including sense of smell, vision, eye movement, face movement, and sensation. Of particular importance are visual disturbances and problems in the motoric aspects of speech (dysarthria).

A frequently encountered neurological finding from an examination of the eyes is homonymous hemianopia. In this condition, a portion of the visual field becomes blind (i.e., nasal half of the field of vision of one eye and temporal half of the other or right-sided or left-sided blindness of the corresponding sides in both eyes). In either situation, there is blindness in one half of each eye with vision unaffected in the other half of each eye (Brust, 2018). This condition results most often from damage to the occipital cortex. With abnormalities of the facial nerve, there are disturbances of facial movements that may cause difficulties in articulation (e.g., poor pronunciation or slurred speech) and produce a functional limitation in speech (dysarthria).

Gait and Station

Disorders of gait and station include disturbances of walking, such as ataxia or gross incoordination of muscle movements, spasticity, or steppage gait (i.e., high-stepping gait so that the toe clears the ground). Gait disturbance causes limitations in the ability to walk, particularly for long distances. If a significant gait disturbance is present, vocational rehabilitation needs to be directed toward work involving limited ambulation (e.g., sedentary work).

Cerebellar Function

The cerebellum controls movement and coordination, and affects cognition (Rapoport, Van Reekum, & Mayberg, 2000). Damage to the cerebellum may manifest as jerky movements, intention tremors (tremors only during deliberate movement), and loss of balance and proprioception (position sense), especially with the eyes closed (Beaumont, 2008). Damage to the posterior cerebellum can result in impairment of executive functions such as planning, set-shifting, verbal fluency, abstract reasoning, and working memory; difficulties with spatial cognition including visual-spatial organization and memory; personality change with blunting of affect or disinhibited and inappropriate behavior; and language deficits including agrammatism and dysprosodia (Schmahmann & Sherman, 1998)

Motor and Sensory Function

During the motor and sensory function evaluation, the neurologist systematically tests reflexes and muscle tone in each group of muscles. For example, the neurologist often uses a nylon monofilament or tuning fork to examine sensory responses. Proprioception, or the ability to tell where one part of the body is in relation to the rest of the body (e.g., my hand is resting on the arm of a chair to the right of my body), is also queried.

The motor system consists of upper motor neurons (nerve connections from the central nervous system to the spinal cord) and lower motor neurons (nerve connections from the spinal cord to muscle fibers in the periphery). Upper motor neuron dysfunction occurs in illnesses involving the cortex and brain stem. This often produces abnormalities involving at least one limb or one-half of the body. There is a characteristic loss of strength, increase in reflexes (hyperreflexia), and spasticity associated with these disorders (Greenberg et al., 2018).

Lower motor neuron diseases involve the nerve roots, peripheral nerves, or both. They cause a smaller area of deficit that affects a specific group of muscles, resulting in abnormal muscle functioning. Characteristically, there is muscle weakness, lack of muscular tone (hypotonicity), and loss of reflexes (areflexia). The sensory system has central and peripheral nervous system components. In disease within the peripheral nervous system, a small area of the skin may show decreased sensation corresponding with abnormality of the specific nerve or nerve root supplying that skin area (Brust, 2018).

Electrophysiology

Electroencephalogram (EEG)

Neurologists and other physicians may request an electrophysiological test called the electroencephalogram (EEG). An EEG involves the use of electrodes placed on the scalp to provide amplification and summation of regional brain activity with exceptional temporal precision. This information is used to explore suspected pathological processes, particularly seizure disorders. In recent years, neuroscientists and neurologists have used a similar approach (i.e., collecting information through the scalp) to record magnetic fields produced by electrical currents occurring naturally in the brain, using very sensitive magnetometers. This high resolution functional neuroimaging method is called magnetoencephalography (MEG), and provides better spatial resolution than conventional EEG.

Electromyography (EMG)

Another physiological test employed in neurology is electromyography (EMG), which involves the insertion of small needles into various muscles to amplify the electrical activity inherent in those muscles. EMG examination reveals abnormalities suggestive of muscle or nerve disease. This procedure aids in diagnosis and location of potential disturbances of a particular nerve, nerve root (radiculopathy), or muscle (myopathy). A nerve conduction study is a test that delivers small electric shocks via electrodes placed on the skin. Electrical stimulation is then followed as it travels along the nerve. Motor and sensory nerve fibers are tested, useful for identifying mononeuropathy (e.g., carpal tunnel syndrome) and peripheral neuropathy.

Neuroimaging Techniques

Advances in neuroimaging technology have allowed physicians to construct detailed visualizations of brain structures and vasculature, blood flow and related metabolic activity, and basic neurochemical composition. Neuropsychological assessments are used in combination with these technologies to help identify impairment and residual functioning.

Computerized Tomography (CT)

Cross-sectional images of the brain and spinal cord are captured via neuroimaging techniques such as computerized tomography (CT) or computerized axial tomography (CAT) scans. These scans employ x-rays directed from different angles through the brain to the x-ray film on the other side. Many images are combined by computational methods to provide a gross overview of brain areas. Relatively inexpensive and widely available, it has limited ability to image abnormalities, and has lower resolution relative to other methods (e.g., magnetic resonance imaging), but tends to be a first-line of inquiry before more advanced and expensive imaging techniques (Kasper et al., 2015).

Magnetic Resonance Imaging (MRI)

An MRI creates a more precise spatial image of the brain by using a powerful magnetic field in which radio waves are used to align the nuclear magnetization of hydrogen atoms. This process allows for greater contrast between soft tissues of the body than CT scans to better detect lesions following a stroke or small areas of damage due to hypertension. MRI provides a high resolution, three-dimensional image of the brain. Recent advances in MRI technology enable mapping of the connections between brain areas (white matter) and is referred to as diffusion tensor imaging (DTI).

Neurological Disabilities

Functional MRI (fMRI)

Functional MRI (fMRI) goes a step beyond showing clear structures of the brain to illustrating brain function. fMRI detects neuronal activity through the haemodynamic response, which is associated with the concentration of oxygen in the blood. fMRI is used to determine which brain areas are most active during a particular cognitive operation by measuring the Blood Oxygenation Level Dependent (BOLD) response of small areas of brain segmented into voxels. Images taken seconds apart can suggest dynamic brain function in association with different cognitive processes. Brain images taken during various stages of a cognitive process are later compared to suggest areas of the brain associated with specific tasks or functions.

Recent advances in fMRI have led to the examination of patterns of connectivity between related brain areas or brain networks, and can be acquired while the patient is resting in the MRI scanner (i.e., resting state functional connectivity) (Grefkes & Fink, 2011). By examining the firing rate or frequency, distant brain areas may be observed working together in unison while the patient performs a particular cognitive or motor operation.

Positron Emission Tomography (PET)

Positron emission tomography scans an image brain function, but at a much slower pace than the fMRI. This technique uses a positron-emitting radionuclide (tracer) to detect regions of greater activity. Further, PET scans may be employed to determine the relative distribution of neurotransmitters (chemical messengers) in the brain.

Abnormalities of the Brain

Clinical data suggest specific behaviors associated with areas of the brain and understanding of these relationships is evolving with advances in neuroscience (Beaumont, 2008; Lezak et al., 2012). Historically, there has been an inherent difficulty in building a sound scientific basis in this area of inquiry. Lesions could not ethically be introduced into the human brain; researchers have to make the best use of the clinical data available to them in the normal course of healthcare.

Recent advances in functional neuroimaging have allowed neuroscientists to test hypotheses in the healthy brain regarding the role of discreet function areas and their associated networks across cognitive domains. Neuroscientists have also begun to use a virtual lesion technique known as Transcranial Magnetic Stimulation (TMS), whereby an innocuous magnetic field is applied to the scalp temporarily disrupting function of the underlying brain area. A related approach, Transcranial Direct Current Stimulation (TDCS), applies a current across two points of contact on the skull (anodal and cathodal poles), exciting and activating brain areas to examine their functional contributions.

Historically, clinical cases and data from advanced neuroscientific methods have provided converging evidence to clarify the function of many brain areas. Yet, most cognitive operations are not performed by any single area of the brain. While elementary operations forming the basis of cognition may be localized to discrete brain areas, many such local operations are involved in any given cognitive task. Thus, a set of distributed brain areas must be evaluated in the performance of even simple cognitive tasks (Brust, 2018). Strict structure to function attributions in the brain are overly simplistic, as the brain operates as a distributed functional network (i.e., distant brain areas cooperate by firing in and out of phase to accomplish distinct cognitive and motor operations). However, generalities regarding functions ascribed to distinct brain areas, as described below, are a good introduction to some aspects of brain function.

Subcortical Structures

Much of what is known about deep subcortical brain function was learned from animal research models. Clinical studies of humans with damage to deep subcortical structures may be difficult, particularly when major functional impairments of consciousness and/or basic drives are typically present. Damage to the brainstem, mesencephalon, and the diencephalon can be catastrophic. A notable exception is research examining the role of the thalamus and basal ganglia; together with frontal and parietal cortex, these areas form a number of interconnected cortical-subcortical circuits involved in such diverse cognitive operations as response selection, learning, attention, and routine motor operations.

Frontal Lobes

Functioning associated with the frontal lobes includes a broad variety of behaviors with a central function related to the management of goal-directed behavior (i.e., executive functions). The frontal lobes are associated with the ability to think abstractly; the ability to form and change mental sets; deconstruct and synthesize the elements of an object or idea; and plan, monitor, and correct on-going goal-directed behaviors. These functions are essential to independent living and work; damage to the frontal lobes can impair these abilities with dramatic consequences. Severe frontal lobe damage can cause dull emotional affect and lack of initiative and spontaneity. Other frontal lobe-related abnormalities include poor self-monitoring (e.g., inattention to personal hygiene) and socially inappropriate and impulsive behavior. These symptoms have been associated with a frontal lobe syndrome that is quite debilitating and may require substantial and long-term care (Kasper et al., 2015).

Four frontal lobe sections are associated with different functional limitations due to injury, beginning from the top of the head and moving down toward the eye orbits. These are the motor and pre-motor cortex, prefrontal cortex, Broca's area, and orbital cortex. Damage to the motor cortex may result in loss of voluntary control over specific parts of the body and possibly fine-motor control (e.g., movements of the hands, fingers, face). Lesions in the pre-motor cortex result in difficulty with coordinating gross body reflexes and movements, verbal and design fluency, and spelling. Lesions in the prefrontal cortex affect planning and programming sequences of behavior, problem-solving, perceptual judgment, memory, and attention (Beaumont, 2008).

Located in the left frontal lobe, Broca's area, when damaged, may result in impairment of expressive communication. Finally, the orbital cortex region of the frontal lobes relates to aspects of personality and social behavior. For example, motor vehicle accidents causing bilateral damage to the orbital cortex results in dramatic personality changes, problems with anger management, and inappropriate social behavior.

Parietal Lobes

Abnormalities of the parietal lobes result in a wide range of symptoms, from misperception of sensory events, loss of or deficits related to attention, and problems with navigation or mapping of the body in relation to the environment. Lesions in the parietal lobes can result in contralateral (side opposite a lesion) or ipsilateral (same-side) loss or alteration of sensation for parts of the body. The loss or change may be total or may only involve a single feature of sensation, such as touch, pressure, temperature, or pain. In addition to sensations perceived by the skin, damage to the parietal lobes may affect ability to perceive information about body position and movement. Parietal lesions cause apraxia (loss of intentional movement) (Beaumont, 2008; Ropper et al., 2014).

Diseases of the left parietal lobe produce problems with language functions, including reading (dyslexia) and writing (alexia), as well as difficulty with recognizing objects visually and through the sense of touch (visual or tactile agnosia). Diseases of the right parietal lobe cause difficulty with mathematical calculations (acalculia), as spatial representation is helpful in solving more complex mathematical problems.

Spatial neglect is a parietal lobe condition associated with failure to pay attention to a particular area of space, typically the half of space opposite the parietal lesion. Most often persistent symptoms of neglect occur following damage to the right parietal lobe. Patients who have spatial neglect may present with scratching and bruising on the side of the body opposite the lesion due to bumping into things on that side. They may shave only one side of the face or forget to completely dress one side of the body.

Bilateral damage to the parietal lobes can result in functional blindness, in which individuals can only perceive one object at a time. This condition, known as Balint's syndrome, is rare but has been important in the examination of higher-order vision and attention.

Temporal Lobes

Damage to the temporal lobes impact many aspects of auditory perception and/or higher-order visual perception; traumatic brain injuries that lead to skull fracture and associated damage in the temporal region cause hearing loss or deafness. The temporal lobes impact some aspects of visual perception. Reception and comprehension of language is associated with Wernicke's area, in the left hemisphere, at the junction of the temporal, parietal, and occipital lobes. Damage to Wernicke's area produces receptive or Wernicke's aphasia, compromising the ability to receive and comprehend written and spoken language.

Lesions in the right temporal lobe cause difficulty with musical ability. The temporal lobes also influence affective, emotional, and personal experience, having close physical connections with the limbic system. Damage to these structures produce personality changes, psychosis, and changes in sexual behavior (Beaumont, 2008).

The temporal lobes, along with some subcortical structures, are involved in encoding and retrieving long-term memory. Typically, lesions in the left temporal lobe impact verbal memory, while lesions in the right temporal lobe impact spatial memory. Korsakoff's disease and Wernicke-Korsakoff syndrome are bilateral diseases of the temporal lobes that create difficulty with retaining new information, or cause anterograde amnesia. Korsakoff's disease is caused by thiamine deficiency often brought about by chronic alcoholism or infection. Wernicke-Korsakoff syndrome is caused by a diffuse disease of the brain called Wernicke's encephalopathy (Beaumont, 2008).

Occipital Lobes

Abnormalities of the occipital lobes affect elementary aspects of visual sensation and perception. Homonymous hemianopsia, visual distortions, and blindness result from lesions in either occipital lobe. Disease of both lobes cause cortical blindness where the pupils remain reactive, but the individual cannot see or react to visual stimuli, called Anton's syndrome, which includes a lack of awareness of the deficit. Smaller areas of damage cause gaps in vision (scotomas). Sometimes, the entire visual field is affected except for the very center or macular region of vision (Beaumont, 2008; Lezak et al., 2012).

Disorders of the Central Nervous System

Disorders of the central nervous system (CNS) are diverse and complex. Disorders reviewed elsewhere is this text include traumatic brain injury, spinal cord injury, multiple sclerosis, intellectual disability, cerebral palsy, and epilepsy. A few remaining disorders of the central nervous system are reviewed here, including dementias, aphasias, Parkinson's disease, Huntington's disease, and motor neuron disease.

Dementias

Dementias involve the decline of general cognitive ability, particularly memory and executive function typically in older adulthood. They can be degenerative or nondegenerative.

Nondegenerative Dementias

Nondegenerative dementias have a number of causes, including infection, chronic drug or alcohol abuse, cerebrovascular accidents (strokes), and autoimmune disease (e.g., lupus). Various types of infection affect the CNS. Patterns of infection include a focal inflammation site (cerebritis) or abscess, most frequently bacterial in origin. Bacterial and viral inflammations of the meninges (membranes enveloping the brain and spinal cord) cause meningitis. Meningoencephalitis, usually viral in origin, affects the brain and meninges. Most CNS infections result in residual deficits, such as personality change, sleep disturbance, decreased cognition, and seizures. When complications occur, damage to cranial nerves and brain tissue result in permanent deficits.

Hardening of the arteries (arteriosclerosis) and hypertension (high blood pressure) are disorders which predispose an individual to arterial vessel abnormalities that may result in blockage or rupture causing a cerebrovascular accident (CVA) or stroke. Functional impairment depends upon the location and size of the area affected. Depending on the type of vascular compromise, strokes can produce either focal or diffuse brain damage. Based on severity, CVAs result in loss or diminished use of one side of the body due to paralysis (hemiplegia); the majority of CVAs occur on one side of the brain (left or right). Speech disturbance often occurs with damage to the left hemisphere of the brain (see Aphasias). Even in mild cases, many individuals have loss of stamina and incoordination on the affected side (hemiparesis). Improvement after stroke occurs over three to six months. Once stabilized, individuals with CVA benefit from rehabilitation evaluation, beginning with an assessment of functional limitations and capabilities, both physical and psychological.

A variety of chemicals and drugs affect the CNS. These substances cause a multiplicity of effects and reactions. Abnormalities include cognitive and behavioral deficits, seizures, and peripheral neuropathies. Predictable effects related to drug (both legal and illegal) intoxication and idiosyncratic reactions to medication are two areas related to drug and chemical effects on the nervous system. Predictable effects are linked to drug dosage. Idiosyncratic reactions are peculiar to an individual and are unpredictable and unrelated to the amount of drug taken. Cocaine, for instance, can cause a CNS vasculitis (inflammation of the vessels) that leads to small strokes. These people generally have diffuse brain involvement, and may have decreased cognition and deteriorated intellectual functioning. Chronic alcohol abuse causes several specific neurological problems such as peripheral neuropathy, cerebellar degeneration, and alcohol-related dementia. With abstinence, improved nutrition, and rehabilitation, these are partially reversible (Ropper et al., 2014).

Degenerative Dementias

Degenerative dementias are caused by the death or reduction in the numbers of neurons essential to the CNS. Alzheimer's disease (AD) is classified within this category. The hippocampus, a structure critical to memory, is often greatly impacted by AD and is characterized by marked atrophy. Found first in the hippocampus, neurofibrillary tangles spread throughout the brain as the disease progresses. There is an early onset variant of AD occurring in 5-10% of all AD cases that affects people between ages 28 to 60 years. Individuals with Down syndrome are more susceptible to AD relative to others their age due to its relationship with chromosome 21. While there is no single cure for dementia, lifestyle changes and medication may act to slow the progression of symptoms.

Tumors

The presence of a brain tumor often denotes a poor prognosis with progressive deterioration. Brain tumors include primary tumors. Metastatic disease (cancer) comprises the largest percentage of brain tumors; primary brain tumors are less common. Generally, brain tumors grow and cause local destruction within the brain. Rate of growth is variable, at times rapid, with death ensuing after several months, or sometimes more slowly with the person living for several years. For individuals with brain tumors, attempts at continuing current employment may be appropriate, depending on the symptoms, deficits, and rate of tumor growth. Occasionally, very slow growing tumors are found in younger people. In these cases, the counselor should obtain information regarding prognosis (Kasper et al., 2015).

Aphasias

Language function can be associated with focal areas of the cortex or the connections between key functional nodes. Advances in neuroscience suggest that language functioning spreads across a large area of the cortex (Beaumont, 2008). For right-handed people, a significant portion of language functioning is in the left hemisphere. In the case of left-handed people, very few actually have right (contralateral) hemisphere dominance in language; most have the same brain functioning as right-handed people, and a smaller percentage have bilateral representation of language functioning (Carter, Hohenegger, & Satz, 1980).

Disorders of the language system are called aphasias. Classification of aphasias is "one of the most hotly contested issues in the history of neuropsychology, and there is yet no firm agreement" (Beaumont, 2008, p. 136). The most widely accepted paradigm divides aphasias into several categories. Global aphasia involves massive and severe disturbance in language functioning. Some of these also involve alexia (a specific disorder of reading) and agraphia (a specific disorder of writing).

Broca's aphasia (expressive aphasia) manifests as impaired ability to express oneself verbally. Speech may omit articles, adverbs, and adjectives, or in more extreme cases muteness occurs. Prompting with sounds or contexts assists people with less severe forms of the disorder; some may not realize their problem. Difficulties occur while language comprehension is unimpaired, where people understand what is being said and can read. Broca's area was described above as one of the language centers of the brain, located typically in the left rear frontal lobe.

Wernicke's aphasia (receptive aphasia) is characterized by a severe deficit in auditory comprehension. Impaired reading and writing often accompany it, and while most individuals are capable of expressive speech, because of the comprehension deficit that impairs self-monitoring of speech production, speech may contain substituted but related words or sounds, resulting in a word salad that is not always intelligible. Wernicke's area is located in the left temporal lobe.

With conduction aphasia, people comprehend both speech and writing and produce nearly-normal speech, but at times substitute one sound for another (phonemic paraphasia). As an example, one might substitute fable for table. Severe impairment may be noted when the person is asked to repeat a phrase that is spoken or while reading aloud. It has been hypothesized that this type of aphasia results from problems with communication between Broca's and Wernicke's areas.

The most common form of aphasia is anomic aphasia, which may exist in residual form while one recovers from other types of aphasia. The key element is difficulty with name finding, especially for nouns. Those recovering from it may substitute related words as a means of coping with the difficulty, so it may go undetected in spontaneous speech.

The last two types of aphasia reviewed here are transcortical motor and sensory aphasias. In the worst case of combined motor and sensory aphasia (which is very rare), the person cannot understand speech or read, is totally nonfluent in speech, speaks only when spoken to, and usually cannot write. In transcortical motor aphasia, most evident is the impairment of speech output. In trancortical sensory aphasia, language reception is usually severely affected, while the ability to repeat is preserved, even though little is understood of what is repeated or read (Brust, 2018).

Parkinson's Disease

Parkinson's disease (PD) is a degenerative disorder that results in the loss of neurons in subcortical structures that serve movement and certain cognitive operations such as set switching (i.e., flexibly modifying responses when a change in the rule or contingencies occur). Its major effects include loss of motor control and problems with initiation of motor operations (freezing). Symptoms involve tremor, slowness (bradykinesia) or rigidity in movement, a shuffling gait, loss of associated movements (e.g., arms moving as one walks), and loss of emotional expression (masked face). With PD, there may be specific or general psychological impairment, including difficulties with executive functioning, memory, and visual spatial skills, as well as depression. Treatment with dopaminergic drug therapy has been helpful (Brust, 2018; Pfeiffer, Wszolek, & Ebadi, 2012).

Huntington's Disease

Sometimes referred to as a subcortical dementia, Huntington's disease (HD) affects the integrity of the basal ganglia. Persons having either parent with HD have a 50% chance of inheriting the disorder. HD is a neurodegenerative disorder that begins midlife with the onset of involuntary body movements. Dysarthria, difficulty with upper limb movements, abnormal gait, and progressive loss of mental functioning occurs, including disinhibition, depression, personality change, and even schizophrenia-like symptoms. Ultimately, problems with physical functioning lead to death within 15 to 20 years. There is no cure for HD; medications are used to treat symptoms (Quarrell, 2008).

Motor Neuron Disease

Amyotrophic lateral sclerosis (ALS), also known as Lou Gehrig's disease (a famous New York Yankees' baseball player) affects the upper and lower motor neurons. It is a disease of the alpha motor neurons involving specific cells in the brain stem and spinal cord. This disease is degenerative, of unknown etiology, and rapidly progressive. There is loss of strength with hyperflexia and fasciculation (involuntary small movement of muscles). ALS is progressive and individuals eventually require wheelchairs for mobility. At times, the downhill progression is such that the person cannot eat or swallow within a year of initial onset (Papadakis et al., 2017).

Diseases of the Peripheral Nervous System

Peripheral nervous system (PNS) disease involves the nerves and nerve roots (neuropathies) and associated muscles. These diseases may be progressive or nonprogressive.

Diseases of the Muscle

Muscular Dystrophies

Muscular dystrophies are inherited or genetically determined illnesses involving a progressive weakening of muscles. Particular types are described based on the muscle groups involved; etiology is unknown. These diseases usually begin in childhood or in the teen years and are slowly progressive. Individuals with muscular dystrophy usually require sedentary work, either because of current limitations or future anticipated impairments. Because muscular dystrophy progresses, short-term goals need to be established; periodic reevaluation and modification of these goals is necessary. The more sedentary the work activity, the longer the individual will be physically able to maintain employment. Prescribed exercise is recommended as prolonged inactivity leads to worsening of the disease state.

Primary Myopathies

These are a rare group of diseases with histological abnormalities involving muscle fiber or muscle cell mitochondria. They produce mild diffuse weakness and a decrease in stamina. The abnormalities are slowly progressive, although life expectancy is not significantly affected. No specific treatment is available. Individuals with primary myopathies do best in light and sedentary types of employment.

Neuropathies

Cranial Neuropathies

The 12 cranial nerves manifest their own specific symptomatology when involved in a disease process. Abnormalities involving eye and face movements present significant barriers to employment. Cranial nerves three, four, and six control eye movements. Abnormalities of these cranial nerves cause variations of eye movement, including diplopia (double vision). Often, the physician prescribes an eye patch for this condition, leaving the person monocular as long as the patch is worn. Seventh nerve (the facial nerve) abnormalities cause difficulty moving facial muscles and closing the eyes. Individuals with this problem need protective glasses and must avoid environments where particles of dust can irritate the eyes. They may have some degree of dysarthria (difficult and defective speech). Eighth nerve or auditory nerve abnormalities are associated with hearing deficits and vertigo.

Radiculopathy

Radiculopathy refers to an abnormality of a nerve root that produces pain in the affected region of the spine. This is accompanied by limited motion of the spine, muscle spasm, and nerve root pain radiating down an extremity. Sensory and motor losses occur in the affected area. There are various causes for radiculopathy, including degenerative changes in the spine with the formation of bony osteophytes (outgrowths). A ruptured or bulging disc is a frequent cause. Pain generally is experienced below the knee in lumbar radiculopathy.

Individuals with radiculopathies may require surgery to help alleviate symptoms. Work limitations for individuals with radiculopathy frequently involve limitation to light or sedentary work. Since many sedentary jobs involve extended sitting, workers may need accommodation allowing them to alternate positioning between sitting and standing. Generally, it is beneficial to avoid either prolonged sitting or standing.

Back and neck pain are major employment problems in industrialized countries. Workers frequently have chronic back and neck pain complaints without objective findings. Often, there is an initial injury, possibly a strain, with ongoing complaints of severe pain. For rehabilitation purposes, one must distinguish between actual physical limitations and pain complaints. A thorough medication history should be obtained with particular attention to addicting or sedating drugs (Brust, 2018).

Peripheral Neuropathy

Peripheral neuropathy is a disease that can affect any of the nerves within the body. Often, peripheral neuropathy affects lower extremity nerves more than the nerves of the upper extremities. Weakness, sensory loss, and incoordination occur. There are multiple causes of peripheral neuropathy. Approximately one-third are due to systemic disease, such as diabetes. Another third of the cases are due to autoimmune inflammation. The final third have multiple causes, both inherited and degenerative.

Despite successful medical treatment, some mild residual symptoms may persist, with symptoms such as mild incoordination, weakness, diminished stamina, and decreased sensation in the extremities. These individuals require lighter types of employment that do not involve frequent use of fine coordination and manual dexterity. At the time of referral for rehabilitation, the level of dysfunction should be stable and not anticipated to change, thereby permitting the counselor to provide vocational rehabilitation services based on current limitations (Greenberg et al., 2018).

Mononeuropathy

Mononeuropathy involves injury or disease of a single nerve. This usually results from compression of a nerve in a specific area of the body (segmental mononeuropathy). The most frequently seen mononeuropathies involve the medial nerve of the wrist (carpal tunnel syndrome), ulnar nerve at the elbow (cubital tunnel syndrome), and peroneal nerve at the head of the fibula.

Carpal tunnel syndrome. This condition involves compression of the median nerve in the carpal tunnel of the wrist. It causes numbness and pain in the thumb, palm, and second through fourth fingers. The person may experience radiating pain and pain during the night. Repetitive wrist motion, sustained grip and pinch activities, continuous wrist angulation, poor posturing, repetitive vibration, and physical injury cause carpal tunnel syndrome. There is weakness in the affected hand and loss of grip strength. Individuals with carpal tunnel syndrome need to avoid frequent pronation, supination, and extension of the wrist. Repetitive activities, such as using a screwdriver for long periods of time, operating a typewriter or computer terminal, need to be modified or avoided.

Ulnar neuropathy. Individuals with ulnar neuropathy have decreased strength in the muscles of the hand. There is weakness of grasp and frequently a decreased coordination of the hand. Sensory disturbance occurs in the fourth and fifth fingers. Usually, the nerve is injured at the elbow level; the individual should avoid activities where the elbow rests on a firm surface or in which minor trauma to the elbow occurs repetitively.

Peroneal neuropathy. In the lower extremity, peroneal neuropathy causes a foot drop. The person is unable to lift the foot against gravity and walks with a peculiar gait termed a steppage gait. A brace is used to maintain a 90° angle of the foot with the ankle. Individuals with peroneal neuropathies have difficulty walking and climbing stairs; they require sedentary work.

Rehabilitation potential for persons with mononeuropathies is generally good. Functional disability is limited to one specific area of the body. These conditions are often stable and improve with treatment; they typically do not worsen over time. Yet, temporary exacerbation frequently is experienced. Rehabilitation counselors working with people who have these conditions need to consider job modification with the current employer, whenever possible (Ropper et al., 2015).

Rehabilitation Case Planning

Knowledge of the history, onset, and course of the disease process is significant in rehabilitation. To maintain employment or return a person to work, the neurological disorder must be stabilized or slowed in its progression. If an individual has had an acute episode that has run its course and reached maximum improvement, the counselor can formulate a rehabilitation plan based on the knowledge that the deficit will not deteriorate further. When an individual is under optimal medical control, but continues to have debilitating neurological symptoms, frequency and intensity of these events help determine the feasibility of providing vocational rehabilitation services (Greenberg et al., 2018).

Case Study

Ms. Nancy Smith is 48 years of age, African-American, and married. The Smith's have three children, two living at home and dependent on their parents' support, and one married and living in the same community. Mr. Smith works full time. After graduating from high school, Ms. Smith attended a community college and received an Associate of Science degree in nursing. She has been a grocery checker for the past 12 years.

Before this job, Ms. Smith worked for three years as a nursing assistant in a convalescent home, and for four years as a pharmacy technician in a retail drugstore. Her first experience in employment was as a house cleaner, which Nancy performed for two years. The work of a nursing assistant involves lifting of 25 pounds repetitively and up to 50 pounds occasionally. A pharmacy technician lifts up to 15 pounds and stands or walks one half of the work shift. Ms. Smith's job as a house cleaner required lifting and carrying up to 40 pounds on an occasional basis with repetitive lifting and carrying of 20 pounds or less.

For the past year, Ms. Smith has had complaints of pain and numbness in her left nondominant hand, primarily the second through fourth fingers. She has night pain and pain radiating into the left shoulder. There is hand weakness and a slight loss of grip strength. Dr. Elizabeth Kim stated that Ms. Smith has a mononeuropathy involving compression of the median nerve in the wrist. Recently, Nancy has complained of low back pain, and feels she is unable to lift and carry more than 25 pounds without experiencing mild pain.

Currently, Ms. Smith receives physical therapy three times a week at 5:00 p.m. on Monday, Wednesday, and Friday. Work hours for a grocery checker on her shift are 8:00 a.m. to 5:00 p.m. Nancy leaves work early at 4:30 p.m. to attend physical therapy. Her employer has expressed concerns about her missing 1½ hours of work each week.

Currently, she is seeing an occupational therapist (OT) for therapy on her hand. The OT suggested to Ms. Smith that she see a rehabilitation counselor. Nancy followed through with this suggestion. You have been assigned this case.

Questions

1. Assign Ms. Nancy Smith a vocational profile, including age category, educational level, and work history (skill and exertional levels).
2. What medical conditions do Nancy's symptoms indicate she may have?
3. Describe Ms. Smith's functional limitations in regard to her job.
4. Should she attempt to continue working as a grocery checker for her current employer? Explain.
5. If you recommend she continue her employment, what advice would you give Nancy and the employer regarding reasonable accommodation?
6. Describe the occupationally significant characteristics (worker traits) and possible transferable skills of Ms. Smith.
7. Suggest rehabilitation possibilities, including use of transferable skills from previous work and possible training programs if Nancy does not continue working for this employer. Remember this client has a college degree.

References

Beaumont, J. G. (2008). *Introduction to neuropsychology* (2nd ed.). New York, NY: Guilford.

Biller, J., Gruener, G., & Brazis, P. (2017). *DeMyer's the neurological examination: A programmed text* (7th ed.). Columbus, OH: McGraw-Hill.

Brust, J. C. M. (2018). *Current diagnosis and treatment neurology* (3rd ed.). Columbus, OH: McGraw-Hill Professional.

Carter, R. L., Hohenegger, M., & Satz, P. (1980). Handedness and aphasia: An inferential method for determining the mode of cerebral speech specialization. *Neuopsychologia, 18*, 569-574.

Greenberg, D. A., Aminoff, M. J., & Simon, R. P. (2018). *Clinical neurology* (9th ed.). Columbus, OH: McGraw-Hill.

Grefkes, C., & Fink, G. R. (2011). Reorganization of cerebral networks after stroke: New insights from neuroimaging with connectivity approaches. *Brain, 134*(5), 1264-1276.

Hauser, S. L., & Josephson, S. (2016). *Harrison's neurology in clinical medicine* (4th ed.). Columbus, OH: McGraw-Hill.

Kasper, D. L., Fauci, A. S., Hauser, S. L., Longo, D. L., Jameson, J. L., & Loscalzo, J. (2015). *Harrison's principles of internal medicine* (19th ed.). Columbus, OH: McGraw-Hill.

Lezak, M. D., Howieson, D. B., Bigler, E. D., & Tranel, D. (2012). *Neuropsychological assessment* (5th ed.). New York, NY: Oxford University.

Papadakis, M. A., McPhee, S. J., & Rabow, M. W. (Eds.). (2017). *Current medical diagnosis and treatment* (56th ed.). Columbus, OH: McGraw-Hill.

Pfeiffer, R. F., Wszolek, Z. K., & Ebadi, M. (Eds.). (2012). *Parkinson's disease* (2nd ed.). Boca Raton, FL: CRC Press Book.

Quarrell, O. (2008). *Huntington's disease* (2nd ed.). New York, NY: Oxford University.

Rapoport, M., Van Reekum, R., & Mayberg, H. (2000). The role of the cerebellum in cognition and behavior: A selective review. *Journal of Neuropsychiatry and Clinical Neurosciences, 12*(2), 193-198.

Ropper, A. H., Samuels, M. A., Klein, J. P., & Prasad, S. (2015). *Adams and Victor's principles of neurology* (11th ed.). New York, NY: McGraw-Hill.

Schmahmann, J. D., & Sherman, J. C. (1998). The cerebellar cognitive affective syndrome. *Brain, 121*(4), 561-579.

About the Authors

David B. Peterson, PhD, is a licensed clinical psychologist, Certified Rehabilitation Counselor, and Professor at California State University, Los Angeles. He contributed to the development of the World Health Organization's International Classification of Functioning, Disability, and Health, and published a text addressing psychological aspects of the same. Additionally, Dr. Peterson is on the Panel of Medical Experts of the Office of Hearing Operations, Social Security Administration, where he provides psychological expert testimony.

Thomas Van Vleet, PhD, is a licensed Clinical Neuropsychologist and Research Neuropsychologist specializing in the development of *neurotherapeutics* - behavioral interventions for the treatment of brain dysfunction following injury, degeneration, or psychiatric illness at the Veterans Affairs (VA) Medical Center, Northern California Health Care System in Martinez, California. Also, he is employed by the Posit Science Corporation in San Francisco, California. Dr. Van Vleet is a Visiting Scholar at the University of California, Berkeley, and Principal Investigator on several research projects supported by the National Institutes of Health (NIH), the VA, and Defense Advanced Research Projects Agency (DARPA), examining the use of neurotherapeutic treatments in clinical populations.

Chapter 16

SPINAL CORD INJURY

Gonzalo C. Centeno, MS
Nancy M. Crewe, PhD
James S. Krause, PhD

Introduction

Compared with many other disabling conditions, spinal cord injury (SCI) affects a relatively small number of people; each year, about 17,000 new diagnoses are added to the current United States total of approximately 285,000 people with this condition. Yet, it commands the attention of rehabilitation counselors and other health care professionals because SCI causes profound changes in virtually all physical systems and functional abilities. Further, the majority of people who sustain new spinal cord injuries are young adults with a lifetime of experiences ahead of them. Over half these individuals are in the 16-30 year age group; however, as of 2010, the average age at injury was 42.6 years. Males account for 80% of these spinal cord injuries (National Spinal Cord Injury Statistical Center [NSCISC], 2017).

Spinal cord injury brings about drastic and overwhelming changes in physical, psychological, and social functioning. Individuals with SCI require multidisciplinary medical and rehabilitation services to rebuild their lives and contemplate the opportunity for an independent and productive future (Falvo & Holland, 2018). This chapter provides essential information on physiological, functional, and psychosocial characteristics pertinent to people with SCI, along with important factors contributing to their rehabilitation needs and potentials.

The public views the inability to walk as the primary consequence of SCI. Although walking is impacted, SCI also affects such areas as arm and hand strength and dexterity, bowel and bladder control, sexual function, temperature regulation, susceptibility to infections, and even the ability to breathe. The most common causes of death post-injury are pneumonia and septicemia (NSCISC, 2017). To understand these various consequences, it is necessary to become familiar with the anatomy and physiology of the central nervous system.

Anatomy and Physiology

Spinal Cord Structure

Voluntary motion takes place when nerve impulses travel from the brain down the spinal cord and out to the body through peripheral nerves. Sensory stimuli are carried from the peripheral nerves through the spinal cord to the brain. The full circuit enables tactile perception and coordinated movements. As a result, damage to the spinal cord can result in both loss of voluntary movement (paralysis) and loss of sensation.

The spinal cord extends from the brain stem to a point in the lower back called the conus medularis. Beyond that point, nerve fibers known as the cauda equina (horse's tail) fan out. The spinal cord is encased in a protective canal that is formed by the spinal vertebrae. At each vertebral junction, a pair of spinal nerves exit from the spinal cord and innervate specific muscles, and sensory nerve filaments enter the spinal cord. The vertebrae and nerves are classified into several sections beginning in the neck region with seven cervical vertebrae, seven pairs of nerve roots that exit above each of those vertebrae, and an eighth pair that exits below the seventh vertebra.

Below the cervical vertebrae are 12 thoracic vertebrae and 12 pairs of spinal nerves. In the lower back, there are five lumbar vertebrae and nerve roots and five fused sacral vertebrae with five nerve roots. The lowest part of the spinal column is a single bone called the coccyx. The vertebrae and nerves are numbered from the top with a letter that corresponds to the spinal section. For example, the first vertebra below the skull is C-1, whereas T-1 is the first vertebra in the thoracic section.

Nerves for the voluntary motor system originate in the motor cortex of the brain and extend down through the basal ganglia to the brain stem. At this point, they cross over to the opposite side and continue to descend in the spinal cord until they synapse at the point where they are about to exit from the spinal cord. The nerves that originate in the motor cortex of the brain's left hemisphere cross over to innervate the right side of the body, and those from the right hemisphere cross over to the left side. These are known as upper motor neurons. Beyond the synapse, the lower motor neurons exit the cord and extend to their particular muscle destination.

When the spinal cord is damaged, communication is disrupted between the brain and parts of the body that are innervated at or below the lesion. The lesion may be complete (no nerve fibers functioning below the level of injury) or incomplete (one or more nerve fibers are secure). The cord need not be completely severed to result in a complete injury; the nerve cells may be destroyed as a result of pressure, bruising, or loss of blood supply, and if they die they do not regenerate. The amount of functional loss depends on the level of injury (the higher the damage, the more of the body that is affected) and the neurological completeness of the injury. Individuals with neurologically complete injuries have more severe and more predictable patterns of functional impairment.

The level of SCI damage is determined in two ways. The first method specifies the level of bony damage as indicated by x-rays. The more useful approach, however, indicates the level of neurological damage, measured by careful testing of an individual's ability to perceive pinprick. Skin surface has been mapped into segments called dermatomes (see Figure 1); each dermatome is known to be innervated by sensory nerves at a particular spinal level. Testing the skin, therefore, can reveal the level at which the spinal cord has been damaged.

Spinal Cord Function

Individuals who sustain damage at the cervical level will have impaired function in both their upper and lower extremities, a condition known as tetraplegia (previously classified as quadriplegia). The most current type of spinal injuries are incomplete tetraplegia (NSCISC, 2017). Those who are injured at or below the thoracic level will have paraplegia, with function maintained in their upper extremities with some degree of impairment in the trunk and lower extremities.

The American Spinal Injury Association (ASIA) developed a system for describing the severity of injury that is widely used in the medical community using letters that pertain to the extent of injury (usually A through D) (Young, 2006). ASIA A injuries are complete, with no motor or sensory function preserved below the neurological level of injury, including the sacral segments S4-S5. ASIA B injuries are incomplete, with sensory but no motor function preserved below the neurological level of injury. ASIA C and D classifications refer to incomplete injuries with increasing degrees of motor function preserved below the neurological level of injury.

Certain incomplete spinal cord injuries produce unusual patterns of deficits. If the damage occurs within the central part of the cervical cord, leaving the outer ring of fibers intact, the individual will have greater weakness in the upper limbs than in the lower limbs, and sacral sensation may be spared. Brown-Sequard syndrome is a lesion that affects only one side of the spinal cord. This causes paralysis on the same side of the body as the lesion, and loss of pain and temperature sensation on the opposite side of the body.

Acute Medical and Rehabilitation Care

Approximately 38% of spinal cord injuries are the result of motor vehicle accidents; other major causes include falls, acts of violence, and sports/recreational accidents (NSCISC, 2017). In a study conducted to review traumatic and non-traumatic SCI injuries, 30.1% were the result of fractures resulting from falls versus 3.2% resulting from gunshot wounds (Ge et al., 2017). Recent reports suggested that the number of new injuries due to violence have decreased from 24.8% during the 1990s to 13.5% reported in 2017. However, acts of violence with specific mention of gunshot wounds remain the primary cause of SCI among some minority populations in the 16-30 age category, with African Americans and Hispanics being the most affected (Chen, Tang, Vogel, & DeVivo, 2013). The number of spinal injuries stemming from motor vehicle accidents has diminished over the last few decades, probably as a result of air bags and other improvements in automobile safety.

Medical emergency procedures executed at the scene of an injury have improved over the years, with careful stabilization of the neck and spine from the injury scene to the hospital, the availability of emergency transportation, and an increasing tendency to utilize specialized trauma hospitals. Damage to the spinal cord from trauma, bleeding, swelling, and oxygen deprivation are also crucial factors during injury. The damage is quickly compounded by the body's release of free radicals and other toxic substances, which leads to inflammation and scarring (Hagan, 2015).

Neuroprotective agents, such as methylprednisolone, are often administered soon after injury in an attempt to disrupt this cascade of events and prevent further cell death. Although use of these agents is controversial, the goals of medications, such as methylprednisolone, are to reduce the possibility of secondary injuries to the nerves resulting from toxic substances. There are two other drugs which are still undergoing clinical trials but have been showing significant promise. Riluzole has been approved by the United States Food and Drug Administration (FDA) and is currently being used in the treatment of amyotrophic lateral sclerosis (Cifra, Mazzone, & Nistri, 2013). The second drug, Minocycline, is currently being used for the treatment of acne, rosacea, and rheumatoid arthritis. According to studies, it contributes to functional improvement and recovery of motor function (Sonmez et al., 2013).

During hospitalization, physicians may determine that the spinal column is unstable and further neurological damage could ensue. In this case, surgery may be recommended to fuse the spine at the point of injury or otherwise stabilize it with rods or other surgical hardware. The individual may be fitted with a halo or body cast to maintain immobility of the fracture site without being confined to bed for excessive periods of time (Hagan, 2015). Approximately 75% of these patients have one of the following spinal cord stabilizing procedures: laminectomy, neural canal restoration, open reduction, spinal fusion, or internal fixation of the spine (NSCISC, 2017).

When the need for acute medical services has passed, the individual is usually transferred to a rehabilitation unit for multidisciplinary services to help build strength, redevelop skills in activities of daily living, identify and obtain adaptive equipment, and prepare for a return to home and community. An SCI rehabilitation team typically includes one or more physicians, nurses, physical therapists, psychologists, occupational therapists, rehabilitation counselors, and social workers.

A network of comprehensive Model SCI Centers has been established across the country, providing medical services, as well as research on medical and psychosocial aspects of SCI. Studies have demonstrated that the post-discharge support system takes into account involvement in social and recreational activities, perceived ability to move about in the community, and the degree of comfort within the family and with other relationships (Hitzig, Romero Escobar, Noreau, & Craven, 2012). This is probably the most important time for the person affected by SCI because the process of assimilation of new body limitations is not only difficult, but sets the stage for physical and psychological growth.

Changes in the health care system have greatly reduced the length of time needed to complete rehabilitation. Decades ago, a person with SCI would receive most of the rehabilitation as an inpatient before going home and out into the community; it was not unusual for a person to be in hospital and rehabilitation center for six months or more before being discharged. The average length of stay in a hospital for individuals with SCI from 1973-1979 was 142 days, which significantly dropped to 52 days from 1995-2011 (NSCISC, 2017).

Levels of Injury and Functioning

Table 1 summarizes the functions of the nerves at various spinal levels. For individuals with complete lesions, patterns of functional loss and preservation are fairly consistent from person to person. The most dramatic changes in function are apparent between adjacent neurological levels in the cervical area. For example, nerves that innervate the diaphragm are at cervical level 3-4, requiring many persons with injuries at or above C-3 to use ventilator assistance to breathe. Most individuals with C-4 injuries regain breathing capacity, but do not have usable function in their upper extremities. As a result, they need assistance with activities of daily living (ADL).

Individuals with injuries at the C-5 level usually have function in the deltoid and bicep muscles, allowing them to bend the arm at the elbow. Some have the ability to develop a weak pinch by using an automatic motion known as tenodesis (when the wrist is extended, the thumb and index finger come together). This makes it possible to hold a light object (such as a washcloth) and carry out some self-care activities. Most people with C-5 injuries use power wheelchairs for mobility.

Many individuals with C-6 injuries use manual wheelchairs, particularly if the chairs are equipped with plastic wheel rims and projection knobs. Most people with C-6 tetraplegia can move independently with the use of appropriate equipment. Assistive devices (e.g., tableware with built-up handles) make many activities of daily living possible. Individuals who have limited manual dexterity may use hand braces (e.g., ratchet splint) that enable grasping items with their hands, such as a pencil or toothbrush.

People who have C-7 and C-8 levels of injury are almost fully independent in their daily lives. They have the use of triceps muscles (which allow them to straighten and lock their arms for transfers from wheelchair to automobile or chair) and finger extensors (which allow them to open their hands).

At the thoracic levels, the nerves innervate muscles that provide control of the trunk; injuries below this level allow for some balance and trunk stability. Control over hip muscles is maintained at the lumbar level, so individuals with injuries below T-12 are sometimes able to ambulate using crutches and braces. This takes a great amount of effort, however, and most people choose to use wheelchairs for mobility, particularly when traveling distances.

Injuries at the lumbar level often result in paraplegia. Persons with L1 and L2 injuries may be capable of standing and walking with braces. Yet, this involves a great amount of energy and a wheelchair is needed for mobility of long distances. Those with L3 and L4 injuries may be able to walk with the assistance of orthotic devices.

Innervation for bowel, bladder, and sexual functioning occur at the sacral level. Persons who have injuries at the cervical or thoracic level have sustained damage to all the upper motor neurons that innervate the body at or below the point of injury. This results in loss of voluntary control of bowel and bladder function. Fortunately, an intact lower motor neuron reflex arc may be retained from these muscles to the synapse in the spinal cord and back. This enables the possibility of retraining the body to respond to direct stimulation (for example, tapping on the lower abdomen to trigger voiding), and provides some degree of control over bowel functions. Individuals who have sacral injuries, on the other hand, may have direct injury to the lower motor neurons in this area. Thus, they may not have the ability to develop these reflexive responses.

Following SCI, most individuals lose voluntary control of bowel and bladder function and need to develop ways to manage these functions (Hagan, 2015). The bowel can be trained to empty at regular intervals by using a suppository and/or digital stimulation. For people who are working, the time that is required to complete the bowel program (up to two hours) can affect productivity. People need to carefully monitor the food they eat and avoid items which cause irregularity or intestinal irritation. If bowel management becomes highly problematic, physicians may recommend a colostomy (surgical procedure that provides for emptying fecal contents through an abdominal stoma). This procedure may reduce the amount of time required for bowel care and serve to prevent accidents.

TABLE 1
Muscles Supplied and Functions Served by Spinal Nerve Motor Roots

Root Segment	Representative Muscles	Functions Served
Cervical		
C1 & C2	High neck muscles	Aid in head control
C3 & C4	Diaphragm	Inspiration (breathing in)
C5 & C6	Deltoid Biceps	Shoulder flexion, abduction (arms forward, out to side) Elbow flexion (elbow bent)
C6 & C7	Extensor Carpi Radialis Pronator Teres	Wrist dorsiflexion (back of hand up) Wrist pronation (palm down)
C7 & C8	Triceps Extensor Digitorum Communis	Elbow extension (elbow straight) Finger extension (knuckles straight)
C8 & T1	Flexor Digitorm Superficialis Opponens Pollicis Interossei (intrinsics)	Finger flexion (fist clenched) Thumb opposition (thumb brought to little finger) Spreading and closing the fingers
Thoracic		
T2—T6	Intercostals	Forced inspiration (breathing in) Expiration (breathing out, coughing)
T6—T12	Intercostals—Abdominals	Forced inspiration (breathing in); aid in expiration (coughing); aid in trunk flexion (sitting up)
Lumbar		
L1, L2, & L3	Iliopsoas Adductors	Hip flexion (thigh to chest); hip adduction, thigh to midline (legs together)
L3 & L4	Quadriceps	Knee extension (knee straight)
L4, L5, & S1	Gluteus Medius Tibialis Anterior	Hip abduction (thigh out to side, legs apart) Foot dorsiflexion (foot up, walk on heels)
L5, S1, & S2	Gluteus Maximus Gastrocneumius	Hip extension (thigh in line with trunk, hips straight, e.g., standing); foot plantar flexion (foot down, walk on toes)
Sacral		
S2, S3, & S4	Anal Sphincter Urethral Sphincter	Bowel function (fecal continence) Bladder control (urinary continence)

Source: Stolov, W. C., & Clowers, M. R. (1981). *Handbook of severe disability.* Washington, DC: U.S. Government Printing Office.

Bladder and kidney functioning is a complex issue following SCI. Persons who retain reflexive function in the bladder may be able to initiate voiding through direct stimulation by tapping on the bladder around the pubic area. This will cause the sphincter muscle to relax and the bladder to drain. However, those who have a flaccid bladder need catheterization or external pressure to void (NSCISC, 2017).

Many people have recurrent episodes of urinary tract infections that cause fever and other symptoms. Infections develop because the bladder does not empty often enough or completely, allowing bacteria to multiply. Without sensation, a person does not receive automatic signals indicating the bladder needs to be emptied. If the bladder becomes overly full, urine backs up into the kidneys (a condition known as reflux) and causes damage. For many years, renal problems were the major cause of premature death among persons with SCI, but antibiotics and better preventive care have reduced this danger.

Functional Complications and Limitations

Sexual Dysfunction

Researchers continue to try to find ways to enhance the sexual lives of individuals with SCI and to diminish the impact of injury on sexual functioning. This area merits additional research and also counseling because of its importance within marriage, and as a component of personal identity and self-esteem. The connection between sexual arousal, which occurs in the brain and genital organs, is usually broken, making it impossible for most men to attain an erection or women to produce lubrication in response to psychological arousal. Yet, if the lower motor neuron reflex arc is intact, a physical response may be produced by direct stimulation. For men with SCI between T6 and L5, sildenafil (Viagra) has been shown to significantly improve the quality of erections and lead to higher levels of satisfaction (Rahimi-Movaghar & Vaccaro, 2012). Other techniques have been developed to enable intercourse, including penile implants and injections.

For men, fertility is a more difficult challenge. Ejaculation typically does not occur after SCI, or semen may be deposited into the bladder rather than being discharged externally. Sperm motility may be low so that pregnancy is unlikely to occur. In recent years, clinicians have successfully used techniques, such as electrical stimulation, to induce ejaculation or artificial insemination. Studies have demonstrated the importance of erectile function for a satisfactory sexual life (Gomes et al., 2017).

A woman who has SCI frequently does not have a menstrual period for several months after the trauma. Many women with SCI remain fertile and can become pregnant. A woman will require prenatal and delivery care from a physician knowledgeable in SCI to avoid complications resulting from the pressure that a growing fetus places on her lungs, bladder, skin, and circulatory system. Special issues may arise during childbirth, in part because she may not experience the typical sensations that signal the onset of labor. Care must be taken to manage any occurrence of autonomic hyperreflexia during labor. A woman with tetraplegia needs to plan the way in which she will be able to care for a baby - perhaps with help from a personal care assistant.

Autonomic Hyperreflexia

Autonomic hyperreflexia is potentially life-threatening for persons with injuries above the level of T-6. As a result of the SCI, this is a response to a noxious stimulus (e.g., a urinary tract infection, a blocked catheter, or even wrinkled clothing that is irritating the skin), where blood pressure drastically increases, producing symptoms of a crashing headache, dizziness, and sweating. Unless treated quickly, the individual is at risk of seizures, stroke, or possibly even death (Boudakian, Berliner, & Ahn, 2017).

Spasticity

Immediately after SCI, the muscles that would be innervated by neurons below the lesion are usually flaccid. The upper motor neurons that were destroyed do not recover, so voluntary motor function will not return. The lower motor neurons some distance below the lesion may not have been directly injured; however, as the initial shock passes, they may begin to conduct signals in a reflex arc from the peripheral nerves to the synapse in the spinal cord and then back to the stimulated muscle. In an intact nervous system, the signal goes to the brain and the brain modulates the body's response. A lesion blocks that pathway and sets up, in effect, a reverberating circuit. Resulting spasticity is disruptive and may cause pain and possible embarrassment for the individual.

A positive side of spasticity is that it serves to help maintain tone in paralyzed muscles and may be functionally useful in some instances, such as in facilitating wheelchair transfers. Psychoactive medications are now available to control spasticity. Other procedures, such as motor point blocks (to block nerve impulses) and surgery, are tried when other means of control are ineffective. Non-medication treatments for spasticity include stretching and similar activities (Strommen, 2013).

Contractures

Joints and muscles not regularly moved through their full range of motion shorten into permanently flexed positions known as contractures. The reduction of range of motion caused by contractures makes everyday life functions difficult; the use of an elevator or simply turning a light switch on and off is difficult because of an inability to reach. Hygiene is made difficult by permanent contractures and any functional capacities that the individual may possess become compromised. Rehabilitation nurses and physical therapists make a concerted effort to avoid development of contractures; range of motion exercises need to be a daily routine.

Pressure Sores

Decubitus ulcers, also known as pressure sores, are a frequent, dangerous, and costly problem for individuals with impaired sensation. This condition is a severe medical complication of SCI. Whereas people with intact nervous systems shift their positions at frequent intervals due to signals of discomfort, those with SCI need to train themselves to shift their weight regularly. Pressure sores are "a common medical complication" that affects individuals with an incidence of 25% in the first year after injury (NSCISC, 2017). Essential to the prevention and management of pressure sores is on-going education for anyone at risk of acquiring them, including patients with acute injuries and individuals aging with SCI.

Subsequent Injuries

Subsequent injuries are those that occur in the years and decades after the initial SCI. In one study, 19% of individuals in a sample of 1,391 participants reported at least one other injury during the previous year that required medical attention (Krause, 2004). Of those with one or more injuries, 27% reported at least one injury-related hospitalization during the same timeframe. Sensation seeking, heavy drinking, prescription medication used for pain, spasticity, depression, and lack of sleep were all associated with an elevated risk of subsequent injuries (consistent with the risk factors for the initial SCI). Brotherton, Krause, and Neitert (2007) surveyed 119 participants with ambulatory SCI where 75% reported at least one fall the previous year. Of those who had at least one fall, 18% had fractures and 45% noted decreased participation in community activities as the result of the fall.

Bone Changes

Almost immediately after SCI, osteoporosis begins to develop. Part of the reason for bone loss is the increased bed rest needed and general disuse that follows trauma. The loss occurs throughout the body, but initially affects areas below the pelvis, especially the knees. Decreased bone density makes a person vulnerable to future fractures.

Another sequela of trauma is heterotopic ossification, a condition in which the body begins to develop pieces of bone in soft tissue. This condition affects individuals with SCI below the level of neurological injury, often affecting range of motion of knees, shoulders, elbows, and hands. Besides being painful, this phenomenon interferes with functioning, sometimes to the point where joints fuse. Surgery is used to treat severe cases of heterotopic ossification.

Respiratory Function

Persons with complete SCI above the level of C-4 are likely to need ventilators to help them breathe. Questions have been raised about quality of life experienced by people with tetraplegia who are ventilator dependent. Interestingly, studies have shown that individuals with such conditions consistently rate their lives as more satisfying than health care professionals predicted (Bach & Tilton, 1994). With sufficient support and assistive technology, these individuals may be capable of working, socializing, and living rewarding lives.

Respiratory function is often a matter of concern for individuals who are not placed on ventilators. Because of weakened chest muscles, people with tetraplegia and those with high thoracic injuries may not be able to cough with sufficient force to clear their lungs of irritants and mucus, and are prone to pneumonia. This is especially dangerous if they have developed immunity to several antibiotics because of frequent use in combating other infections. Pneumonia is the most common cause of death among people with SCI. Pulmonary embolism is another serious condition that occurs at greatly increased rates for this population (NSCISC, 2017).

Cardiac Issues

Among people with SCI, heart problems triggered by neurogenic shock resulting from hypotension and persistent bradycardia causes blood pressure to drop to dangerous levels. Furthermore, cardiac insufficiency may contribute to reduced energy and strength and can lead directly or indirectly to the development of other secondary disorders, such as pressure ulcers. Paralysis poses formidable barriers to exercise and the maintenance of cardiovascular fitness.

Chronic Pain

The majority of people with SCI experience neuropathic pain that affects functioning and quality of life (Finnerup, 2012). They may report a sharp, stabbing pain below the level of injury that occurs intermittently, or a dull, aching pain that persists for long periods of time and becomes worse with activity. The cause for pain is not well understood and there may be no means of relief available.

Another source of pain comes from overuse of shoulders and upper extremities needed to propel a wheelchair and transfer from one surface to another. According to Finnerup (2012), pain which did not respond to ordinary therapies was treated and relieved with complimentary treatments, such as warm baths, physical activities, and finding a balance between activity and rest.

Psychosocial Aspects of SCI

Adequately describing the psychological and social consequences of SCI is complex. People experiencing objectively similar levels of trauma respond in entirely different ways as a result of differing personalities, social support systems, cultural and ethnic backgrounds, available resources, age, education, and intellect. Every aspect of a person is affected by the injury; thus, rehabilitation efforts need to address the whole person.

There are some characteristics of SCI that play a role in the adjustment process, including:

- SCI usually involves sudden and unexpected onset. In a moment's time, life is irretrievably altered. With no opportunity for preparation, the entire adjustment process takes place after onset. In past years, hospital stays were six months to a year after SCI, allowing time for gradual assimilation to the injury and with the support of a rehabilitation team. Currently, SCI patients are discharged much sooner and have less time to comprehend and plan for the future within a supported environment.

- The person with SCI experiences loss in many areas of life, including the inability to participate in valued activities, financial losses related to interruption or discontinuance of work, and the burden of new expenses. Eventually, most people perceive gains stemming from the injury (e.g., deepening of family relationships, personal growth, and new educational or vocational opportunities).

- One of the most profound changes following SCI is the loss of independence in daily living. The individual with tetraplegia needs to rely on another person to provide basic care, including toileting, bathing, and feeding.
- Individuals with SCI must be aware of non-accessibility when in the community. The Americans with Disabilities Act (ADA) and other legislation have helped in increasing the number of public places that are wheelchair accessible.
- The bodies of persons with SCI are a further source of insecurity because of the loss of voluntary control of functions. A bowel or bladder accident or even a bout of spasticity brings unwanted attention and embarrassment. Some people choose to stay at home rather than risk such occurrences.
- The person with SCI is subject to attitudinal barriers of people who are uncomfortable with or biased against individuals with disabilities. Many persons have reported that pre-injury friends drift away and new acquaintances must be made to avoid isolation. The incidence of marriage is lower and that of divorce somewhat higher among individuals with SCI compared with the general population (Crewe & Krause, 1992; DeVivo, Hawkins, Richards, & Go, 1995).
- Some individuals with SCI must cope with additional barriers, such as substance abuse. Up to half the people admitted to emergency rooms with severe trauma, including SCI, were intoxicated at the time of injury (Heinemann, Doll, Armstrong, Schnoll, & Yarkony, 1991). Thus, people who abuse substances are more likely to engage in risky behavior that leads to injury. Furthermore, substance abuse may be a coping strategy subsequent to injury.
- The rate of depressive disorders is approximately three times higher among people with SCI than in the general population. Between 20-40% of individuals with this disability suffer from depression (Kemp, Kahan, & Krause, 1999; Weingardt, Hsu, & Dunn, 2001). Depression can interfere with health, psychosocial functioning, and lead to suicide.
- People are resilient in their abilities to cope with the challenges of SCI. Psychological adjustment (as measured by satisfaction with life and involvement in work and social activities) continues to improve for many years after injury. Without denying that SCI is a tragic event, most survivors rate their quality of life as good to excellent years after the event.

Veterans with SCI

In the United States, many veterans return home with spinal cord injuries. Studies reflecting the challenges experienced by veterans are focusing on highlighting treatment models post-injury to improve satisfaction with life and enhance overall quality of life. According to Fortmann et al. (2013), veterans compose 10% of the U.S. population of which 20% of this number are affected by acquired SCI. Therefore, organizations such as the Wounded Warrior Project are focusing on the needs of this population and searching for improved ways of providing support, guidance, and independence.

Challenges affecting veterans with SCI are depression, post-traumatic stress disorder (PTSD), substance abuse, among others. Psychological ramifications of these contributing conditions significantly hinder quality of life (deRoon-Cassini, Hastings, de St-Aubin, Valvano, & Brasel, 2013). Among the job counseling and job services provided, the philosophy is that employment is possible regardless of severity of disability.

Employment

The most prominent benefits of employment are financial. However, employment is also related to other favorable outcomes. For example, individuals who are employed after SCI consistently report greater satisfaction in nearly all areas of life (Krause, 2003). Return to gainful employment is associated with a significantly greater likelihood of surviving SCI over an extended period.

Employment Rates

According to the NSCISC (2017), 57.6% of those affected by SCI were working full time when injured, whereas 15.6% were unemployed. Among those who returned to work after SCI, it took an average of about five years to return to the first post-injury job, and just over six years to return to the first full time job (Krause, 2003).

Return-to-Work Approaches

There are two separate tracks to employment - a fast track, defined by return to the pre-injury job or having worked as a professional prior to injury, and a slow track, reflecting the absence of these characteristics. Those in the fast track required substantially less time to return to both their first job (2.1 years compared to 5.5 years) and their first full time job (3.3 years compared to 7.1 years). Differences between those with cervical and non-cervical injuries were observed only for the slow track. These findings suggest there is a window of opportunity shortly after SCI onset where there is greater likelihood of return to work if the preinjury employer is willing to rehire or if preinjury education and work skills can be applied to a new position. An assertive approach may maximize employment opportunities when compared with the frequent practice of delaying discussion of employment issues until after the person returns to the community and has had time to adapt to the injury (Krause, 2003; Sinnott, Cheng, Wagner, Goetz, & Ottmanelli, 2011).

Employment Outcomes

Primary factors associated with post-injury employment are race-ethnicity, age, severity of injury, etiology, duration of SCI, pre-injury employment status, and years of education. The highest employment rates were obtained by participants who had the following characteristics: Caucasian, 25 years of age and younger at time of injury, ASIA D severity, not injured as the result of violence, had been injured 20 years earlier, were working at time of injury, and had completed 16 or more years of education.

Being employed at the time of injury was associated with a greater probability of employment, but only during the first few years following the injury, after which time this factor was unrelated to work status. The employment rate of those working at injury ranged from 18-31% at one, two, and five years post-injury, compared with a range of 6-16% over the same timeframe for those unemployed at injury. However, by ten years post-injury the trends had reversed (33% compared with 40%) (NSCISC, 2017).

Severity of Disability

Although severity of injury and functional limitations play a role in return to work, the relationship is not simple. For example, if jobs require manual dexterity, but not lower extremity function, a person with paraplegia is more likely than someone with tetraplegia to return to the position. Another reason why people with tetraplegia find it more difficult to return to work is that they are likely to have higher medical costs, including medications, supplies, and especially personal care assistance. Medicaid often covers these costs; eligibility for Medicaid generally is lost when a person begins earning more than about $1,321 per month. Enactment of Ticket to Work legislation in 1999 represented an effort to change public policy to remove this disincentive to employment.

Education

It is rare for persons with less than 12 years of education to return to work after SCI, and even more uncommon for them to retain employment. For example, the NSCISC (2017) reported that 51.5% of those surveyed had completed high school or GED, and 6.8% completed a bachelor's degree; only 23.7% completed less than 12 years of education at time of injury.

The significance of education is best demonstrated in conjunction with injury. Education mediates the extent to which severity of injury is associated with diminished labor force participation. Among those with 12 years of education, only 8% of participants with C1-C4, ASIA A-C were currently working, compared to 33% for those with motor function injuries (i.e., ASIA D, all levels). However, the differences disappeared among those at the Master's-PhD level. The benefits of further education were most dramatic for those with the most severe SCI, as the employment rate for the C1-C4 group was nearly eight times greater between high school and Master's-PhD level education compared with less than two times the increase for those with ASIA D. In fact, the employment rate for those with ASIA D injuries flattened, starting at an Associate's degree, but continued to increase for those with C1-C4 ASIA A-C, all the way through the Master's-PhD (increasing from 36% with a four-year degree to 61% with a master's or higher degree). In summary, education is the great equalizer of employment opportunities for people with SCI (Krause, 2003).

Search for a Cure

Writings from ancient Egypt described SCI as a condition that was untreatable. Survival prospects for those injured did not improve significantly until the discovery of antibiotics in the early 1940s. Cells within the central nervous system do not regenerate once they have been destroyed so medical treatment and rehabilitation have always focused on preventing complications and maximizing residual functional capacities. Today, researchers have been working with increased intensity to find ways to stimulate regrowth of nerve cells, to block the processes that serve to inhibit growth, and to promote connections across the site of injury.

Aside from medications that help prevent cellular destruction at time of injury, there are further advances in stem cell research to aid in the nerve regeneration process (Boudakian et al., 2017). From laboratory studies on animals, stem cell research is offering hope and evidence for a cure. Additionally, repair through transplantation of nerve cells is being studied and many believe that a breakthrough may be achieved in the foreseeable future. "The ultimate goal in spinal cord injury treatment is the repair of altered neural function and restoration of normal physiology" (Boudakian et al., p. 553). Until that time, it is important to remember that thousands of people are experiencing fulfilling and productive lives with severe disability.

Conclusion

A spinal cord injury usually begins with a sudden, traumatic impact on the spine that fractures or dislocates vertebrae. An injury to the spinal cord can damage a few to almost all axons in a particular area. There will be almost total recovery from some injuries, while other injuries result in complete paralysis. Improved emergency care for people with spinal cord injuries and aggressive treatment and rehabilitation can minimize damage to the nervous system and restore function. Rehabilitation programs combine physical therapy with skill-building activities and counseling to provide social and emotional support.

Spinal cord injuries are classified as either complete or incomplete. People with incomplete injuries retain some motor or sensory function below the injury. Complete injuries cause a total lack of sensory and motor function below the level of injury. People who survive spinal cord injuries will most likely have medical complications such as paralysis, chronic pain, bladder and bowel dysfunction, along with increased susceptibility to respiratory and heart problems. Successful recovery depends upon how well these chronic conditions are handled on a daily basis. Severity of disability and education has a profound impact on resuming employment.

Case Study

John Reno is a 27-year-old former firefighter who was injured on the job when he fell off a ladder during an emergency call at an abandoned warehouse. The impact of the fall caused John to damage his spinal cord at the T10-T11 vertebrae, and as a result he has been diagnosed with paraplegia and is now a wheelchair user. At the time of injury, John had just married and was expecting a child; he continues to be married and has a one-year-old son.

After graduating from high school, John attended community college where he completed his general education before enrolling in the Fire Technology Associate of Arts (AA) degree program. The courses that were required for the completion of his program included Fire Protection Organization, Fire Protection Equipment, Fire Behavior and Combustion, and Fire Tactics and Strategy. Additionally, John enrolled in classes that further prepared him for the fire technology field, such as a certificate of achievement course in Emergency Medical Technician.

Prior to the injury, John had obtained employment with the Los Angeles Fire Department for approximately two years where aside from the typical duties of an active fire fighter, he incorporated his public relations experience to participate in community events as an educator and trainer. The essential functions of his position for the fire department required much physical strength and stamina as the exertion level is very heavy.

John's physical condition at the time of the injury was excellent and this aided him in maintaining a good prognosis when discharged from the hospital. In addition to the protection of the public, John coordinated monthly CPR classes for the community through a locally funded program sponsored by the City Mayor's Office. This not only provided a much needed service to the community, but it created a positive outlook on the image of the department and the other firefighters.

The spinal cord injury acquired by Mr. Reno has limited him from being able to return to his former position in the fire department as he is no longer able to perform the physical requirements of the position. He has fully functional manual dexterity which enables him to independently maintain his bladder and bowel program. However, John's level of education and his experience in the field make him an excellent candidate for rehabilitation in the same field.

Questions

1. Provide a vocational profile for Mr. Reno, including age category, educational level, and work history (skill and exertional levels).
2. Does this client possess transferable skills? If so, what are they and what vocational alternatives might provide an opportunity to use them?
3. What kinds of adaptive equipment would you recommend to increase independence?
4. How would you learn more about John's psychological adjustment to his disability? What services would be appropriate for him?
5. Will you involve his family in rehabilitation counseling? Discuss.
6. Outline a comprehensive rehabilitation plan for this client.

References

Bach, J. R., & Tilton, M. C. (1994). Life satisfaction and well-being measures in ventilator-assisted individuals with traumatic tetraplegia. *Archives of Physical Medicine and Rehabilitation, 75,* 626-632.

Boudakian, C., Berliner, J., & Ahn, J. (2017). Spinal cord injury. In A. Moroz, S. R. Flanagan, & H. H. Zaretsky (Eds.), *Medical aspects of disability for the rehabilitation professional* (5th ed., pp. 553-569). New York, NY: Springer.

Brotherton, S. S., Krause, J. S., & Nietert, P. J. (2007). Falls in individuals with incomplete spinal cord injury. *Spinal Cord, 45,* 37-40.

Chen, Y., Tang, Y., Vogel, L. C., & DeVivo, M. J. (2013). Causes of spinal cord injury. *Top Spinal Cord Injury Rehabilitation, 19,* 1-8.

Cifra, A., Mazzone, G., & Nistri, A. (2013). Riluzole: What it does to spinal and brainstem neurons and how it does it. *The Neuroscientist, 19,* 137-144.

Crewe, N. M., & Krause, J. S. (1992). Marital status and adjustment to spinal cord injury. *Journal of the American Paraplegia Society, 15,* 14-18.

deRoon-Cassini, T. A., Hastings, J., de St-Aubin, E., Valvano, A. K., & Brasel, K. J. (2013). Meaning-making appraisals relevant to adjustment for veterans with spinal cord injury. *Psychological Services, 10,* 186-193.

DeVivo, M. J., Hawkins, L. N., Richards, J. S., & Go, B. K. (1995). Outcomes of post-spinal cord injury marriages. *Archives of Physical Medicine and Rehabilitation, 76,* 130-138.

Falvo, D. R., & Holland, B. E. (2018). *Medical and psychosocial aspects of chronic illness and disability* (6th ed.). Burlington, MA: Jones and Bartlett Learning.

Finnerup, N. B. (2012). Pain in patients with spinal cord injury. *International Association for the Study of Pain, 12,* 1-6.

Fortmann, A. L., Rutledge, T., McCulloch, R. C., Shivpuri, S., Nisenzon, A. N., & Muse, J. (2013). Satisfaction with life among veterans with spinal cord injuries completing multidisciplinary rehabilitation. *International Spinal Cord Society, 51,* 482-486.

Ge, L., Arul, K., Ikpeze, T., Baldwin, A., Nickels, J.L., & Mesfin, A. (2018). Traumatic and non-traumatic spinal cord injuries. *World Neurosurgery, 111,* e142-e148.

Gomes, C. M., Miranda, E. P., de Bessa, Jr., J., Suzuki Bellucci, C. H., Battistella, L. R., Najjar Abda, C. H., . . . Mulhall, J. P. (2017). Erectile function predicts sexual satisfaction in men with spinal cord injury. *Sexual Medicine, 5*(3), e148-e155.

Hagan, E. M. (2015). Acute complications of spinal cord injuries. *World Journal of Orthopedics, 6*(1), 17-23.

Heinemann, A. W., Doll, M. D., Armstrong, K. J., Schnoll, S., & Yarkony, G. M. (1991). Substance use and receipt of treatment by persons with long-term spinal cord injuries. *Archives of Physical Medicine and Rehabilitation, 72,* 482-487.

Hitzig, S. L., Romero Escobar, E. M., Noreau, L., & Craven, B. C. (2012). Validation of the Reintegration to Normal Living Index for community-dwelling persons with chronic spinal cord injury. *Archives of Physical Medicine and Rehabilitation, 93,* 108-114.

Kemp, B., Kahan, J., & Krause, J. S. (1999). The effects of treatment of depression on symptoms, community activities, and life satisfaction in persons with SCI: A controlled study. *Journal of Spinal Cord Medicine, 22,* 58-61.

Krause, J. S. (2003). Years to employment after spinal cord injury. *Archives of Physical Medicine and Rehabilitation, 84*(9), 1282-1289.

Krause, J. S. (2004). Factors associated with risk for subsequent injuries after the onset of traumatic spinal cord injury. *Archives of Physical Medicine and Rehabilitation, 85*(9), 1503-1508.

National Spinal Cord Injury Statistical Center (NSCISC). (2017). *Annual report for the model spinal cord injury care systems.* Birmingham, AL: Author.

Rahimi-Movaghar, V., & Vaccaro A. R. (2012). Management of sexual disorders in spinal cord injured patients. *Acta Medica Iranica, 50,* 295-299.

Sinnott, P. L., Cheng, A., Wagner, T. H., Goetz, L. L., & Ottomanelli, L. (2011). Cost-effectiveness analysis of the spinal cord injury vocational integration program. *Top Spinal Cord Injury Rehabilitation, 16,* 80-88.

Sonmez, E., Kabatas, S., Ozen, 0., Karabay, G., Turkoglu, S., Ogus, F., . . . Altinors, N. (2013). Minocycline treatment inhibits lipids peroxidation, preserves spinal cord, ultrastructure, and improves functional outcome after traumatic spinal cord injury in the rat. *Spine, 38,* 1253-1259.

Stolov, W. C., & Clowers, M. R. (Eds.). (1981). *Handbook of severe disability.* Washington, DC: U.S. Government Printing Office.

Strommen, J. (2013). Management of spasticity from spinal cord dysfunction. *Neurologic Clinics, 31,* 269-286.

Weingardt, K. R., Hsu, J., & Dunn, M. E. (2001). Brief screening for psychological and substance abuse disorders in veterans with long-term spinal cord injury. *Rehabilitation Psychology, 46(3),* 271-278.

Young, W. (2006). *Spinal cord injury levels and classification.* Retrieved from http://www.sci-info-pages.com/levels.html

About the Authors

Gonzalo C. Centeno, MS, attended the Master of Science degree program in Counseling, option in Rehabilitation Counseling, at California State University, Los Angeles. Currently, he is Director of the Office for Students with Disabilities at Cal State LA. Mr. Centeno previously worked as a Disability Management Specialist from 1995 to 2014. In 1979 at age 13, he acquired a spinal cord injury at the C5-C6 level and was diagnosed with incomplete tetraplegia; he has since been a wheelchair user. Mr. Centeno received the California State Department of Rehabilitation's 50 Notable People in Rehabilitation.

Nancy M. Crewe, PhD, was a Professor in the Department of Physical Medicine and Rehabilitation at Michigan State University in East Lansing, Michigan. She coordinated the Master's Degree Program in Rehabilitation Counseling. For more than 25 years, Dr. Crewe conducted longitudinal research on psychosocial adjustment to spinal cord injury.

James S. Krause, PhD, is a Professor, Associate Dean for Research, and Director of the Center for Rehabilitation Research in Neurological Conditions in the College of Health Professions, Medical University of South Carolina. Prior to this, Dr. Krause worked as a rehabilitation psychologist and served as principal investigator on six federally funded research grants; previously, he was a visiting scientist at the Centers for Disease Control and Prevention (CDC) in Atlanta, Georgia.

Chapter 17

CEREBRAL PALSY

Angie Juàrez, EdD
Sherwood J. Best, PhD

Introduction

Most people recognize the words cerebral palsy but few are able to describe this heterogeneous and complex disorder. Ancient art and medical descriptions of cerebral palsy symptoms by Egyptian, Greek, and Roman scholars reflected interest in this condition (Panteliades, Panteliadis, & Vassilyadi, 2013). In the 1800s, several European physicians reported on the relationship between brain lesions and motor abnormalities. In 1853, Dr. William John Little (1810-1894) published a monograph entitled "On the Nature and Treatments of the Deformities of the Human Frame." He proposed a direct relationship between motor disabilities in children and circumstances of prematurity, difficult delivery, and infant asphyxia (Panteliades et al.). Later research by Sigmund Freud in the 1890s and Winthrop Phelps in the 1940s resulted in a motor classification system of cerebral palsy symptoms that is used today. Called Little's Disease for decades, the term cerebral palsy was first used in 1937 (Fairhurst, 2012). Each individual with cerebral palsy is unique with clinical, educational, rehabilitative, and vocational needs and outcomes that are not easily predictable.

Cerebral palsy (CP) cannot be cured by medical or educational interventions. As children with cerebral palsy grow into adulthood, they are faced with a variety of challenges related to physical and emotional maturation. Advances in medical and therapeutic treatments and changes in assistive technology have done much to improve quality of life of persons with CP. The limitations imposed by cerebral palsy no longer define their educational or career aspirations and outcomes.

Definition

Cerebral palsy is defined as:

> A group of permanent disorders of the development of movement and posture, causing activity limitations, which are attributed to non-progressive disturbances that occurred in the developing infant or fetal brain. The motor disorders of cerebral palsy are often accompanied by disturbances of sensation, perception, cognition, communication, and behavior, including epilepsy and secondary musculoskeletal problems (Moreno-De-Luca, Ledbetter, & Martin, 2012, p. 283).

Components of this complex definition contain the following features: (1) permanent movement and posture disorders that reduce activity; (2) early onset; (3) lack of underlying progressive pathology; and (4) numerous co-occurring deficits. Cerebral palsy is not a disease but the result of damage to areas of the developing brain that control motor function. The damage is referred to as static; it does not worsen. However, the dysfunction that results from muscle imbalance over time, combined with co-occurring characteristics of CP, contributes to more severe disability as the person ages (Cremer, Huvitz, & Peterson, 2017). Individuals may develop scoliosis (curvature of the spine), hip dislocation, early degenerative arthritis, hypertension, obesity, asthma, uneven bone growth, and chronic pain. These all contribute to reduced activity, functionality, and quality of life.

In addition to posture and motor disorders, people may have secondary outcomes of brain damage, including epilepsy, intellectual disability, sensory and cognitive impairments, and orthopedic complications

(Best & Bigge, 2010). Communication impairments that include disorders of speech and language occur in individuals with CP (Schölderle, Staiger, Lampe, Strecker, & Ziegler, 2016; Smith & Hustad, 2015). It is estimated that approximately "… 20% of individuals with cerebral palsy have psychosocial and behavioural problems" (Moreno-De-Luca et al., 2012, p. 284). However, not everyone will experience each of these associated impairments.

The prevalence of CP is reported to be between 1.4 to 3.0 per 1,000 live births (Bear & Wu, 2016; Maennar et al., 2016). Increases in both incidence and prevalence of cerebral palsy have been attributed to improved documentation, advances in obstetrics, and medical interventions that save the lives of infants and children while failing to prevent central nervous system damage. A recent phenomenon has been the occurrence of multiple births resulting from assisted reproduction. Children who are the products of multiple births, or who are very premature, are more likely to have CP than children who do not experience these intrauterine and birth conditions. The most commonly occurring type of cerebral palsy in persons born prematurely is spastic diplegia.

Etiology

Many factors are associated with a diagnosis of cerebral palsy. Cerebral palsy can occur before birth (prenatal), during the birth process (perinatal), or after birth (postnatal). Prematurity, genetic factors, low birthweight, exposure to maternal infection, metabolic disorders, anoxia (lack of oxygen) due to problems with the placenta, and multiple births are all potential prenatal contributors. Although anoxia during the birth process was historically proposed as the leading contributor to CP, it is now understood that prenatal contributors pose a greater risk (Moreno-De-Luca et al., 2012). Finally, postnatal trauma can include infections, exposure to toxic substances, and trauma such as child abuse. Gladstone (2010) proposed that postnatal causes, especially in relation to diseases such as cerebral malaria and meningitis, are more likely to occur in what he called resource-poor settings than would occur in Western countries, where CP is more highly related to premature birth. Impairments that co-occur with CP, including intellectual disability, seizures, and sensory impairments, help explain why this condition is so complex and varied.

Approximately 2.5% of every 1,000 infants born in the world every year have CP (Rana, Upadhyay, Rana, Durgapal, & Jantwal, 2017). Brain malformation, genetic syndromes, maternal infection, and anoxia are causes during the prenatal (pre-birth) period. Prenatal brain malformation resulting in CP may be due to genetic syndromes and acquired injuries from infections, such as cytomegalovirus and mutations. Premature infants whose birthweights are very low are at risk of injury to the white matter within the brain. Asphyxia (loss of oxygen) during the latter prenatal period may damage deep structures in the brain, leading to dyskinetic cerebral palsy. Multiple births place stress on the uterine environment and heighten the possibility of preterm birth. Maternal infection during pregnancy is also associated with higher incidence of CP (Bear & Wu, 2016).

The birth process itself can result in cerebral palsy. Risk factors such as maternal bleeding, problems with the placenta, maternal infection (such as herpes), and obstetrical complications such as prolonged labor, use of forceps, prolapsed cord, and abnormal presentation of the infant can all result in brain injury, either from direct insult to the brain or from anoxia.

After birth, the brain can be damaged through direct injury due to lack of oxygen (Best & Bigge, 2010). Infections to the central nervous system from encephalitis, poison, near drowning, suffocation, electrocution, and other traumatic events can result in CP. One entirely preventable cause of postnatal CP is physical abuse; infants and young children can suffer severe head injury from shaking and/or hitting. Another preventable cause of brain injury occurs when infants and children are not properly secured in automobiles.

Diagnosis

Due to the complexity of causes and risk factors associated with cerebral palsy, many infants may not be diagnosed for several years. To make a diagnosis, physicians rely on clinical judgment and comparison of infant function to their knowledge of typical infant development. Scales of early development are heavily focused on motor skills, which may be absent, delayed, or distorted in infants with cerebral palsy. However, the presence of certain abnormal general movements in infants have been found to be associated with a diagnosis of CP (Hamer, Bos, & Hadders-Algra, 2016).

Physicians and other professionals look for the presence of certain reflexive motor behaviors to assist in diagnosis. These reflexive behaviors, common to all infants, appear and disappear at predictable times during the course of development. They are involuntary and largely mediated through the brain stem. As infants mature, these motor behaviors are subsumed by higher brain development and become controlled by voluntary movement. Since human development is logical and predictable, the presence of these reflexive motor behaviors past the time when they should no longer be predominant is a strong indicator of brain damage and possible CP.

Although it is difficult to predict developmental outcomes in young children with CP, understanding the developmental trajectory of infants and young children assists in implementing services and interventions. Professionals need to work collaboratively with parents for information which will assist in providing optimal treatment. Practitioners need a thorough understanding of available treatments and their efficacy for treating symptoms.

Classification

Cerebral palsy has been classified in several ways, including: (1) type of movement disorder (spastic, dyskinetic, ataxic, and mixed); (2) limb involvement (topographical); and (3) motor limitations and functional abilities (Moreno-De-Luca et al., 2012). The most common form of movement disorder is spasticity, which is presumed to occur when there is damage to the cerebral cortex and pyramidal tracts (nerve fibers that originate in the nerve cells in the cerebral cortex and descend to the limbs to provide voluntary control of muscles). In spastic CP, limb muscles contract (tighten) abnormally, resulting in movement that is stiff and jerky. Over time, spastic muscles become shorter and exert differential pull around joints. The result is skeletal deformity, as the limbs, pelvis, and spine become misaligned. The movement disorder of dyskinesia is associated with damage in the extrapyramidal tracts (cells in the deep structures of the brain called the basal ganglia).

In dyskinetic CP, purposeful movement is distorted and muscles move randomly and involuntarily, especially in the arms, hands, and face. Movement may range from writhing to jerking to tremor, depending on the type of dyskinesia. Muscle tone may be more normal when the individual is asleep. Finally, ataxia is associated with damage in the cerebellum (tissue at the base of the brain that controls balance and coordination). Persons with ataxia may have great difficulty stabilizing their gait, and walk with feet wide

FIGURE 1
Classification of Cerebral Palsy by Location (Topography)

Limb Involvement	Description
Monoplegia	Single limb involvement. Uncommon in cerebral palsy.
Paraplegia	Legs only are involved.
Hemiplegia	Limbs on one side of the body are involved. The arm is usually more involved than the leg.
Triplegia	Three limbs are involved, usually both legs and one arm.
Quadriplegia or Tetraplegia	All four limbs are involved. The trunk is often involved.
Diplegia	Greater involvement of the lower limbs than the upper limbs.
Double Hemiplegia	More involvement in the upper limbs than the lower limbs. One side of the body may be more involved than the other.

apart while holding the arms out for balance. Rarely do these types of cerebral palsy exist in pure forms. Frequently, for example, persons have both spasticity and dyskinesia, referred to as mixed CP.

In addition to classification by type of movement disorder, CP also is classified by location of limb involvement, as follows:

Classifying CP by location of damage and quality of movement may not help the practitioner to understand the functional capabilities of persons with CP. Three classification systems defined by function are the Gross Motor Classification System (GMCS), the Manual Ability Classification System (MACS), and the Communication Function Classification System (CFCS). Each system is divided into five levels of mobility, hand/arm use, and communication. These systems have been found to be objective, reliable, and useful for practitioners (Fairhurst, 2012). A synopsis of the systems is provided in Figure 2.

Treatment

Persons with cerebral palsy have been the recipients of a variety of medical and therapeutic treatments. These treatments do not cure this condition, but are primarily employed to manage symptoms. Because symptoms associated with CP range in severity, location, and form among different persons, treatments may be more useful for some persons than for others. Close communication with health providers, as well as patient and caregiver attention to treatments, ensure the best outcomes.

FIGURE 2
Classification of Cerebral Palsy Using the GMCS, MACS, and CFCS

Level	Gross Motor	Manual Ability	Communication Function
I	Walks without limitations	Handles objects easily and successfully; some limitations with manual tasks requiring speed & efficiency	Effective sender & receiver with familiar & unfamiliar communication partners
II	Walks with limitations (long distances & balancing)	Handles most objects but with reduced quality & speed; may avoid some tasks or seek alternative ways to perform	Effective but slower paced sender & receiver with unfamiliar & familiar communication partners
III	Walks using a hand-held mobility device; uses wheelchair for community use	Handles objects with difficulty; needs help to prepare or modify activities	Effective sender & receiver with familiar communication partners
IV	Functions while sitting but self-mobility is limited; may use powered mobility	Handles a limited selection of easily managed objects in adapted situations; needs continuous support	Inconsistent sender & receiver with familiar communication partners
V	Severe head/trunk control limitations; transported using a manual wheelchair	Does not handle objects; severely limited to perform simple actions; requires total assistance	Seldom effective sender & receiver even with familiar communication partners

Medications

Medications are used to treat associated conditions, such as epilepsy or more direct treatment of muscle spasticity. Two medications used to relax tight muscles are intramuscular botulinum neurotoxin (BoNT) and intrathecal baclofen (Lioresal). Both medications have been used successfully with children and adults (Zdolsek, Olesch, Antolovich, & Reddihough, 2011).

Botulinum neurotoxins (BoNT) reduces muscle spasticity (Kahramam, Seyhan, Deger, Kutlutürk, & Mutlu, 2016). BoNT is injected into spastic muscles to release tension in the feet, upper limbs, pelvis, and back, which assists in more functional walking and sitting. It is also effective in reducing muscle spasms and migraine, back, knee, pelvic, and foot pain, as well as excessive drooling (Hay & Penn, 2011). The effect is temporary but injections may safely be repeated.

Baclofen inhibits spinal reflexes and is administered orally or via a pump that is worn externally or inserted under the skin. Oral Baclofen can result in side effects such as drowsiness, confusion, and nausea, so it is more efficiently and effectively delivered from the pump through a catheter to the cerebral spinal fluid in the lower back. Baclofen has been successful in reducing spasticity in the legs and also improving intelligible speech (Pin, McCartney, Lewis, & Waugh, 2011). "The most common negative side effects have been pump malfunction, catheter displacement, and infection at the pump site or within the central nervous system" (Zdolsek et al., 2011, p. 208).

Surgical Treatments

The goals of surgical intervention are to correct defects, prevent or reduce deformity, and optimize functionality. A variety of surgical procedures are used to treat symptoms. One neurosurgical procedure is selective dorsal rhizotomy (SDR). Selected nerve rootlets in the lumbar and sacral areas of the back are exposed. After electrical stimulation is applied to elicit muscle response, some rootlets are cut (Al-Shaar, Imtiaz, Alhalabi, Alsubaie, & Sabbagh, 2017; Sharan, 2017). The best candidates for SDR are young persons with lower limb spasticity who have ambulation before surgery. Following surgery, physical therapy is provided to maintain limb flexibility and improved function. However, long-term physical and psychosocial benefits of SDR may not be superior than less invasive approaches (Munger, Aldahondo, Krach, Novacheck, & Schwartz, 2017).

Orthopedic surgery is complementary to treatment such as IBT or SDR. It is frequently performed to release contracted muscles and improve standing and walking, as well as reduce pain, prevent joint dislocations, enhance comfort, and ease caregiver issues. Surgeries may be performed on the upper limbs, spine, hips, knees, ankles, and feet. The majority of surgery is performed for children younger than ten years to avoid damage due to continued use of deformed joints. These involve minimally invasive procedures and rely on external fixation such as pins instead of internal plates and screws to stabilize bone and reduce bony deformities by restoring joint function (Sharan, 2017).

Occupational Therapy and Physical Therapy

Occupational and physical therapists work with physicians to facilitate motor development and management. Physical therapists (PT) work to normalize the quality of patient movement through program planning for posture and balance, deformity prevention, and gross motor function, including walking. They work to align the spine, legs, and feet, provide postoperative rehabilitation, assist with physical management at home, and are responsible for fitting and monitoring positioning equipment, braces, prostheses, and casts.

Occupational therapists (OT) focus on development of functional skills for performance of activities in daily life. They work on eye-hand coordination skills, use of hands and arms for functional activities such as keyboarding, feeding, and writing; assess and remediate perceptual skills; evaluate the ability to organize and respond to incoming sensory information; and perform prevocational assessments (Best & Bigge, 2010). While physical therapists are more focused on motor abilities in the lower extremities, occupational therapists are focused on abilities in the upper extremities; the disciplines complement each other.

Many systems of treatment have developed in physical and occupational therapy, based on different theories of motor learning. Two of the most widely recognized approaches are neurodevelopment treatment and sensory motor integration. Neurodevelopment treatment is based on the work of Karel and Bertha Bobath from the 1940s. It features the use of positioning to inhibit inappropriate reflexive movements and enhance postural control. Movement potential is maximized while musculoskeletal complications are reduced. Therapy is applied within the context of functional activities that promote motivation and participation.

In the 1970s, Anna Jean Ayers developed sensory integration. It is not designed to teach specific skills but "to improve the child's ability to process and integrate sensory information (visual, auditory, tactile, and kinesthetic)... to allow improved functional capabilities in daily life" (Feferman, Harro, Patel, & Merrick., 2011, p. 335). Children may have dysfunction of sensory-motor integration because they lack normal motor control and therefore do not experience what normal movement feels like. Occupational therapists engage children in play activities in a sensory-rich environment to enhance body awareness, stimulate the vestibular system, and support perceptual and fine motor skills.

A critical aspect of therapy support is assessment and use of orthotic devices, which include custom-made braces, splints, and other appliances. Orthotic devices are prescribed after surgery to hold muscles in correct positions and avoid contractures. They also support weak muscles and aid the person in walking. Modern orthotic devices are made of lightweight plastic and are worn with regular shoes.

Physical and occupational therapists also assess and recommend equipment for positioning and mobility (Best & Bigge, 2010). This equipment is selected for function, comfort, durability, safety, as well as acceptance by individuals with CP and their families. Equipment to assist with sitting, standing, and lying on the side may be prescribed. Physical therapists assess and recommend mobility equipment, including wheelchairs, walkers, canes, and crutches. Wheelchairs are customized individually and include specialized wheelchairs for street mobility, road racing, and beach use.

Exercise is an area of physical activity that is often limited for persons with CP. It is planned and structured, which differentiates it from general energy expenditure which occurs through walking and other movement. Exercise strengthens muscles, supports physical fitness, and provides opportunities for social interaction. Practitioners recommend strength training, resistance training, and aquatic exercise. Strength training has enhanced outcomes for walking, running, and jumping in some individuals (Gillette, Boyd, Carty, & Barber, 2016). Resistance training is effective when compared to treadmill (endurance) exercise (Avraham, Harries, Namourah, Amro, & Bar-Haim, 2017).

Aquatic exercise is especially appealing because water helps eliminate pressure on joints and reduces the influence of gravity. The resistance offered by water promotes improved outcomes in aerobic activity, muscle strengthening, and toning. Aquatic therapy has no adverse effects and has value for improving motor function and physical activity enjoyment, even in more severely involved persons (Lai et al., 2015; Roostaei, Baharlouei, Axadi, & Fragala-Pinkham, 2017).

Alternative Therapies

Many therapies have been used to treat symptoms of CP. Some are not commonly used in the United States, but have gained popularity in other countries. These are categorized as examples of complementary and alternative medicine (CAM), defined as "a group of diverse medical and health care systems, practices, and products that are not presently considered to be part of conventional medicine" (Weisleder, 2010, p. 7). Complimentary therapies add a therapeutic component to activities that children would otherwise normally perform, like riding a horse, swimming, and skiing. Alternative therapies are separate from traditional therapies and are frequently based on different and "at best, anecdotal evidence and at times unusual ideas of the biology of the condition to which they are being applied" (Rosenbaum, 2003, p. s91). Selected examples of CAM include equine therapy, patterning, conductive education, the Adeli suit, hyperbaric oxygen therapy, and stem cell therapy.

Equine Therapy

Hippotherapy (horse-assisted therapy) improves balance, posture, and coordination in persons with CP as they adjust to the movement of the horse beneath them. Riders must keep the head and trunk controlled while astride the horse; horseback riding provides incentive for these tasks. Several studies have found improvements in muscle symmetry and balance, as well as dynamic activities, such as walking, running, and jumping (Stergiou, Tzoufi, Ntzani, Beris, & Ploumis, 2017; Whalen & Case-Smith, 2012).

Patterning

The premise of patterning is to recapitulate the physiological stages of motor development through exercises, by putting the person through a series of daily repetitive motor sequences. There is a lack of evidence that patterning leads to lasting changes in motor ability.

Conductive Education

The goal of this therapeutic and educational intervention is enhanced independent functioning through repetitive movements supported by specific verbal guidance by a conductor. The combinations of motor repetitions and active cognitive participation, coupled with simple adaptive equipment, makes conductive education an appealing therapy.

Hyperbaric Oxygen Therapy

The assertion of hyperbaric oxygen therapy (HBOT) is that regions of the brain near damaged areas can be re-activated with oxygen added in increased concentrations via a hyperbaric chamber (Feferman et al., 2011). HBOT has been successfully used to treat carbon monoxide poisoning, decompression sickness, and infections that receive poor blood supply. Scientific evaluations of this therapy have not resulted in any lasting results other than the positive effect of being involved in clinical trials.

Stem Cell Therapy

Stem cells "are naturally occurring cellular elements that retain the capacity to differentiate into various cell lines including neural cells" (Bell et al., 2011, p. 19). The proposed injection of stem cells to replace lost or damaged neurons is an enticing prospect that has resulted in a proliferation of clinics outside the United States. There is no current evidence of the efficacy of this approach for improving motor performance in persons with CP (Dan, 2016; Fairhurst, 2012; Feferman et al., 2011). Weisleder (2010) noted that many families turn to Complementary and Alternative Medicine (CAM) when "western medicine fails to address their needs" (p. 8). The combination of testimonial data and appealing web-based advertising result in continued pressure to try various CAM treatments.

Educational and Psychosocial Implications

Early Intervention

Whatever medication, surgical, and therapeutic experiences the child encounters is secondary to the fact that the typical experiences of childhood are necessary for growth and development. Early intervention provides many opportunities for development of the young child with cerebral palsy. Supported by federal law since 1986, early intervention is available for families of infants and young children. It provides opportunities for the child to develop in the domains of gross/fine motor skills, self-care, social/emotional, communication, and cognition.

Play is a crucial activity that enhances learning in children. Many fine and gross motor skills are practiced and refined during play. Children engage in symbolic play when they practice adult activities, such as cooking and fantasy play. Play fulfills social needs as children learn to take turns, explore roles, and learn to cooperate. Because it is intrinsically motivating, play is a pleasant activity undertaken for its own value rather than for a particular outcome.

Many children with CP cannot play in typical ways. Their motor impairments prevent them from grasping and manipulating toys. If they have visual or auditory deficits, their interactions with toys is more limited. The intensity of their motor needs may prevent others from engaging them in play activities. The outcomes of reduced play experiences affect not only the child's motor and cognitive development, but reduce the potential for social competence. Very young children benefit from toys on which they can ride and propel themselves until power-assisted wheelchairs become available to them. Commercial riding toy cars can be equipped with a switch interface that moves the car forward and hand controls for gripping.

These toys have been adapted for hospital use and can accommodate children who travel with oxygen, ventilators, and even intravenous poles (Martin & Dischino, 2017).

Play materials and activities can be effectively adapted for young children. Non-slip mats, Velcro® strips, and magnets can be used to stabilize play materials. Foam padding can be attached to handles or knobs to facilitate grasp. Battery-operated toys can be attached to switches for easy activation.

Assistive Technology in Elementary and Secondary School Programs

In recent years, assistive technology (AT) has opened new worlds of exploration and interactions for children and youth. The Individuals with Disabilities Education Improvement Act (IDEIA) defined assistive technology as " any item, piece of equipment, or product system, whether acquired commercially off the shelf, modified, or customized, that is used to increase, maintain, or improve the functional capabilities of a child with a disability" (20 U.S.C., 1401§ 602[1]). This means that AT is as simple as a pencil with a thicker handle for easier grasping, a book podium to adjust height and angle of reading materials, or as complex as a computer and its peripheral elements.

Children can learn to operate computer software using switch interface to replace a hand-controlled mouse. A head mouse is available that is mounted on spectacles. Head movement controls the cursor, and maintaining the head in a steady position (dwelling) acts to click the mouse. Voice-controlled software programs are available for the individual whose speech is adequate but hand use is not.

An exciting variation of environmental control for children and adolescents with CP is virtual reality technology. Virtual reality technology immerses the child in an experience and allows levels of interaction otherwise prevented by the disability. For example, a child engaged in a virtual reality artistic experience can draw, play paintball or sports, and even play a musical instrument. Active video games can replace sedentary screen activities such as television or internet searching as teaching and rehabilitation tools. Applications of virtual reality enhance activities of daily living, social participation, mobility, and cognition. Children who engaged in Wii-Fit® balance-based video games had better motor outcomes than a control group who participated in more conventional therapy (Taracki, Huseyinsinoglu, Taracki, & Ozdincler, 2016).

Psychosocial Implications of Cerebral Palsy

Although breakthroughs in technology have liberated people with CP from some of the physical constraints of their motor and speech impairments, non-physical aspects of functioning such as psychological, social, and environmental factors are equally important for maintaining well-being (Cheong, Lang, Hemphill, & Johnston, 2016). Adults with CP reported that receiving support to manage their physical needs resulted in stigma associated with feeling different (Read, Morton, & Ryan, 2015). A lack of reciprocated friendships and fewer social behaviors/interactions can lead to feelings of isolation. Even as the Internet and social media have created physical and social access opportunities, they also provide an avenue for cyber-bullying and other forms of victimization.

For children and youth, school provides a venue for implementing social support strategies and boosting self-perceived competence. These include structured disability awareness training for peers and school personnel, direct and firm adult responses to bullying, creation of peer support networks, and greater efforts by teachers for curricular and social integration in school environments (Lindsay & McPherson, 2011).

A unique approach for adolescents was the creation of an online social support intervention. Youth with cerebral palsy were able to contact adult mentors with disabilities, as well as psychologists through message boards and email. Structured meetings in chat rooms addressed topics including health concerns, bullying, making friends, career planning, recreation and leisure, and relationships. Participants reported enhanced peer contacts, friendships, social acceptance, self-awareness, family interaction, and reduced loneliness.

Rehabilitation and Vocational Outcomes

Rehabilitation

Persons with cerebral palsy do not acquire their disability as a result of disease, accident, or other experience later in life. Cerebral palsy is a developmental disability, a condition that begins before, during, or shortly after birth or during early childhood. Therefore, the concept of rehabilitation is actually one of habilitation, with professionals, family members, and the person focused on maximizing physical, intellectual, emotional, and social potential from the time of diagnosis. Previous discussion of medical and therapeutic treatments indicates the need for early intensive intervention. However, medical and therapeutic interventions can complicate attainment of an appropriate and complete educational experience. Recuperation from surgeries, therapy sessions, and other necessities such as orthotic evaluations and medication regimens all contribute to lost time from school. Teachers who lack training to adequately address the needs of students with CP, coupled with lack of appropriate assistive technology, diminish the educational experience.

Vocational Potential and Outcomes

Vocational potential for individuals with cerebral palsy is broad and varied. Becoming and staying employed is a strong indicator of successful rehabilitation and adult achievement. However, lack of adequate school-based vocational preparation represents an additional hurdle to successful employment. Fewer adults with CP are employed than their counterparts who do not have disabilities. When individuals with CP are employed, the rate of employment drops when they are in their 40s. Changes in health status associated with age, increased fatigue, need for medical services, and pain may account for workplace loss (Benner, Helberink, Veenis, van der Slot, & Roebroeck, 2017).

Research on disability and employment strongly suggests that higher educational achievement is associated with greater employment and may mediate other factors that result in early employment loss (Huang et al., 2013). Unfortunately, disability entitlements (Social Security, Medicare) received by non-working persons with disabilities may eclipse the wage rate for unskilled employment. In addition, lower paying jobs are more physical in nature and often not possible for persons with CP. Maintaining people in the workplace should include knowledge about age-related physical changes, anticipation of changes with appropriate accommodations, and improved workplace and job efficiency.

Direct training related to life skills provides support for successful adult outcomes. Participation in an immersive residential life skills program contributes to higher employment, independence, and overall life satisfaction by graduates. The content of the program included peer mentorship, real-life experiences, facilitated goal-setting, trial and error learning, calculated risk taking, and coaching based on themes of choice, responsibility, and control. Graduates commented positively on their social networks and understanding of their personal strengths and weaknesses. Vocational rehabilitation services enhance employment outcomes. Research (Huang et al., 2013) found that on-the-job training, job placement assistance, on-the-job support, maintenance services, and rehabilitation technology predicted successful employment outcomes.

People with cerebral palsy may be judged more on physical appearance and motor limitations than either education or vocational motivation. Although cognitive limitations frequently accompany CP, they are not synonymous conditions. Severity of CP is not a predictor of intellectual ability or limitation. While physical barriers can be eliminated through legislation and its enforcement, attitude is more difficult to manage. Tangible benefits can be derived from hiring a person with CP that far outweigh the effort to provide accommodations. The key is to believe that the individual can make a valuable workplace contribution.

Essential re-adjustment in attitude is one that places responsibility for making accommodations within the community, rather than viewing the person with CP as someone who needs to meet the challenge of disability. Incorporating universal design into living, education, and work is an example of adaptation that meets the physical needs of all persons, including persons with CP. When all people benefit from physical barrier reduction, such as incorporation of ramps, elevators, and other devices into physical structures, or less tangible accommodations such as flexible work schedules and cyber-commuting, the partition between persons with disabilities and those without disabilities decreases. The concept of universal design needs to be accompanied by services that are individualized and flexible to make a best fit between the person and work environment (Drnach, Magill-Evans, & Galambos, 2010).

Assistive Technology

The role of AT in providing educational and vocational access is clear. Within the broad arena of AT is a sub-category known as augmentative and alternative communication (AAC). AAC attempts to compensate, either temporarily or permanently, for the impairment and disability patterns of individuals with severe expressive communication disorders. It can augment speech that is present but difficult to understand, or be an alternative for speech that is absent. AAC is a revolutionary breakthrough for persons who previously were unable to express their thoughts and feelings. These systems can be simple, such as two-dimensional picture-based communication boards that are accessed by pointing. It can be complex electronic, dedicated communication devices that store and retrieve entire messages and output them through synthesized voice. These high tech devices frequently interface with computers. The communication possibilities with AAC are significant (Best & Bigge, 2010).

Persons who use AAC face unique issues of employment and co-worker interaction. Discussion with a group of AAC users who were fully employed in competitive job situations included three themes: (1) barriers to employment; (2) necessary supports for employment; and (3) recommendations for improving employment outcomes for persons who use AAC. Barriers to employment activities include negative attitudes of others, poor educational attainment, lack of technological training, policy and funding shortfalls, inadequate personal care/support services, and transportation problems. Supports for employment include the user's personal characteristics, education, work experience, family assistance for transportation and personal care, ability to use technology, the presence of workplace mentors, and legislative supports, such as the Americans with Disabilities Act (ADA) and Section 504 of the Rehabilitation Act of 1973. Many avenues of funding exist for the assessment and purchase of AAC systems. Children may be eligible through their schools, therapy providers, or private insurance, while adults can consult with state vocational rehabilitation agencies.

Quality of Life

Quality of life extends beyond employment and encompasses the opportunity to be an active part of one's community and engage in interactions crucial to personal well-being. In addition to objective factors such as physical health and material security, it includes subjective factors such as personal satisfaction and feelings of competence and empowerment.

Like anyone else, persons with cerebral palsy have interests in life fulfillment beyond a good education and employment satisfaction. Attainment and maintenance of physical and material well-being, social relations, participation in community and civic activities, personal development and fulfillment, and recreation all indicate an enhanced quality of life (Best, 2010). These more inclusive outcomes should be the goal for educators, rehabilitation counselors, and other professionals who assist persons with CP reach their full potential.

Case Study

Justin is 20 years old and graduated high school last year. At two years of age, he was diagnosed with cerebral palsy. The CP involvement was later diagnosed as quadriplegia (involving all four limbs), and Level IV on the Gross Motor Classification System. In his early years of school, Justin was enrolled in a special class for students with orthopedic impairments. During the four years from kindergarten through third grade, Justin was frequently hospitalized for respiratory problems and other illnesses associated with his physical impairments. This led to him falling increasingly further behind in school. While he was not unhappy in the environment, his parents felt that Justin would be challenged to excel at a higher level, both academically and socially, if he were transferred to general education classes with his non-disabled peers. His teachers agreed.

From the third grade (which he repeated) until graduation from high school, Justin was included in age-appropriate general education classes with support from special education. Primarily, Justin's special education support involved the provision of physical therapy to assist in increasing his mobility, and speech and language therapy using augmentative communication devices to help in developing communication skills. Special education teachers provided assistance in developing computer skills and helping him learn appropriate computer interface, as well as other assistive technology to negotiate his campus and acquire independent self-care skills.

Justin maintained average achievement from elementary through high school. Since elementary school, Justin has been non-ambulatory and has used a motorized wheelchair. The wheelchair has a special tray designed to carry a laptop computer. With support from a paraprofessional assistant who helps with personal care and eating, Justin is able to perform all the learning activities required in school.

Justin is sure he will be able to succeed in work. His goal is to obtain a job in the computer field and work while attending university classes part-time until he graduates with a degree in computer science. Using several different assistive technology devices, Justin has developed a high level of proficiency with the computer. Throughout school, he was a member of a group of young men and women who frequently met during high school to play computer games. Justin was able to alter many of the games to make them more challenging and entertaining.

In the past year, one of Justin's friends from the group found a position with a computer game manufacturer as a programmer in research and development. This friend assured Justin that the company would be interested in hiring him also. The pay is excellent and includes benefits; Justin feels that he is even more knowledgeable than his friend in this particular area. He could not think of a single reason not to seek employment with this company – until he spoke to his parents.

His parents explained that, while they wanted to join in his excitement, they were concerned that Justin complete college before becoming employed. They reminded him that technology is developing at a phenomenal pace and many technology companies are unable to keep pace and have layoffs or declare bankruptcy. Without a college degree, Justin could find himself out of work with no prospects for finding another job.

Justin is sure of what he wants to do. The Americans with Disabilities Act provides some workplace protections against discrimination based on disability and Justin is aware of this. Although he respects his parents and knows they have his best interests at heart, he believes this job is an opportunity of a lifetime. Justin reached a compromise with his parents by agreeing to speak to his rehabilitation counselor at the Department of Rehabilitation and seek advice. Both Justin and his parents agreed to seriously consider the counselor's ideas.

Questions

1. The vocational rehabilitation counselor needs to have basic information about the client to recommend a realistic vocational goal. Identify several examples of this information.
2. As the counselor, identify how you will handle the dilemma regarding Justin's potential job and his completion of college.
3. Are the career goals of Justin and those of his parents realistic and compatible with his capabilities and limitations?
4. Identify other possibilities for Justin as a client of the Department of Rehabilitation.
5. What obstacles to employment may Justin encounter? How limiting is his disability and society's perception of him, including potential employers? Include a discussion of the concept of a disabling environment.

References

Al-Shaar, H. A., Imtiaz, M. T., Alhalabi, H. Alsubaie, S. M., & Sabbagh, A. J. (2017). Selective forsal rhizotomy: A multidisciplinary approach to treating spastic diplegia. *Asian Journal of Neurosurgery, 12*, 454-465.

Avirham, R., Harries, N., Namourah, I., Amro, A., & Bar-Haim, S. (2017). Effects of a group circuit progressive resistance training program compared with a treadmill training program for adolescents with cerebral palsy. *Developmental Neurorehabilitation, 20*(6), 347-354.

Bear. J. J., & Wu, Y. W. (2016). Maternal infections during pregnancy and cerebral palsy in the child. *Pediatric Neurology, 57*, 74-79.

Bell, E., Wallace, T., Chouinard, I., Shevell, M., & Racine, E. (2011). Responding to requests of families for unproven interventions for neurodevelopmental disorders: Hyperbaric oxygen "treatment" and stem cell "therapy" in cerebral palsy. *Developmental Disabilities Research, 17*, 19-26.

Benner, J. L., Helberink, S. R., Veenis, T., van der Slot, W. M., & Roebroeck, M. E. (2017). Course of employment of adults with cerebral palsy over a 14-year period. *Developmental Medicine and Child Neurology, 59*(7), 762-768.

Best, S. J. (2010). Understanding individuals with physical, health, and multiple disabilities. In S. J. Best, K. W. Heller, & J. L. Bigge, *Teaching individuals with physical or multiple disabilities* (6th ed., pp. 3-31). Upper Saddle River, NJ: Pearson.

Best, S. J., & Bigge, J. L. (2010). Cerebral palsy. In S. J. Best, K. W. Heller, & J. L. Bigge. *Teaching individuals with physical or multiple disabilities* (6th ed., pp. 59-81). Upper Saddle River, NJ: Pearson.

Cheong, S. K., Lang, P. L., Hemphill, S. A., & Johnston, L. M. (2016). What constitutes self-concept for children with CP? A Delphi consensus study. *Journal of Developmental and Physical Disabilities, 28*, 333-346.

Cremer, N., Huvitz, E. A., & Peterson, M. D. (2017). Multi mobidity in middle-aged adults with cerebral palsy. *American Journal of Medicine, 130*(6), 9-15.

Dan, B. (2016). Stem cell therapy for cerebral palsy. *Developmental Medicine and Child Neurology, 58*(5), 424.

Drnach, M., O'Brien, P. A., & Kreger, A. (2010). The effects of a 5-week therapeutic horseback riding program on gross motor function in a child with cerebral palsy: A case study. *Journal of Alternative and Complimentary Therapy, 16*(9), 1003-1006.

Fairhurst, C. (2012). Cerebral palsy: The whys and hows. *Archives of Disease in Childhood, 97*(4), 122-131.

Feferman, H., Harro, J., Patel, D. R., & Merrick, J. (2011). Therapeutic interventions in cerebral palsy. *International Journal of Child and Adolescence Health, 4*(4), 333-339.

Gillette, J. G., Boyd, R. N., Carty, C. P., & Barber, L. A. (2016). The impact of strength training on skeletal muscle morphology and architecture in children and adolescents with cerebral palsy: A systematic review. *Research in Developmental Disabilities, 56*, 183-196.

Gladstone, M. (2010). A review of the incidence and prevalence, types, and aetiology of childhood cerebral palsy in resource-poor countries. *Annals of Tropical Paediatrics, 30*, 181-196.

Hamer, E. G., Bos, A. F., & Hadders-Algra, M. (2016). Specific characteristics of abnormal general movements associated with functional outcome at school age. *Developmental Medicine and Child Neurology, 95*, 9-13.

Hay, N., & Penn, C. (2011). Botox® to reduce drooling in a paediatric population with neurological impairments: A Phase I study. *International Journal of Language and Communication Disorders, 54*(5), 550-563.

Huang, I-C., Holzbauer, J. J., Lee, E-J, Chronister, J., Chan, F. & O'Neill, J. (2013). Vocational rehabilitation services and employment outcomes for adults with cerebral palsy in the United States. *Developmental Medicine and Child Neurology, 55*, 1000-1008.

Individuals with Disabilities Education Improvement Act (IDEIA) of 2004, 1401§ 602.

Kahramam, A., Seyhan, K., Deger, U., Kutlutürk, S., & Mutlu, A. (2016). Should botulinum toxin A injections be repeated in children with cerebral palsy? A systematic review. *Developmental Medicine and Child Neurology, 58*, 910-917.

Lai, C-J., Liu, W-Y., Yang, T-S., Chen, C-L., Wu, C-Y, & Chan, A-C. (2015). Pediatric aquatic therapy on motor function and enjoyment in children diagnosed with cerebral palsy of various motor severities. *Journal of Child Neurology, 32*(2), 200-208.

Lindsay, S., & McPherson, A. C. (2011). Strategies for improving disability awareness and social inclusion of children and young people with cerebral palsy. *Child Care, Health, and Development, 38*(6), 809-816.

Maennar, M. J., Blumberg, S. J., Kogan, M. D., Christensen, D., Yeargin-Allsopp, M., & Schieve, L. A. (2016). Prevalence of cerebral palsy and intellectual disability among children identified in two national surveys, 2011-2013. *Annals of Epidemiology, 26*, 222-226.

Martin, M. R., & Dischino, M. (2017). Go baby go! The freedom of movement. *Palaestra, 31*(3), 14-17.

Moreno-De-Luca, A., Ledbetter, D. H., & Martin, C. L. (2012). Genetic insights into the causes and classification of the cerebral palsies. *Lancet, 11*, 283-292.

Munger, M. E., Aldahondo, N., Krach, L. E., Novacheck, T. F., & Schwartz, M. H. (2017). Long-term outcomes after selective dorsal rhizotomy: A retrospective matched cohort study. *Developmental Medicine and Child Neurology, 59*(11), 1196-1203.

Panteliades, C., Panteliadis, P., & Vassilyadi, F. (2013). Hallmarks in the history of cerebral palsy: From antiquity to mid-20th Century. *Brain and Development, 35*, 285-292.

Pin, T. W., McCartney, L., Lewis, J., & Waugh, M. C. (2011). Use of intrathecal baclofen therapy in ambulant children and adolescents with spasticity and dystonia of cerebral origin: A systematic review. *Developmental Medicine and Child Neurology, 53*(10), 885-895.

Rana, M., Upadhyay, J., Rana, A., Durgapal, S., & Jantwal, A. (2017). A systematic review of etiology, epidemiology, and treatment of cerebral palsy. *International Journal of Nutrition, Pharmacology, and Neurological Diseases, 7*(4), 76-83.

Read, S. A., Morton, T. A. & Ryan, M. K. (2015). Negotiating identity: A qualitative analysis of stigma and support seeking for individuals with cerebral palsy. *Disability and Rehabilitation, 37*(13), 1162-1169.

Roostaei, M., Baharlouei, H., Axadi, H., & Fragala-Pinkham, M. A. (2017). Effects of aquatic intervention on gross motor skills in children with cerebral palsy: A systematic review. *Physical and Occupational Therapy in Pediatrics, 37*(5), 496-515.

Rosenbaum, P. L. (2003). Controversial treatment of spasticity: Exploring alternate therapies for motor function in children with cerebral palsy. *Journal of Child Neurology, 18*(9), s89-s94.

Schölderle, T., Staiger, A., Lampe, R., Strecker, K., & Ziegler, W. (2016). Dysarthria in adults with cerebral palsy: Clinical presentation and impacts on communication. *Journal of Speech, Language, and Hearing Research, 59*, 216-229.

Sharan, D. (2017). Orthopedic surgery in cerebral palsy: *Indian Journal of Orthopedics, 51*, 240-255.

Smith, A. L., & Hustad, K. C. (2015). AAC and early intervention for children with cerebral palsy: Parent perceptions and child risk factors. *Augmentative and Alternative Communication, 31*(4), 336-350.

Stergiou, A., Tzoufi, M., Ntzani, D., Beris, A., & Ploumis, A. (2017). Therapeutic effects of horseback riding interventions: A systematic review and meta-analysis. *American Journal of Physical Medicine and Rehabilitation, 96*(10), 717-725.

Taracki, D., Huseyinsinoglu, B. E., Taracki, E., & Ozdincler, A. R. (2016). Effects of Nintendo Wii-Fit® video games on balance in children with mild cerebral palsy. *Pediatrics International, 58*, 1042-1050.

Weisleder, P. (2010). Unethical prescriptions: Alternative therapies for children with cerebral palsy. *Clinical Pediatrics, 49*(1), 7-11.

Whalen, C. N., & Case-Smith, J. (2012). Therapeutic effects of horseback riding therapy on gross motor function in children with cerebral palsy: A systematic review. *Physical and Occupational Therapy in Pediatrics, 32*(3), 229-242.

Zdolsek, H. A., Olesch, C., Antolovich, G., & Reddihough, D. (2011). Intrathecal baclofen therapy: Benefits and complications. *Journal of Intellectual and Developmental Disability*, *36*(3), 207-213.

About the Authors

Dr. Angie Juàrez is Program Specialist in the Alhambra Unified School District and a Lecturer in the Division of Special Education and Counseling at California State University, Los Angeles. She has taught as a special day program teacher and itinerant support provider for students with orthopedic, health, and multiple disabilities for over 16 years. Currently, Dr. Juarez is President of the National Division for Physical, Health, and Multiple Disabilities (DPHMD) of the Council for Exceptional Children and Vice President of California Association for Physical and Health Impairments (CAPHI).

Dr. Sherwood J. Best is Professor and Coordinator of the program for Physical and Health Impairments in the Division of Special Education and Counseling at California State University, Los Angeles. Dr. Best has presented at many local, state, and national professional conferences, and is Past-President of DPHMD of the Council for Exceptional Children and CAPHI.

Chapter 18

MUSCULAR DYSTROPHY

Roy K. Chen, PhD, CRC

Introduction

Muscular dystrophy (MD) is a group of over 40 forms of neuromuscular diseases and related myopathies. Neuromuscular disorders are the result of single gene or complex genetic mutations (Amato & Russell, 2016). Persons with MD differ in terms of age of onset, etiology, severity of progression, locations of the muscles affected, and mode of inheritance (Che Ismail & Othman, 2016; Mathews, 2003). One common characteristic present in the wide array of neuromuscular disorders is the gradual weakening and progressive degeneration of the skeletal muscles that control voluntary movements. Despite recent advances in the molecular diagnosis of defective genes and the continuing breakthroughs in curative treatments over the last decade, MD still remains an incurable disease.

This disabling illness impacts the quality of life for people affected by it, along with their families. Ouyang, Grosse, and Kenneson (2008) calculated the average medical expenditures for individuals with MD and found their costs to be 10 to 20 times higher than for individuals without MD. In addition to learning to cope with the functional limitations associated with this progressively deteriorating physical condition, these individuals encounter attitudinal and architectural barriers to living independently and obtaining gainful employment. Collectively, they experience higher unemployment and underemployment rates as well as a lower acceptance rate for vocational rehabilitation counseling services than those with other disabilities (Fowler et al., 1997). There is an imperative need to improve the effectiveness of rehabilitation services provided for clients with this disease.

The purpose of this chapter is to review clinical and psychosocial aspects involving MD and to offer suggestions for developing and implementing rehabilitation plans for adults with MD from a holistic perspective. This holistic approach includes addressing the disability (functional limitations and capabilities), psychological and emotional factors, education, vocational histories, social resources, and belief systems. Through the use of a holistic approach, counselors can help clients maximize their rehabilitation potential.

Prevalence of MD

Although no exact incidence figures for persons with MD are available, based on the 2005 world population (6 billion, 451 million people) and the prevalence of neuromuscular disorders, it is estimated there are at least 1.26 million children and adults with MD worldwide. In the United States, more than 250,000 Americans have been diagnosed with one of the 40 types of MD (Centers for Disease Control and Prevention [CDC], 2018; Shannon, 2004); about two-thirds of them are children (Siegel, 1999). Premature death among children with Duchenne MD (DMD) is common. These individuals rarely live past their second decade of life due to the irreversible and continuous weakening of involuntary muscles affecting various body systems and organs such as the cardiovascular system, pulmonary system, and gastrointestinal system.

The American public tends to view MD as a disease affecting only children, in part due to the huge success of the annual Muscular Dystrophy Association (MDA) Jerry Lewis Telethon held on Labor Day.

While it is commendable of Jerry's "poster boys and girls" and their parents to come forth on national television in an effort to share their courageous personal stories and to entreat to television viewers for generous financial support, adults with MD often go unnoticed. There are several reasons why adults with MD as a group fail to generate strong public interest. First, the debilitating physical condition impedes many people from actively participating in and organizing grass roots support groups. Mobility and transportation difficulties present major challenges for persons who do not drive. Children with MD experience a reduced life expectancy; consequently, the number of persons with MD declines as age advances.

Based on the estimates provided by the CDC (2018) and Shannon (2004), the total number of adult Americans with MD is about 83,000 – a number far fewer than the number of people with AIDS, visual impairments, or psychiatric disabilities. Additionally, due to the early onset of disability, the education of children with MD is often interrupted by frequent hospitalizations and a decline in general health. Consequently, people with MD do not always have the necessary education and vocational training to assume leadership positions in professional fields. There are no prominent public figures or celebrities with MD to advocate for the cause and rights of this community. Michael J. Fox and Mohammed Ali are high profile spokespersons for Parkinson Disease. Christopher Reeves was the charismatic ambassador for people with spinal cord injuries. Elton John is a steadfast ally for HIV/AIDS. The Kennedy family has been a long-time crusader for people with developmental disabilities. In comparison with other interest groups, there is an absence of strong political representation for MD to facilitate advocacy for more medical research funding (Sirotkin-Roses, 1991).

Major Types of MD

The three most common procedures used by physicians to confirm the presence of MD are blood testing, electromyography (EMG), and biopsy (Angelini, 2014). MD is a taxonomy of several types of hereditary, mostly X chromosome-linked, progressive muscular disorders characterized by gradual degeneration and wasting away of the muscle cells and fibers (Siegel, 1999). The subsequent discussion examines some of the most commonly seen types.

Duchenne Muscular Dystrophy (DMD)

DMD, named after French physician Guillaume Duchenne de Boulogne, is by far the most common and severe form of MD in childhood (Angelini, 2014; Huml, 2015), with a total incidence of 63 per million people (CDC, 2018). It is estimated to occur in three out of every 10,000 male births (Bray, Bundy, Ryan, & North, 2017). The average onset of the disability is between two and five years of age. Most children diagnosed with DMD lose their ambulatory function during elementary school. Improper sitting positions in a wheelchair for prolonged periods of time may cause scoliosis (curvature of the spine). Early signs of the disease include frequent falls and difficulty running, trouble changing from a squatting or sitting position, and problems climbing stairs. Initial weakness occurs in proximal muscles – particularly in the hip and shoulder.

In contrast to the atrophy of muscles, enlargement of the calf muscles, a sign of pseudohypertrophy, may occur. A significant number of children with DMD do not survive into adulthood (age 20) due to the failure of respiratory and cardiac muscles. Like the wide range of intelligence levels exhibited in the general population, people with MD vary in their cognitive abilities. However, researchers have no explanation as to why people with DMD tend to have lower intelligence scores compared to people with other types of MD (McDonald et al., 1995a; Ouyang et al., 2012). Reading disability due to poor simultaneous and sequential information processing has been observed in children with DMD.

Becker Muscular Dystrophy (BMD)

In 1956, Peter Emil Becker, a German physician, was the first person to recognize this mild, variant form of DMD. The clinical presentations of BMD are similar to that of DMD. However, the time of initial diagnosis usually appears much later (as late as 25 years) and has a slower rate of muscle deterioration. The prevalence figure of BMD is about 24 per million people (CDC, 2018; Shannon, 2004). The absence of a vital protein surrounding muscle fiber called dystrophin distinguishes DMD from BMD. Dystrophin is needed to allow muscle cells to work properly. The dystrophin produced in people with BMD is often inadequate and of poor quality. As with people with DMD, the body simply fails to manufacture this protein. Muscle weakness begins in the lower extremities and gradually includes the upper body. Due to the late onset of the disease, individuals with BMD often ambulate until about age 30, after which they may need to use a wheelchair. The major risk in BMD is from cardiac, as opposed to pulmonary complications (McDonald et al., 1995b). Death can occur in the 20s or 30s, yet some patients live beyond this age range. Persons with BMD have longer life expectancies than those who have DMD.

Facioscapulohumeral Muscular Dystrophy (FSHMD)

Facioscapulohumeral muscular dystrophy is the third most frequent form of myopathy (Angelini, 2014). Face, shoulders, and upper arms are the three groups of musculatures affected by this progressive myopathy. FSHMD is characterized by persons having difficulty raising the arms, closing the eyelids, sucking from a straw, and swallowing food. Speech may become indistinct if facial muscles continue to weaken. Asymmetric scapular winging is commonly observed (Angelini, 2014). FSHMD affects both sexes and its usual onset is between the ages of 20 and 30. Yet, persons with FSHMD are expected to have near-normal life expectancies. The prevalence is estimated at 10 to 20 per million (Shannon, 2004). As one of the least threatening forms of MD, this disease does not affect pulmonary and cardiac functions. Because the severity is mild in comparison to DMD and LGMD, most people do not develop pelvic muscle problems and retain an ability to walk throughout their lifetimes (Chen & Crewe, 2009).

Limb-Girdle Muscular Dystrophy (LGMD)

The prevalence of LGMD is estimated to be 20 to 40 per million people (Shannon, 2004). Shoulder and pelvic girdle muscles are the primary areas affected. These individuals have weakness in their proximal muscles with a moderate rate of deterioration; the onset of disability occurs in late adolescence or early adulthood. The typical pattern of muscle deterioration begins in the hip girdle and moves toward the arms and shoulders. As a result, individuals with LGMD require the use of both hands when rising from lying or sitting positions (Angelini, 2014). Weakness in the legs advances more rapidly than weakness in the arms because lower extremities bear more stress from their constant involvement in maintaining posture. In all cases, people who have LGMD will lose their ability to ambulate and require the use of a wheelchair. Life expectancy is somewhat reduced.

Autosomal diseases like LGMD are characterized by gene mutations in any of the first 22 pairs of non-sex-determining autosomal chromosomes (Mathews, 2003). A person with an autosomal dominant disorder usually has one parent who carries mutated genes. Someone with an autosomal recessive disorder has two unaffected parents each carrying defective genes.

Myotonic Muscular Dystrophy (MMD)

The most prominent difference between MMD and other types of MD is that the distal muscles instead of the proximal muscles are affected first. A major characteristic symptom is the delay in timed motor performance. Persons with MMD lack strong small muscles in their hands and have difficulty relaxing a handgrip. Due to stiffness in their hands, it takes them longer to let go of an object. The onset of disability ranges from early childhood to adulthood. MMD has an estimated prevalence of 1 in 8,000 people, similarly affecting males and females (Yu, Blankenship, Yang, & Lee, 2006).

Noticeable muscle deterioration in the neck and face, forearms and lower legs, cardiac dysrhythmias, endocrine problems, frontal baldness, and cataracts of the eyes are common complications of MMD. The severity of this condition increases from one generation to the next. Children with MMD who inherit genetic defects show far more serious conditions than their affected parents.

Functional Limitations

Physical impairments caused by MD have an adverse effect on a person's ability to function in the overall environment. Rehabilitation counselors may encounter difficulty pinpointing functional limitations associated with MD because there is no uniform symptom and severity experienced (Chen & Crewe, 2009). Depending on the type of MD, its effect on quality of life varies. Counselors need to evaluate each client individually, as these muscular diseases vary greatly in terms of their symptoms, complications, limitations, and progression. Swenson (2000) suggested examining a client's functional capacity in the following areas: cognitive, social, physical, vocational, and emotional.

Cognitive Functioning

There is lack of consensus among researchers regarding cognitive deficits in people with DMD. Studies have shown that lower intelligence is one of the primary manifestations (McDonald et al., 1995a; Ogasawara, 1989). However, some investigators have argued that the correlation between low intelligence levels and the presence of DMD is a consequence of experiential conditions (insufficient early education due to illness) rather than being an inherent nature of the disorder. Mean intelligence scores of people with LGMD and FSHMD measured by full scale IQ did not significantly differ from those of the general population (Kilmer et al., 1995; McDonald et al., 1995c).

Social Functioning

Quality of social interaction suggests a person's capability in interacting with the environment. People with pleasing physiques often have higher self-esteem and egos because they have been receiving praise since an early age. Freud (1963) believed that body image is formed in conjunction with the development of the ego, and interpersonal relationships are reflections of body attitude. Disability alters not only physical functioning but also reciprocity of human actions and reactions (Marini, Chen, Feist, Flores-Torres, & Castillo, 2011). Walkers, wheelchairs, respiratory ventilators, and other assistive devices often evoke discomfort and fear in others. Not wanting to cause embarrassment or not knowing how to respond to the person's altered physical status, friends and associates may be hesitant regarding how to interact appropriately (Brodwin & Chen, 2000). Opportunities for casual friendly gatherings and dating are further diminished due to architectural barriers and the unavailability of transportation (Miller, Chen, Graf, & Kranz, 2009).

Physical/Vocational Functioning

Limited range of motion in the upper and lower extremities is a common complication in clients with LGMD, FSHMD, and MMD. The occurrence of muscle contractures in the legs and heels, due to the shortening of muscle fibers and fibrosis of the connective tissues, limit ambulatory function. In most cases, hand function is maintained long after leg function ceases. Yet, raising the arms above shoulder level and lifting the feet off the ground become difficult. Buttoning shirts, twisting jar tops, tying neckties, and gripping pens pose difficulties as a result of loss of gross and fine motor movements. As muscles grow weaker, personal attendant care may be needed for hygiene and dressing. Lifting, carrying, and walking on uneven surfaces may not be possible and can require accommodation at the worksite. Clients with dystrophy affecting their hips and joints tend to find squatting and kneeling positions difficult or impossible. Fatigue and physical exhaustion occasionally interrupt workflow for brief moments, as people with MD often require short rest breaks to replenish their energy levels.

Emotional Functioning

To revert from a self-reliant person to a dependent person needing assistance is traumatic and emotionally painful. Role reversal inflicts emotional distress. Furthermore, physical inadequacy produces self-doubts as adults with late onset MD come to terms with the reality that functional losses are inevitable, progressive, and irreversible. Having MD greatly impacts self-identity. It is not unusual for someone who has been performing a particular job for years to lose the identity associated with that profession when no longer able to perform the work. The self-perception of people with MD varies in accordance with the status of their ever-changing physical condition.

Employment Profiles for Persons with MD

Of the 54 million Americans with disabilities, 26 million of them have severe disabilities (Roessler, Rubin, & Rumrill, Jr., 2017). Evidence has shown that disability has a negative effect on employment prospects and earnings among persons within the disability community. In 2000, the employment rate for working age (21 to 58) individuals with disabilities was 46% lower than individuals without disabilities (Hotchkiss, 2004). Median monthly earnings for nondisabled male workers between the ages of 35 to 54 were $2,566, compared to $1,568 among those with severe disabilities. Not surprisingly, people with neuromuscular diseases frequently are near the bottom level of income. There are several reasons for the disproportionate numbers of people with disabilities and why they are unrepresented in the workforce. In the ensuing paragraph, the author discusses those reasons from the perspectives of both the client and rehabilitation provider.

Education has long been regarded as a necessary requisite for entry into the labor force. Chronic medical conditions often create insurmountable obstacles for receiving the quality education needed in today's labor market. Inadequate job preparation due to insufficient education is of great concern to rehabilitation counselors. About 40% of people with disabilities never finish high school and 69% never attend college (Mackelprang & Salsgiver, 1999). Another factor that affects employment level is the type of MD. In a study of employment status of rehabilitation clients, Fowler and his colleagues (1997) found a significant difference in employment across MD types. Specifically, 49% of individuals with BMD and FSHD were employed at the time of the survey, compared to 26% of LGMD patients and 31% of MMD individuals.

The unfamiliarity with MD among rehabilitation service providers decreases the referral and acceptance rates for vocational rehabilitation services. Rehabilitation counselors at state agencies generally do not possess sufficient knowledge regarding MD, which in turn has led to a higher denial rate for services (Fowler et al., 1997). Due to the unpredictability of the pace of deterioration in MD, counselors may see little vocational potential in those affected. Negative attitudes toward MD on the part of rehabilitation counselors inevitably produce unsatisfactory rehabilitation outcomes. It is, therefore, understandable that people with this condition underutilize rehabilitation.

Holistic Interventions

To increase rehabilitation efficacy, counselors must distinguish the type of MD when developing vocational plans. It is a great disservice to clients if rchabilitation counselors lay out generic plans without regard to the nature of MD. Due to shortened life expectancy and progressive deterioration, mapping out a long-term career plan for clients with DMD will not always be realistic, practical, or appropriate. The complex nature of MD makes it difficult for rehabilitation counselors to understand the general well-being of these clients. A multidisciplinary team approach draws on expertise from different professionals, such as occupational therapists, psychologists, neurologists, physical therapists, rehabilitation counselors, and orthopedists. Bartalos (1990) identified key areas of quality of life that are of great concern to people with neuromuscular disorders: physical symptoms, medical complications, functional limitations, emotional symptoms, interpersonal relations, work adjustment, leisure activities, and sexual function. The following section recommends several interventions to ameliorate the debilitating effects of MD in various areas.

Psychosocial Counseling Considerations

Clinicians have long believed that persons with MD go through stages of emotional distress similar to persons faced with dying, as described by Dr. Elizabeth Kubler-Ross. These stages include denial, anger, bargaining, depression, and eventual acceptance. When considering stage theories, one needs to keep in mind that no two people react in the same way to the diagnosis of a severely disabling condition, nor is progression through the stages necessarily linear. Adaptation to disability is an ongoing lifelong developmental process.

Rehabilitation clients with MD face loss of mobility, reduced opportunities for employment, changes in living arrangements, and diminished social interaction. Clients with these conditions are at considerably higher risk for mental health issues; depression is a common problem among people with neuromuscular diseases (Fowler et al., 1997). In addition to social stigma, environmental restrictions, such as architectural barriers, unfriendly terrain, and lack of availability of suitable means of transportation further impede persons with MD from establishing meaningful relationships with others (Chen, Miller, Seo, & Mendoza, 2010).

To improve self-esteem and self-concept for people with disabilities, rehabilitation counselors must listen to their clients' problems with empathy and provide encouragement and support. In a multicultural society like the United States, people practice different religions and beliefs to draw upon sources of power to sustain psychological growth. Research has shown that spiritual well-being is positively correlated with life satisfaction (Chen & Crewe, 2006). Rehabilitation counselors need to show sensitivity toward religious beliefs that are unfamiliar to them. Because the impact of disability influences the lives of clients and their families, counseling outcomes will be more positive if the healing process invites family members to share their own views and expectations (Smart, 2016).

Vocational Counseling

Formulating feasible vocational objectives requires collaborative efforts between clients and rehabilitation counselors. In addition to teaching job search and interviewing skills, counselors need a thorough understanding of their clients' existing functional capabilities. Without knowing the functional limitations, it is difficult to match clients' physical exertion levels with jobs they can successfully perform. Counselors can take a proactive approach to educating prospective employers about neuromuscular diseases and recommend necessary accommodations. Hicks (1998) suggested several adaptive techniques and mobility devices to help people with MD increase their functional capacities. As an example, using an elevated seat cushion or a high stool can help a client with LBMD more readily get on and off a chair.

American society measures success by one's earning power and job status. Holding gainful employment is a way to earn peer respect and command social acceptance and high regard. The myths regarding people with disabilities and unwarranted fears of increases in medical insurance costs can dissuade prospective employers from considering hiring qualified job candidates with MD. Self-employment empowers clients by providing financial independence. Another advantage of being one's own boss is the flexibility of arranging convenient work hours.

While self-employment presents a viable alternative for some rehabilitation clients to secure financial security and independence, it is by no means a decision to be made casually in light of the high business failure rate of new entrants. Counselors can consult with their local Small Business Administration (SBA) to evaluate a client's prior work experience, level of educational attainment, complexity of business, technical training, and availability of start-up business financing capital.

As the business world moves in the direction of telecommunication and computer technology, the traditional work setting of an office environment is no longer the only option. Electronic transmission of data via the Internet allows for working from home. For those clients who prefer to use personal transportation or for whom telecommunication is not feasible, rehabilitation counselors can direct their clients to contact special driving schools for individuals with disabilities, and to locate engineers who perform vehicle modifications. In addition, major automobile manufacturers can provide financial assistance for clients with disabilities to modify their new vehicles. Having accessible transportation is a crucial step toward making people with MD more employable.

Medical Counseling Considerations

Proper physical therapy and suitable orthopedic footwear can effectively prolong the duration of a client's ability to walk. Being able to ambulate independently is a strong psychological boost for someone with a prognosis that he or she will eventually need to use a wheelchair. To extend productivity in life, clients need to anticipate the inevitability of the disease and find ways to enrich their quality of life as physical functioning diminishes (Chen & Crewe, 2009; Chen, Miller, Seo, & Mendoza, 2010). Although clients may initially find assistive devices to be awkward and embarrassing, rehabilitation counselors nevertheless should elucidate the advantages of using a walker, wheelchair, and scooter.

Decline in daily physical activities as a result of muscle deficiency is a substantial problem in the MD population. People with sedentary lifestyles are prone to developing adverse medical conditions including coronary artery disease, osteoporosis, obesity, anxiety, depression, and musculoskeletal impairments (Matthews, 2003). Healthy bodies need regular exercise to maintain toned and conditioned muscles. Paradoxically, people with MD are at greater risk of damaging muscle fibers when they undergo exercise regimens because the dystrophin protein cannot function properly to repair injured muscles. Hence, it is advised that patients consult neurologists and physiotherapists familiar with MD before beginning an exercise regimen.

Improved pain management serves to enhance quality of life. BMD and DMD are known to cause uncomfortable muscle cramps and painful stiffness. Ruptured and swollen connective tissues set off prolonged painful and irritating spasms that may persist during sleep. Lethargy in the daytime attributed to poor quality of sleep seriously affects concentration and productivity at work. Weakening in the pulmonary muscles in people with neuromuscular failure requires respiratory support to regulate the inhalation of oxygen and exhalation of carbon dioxide. To minimize sleep disruption, suitable ventilators must be chosen to meet the unique needs of individuals with MD to ensure that respiratory mechanics function to maximum capacity (Fanfulla, Delmastro, Berardinelli, Lupo, & Nava, 2005).

Leisure and Recreational Issues

Exercise for persons with MD has been somewhat controversial due to dystrophin deficiency and decreased muscle contractile properties (Hicks, 1998). Nonetheless, an appropriate amount and intensity of exercise is recommended, depending on disease progression. While there is a benefit in conditioning muscles, precautionary measures need to be taken to avoid excessive muscular tissue damage that will accelerate the deterioration process. Aquatic therapy and hippotherapy (horseback riding) are ideal exercises for persons with neuromuscular diseases. Resistance in water allows the body to harden its flex and reflex movements with minimal risk of injuring muscles.

Sexual and Reproductive Concerns

For many people with disabilities, rehabilitation counselors are often the first persons they confide in about their anxiety over sexual issues (Vash & Crewe, 2004). Prior to providing counseling on sexual issues, counselors must first examine their own attitudes. If the counselor feels apprehensive about discussing intimate and sensitive questions with clients, appropriate referrals should be made. Rehabilitation professionals can serve as vital information sources to alleviate clients' anxieties and doubts about their sexuality (Brodwin & Chen, 2000). The onset of LGMD and MMD often occurs at the time when young boys and girls are entering puberty. The severity of disability and its subsequent impact on social interaction deprive young people of the chance to experience sexual intimacy. To project a warm and amicable image, clients with MD should learn about proper social etiquette and maintaining positive attitudes toward other people.

Inheritable disorders are a legitimate concern when planning a family. Individuals with MD often do not recognize the hereditary nature of their disease due to a recessive inheritance pattern, spontaneous mutation, and false paternity (Amato & Russell, 2016). DNA testing and analysis of cell mutations provide information to predict the likelihood of passing on inherited diseases to offspring. The desire to have children can be carefully weighed against the possibility of passing mutant genes to offspring. As one example, research has shown that Japanese couples often choose to terminate fetuses with chromosomal abnormalities, succumbing in part to the enormous pressure to conform to societal expectations (Suzumori, Kumagai, Goto, Nakamura, & Sugiura-Ogasawara, 2015).

Deviations from strictly observed social norms are neither encouraged nor accepted in a culture that prizes homogeneity, perfection, and cohesiveness. In addition, religious values and personal beliefs can shape an individual's views on disability (Smart, 2016). Whether the parents see the disability as a curse or a blessing from God is a key factor in determining if they will love and embrace their child. Research with Muslim parents of children with Down syndrome in Pakistan has revealed that they routinely draw strength and guidance from the teachings of the Koran to help them cope with a disability in the family (Ahmed, Bryant, Ahmed, Jafri, & Raashid, 2013).

The purpose of genetic counseling is to provide a person with MD and his or her spouse with knowledge of the nature of the genetic disorder, its transmission, and the risk of occurrence in potential offspring. Depending on the type of disorder, the probabilities of genetic risks range from one in two people (with a dominant gene) and one in four people (with a recessive gene) (Gustavson, 1999). While the responsibility of explaining family planning rests on rehabilitation and medical professionals, clients with MD and their families are responsible for the decision as to whether or not to have children.

Conclusion

MD is a group of neuromuscular diseases that gradually lead to the deterioration and erosion of muscles. Although there is no cure, people with this condition do not have to hold a bleak view of their future. When preparing a rehabilitation program or plan, it is imperative for rehabilitation counselors to acquire both knowledge of the client's capacity to handle tasks and knowledge of what the client is unable to manage. Because of the wide range of differences, each client needs careful, individualized evaluation. Fear and uncertainty about the future may induce clients to believe they are living on "borrowed time" because they have no control over the progressive weakening process (Chen et al., 2010).

When helping clients implement planning, rehabilitation counselors are wise to consider holistic interventions, i.e., psychological counseling considerations, vocational counseling advice, medical counseling issues, leisure and recreational issues, and sexual and reproductive concerns. Compassion is an imperative aspect in building a strong and mutually respectful rapport between client and counselor. Rehabilitation counselors should neither communicate an overly pessimistic outlook nor raise false hopes. By formulating realistic and practical goals with input from clients, counselors will attain better rehabilitation outcomes.

Case Study

Mindy Lam is a 20-year-old immigrant who came to the United States from Hong Kong one year ago. She lives with her parents and one older sister in an apartment adjacent to Chinatown in Los Angeles, California. Before arriving in the United States, Mindy finished the 11th grade in her home country, learned a basic command of conversational English, and worked for two years as an apprentice tailor. Mindy is a referral to the Department of Rehabilitation from a Muscular Dystrophy Association (MDA) support group. Miss Lam has been working at a clothing factory as a children's apparel seamstress since arriving in this country.

At age 19, Miss Lam was diagnosed with facioscapulohumeral muscular dystrophy (FSHMD) and was treated at a public hospital in Hong Kong. Despite the presence of FSHMD, Mindy has been able to care for herself. Since her arrival in the United States, Mindy has been working for the same employer. Job evaluations indicate she is a reliable employee and gets along well with co-workers and supervisors. Four months ago, Mindy noticed her productivity steadily decreasing. Dust from cutting and sewing textiles irritated her eyes. She had difficulty sewing with precision and maintaining productivity. Her arms quickly became sore and tired after working on the sewing machine for a short time. To meet the daily quota, Miss Lam took fewer breaks and a shorter lunch. Mindy often could not finish her lunch in the designated time due to swallowing difficulties; she does not have this problem when she eats slowly.

This client feels she is on the verge of a nervous breakdown. The fast pace of garment factory work is difficult for her, both mentally and physically. She does not want to be a burden to her family and desires to continue working. Mindy is experiencing mild depression because of social isolation. Typically, she spends her time watching television and cooking for her family. Occasionally, they have dinner out. Presently,

Mindy is living with her parents and has doubts about dating due to her physical condition. In addition, her father does not approve of interracial dating. At a co-worker's invitation, Mindy attended a local Chinese-speaking church on several occasions. However, her Buddhist parents prefer that Mindy not attend this particular church.

Before taking a few weeks of sick leave because of muscular dystrophy symptoms, Mindy was considered the top candidate for promotion to floor supervisor. Additionally, the company is in the process of computerizing the production lines. Miss Lam has expressed a strong interest in learning the new computer-aided fashion design software to sketch clothing designs, a position available at her employer. However, she is pessimistic about the likelihood of being promoted to a designer position due to her lack of education, limited computer experience, and because her employer now is aware that she has MD. Except for a brief period of sick leave, Mindy has been working full time. Additional employment interests of Miss Lam include child care, counseling, and working with people who have disabilities. Due to a family business failure, Mindy had to leave high school at the beginning of the 12th grade; she immediately secured employment in the clothing industry and never returned to school.

Questions

1. Identify some problems persons with MD encounter in society and in seeking and maintaining employment.
2. As Miss Lam's counselor, what possible physical and emotional limitations would you take into consideration when planning vocational rehabilitation services?
3. If you recommend continued employment with her employer, what advice would you give concerning reasonable accommodation? Would you recommend one of the two positions available, one being a floor supervisor and the other as a computer-aided fashion designer?
4. How would you suggest Mindy expand her social activities without creating tension with her parents? Provide your rationale within a cultural context.
5. As a career counselor, provide a career path for this individual. Remember that Los Angeles is a garment-manufacturing center. Take into consideration her particular type of muscular dystrophy.

References

Ahmed, S., Bryant, L. D., Ahmed, M., Jafri, H., & Raashid, Y. (2013). Experiences of parents with a child with Down syndrome in Pakistan and their views on termination of pregnancy. *Journal of Community Genetics, 4*(1), 107-114.

Amato, A. A., & Russell, J. A. (2016). *Neuromuscular disorders* (2nd ed.). New York, NY: McGraw-Hill Education.

Angelini, C. (2014). *Genetic neuromuscular disorders: A case-based approach.* New York, NY: Springer.

Bartalos, M. K. (1990). Muscular dystrophy: Assessing the impact of a diseased state. *Loss, Grief and Cure, 4*(3/4), 63-73.

Bray, P., Bundy, A. C., Ryan, M. M., & North, K. N. (2017). Can in-the-moment diary methods measure health-related quality of life in Duchenne muscular dystrophy? *Quality of Life Research, 26*(5), 1145-1152.

Brodwin, M. G., & Chen, R. K. (2000). Marital and sexuality issues in clients with disabilities. In L. Vandecreek & T. L. Jackson (Eds.), *Innovations in clinical practice: A source book* (vol. 18, pp. 459-470). Sarasota, FL: Professional Resource Press.

Centers for Disease Control and Prevention (CDC). (2018). *Muscular dystrophy.* Retrieved from https//www.cdc.gov/ncbddd/musculardystrophy/data.htm/

Che Ismail, E. H., & Othman, N. (2016). From diagnosis to treatment of muscular dystrophy: Psychology meets medicine. *International Journal of Psychological Studies, 8*(1), 85-91.

Chen, R. K., & Crewe, N. M. (2009). Life satisfaction among people with progressive disabilities. *Journal of Rehabilitation, 75*(2), 50-58.

Chen, R. K., Miller, E., Seo, W. S., & Mendoza, E. (2010). Living with uncertainty: Impacts of a progressive disability on life perspectives. *Australian Journal of Rehabilitation Counseling, 16*(2), 85-98.

Fanfulla, F., Delmastro, M., Berardinelli, A., Lupo, N., & Nava, S. (2005). Effects of different ventilator settings on sleep and inspiratory effort in patients with neuromuscular disease. *American Journal of Respiratory and Critical Care Medicine, 172*(5), 619-624.

Fowler, W. M. (2002). Role of physical activity and exercise training in neuromuscular diseases. *American Journal of Physical Medicine and Rehabilitation, 81*(11 Suppl.), S187-S195.

Fowler, W. M., Abresch, R. T., Koch, T. R., Brewer, M. L., Bowden, R. K., & Wanlass, R. L. (1997). Employment profiles in neuromuscular diseases. *American Journal of Physical Medicine and Rehabilitation, 76*(1 Suppl.), S26-S37.

Freud, S. (1963). *General psychological theory: Papers on metapsychology*. New York, NY: Collier Books.

Gustavson, K. H. (1999). Muscular dystrophy: Genetic counseling and family planning. *Scandinavian Journal of Rehabilitation Medicine, 39*(Suppl.), 38-41.

Hicks, J. E. (1998). Role of rehabilitation in the management of myopathies. *Current Opinion in Rheumatology, 10*(6), 548-555.

Hotchkiss, J. L. (2004). A closer look at the employment impact of the Americans with Disabilities Act. *Journal of Human Resources, 39*(4), 887-911.

Huml, R. A. (2015). *Muscular dystrophy: A concise guide*. New York, NY: Springer.

Kilmer, D. D., Abresch, R. T., McCrory, M. A., Carter, G. T., Fowler, W. M., Johnson, E. R., & McDonald, C. M. (1995). Profiles of neuromuscular diseases: Facioscapulohumeral muscular dystrophy. *American Journal of Physical Medicine and Rehabilitation, 74*(5 Suppl.), S131-S139.

Mackelprang, R. W., & Salsgiver, R. O. (1999). *Disability: A diversity model approach in human service practice*. Pacific Grove, CA: Brooks/Cole.

Marini, I., Chen, R. K., Feist, A. M., Flores-Torres, L., & Castillo, A. (2011). Student attitudes toward intimacy with persons who are wheelchair users. *Rehabilitation Research, Policy, & Education, 25*(1), 15-26.

Mathews, K. D. (2003). Muscular dystrophy overview: Genetics and diagnosis. *Neurologic Clinics, 21*(4), 795-816.

McDonald, C. M., Abresch, R. T., Carter, G. T., Fowler, W. M., Johnson, E. R., Kilmer, D. D., & Sigford, B. J. (1995a). Profiles of neuromuscular diseases: Duchenne muscular dystrophy. *American Journal of Physical Medicine and Rehabilitation, 74*(5 Suppl.), S70-S92.

McDonald, C. M., Abresch, R. T., Carter, G. T., Fowler, W. M., Johnson, E. R., & Kilmer, D. D. (1995b). Profiles of neuromuscular diseases: Becker's muscular dystrophy. *American Journal of Physical Medicine and Rehabilitation, 74*(5 Suppl.), S93-S103.

McDonald, C. M., Johnson, E. R., Abresch, R. T., Carter, G. T., Fowler, W. M., & Kilmer, D. D. (1995c). Profiles of neuromuscular diseases: Limb-girdle syndromes. *American Journal of Physical Medicine and Rehabilitation, 74*(5 Suppl.), S117-S130.

Miller, E., Chen, R. K., Graf, N. M., & Kranz, P. L. (2009). Willingness to engage in personal relationships with persons with disabilities: Examining category and severity of disability. *Rehabilitation Counseling Bulletin, 52*(4), 211-224.

Ogasawara, A. (1989). Downward shift in IQ in persons with Duchenne muscular dystrophy compared to those with spinal muscular atrophy. *American Journal on Mental Retardation, 93*(3), 544-547.

Ouyang, L., Grosse, S. D., Fox, M. H., & Bolen, J. (2012). A national profile of health care and family impacts of children with muscular dystrophy and special health care needs in the United States. *Journal of Child Neurology, 27*(5), 569-576.

Ouyang, L., Grosse, S. D., & Kenneson, A. (2008). Health care utilization and expenditures for children and young adults with muscular dystrophy in a privately insured population. *Journal of Child Neurology, 23*(8), 883-888.

Roessler, R. T., Rubin, S. E., & Rumrill, Jr., P. D. (2017). *Case management and rehabilitation counseling: Procedures and techniques* (5th ed.). Austin, TX: Pro-ed.

Shannon, J. B. (2004). *Muscular dystrophy sourcebook*. Detroit, MI: Omnigraphics.

Siegel, I. M. (1999). *Muscular dystrophy in children: A guide for families*. New York: Demos Medical.

Sirotkin-Roses, M. (1991). Psychosocial issues and case management in myotonic muscular dystrophy. *Loss, Grief and Care, 4*(3/4), 43-61.

Smart, J. (2016). *From disability, society, and the individual* (3rd ed.). Austin, TX: Pro-Ed.

Suzumori, N., Kumagai, K., Goto, S., Nakamura, A., & Sugiura-Ogasawara, M. (2015). Parental decisions following prenatal diagnosis of chromosomal abnormalities: Implications for genetic counseling practice in Japan. *Journal of Genetic Counseling, 24*(1), 117-121.

Swenson, T. S. (2000). Chronic fatigue syndrome. *Journal of Rehabilitation, 66*(1), 37-42.

Vash, C. L., & Crewe, N. M. (2004). *Psychology of disability*. New York, NY: Springer.

Yu, A. J., Blankenship, L. D., Yang, R. Y., & Lee, M. Y. (2006). Myotonic dystrophy. *American Journal of Physical Medicine and Rehabilitation, 85*(6), 551.

About the Author

Roy K. Chen, PhD, CRC, is Professor, School of Rehabilitation Services and Counseling, University of Texas, Rio Grande Valley. He received his doctorate in rehabilitation counselor education from Michigan State University in East Lansing, Michigan. His current research interests include disability-related employment issues, psychosocial aspects of disabling conditions, quality of life, multicultural rehabilitation, neuromuscular and neurological disorders, and special education.

Chapter 19

MULTIPLE SCLEROSIS

Roxanna N. Pebdani, PhD, CRC

Introduction

Despite being one of the most common neurological disorders in the world, affecting 2.3 million people worldwide (Browne et al., 2014), and being one of the most commonly studied neurological disorders, our understanding of multiple sclerosis (MS) continues to need further development. A single causal factor for MS has not been identified. It is likely there are both genetic and environmental factors which cause MS (Noseworthy, Lucchinetti, Rodriguez, & Weinshenker, 2000).

MS is more prevalent in women than in men (Dilokthornsakul et al., 2016). It is most commonly diagnosed around 30 years of age and is most often seen in Caucasian populations (Ascherio & Munger, 2016).

Multiple Sclerosis Defined

MS is primarily considered to be an autoimmune disorder, which means that in individuals with MS, their immune system attacks their otherwise healthy central nervous system (the brain and spinal cord). These immunological attacks damage the myelin sheath - the protective part of the brain that surrounds a person's nerves - leading to plaque or lesions on the brain and spinal cord (Popescu, Pirko, & Lucchinetti, 2013). This damage to the myelin sheath leads to scar tissue called sclerosis, the medical term for the hardening of tissue. The result of these lesions is physical and neurological symptoms and, in some cases, mental health issues.

Prevalence

As indicated, MS affects 2.3 million people worldwide with significant variations from country to country. It is more common in western Europe and North America, Australia, New Zealand, and Japan, and less in the Middle East, Asia, and Africa (Browne et al., 2014). Historically, the thought has been that the prevalence of MS increases as one lives further from the equator (Ascherio & Munger, 2016; Dilokthornsakul et al., 2016), though some recent research disputes this claim (Koch-Henriksen & Sørensen, 2010).

MS is at least twice as common in women as men (Dilokthornsakul et al., 2016). Diagnosis of MS may occur at any time in one's life, but most commonly between 25 and 35 years of age.

Risk Factors

Risk factors are difficult to assess as a singular cause of MS has not been determined. Instead, it is widely recognized that some combination of genetic factors which exist when a person is born plus environmental factors increase a person's risk of MS. Genetic factors are seen in identical twins and when a person has a family member with the disorder. Genetics factors also include ethnicity and gender, with MS being highest in white women. Environmental factors include geographic location, exposure to sunlight and vitamin D, having had the Epstein-Barr virus, and smoking (O'Gorman, Lucas, & Taylor, 2012).

What is known about environmental risk factors indicates that geographic latitude (being further from the equator) has historically been shown to be a risk factor for MS (Ascherio & Munger, 2016; Dilokthornsakul et al., 2016). Sunlight and vitamin D are thought to reduce one's susceptibility to developing this disease. Having had the Epstein-Barr virus, a virus that causes mononucleosis, greatly increases the risk of MS, as does smoking (O'Gorman et al., 2012).

Diagnosis and Progression

Process of Diagnosis

Receiving a diagnosis of MS is often a long and difficult process. In many cases, people experience neurological symptoms for which they will see their primary care physicians. They will take a medical history and likely run a series of tests, including a blood test and any other test to rule out easier-to-diagnose illnesses. They may be referred to a series of other physicians who are unable to determine a cause for their symptoms. If referred to a neurologist, that physician will likely order imaging of the brain (e.g., Magnetic Resonance Imaging – [MRI]), a spinal tap, blood tests, and any other tests to rule out other reasons for the symptoms. Unfortunately, MS is a diagnosis that is made when other diagnoses are ruled out, meaning the diagnostic process is often extensive and complicated (National Multiple Sclerosis Society, n.d.-b).

Types of Multiple Sclerosis

MS presents itself in a multitude of ways, which are divided into four clinical categories or phenotypes. However, prior to reaching that stage, individuals are known to experience Clinically Isolated Syndrome (CIS), which is a person's first experience of inflammation and damage to the myelin sheath. However, not everyone who experiences CIS goes on to fully develop MS. When MS is developed post-CIS, it is classified in the following ways: Relapsing Remitting Multiple Sclerosis, Primary Progressive Multiple Sclerosis, and Secondary Progressive Multiple Sclerosis. Each of these diagnoses affects individuals differently, and a person can (and often will) move from one phenotype to another (Lublin et al., 2014).

Clinically Isolated Syndrome (CIS)

As stated above, CIS does not necessarily lead to a diagnosis of MS. Neurological symptoms demonstrate that the myelin sheath is inflamed and eventually damaged. However, when CIS is accompanied with brain lesions (diagnosed with an MRI), this greatly increases a person's chance of being diagnosed with MS (Lublin, 2014; Lublin et al., 2014).

Relapsing Remitting Multiple Sclerosis (RRMS)

Relapsing Remitting MS is the most common phenotype of MS. In RRMS, people have periods of time in which their illness relapses, meaning their neurological function worsens. However, in RRMS, the symptoms remit, and there is some level of lessening of neurological problems. Between relapses and subsequent lessening of symptomology, disease progression is stable until the next relapse occurs.

Primary Progressive Multiple Sclerosis (PPMS)

As opposed to RRMS, PPMS occurs without remissions. PPMS is progressive from the onset, though there are occasions where symptomology may plateau and individuals may improve temporarily. Ultimately, PPMS results in a constant increase in symptomology without any relapse.

Secondary Progressive Multiple Sclerosis (SPMS)

Secondary Progressive MS occurs in individuals who started their MS progression with RRMS. Eventually the relapses stop and the disease moves into a progressive course with more minor remissions, plateaus in disease progression, and a possible lack of remissions.

Adjustment to Disability

Given the long and drawn out process that is common in MS, when individuals finally receive a positive diagnosis, they may feel a sense of relief in response to finally having an answer for the symptoms they have been experiencing. Other feelings include shock, anger, fear, and denial (Kalb, 2015). MS is progressive; the progression does not necessarily occur on a linear trajectory. Therefore, adjustment to MS may happen cyclically, with people readjusting to their diagnosis or prognosis as the symptoms progress. This uncertainty complicates adjustment to the disability. Similarly, experiencing high stress (MS-related and in general) leads to worse adjustment (Dennison, Moss-Morris, & Chalder, 2009).

Positive coping strategies have been shown to improve adjustment to disability. Strategies that individuals with MS use to cope with disability include: seeking social support, problem-focused coping (focusing on a particular problem or stressor and efforts to reduce that stress), and positive reappraisal (reframing the negative to more positive). Each of these showed a positive impact on adjustment to disability. On the other hand, coping skills such as wishful thinking and avoidance coping were related to worse adjustment to disability (Dennison et al., 2009).

Self-efficacy, an individual's belief that he or she is capable of control over one's life, has shown that a higher level of self-efficacy may lead to better adjustment to disability. Similarly, optimism, hope, and spirituality have been shown to improve adjustment to disability, as have positive health behaviors such as exercising, a healthy diet, and stress management in general (Dennison et al., 2009). Ultimately, while professionals may know factors that can improve adjustment to disability for individuals with MS, these factors vary from individual to individual. One cannot assume that because a person is undertaking these protective factors that adjustment will necessarily improve.

Symptoms

The most common symptom of MS is a feeling of overwhelming fatigue, which occurs in 80% of individuals. Other symptoms include difficulties with balance and walking, weakness or paralysis, numbness or tingling, bladder problems, spasticity, bowel problems, memory issues, depression, pain, emotional lability (sudden changes in mood), vision issues, shaking, speech difficulties, and trouble with problem solving (Kraft, Freal, & Coryell, 1986; Krupp, Alvarez, LaRocca, & Scheinberg, 1988).

Symptoms change in severity as the disease progresses. In RRMS, for example, symptomology may increase and then temporarily remit, and further increase during the next relapse. Similarly, not everyone experiences all these symptoms, nor do they experience the symptoms at the same level of severity. The symptoms and severity an individual experiences vary from person to person.

Supports for Multiple Sclerosis

There are many avenues through which individuals can receive care. In some geographic areas, people have access to comprehensive care centers, where many healthcare providers work in one building to provide care for individuals with MS. In other areas, people with MS have to work to build a team of providers who can deliver the various services needed for continuity of care.

Medical Professionals

Prior to an official diagnosis, when individuals are experiencing unexplainable neurological difficulties, they will likely see their primary care physicians. Yet, the ideal care for an individual with MS is for a team of physicians who specialize in treating this condition.

The head of a comprehensive MS team is a neurologist. Other team members include physiatrists (physicians who specializes in rehabilitation and physical medicine), rehabilitation professionals (e.g., occupational therapists, physical therapists), mental health professionals (neuropsychologists, psychologists, counselors, social workers), among other healthcare professionals. Lastly, nurses may act as medical professionals, case managers, and emotional support for individuals diagnosed with MS (National Multiple Sclerosis Society, n.d.-a).

Other Supports

A definitive diagnosis leads to complicated emotions in many cases; in some cases, individuals may feel relief, finally having an answer or reason for their symptoms; in others shock, anger, fear, or denial occur (Kalb, 2015). There are a number of resources to help navigate negative feelings or to find support as one progresses. There are both in-person and online support groups, online discussion boards, and peer-to-peer mentoring programs that people with MS can join for support.

Treatment

There is no cure for MS. The National Multiple Sclerosis Society funds research that aims to diminish the disease and its symptomology, reverse lost functioning, and find a cure (National Multiple Sclerosis Society, n.d.-c). The federal government provides funding for rehabilitation research and training centers that study different aspects of MS. This condition is one of the most commonly researched neurological disorders. Treatment has advanced over the years (Comi, Radaelli, & Sørensen, 2017).

Treatment is different for each individual; some treatments work more effectively than others, depending on the person and disease characteristics. Medications serve multiple functions - some work to modify the course of the disease (called Disease Modifying Therapies), and others work to prevent relapses. These medications function in different ways; some suppress the immune system, while others reduce inflammation. Some medications have a more targeted response within the body (Comi et al., 2017). Other medications are used for symptom management to help people cope with symptoms such as fatigue, pain, bowel and bladder difficulties, among others.

Mental Health Concerns

There are a number of mental health difficulties that are more frequently seen in individuals with MS. Depression and anxiety are common. Recent research shows that this depression may indirectly be influenced by pain - which in turn increases fatigue, anxiety, and difficulties in sleep, and may increase depression (Amtmann et al., 2015).

Sexual Dysfunction and Pregnancy

Sex Issues

Many individuals with MS experience sexual dysfunction. This dysfunction is a symptom of the disease, and affects both men and women. Despite this, healthcare providers often ignore the sexual concerns of their patients with MS. Some say that up to 80% of women with MS experience some type of sexual dysfunction, whether decreased sexual desire, diminished arousal, reduced lubrication, and difficulties in orgasm which may be attributed to levels of disability, pain, and illness duration in these women. Men also experience sexual dysfunction, often manifesting itself in erectile dysfunction, difficulty reaching orgasm or ejaculation, and a decrease in overall sexual desire (Lew-Starowicz & Rola, 2014).

Pregnancy

For many years, pregnancy was thought to increase symptomology in women with MS. Yet, recent research shows that women with MS have a decrease in MS relapses during pregnancy, though after the child is delivered, the risk of relapse in women increases (Miller, Fazekas, & Montalban, 2014; Pebdani, Johnson, Amtmann, Bamer, & Wundes, 2015; Wundes, Pebdani, & Amtmann, 2014).

Though MS likely has no impact on a woman's fertility, a woman who is contemplating pregnancy should speak with her neurologist and treatment team prior to conception. This occurs in only about 20% of pregnancies of women (Pebdani et al., 2015). While the research on Disease Modifying Therapies during pregnancy is scarce, physicians use information available to determine the course of medical treatment during pregnancy. Physicians and healthcare providers self-report being supportive of their patients with MS becoming pregnant, though women report receiving negative messages about pregnancy, including from their physicians (Prunty, Sharpe, Butow, & Fulcher, 2008). This discrepancy speaks to the need for other providers to voice their support for pregnancy for women with MS to help them feel supported throughout the process.

Employment

Given that this condition is often diagnosed between 25 and 35 years of age, many individuals have recently begun their careers at the time of diagnosis. They may have taken time from work to see physicians and obtain a diagnosis, and may have had to take time off to manage their developing neurological symptoms. A person who has recently received a diagnosis will likely stop working within five years after diagnosis. Research shows that approximately 60% of individuals with MS are unemployed (Bishop & Rumrill, 2015; Uccelli, Specchia, Battaglia, & Miller, 2009). As individuals age, they are less likely to be employed, often due to the increase in severity and impact of disability as they age (Roessler, Rumrill, Li, & Leslie, 2015).

Rehabilitation Potential

Despite the high rate of unemployment for individuals with MS (Bishop & Rumrill, 2015; Uccelli et al., 2009) and the high likelihood that people with MS will leave their jobs within five years of diagnosis, the fact that diagnoses come later in life means that individuals are likely to have had work experience. Counselors can draw on this employment experience to help place their clients by using possible transferable skills.

Barriers to Employment

Individuals with MS experience symptoms which make employment difficult. For example, overwhelming fatigue, one of the most common symptoms of MS, can affect a person's employment, and if individuals have varying levels of fatigue that are unpredictable, it may be difficult for an employer to provide accommodations on this varying basis. Other barriers include managing the cognitive changes, including forgetfulness, attention deficits, memory problems, inability to multitask, among others. Similarly, heat sensitivity, difficulties in mobility, and vision problems are barriers to employment, along with depression and anxiety (Johnson & Fraser, 2005).

Accommodations

Individuals with MS report needing on-the-job training, accommodations, and potential job reassignment to mediate the impact of their disability on work (Bishop & Rumrill, 2015). Accommodations should be determined based on the particular barrier. For example, fatigue may be mitigated by tracking the timing of fatigue and planning particular work activities around times of major fatigue. Cognitive changes, such as memory impairments, may be managed by reducing distractions and developing set routines. Symptoms such as heat sensitivity can be managed through the use of fans, personal air conditioners, and minimizing time in hot areas (Johnson & Fraser, 2005).

Accommodations for ambulation include the use of mobility devices and preferential parking. Vision difficulties may be eased by changes in lighting, devices for magnification, and specialized computer programs. Some may be reluctant to disclose their disability or their need for accommodations for various reasons (Johnson & Fraser, 2005), despite the fact that disclosing one's MS status makes it more likely to remain employed (Kork-Brown, Van Dijk, & Simmons, 2013). Individuals who decide not to disclose may need support to self-accommodate within the workplace.

Conclusion

Multiple sclerosis is a complex illness. It is difficult to obtain a definitive diagnosis, challenging to manage, with an unknown progression and variability from individual to individual. It often co-occurs with depression and anxiety, which complicate adjustment to disability. MS is most common in women and often diagnosed between ages 25 and 35, which impacts relationships, childbearing, and employment, among other life activities. It is essential that rehabilitation counselors be aware of these potential impacts and ways to manage or mediate them.

Case Study

Sasha is a 28-year-old married Caucasian woman, born and raised in Seattle, Washington. She leads a healthy and outdoor lifestyle riding a bicycle six miles each way to and from her job at Amazon, hiking on weekends, and running regularly. Recently, Sasha has been arriving at work exhausted after her six-mile ride. During these times, she experienced intermittent tingling in her hands and feet. After ruling out a vitamin deficiency and poor circulation as possible causes, her primary care physician referred her to a neurologist to help determine the cause of her fatigue and the tingling.

Sasha's treating neurologist asked about the fatigue and tingling. By asking more specific questions, Patricia Manukyan, MD, concluded that Sasha is also experiencing tremors in her left arm and intermittent vision problems and dizziness. Dr. Manukyan, suspecting multiple sclerosis, sent her for an MRI (magnetic resonance imaging) and spinal tap. The MRI results showed a number of lesions within the brain; the spinal tap showed antibodies indicative of multiple sclerosis. Based on the test results, Sasha's symptoms, and the progression of her illness, her neurologist diagnosed her with Relapsing Remitting Multiple Sclerosis.

At Amazon, Sasha is a recruitment manager. Her staff recruits recent college graduates for programming positions within Amazon at their West Coast locations. To oversee recruitment teams at each location, she regularly travels to other cities in Washington, Oregon, California, and Nevada. Sasha's occupation consists of travel approximately 50% of the time. Much of her other work activities are done within an office setting, on the computer and telephone.

Married for two years, Sasha and her wife have been taking steps towards artificial insemination. They have been saving money for three years in anticipation of this expensive procedure. They planned that Sasha will carry the baby; over the past several months, Sasha has been preparing herself physically for this procedure and subsequent pregnancy.

Dr. Manukyan referred her to you for counseling related to her diagnosis. Sasha is worried about her health, work life, and home life. Concerned about the future, she came to you anxious and depressed.

Questions

1. Given Sasha's diagnosis of Relapsing Remitting Multiple Sclerosis, how do you anticipate her illness progressing?

2. Propose employment factors you need to discuss with this client? What might you want to consider in terms of her employment situation, accommodations, and likely disclosure of her newly diagnosed disability?
3. Suggest accommodations Sasha may need given the symptoms she is currently experiencing.
4. What psychosocial issues might help or hinder Sasha's adjustment to her recent diagnosis?
5. Identify lifestyle factors which may change for Sasha as she progresses with her condition.
6. Specify possible concerns which need to be identified regarding Sasha's intended pregnancy.

References

Amtmann, D., Askew, R. L., Kim, J., Chung, H., Ehde, D. M., Bombardier, C. H., . . . Johnson, K. L. (2015). Pain affects depression through anxiety, fatigue, and sleep in multiple sclerosis. *Rehabilitation Psychology, 60*(1), 81-90.

Ascherio, A., & Munger, K. L. (2016). Epidemiology of multiple sclerosis: From risk factors to prevention - An update. *Seminars in Neurology, 36*(2), 103-114.

Bishop, M., & Rumrill, P. D. (2015). The employment concerns of Americans with multiple sclerosis: Perspectives from a national sample. *Work, 52*(4), 735-748.

Browne, P., Chandraratna, D., Angood, C., Tremlett, H., Baker, C., Taylor, B., & Thompson, A. J. (2014). Atlas of multiple sclerosis 2013: A growing global problem with widespread inequity. *Neurology, 83*(11), 1022-1024.

Comi, G., Radaelli, M., & Sørensen, P. S. (2017). Evolving concepts in the treatment of relapsing multiple sclerosis. *The Lancet, 389*, 1-7.

Dennison, L., Moss-Morris, R., & Chalder, T. (2009). A review of psychological correlates of adjustment in patients with multiple sclerosis. *Clinical Psychology Review, 29*(2), 141-153.

Dilokthornsakul, P., Valuck, R. J., Nair, K. V., Corboy, J. R., Allen, R. R., & Campbell, J. D. (2016). Multiple sclerosis prevalence in the United States commercially insured population. *Neurology, 86*(11), 1014-1021.

Johnson, K. L., & Fraser, R. T. (2005). Mitigating the impact of multiple sclerosis on employment. *Physical Medicine and Rehabilitation Clinics of North America, 16*(2), 571-582.

Kalb, R. C. (2015). *Multiple sclerosis and your emotions*. New York, NY: National Multiple Sclerosis Society.

Koch-Henriksen, N., & Sørensen, P. S. (2010). The changing demographic pattern of multiple sclerosis epidemiology. *Lancet Neurology, 9*(5), 520-532.

Kork-Brown, A. K., Van Dijk, P. A., & Simmons, R. D. (2013). Disclosure of diagnosis of multiple sclerosis in the workplace positively affects employment status and job tenure. *Multiple Sclerosis Journal, 20*(7), 871-876.

Kraft, G. H., Freal, J. E., & Coryell, J. K. (1986). Disability, disease duration, and rehabilitation service needs in multiple sclerosis: Patient perspectives. *Archives of Physical Medicine and Rehabilitation, 67*, 164-168.

Krupp, L. B., Alvarez, L. A., LaRocca, N. G., & Scheinberg, L. C. (1988). Fatigue in multiple sclerosis. *Archives of Neurology, 45*, 435-437.

Lew-Starowicz, M., & Rola, R. (2014). Sexual dysfunctions and sexual quality of life in men with multiple sclerosis. *Journal of Sexual Medicine, 11*(5), 1294-1301.

Lublin, F. D. (2014). New multiple sclerosis phenotypic classification. *European Neurology, 14*(72), 1-4.

Lublin, F. D., Reingold, S. C., Cohen, J. A., Cutter, G. R., Sørensen, P. S., Thompson, A. J., . . . Polman, C. H. (2014). Defining the clinical course of multiple sclerosis. *Neurology, 83*, 278-286.

Miller, D. H., Fazekas, F., & Montalban, X. (2014). Pregnancy, sex, and hormonal factors in multiple sclerosis. *Multiple Sclerosis Journal, 20*(5), 527-536.

National Multiple Sclerosis Society. (n.d.-a). *Developing a healthcare team*. Retrieved from https://www.nationalmssociety.org/Treating-MS/Comprehensive-Care/Deveoping-a-health-care-team

National Multiple Sclerosis Society. (n.d.-b). *Diagnosing MS*. Retrieved from https://www.nationalmssociety.org/Symptoms-Diagnosis/Diagnosing-MS

National Multiple Sclerosis Society. (n.d.-c). *Research we fund*. Retrieved from https://www.nationalmssociety.org/Research/Research-We-Fund

Noseworthy, J. H., Lucchinetti, C., Rodriguez, M., & Weinshenker, B. G. (2000). Multiple sclerosis. *New England Journal of Medicine, 343*, 938-952.

O'Gorman, C., Lucas, R., & Taylor, B. (2012). Environmental risk factors for multiple sclerosis: A review with a focus on molecular mechanisms. *International Journal of Molecular Sciences, 13*(9), 11718-11752.

Pebdani, R. N., Johnson, K. L., Amtmann, D., Bamer, A. M., & Wundes, A. (2015). Experiences and perspectives of pregnancy in women with multiple sclerosis. *Sexuality and Disability, 33*, 47-52.

Popescu, B. F., Pirko, U., & Lucchinetti, C. (2013). Pathology of multiple sclerosis: Where do we stand? *Continuum: Lifelong Learning in Neurology, 19*(4), 901-921.

Prunty, M., Sharpe, L., Butow, P., & Fulcher, G. (2008). The motherhood choice: Themes arising in the decision-making process for women with multiple sclerosis. *Multiple Sclerosis, 14*(5), 701-704.

Roessler, R. T., Rumrill, P. D., Li, J., & Leslie, M. J. (2015). Predictors of differential employment statuses of adults with multiple sclerosis. *Journal of Vocational Rehabilitation, 42*, 141-152.

Uccelli, M., Specchia, C., Battaglia, M., & Miller, D. (2009). Factors that influence the employment status of people with multiple sclerosis: A multi-national study. *Journal of Neurology, 256*(12), 1989-1996.

Wundes, A., Pebdani, R. N., & Amtmann, D. (2014). What do healthcare providers advise women with multiple sclerosis regarding pregnancy? *Multiple Sclerosis International,* Article ID 819216.

About the Author

Roxanna Nasseri Pebdani, PhD, CRC is a faculty member, Discipline of Rehabilitation Counseling, Faculty Health Sciences, University of Sydney in Sydney, Australia. Prior to that position, she was an assistant professor in the Master of Science degree program in Counseling, Option in Rehabilitation at California State University, Los Angeles. Dr. Pebdani obtained her Bachelor's degree in psychology from the American University of Paris, her Master of Science degree in Rehabilitation Counseling from Syracuse University, and her PhD in Counselor Education from the University of Maryland. Upon earning her PhD, she completed a two-year post-doctoral fellowship at the University of Washington, where she studied psychosocial aspects of multiple sclerosis, spinal cord injury, and other disabilities. Dr. Pebdani's research focuses on sexuality and disability, pregnancy and fertility in disability, and multiple sclerosis.

Chapter 20

RHEUMATIC DISEASES

Penny J. Chong, MD
Constance A. Richard, MFA, MS, CRC

Introduction

Over 100 degenerative, inflammatory, and autoimmune conditions make up rheumatic diseases, which is a blanket term for conditions affecting connective tissue and joints. Currently, arthritis affects about one out of every five Americans and is the leading cause of disability. Close to 24 million adults reported they have some limitations in various activities of daily life (Barbour, Helmick, Boring, & Brady, 2017). Physicians who specialize in rheumatic disease, rheumatologists, are found in all major urban areas in the United States, but only 7% of rheumatologists practice in rural areas where one out of every five Americans live (Arthritis Foundation, 2017a).

Definition

Rheumatic diseases are a group of conditions affecting the supporting structures of the body, including the joints and periarticular tissues, connective tissues of the skin, bones, muscles, and diseases of the immune system. Fundamental features of rheumatic diseases are the signs of inflammation: warmth, swelling, redness, pain, and loss of motion. The onset of rheumatic disease, especially inflammatory diseases such as rheumatoid arthritis or other connective tissue disease, are often times insidious. One sees a subtle and gradual progression that leads from signs of inflammation, such as stiff hands in the morning to abnormalities of mobility and joint deterioration. Connective tissue diseases are characterized by exacerbations and remissions, and resistant to medical therapy (there are no cures, only palliative treatment).

Individuals with rheumatic disease have complaints of pain, loss of energy, easy fatigability, stiffness, and limitations of joint motion. The most prominent and challenging symptom is that people feel overwhelming fatigue. These symptoms affect endurance and capacity; with severe involvement, activities of daily living and mobility become impaired.

Arthritis and Myositis

The common rheumatic diseases that affect the joints are called arthritis, those that affect the muscles are termed myositis, and soft tissue rheumatism is present when soft tissues (tendons, ligaments, bursa, and muscles) are involved, accompanied by associated stiffness and pain. There are more than 100 rheumatic diseases. Typical symptoms include pain, stiffness, and functional impairment. Some of the more common diseases are osteoarthritis (the most common rheumatic disease), rheumatoid arthritis (the highest rate of disability), gout, bursitis, tendonitis, fibromyalgia, systemic lupus erythematosus, scleroderma, and ankylosing spondylitis. Less common types of rheumatic diseases include myositis (polymyositis and dermatomyositis), scleroderma, and arteritis (Firestein, Budd, Gabriel, McInnes, & O'Dell, 2017; Klippel, Stone, Crofford, & White, 2008).

Arthritis and Rheumatic Disorders

Musculoskeletal diseases, which include arthritis and other rheumatic disorders, are the leading causes of disability and absence from work (Firestein et. al, 2017). They are the second most common reason why people see physicians, affecting 22% of the adult population. Arthritis and the other rheumatic diseases are difficult to diagnosis due to the subtlety of physical signs, the tendency for symptoms to overlap with other medical problems, and the scarcity of diagnostic clinical and laboratory tests. Symptoms tend to develop gradually, respond slowly to treatment, and require long-term care.

Impact and Prevalence

The impact of arthritis in the United States is great. Fifty percent of adults 65 years of age and older reported a diagnosis of arthritis. The Centers for Disease Control and Prevention (CDC) (2017), using information from the National Health Interview Survey, years 2013-2015, estimated that 54.4 million Americans had a diagnosis of arthritis. Of these, about 294,000 were under age 18; this represents one in every 250 children. Barbour, Boring, Helmick, Murphy, and Qin (2016) estimated that 64% of adults with arthritis are younger than 65 years of age. In 2015, 23.7 million individuals had physical limitations due to arthritis.

In the United States, one in every four people or 25% of the population has an arthritic condition (Barbour et al., 2017). Currently, over eight million Americans are disabled by arthritis. Annually, arthritis accounts for 500 million days of restricted activities and 172 million days of lost work. It is the leading cause of absenteeism in business and industry and the second leading cause of disability payments (following heart disease); osteoarthritis accounts for an estimated 100 billion dollars annually.

Gout involves inflammation and painful flares of arthritis that develops in some people who have high levels of uric acid in the blood. The acid can form needle-like crystals in a joint and cause sudden, severe episodes of pain, tenderness, redness, warmth, and swelling. The common site of gout attack occurs in the large joint of the big toe; however, other joints can also be affected. The pain may last hours or weeks and make it difficult to perform daily activities. It is the most common cause of inflammatory arthritis among adults in the U.S., with 8.3 million individuals affected by gout. Men are nearly three times more likely to develop gout than women (American College of Rheumatology [ACR], 2017a).

Categories of Rheumatic Disease

There are three categories of rheumatic diseases that the rehabilitation professional is most likely to encounter. First, are the diffuse connective tissue diseases (rheumatoid arthritis, systemic lupus erythematosus, scleroderma, and polymyositis). This category has the most severe and highest prevalence of disability. Second is osteoarthritis, the most common form of arthritis, accounting for the largest number of lost days of work. The third category is ankylosing spondylitis, which causes severe back pain and often is confused with other causes of back pain.

Rheumatoid Arthritis

Explanation of Disease State

Rheumatoid arthritis (RA) is a systemic disorder of the connective tissues of the body, characterized by exacerbations and remissions. Its primary targets are the joints and adjacent supporting structures. The lining of the joint (synovium) is the site of chronic inflammation. Synovial tissues proliferate and lymphocytes (white blood cells) and other chronic inflammatory cells invade its interstices (spaces or gaps in tissues). This inflammatory process produces pain, heat, swelling, and loss of joint motion. The process is locally invasive; rheumatoid tissue erodes cartilage, bone, and ligaments.

Incidence

RA is a common disorder affecting approximately 1% of the adult population. It has a high rate of disability (Arthritis Foundation, 2017a). This disability rate is higher than the next three most common conditions: heart disease, back impairment, and hypertension. In addition, people diagnosed with rheumatoid arthritis utilize more medical services (physicians and hospitals) than patients with osteoarthritis, back pain, or tendonitis. Rheumatoid arthritis is three times more likely to affect women than men and has its peak onset between the ages of 20 and 30. The incidence of RA has declined over the years. Because of its chronicity and severe consequences, it is a primary focus of arthritis research (Vonkeman & van de Laar, 2013).

Effects

The primary effects of this type of arthritis are pain, swelling, loss of joint motion, joint deformities, and subsequent loss of function. The disease is one of exacerbations and remissions, but the overall course is progressive. The Arthritis Foundation (2017a) reported approximately 20% to 70% of adults working at the inception of their rheumatoid arthritis were disabled after seven to ten years. For employees with early-stage rheumatoid arthritis, a 39% prevalence rate of work disability was found after ten years. Wolfe and Michaud (2009) reported that 44% of patients with rheumatoid arthritis had problems paying medical and medication expenses after insurance payments.

People with RA have a symmetrical arthritis affecting multiple joints. Initially, small joints of the body are affected, but eventually all joints can be impacted. The initial symptoms occur in the small joints of the hands and feet with symptoms of pain, swelling, and joint stiffness. Individuals commonly experience fatigue, morning stiffness, and may have weight loss. As the disease progresses, more joints are affected and the degree of disability increases. Development of characteristic deformities of the hands typically occurs with rheumatoid arthritis. These deformities limit performance of employment and leisure activities. Restriction of range of joint motion frequently accompanies the deformities. Additionally, individuals become self-conscious about the appearance of their hands and feet, restrict their activities, and tend to wear concealing clothing (Klippel et al., 2008).

Diagnosis

Diagnosis is established through clinical features and laboratory testing. To establish a diagnosis, the arthritis must be polyarticular (i.e., involve more than one joint) and be at least six weeks in duration. Synovial joints are involved in a symmetrical manner. Initially affected are the small joints of the hands and feet. Joints are swollen, tender, with increased synovial fluid. People with more severe disease may have inflammation of the lining of the lungs and heart, lung involvement with fibrosis (scar tissue formation) and nodules, as well as inflammatory vessel disease of the skin and other organs. Dryness of the eyes and mouth is common, as are compression of peripheral nerves adjacent to joints (e.g., causing carpal tunnel syndrome).

The ACR-EULAR (American College of Rheumatology-European League against Rheumatism, 2017a) classification criteria for RA is based on the size and number of joints with clinical evidence of synovitis. In early disease, x-rays show loss of bone density (osteoporosis) and soft tissue swelling about the joints. X-rays of individuals with more advanced arthritis show loss of articular cartilage, erosion of bone adjacent to joints, and associated deformity (Firestein et al., 2017).

Treatment

Currently, there is no cure for RA, although there are effective palliative measures that can ameliorate symptoms or induce remission for extended periods. A three-pronged approach to treatment should be considered with 1) non-steroidal anti-inflammatory drugs (NSAIDS) and/or low dose oral and/or intra-articular steroids, 2) disease-modifying antiheumatic drugs (DMARDS), and 3) biologic agents (National Rheumatoid Arthritis Society, 2014; Smolen, Landewe, & Breedveld, 2010).

By diminishing inflammation, NSAIDS and steroids reduce pain and swelling and improve range of motion and strength. NSAIDS (e.g., ibuprofen) are generally preferred because they have fewer side effects, although steroids are more potent. NSAIDs and steroids can be taken together.

DMARDS, including methotrexate, have been the medication of choice to initiate therapy in RA. Methotrexate has been demonstrated to be very effective alone or in combination with the biologic agents (Smolen et al., 2010). These agents are slow acting and may require up to six months to achieve a therapeutic response. By potentially reducing the inflammatory hyperplastic synovium and reversing erosions of bone and nodules, early use can slow progression of RA and improve overall prognosis.

The biological agents are the newest line of treatment and, like DMARDS, take weeks to months to have discernible effects. They have very diverse mechanisms of action, including inhibition of tumor necrosis factor (TNF) and depletion of B-lymphocytes. Biological agents are more effective than methotrexate at slowing radiographic progression. The biologic agents, however, do have significant potential side effects, such as increased susceptibility to serious infections (Arthritis Foundation, 2017a).

Total joint replacement is a standard treatment for advanced joint disease that is progressive, symptomatic, and unresponsive to pharmacologic treatment. Through joint replacement, the diseased joint is surgically replaced with an artificial joint. Surgery relieves pain and frequently improves mobility. Resumption of work and recreational activities may occur after joint replacement. Successful joint replacements have been achieved in the hands, wrists, shoulders, hips, and knees with the greatest level of satisfaction with hip and knee replacements.

Functional Limitations

Functional limitations for individuals with rheumatoid arthritis are of primary concern. As the disease progresses and the years pass, functional loss becomes progressive. The American College of Rheumatology established criteria that physicians use to describe functional status. These criteria are illustrated in Table 1 and include Functional Class I (normal function) through Functional Class IV (unable to perform self-care activities). People referred for vocational rehabilitation are usually in Functional Classes II and III. Functional limitations are stated relating to the stage of the disease and areas of the body involved (Hochberg et al., 1992).

TABLE 1
Functional Status in Rheumatoid Arthritis

CLASS I	Able to perform all usual activities of daily living.
CLASS II	Able to perform all usual self-care and vocational activities. Limited in avocational activities.
CLASS III	Able to perform all usual self-care activities. Limited in vocational and avocational activities.
CLASS IV	Unable to perform usual self-care, vocational, and avocational activities.

Source: American College of Rheumatology (ACR) (2017b). *The use of anti-cyclic citrullinated pepetide (anti-CCP) antibodies in RA*. Retrieved from http:www.rheumatology.org/

Chronic Pain

Individuals diagnosed with rheumatoid arthritis have pain that is chronic in nature and exacerbated by movement of the affected joints. Many people have stiffness of the entire body, which is primarily a morning phenomenon and may last from minutes to hours. Specific functional disabilities occur in each individual, depending on the stage of disease and body areas affected. This disorder causes loss of motion and pain on motion; there is weakness, decreased strength, and diminished endurance. If the hands and upper extremities are involved, pain and loss of motion results in decreased capacity to perform grasping, fine dexterity hand activities, and overhead reaching. With lower extremity involvement, decreased capability to stand and walk for long distances occurs (National Rheumatoid Arthritis Society, 2014).

Emotional and Intellectual Factors

People with rheumatoid arthritis have no emotional limitations except those imposed by a disorder associated with chronic illness, pain, and loss of motion. There is an increased incidence of depression; however, it is not greater than would be expected for any chronic, progressive disorder. Matcham, Raynor, Steer, and Hotopf (2013) estimated that about 16.8% of individuals with RA also have depression. Intellectual capacity is not affected and ability to interact on a social level is unimpaired. Occasionally, because of the deforming nature of the disease, embarrassment is experienced concerning deformities of the hands and feet, as well as use of ambulatory aids such as canes, walkers, and wheelchairs.

Vocational Considerations

If rheumatoid arthritis is not well controlled or of long duration, there may be chronic pain, stiffness, fatigue, and weakness, all of which influence the capability to work (Gunnarsson, Chen, Ladapo, Naim, & Lofland, 2015). The ability and stamina needed to focus on work may be diminished. Yet, during the first years of the disease, most people obtain good control with first and second line medications, and vocational limitations are a consequence of the specific area of the body affected. Because of a reduction in strength and involvement of articulations effecting movement, most individuals are unable to perform heavy and very heavy work activities. Employment in the exertional categories of light and sedentary exertion is preferred. If a person, before acquiring rheumatoid arthritis, was performing medium work, it is likely that employment eventually will require modification to lighter work (Drenkard, Bao, Dennis, Molta, & Lin, 2014).

Upper Extremity Involvement

Hand and wrist involvement results in decreased power grip; most people with rheumatoid arthritis are assessed below the 5th percentile for grip strength. Additionally, pinch, grasp, and manual dexterity are reduced. If there is involvement of the hands, wrists, elbows, and shoulders, activities involving reaching and rapid movements of the upper extremities are diminished.

Lower Extremity Involvement

Disease in the lower extremities results in impaired ability to rise from a sitting position, stand, and walk for long periods of time. Work activities should accommodate the specific deformities and symptoms of the individual. If the arthritis affects standing and walking, the person may be limited to sedentary work activity.

Other Factors

Some people with rheumatoid arthritis require special considerations because of deformities, weakness, and loss of joint range of motion. Adaptations, such as higher chairs, raised toilet seats, and curb cuts accommodate lower extremity impairments. Occasionally, individuals have other health problems related to rheumatoid arthritis. For example, multisystem involvement from rheumatoid disease usually results in generalized fatigue with decreased strength and endurance (Hammand et al., 2017).

Rehabilitation Potential

Rheumatoid arthritis does not affect intellectual capabilities. Life expectancy for a person with this disease is shortened by a few years. Therefore, if retraining is required, counselors may consider more extensive training and educational programs. The disease is progressive; yet, it is slowly progressive and functional impairments increase at a gradual rate. Most people need accommodation or training for work that requires less exertion, perhaps one or two exertional levels less than prior work activities. Hence, heavy work activities prior to diagnosis will likely need to be restructured to activities involving medium or light work, and performance at the light level will need modification to sedentary work. No matter how severe the disability, the person with rheumatoid arthritis with work modifications should be able to do sedentary work activity.

Studies on return to work indicated that work disability is related to age, number of involved joints, and a desire to remain gainfully employed. Control of pace and work activities was not significant (Reisine, McQuillan, & Fifield, 1995). The United Kingdom's National Rheumatoid Arthritis Society provided examples of typical accommodations that an individual might use: flexible work schedule for fatigue and flares, ergonomic telephone handsets and computer keyboards, accessible parking spots, ramps, and elevators. Another study from the United Kingdom suggested that vocational rehabilitation training and counseling early in the disease enhances job retention (Hammond et al., 2017). Educational level, severity of disability, and financial status had no relationship to the outcome of vocational rehabilitation. As a result, rehabilitation counselors should persist with retraining, re-education, and vocational placement for people with rheumatoid arthritis who are not able to work at their current or prior positions.

Continued consultation with the physician, allied health professionals (i.e., occupational and physical therapists), and a work environmental specialist can help accommodate needs in the work environment. Prognosis for work is enhanced for individuals who have higher education levels because, in general, work environments for employees with higher levels of education require less physical exertion and mobility. Since intellectual functioning is not affected by RA and the expected lifespan is only a few years less than normal, rehabilitation counselors need to make every effort to return people diagnosed with this condition to the workforce.

Osteoarthritis

Explanation of Disease State

Osteoarthritis (OA) is a degenerative disease affecting the articular cartilage lining of the surfaces of joints. It is a localized disease and does not have systemic manifestations. This condition refers to a group of overlapping distinct diseases with different etiologies, but similar biologic and clinical outcomes. OA affects the entire joint, including the subchondral bone, ligaments, capsule, synovial membrane, and periarticular muscles. Pathophysiologically, there is degeneration of the articular cartilage with fibrillation, fissures, ulceration, and a loss of joint surface.

Effects

Osteoarthritis is the most common arthritis in the United States, more often affecting women. Virtually everyone over 65 years of age will have x-ray evidence of osteoarthritis; yet, most people do not have symptoms. There is a characteristic wearing away of the surface cartilage at the joint, resulting in pain, swelling, stiffness (particularly with activities), and loss of motion.

This disorder primarily affects the joint cartilage; yet, secondary inflammation involving the joint lining is common. Surface cartilage is disorganized, lost, and adjacent bony growth at the joint margins occurs. Marginal bony spurs are characteristic of OA. Diagnosis is primarily based upon symptoms and characteristic x-ray changes, which include loss of cartilage, increased bone density, and bone overgrowth at the joint margin.

Treatment

Many people benefit from nonpharmacological interventions such as exercise, weight loss, modifying activities of daily living, physiotherapy, braces, and use of a cane and orthotics. For OA in the hand, the ACR recommends topical NSAIDS and topical capsaicin. If these do not work, oral NSAIDS and tramadol are the next steps. In cases of knee OA, ACR recommends acetaminophen, oral and topical NSAIDS, and tramadol. More advanced cases can benefit from intra-articular steroid injections (Hochberg et al., 2012). Other patients require the use of narcotic analgesics for pain relief. Joint prostheses (total artificial joints) are effective for advanced OA when lesser treatments prove ineffective (Arthritis Foundation, 2017b).

Functional Limitations

People with OA do not exhibit systemic features; no other organ systems are involved, and there are no emotional or intellectual consequences. The disorder is localized and may be symptomatic with severe functional problems; more commonly, it does not create major physical limitations. Most people with osteoarthritis are older; many are no longer in the workforce and are not candidates for vocational rehabilitation. Those who are in the workforce have functional limitations that are specific to the areas of the body involved.

If the small digits of the hands are affected, there will be stiffness and loss of motion that interfere with finger dexterity. Pinch and grip may be decreased. Other common areas affected by OA are the cervical and lumbar spine, resulting in pain and loss of motion with rotation of the body and with bending. The weight bearing joints of the lower extremities, especially the hips and knees, are commonly involved and have the highest incidence of disability. People with osteoarthritis of the hips or knees have pain, particularly with standing and walking. Additionally, there is loss of range of motion and stiffness with the initiation of activities (Klippel et al., 2008).

Vocational Considerations

Emotional, intellectual, organ systems, and other health factors do not limit the vocational rehabilitation process. For individuals who have OA of the lumbar spine, ability to bend and lift is reduced by one or more exertional levels. When the knees and hips are involved, tolerance for bending, squatting, ladder or stair climbing, long distance ambulation, and lengthy periods of standing are reduced. With OA of the hands, fine manual dexterity and strength are reduced.

Rehabilitation Potential

Persons with localized osteoarthritis and the lack of systemic features are good candidates for rehabilitation. Both short-term and long-term training and educational programs are realistic. Movement is affected, while strength is preserved. Communication skills, social skills, behavioral abilities, the capacity to learn, comprehend, and other intellectual skills are unchanged. Because of the lack of systemic features of this illness and involvement of only particular joints, rehabilitation potential usually is strong.

Systemic Lupus Erythematosus

Explanation of Disease State

Systemic lupus erythematosus (SLE), commonly called lupus, is a disorder of the immune system, resulting in inflammation of the connective tissue. The disease is characterized by the presence of autoantibodies against the DNA and RNA/protein complexes. Some patients form pathogenic immune complexes (National Institute of Arthritis and Musculoskeletal and Skin Diseases, 2017). Seventy percent of all lupus cases are systemic lupus erythematosus.

Incidence

This disorder primarily affects women. It is nine times greater in women than in men (Lee, Rosenthal, & Abramson, 2017). It has an increased incidence in African-Americans, Hispanics, and Asian Americans. SLE is more common in urban areas than rural areas. In this country, the incidence of SLE is 3.5 per 100,000 per year in whites, and 9.2 per 100,000 per year in African-Americans. Prevalence of SLE is 40-50 per 100,000 population with a total of 239,000 Americans affected. African-American females account for the most prevalent group. Eighty-six percent of people with lupus are women. Peak onset of this disease is during the most productive part of a woman's life, between the ages of 20 to 30 (Firestein et al., 2017). Drenkard et al. (2014) indicated that four studies from the last 20 years gave percentage rates of 15% to 40% of systemic lupus erythematosus patients are unemployed within five years of diagnosis.

Effects

Systemic features of fatigue, fever, weight loss, and joint pain characterize the disease. All individuals have joint pain as a predominant symptom; yet, the major disability is not related to the joints, but rather to systemic involvement. The characteristic clinical course is one of exacerbation and remission; remissions may last for many years. Typically, SLE affects multiple organ systems but not all at the same time. Joint pain is the most common symptom with small joints being most affected. When compared to rheumatoid arthritis, there is no morning stiffness and joint deformity is rare. Some people have skin rashes, especially in sun-exposed areas of the body. There may be inflammation of the lining of the heart and lungs, and acute or chronic renal disease that can progress to kidney failure. Central nervous system involvement manifests itself as stroke, psychosis, or depression for some individuals. Anemia is a common problem (Lee et al., 2017).

Diagnosis

The onset of lupus is insidious. Individuals may have non-specific symptoms, such as fever, fatigue, weight loss, blood clots, hair loss, heart burn, and stomach complaints. The diagnosis of SLE requires at least four of eleven criteria (at any point in time, not necessarily all at once) that the American College of Rheumatology has set forth (Hochberg et al., 2012). These criteria include the presence of a malar rash, discoid rash, photosensitivity (skin rash from the sun), mouth ulcers, nonerosive arthritis, serositis, renal disorder, neurological disorder (seizures or psychosis), hematologic disorder (hemolytic anemia, leucopenia, lymphopenia, thrombocytopenia), immunologic disorder, and antinuclear antibody. Prognosis depends on the organs involved and is most guarded when there is renal and central nervous system involvement.

Treatment

Treatment is a function of the organ systems involved. Musculoskeletal symptoms (arthralgias, myalgias) are treated with NSAIDS. Corticosteroids are generally reserved as temporary measures when symptoms are resistant to NSAIDS (Dooley & Ginzler, 2006). More recently, the biological agents have assumed a prominent role in the treatment of SLE. Beluminab (Benlysta), a biologic agent, inhibits B lymphocyte stimulation and decreases SLE activity. Rituximab, a B cell inhibitor, has been shown to be effective for CNS vasculitis and thrombocytopenia, but has not been successful for generalized lupus. The biologics, Epratuzumab and Toclizunab, which have been efficacious in RA, have shown promise for the treatment of SLE (Drenkard, et al., 2014).

Functional Limitations

Fatigue is a major symptom of SLE and a prominent consideration in job placement. It is particularly apparent during periods of exacerbation, also known as flares, but not during remissions. In contrast to other forms of inflammatory arthritis (e.g., rheumatoid arthritis), there are no problems with mobility, motor strength, or control. Limitations are dependent upon the organ systems affected; pulmonary and cardiac involvement causing shortness of breath limits exertional activities. Persons who have central nervous system involvement may be limited by emotional problems and chronic depression. An individual who has had a stroke may have residual problems of hemiparesis (muscle weakness on one side of the body), which interferes with ambulation and motor skills in the involved extremities. Up to 80% of individuals with SLE have cognitive dysfunction, brain fog that may interfere with memory and focus.

Vocational Considerations

Expected lifespan of people with SLE is good, unless there is involvement of the central nervous system or the kidneys; hence, a counselor can consider educational and training programs that are longer in duration. Special environmental factors involve avoidance of cold environments, as vasospasm of fingers and toes may occur when exposed to cold objects and environments. Sun intolerance (excessive ultraviolet light exposure) can worsen the illness; jobs with excessive exposure to sun are inadvisable. Most people are restricted to light or sedentary exertion because of fatigue (Drenkard et al., 2014).

Rehabilitation Potential

When SLE is in remission, either naturally occurring or medication induced, the individual will have no physical or emotional impairments. This disorder may remain in remission for years; persons diagnosed with lupus are good candidates for re-training and educational programs. Motor and physical limitations are not a common consequence of this disease.

Scleroderma

Explanation of Disease State

Scleroderma is a chronic disorder of the connective tissue in which there is inflammation of multiple organs of the body, resulting in increased deposits of collagen. Primary target organs are the skin, joints, lungs, gastrointestinal tract, and heart. The etiology is unknown.

Effects

There may be extensive fibrosis and tightening, particularly of the hands, face, chest, and feet. Inflammation may cause sclerosis (scarring) of the lungs, heart, and gastrointestinal tract. People with scleroderma have great intolerance to cold; cold temperatures cause spasm of the peripheral vessels that may result in gangrene in the tips of the fingers and even loss of entire digits. Deformities are not a common part of this disease. General fatigue, weakness, and loss of motion related to fibrosis about the joints and skin are common consequences.

Treatment

Treatment is only palliative and symptomatic; non-steroidal anti-inflammatory drugs are given for inflammation and pain. Second line drugs have beneficial effects on interstitial lung disease and renal involvement if given over long periods of time. Biologics have been shown to diminish symptoms. Pulmonary artery hypertension is the major cause of death in patients with scleroderma (Firestein et al., 2017).

Functional Limitations and Vocational Considerations

Scleroderma causes impairment of fine motor activities of the hands, as well as manipulations requiring hand strength (Lim et al., 2014). Grip and pinch are markedly reduced and the ranges of motion of the wrists, elbows, and shoulders may be mildly decreased. There is no intellectual or cognitive impairment; mobility is usually fine. Individuals with pulmonary involvement have fatigue and restricted activity because of shortness of breath upon exertion. Physicians recommend jobs within the light and sedentary exertional categories. Preferred work environments for persons diagnosed with scleroderma are ones that are warm and not subject to extremes or changes in temperature. Job activities should not involve repeated trauma to the hands, since trauma and cold temperatures can result in vasospasm, gangrene, and even loss of fingers.

Rehabilitation Potential

Many individuals with scleroderma have minimal limitations. In more severe cases, there are problems with manual dexterity, stamina, and working in cold environments. Rehabilitation potential usually is good, with most workers being able to stay on their jobs with possible minor accommodation.

Polymyositis and Dermatomyositis

Explanation of Disease State

Polymyositis and dermatomyositis are uncommon, having an incidence of 0.9 to 9.3 new cases a year per million people. This is an autoimmune disorder of skeletal muscle in which the muscles are inflamed and lose strength. The usual course of polymyositis is a sudden onset of severe weakness and then recovery. Remissions can last for many years with few exacerbations. There is a biomodal distribution of the onset of polymyositis - at ages 10 to 15 and then ages 45 to 60 (Firestein et al., 2017). Dermatomyositis is a condition similar to polymyositis, but one in which a skin rash is present in addition to inflammation of the muscles.

Effects

The proximal muscles of the extremities are most involved; hence, patients have major involvement of the muscles about the shoulder and hip regions. Symptomatically, there occurs difficulty in raising the arms above the head, arising from sitting, and climbing stairs. For those who do not have full return of strength, there is partial return of strength that can be maintained for years. Only a small percentage of individuals have continued loss of strength.

Treatment

Most individuals diagnosed with these conditions are treated with high doses of corticosteroids until muscle enzymes normalize. Steroids are tapered slowly over a six month period. It is estimated that 90% will have a positive response, and 50% to 75% will go into remission. Those who do not respond well are treated with second line medications, such as azathioprine and methotrexate, either alone or in combination. Alternatively, intravenous immune globulin (IVIg) has been shown to be effective (Dalakas et al., 1993). More recently, it has been demonstrated that Rituximab is an effective treatment in refractory cases, showing an increase in muscle strength.

Functional Limitations and Vocational Considerations

When there is not a full recovery, there is either a minor degree of motor weakness (i.e., arising from a chair) or major motor problems (i.e., inability to stand or walk, and capacity to do only activities involving the musculature of the forearms and hands). Individuals in this latter group have functional capacities similar to persons with paraplegia (lower extremity involvement). Those with severe lower and upper extremity limitations have a functional capacity similar to quadriplegia. Fortunately, severe extremity complication occurs in only a few individuals with this condition. People with polymyositis who have significant weakness of the lower or upper extremities require jobs within the lowest exertional categories, light and sedentary activities. These persons may require walking aids or wheelchairs; therefore, workstations need modification to accommodate these assistive devices. Once the disability is established, it is usually static.

Rehabilitation Potential

For the majority of persons with polymyositis, medication effectively controls symptoms. After treatment with various medications, most are able to return to work. Rehabilitation potential, therefore, is positive. For the few who do not respond well to medications, potential for rehabilitation may be poor; alternatively, the individual may have the capacity to do sedentary work activity.

Ankylosing Spondylitis

Explanation of Disease State

Ankylosing spondylitis (AS) is a chronic inflammatory disorder of the synovial joints and entheses (points at which tendons insert into bones) of the spine. Primarily a disorder affecting men, the incidence is nine times greater for men than women. Initial onset occurs during the second and third decades of life and causes pain, stiffness, and loss of motion of the lower back. Frequently, the disorder is mistaken for low back pain of a mechanical or degenerative nature. AS affects up to 1% of the population, an estimated 1.7 million people (Reveille, Witter, & Weisman, 2012). Other related diseases include Reiter's syndrome, psoriatic arthritis, and enteropathic (i.e., bowel associated) arthritis. These disorders have similar symptomatology and disability patterns. They are known collectively as spondyloarthropathies (Chakravarty & Paget, 2012).

Effects

This disorder is slowly progressive and, in its full expression, involves the entire spine from the skull to the pelvis. The sacroiliac joints (posterior pelvic joints) are initially involved. Also affected are the synovial joints of the back and ligamentous insertions that join the vertebral bodies. These areas become inflamed resulting in pain, swelling, and loss of motion. Approximately 20% of patients with ankylosing spondylitis have involvement of the peripheral joints, primarily the hips and shoulders. To a lesser extent, there is involvement of the more peripheral joints of the lower extremities and hands.

Symptoms

Pathology of AS involves inflammation of the lining of the posterior joints of the back and ligamentous connections between vertebral bodies. With progression of the disease, there is fibrous ankylosis (fusion) and later, bony ankylosis of the affected joints with consequent loss of all motion in the back. Pain is the main symptom, along with stiffness and gradual progressive loss of motion. When ankylosis is complete, the pain stops but loss of motion in the spine remains.

Treatment

Treatment of AS is symptomatic, primarily with NSAIDS. It is thought that a trial of two or more NSAIDS over a four-week period coupled with physical therapy is the best first-line therapy. Exercise helps retain range of motion. In some cases, sulfasalazine is useful in reducing the length and severity of morning stiffness and pain. Physical therapy with maintenance of proper posture can prevent development of a bent fixed flexion posture of the spine (Klippel et al., 2008). If symptoms last more than four weeks, TNF alpha therapy should be instituted. Currently, there are several FDA approved agents which work on both the spine component and the non-spine inflammatory components. In one study, remission was achieved in 55.6% of patients (Chakravarty & Paget, 2012).

Functional Limitations

AS does not have systemic features; occasionally, patients have involvement of the aortic valve of the heart and pulmonary fibrosis with resultant symptoms. Systemic features are not correlated with loss of work capacity. For most, functional limitations are related to loss of motion of the spine. Bending, twisting, and rotational motions of the lumbar and cervical spine are impaired. If the hips and shoulders are affected there will be pain, loss of motion, and development of flexion contractures in those areas. Involvement of hips, shoulders, and peripheral joints commonly lead to loss of ability to work.

Vocational Considerations

Intellectual functioning is unimpaired. Aptitudes, interests, and communication skills are similar to the normal population and life expectancy is unchanged, unless there is cardiac or pulmonary involvement. There are no special environmental needs.

Early in the disease, there is chronic pain, but little impairment in range of motion in the cervical and lumbar spine. Anti-inflammatory medications and analgesics control this; hence, little modification of the work environment is needed. Most individuals require reduction of exertion in work activities. As the disease progresses, some persons become unable to perform work that is within the higher exertional categories because of pain and loss of mobility of the lumbar spine, including an ability to bend forward (Firestein et al., 2017). Life expectancy is not affected by AS; most people have full, productive lives. Social and behavioral skills are unimpaired, learning comprehension is unchanged and, with the exception of the few who have cardiac involvement, there are no other health problems associated with this condition (Chakravarty & Paget, 2012).

Rehabilitation Potential

Rehabilitation potential for persons with this rheumatic disease generally is strong. With work accommodation for those individuals who have heavier jobs, most maintain productive employment for many years as long as they stay within the lifting and carrying restrictions recommended, usually within the light and sedentary levels. Persons with chronic back pain from ankylosing spondylitis may need jobs that do not involve undue emotional stress. With these factors in mind, the counselor can effectively rehabilitate the majority of people with this disorder.

Case Study

Fernanda Rivas is 25 years of age and has had juvenile-onset rheumatoid arthritis (RA) for 17 years. During this time, she has had lengthy periods of illness where she was confined to her home and, as a result, has just completed her first semester of college. At the present, Fernanda's RA is well controlled and she has not missed any school for the past six months. Three times a day, she takes oral medication. Twice a week, Fernanda self-administers subcutaneous injections of a biologic medication, and visits her physician on a monthly basis to attempt to keep the disease in remission.

To maintain ambulation, Ms. Rivas needed surgery. This involved a hip replacement and knee reconstruction. Presently, Fernanda is able to walk about the house unassisted; she uses a motorized wheelchair when going out into the community. At the current time, Fernanda experiences morning stiffness; she has arranged to take classes at school no earlier than 10:00 AM. On occasion, she has pain in multiple joints including her feet, shoulders, wrists, and the small joints of her hands. In addition to her limited ambulation, she requires assistance from her mother to shampoo her hair, has a bilateral grip strength of 20 pounds, and pinch strength of five pounds. Dr. Margaret Garcia prescribed pool exercise.

Fernanda is the first child of a second generation Hispanic family; she is bilingual in Spanish and English. Her father passed away and general relief and contributions from the children, including Fernanda's Social Security Insurance (SSI) payments, currently support her mother. Fernanda's mother speaks only limited English and has never worked outside the home; she sees her life's role as her daughter's care provider. The relationship between Fernanda and her mother is close; it has been criticized by the health care team as one that promotes a dependent relationship, rather than independence.

Psychological testing showed that Ms. Rivas has high average intelligence, social immaturity, and mild depression. The health care team feels that Fernanda had been an underachiever in school and relies on her mother and siblings rather than taking initiative. Fernanda does not drive. The primary source of emotional support is family.

The college Office for Students with Disabilities referred Fernanda for vocational counseling. Presently, she is taking general education requirements and does not have a major. Ms. Rivas did well in high school and particularly enjoyed the sciences, receiving a senior prize in biology. At the current time, she is unsure about staying in college. A younger sister is the assistant manager at the college bookstore, and has assured Fernanda that she can get her a cashiering job within the store. Fernanda's mother is opposed to Fernanda securing employment, and feels she should stay home and babysit for her nieces, nephews, and the neighborhood children.

Questions

1. Is this individual a suitable candidate for vocational rehabilitation counseling services? What additional medical information is needed from her healthcare team?
2. If you feel Ms. Rivas is a suitable candidate for counseling and rehabilitation, what programs would give her the greatest opportunities for long-term employment? Is additional education indicated?
3. Discuss whether employment as a cashier in the college bookstore with her sister is a practical and realistic choice for employment.
4. How might her counselor handle Fernanda's inability to drive and her dependence upon her mother? Is use of public transportation an option? Consider the impact of her motorized wheelchair on further education, training, transportation, and work.
5. How will Fernanda's current illness, physical limitations, and psychological status influence a decision about higher education? Should vocational training, further higher education, or on-the-job training be considered?
6. What physical problems need to be considered if job placement is to be conducted? Indicate the impact upon Fernanda's ability to obtain and maintain employment.

7. List Ms. Rivas' strengths and functional limitations from both a physical and psychosocial perspective that need evaluation when formulating vocational plans.
8. Discuss any cultural implications relevant to this case.

References

American College of Rheumatology. (ACR; 2017a). *Diseases and conditions.* Retrieved from https://www.rheumatology.org/I-Am-A/Patient-Caregiver/Diseases-Conditions

American College of Rheumatology (ACR; 2017b). *The use of anti-cyclic citrullinated pepetide (anti-CCP) antibodies in RA.* Retrieved from http:www.rheumatology.org/Antinuclear-Antibodies-ANA

Arthritis Foundation. (2017a). *Arthritis by the numbers.* Retrieved from https://www.arthritis.org/Documents/Sections/About-Arthritis/arthritis-facts-stats-figures.pdf

Arthritis Foundation. (2017b). *Arthritis treatment options.* Retrieved from http://www.arthritis.org/living-with-arthritis/treatments/

Barbour K. E., Boring, M., Helmick, C. G., Murphy, L. B., & Qin, J. (2016). Prevalence of severe joint pain among adults with doctor-diagnosed arthritis – United States, 2002-2014. *Morbidity and Mortality Weekly Report, 65*(39), 1052–1056.

Barbour K. E., Helmick, C. G., Boring, M., & Brady, T. J. (2017). Vital signs: Prevalence of doctor-diagnosed arthritis and arthritis-attributable activity limitation – United States, 2013-2015. *Morbidity and Mortality Weekly Report, 66*(9), 246-253. .

Chakravarty, S. D, & Paget, S. A. (2012). Ankylosing spondylitis: Pathogenesis, diagnosis, and therapy. *Rheumatology Practice News Special Edition, 3,* 39-43.

Centers for Disease Control and Prevention. (CDC). (2017). *Arthritis related statistics.* Retrieved from https://www.cdc.gov/arthritis/data_statistics/arthritis-related-stats.htm

Dalakas, M. C., Illa, I., Dambrosia, J. M., Soueidan, S. A., Stein, D. P., Otero, C., . . . McCrosky, S. (1993). A controlled trial of high-dose intravenous immune globulin infusions as treatment for dermatomyositis. *New England Journal of Medicine, 329,* 1993-2000.

Dooley, M. A., & Ginzler, E. M. (2006). Newer therapeutic approaches for systemic lupus erythematosus: Immunosuppressive agents. *Rheumatic Disease Clinics of North America, 32,* 91-102.

Drenkard, C., Bao, G., Dennis, G., Molta, C. T., & Lin, S. S. (2014). Burden of systemic lupus erythematosus on employment and work productivity: Data from a large cohort in the Southeastern United States. *Arthritis Care and Research, 66*(5), 878-887.

Firestein, G. S., Budd, R. C, Gabriel, S. E., McInnes, R., & O'Dell, J. R. (Eds.). (2017). *Firestein & Kelley's textbook of rheumatology* (10th ed.). Philadelphia, PA: Elsevier Saunders.

Gunnarsson C, Chen, J., Ladapo, J. A., Naim, A., & Lofland, J. H. (2015). The employee absenteeism costs of rheumatoid arthritis: Evidence from U.S. National Survey Data. *Journal of Occupational and Environmental Medicine, 57*(6), 635-642.

Hammond, A, O'Brien, R., Woodbridge, S., Bradshaw, L., Prior, Y., Redford, K., . . . Pulikottil-Jacob, R. (2017). Job retention vocational rehabilitation for employed people with inflammatory arthritis (WORK-IA): A feasibility randomized controlled trial. *BMC Musculoskeletal Disorders, 18,* 315.

Hochberg, M., Altman, R. D., April, K. T., Benkhalti, M., Guyatt, G., McGowan, J., . . .Towheed, T. (2012). American College of Rheumatology 2012 recommendations for the use of nonpharmacologic and pharmacologic therapies in osteoarthritis of the hand, hip, and knee. *Arthritis Care and Research, 64*(4), 465-474.

Hochberg, M., Chang, R., Dwosh, S., Lindsey, T., Pincus, T., & Wolfe, F. (1992). American College of Rheumatology 1991 Revised Criteria for the Classification of Global Functional Status in rheumatoid arthritis. *Arthritis and Rheumatism, 35,* 498-502.

Klippel, J. H., Stone, J. H., Crofford, L. J., & White, P. H. (Eds.). (2008). *Primer on the rheumatic diseases* (13th ed.). New York, NY: Springer.

Lee, S. H., Rosenthal, P. B., & Abramson, S. B. (2017). Rheumatic diseases. In A. Moroz, S. R. Flanagan, & H. H. Zaretsky (Eds.), *Medical aspects of disability for the rehabilitation professional* (5th ed., pp. 533-552). New York, NY: Springer.

Lim, S. S., Bayakly, A. R., Helmick, C. G., Gordon, C., Easley, K., & Drenkard, C. (2014). The incidence and prevalence of systemic lupus erythematosus: The Georgia Lupus Registry. *Arthritis Rheumatology, 66*(2), 357-368.

Matcham F, Rayner, L., Steer, S., & Hotopf, M. (2013). The prevalence of depression in rheumatoid arthritis: A systematic review and meta-analysis. *Rheumatology, 52*(2), 2136–2148.

National Institute of Arthritis and Musculoskeletal and Skin Diseases (NIAM). (2017). *Arthritis and Rheumatic Diseases.* Retrieved from https://www.niams.nih.gov/health-topics/arthritis-and-rheumatic-diseases

National Rheumatoid Arthritis Society. (2014). *Invisible disease: Rheumatoid arthritis and chronic fatigue survey.* Retrieved from https://www.nras.org.uk/invisible-disease-rheumatoid-arthritis-and-chronic-fatigue-survey

Reisine, S., McQuillan, J., & Fifield, J. (1995). Predictors of work disability in rheumatoid arthritis patients. *Arthritis and Rheumatism, 38*(11), 1630-1637.

Reveille, J. D., Witter, J. P., & Weisman, M. H. (2012). Prevalence of axial spondylarthritis in the United States: Estimates from a cross-sectional survey. *Arthritis Care & Research, 64*(6), 905–910.

Smolen, J. S., Landewe, R., & Breedveld, F. C. (2010). EULAR recommendations for the management of rheumatoid arthritis with synthetic and biologic disease-modifying antirheumatic drugs. *Annals of Rheumatic Diseases, 69*(6), 964-975.

Vonkeman, H. E., & van de Laar, M. (2013). The new European League against Rheumatism. American College of Rheumatology Diagnostic Criteria for Rheumatoid Arthritis: How are they performing? *Current Opinion in Rheumatology, 25*(3), 354-359.

Wolfe, F., & Michaud, K. (2009). Out-of-pocket expenses and their burden in patients with rheumatoid arthritis. *Arthritis Rheumatism, 61,* 1563–1570.

About the Authors

Penny J. Chong, MD is Medical Director of Cigna Healthcare in Glendale, California. She is a licensed medical practitioner in California, specializing in rheumatology and internal medicine. Prior to Cigna Healthcare, Dr. Chong was Co-Director of Reproductive Immunology Associates in Van Nuys, California, and Assistant Clinical Professor of Medicine at the University of California, Los Angeles.

Constance A. Richard, MFA, MS is a Certified Rehabilitation Counselor. Currently teaching at California State University, Los Angeles, she specializes in disability studies, rehabilitation, professional writing, and fieldwork supervision. Ms. Richard is a lead vocational trainer for CaPROMISE, a federally-funded transitional training program for Supplemental Security Income (SSI) recipients in California.

Chapter 21

PSYCHIATRIC DISABILITIES

David B. Peterson, PhD, CRC, NCC, LCP
Heidi Paul, PhD, CRC, CLCP, LPCC

Introduction

This chapter begins with the definition of psychiatric diagnosis, followed by a review of the competencies necessary for rehabilitation counselors to work effectively with people presenting with psychiatric disabilities. It continues with an overview of the prevalence of psychiatric disabilities and the systems commonly used to classify them, the Diagnostic and Statistical Manual of Mental Disorders, Fifth Edition(DSM-5) (American Psychiatric Association [APA], 2013), and the International Classification of Diseases, Tenth Revision, Clinical Modification(ICD-10-CM) (World Health Organization [WHO], 2018). Next, psychiatric disability is defined using the World Health Organization's model of health (WHO, 2001).

The chapter continues with a discussion of the evolution of the DSM, first with a brief overview of the Diagnostic and Statistical Manual of Mental Disorders, Fourth Edition, Text Revision (DSM-IV-TR) (APA, 2000), as rehabilitation professionals will need to be familiar with it when evaluating medical records generated prior to the release of the DSM-5 (APA, 2013). Next, this chapter provides an introduction to the DSM-5, followed by highlights of changes from the IV-TR to the 5th edition. It concludes with a review of general diagnostic categories of psychiatric diagnoses, a discussion on stigma and the recovery model of psychiatric rehabilitation, and a case example illustrating the issues rehabilitation counselors may face in working with someone with the diagnosis of major depressive disorder, recurrent, severe, with psychotic features.

Psychiatric Diagnoses Defined

Psychiatric diagnoses are *mental disorders* that manifest certain symptoms or diagnostic criteria that significantly impair psychological functioning. The American Psychiatric Association (2013) defines a *mental disorder* as:

> . . . a syndrome characterized by clinically significant disturbance in an individual's cognition, emotion regulation, or behavior that reflects a dysfunction in the psychological, biological, or developmental processes underlying mental functioning. Mental disorders are usually associated with significant distress or disability in social, occupational, or other important activities (p. 20).

It goes on to say that a mental disorder is not . . .

> [. . .] an expectable or culturally approved response to a common stressor or loss, such as the death of a loved one… socially deviant behavior (e.g. political, religious, orsexual) and conflicts that are primarily between the individual and society . . . unless the deviance or conflict results from a dysfunction in the individual as described above (p. 20).

Advances in science suggest that boundaries between psychiatric diagnoses are less clear than once thought, and that most conditions can be placed on a spectrum with closely related diagnoses that share symptoms, genetic and environmental risk factors, and probable biological bases of behavior (APA, 2013). To understand psychiatric diagnoses, the clinician must be able to distinguish between normal life variations and transient responses to stress, and serious symptomatology manifested as disturbances in behaviors, cognition, personality, physical signs, and syndrome combinations.

Accurate diagnosis of psychiatric conditions lead to appropriate referrals, selection of the most appropriate evidenced-based treatments, and ultimately amelioration or elimination of problematic symptoms that negatively impact health and functioning (Peterson, 2011). Practitioners have learned a great deal about psychiatric diagnoses in the last two decades. This new information continues to grow with advances in science and enhances the understanding of psychiatric diagnoses, reduces social stigma associated with them, and improves treatment outcomes (APA, 2013).

Competency in Psychiatric Disabilities

This section of the chapter provides rehabilitation counselors with an overview of the knowledge, skills, and competencies necessary to understand psychiatric disabilities, knowledge that is essential to optimize the mental health and functioning of consumers of rehabilitation services. A single book chapter is insufficient to train counselors to identify psychiatric diagnoses, but is very useful in highlighting the depth and breadth of knowledge required to do so effectively in practice.

While many consumers of rehabilitation services will begin work with counselors, having already been diagnosed with a psychiatric condition, a rehabilitation counselor may be the first mental health professional to have established any type of therapeutic relationship with them. A rehabilitation counselor may be the first allied health professional to accurately identify a psychiatric diagnosis for a consumer, and make appropriate referrals for psychiatric treatment. After a consumer begins vocational training, an educational program, or job placement, he or she may encounter significant stressors and circumstances that lead to the development, recurrence, or exacerbation of psychiatric symptoms, which rehabilitation counselors need to identify and plan for occurring in the counseling relationship.

Psychiatric Rehabilitation Defined

The definition of psychiatric rehabilitation as approved by the United States Psychiatric Rehabilitation Association is as follows:

> Psychiatric rehabilitation promotes recovery, full community integration, and improved quality of life for persons who have been diagnosed with any mental health condition that seriously impairs their ability to lead meaningful lives. Psychiatric rehabilitation services are collaborative, person directed, and individualized. These services are an essential element of the health care and human services spectrum, and must be evidence-based. They focus on helping individuals develop skills and access resources needed to increase their capacity to be successful and satisfied in the living, working, learning, and social environments of their choice (Anthony & Farkas, 2009, p. 9).

Competencies Required

Specifically, rehabilitation counselors need training and supervision in several key areas to work effectively with consumers who have psychiatric disabilities. First, training and supervision in the assessment of psychological functioning is essential to understanding information used in the diagnostic process. Counselors need familiarity with the contemporary classification of diagnoses and related functioning, including the 22 diagnostic categories in the DSM-5 and the WHO's family of classifications. A thorough understanding of the evidenced-based psychotherapeutic and psychopharmacologic treatments is necessary for the elimination or amelioration of functional difficulties and barriers to gainful employment and independent living (CACREP, 2016; CORE, 2013).

One needs a conceptual framework from which to draw when conceptualizing a case in psychiatric rehabilitation counseling. A framework that works effectively with psychiatric diagnoses is the World Health Organization's model of health, as operationalized in the International Classification of Functioning, Disability, and Health (WHO, 2001; Peterson, 2011). This chapter presents a conceptualization of psychiatric disability.

Prevalence of Psychiatric Diagnoses

The National Alliance on Mental Illness (NAMI) (2017) provides a compendium of mental health statistics based upon data spanning the years 2006 to 2017, where they suggest that in any given year, one in five adults in the United States (over 43 million people), experience mental illness, and almost 10 million of those have significant limitations in one or more major life activities. The U.S. Census Bureau's American Community Survey (ACS) of 2008 estimates that over one-third of those seeking rehabilitation services may have a psychiatric diagnosis affecting cognitive functioning (Brault, 2009). The National Comorbidity Survey Replication (NCS-R) conducted by Kessler, Chiu, Demler, and Walters (2005), which surveyed the prevalence, severity, and comorbidity of twelve-month duration DSM-IV disorders, estimated that over one quarter of the population presents with psychiatric diagnoses in any given year, and 57.4 percent will have a psychiatric diagnosis within their lifetime; nearly half of those diagnosed will likely have more than one psychiatric diagnosis.

Diagnostic Systems

DSM-5

The most contemporary diagnostic system available for psychiatric diagnoses is the Diagnostic and Statistical Manual of Mental Disorders, Fifth Edition (DSM-5; APA, 2013). The intent of the latest revision of the DSM was to be useful to mental health professionals, consumers of mental health services and their families, and researchers, by providing clear and concise descriptions of psychiatric diagnoses. Each diagnosis provides explicit diagnostic criteria, dimensional measures that cut across diagnoses, and a concise overview of a given diagnosis, risk factors, associated features, related research, and possible manifestations of the diagnosis.

ICD-10-CM

The system more commonly used throughout the world than the DSM is the International Statistical Classification of Diseases and Related Health Problems, Tenth Revision (ICD-10; WHO, 1992), recently updated as the International Classification of Diseases, Tenth Revision, Clinical Modification (ICD-10-CM; WHO, 2018). Within the U.S., clinicians use the clinical modification of the 9th revision of the ICD (ICD-9-CM; WHO, 2011). There have been efforts to *harmonize* the DSM-5 revision with the ICD-11 revision (APA, 2013, p. xli). The DSM-5 references both the ICD-9-CM codes and ICD-10-CM codes as they relate to the DSM's current diagnoses.

Psychiatric Disability Defined: The ICF

The most contemporary definition of disability to date can be found within the WHO's conceptualization of health (ICF, WHO, 2001). The ICF is the latest addition to the WHO family of classifications. While the ICD provides an etiological classification of health conditions (e.g., diseases, disorders, injuries), the ICF provides information on functioning associated with a broad array of health conditions (Peterson, 2011; Peterson & Elliott, 2008; Peterson, Mpofu, & Oakland, 2010; Peterson & Paul, 2009). The ICF is a significant development in healthcare, as it can be used as a standard for defining concepts, building constructs, hypothesizing relationships, and proposing new theories that will further research and practice (WHO).

The conceptual framework of the ICF provides an intuitive model of functioning, disability, and health. The WHO model of health as defined in the ICF conceptual framework describes interrelated, reciprocally interacting factors related to a person in the environment. The framework is comprised of two parts, each with two components. The first part addresses the person; the two components are body structures and functions. The person is described physically with respect to *body structure*, which for psychiatric diagnoses involves the brain and nervous system. *Body function* describes a change in function as a result of a change in *body structure*. For example, a lack of a specific neurotransmitter in the brain, serotonin, could result in a change in the neurochemistry of the brain. The related change of function could be unremitting depressive symptoms.

The second part involves one's potential to function, or *activity*, in comparison with one's actual functioning within a current context, or *participation*. In the case of depression, a person's depressive symptoms may include psychomotor slowing that would impact the ability to keep pace in a work environment. If within a specific context the person has access to effective medication in the form of antidepressants, psychomotor slowing could improve. The provision of medication in this *context* can impact a person's ability to *participate* effectively, in this case keep pace in the work environment. Interventions like medication or reasonable accommodations in a work setting target disparities between a person's potential (activity) and actual performance (participation) in a given context.

Psychiatric disability then, according to the WHO model of health, can be defined as a function of how a person's impairment manifests within a context. The contextual or second part of the ICF is comprised of the *environment* and also *personal factors*. The environment addresses the immediate context and more distant but impactful societal contexts. Personal factors address a long list of diversity-related issues that could impact functioning. A mental health professional can target disparities between someone's potential and current functioning because of environmental factors, to maximize potential function and minimize the impact of disability. All interventions should be sensitive to an individual's context as defined in *personal factors* of the framework.

What determines whether a disability is clinically significant? Both the APA and WHO have attempted to separate the constructs of mental disorder from disability (APA, 2013). Mental disorders fall under the ICD WHO classifications of disease. The point has been made that disability does not manifest functional impairment consistently across individuals. The impact of the impairment on someone's health and functioning in a specific context is classified using the ICF (WHO, 2001). The WHO Disability Assessment Schedule (WHODAS 2.0) (WHO, 2011) is based upon the ICF, and is proposed for use within the DSM-5 as a standardized measure of disability. However, many psychiatric diagnoses lack reliable measures of severity to inform the use of the WHODAS. The clinical significance of a psychiatric diagnosis remains a matter of clinical judgment as to whether "the disturbance causes clinically significant distress or impairment in social, occupational, or other important areas of functioning" (APA, 2013, p. 21).

Evolution of the DSM

The American Psychiatric Association began classifying *institutionalized mental patients* in 1844 (APA, 2013), and the resulting DSM system has been through five revisions. To help manage the co-existence of the DSM-IV-TR and the DSM-5 during the two-year trial period and beyond, this chapter reviews the structure of the DSM-IV-TR.

The Multiaxial Assessment Format of the DSM-IV-TR

The DSM-IV-TR consists of five component axes (APA, 2000). The first, Axis I, Clinical disorders and other conditions that may be a focus of clinical attention, involves most psychiatric disorders in the system. Axis II, Personality disorders and mental retardation, may be conceptualized as a group of conditions that are less temporal and more enduring than many Axis I diagnoses.

Axis III, General medical conditions, provides an opportunity to consider how physical condition affects psychological functioning. Axis IV, Psychosocial and environmental problems, provides a list of possible contextual factors that may impact overall psychological functioning, including interpersonal problems, family discord, death of a family member, and educational, occupational, housing, economic, healthcare, and legal issues. Finally, Axis V, Global Assessment of Functioning or GAF, provides a numeric scale to estimate level of impairment and/or the impact of a diagnosis on functioning. The scores on this scale ranged from 1 to 100, with "0" indicating inadequate information. A score in the 1 to 10 range indicates extremely low functioning, and the 90 to 100 range denotes superior functioning. Ultimately, the GAF was eliminated due to inconsistency in its application in practice. The multiaxial system brought attention to a biopsychosocial model of health and functioning comprised not only of physical and mental illness, but also the person within his or her social and environmental context (Peterson, 2011).

The DSM-5

The DSM-5 (APA, 2013) is made up of three sections. Section I reviews the history and developmental process of the latest revision of the DSM, and provides a guide to the basics of DSM-5 clinical diagnosis. Section II contains the diagnostic criteria and codes, classifying psychiatric disorders into 22 major categories, an expansion of the DSM-IV-TR's 17 major categories:

1. Neurodevelopmental Disorders
2. Schizophrenia Spectrum and Other Psychotic Disorders
3. Bipolar and Related Disorders
4. Depressive Disorders
5. Anxiety Disorders
6. Obsessive-Compulsive and Related Disorders
7. Trauma- and Stressor-Related Disorders
8. Dissociative Disorders
9. Somatic-Symptom and Related Disorders
10. Feeding and Eating Disorders
11. Elimination Disorders
12. Sleep-Wake Disorders
13. Sexual Dysfunctions
14. Gender Dysphoria
15. Disruptive, Impulse-Control, and Conduct Disorders
16. Substance-Related and Addictive Disorders
17. Neurocognitive Disorders
18. Personality Disorders
19. Paraphilic Disorders
20. Other Mental Disorders
21. Medication-Induced Movement Disorders and Other Adverse Effects of Medication
22. Other Conditions that May Be a Focus of Clinical Attention

The primary purpose of Section II of the DSM-5 is "to assist trained clinicians in the diagnosis of their patients' mental disorders as part of a case formulation assessment that leads to a fully informed treatment plan" (p. 19). Section III, Emerging Measures and Models, provides new assessment measures, cultural formulations, an alternative model for disorders of personality, and conditions for further study. The contents of Section III are suggested to require further study before full implementation with Section II of the manual, but users are encouraged to use them to enhance clinical decision-making (APA, 2013).

Changes from DSM-IV-TR to DSM-5

Organization of the diagnostic categories in the DSM-5 was changed to harmonize with the most recent version of the Mental and Behavioral Disorders section of the ICD (versions 10 and 11). This was done to minimize the impact of having two different diagnostic systems affecting the collection of health statistics and future research replication. Advances in neuroscience are reflected in expanded diagnostic categories and subtypes of neurocognitive disorders.

The DSM-5 has transitioned away from the multiaxial system of diagnosis, to a non-axial system. Axes I and II are combined, and Axis III, physical conditions, if they affect psychological functioning, are to be noted along with the psychiatric diagnoses. Axis IV was eliminated, as the DSM-5 task force decided not to further develop its own psychosocial and environmental problems classification schema (APA, 2013, p. 16).

With the elimination of the axial system, the order of diagnoses presented in the DSM-5 reflects a developmental and lifespan perspective.

Axis V, Global Assessment of Functioning or GAF score, has been eliminated. In its place, within section III of the DSM-5, Emerging Measures and Models, and related to the prior ICF discussion, the WHODAS 2.0 (WHO, 2011), a derivative of the ICF, provides a new standard method for assessing global disability levels for mental disorders. The WHODAS conception of disability replaces the GAF and specifically addresses *disability* (APA, 2013). Also included in section III are 13 symptom domains with dimensional measures of severity proposed for all DSM diagnostic groups.

The frequently used "not otherwise specified" or "NOS" qualifier for DSM-IV-TR, which meant a diagnosis came close to but did not satisfy all the diagnostic criteria required for the formal diagnosis, has been changed to one of two new options. *Other specified disorder* is used to highlight the specific reason why a set of symptoms does not meet diagnostic criteria. *Unspecified disorder* is the qualifier used if the clinician decides not to highlight the specific reason. Clinical judgment is used in determining whether there is sufficient evidence to use *other specified* versus *unspecified disorder*.

The DSM-5 has online supplemental information, including more symptom and functional impairment severity measures that cut across diagnostic categories. To enhance cultural sensitivity of DSM diagnoses, the *Cultural Formulation Interview* is provided with supplements (see www.psychiatry.org/dsm5). Pages 14 and 15 of the DSM-5 provide an overview of the myriad of cultural and gender issues that affect the boundary between normality and pathology, and the systems in which healthcare is provided.

Some of the diagnostic changes in the DSM-5 include the pervasive developmental disorders combined into an *autism spectrum disorder*; the term mental retardation has been replaced by *intellectual disability* (or intellectual developmental disorder). Severity of these conditions is estimated using measures of adaptive functioning rather than measures of IQ. The various learning disorders have been combined into one *specific learning disorder* diagnosis. Substance abuse and dependence are now described as *substance use disorders*, and the distinction between tolerance and withdrawal (formerly associated with dependence) and addiction is made clear. The subtypes of schizophrenia have been removed due to their lack of clinical utility. The commonly used cognitive disorder *not otherwise specified* is now *neurocognitive disorder*.

Diagnostic Groups

This section provides overviews of some of the diagnostic groups within the DSM-5 (and related diagnostic groups in the ICD-9-CM and the ICD-10-CM). This text contains stand-alone chapters that focus on specific diagnostic categories within the DSM, such as alcoholism and addictions, intellectual disability, specific learning disorders, neurological diagnoses, and acquired brain injury (related to neurodevelopmental and neurocognitive disorders).

The brief descriptions of diagnostic groups do not replace the direct use of the DSM-5; readers are encouraged to refer directly to it for specific diagnostic criteria. In contrast, the ICD-10-CM is a free system available online at the World Health Organization's homepage. The brief descriptions of diagnoses in this chapter can be referenced back to these ICD systems; the most recent versions 10 and 11 have been and are being harmonized with the DSM-5 system (WHO, 2018). Next, are reviews of specific diagnostic groups commonly encountered in rehabilitation counseling.

Anxiety Disorders

Anxiety disorders are among the most commonly occurring psychiatric diagnoses, with a lifetime prevalence of 31.2%. In a given year, about 40 million American adults age 18 and older, or 18.1% of people in this age group, have anxiety disorders (Kessler et al., 2005). These statistics were calculated while the DSM-IV-TR was in use, and when posttraumatic stress disorder (PTSD) was within this category; it has since been moved to the Trauma-and Stressor-Related Disorders category.

Anxiety symptoms include nervousness, trembling, muscular tension, sweating, lightheadedness, palpitations, dizziness, epigastric discomfort, and various forms of worries and forebodings. This diagnostic category includes separation anxiety disorder, selective mutism, specific phobia, social anxiety disorder, panic disorder, agoraphobia, generalized anxiety disorder, and substance/medication-induced anxiety disorder. Specific diagnoses selected within the DSM-5 are what may have caused the anxiety (e.g., substance or medication-induced, a medical condition), when it occurred, and duration (APA, 2013). For this diagnostic group, features of generalized anxiety disorder, panic disorder, agoraphobia, and social anxiety disorder (social phobia) are highlighted. According to the NIMH study, the comorbidity of anxiety disorders with both depression and substance use is high (Kessler et al., 2005).

Generalized Anxiety Disorder

This condition involves excessive anxiety or worry that is pervasive and chronic, lasting at least six months. Symptoms include anxiety and worry that is far out of proportion for the context. Other symptoms include: restlessness, feeling on edge, easily fatigued, concentration problems, irritability, muscle tension, and difficulty with sleep. Some have reported that they struggled with such symptoms for years before seeking treatment.

Panic Disorders

Panic disorders involve the presence of sudden panic attacks and intense experiences of psychological fear and physiological arousal. A panic attack starts suddenly with a feeling of severe apprehension, fearfulness, or terror associated with feelings of impending doom. During an attack, the individual experiences physiological symptoms like shortness of breath, rapid or skipped heartbeats, chest pain or discomfort, and choking or smothering sensations. There is a fear of losing control or even dying.

Agoraphobia

In the DSM-IV-TR, panic disorders were classified as with or without agoraphobia, but agoraphobia is no longer associated with panic disorder; it stands on its own as a marked fear of social situations. Individuals fear or avoid social situations because they believe escape might be difficult in the event of an embarrassing situation (e.g., panic attack, falling asleep in public, incontinence).

Social Anxiety Disorder, Specific Phobias

Social anxiety disorder, or social phobia, consists of a marked fear or anxiety about one or more social situations where one might be scrutinized. Approximately 15 million adults in the U.S., or 6.8%, have social phobia in a given year, with a 12.1% lifetime prevalence (Kessler et al., 2005; NAMI, 2017).

Treatment of Anxiety Disorders

Medication, psychotherapy, or combinations of both methods are effective means to treat anxiety disorders. Temporary relief is available from a class of medications called benzodiazepines, which provide rapid relief, but are addictive. Antidepressant medications are a better long-term medical treatment for anxiety, and most effective with psychotherapeutic techniques that provide behavioral and cognitive strategies for managing anxiety (Preston, O'Neal, & Talaga, 2017). Consumers of rehabilitation services may have struggled with anxiety their entire lives and coped with it using substance abuse or avoidance of anxiety provoking situations. There is a high comorbidity between anxiety disorders and alcoholism and other substance use (Sadock, Sadock, & Ruiz, 2014). The rehabilitation counselor may need to make appropriate treatment recommendations to minimize debilitating anxiety in the rehabilitation process, and to help teach new and functional coping skills for anxiety.

Mood Disorders

Bipolar and depressive disorders, whose primary impairment is disturbance in mood are commonly diagnosed conditions. Depressive disorders involve only depressive episodes, while bipolar disorders involve both manic or hypomanic (elevated mood) and depressive episodes.

According to NCS-R, 20.9 million American adults, or 9.5% of the U.S. population age 18 and older in a given year have mood disorders, which may include major depressive disorder (the leading cause of disability in the U.S. for ages 15 to 44) (WHO, 2004), dysthymic disorder (affecting 1.5% of the U.S. population age 18 and older in a given year), and bipolar disorder (affecting 2.6% or 5.7 million adults age 18 and older) (Kessler et al., 2005).

Depressive Disorders

The DSM-5 reported that the one-year prevalence of Major Depressive Disorder is 7% in the United States, with higher rates for younger individuals and women (APA, 2013). Depressive disorders often occur comorbidly with anxiety and substance-related disorders (Kessler et al., 2005). The depressive disorders in the DSM-5 and ICD-10 have in common moods that are sad, empty, or irritable, with somatic and cognitive effects on health and functioning. The specific depressive diagnosis selected within the DSM-5 is a matter of what caused the mood disturbance (e.g., substance or medication-induced, a medical condition, bereavement, etc.), when it occurred, and for how long.

Depression may manifest as anhedonia, or a lack of interest in pleasurable activities. Depression makes it hard to fall asleep, or causes early morning awakening, adversely impacting restorative sleep. It can increase or decrease appetite. The person may demonstrate psychotic features, such as hallucinations or delusions. Depression often is accompanied by anxiety. There is a high prevalence of alcohol and substance abuse with individuals who have mood disorders so it is common to encounter clients with dual diagnoses (Sadock et al., 2014). Persons with mood disorders may use alcohol or other substances as self-medication (i.e., for their sedative, disinhibiting, or stimulating effects). Historically, more than 87% of those who end their life had a diagnosable mental disorder (Stack, 2014).

Severe depression causes difficulty with concentration, the ability to persist on a job, keeping appropriate pace due to psychomotor slowing, or fatigue, resulting in both personal and occupational difficulties. Disturbance in mood adversely impacts social functioning as well, has an impact on where an individual can find employment, and how one interacts with the system of social support. Self-esteem and confidence diminish.

Treatment of Depression

Major depressive disorder is treated using medication, psychotherapy, or a combination. Response to treatment takes several weeks with antidepressants. Symptoms can be unresponsive to medication. Dosage or type of medication often needs periodic adjustment, or symptoms may remit and return as a matter of course or in response to stressful life situations. There are adjunctive therapies using atypical antipsychotic medications when antidepressant medications alone are ineffective. Longitudinal research suggests that psychotherapy and medication combined are more effective than either treatment alone (Preston et al., 2013).

People experiencing depression often consider their symptoms to be related to physical illness rather than psychiatric illness, so they may seek help from general health care professionals (Sadock et al., 2014). Mental health professionals, including counselors, provide collaborative support to other health professionals to maximize treatment efficacy.

Bipolar Disorders

The lifetime prevalence of people with any type of bipolar disorder is 4.4% (NAMI, 2017). People with bipolar disorders were historically referred to as being *manic-depressive*. In contrast with depressive disorders, bipolar disorders involve depression and either a manic (elevated mood) or hypomanic (less severe mood elevation) episode. Depression, in this condition, is defined the same as for depressive disorder. According to the DSM-5, Bipolar I disorder manifests both depression and mania. Bipolar II disorder manifests depression and hypomania (APA, 2013).

During mania or a manic episode, a person demonstrates a distinct period of abnormally and persistently elevated, expansive, or irritable mood. Oftentimes, the person feels euphoric, has inflated self-esteem, or becomes extremely gregarious, talkative, and overly active socially or occupationally. They feel that their thoughts are racing, and become very distractible or impulsive. The person appears overly energetic with a decreased need for sleep. Severe cases of bipolar disorders may experience hallucinations and delusions (APA, 2013).

Persons experiencing manic symptoms often do not recognize that something is wrong. They seek help only at the insistence of family members or employers who find their behaviors disturbing. They may be brought in by law enforcement officers for unruly or bizarre behaviors in public, or for engaging in activities that are dangerous to themselves or others. Features include poor judgment, risky business ventures, disregard for ethical concerns, and engaging in antisocial behaviors. Substance abuse and other risk taking behaviors can accompany a manic or hypomanic episode.

Treatment of Bipolar Disorders

People with bipolar disorders require medication for mood stabilization, which include antidepressants, atypical antipsychotics, anti-seizure medication (which have a mood stabilizing effect), and lithium. Unfortunately, manic and hypomanic episodes may be accompanied by the belief that one is *cured*, and the person stops medication compliance, resulting in exacerbations in mania and depression. Many cases of bipolar disorder require lifetime medication management. Psychotherapy can be of limited use when someone is in a manic state, but pharmacotherapy is very useful for overall mental health and functioning (Preston el al., 2013).

Trauma- and Stress-Related Disorders

This category is new to the DSM-5; all disorders share in common the exposure to a traumatic event, and the variable psychological distress that ensues. Within this group are the following diagnoses: reactive attachment disorder, disinhibited social engagement disorder, posttraumatic stress disorder (PTSD), acute stress disorder, and adjustment disorder (APA, 2013). This section focuses on three diagnoses: PTSD, Acute Stress Disorder, and Adjustment Disorders.

Posttraumatic Stress Disorder (PTSD)

Formerly, one of the anxiety disorders, PTSD, gained significant attention during the Vietnam War; the more recent conflicts in Afghanistan and Iraq brought further attention to the diagnosis. A study reported in the *New England Journal of Medicine* (Hoge et al., 2004) indicated that among those in combat in Iraq, the prevalence of PTSD is 9.3% for those who had experienced one to two firefights, 12.7% for those with three to five firefights, and 19.3% for those with more than five firefights. Similar rates were found for those deployed to Afghanistan.

PTSD is a diagnosis associated with a delayed and/or protracted response following exposure to stressful or traumatic events. Traumatic events that lead to the development of PTSD are as varied as the human experience. Examples of such events include natural or man-made disasters, serious accidents, witnessing the violent death of another, and being a victim of violence.

Related symptoms include reliving the trauma in intrusive memories (flashbacks) or dreams, feeling detached or emotionally numb, or diminished interest or participation in social or daily activities (WHO, 2018). Other persistent symptoms include increased arousal, insomnia, irritability, emotional outbursts, difficulty concentrating, hypervigilance, and exaggerated startle response. Symptoms can be triggered by events in the environment that remind one of the distressing event.

Acute Stress, Adjustment Disorders

Acute stress disorder is a stress reaction shorter in duration than PTSD, lasting less than one month. The diagnosis is changed to PTSD if symptoms persist beyond a month. Adjustment disorder is a state of distress and emotional disturbance resulting from a significant life change or stressful event that interferes with personal, social, or occupational functioning (WHO, 2011). Related symptoms manifest as anxiety, depressed mood, and disturbance in conduct.

Treating Trauma- and Stress-Related Disorders

Psychopharmacological treatment is useful in treating debilitating anxiety associated with stress and trauma. Alpha blockers and blood pressure medications help diminish night terrors and nightmares in military personnel with PTSD. Antidepressants, antianxiety, and atypical antipsychotic medications are effective in managing mood instability associated with stress and trauma-related symptoms. Behavioral and cognitive approaches in psychotherapy help manage the body's reaction to symptoms, and provide compensatory strategies for troubling thoughts and recollections (Lambert, 2013; Preston et al., 2013).

Schizophrenia Spectrum Disorders

Based on nearly 200 studies from 46 nations, international lifetime prevalence rates for schizophrenia are less than 0.005% (Bhugra, 2005), much lower than the 1% reported in the DSM-IV-TR (APA, 2000). Small numbers notwithstanding, schizophrenia and related spectrum disorders are often chronic and severe conditions that require specific clinical skills of the rehabilitation professional.

Based upon the ICD-10-CM (WHO, 2018), *schizophrenic disorders* are characterized by fundamental and characteristic distortions of thinking and perception, and by inappropriate or blunted (unusually unexpressive) affect. Hallucinations, delusions, and gross behavioral disturbances may be present when people are diagnosed. Noncompliance with medication and subsequent psychotic episodes can lead to irreversible changes in brain structure resulting in cognitive deficits (Preston et al., 2013).

Key Features of Psychotic Disorders

The DSM-5 (APA, 2013) defined five key features of psychotic disorders. Included are delusions, hallucinations, disorganized thinking (speech), grossly disorganized or abnormal motor behavior (including catatonia), and negative symptoms. *Delusions* are false beliefs and can include the idea that an external force is remotely controlling one's actions or that one's thoughts are being monitored by some kind of transmitter. These ideas are often bizarre and clearly discerned to be without grounds by practically everyone else. *Hallucinations* are sensory perceptions not based on external stimuli. As an example, the person may hear voices when there is no one speaking.

Disorganized thinking is manifest through speech that reveals incoherent or tangential thought processes difficult to understand. *Disorganized* or *abnormal motor behavior* ranges from silliness to unpredictable agitation and socially inappropriate behavior. An individual may act in an eccentric manner or demonstrate a marked decrease in reactivity to the environment (catatonia). *Negative symptoms* relate primarily to diminished emotional experience, and a decrease in motivated, self-initiated, purposeful activity. Persons with psychotic or negative symptoms of schizophrenia may appear irrational, incoherent, withdrawn, or engage in inappropriate behavior. The onset of symptoms typically occurs during young adulthood. Complete recovery is unlikely (Sadock et al., 2014).

Diagnoses within Schizophrenia Spectrum Disorders

The DSM-IV-TR (APA, 2000) identified five major types of schizophrenia: paranoid type, disorganized type, catatonic type, undifferentiated type, and residual type; these categories no longer exist in the DSM-5 (APA, 2013). The first three types are characterized by their most prominent symptoms, namely paranoia, disorganization, and catatonic behavior, respectively. Undifferentiated type refers to a form of schizophrenia that currently does not display the specific criteria for any of these three dominant symptoms. Residual type is diagnosed in individuals who once had an active diagnosis of schizophrenia but currently do not show any major symptoms.

Within the DSM-5, diagnoses in this category are organized along a gradient of severity of psychopathology (APA, 2013). First, schizotypal personality disorder is mentioned (but defined elsewhere among the personality disorders group) as a condition manifesting social and interpersonal deficits, which may include milder forms of bizarre thinking, behavior, or psychoses. Next, is brief psychotic disorder, symptoms remitting within a month. Schizophreniform disorder may ultimately develop into schizophrenia with sufficient duration of symptoms. Schizophrenia may be diagnosed if lasting at least six months in duration. Finally, schizoaffective disorder shares features of schizophrenia and a major mood (depression or mania) episode (APA, 2013).

Treatment of Schizophrenia Spectrum Disorders

Schizophrenia is typically treated with psychotropic medication; psychotherapy has proven useful with some promise shown for family systems-based psychotherapy and assertive community-based treatment (Lambert, 2013). Unless they have an adequate support network of family members and helping professionals, individuals with more severe forms of schizophrenia spectrum disorders face chronic unemployment and related financial problems. People with diagnoses of schizophrenia account for a portion of the homeless population (Sadock et al., 2010).

Medication may be essential in controlling the symptoms of schizophrenia and preventing relapse; side effects present a major health concern. Typical and atypical antipsychotic medications have neurological and other side effects, including involuntary movements of the tongue, jaw, and extremities; muscular rigidity; Parkinsonian tremors; weight gain; new onset Type II diabetes mellitus; and for some the risk of sudden cardiac death (Preston et al., 2013; Sadock et al., 2010). The consequences of not taking prescribed medication can be dire.

Personality Disorders

Personality disorders are defined in the ICD-10-CM as clinically significant conditions and behavior patterns that may be a persistent expression of one's lifestyle and mode of relating to self and others. The various types of personality disorders all share deeply engrained and enduring behavior patterns that manifest as inflexible and maladaptive responses to a broad range of personal and social situations. This causes personal distress that results in significant problems (WHO, 2011).

DSM-IV-TR and DSM-5 Clusters

The specific diagnoses of personality disorders do not match perfectly between the DSM and the ICD systems. In the DSM revision, those diagnoses that existed in DSM-IV-TR remain in the 5th revision. The 12 personality disorder diagnoses can be summarized into three clusters. Cluster A diagnoses share odd or eccentric behavior; Cluster B diagnoses share dramatic, emotional, or erratic presentations; and Cluster C diagnoses share in common a fearful or anxious presentation (APA, 2013).

Effect of Personality Disorders

Personality disorders play a role in the potential development of other psychiatric diagnoses, and also as factors affecting the treatment of co-existing conditions. One psychiatric diagnosis can cause exaggeration of a preexisting personality trait, which appears to be a personality disorder, but resolves once the related diagnosis is resolved. Also, many psychiatric diagnoses evolve over time and at first appear to be personality disorders. Certain personality disorders predispose an individual to increased risk of developing another psychiatric diagnosis, or complicate the treatment of a co-occurring condition.

Stigma and Psychiatric Diagnoses

Stigma is a . . . "mark of shame or discredit" (Merriam-Webster Online, 2017). The definition has expanded to include . . . " negative judgments we levy against each other based on devalued group identities" (Scheyett, as cited in Lucksted & Drapalski, 2015, p. 99). Stigma takes three forms: social stigma, internalized stigma, and stigma by association. A major challenge for people with mental health disabilities is living with the stigmas of mental illness.

The media has had significant influence over public perceptions of mental illness. Most people receive information about mental illness from either the news media (print, television, and electronic) or movies. After a mass shooting, the news media seeks reasons for the incident, most often inquiring about the mental health state of the individual responsible for the violence. Some movies depict people with mental illness as violent, dangerous, and unpredictable. The greater negative coverage the media presents to the public, the more likely people will think negatively about mental illness. Negative cognitions create adverse emotions, such as fear and revulsion. Deleterious emotions adopted by society can be internalized by a person with mental illness, a phenomena known as self-stigma.

Self-stigma occurs when ". . . stigmatized individuals believe that stigmatizing attitudes are true of them" (Hoffner, Fuijoka Cohen, & Seate, 2017, p. 10). If people in society see themselves negatively, they will believe that others view them adversely. Self-stigma creates behaviors such as avoidance, blaming, and exclusion. Another serious consequence of self-stigma is that it prevents people from seeking treatment and potential improvement or recovery because of the belief they will be found out, lose friends, careers, and family relationships. Avoiding treatment may lead to self-destructive behaviors such as self-medicating or illegal drug use or to more serious adverse consequences such mental deterioration and possible suicide (Yeh, Jewell, & Thomas, 2017).

Individuals who have a relationship with a person who has mental illness, such as a family member, friend, or teacher, may themselves be stigmatized. This type of stigma is known as *stigma by association* (SBA) (van der Sanden, Pryor, Stutterheim, Kok, & Bos, 2016). SBA may cause people who associate with the person with mental illness to be viewed negatively. The adversity may be severe enough to cause friends or family members to distance themselves from the person with mental illness, leading to social isolation and lack of meaningful relationships causing poor psychological well-being. Van der Sanden, Bos, Stutterheim, Pryor, and Kok (2013) found that SBA was positively correlated with greater psychological distress and less perceived closeness.

Stigma adversely affects persons with mental illness, as well as family and friends. This in turn inhibits their ability to form and maintain satisfying relations, rewarding careers, and appropriate medical treatment. The lack of positive social integration and satisfying relationships has a lasting negative effect on the psychological well-being for the person (van der Sanden et al., 2013).

The Recovery Model in Psychiatric Rehabilitation

The origin of this model is the recovery approach defined within psychiatric rehabilitation. This is a comprehensive model with many elements, one of which is to help clients manage and live with mental disorders, rather than expecting or waiting for them to be symptom free before returning to full participation in society. This model emphasizes self-determination and input from clients and their family members in the recovery process, and in the design and operation of the mental health service system. Rehabilitation counselors working in public mental health settings with clients need to be familiar with the recovery model approach for intervention planning (Anthony & Farkas, 2009).

The psychiatric rehabilitation process as defined by the Boston University Center for Psychiatric Rehabilitation is an evidence-based approach with specific job descriptions, record keeping formats, and quality assurance mechanisms that require intensive training and supervision over time to implement. The approach stemmed from the deinstitutionalization movement that began in the 1950s, which discharged large numbers of patients from state hospitals into communities that were not prepared or unwilling to provide appropriate support. Essential services provided within a recovery-oriented system include treatment for symptom relief, crisis intervention, case management, rehabilitation goals, enrichment activities for self-development, rights protection for equal opportunity, and support for healthy lifestyle, empowerment, and basic support of essential needs (Anthony & Farkas, 2009).

Case Study

Mr. Robert Arsenije is a 19-year-old immigrant from Kosovo with a diagnosis of major depressive disorder, recurrent, severe, with psychotic features. He was first diagnosed at age 18. Throughout his adolescence in Kosovo, he presented as a rather sullen and pessimistic individual who frequently reported feeling down and wondering what was the worth of living. When Robert was 16, his family moved to the United States; at this time, his symptoms intensified. His family became increasingly concerned with his deteriorating condition, and finally convinced him to see a psychiatrist just after his 18th birthday.

Robert is the second of three children of an intact family. Prior to the onset of his symptoms of depression, he had no history of psychiatric treatment and maintained an average level of academic performance. Robert's symptoms first began in Kosovo. His family observed that he was sad for most of the day, nearly every day of the week. He became tearful when confronted with stressful situations. They tried to be encouraging but did not force any discussion, and Robert was maintaining his academic performance in high school. When his family relocated to the U.S., although in his home of origin his education was completed, he learned that he had another year of education to complete and graduate within the U.S. system. When he reluctantly began this last year of study, he expressed a sadness and empty feeling inside, missing the few friends he had in Kosovo and their former way of life.

The month of his graduation Robert demonstrated a diminished interest in most of his daily routine, apart from private time in his room. When asked by the school counselor about his future plans for college or employment, Robert said he did not have much hope for the future, as he could not imagine what worth he would bring to any specific job or college program. The school counselor was concerned about the expressed hopelessness that Robert was experiencing and contacted his family to recommend counseling and evaluation.

Robert delayed seeking any mental health assistance until his 18th birthday, when he finally acquiesced to his family's request that he seek treatment. During the intake, Robert disclosed frequent thoughts of ending his life, but he had neither a specific plan nor ready means for suicide. He was diagnosed with major depressive disorder, recurrent, moderate. The psychiatrist recommended therapy and medication, and referred Robert to see a rehabilitation counselor with the state agency for assistance.

With the help of his counselor, Robert obtained employment in a large retail store as a sales associate and cashier. Robert was compliant with his first two weeks of therapy appointments and regular dosing of medication, but therapy was causing him to think of issues that made him feel worse, and the medication was not yet changing how he felt. Robert began his employment during the busy holiday season. After two weeks of stressful holiday retail employment, Robert's symptoms of depression worsened. He became irritable with his family and cried more frequently.

Robert began hearing a voice telling him negative thoughts. At times, this voice suggested he walk out to the bridge down the road and jump into the river to end his life. He had biweekly appointments arranged with his vocational rehabilitation counselor while he began new employment. During an appointment, Robert disclosed his worsening depressive symptoms, the beginning of auditory hallucinations, and thoughts of suicide. His rehabilitation counselor suggested that she accompany him to the emergency room where they could get in touch with his psychiatrist and address his deteriorating mental health.

On the way to the hospital, Robert's counselor assured him that sometimes in psychotherapy, issues occur that make one feel worse before feeling better. She also assured Robert that the medication he was prescribed for his depression takes four to six weeks to become effective, and that with patience and adjustments of medication by his psychiatrist his treatment would likely be helpful. Also, she surmised that perhaps the intensity of retail work around the holidays was not effective for Robert. By encouraging him, she reassured Robert not to give up on being compliant with his therapy, and that they would continue to work together on an employment opportunity that suited his interests and abilities.

Robert felt better with these assurances. While in the emergency room, Robert's diagnosis was modified to major depressive disorder, recurrent, severe, with psychotic features. He continued to work with his psychiatrist, psychotherapist, and rehabilitation counselor to ameliorate his symptoms, explore his interests, and expressed an interest in a community college training program to become an x-ray technician.

Questions

1. Based on this chapter review and the WHO's model of health, what does a rehabilitation counselor need to conceptualize for this case?
2. Assign Robert a vocational profile including age category, educational level, and work history.
3. What vocational alternatives can you recommend?
4. How should a rehabilitation counselor help Robert establish and achieve realistic educational goals?
5. What counseling techniques can you use to help Robert comply with his prescribed treatment?
6. Discuss prejudice and discrimination toward persons with psychiatric disabilities and how these can be diminished in the workplace.

References

American Psychiatric Association (APA). (2000). *Diagnostic and statistical manual of mental disorders (4th ed., text rev.)*. Washington, DC: Author.

American Psychiatric Association (APA). (2013). *Diagnostic and statistical manual of mental disorders (5th ed.)*. Washington, DC: Author.

Anthony, W. A., & Farkas, M. D. (2009). *A primer on the psychiatric rehabilitation process*. Boston, MA: Boston University Center for Psychiatric Rehabilitation.

Bhugra, D. (2005). The global prevalence of schizophrenia. *PLoS Medicine, 2*(5), 151.

Brault, M. W. (2009). *Review of changes to the measurement of disability in the 2008 American Community Survey*. Washington, DC: United States Census Bureau.

Council for Accreditation of Counseling & Related Education Programs (CACREP). (2016). *CACREP Standards*. Retrieved from http://www.cacrep.org/for-programs/2016-cacrep-standards/

Council on Rehabilitation Education (CORE). (2013). *Accreditation manual for masters level rehabilitation counselor education programs*. Schaumburg, IL: Author.

Hoffner, C.A., Guijioka, Y., Cohen, E.L., & Seate, A. (2017). Perceived media influence, mental illness, and response to news coverage of a mass shooting. *Psychology of Media Culture 6*(2), 159-173.

Hoge, C. W., Castro, A. A., Messer, S. C., McGurk, D., Cotting, D. I., & Koffman, R. L. (2004). Combat duty in Iraq and Afghanistan, mental health problems, and barriers to care. *New England Journal of Medicine, 351*, 13-22.

Kessler, R. C., Chiu, W. T., Demler, O., & Walters, E. E. (2005). Prevalence, severity, and comorbidity of twelve-month DSM-IV disorders in the National Comorbidigy Survey Replication (NCS-R). *Archives of General Psychiatry, 62*, 617-627.

Lambert, M. J. (Ed.) (2013). *Bergin & Garfield's handbook of psychotherapy and behavior change* (6th ed.). Hoboken, NJ: Wiley.

Lucksted, A. & Drapalski, A.L. (2015). Self-stigma regarding mental illness: Definition, impact, and relationship to societal stigma. *Psychiatric Rehabilitation Journal, 38*(2), 99-109.

Merriam-Webster Dictionary Online. (2017). Stigma. Retrieved from https://www.merriam-webster.com/dictionary/stigma

National Alliance on Mental Illness (NAMI). (2017). *Mental health by the numbers*. Retrieved from https://www.nami.org/Learn-More/Mental-Health-By-the-Numbers

Peterson, D. B. (2011). *Psychological aspects of functioning, disability, and health*. New York, NY: Springer.

Peterson, D. B., & Elliott, T. R. (2008). Advances in conceptualizing and studying disability. In S. Brown & R. W. Lent (Eds.), *Handbook of counseling psychology* (4th ed., pp. 212-230). Hoboken, NJ: Wiley & Sons.

Peterson, D. B., Mpofu, E., & Oakland, T. D. (2010). Concepts and models in disability, functioning, and health. In E. Mpofu & T. Oakland (Eds.), *Rehabilitation and health assessment: Applying ICF Guidelines* (pp. 3-26). New York, NY: Springer.

Peterson, D. B., & Paul, H. (2009). Using the International Classification of Functioning, Disability & Health (ICF) to conceptualize disability and functioning in psychological injury and law. *Psychological Injury and Law, 2*(3-4), 205-214.

Preston, J. D., O'Neal, J. H., & Talaga, M. C. (2017). *Handbook of clinical psychopharmacology for therapists* (8th ed.). Oakland, CA: New Harbinger.

Sadock, B. J., Sadock, V. A., & Ruiz, P. (2014). *Kaplan and Sadock's synopsis of psychiatry: Behavioral Sciences/Clinical Psychiatry* (11th ed.). Philadelphia, PA: Lippincott Williams and Wilkins.

Stack, S. J. (2014). Mental Illness and suicide. *Wiley Blackwell Encyclopedia of Health, Illness, Behavior, and Society*. 1618–1623.

van der Sanden, R. L. M., Bos, A. E. R., Stutterheim, S. E., Pryor, & J. B., & Kok, G. (2013). Experiences of stigma by association among family members of people with mental illness. *Rehabilitation Psychology, 58*(1), 73-80.

van der Sanden, R. L. M, Pryor, J. B., Stutterheim, S. E., Kok, G. & Bos, A. E. R. (2016). Stigma by association and family burden among family members of people with mental illness: The mediating role of coping. *Social Psychiatry and Psychiatric Epidemiology, 51*, 1233-1245.

World Health Organization (WHO). (1992). *International statistical classification of diseases and related health problems* (10th revision) (ICD-10). Geneva, Switzerland: Author.

World Health Organization (WHO). (2001). *International classification of functioning, disability, and health: ICF*. Geneva, Switzerland: Author.

World Health Organization (WHO). (2004). *The World Health Report 2004: Changing history, annex table 3. Burden of disease in DALYs by cause, sex, and mortality stratum in WHO regions, estimates for 2002*. Geneva, Switzerland: Author.

World Health Organization (WHO). (2011). *Measuring health and disability: Manual for WHO Disability Assessment Schedule (WHODAS 2.0)*. Geneva, Switzerland: Author.

Word Health Organization (WHO). (2018). *International classification of disease* (10th revision). Clinical Modification (ICD-10-CM). Geneva, Switzerland: Author.

Yeh, M., Jewell, R. D., Thomas, V. L. (2017). The stigma of mental illness: Using segmentation for social change. *Journal of Public Policy, 36*(1), 97-116.

About the Authors

David B. Peterson, PhD, is a licensed clinical psychologist, Certified Rehabilitation Counselor, National Certified Counselor, and Professor in the Rehabilitation Counseling option of the Master of Science in Counseling at California State University, Los Angeles. He has contributed to the development of the World Health Organization's International Classification of Functioning, Disability, and Health, publishing a text addressing psychological aspects of the same. Also, Dr. Peterson is on the Panel of Medical Experts of the Office of Hearing Operations, Social Security Administration, where he provides psychological expert testimony.

Heidi Paul, PhD, CRC, CLCP, LPCC, is Associate Professor at California State University, Los Angeles, where she is Coordinator of the Rehabilitation Counseling program option within the Master of Science in Counseling. In addition to being a Licensed Professional Clinical Counselor and a Certified Rehabilitation Counselor, Dr. Paul volunteers for the Red Cross as a disaster mental health counselor. As a vocational expert for the Office of Hearing Operations, Social Security Administration, she testifies on disability. Her research concentrates on trauma counseling and creative and effective teaching techniques in graduate education.

The authors wish to acknowledge the contribution of Dr. George K. Hong to previous editions of this chapter.

Chapter 22

SEXUAL HEALTH AND DISABILITY

Leo M. Orange, MS

"After surviving a battle with cancer and an automobile accident which left me paralyzed with quadriplegia, I wondered if anyone would ever see me as a sexual human being and want to love me again" (Leo M. Orange).

Introduction

Sexual health is having the ability to communicate, enjoy, and embrace your sexuality. Understanding your sexuality means understanding that you are a sexual human being no matter what others may think about you. As long as your desire to love and be loved is true, you will have the opportunity to enjoy a healthy sexual relationship with another person.

It requires a positive and respectful approach to your sexuality and sexual relationships, and an understanding that sexuality is a natural part of life that involves more than sexual behavior. Sexual health is a state of mental, physical, and social well-being in relation to one's sexuality. It is a significant part of our emotional and physical health and can shape a person's thoughts, relationships, and experience with others. Being sexually healthy means recognizing and respecting the sexual rights we all share. All of us have the right to love and be loved by who we choose to share life.

Sexuality refers to the expression of sexual sensation and related intimacy between human beings and the expression of identity through sex. Sexuality comprises a broad range of behaviors and processes, including those that are biological, psychosocial, emotional, spiritual or religious, cultural, and political. Beginning with how we see ourselves, it extends to influence and encompass our relationships with others (Best, 1993).

Sexuality goes above and beyond intercourse. It is also about feelings and attractions. The most widely recognized labels people use to identify their sexuality are as follows (LGBTQIA):

Heterosexual: Attracted mostly to people of the opposite sex or gender.

Lesbian: Attracted mostly to people of the same sex or gender (usually used by women).

Gay: Attracted mostly to people of the same sex or gender (usually used by males).

Bisexual: Attracted to both men and women.

Transsexual: Identify as a member of the sex opposite to that assigned at birth and desire to live as such.

Questioning: Uncertain and still exploring one's sexuality or gender.

Intersexual: Being of any of several variations in sex or gender characteristics.

Asexual: Without sexual feelings or associations.

As of June 26, 2015, same-sex marriage is legally recognized in the United States. The recognition of people of non-traditional identities as members of society is a first step in the process of integration or allowing all people to express themselves sexually. Increased access to information and educational material is integral to affirming this process. Because sexuality is both physiological and psychological, so too are the societal obstacles that people with disabilities encounter regarding sexual expression. From a psychological perspective, sexuality involves expressions of intimacy, affection, caring, and love.

Although recent laws have officially recognized members of non-traditional sexual identities, they do nothing for people with disabilities, who are still largely thought of as non-sexual (Brodwin & Orange, 2014; Brodwin, Orange, & Chen, 2004). In recent years, representations of people with disabilities in the media have improved; people with disabilities are beginning to be portrayed as legitimate beings with desires, needs, and capabilities for success. Either as a consequence or a precursor to this portrayal, the lives of people with disabilities have improved. Hahn (1991) illustrated these changes when he wrote that people with disabilities, despite having experienced isolation, alienation, and rejection, have been able to enjoy the pleasures of intimate relationships, marriage, and child rearing.

Gender and Sexuality

Any discussion about people with disabilities having sex is guaranteed to raise a few eyebrows. An individual in a wheelchair is often viewed as an object of pity, not of desire. In our society, the existence of a physical, mental, or intellectual disability has implications of assumed asexuality. For example, for many men, a spinal cord injury that results in impotence is seen as the end of their sexuality. Often, even less dramatic disabilities cause individuals to shut themselves off sexually due to feelings of inadequacy and a fear of rejection (Gill, 1996).

Women with disabilities face multiple barriers to social inclusion. Some experience what is known as *double discrimination*, or being socially judged based upon both their disability and gender. Women with disabilities marry less often and those who acquire disability during marriage have higher rates of separation and divorce (Brodwin & Frederick, 2010). People with disabilities do not fit the image of beauty in society and, therefore, are thought to be incapable of being supportive partners or parents.

Psychological Perspectives

People with disabilities may experience reduced sexual functioning and feeling, concerns about body image, and doubts as to how to negotiate the sexual act because of lack of knowledge or physical capacity (Cash & Hrabosky, 2004). People with disabilities may also have reduced sexual opportunities because of lack of transportation and privacy, necessitated by the disability or chronic illness. Finding ways to express one's sexuality can thus be a vital part of rehabilitation, especially for adults who acquire disabilities.

The inability to move or perform in the same manner as before the onset of a disability does not imply an inability to please or to receive pleasure. The absence of sensation does not correspond with an absence of feeling. Persons with disabilities still feel desire even though their cognitive abilities, physical lower or upper body extremities, or genitals function differently. The ability to enjoy intimacy, passion, and closeness persists despite an inability to perform certain sexual activities.

Persons with disabilities may feel unattractive, or even less worthy of sexual partnerships or relations because they think they cannot live up to the idealized image today's society has set. If the disability happens later in life, individuals may recall how they appeared in the past and now may feel unattractive by comparison.

The ability to enjoy intimacy, passion, and closeness persists even with an inability to perform certain sexual activities. Although it may be different from the one shared prior to the disability or chronic illness, individuals with disabilities can still enjoy loving, close, and intimate relationships. Psychological factors such as emotional stress, depression, and grief may diminish interest in sex and create performance anxiety. Pressures of not being able to work or feelings of being a burden affect one's feelings of sexuality. An individual may believe that the disability or illness has changed the way he or she looks and feels causing that person to be less independent with a restricted ability to play the *traditional* role in the relationship.

For others, pain can make sexual response unpredictable and make uncomfortable what once felt stimulating. Bladder or bowel incontinence causes embarrassment and anxiety, and an indwelling catheter diminishes sexual interest. In addition, weakness, fatigue, and breathing difficulties become barriers to sexual activity (Thomas, 1992; Wetchler & Hecker, 2015). To enjoy one's sexuality, an individual must have the opportunity to share and communicate feelings with others. The potential to experience and enjoy one's sexuality becomes broadened when one desires to engage sexually with another person.

People with disabilities learn new ways of viewing relationships (Miller, Chen, Glover-Graff, & Kranz, 2009). With the intervention of medicine and sexual aides such as injections, implants, and pharmaceuticals such as Viagra, a man with a disability has greater chances of having an erection and intercourse. Regardless of medical intervention, however, a person cannot enhance a relationship unless he or she surpasses the fears and insecurities that occur with newly acquired physical limitations.

Men rarely discuss sexual difficulties with friends, acquaintances, or physicians (Moore, Davidson, & Fisher, 2009). It is often the case that a man requests treatment from an urologist at the insistence of a partner, perhaps after years of repressed depression, decreased self-esteem, and denial (Nusbaum & Hamilton, 2002). During classic denial, the emotional pain of the perceived loss of *manhood* may be too great to face or express. Perhaps what is at issue is not the male sex drive or sexuality, but the fact that men are raised to believe that there are specific ways to express their emotions. Sexual intercourse may be one of the few permissible ways for a man to be close to someone. Due to cultural values and belief systems, for many men it is the only acceptable place to express feelings of love. This may be the result of deep cultural fears of women's sexual passion, non-traditional roles, culture, and issues of power and status.

Women who have disabilities, on the other hand, are often viewed as unfit to fulfill the traditional roles of mother, wife, homemaker, nurturer, and lover, and are seen as asexual (Fine & Asch, 1988; Miller et al., 2009). Although the traditional image of the mother as the sole caretaker and nurturer of her children is changing, it remains the predominant social conception. Since women with disabilities are seen as helpless, dependent, and in need of being taken care of, it is difficult for many to accept a woman with a disability as a potential mother and provider (Brodwin & Frederick, 2010).

Social Components of Sexuality

One of the major difficulties facing the study of sexuality and disability has been the tendency to view disability strictly from a clinical or biological perspective rather than a social one. Although there has been much discussion about social issues in the literature on disability, most have been limited to exploring the impacts of particular physical impairments on sexuality (Goffman, 1963). Since the concept of disability encompasses social as well as physical components, there is a need to devote increased attention to the social problems that may affect sexual relationships involving people with disabilities.

Beauty and strength are perceived as integral, beneficial components of life in American culture (Esmail, Darry, & Knupp, 2010). At the interpersonal level, persons who are physically attractive are evaluated on the basis of their sexuality. A physical disability thus leads to the categorization of a person as abnormal. When it is used to discredit an individual in this stereotypical manner, it becomes a source of stigmatization.

Pervasive social norms reinforce taboos against sexual contact and interaction with people who have disabilities (Brodwin & Orange, 2014). Often, physical attractiveness alone is considered paramount in the development of relationships. This emphasis may reflect traditional values that are attached to physical strength, power, beauty, and grace. There is a coexisting significance to the terms the *whole body*, or the *body beautiful*, and the narcissistic anxiety that is easily aroused in many people who are plagued by doubts about their own supposed physical flaws and defects.

Sexual Identity

Sexual identity is at the core of one's sexuality. As with other aspects of identity, including gender, age, and ability, sexual identity involves self-perception and expression. Like age, sexual identity is not static, but changes over time.

Sexual behaviors, like dating, often involve physical skills that are beyond the capacity of people with major disabilities. As a result, the person with a disability and the non-disabled individual in a relationship may face negative feelings and attitudes from others, including parents and friends who regard the relationship as inappropriate or inadvisable (Miller et al., 2009). Those who are able to overcome the effect of adverse attitudes and taboos against physical contact between persons with and without disabilities must still confront the handicaps resulting from ambiguous social values and dating norms. Social customs, perhaps more than physical differences, are powerful deterrents to these relationships.

Many professionals are implicitly or explicitly aware of the social problems restricting the sexuality of people with disabilities; these problems increase vulnerability. Reduced prospects for forming sexual and marital relationships poses a serious threat to the natural instinct of all human beings to find love and establish stability (Brodwin & Chen, 2000). Although professionals who work with people with disabilities may be cognizant of the reduced probability that their clients will achieve sexual and marital relationships, they often appear reluctant to acknowledge and discuss these subjects.

Self-Esteem

One of the most difficult accomplishments in life is being courageous enough to take chances with love, as it requires not only loving oneself but caring for another person. Self-esteem helps people with disabilities maintain positive attitudes. Research indicates that almost every aspect of our lives including personal happiness, success, relationships, achievements, creativity, and sexuality are dependent upon positive self-esteem (Ivey, Ivey, & Zalaquett, 2018; Miller et al., 2009). With positive self-esteem, a person is more effective, productive, and responsive to others in healthy and affirmative ways.

Pebdani's (2013) study of 312 Master's degree students in CORE-accredited rehabilitation counselor education programs reported that rehabilitation counseling students had negative attitudes toward sex and disability, and low levels of comfort if they were asked to discuss sexuality with prospective clients. This researcher concluded that these issues need to be a part of rehabilitation counselor training programs to increase students' knowledge and comfort level needed to discuss sexuality with clients.

Anxiety due to disability may cause an individual to withdraw and, as a result, lead to depression and loneliness (Vash & Crewe, 2004). This loneliness or depression is often a symptom of frustration. If the frustrated individual is unable to socialize, he or she may become anxious and withdrawn. Increased loneliness, anxiety, and depression makes it problematic for people with disabilities to recognize their role in society.

Body Image

Body image encompasses perceptions and attitudes about one's physical appearance (Wiederman, 2012). The role of body-image and attitudes in human sexual functioning include one's appearance-related thoughts, emotions, and behaviors. Specifically, body dissatisfaction and excessive psychological investment in one's physical appearance may lead to physical self-consciousness and avoiding body exposure during sexual relations, which in turn may impair sexual desire, enjoyment, and performance.

Most body image research has focused on eating disturbances among women (Cash & Hrabosky, 2004; Cash & Smolak, 2012). Clearly, body image has implications for other facets of psychosocial functioning in both sexes, and can influence one's interest in and experiences during sexual activities. Wiederman (2012) found that body dissatisfaction may inhibit sexual behavior and interfere with the quality of sexual experiences.

Western civilization has historically defined its standard of beauty and health by the image of an impeccable and physically fit body (Brodwin & Frederick, 2010; Brodwin & Orange, 2014). Persons with disabilities may feel unattractive, or even *less worthy* of sexual partnerships, because they cannot live up to the idealized image. If the disability was acquired later in life, the person may remember how they used to look and feel unattractive by comparison. Talking with others who have overcome their body image problems is helpful (Bailey, Gammage, van Ingen, & Ditor, 2015).

Embedded in the ideal appearance for both men and women with disabilities is the assumption of having an able body, implying anyone who has a physical disability can never attain the ideal. The psychological feelings of being different may lead to more negative body image as individuals move further from the ideal.

Sexual Violence and Abuse

To express and enjoy one's sexuality, a person must be able to grow in a healthy, nurturing, and loving environment. Sexual violence and abuse refer to a completed or attempted sexual activity without the willful consent of the victimized individual or involving a victim who is unable to consent or refuse due to age, disability, unconsciousness, or being under the influence of drugs or alcohol. Sexual abuse of individuals with disabilities is a problem of epidemic proportions that is only beginning to attract the attention of researchers, service providers, and funding agencies. People with disabilities are more at risk of abuse and neglect than individuals without disabilities (Siu & Brodwin, 2014). Adults with disabilities who have been sexually assaulted may have experienced sexual assault or abuse during childhood, as adults, or both.

Factors that place these individuals at higher risk include: societal misconceptions about people with disabilities, especially children (including family members and non-family caregivers); factors that relate to the particular disability itself; and program policies and procedures governing the care of individuals with disabilities (Orange & Brodwin, 2005a).

Spirituality

Spirituality is a basic construct that subsumes religious involvement. The highest level of our development is affected by the ability to appreciate the sacred in life and to find a sense of meaning and purpose. The essence of spirituality is the search to know our real self, to discover the true nature of consciousness and why we exist (Brodwin & Orange, 2014). Spirituality invites people with disabilities to live fully in the present. According to Havranek (2003), people, in particular individuals with disabilities, depend on spirituality and religion as an important, if not primary, method of coping with physical health problems and life stressors.

Spirituality concerns issues of inner beliefs and feelings, and is closely associated with religion and philosophy. Its various forms shed light on the human experience of reality, purpose, and meaning of life. Many people who have acquired their disability later in life and who are spiritual believe their disability happened for a reason and that it is connected to their spirituality. If there is a reason for their disability, there must be a reason for their existence. It is the author's belief that it is through pain and suffering that individuals become closer in touch with their spiritual self and understanding with God (Brodwin & Orange, 2014).

Spirituality concerns issues of inner beliefs and feelings, and is closely associated with religion and philosophy. In its various forms spirituality sheds light on the human experience of reality, purpose, and existence.

Multicultural Perspectives

Culture encompasses the socially transmitted behavior patterns characteristic of a community or population (Ivey et al., 2018; Moore et al., 2009). People with disabilities have developed a culture as a result of characteristics that are part of the environment in which they live (Orange, 1995). Counselors may attempt to understand these characteristics, which are often viewed as peculiarities, without seeing their own cultural biases. This is true of sexuality and disability. With regard to sexuality, people with disabilities are seen as needing to be corrected to fit into the dominant, non-disabled culture. Professional services always reflect the dominant culture.

To provide appropriate services when counseling ethnic minorities about issues related to sexuality and disability, counselors need to understand both the meaning of disability in their lives and the cultural context within which they live. Ideas about sexuality are part of a larger culturally-based belief system. All cultures have shared ideas of what makes people sexy, appealing, and helps them maintain health through time (Esmail et al., 2010; Orange & Brodwin, 2005b). These beliefs help people understand their sexuality and make sense of the world around them. All cultures have beliefs about the *appropriate* type of sexuality;

cultural and ethnic beliefs describe how people view what is sexually desirable. Defining sexuality from a multicultural perspective is particularly important for people with disabilities. Counselors need the understanding that people are all sexual beings, young or old, married or single, heterosexual, lesbian, gay, bisexual, transsexual, questioning, intersexual, or asexual. As people change, their sexuality changes which remains a lifelong process no matter what the disability, culture, ethnic background, or sexual orientation.

Heterosexual relationships are not the sole form of interpersonal attraction. As more people are feeling comfortable acknowledging their sexual orientation, these relationships have gained wider acknowledgement and acceptance. With the gradual subsidence of homophobia over the last several decades, individuals with disabilities with same sex gender orientations are becoming less intimidated from expressing their true sexuality.

Conclusion

Sexuality is a form of communication, a way of expressing part of one's personality to another individual. The way people present themselves largely depends on how they see and feel about themselves. Sexuality is a very intimate area of an individual's personal life and is usually shared among a few people who care and respect one another. Relationships are developed between people sharing their experience and insights concerning their sexuality and learning to appreciate each other for who they truly are as unique human beings.

Learning to appreciate one's sexuality is a lifelong process that takes courage and understanding, with or without a disability.

"I feel extremely privileged to wake up each morning knowing that I have the ability to love and be loved. My beautiful wife, Marie, and our two sons, Leo Jr. age 25, and Brandon age 21, fill each day and moment of my life with joy, happiness, and a passion for living. My professional life is filled with many rewarding challenges as Coordinator of Disabled Student Services at Oxnard College in Oxnard, California. One must never lose sight of the ability and opportunity to live and love" (Leo M. Orange).

Case Study

Three years ago, Larry Young, a 28-year-old male, sustained an incomplete spinal cord injury at the C-5 level. While on vacation from work, he was injured in a swimming accident. Flown to a nearby trauma center, Mr. Young received six weeks of neurosurgical care before being transferred to a rehabilitation center in his home community. During the next two months, Larry received interdisciplinary rehabilitation and was then transferred to his parents' home where he still resides. There is a permanent and significant diminished functioning in all four extremities; Larry must use a wheelchair for ambulation. There is a 50% loss of function in both upper extremities, with a capacity for some gross and fine hand dexterity.

Since leaving the rehabilitation center, Mr. Young has spent the majority of time in his room watching television, using the Internet, and reading; his mother provides his personal care. His fiancé and friends visit infrequently and, although he had been socially active and well liked in the community, he is now alone much of the time. Recently, Mr. Young has been dissatisfied with his life and is now seeking rehabilitation counseling services to help plan for a possible return to college and a career. Prior to his accident, Larry held various positions at his parents' retail computer store involving sales, computer repair, stock work, and cashiering. Mr. Young had planned on marrying his fiancé and someday taking over the family business, but he believes this is no longer possible due to his physical limitations.

Questions

1. What are some issues that need to be addressed in regard to Larry's sexuality?
2. How would you try to learn about Mr. Young's psychosocial issues and how he feels about his body, sexual activity, and social interaction? If Larry wants counseling in this area, will you, as his rehabilitation counselor, provide it? Discuss.

3. What kind of adaptive equipment and devices would you recommend to increase Mr. Young's independence?
4. Does Larry possess transferable skills? Explain.
5. As his counselor either at a college or state rehabilitation agency, discuss educational and vocational counseling services and planning which you will provide.
6. Would you have Larry consider a possible return to work in his family's business?

References

Bailey, K. A., Gammage K. L., van Ingen C., & Ditor, D. S. (2015). "It's all about acceptance:" A qualitative study exploring a model of positive body image for people with spinal cord injury. *Body Image, 15*, 24–34.

Best. G. A. (1993). Sexuality and disability. In M. G. Brodwin, F. Tellez, & S. K. Brodwin (Eds.), *Medical, psychosocial, and vocational aspects of disability* (pp. 79-90). Athens, GA: Elliott and Fitzpatrick.

Brodwin, M. G., & Chen, R. K. (2000). Marriage and sexuality issues in clients with disabilities. In L.Vandecreek & T. L. Jackson (Eds.), *Innovations in clinical practice: A source book* (Vol. 18) (pp. 459-470). Sarasota, FL: Professional Resource Press.

Brodwin, M. G., & Frederick, P. C. (2010). Sexuality and societal beliefs regarding persons living with disabilities. *Journal of Rehabilitation, 76*(4), 37-41.

Brodwin, M. G., & Orange, L. M. (2014). Attitudes toward disability. In J. D. Andrew & C. W. Faubion (Eds.), *Rehabilitation services: An introduction for the human services professional* (3rd ed., pp. 164-185). Linn Creek, MO: Aspen Professional Services.

Brodwin, M. G., Orange, L. M., & Chen, R. K. (2004). Societal attitudes toward the sexuality of people with disabilities. *Directions in Rehabilitation Counseling, 15*, 45-52.

Cash, T. F., & Hrabosky, J. I. (2004). The treatment of body-image disturbances. In J. K. Thompson (Ed.), *Handbook of eating disorders and obesity* (pp. 515-541). Hoboken, NJ: Wiley.

Cash, T. F., & Smolak, L. (2012). *Body image: A handbook of science, research, and practice* (2nd ed.). New York, NY: Guilford.

Esmail, S., Darry, K., & Knupp, H. (2010). Attitudes and perceptions towards disability and sexuality. *Disability and Rehabilitation, 32*, 1148-1155.

Fine, M., & Asch, A. (Eds.). (1988). *Women with disabilities: Essays in psychology, culture, and politics.* Philadelphia, PA: Temple University.

Gill, C. J. (1996). Dating and relationship issues. *Sexuality and Disability, 14*(3), 183-190.

Goffman, E. (1963). *Stigma.* Englewood Cliffs, NJ: Prentice-Hall.

Hahn, H. (1991). The social component of sexuality and disability: Some problems and proposals. *Sexuality and Disability, 4*, 220-233.

Havranek, J. E. (2003). The spirituality exploration guide: A means to facilitate discussion of spiritual issues in the rehabilitation counseling process. *Journal of Applied Rehabilitation Counseling, 34*(1), 38-43/55-56.

Ivey, A. E., Ivey, M. B., & Zalaquett, C. P. (2018). *Intentional interviewing and counseling: Facilitating client development in a multicultural society* (9th ed.). Boston, MA: Cengage Learning.

Miller, E., Chen, R. K., Glover-Graff, N. M., & Kranz, P. (2009). Willingness to engage in relationships with people with disabilities. *Rehabilitation Counseling Bulletin, 52*, 211-224.

Moore, N. B., Davidson, J. K., & Fisher, T. D. (2009). *Speaking of sexuality: Interdisciplinary readings* (3rd ed.). Oxford, England: Oxford University.

Nusbaum, M. R., & Hamilton, C. (2002). The proactive sexual health inquiry: Key to effective sexual health care. *American Family Physician, 66*, 705-712.

Orange, L. M. (1995). Skills development for multicultural counseling: A quality of life perspective. In S. Walker, K. A. Turner, M. Haile-Michael, A. Vincent, & M. D. Miles (Eds.), *Disability and diversity: New leadership for a new era* (pp. 59-65). Washington, DC: President's Committee on Employment of People with Disabilities.

Orange, L. M., & Brodwin, M. G. (2005a). Assessment and treatment of children with disabilities who have been abused. In L. Vandecreek, & J. B. Allen (Eds.), *Innovations in clinical practice: A source book* (pp. 131-142). Sarasota, FL: Professional Resource Press.

Orange, L. M., & Brodwin, M. G. (2005b). Childhood sexual abuse: What rehabilitation counselors need to know. *Journal of Rehabilitation, 71*(4), 5-11.

Pebdani, R. N. (2013). Rehabilitation counselor knowledge, comfort, approach, and attitude toward sex and disability. *Rehabilitation Research, Policy, and Education, 27*(2), 32-42.

Siu, F. W., & Brodwin, M. G. (2014). Abuse and neglect of people with disabilities. In J. D. Andrew & C. W. Faubion (Eds.), *Rehabilitation services: An introduction for the human services professional* (3rd ed., pp. 146-163). Linn Creek, MO: Aspen Professional Services.

Thomas, M. B. (1992). *An introduction to marital and family therapy: Counseling toward healthier family systems across the lifespan.* New York, NY: Merrill.

Vash, C. L., & Crewe, N. (2004). *Psychology of disability* (2nd ed.). New York, NY: Springer.

Wetchler, J. L., & Hecker, L. L. (Eds.). (2015). *An introduction to marriage and family therapy.* New York, NY: Routledge.

Wiederman, M.W. (2012). Body image and sexual functioning. In T. F. Cash (Ed.), *Encyclopedia of body image and human appearance* (pp. 148-152). Philadelphia, PA: Elsevier.

About the Author

Leo M. Orange, MS, is the Coordinator of Disabled Student Services at Oxnard College in Oxnard, California. Mr. Orange has various book chapters and article publications in rehabilitation and counseling journals addressing attitudes towards disability, reasonable accommodation, childhood abuse issues, multicultural counseling, sexuality of people with disabilities, and psychosocial aspects of disability. Additionally, he has presented numerous professional papers and workshops on various topics of disability studies at local, state, regional, and national conferences.

Chapter 23

SUBSTANCE-USE DISORDERS

Carol M. Calandra, MS

Introduction

According the National Center on Addiction and Substance Abuse (2017), addiction is defined as a complex disease of the brain and body that involves compulsive use of one or more substances despite serious health and social consequences. Addiction disrupts regions of the brain that are responsible for reward, motivation, learning, judgment, and memory. It damages various body systems as well as families, relationships, schools, workplaces, and neighborhoods. Addiction, despite serious health and social consequences, crosses all cultures, socio-economic statuses, ethnicities, ages, sexual identifications, and has the ability to affect not only those alive today, but future generations as well.

Because it is difficult to overcome addictions, people with substance use disorder often need help from a myriad of resources. A combination of counselors, physicians, family members, friends, and support groups, and treatment programs are valued resources in helping people with drug use disorder and those in recovery.

According to the fifth edition of the *Diagnostic and Statistical Manual of Mental Disorders* - DSM-5 (American Psychiatric Association [APA], 2013), there are ten substance-related classes of drugs (some of which are legal): alcohol, caffeine, cannabis (marijuana), hallucinogens, inhalants, opioids, sedatives (hypnotics and anxiolytics), stimulants, tobacco, and other (unknown) substances.

Ceasing the use of an addictive substance and beginning the recovery process needs to be tailored to each person's needs, background, and history of substance use. The treatment plan should also address secondary effects substance use disorder has on others including family, friends, and co-workers. The goal is for recovered users to lead productive, enjoyable, and satisfying lives.

History

In 1849, Swedish physician Magnus Huss described a disease resulting from chronic alcohol consumption, which he called "Alcoholismus Chronicus." This was the first use of the term "alcoholism." In 1864, New York state opened the first American treatment center, then known as an "inebriate asylum." While the asylum primarily treated alcoholism, a growing number of other addictive substances were also treated, including opium, morphine, and cocaine (White, 2014). Changing laws and the emergence of new and novel substances have altered the number and rate of addictions in the population at any one time. According to the Centers for Disease Control and Prevention (CDC, 2015, 2016) drug overdose deaths and opioid-involved deaths continue to increase in the U.S. The majority of drug overdose deaths (more than six out of ten) involve an opioid (Rudd, Seth, David, & Scholl, 2016). Since 1999, the number of overdose deaths involving opioids (including prescription opioids and heroin) quadrupled (CDC, 2016).

Prevalence

Alcohol is one substance of frequent use that has been linked with a high rate of mortality. The CDC reports that excessive alcohol use has led to approximately 88,000 deaths and 2.5 million years of potential life lost each year in the U.S. from 2006 to 2010, shortening the lives of those who died by an average of 30 years (CDC, 2017; Stahre, Roeber, Kanny, Brewer, & Zhang, 2014). Further, excessive drinking was responsible for one in ten deaths among working-age adults aged 20-64 years (Sacks, Gonzales, Bouchery, Tomedi, & Brewer, 2015). Daily, at least 28 people in the U.S. die in motor vehicle crashes that involve an alcohol-impaired driver. This averages one death every 51 minutes. The annual cost of alcohol-related crashes totals more than $44 billion annually.

Drug use disorder is a public health issue costing the U.S. approximately $484 billion annually. This includes $138 billion in smoking-related costs, $161 billion in drug-related costs, and $185 billion in alcohol-related costs. Greater than two million people within the U.S. are currently incarcerated in state and federal facilities for addiction-related charges, making the U.S. the world leader in this category. An estimated 6.8 million Americans have substance use disorder and dependency. The growth of the incarcerated populations continues to be driven by addiction-related offenses. From 2000 to 2015, more than half a million people died from drug overdoses. Every day, 91 Americans die from opioid overdose (CDC, 2016; Drug War Facts, 2017).

When a parent or partner has substance use disorder, the risk of domestic violence and child abuse rise roughly two-thirds. An estimated 40,000 babies with Fetal Alcohol Syndrome are born yearly in the U.S. (CDC, 2015; Drug War Facts, 2017). About 50-80% of all child abuse and neglect cases involved substance abuse of at least one parent (or guardian). Approximately 38% of homeless individuals and families have substance use disorders (CDC, 2016; Substance Abuse and Mental Health Services Administration [SAMHSA, 2007]).

The consequences of addiction are not limited to the user: family, friends, work, and society in general are impacted. Addictions cross all boundaries and have a powerful impact not only on the person with a substance use disorder but on society as a whole.

Some addictions develop slowly, while others impact individuals quickly. While there are still many unanswered questions among scientists about how and why addiction develops, the general consensus involves neurological changes that may begin early on during use of the substance. Alcoholism and addiction are chronic and complex diseases that changes both brain and body structures, and involve obsessive use despite deleterious consequences on one's health, well-being, family, and social consequences.

Etiology

Genetics and environmental factors such as abuse and trauma play a role in the development of a substance use disorder. Once the physical addiction is established, the addiction causes changes to the body and brain. Changes in personality will most likely develop during addiction causing substance seeking behaviors to emerge. There is a correlation between prior addictions and family histories of addiction that are strong predictors of continued substance abuse. Certain risk factors increase the likelihood that an individual will develop an addiction. Some of the more common factors include psychological problems, such as attention-deficit/hyperactivity disorder, post-traumatic stress disorder, behavioral disorders, depression, anxiety, and a history of exposure to trauma.

Alcohol Use Disorder Defined/Alcoholism

The National Institute on Alcohol Abuse and Alcoholism (NIAAA) of the National Institutes of Health (2013) defined alcohol use disorder as a maladaptive pattern of drinking that leads to clinically significant impairment or distress. An individual diagnosed with alcohol use disorder drinks despite alcohol-related physical, social, psychological, academic, or occupational problems. Alcohol use disorder does not necessarily involve a consistent pattern of heavy drinking, but is defined by the adverse consequences associated with the drinking pattern. These include failure to fulfill major obligations at work, school, or home (e.g., repeated absences or poor work performance related to substance use, substance-related absences, suspensions or expulsions from school, neglect of children or household). The American Society of Addiction Medicine (ASAM) (2011) and the National Council on Alcoholism and Drug Dependence (NCADD, 2007) defined alcoholism as a primary, chronic disease that is often progressive and can be fatal.

Historically, alcoholism refers to any condition that results in the continued consumption of alcoholic beverages despite negative personal and social consequences. The National Institute on Alcohol Abuse and Alcoholism (NIAAA, 2013) stated that alcoholism is characterized by the following four symptoms: (1) craving (i.e., a strong need or urge to drink), loss of control (i.e., not being able to stop drinking once drinking has begun), physical dependence (i.e., the occurrence of withdrawal symptoms, such as nausea, sweating, shakiness, and anxiety after stopping drinking), and tolerance (i.e., the need to drink greater amounts of alcohol to become intoxicated) (Carlos, 2014).

Substance Use Disorder/Addiction Defined

According to the American Society of Addiction Medicine (2011), addiction is primarily a chronic disease characterized by dysfunction of the brain circuits involved with reward, motivation, and memory. This dysfunction is manifested biologically, psychologically, and socially. Those who are addicted to a substance are not only unable to stop using the substance but suffer from impaired behavioral control, craving, cycles of relapse and remission, diminished recognition of significant problems with one's behaviors and interpersonal relationships, and a dysfunctional emotional response. While the media and the public tend to associate addictions mainly with illicit drugs, the reality of misuse of legal drugs, such as alcohol, medical prescriptions, and over-the-counter substances can be equally dangerous.

The Diagnostic and Statistical Manual of Mental Disorders (*DSM-5*, APA, 2013) includes two groups of substance-related disorders: (a) substance use disorders and (b) substance-induced disorders. Substance use disorders refers to the collection of cognitive, behavioral, and physiological indicators signifying that the person continues to use the substance regardless of significant substance-related issues. Conditions associated with substance-induced disorders, or the symptoms that arise from continued or excessive use of the substance, include psychosis, anxiety, bipolar, depressive, neurocognitive or obsessive-compulsive disorders, sleep disorders, sexual dysfunctions, and delirium.

Co-Occurring Disorders or Dual-Diagnosis

Co-occurring disorders occur when an individual is affected by both addiction and mental illness. These disorders, previously referred to as dual diagnoses, can be difficult to diagnose due to the complexity of symptoms. These disorders cause a plethora of challenges by disguising symptoms, creating multiple interacting illnesses, and interfering with a singular treatment plan. In many cases, an individual may receive treatment for one disorder while the other disorder remains untreated. This may occur because both mental and substance use disorders have multiple components (i.e., biological, psychological, and social). According to SAMHSA's 2014 National Survey on Drug Use and Health, approximately 7.9 million adults in the United States had co-occurring disorders in 2014 (NSDUH, 2014).

Alcohol and the Brain

Alcohol clearly affects the brain with both short- and long-term impairments, including difficulties in motor skills, blurred vision, slurred speech, and impaired memories. Some of these impairments are detectable after only one or two drinks and quickly resolve when drinking stops. However, a person who drinks heavily over a long period of time may have brain deficits that persist well after he or she stops drinking. Exactly how alcohol affects the brain and the likelihood of reversing the impact of heavy drinking on the brain remain hot topics in research today. Heavy drinking has extensive and far-reaching effects on the brain, ranging from simple "slips" in memory to permanent and debilitating conditions that require lifetime custodial care.

Even moderate drinking leads to short term impairment, as shown by extensive research on the impact of drinking and driving. A number of factors influence how, and to what extent, alcohol affects the brain, including how much and how often a person drinks. These factors include age at which drinking started; length of time a person has been drinking; age, education level, gender, genetics, and family history of alcoholism; whether the individual is at risk as a result of prenatal alcohol exposure; and general health status (CDC, 2017).

Alcohol and the Body

Most people realize that heavy, long-term drinking damages the liver, the organ chiefly responsible for breaking down alcohol into harmless byproducts and eliminating it from the body. Prolonged liver dysfunction, such as liver cirrhosis resulting from excessive alcohol consumption, can harm the brain, leading to a serious and potentially fatal brain disorder known as hepatic encephalopathy. This disorder is caused by a buildup of toxins in the brain which can occur with advanced cirrhosis. Hepatic encephalopathy causes changes in sleep patterns, mood, and personality; psychiatric conditions such as anxiety and depression; severe cognitive effects such as shortened attention span; and problems with coordination such as a flapping or shaking of the hands (called asterixis). In the most serious cases, a patient may slip into a coma (i.e., hepatic coma), which can be fatal.

New imaging techniques have enabled researchers to study specific brain regions in patients with alcoholic liver disease, giving them a better understanding of how hepatic encephalopathy develops. These studies have confirmed that at least two toxic substances, ammonia and manganese, have a role in the development of hepatic encephalopathy. Alcohol-damaged liver cells allow excess amounts of these harmful byproducts to enter the brain, thus harming brain cells.

Addiction and the Brain

Drugs can alter critical brain areas necessary for life-sustaining functions, and drive the compulsive drug use that marks addiction. The reason addiction is considered a brain disease is because the drug changes the brain, both structurally and functionally. As the neurotransmitters cross the synapse, they attach to proteins called receptors on the receiving brain cell. These changes can be long lasting and lead to harmful behaviors (Connors, DiClemente, Velasquez, & Donovan, 2013).

Addiction and the Body

Because of their chemical structure, different substances and the manner in which they are used (i.e., by injection, inhalation, or ingestion) affect the body in various ways. Some substances change a person's body and brain in ways that last long after the person has stopped taking drugs and may be permanent.

Results from the National Survey on Drug Use and Health (2014) performed by the Substance Abuse and Mental Health Administration show the impacts of substance use disorder can be far-reaching, affecting almost every organ in the human body. These impacts include:

- A weakening of the immune system, increasing susceptibility to infections.
- Cardiovascular conditions ranging from abnormal heart rate to heart attacks.
- Collapsed veins and infections of the blood vessels and heart valves.
- Nausea, vomiting, and abdominal pain.
- Liver damage or failure.
- Seizures, stroke, and brain damage.

Global body changes such as breast development in men, dramatic fluctuations in appetite, and increases in body temperature impact a variety of health conditions. Substance abuse causes behavioral problems, such as paranoia, aggressiveness, hallucinations, impaired judgement, impulsiveness, and loss of self-control.

Treatment for Alcoholism

There are a variety of treatments for alcoholism. Those who approach alcoholism as a medical condition or disease recommend different treatments than those who approach the condition as one of social choice. In general, most treatments focus on helping people discontinue the intake of alcohol. These treatments include life training and/or social support strategies to help the individual avoid a return to alcohol use. Since alcoholism involves multiple factors that encourage a person to continue drinking, each must be addressed individually to successfully prevent a relapse once drinking is stopped (McDonald, 2013).

Detoxification

Alcohol detoxification is only the first step in recovery. Although symptoms of withdrawal are treatable, addiction, which has both physical and mental characteristics, must be treated over an extended period of weeks or months. While some alcoholics can stop drinking for a period of time, alcoholic drinking generally recurs. Rarely are people who show signs of alcoholism capable of maintaining prolonged abstinence without assistance (McDonald, 2013). For most people with alcoholism, it is a life-long problem requiring comprehensive treatment. Because a return to asymptomatic drinking is unlikely, the commitment to long-term abstinence is needed to prevent further alcohol-related problems. Sobriety is achieved by many through regular participation in recovery programs, such as Alcoholics Anonymous (Alcoholics Anonymous, 1981, 2001).

Withdrawal ranges from mild to severe (life threatening) and sedative hypnotics decrease the symptoms of withdrawal. Hangovers are the mildest form of alcohol withdrawal syndrome, also consisting of nausea, headache, thirst, and dysphoria (exaggerated feelings of depression and unrest). Moderate withdrawal symptoms include severe agitation, tremulousness, irritability, insomnia, difficulty concentrating, anxiety, and increased dysphoria. Symptoms arise as early as two to four hours after the last drink and reach a peak within 12 to 72 hours (Weiss, 2012).

The most severe form of alcohol withdrawal syndrome is delirium tremens (DTs). This consists of delirium, increased pulse rate, elevated blood pressure and body temperature, and severe agitation. Delirium tremens has a mortality rate of about ten percent; early and intensive medical intervention is required to prevent death. Cardiac arrhythmias may occur during withdrawal from alcohol. Symptoms of mild withdrawal usually last for two to three days; more severe withdrawal symptoms last much longer (White, 2014).

Detoxification treats withdrawal symptoms but does not resolve the illness of alcoholism or alcohol abuse (Carson-DeWitt, 2003). Rapid recovery usually occurs during the first week of abstinence manifesting in physical and cognitive improvements. Recovery is affected by factors such as severity and duration of alcohol dependence, age, concurrent emotional and physical diseases, and intensity of medications used to help the person withdraw from alcohol.

Alcoholics Anonymous

Alcoholics Anonymous (AA) is a fellowship of men and women who share their experiences of strength and hope with each other to resolve their common problem and help others recover from alcoholism. The only requirement for membership is a desire to stop drinking. There are no dues or fees for AA membership; it is self-supporting through voluntary contributions. Our primary purpose is to stay sober and help others achieve sobriety. – Alcoholics Anonymous (2001)

Of great importance in AA is service to other alcoholics and practicing a program of complete honesty, tolerance, and service in daily living. Recovery in AA is viewed as a life-long process, requiring consistent effort and regular involvement in the organization. Its effectiveness as a recovery program is widely accepted by the helping professions and the judiciary. Hundreds of thousands of sober alcoholics worldwide attribute their lives to AA (Alcoholics Anonymous, 2001).

Treatment for Drug Abuse

Comprehensive Treatment

The 1990 Americans with Disabilities Act (ADA) qualifies a person with a history of illegal drug use as having a disability when the individual (a) has successfully completed a supervised rehabilitation program; (b) is participating in such a program and no longer engaged in the illegal use of drugs; or (c) is regarded erroneously as an illegal drug user. People with substance use disorder are protected by the ADA if they are not using and are qualified to perform the essential functions of the job. However, an employer can discipline, discharge, or deny employment to such a person when use of substances adversely affects job performance or conduct.

Many people with substance use disorder face challenges in obtaining and maintaining careers. Therefore, it is imperative that assessment for rehabilitation services includes physical abilities and limitations, medical concerns including any treatment program, and current support systems using a holistic approach. One of the key components of assessment for rehabilitation is sobriety. Physical and emotional withdrawal symptoms from each substance differs, and the rehabilitation counselor must be mindful of such. According to the National Institute on Drug Abuse (NIDA) (2012), effective treatment includes a combination of services targeting not only the repercussions of addiction but the disease as well. Figure 1:

FIGURE 1
Components of Comprehensive Drug Abuse Treatment

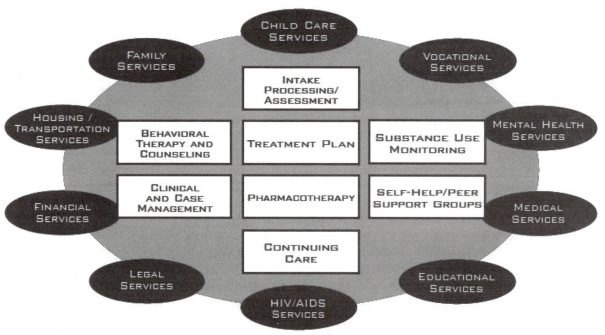

Source: National Institute on Drug Abuse. (2012). *Principles of drug addiction treatment: A research-based guide*.

Components of Comprehensive Drug Abuse Treatment illustrates a multitude of services that may be necessary for clients to access during the recovery process.

Many service delivery models are employed to help recovering addicts obtain and retain employment. Four of the most common models utilized among drug rehabilitation agencies are the following:

- **Work as positive outcome** - obtaining employment after completion of treatment.
- **Work infusion** - integrates vocational services within treatment.
- **Contingent sanctions** - has punitive consequences for not obtaining and maintaining employment.
- **Work as reinforcement** - utilizes employment as a positive outcome for remaining abstinent.

Medication-Assisted Treatment

More than two million individuals in the U.S. are addicted to opioids (Drug War Facts, 2017). Medication-assisted treatment (MAT) provides a treatment option for these people. This treatment option involves the use of FDA-approved medications, in combination with counseling and/or behavioral treatments to provide a "whole-patient" approach to the treatment of opioid addictions. There are three medications: methadone, naltrexone, and buprenorphine that can be used for opioid addiction to opioids, such as heroin and prescription pain relievers which contain opiates. They block the euphoric effects, relieve physiological cravings, and normalize body functions. MAT goals and treatment approach has been shown to (SAMHSA, 2015, 2018):

- Improve patient survival
- Increase retention in treatment
- Decrease illicit opiate use
- Enhance the ability to gain and maintain employment
- Improve birth outcomes among pregnant women who have substance use disorders

The two options for pharmacological maintenance treatment for opioid addiction are buprenorphine and methadone, opioid agonists. These are provided in combination with psychosocial or other support services, including peer support. SAMHSA (2018) has reported positive recovery results for these treatment methodologies.

Functional Limitations

Physicians knowledgeable about addictions help determine what residual functional limitations, emotional and physical, are present in individuals who are recovering from substance abuse (O'Brien, 2013; Weiss, 2012). The rehabilitation counselor needs to assess a person's (a) ability to work effectively with others, including supervisors, (b) limitations due to mood or emotional disorders (dual diagnosis), (c) ability to work independently without close supervision, and (d) capacity to tolerate stress.

Some late-stage substance users become overly dependent on others and are unable, at least for a time, to work independently. These individuals benefit from more structured work settings to make the successful transition to gainful employment. The recovering person also faces a decreased tolerance for stress during the first months of return to work, and this may continue for up to two years of sobriety. Employment involving low stress during the early months of a person's sobriety is likely to result in a more successful transition.

Although complete recovery from addiction leaves few specific functional limitations, the recovery to maximum functioning is slow and gradual, occurring over several years. A return to productive employment improves one's overall recovery by enhancing self-esteem and beginning the process of resolving financial difficulties. It is for this reason that some recovery programs emphasize an early return to some type of work, generally beginning after one month of participation and sobriety (Carlos, 2014).

Rehabilitation Potential

Assessment of the potential for rehabilitation is a challenging task for counselors. Many factors affect rehabilitation potential including age, educational background, prior work history, functional limitations, and motivation to work. Though not always immediate, most recovering substance abusers are able to return to productive employment. Factors likely to affect the potential for effective participation in vocational rehabilitation include: (a) length of sobriety and active participation in a recovery program, (b) history of relapses and their frequency, (c) commitment to maintaining sobriety, and (d) residual functional limitations (physical, cognitive, and emotional) resulting from the alcoholism and other chronic conditions (Carson-DeWitt, 2003). Once sober, the recovering addicts and alcoholics need to demonstrate the same traits as any other person in rehabilitation, including willingness to accept responsibility for behavior, personal well-being, capacity to meet vocational expectations, and personal determination to succeed (Boyle et al., 2013; Carlos, 2014).

Vocational Rehabilitation

During all the stages of recovery, a counselor needs to work with the individual, as work levels may need to be adjusted and appropriate employment goals be set. It is imperative to provide the individual with information necessary to obtain and maintain successful employment, including types of stressors and rewards, problem solving, and coping skills associated with different career opportunities. Development of realistic views of an individual's skills, abilities, and limitations during the stages of recovery assist the counselor in maintaining successful employment goals. Other options in vocational rehabilitation include participation in educational opportunities and services, job training, and continual recovery support systems, such as Narcotics Anonymous and Alcoholics Anonymous.

Reasonable Accommodation

Workers currently engaging in the illegal use of drugs are not protected by the Americans with Disabilities Act of 1990 (ADA). As stated, ADA qualifies individuals who (1) have been rehabilitated successfully and are no longer engaging in drug use, (2) are participating in a supervised rehabilitation program and are no longer engaging in such use, or (3) are erroneously regarded as engaging in drug use, but are not engaging. Only these individuals have employment rights to receive reasonable accommodation. Depending on the individual's needs, the array of accommodations varies greatly and should be individualized. Most employers refer such individuals to their Employee Assistance Programs (EAPs) for counseling and support, if available. The ADA's confidentiality provisions do not permit employers' disclosures of any employee receiving reasonable accommodation (Payo & Siu, 2014). The Rehabilitation Act Amendments of 1992 also protect individuals with addiction issues.

Conclusion

Substance use disorders are treatable with appropriate interventions when using the holistic approach. Addictions are a disease and when compounded with mental health issues, recovery can be a lifelong process. With determination and support, people with substance use disorder can lead healthy, satisfying, and productive lives.

Case Study

As a case manager/counselor working in a supportive program at a community college you are responsible for offering case management, referrals, and supportive services for students by using the holistic approach with the objective of helping students with their educational goals.

Immediately after graduating high school, Joseph joined the United States Marine Corps. Upon completion of basic training, he was deployed as an infantryman to Iraq in support of Operation Iraqi Freedom during some of the heaviest fighting of the war. Joseph was on patrol in Iraq when a roadside bomb exploded within inches of him. His treatment in the field included massive amounts of morphine. He was transported to the military hospital in Germany, where Joseph was kept in a drug-induced coma while his physicians evaluated the extent of his injuries. Due to the severity of his injuries, he was transported to a military hospital in the United States where he stayed for almost two years.

During his hospitalization, he underwent over 35 surgeries, consisting of skin grafts, reconstructing his shoulder, arm, and leg as well as numerous eye operations. Joseph lost sight in one of his eyes, hearing in one of his ears, and his body is covered in burnt scar tissue; he has limited use of his nondominant arm, a traumatic brain injury, and post-traumatic stress disorder. Upon his release from the hospital, Joseph was addicted to opioids. In the years to follow and under the care of the Veterans Administration, Joseph was able to convince the doctors that he was in constant pain which lead to unlimited prescriptions of opioids and numerous other medications enabling him to continue his addiction for three more years. As Joseph's drug seeking behaviors became more aggressive and the prescribed opioids were insufficient, he began to experiment with heroin.

Within a few months, Joseph was addicted to heroin. His addiction caused him alienation from his previously supportive family and friends. In the deepest and darkest days of his addiction, he was living on the streets or in drug-dens with other addicts where the only daily objective was to obtain heroin. When the addiction and circumstances of daily living became overwhelming, he would check himself into the Veterans Administration's inpatient treatment programs. This offered some relief, but he found himself using again each time he was released. He had been to various rehabilitation programs before he ended up in the county jail for a year.

Even while incarcerated, he was able to obtain drugs and learned new methods of making jailhouse alcohol. He was able to use his status as an injured combat Marine to manipulate the medical staff and other inmates to support his addictions while in jail. Trying to be a model inmate and hoping for a reduction in time, he attended some of the Narcotics/Alcoholics Anonymous meetings in jail but felt it was a waste of time. Instead, he became a drug dealer resource once he was released. Within a few hours after his release from jail, he used his drug dealer's resource list to procure heroin. Joseph estimates that he spent approximately $250,000 for drugs during the height of his drug years.

Joseph participated in a year-long inpatient treatment program at the Veterans Administration Combat Veterans Center that not only focused on addiction but also addressed his post-traumatic stress and traumatic brain injury. After successfully completing the program, Joseph is eager to begin his educational journey using his Veterans Educational Benefits which affords him the opportunity to obtain a college education. He is interested in becoming an environmental scientist with a primary focus in oceanography.

Prior to his injuries and addictions, he was an avid hiker and runner but is apprehensive to join any of the local hiking/running groups. He has a new found interest in horseback riding, surfing, and yoga. Joseph regularly attends Narcotics/Alcoholics Anonymous meetings and a Combat Veteran Wellness Group at his local Veterans Center.

Questions

1. As Joseph's case manager at the college, which programs would be most beneficial for developing an educational support system for this client?
2. Identify holistic approaches in helping Joseph reintegrate from military to civilian and student life.
3. Identify the type of services, accommodations, and/or assistive technology you could offer Joseph to meet his educational goals?
4. Identify possible career options for this client and create a vocational rehabilitation plan.
5. What factors are important to reinforce this client's wellness and growth?

# References

Alcoholics Anonymous. (1981). *The twelve steps and twelve traditions*. New York, NY: Author.

Alcoholics Anonymous. (2001). *The story of how many thousands of men and women have recovered from alcoholism* (4th ed.). New York, NY: Author.

American Psychiatric Association (APA). (2013). *Diagnostic and statistical manual of mental disorders* (5th ed., DSM-5). Washington, DC: Author.

American Society of Addiction Medicine. (2011). *Definition of addiction: The voice of addiction*. Retrieved from http://www.asam.org/for-the-public/definition-of-addiction

Americans with Disabilities Act of 1990 (ADA), PL 101-336, 42 U.S.C. §12101 *et seq.*

Boyle, P., Boffetta, P., Lowenfels, A. B., Burns, H., Brawley, O., Zatonski, W., & Rehm, J. (2013). *Alcohol: Science, policy, and public health*. New York, NY: Oxford University.

Carlos, R. (2014). Alcohol-related disorders. In M. G. Brodwin, F. W. Siu, J. Howard, E. R. Brodwin, & A. T. Du (Eds.), *Medical, psychosocial, and vocational aspects of disability* (4th ed., pp. 309-316). Athens, GA: Elliott and Fitzpatrick.

Carson-Dewitt, R. (2003). *Drugs, alcohol, and tobacco: Learning about addictive behavior*. New York, NY: Macmillan.

Centers for Disease Control and Prevention (CDC). (2015). *Wide-ranging online data for epidemiologic research (WONDER)*. Retrieved from http://wonder.cdc.gov

Centers for Disease Control and Prevention (CDC). (2016). *National Center for Health Statistics*. Retrieved from http://wonder.cdc.gov

Centers for Disease Control and Prevention (CDC). (2017). *Alcohol-Related Disease Impact (ARDI) Application*. Retrieved from https://nccd.cdc.gov/DPH_ARDI/default/default.aspx

Connors, G. J., DiClemente, C. C., Velasquez, M. M., & Donovan, D. M. (2013). *Substance abuse treatment and the stages of change: Selecting and planning interventions*. New York, NY: Guilford.

Drug War Facts. (2017). *Drug war facts – Knowledge is power*. Retrieved from http://www.drugwarfacts.org/chapter/drug_prison

McDonald, F. (2013). *The thirteenth step*. Bloomington, IN: Balboa.

National Center on Addiction and Substance Abuse. (2017). *Addiction as a disease*. Retrieved from https://www.centeronaddiction.org/what-addiction/addiction-disease

National Council on Alcoholism and Drug Dependence (NCADD). (2007). *Overview*. Retrieved from http://www.ncaddnj.org/about/default.asp

National Institute on Alcohol Abuse and Alcoholism (NIAAA). (2013). *MADD – Statistics*. Retrieved from http://www.madd.org/statistics/htm

National Institute on Drug Abuse. (2012). *Principles of drug addiction treatment: A research-based guide* (3rd ed.). Bethesda, MD: Author.

National Survey on Drug Use and Health. (2014). *Co-occurring major depressive episode (MDE) and alcohol use disorder among adults*. The NSDUH report. Retrieved from http://www.samhsa.gov/data/2k7/alcDual/alcDual.pdf

O'Brien, P. G. (2013). Substance-related disorders. In P. G. O'Brien, W. Z. Kennedy, & K. A. Ballard (Eds.), *Psychiatric mental health nursing* (2nd ed., pp. 342-369). Burlington, MA: Jones & Bartlett.

Payo, F., & Siu, F. W. (2014). Addictions and related disorders. In M. G. Brodwin, F. W. Siu, J. Howard, E. R. Brodwin, & A. T. Du (Eds.), *Medical, psychosocial, and vocational aspects of disability* (4th ed., pp. 295-308). Athens, GA: Elliott and Fitzpatrick.

Rehabilitation Act Amendments of 1992, 106 Stat. 4344.

Rudd, R.A., Seth, P., David, F., & Scholl, L. (2016). Increases in drug and opioid-involved overdose deaths - United States, 2010–2015. *Morbidity and Mortality Weekly Report, 65*(50-51), 1445-1452.

Sacks J. J., Gonzales, K. R., Bouchery, E. E., Tomedi, L. E., & Brewer, R. D. (2015). National and state costs of excessive alcohol consumption. *American Journal of Preventive* Medicine, *49*(5), e73–e79.

Stahre, M., Roeber, J., Kanny, D., Brewer, R. D., & Zhang, X. (2014). Contribution of excessive alcohol consumption to deaths and years of potential life lost in the United States. *Preventing Chronic Disease, 11*, 130293.

Substance Abuse and Mental Health Services Administration (SAMHSA). (2007). *Results from the 2006 National Survey on Drug Use and Health: National Findings.* Retrieved from https://files.eric.ed.gov/fulltext/ED498206.pdf

Substance Abuse and Mental Health Services Administration (SAMHSA). (2015). *Addiction counseling competencies: Knowledge, skills, and attitudes of professional practice.* Washington DC: Author.

Substance Abuse and Mental Health Services Administration (SAMHSA). (2018). *Medication-assisted treatment.* Retrieved from https://www.samhsa.gov/medication-asistedtreatment:programandcampaigns

Weiss, R. D. (2012). Drug abuse and dependence. In L. Goldman & A. I. Schafer (Eds.), *Goldman's Cecil medicine* (24th ed., pp. 153-159). Philadelphia, PA: Elsevier Saunders.

White, W. (2014). *Slaying the dragon: The history of addiction treatment and recovery in America* (2nd ed.). Bloomington, IL: Chestnut Health System.

About the Author

Carol M. Calandra, MS received her BS degree in rehabilitation services and MS degree in counseling, with an option in rehabilitation counseling from California State University, Los Angeles (CSULA). Currently, she is the Veterans Case Manager/Veterans Center Specialist at Pasadena City College in Pasadena, California, where she provides a holistic approach for veterans transitioning from military to civilian life. Ms. Calandra has been a strong advocate for preventing both veteran homelessness and potential suicide. Also, she is an Adjunct Professor within the Charter College of Education at CSULA.

Chapter 24

LEARNING DISABILITIES

Diane Haager, PhD
Martin G. Brodwin, PhD, CRC
Leila Ansari Ricci, PhD

Introduction

This chapter focuses on the various issues related to the successful habilitation and rehabilitation of persons with specific learning disabilities (LD). Unlike other disabilities, LD can be thought of as an invisible disability in that it may not be physically evident. Defining characteristics are typically evident in cognitive functioning and language processing. There is a common misconception that LD is only a *mild* disability and therefore has little impact on quality of life (Sabornie & deBettencourt, 2004), but a learning disability can occur along a continuum from mild to severe and can have a tremendous impact into adulthood. "Issues of stigma and a lack of awareness and understanding of LD by the general public have contributed to the confusion about their existence and impact" (Cramer & Ellis, 1996, p. xxvii).

Despite a lack of consensus in how to define and measure specific learning disabilities, especially in the adult population, there is no question that the learning and life challenges experienced by individuals with this disorder play a significant role in determining their adult outcomes (Kirsch, Jungeblut, Jenkins, & Kolstad, 1993).

Upon completion of this chapter, the reader will have (a) an understanding of the various dynamics and life implications that people with LD face, and (b) the ability to design effective vocational rehabilitation plans for persons with learning disabilities. Topics covered include: prevalence, definition of LD, diagnosis and evaluation, characteristics of LD, reasonable accommodation, and rehabilitation potential. The chapter concludes with a case study.

Prevalence

LD affects approximately 15% of the United States population; additionally, many people who have learning disabilities are never diagnosed. In 2014-2015, the total number of children and youth ages 3-21 who received special education services was 6.6 million, of whom 35% had specific learning disabilities (U.S. Department of Education, 2017). Getzel and Gugerty (2001) noted that it is estimated that 35% of youth with learning disabilities drop out of high school. Of those students who complete high school, 62% are unemployed a year following graduation. Approximately 56% of students with LD who drop out of high school eventually are arrested. In 2013-2014, 18.1% of students with LD dropped out of high school, which was nearly triple that of 6.5% of all students (Horowitz, Rawe, & Whittaker, 2017). Among adults with LD, only 46% were employed according to 2010 census data, and twice as likely to drop out of the workforce as compared to adults without LD. Only 19% of young adults with LD reported that their employers were aware of their disability, with only 5% reporting that they received reasonable accommodations in the workplace.

The term *learning disabilities*, by federal definition, is a heterogeneous set of conditions that may manifest differently across individuals (Fletcher, Steubing, Morris, & Lyon, 2013). Generally speaking, the term refers to any combination of difficulties in the domains of listening, speaking, reading and writing, mathematics, and reasoning. These disabilities interfere with a person's ability to store, process, and produce information, and are often hidden by the individual's general level of functioning. Learning disabilities may occur with or be complicated by problems involving inadequate attention and inappropriate social skills (Cramer & Ellis, 1996).

As of yet, no single current database exists to determine the prevalence of learning disabilities in the adult population. Although the actual number of adults with LD in this country has not been determined, the 2014-2015 numbers of children and youth with LD suggests the number of adults with LD is likewise substantial (Rubin, Roessler, & Rumrill, Jr., 2016). Estimated prevalence discussed below has been derived from various national data sources.

A 2017 report, "The State of Learning Disabilities: Understanding the 1 in 5," published biennially by the National Center for Learning Disabilities estimated that 39% of students receiving special education have learning disabilities (Horowitz et al., 2017). Surveys of students in post-secondary institutions estimated 2-3% of students had self-reported LD. Another survey of adult literacy in the general population found 3% of adults reported reading-related LD (Vogel, 1998). Thus, the adult population of individuals with this disorder appears to be under-identified.

The United States Employment and Training Administration (1991) reported that between 15% and 23% of Job Training Partnership Act (JTPA) trainees have learning disabilities, while 50% to 80% of adults reading below the 7th grade level have learning disabilities. Additionally, between 10% and 50% of Adult Basic Education students likely have learning disabilities (Adult Education Amendments, 1988).

Regarding gender-related prevalence, it is a common observation that the school-identified LD ratio of males to females is 4:1. In research and self-identified samples, gender ratio was found to be almost equivalent (1:1), very similar to the self-reported numbers described in the National Adult Literacy Survey results (Kirsch et al., 1993; Lyon, 1994). Researchers (Heward, Alber-Morgan, & Konrad, 2017; Sabornie & deBettencourt, 2004) have suggested that the discrepancy between school-identified and self-reported LD gender ratios is related to referral bias in school samples and higher prevalence of attention deficit hyperactivity disorders (ADHD) in males. This increases the likelihood of identification of males in school-age special education programs. According to the U.S. Department of Education (2017), 44% of school-age students receiving special education services for LD were females, with 36% of males receiving services under this category.

Definitions of Learning Disabilities

The earliest and most widely used definition of LD was integrated into federal legislation as the Education for All Handicapped Children Act of 1975. Each subsequent version was incorporated into the Individuals with Disabilities Education Act (IDEA, 1990) and the Individuals with Disabilities Education Improvement Act (IDEIA) of 2004. The earlier definitions included only children. The 2004 definition includes adults with LD, and is written as follows:

The term "specific learning disability" (SLD) means a disorder in one or more of the basic psychological processes involved in understanding or using language, spoken or written, which disorder may manifest itself in an imperfect ability to listen, think, speak, read, write, spell, or do mathematical calculations. SLD includes such conditions as perceptual disabilities, brain injury, minimal brain dysfunction, dyslexia, and developmental aphasia. It does not include a learning problem that is primarily the result of visual, hearing, or motor disabilities; intellectual disabilities; emotional disturbance; and environmental, cultural, or economic disadvantage (IDEIA, 2004).

Adults with LD have legal protection from discrimination under federal statutes, including the Rehabilitation Act of 1973, specifically Section 504; the Americans with Disabilities Act (ADA) of 1990; IDEA (1990); and IDEIA (2004). These statutes acknowledge the lifelong nature of specific learning disabilities. While Section 504 has its greatest impact on educational environments, the ADA concerns employment. These acts protect persons with disabilities from discrimination, provide for equal access to education and employment, and recommend the provision of reasonable accommodation (Heward et al., 2017; Rubin et al, 2016).

Diagnosis and Evaluation

Diagnostic Criteria

Given the complexity and heterogeneity of learning disabilities, it is essential to maintain a database of vocational and other services for adults with LD. The U.S. Department of Education has funded a national longitudinal study since 2001. Newmann et al. (2012) reported that 66.8% of individuals with LD attend some type of post-secondary education up to eight years post high school, with 21% attending a four-year college or university. Aside from individuals with speech and language impairment (66.9%), this is higher than the percentage of any other disability group.

The diagnostic criteria for vocational and post-secondary education services may vary across institutions, but the diagnosis of LD for vocational rehabilitation purposes should directly relate to the criteria established in the Rehabilitation Services Administration (RSA) definition. Major definitional criteria include evidence of a central nervous system processing difficulty and manifest deficits in one or more of the following areas: attention, reasoning, processing, memory, communication, reading, spelling, writing, calculations, coordination, social competence, and emotional maturity.

Psychological evaluation must be preceded by a thorough medical examination; the physician needs familiarity with specific learning disabilities to rule out any systemic organic abnormality that may be causal to the symptoms of a learning disability. A qualified professional conducts a formal evaluation that includes an interview, a cognitive test battery, academic testing, and assessment of information processing skills (Gregg, 2012). There are numerous cognitive batteries that are widely used for this purpose. An overall IQ score is used to determine the individual's overall cognitive functioning, and specific subtests or additional measures are used to examine cognitive processing skills, such as working memory, attention, processing speed, spatial ability, and others.

A multidisciplinary team consisting of a physician, psychologist, and vocational evaluator may participate in the diagnostic evaluation. The vocational evaluator assesses interests, aptitudes, abilities, and work behaviors through inventories, observation, and work samples. Other professionals, including neuropsychologists, speech and language therapists, audiologists, occupational therapists, and medical specialists may serve on the team, depending on the nature of the person's learning disability.

Assessment Practices

The diagnosis needs to focus on overall cognitive processing to rule out an intellectual disability and examination of achievement and specific processing skills. Having an invisible disability, a person with LD may be labeled as bright but bored by his or her parents, "lazy" or "dumb" by teachers, "strange" by peers, and incapable of work by employers (Fletcher et al., 2013).

Hawks et al. (1990) suggested that to appropriately assess areas of potential deficit or need, four essential sources of information need to be used. These are standardized testing, a record review, behavioral observations, and in-depth clinical interviews. The record review, including the person's school and vocational history, previous assessments and results, and the transition plan from high school (if available) must be comprehensive to yield a complete case history specifying previously identified deficits, past interventions, and treatments. Behavioral observations focus on the following considerations: the person's appearance, punctuality, social skills, activity level, attention span, impulse control, reaction to praise, memory, emotionality, language, and persistence. Clinical interviews include gathering information regarding an individual's self-perception of educational, social, vocational, and cognitive processing abilities and limitations, as well as information on family and personal adjustment issues.

Characteristics of Learning Disabilities

As stated previously, the population of adults with learning disabilities is heterogeneous (Fletcher et al., 2013). The nature of this disability and its impact on a person's life is influenced by various personal characteristics and external contextual variables including: (a) the unique individual strengths and needs of the individual; (b) cognitive capacity; (c) the precise and unique nature of the specific learning disability; (d) educational history; (e) current contextual cognitive and psychosocial demands; and (f) the historical pattern of successes, frustrations, and failures. The following section discusses the medical aspects of disability, learning characteristics, social skills/adaptive behavior, and job-relevant characteristics.

Medical Aspects

Physiological factors related to this disorder focus mainly on the information processing mechanisms in the brain. Sensory input is obtained through visual, auditory, and tactile stimuli, thus allowing a person to learn through seeing, listening, touching, and moving the body (Carter, Lane, Pierson, & Glaeser, 2006). Information is sent to the brain for processing (i.e., analysis, integration, and storage). To assimilate information, a person must pay close attention to relevant details, classifying new information efficiently for later retrieval. The brain creates *schemata*, or cognitive organizational files, to classify and store information.

Persons with LD may have difficulty recognizing crucial details and associating new information efficiently with what has previously been learned. This results in an inefficient memory system, making later retrieval of information difficult. Persons with learning disabilities may appear unorganized, especially in terms of their time management skills. Because of the apparent disorganization, a person is often misperceived as lazy, unmotivated, or forgetful. However, learning disabilities are a heterogeneous set of characteristics and these descriptors may or may not apply to a specific individual.

A learning disability is not synonymous with intellectual disability, a common misperception. Learning disabilities occur in individuals irrespective of intelligence level. The learning difficulties experienced are directly related to information processing difficulties involved in cognitive functioning (Osmon, Smerz, Braun & Plambeck, 2006). The majority of persons with LD have difficulties related to reading, but not all individuals with reading difficulties have LD. Between 15% and 20% of school age individuals are affected by specific reading disabilities (Lyon, 1994), ranging from mild to severe while about 5% of the school-aged population has LD. Adults who read below a fourth grade level should be assessed for other indicators of LD. Additionally, many adults with LD have processing deficits that impact mathematics learning, in addition to reading difficulties (Osmon et al., 2006).

Learning Characteristics

Many adults with LD experience reading and other language-related deficits as major barriers to learning and life functioning. Vogel (1985) conducted a major review of the literature to synthesize the reported manifestations of LD in adults attending college. This information remains current. A brief summary of the most significant limitations follows.

Language

Adults with LD often have difficulty perceiving sounds, recognizing syllables within words, and understanding rapid conversation. Frequently, they cannot find the right word or mispronounce words with several syllables. Adults often experience various reading disorders, including inaccurate decoding of words and various kinds of comprehension difficulties. In written language, they may have great difficulty with legible penmanship, grammar, spelling, and organizing and developing ideas on paper.

Reading

Individuals with reading-related learning disabilities have a language-based, auditory processing difficulty that persists even after learning to read and comprehend with accuracy. For such people, rapid and accurate decoding of unfamiliar, multisyllabic, and foreign language words remains inaccurate and the rate of decoding is slow. Although people with LD read slowly, with appropriate intervention some become proficient at reading comprehension, especially in their fields of expertise (Fletcher et al., 2013; Sabornie & deBettencourt, 2004).

Vogel (1998) found that adults with significant reading-related LD are more frequently under-employed, earn significantly diminished wages, and have lower occupational status. These statistics have major implications for vocational rehabilitation. First, young adults with learning disabilities benefit from staying in school, achieving a diploma, and participating in some type of vocational or career planning. Second, upon graduation, students with LD benefit from postsecondary education or vocational training. To facilitate this process, education and rehabilitation professionals need to: (a) create more meaningful secondary school programs for youth with LD; (b) improve the implementation and procedures involved when transitioning youth from high school to postsecondary training and employment; and (c) increase the number of adults with LD who enroll in and complete a variety of adult secondary education programs.

Mathematics

People with LD may exhibit limitations related to mathematics. They have difficulty mastering basic operations of mathematics, remembering the sequence of steps in algorithms, and solving multistep mathematical problems. Significant cognitive processing deficits in the areas of spatial relations and executive function are related to LD mathematics difficulties (Osmon et al., 2006).

Study Skills and Attention

Adults with LD may have trouble organizing their time, note taking, focusing on critical components of assignments, and completing tasks. These various limitations impact effectiveness of daily functioning. Appropriate accommodations help alleviate these obstacles and promote success.

Social Skills Issues and Adaptive Behavior

Friendlessness, social ineptitude, and loneliness are social development patterns that sometimes can result from LD. Having this disorder may significantly impact one's psychological well-being, social functioning, emotional adjustment, achievement, motivation, and self-esteem (Nelson, 2012). Persons with LD often exhibit ineffective adaptive behavior across varying life contexts. If individuals have experienced a history of failure and frustration, they may display patterns of procrastination and lack of initiative, attributing failure to external causes and success to luck. Mithaug and Horiuchi (1983) found that adults are often socially inactive as a result of fear of intimacy. This fear leads to social isolation and loneliness. Loneliness and mild depression may lead to the overuse of prescription mood-altering drugs, alcohol, and illegal substances. Medical consultation, individual or group therapy, and support groups are helpful in minimizing such psychosocial symptoms.

Young adults with LD are at greater risk for depression, anxiety, and even potential suicide. A study of social skills problems and issues of adults with LD indicated that they (Lehtinen-Rogan & Hartman, cited in Rubin et al., 2016):

- Feel responsible to form themselves into likeable and successful people but find this difficult.
- Find social relationships trying. They want and need others but lack the confidence that people will like or respect them.
- Tend to move between despondency and euphoria in relationships because of an underlying level of depression which is diminished by social contact.
- Are overly sensitive and easily hurt while, at the same time, being tense and anxious.

Job-Relevant Characteristics

Non-academic problems, like those described above, often relate directly to employment. Adult employees with LD experience challenges related to cognitive processing difficulties. As previously stated, many individuals experience significant difficulties in the areas of psychosocial functioning and social adaptability. Deficits in social skills are the most debilitating aspect within the workplace. Adults with LD may find it difficult to recognize subtle social cues and misinterpret interpersonal dynamics; they may be *socially incompetent*.

Reasonable Accommodation

The following list was adapted from Vogel (1998, pp. 10-11) describing aspects of reasonable accommodation. Counselors and educators apply reasonable accommodation in schools and employment when assisting individuals who have learning disabilities. Gregg (2012) cited the lack of comprehensive evidence for accommodations in adult education services regarding testing and educational accommodations. With appropriate supports and accommodations, many individuals can be successful in postsecondary education and employment settings (Newman et al., 2012).

- **Reasonable accommodations** in educational environments include equal opportunity for acceptance, providing or modifying equipment, and modifying instructional methodology and examination procedures to ensure that individuals with disabilities have equal opportunities to learn and be evaluated on the basis of knowledge and skills, rather than on the basis of disability.
- **Reasonable** refers to the idea that the suggested accommodations will not create an *undue hardship* on an institution. Undue hardship is defined by the ADA as any action that creates *significant difficulty or expense* for an employer given the size of the employer, the resources available, and the nature of the operation.
- **A person with a disability** is an individual who has a "physical or mental impairment which substantially limits one or more major life activities, has a record of such impairment, or is regarded as having such impairment" (ADA, 1990).
- **Physical or mental impairments** include physical disabilities and mental disabilities (e.g., intellectual disability, organic brain syndrome, emotional or mental illness, and specific learning disabilities [ADA, 1990]).
- **Learning disabilities** are protected under Section 504 of the Rehabilitation Act of 1973, but the learning disability must be significant enough to substantially limit one or more major life activities.
- A **substantial limitation** occurs when a person is unable to perform a task or is significantly restricted because of a disability.
- An **otherwise qualified person** pertains to adults with LD across various settings, such as literacy environments, job training, adult education, adult secondary education classes, and postsecondary institutions meeting the criteria for admission and participation in education programs and activities.
- A **program or activity** refers to all education programs that receive federal subsidies or grants. This includes all public elementary and secondary schools; adult educational environments, such as adult education programs; postsecondary vocational, trade, and military schools; and public (and most private) colleges and universities.

Requests for accommodation must be documented and establish the identified disability as interfering with the person's ability to perform the relevant tasks in a manner similar to persons without disabilities. It is incumbent upon the instructor, employer, or accrediting organization to establish whether or not the proposed reasonable accommodation will modify the essential requirements, standards, or functions of the task. If it is found that the accommodation does modify those essential functions, the request for accommodation can be denied.

Rehabilitation Potential

Characteristics for Success

Despite the unique challenges facing adults with learning disabilities, many experience success in employment and other life circumstances (Newman et al., 2012). A study conducted by Ginsberg, Gerber, and Reiff (1994) investigated 70 adults with LD who were successful in their professions. This study and other research suggested that higher socioeconomic status, greater educational levels, and appropriate intervention maximize the possibilities of successful employment.

Ginsberg et al. (1994) indicated that the overriding factor leading to success with persons who have learning disabilities was *control*. Taking control was categorized into several themes related to internal decisions and external manifestations. Internal decisions included the characteristics of desire, goal orientation, and reframing. External manifestations (i.e., adaptability) were characterized as persistence, goodness-of-fit, learned creativity, and social ecologies. All these characteristics were found to interact with one another to either optimize or reduce a person's potential for success.

Internal Decisions

While desire and motivation to succeed relate to general success, they play a vital role in the success of adults with learning disabilities. Through goal orientation, practical and obtainable aspirations can be established. Reframing involves a reinterpretation of the LD experience from negative and dysfunctional to positive and functional, allowing one to recognize that obstacles can be overcome (Trainor, 2005). Steps in the process of reframing include: (a) recognition of the disability; (b) acceptance of the negative and positive ramifications of having LD; (c) understanding the disability and its implications, as well as one's own strengths and weaknesses; and (d) taking productive action.

External Manifestations/Adaptability

Various aspects of external manifestations/adaptability are key to success. *Persistence*, for example, involves consistently working hard, being willing to sacrifice, and delaying personal gratification. *Goodness-of-fit* involves personal adaptation to surroundings and environments which encourage success. *Learned creativity* incorporates various strategies, techniques, and other mechanisms devised to enhance one's ability to perform. *Social ecology* includes ability to utilize supportive and helpful people, and develop and implement a variety of self-improvement processes. By identifying unique and personal ways to accommodate limitations to accomplish tasks, anticipating possible difficulties, and devising various options for problem-solving, adults are provided with a variety of alternative coping strategies (Fletcher et al., 2013; Heward et al., 2017).

Interventions and Accommodations

Various adult basic education and postsecondary education programs exist to ameliorate functional literacy deficits. Whatever program is chosen, instructional interventions should be individualized to meet area-specific functional literacy needs. Crawford (1998) provided a thorough discussion of the process for developing abilities-based literacy and employment preparation services for adults with learning disabilities.

Assistive Technology (AT)

Another tool utilized to maximize functional literacy skills is assistive technology (Jette, Spicer, & Flaubert, 2017). Various applications and types of AT afford powerful accommodations to ensure the ability to perform competently and successfully despite reading, writing, and organizational problems. For difficulties in written language, assistive devices include word processors, spell checkers, proofreading programs, speech synthesizers, and speech recognition systems. For reading, optical character recognition systems, screen review systems, and tape recorders are options. With organizational or memory compensation deficits, personal data managers and free-form databases are effective. Difficulties in mathematical computations are compensated with use of calculators and simple spreadsheets.

The importance of AT for people with disabilities cannot be overemphasized. Its effective use provides opportunities for enhanced self-sufficiency, increased independence, and greater potential for gainful employment. AT extends into the areas of daily living, social functioning, recreation, and work opportunities, thus diminishing a person's functional limitations and helping to *level the playing field* (Brodwin, Siu, & Cardoso, 2018).

AT is an effective and powerful tool to increase functioning, enhance quality of life, and remove physical and attitudinal barriers for persons with LD. With increased access to the environment and enhanced social integration, individuals can more effectively and readily interact in all phases of society. Through use of AT, people with LD can achieve greater productivity within both education and employment, leading to enhanced self-sufficiency, independence, freedom of choice, and social integration (Brodwin, Boland, Lane, & Siu, 2010).

Job Relevant Skills and Employability

There are several skills related to employment that affect adults with LD (Gregg, 2012; Newman et al., 2012; Rubin et al., 2016). Adults with LD often lack adequate job acquisition skills. Because of cognitive processing difficulties, such as organizational skills and short term memory, and general reading, writing, and mathematics difficulties, individuals may have significant problems going through the steps of acquiring employment. They may have difficulty accessing information about jobs through the Internet and other media, and have problems completing employment applications.

The high level of credentialing and entrance examinations required by vocational and professional jobs are a barrier for adults with LD. These exist despite the ADA mandate for reasonable testing accommodations. Adults often are hesitant to request testing accommodations prior to employment for fear of discrimination by prospective employers.

The interview process is a challenge for many adults with learning disabilities because a positive interview involves the utilization of complex social skills, and the ability to decide whether or not to disclose information pertinent to the learning disability. Job coaches and job preparation workshops can assist people in successfully navigating these job acquisition skills (Trainor, 2005). Through these programs, vocational strategies are devised to optimize work-related assets and minimize disability-related problems (i.e., development of possible reasonable accommodations for a job).

Krishnaswami (1984) identified the following 15 employability factors needed for persons with severe LD to enter the labor market:

1. Hygiene, grooming, and appropriate dress.
2. Ability to relate to supervisors and co-workers.
3. Skills in communication.
4. Increased frustration tolerance.
5. Appropriate responses to criticism.
6. Proper social behavior at work.
7. Punctuality and attendance.
8. Initiative in carrying out work tasks.
9. Awareness of safety and work rules.
10. Increasing stamina/energy levels for work.
11. Organizational skills with job tasks.
12. Consistency in the various aspects of work.
13. Improved speed performance on the job.
14. Enhanced independent functioning with work assignments.
15. Attending to and following up with directions.

Social Competency and Adaptive Behavior

Job skills training should involve careful development and refinement of needed job-related social skills. Adequate social competence is necessary for all jobs, especially as the workplace becomes more collaborative. Classes in social skills, support groups, and individual sessions with a rehabilitation counselor are various ways of enhancing social competence.

Colleagues can provide social assistance help through on-the-job mentoring. Mentors can explain the dynamics of inappropriate behavior, provide tools for overcoming specific problems, and explain unspoken cultural mores. Social skills are inherent for job advancement in higher-level positions, and involve managerial responsibilities that include the ability to work closely with a variety of personnel.

Self-Efficacy

Adults with LD develop self-efficacy as they experience various problem-solving strategies. These perspectives allow individuals to increase means, techniques, and strategies to overcome the challenges presented by learning disabilities (Trainor, 2005). To learn effective coping strategies, persons must cultivate a personal understanding, a process aided by perseverance, creativity, and support. By learning and using effective employment techniques, adults with LD can optimize their potential.

Case Study

Joaquin Martinez is a 34 year-old Latino male with a well-documented learning disability; he is currently unemployed. Because Joaquin has been unable to maintain employment for more than seven months at a time, his job counselor at the employment office referred him to the Department of Rehabilitation (DOR) for further job training.

As the youngest of six children, Joaquin grew up in a working class family in a large, urban city. As an infant, he experienced several serious pneumonia infections and spent much of his first two years of life in and out of the hospital. Eventually, his pediatrician discovered that Joaquin had a genetic autoimmune disorder. Medical records obtained from the family physician supported this information.

During elementary school, Joaquin experienced serious difficulties socially as well as academically. He had trouble learning to read and write. In fourth grade, Joaquin was referred, evaluated, and identified as having a specific learning disability and was placed in a self-contained classroom for students with LD. He remembers being teased by the neighborhood children and his older brother, occasionally being referred to as "dumb" and "lazy." He often spent time alone in the kitchen with his mom helping her cook, while his siblings played outside with friends. Throughout his elementary school experience, Joaquin worked hard to learn to read, write legibly, and master basic mathematics.

Upon entering high school, Joaquin was enrolled in a high school with a full inclusion philosophy and program that resulted in him being placed in general education classes with special education support. His mother and siblings helped him complete reading assignments and written homework, as the reading and writing demands of high school overwhelmed him. Joaquin found much joy in participating in high school football and wrestling. Although proud of Joaquin's participation, the football coach often complained that Joaquin was "clumsy" and "lacked coordination." Standing 6 foot 4 inches and weighing 220 pounds, his nickname became "the Hulk."

After graduating high school, Joaquin obtained a job as a printing-press operator with a small company owned by his buddy in his hometown. Through intervention by the DOR counselor, Joaquin was able to maintain his job as a press operator. Yet, after one year, he quit because of his inability to get along with other employees. He failed to notify his counselor.

Since that time, Joaquin has had several unskilled, general labor jobs. These include a position as a factory worker in the canned food industry, warehouse worker, non-union construction worker, gardener, dishwasher, and janitor in a high school. Keeping a job has been difficult; at times, Joaquin was fired for arriving at work late, cultural insensitivity, and inappropriate comments. Other times, he quit a job because he felt the pay to be insufficient. Joaquin also had disagreements with fellow workers and supervisors. Currently, Joaquin states he wants to "get his act together" and is thinking about acquiring a career which will help him obtain financial stability. Joaquin stated that he is tired of feeling overwhelmed and being unable to provide for his own expenses.

Questions

1. What kinds of services are available and relevant to Joaquin's needs?
2. Describe how you, as the rehabilitation counselor, will proceed with this case.
3. Develop two appropriate and feasible vocational goals for this client. Outline two vocational plans.
4. Are there additional assessments that need to be conducted to better understand the work-related strengths and needs of this client?
5. What kinds of work-related accommodations would you suggest?
6. Discuss Joaquin's problems in getting along with others.

References

Adult Education Amendments of 1988, 20 U.S.C. §1201 *et seq.*

Americans with Disabilities Act of 1990 (ADA), 42 U.S.C. §12101 *et seq.*

Brodwin, M. G., Boland, E. A., Lane, F. J., & Siu, F. W. (2010). Technology in rehabilitation counseling. In R. M. Parker & J. B. Patterson (Eds.), *Rehabilitation counseling: Basics and beyond* (5th ed., pp. 333-367). Austin, TX: Pro-ed.

Brodwin, M. G., Siu, F. W., & Cardoso, E. (2018). Users of assistive technology: The human component. In I. Marini & M. A. Stebnicki (Eds.). *The psychological and social impact of illness and disability* (7th ed., pp. 345-353). New York, NY: Springer.

Carter, E. W., Lane, K. L., Pierson, M. R., & Glaeser, B. (2006). Self-determination skills and opportunities of transition-age youth with emotional disturbance and learning disabilities. *Council for Exceptional Children, 72*(3), 333-346.

Cramer, S. C., & Ellis, W. (Eds.). (1996). *Learning disabilities: Lifelong issues*. Baltimore, MD: Paul H. Brookes.

Crawford, R. (1998). Developing abilities-based literacy and employment services for adults with learning disabilities. In S. A. Vogel & S. Reder (Eds.), *Learning disabilities, literacy, and adult education* (pp. 275-294). Baltimore, MD: Paul H. Brookes.

Education for All Handicapped Children Act of 1975, 20 U.S.C. §1400 *et seq.*

Fletcher, J. M., Steubing, K. K., Morris, R. D., & Lyon, G. R. (2013). Classification and definition of learning disabilities: A hybrid model. In H. L. Swanson, K. R. Harris, & S. Graham (Eds.), *Handbook of learning disabilities* (2nd ed., pp. 33-50). New York, NY: Guilford.

Getzel, E. E., & Gugerty, J. J. (2001). Applications for youth with learning disabilities. In P. Wehman (Ed.), *Life beyond the classroom* (pp. 371-398). Baltimore, MD: Brookes.

Ginsberg, R., Gerber, P. J., & Reiff, H. B. (1994). Employment success for adults with learning disabilities. In P. J. Gerber & H. B. Reiff (Eds.), *Learning disabilities in adulthood: Persisting problems and evolving issues* (pp. 204-213). Boston, MA: Andover Medical.

Gregg, N. (2012). Increasing access to learning for the adult basic education learner with learning disabilities: Evidence-based accommodation research. *Journal of Learning Disabilities, 45*(1), 47-63.

Hawks, R., Minskoff, E. H., Sautter, S. W., Sheldon, K. L., Steidle, E. F., & Hoffmann, F. J. (1990). A model diagnostic battery for adults with learning disabilities in vocational rehabilitation. *Learning Disabilities: A Multidisciplinary Journal, 1*(3), 94-101.

Heward, W., Alber-Morgan, S. R., & Konrad, M. (2012). *Exceptional children: An introduction to special education* (10th ed.). Saddle River, NJ: Pearson/Merrill/Prentice Hall.

Horowitz, S. H., Rawe, J., & Whittaker, M. C. (2017). *The state of learning disabilities: Understanding the 1 in 5*. New York, NY: National Center for Learning Disabilities.

Individuals with Disabilities Education Act (IDEA) of 1990, 20 U.S.C. §1400 *et seq.*

Individuals with Disabilities Education Improvement Act (IDEIA) of 2004, 118 Stat. 2647.

Jette, A. M., Spicer, C. M., & Flaubert, J. L. (Eds.) (2017). *The promise of assistive technology to enhance activity and work participation*. Washington, DC: National Academies Press.

Kirsch, I. S., Jungeblut, A., Jenkins, L., & Kolstad, A. (1993). *Adult literacy in America: A first look at the results of the National Adult Literacy Survey*. Princeton, NJ: Educational Testing.

Krishnaswami, U. (1984). Learning to achieve: Rehabilitation counseling and the learning disabled adult. *Journal of Applied Rehabilitation Counseling, 15*, 18-22.

Lyon, G. R. (Ed.). (1994). *Frames of reference for the assessment of learning disabilities: New views on measurement issues*. Baltimore, MD: Paul H. Brookes.

Mithaug, D. E., & Horiuchi, C. N. (1983). Colorado statewide follow-up survey of special education students. *Exceptional Children, 51*, 397-404.

Nelson, J. M. (2012). General and domain-specific self-concepts of adults with learning disabilities: A meta-analysis. *Learning Disabilities: A Multidisciplinary Journal, 18*(2), 61-70.

Newman, L., Wagner, M., Knokey, A.-M., Marder, C., Nagle, K., Shaver, D., . . . Schwarting, M. (2012). The post-high school outcomes of young adults with disabilities up to 8 years after high school. *A Report from the National Longitudinal Transition Study-2 (NLTS2)* (NCSER 2011-3005). Menlo Park, CA: SRI International.

Osmon, D. C., Smerz, J. M., Braun, M. M., & Plambeck, E. (2006). Processing abilities associated with math skills in adult learning disability. *Journal of Clinical and Experimental Neuropsychology, 28*(1), 84-95.

Rehabilitation Act of 1973, 29 U.S.C. §701 *et seq.*

Rubin, S. E., Roessler, R. T., & Rumrill, Jr., P. D. (2016). *Foundations of the vocational rehabilitation process* (7th ed.). Austin, TX: Pro-ed.

Sabornie, E. J., & deBettencourt, L. U. (2004). *Teaching students with mild and high-incidence disabilities at the secondary level.* Upper Saddle River, NJ: Prentice Hall.

Trainor, A. A. (2005). Self-determination perceptions and beliefs of diverse students with LD during the transition planning process. *Journal of Learning Disabilities, 38*(3), 233-249.

United States Employment and Training Administration. (1991). *The learning disabled in employment and training programs* (Research and Evaluation Series 91-E). Washington, DC: United States Department of Labor.

U.S. Department of Education, National Center for Education Statistics. (2017). *Digest of educational statistics, 2017.* Retrieved from https://nces.ed.gov/programs/coe/indicator_cgg.asp

Vogel, S. A. (1985). Learning disabled college students: Identification, assessment, and outcomes. In D. Duane & C. K. Leong (Eds.), *Understanding learning disabilities: International and multidisciplinary views* (pp. 179-203). New York, NY: Plenum.

Vogel, S. A. (1998). Adults with learning disabilities: What learning disabilities specialists, adult literacy educators, and other service providers want and need to know. In S. A. Vogel & S. Reder (Eds.), *Learning disabilities, literacy, and adult education* (pp. 10-11). Baltimore, MD: Paul H. Brookes.

About the Authors

Diane Haager, PhD, is a professor, researcher, and teacher educator in reading and learning disabilities at California State University, Los Angeles where she instructs special education teachers and graduate students. Dr. Haager has worked in urban schools as a reading specialist and special educator. She has authored numerous professional journal articles, book chapters, and books. Research interests of Dr. Haager include issues related to effective reading instruction for English language learners, students with learning disabilities, and students at risk for reading failure.

Martin G. Brodwin, PhD, CRC, is professor in the Rehabilitation Counselor Education Program at California State University, Los Angeles. He is a vocational expert for the Office of Hearings Operations, Social Security Administration, providing testimony on disability-related issues. As a rehabilitation consultant, Dr. Brodwin provides assessment for long-term disability, case management, and reasonable accommodation. He has published over 100 refereed journal articles, book chapters, and books.

Leila Ansari Ricci, PhD, is an associate professor in the mild/moderate disabilities program of the Division of Special Education and Counseling at California State University, Los Angeles. Dr. Ricci is the program coordinator for the special education pathway of the Los Angeles Urban Teacher Residency Transformation Initiative. Previously, she worked as a special educator in K-12 schools in California. Dr. Ricci has researched, written, and presented on the topics of emergent literacy, reading, mentoring novice special education teachers, and collaboration/co-teaching to meet the needs of children with disabilities.

Chapter 25

INTELLECTUAL DEVELOPMENTAL DISORDERS

Julie Ton Fercho, PhD
Mary A. Falvey, PhD
Kathryn D. Bishop, PhD
Susann Terry Gage, PhD

Introduction

Researchers have found evidence of intellectual developmental disabilities as far back as 1552 B.C.E., during the time of the therapeutic papyri of Thebes (Luxor), Egypt (Ainsworth & Baker, 2004). Through the ages, individuals with intellectual disabilities have faced challenges relative to the customs and beliefs of their culture and time. It was not until John Locke (1690) published An Essay Concerning Human Understanding that the public began to realize that individuals with mental disabilities still maintain a capacity to learn and acquire meaningful skills. He proposed the idea that humans are born with a blank slate (tabula rasa) and learn through experience. Locke suggested that society, rather than an innate mental disorder, was the more likely contributing factor to intellectual disability. This turning point in the conceptual world of intellectual disability inspired the development of new treatment approaches, and improving the cultural perceptions of intellectual disability, ultimately resulting in greater acceptance and contributions of those with intellectual disabilities.

Changes in policies, services, expectations, and personal values over the past several decades have significantly affected quality of life for individuals with intellectual disability. This chapter discusses programs, services, and support systems available for these individuals. The framework of the chapter includes the definition of intellectual disability, prevalence, etiology, normalization, functional limitations, and rehabilitation potential generally observed in people with intellectual disability.

Repeated research has demonstrated that employment has had a positive impact on the lives of those with intellectual disabilities (Steere & Dipipi-Hoy, 2013). Such positive impacts are evidenced by reported increased confidence, independence, and community membership. However, Wehmeyer et al. (2003) asserted that there continues to be challenges associated with employment. As of 2010, over 85% of adults with intellectual disabilities were unemployed and of the 15% of adults who reported employment, less than half of them earned "competitive wages" (rates at or above minimum wage).

Core aspects of successful post-school outcomes should include: transition planning that focuses on functional and job-specific skills (Southward & Kyzar, 2017), self-determination (Shogren, Wehmeyer, Palmer, Rifenbark, & Little, 2015), and ongoing supports within the work setting (Wehman, Chan, Ditchman, & Kang, 2014). The authors of this chapter encourage rehabilitation professionals to consider the information presented in the hope that they may develop improved quality programs, services, and support for their clients.

Definition of Intellectual Disability

Throughout the decades, intellectual disability has been described by the level of mental and functional impairment of an individual's abilities. In recent years, the definition and label of such intellectual and developmental disabilities have been at the forefront of discussion between advocacy organizations, government agencies, and grassroots family movements (Tassé, Luckasson, & Nygren, 2013; Wehmeyer, 2013). In accordance with Rosa's Law (2010) and the Diagnostic and Statistical Manual of Mental Disorders (5th ed.) (American Psychiatric Association, 2013), this chapter uses the term Intellectual Disability and Intellectual Developmental Disorder versus the previous diagnostic category, Mental Retardation.

In 2010, the United States Congress officially struck the term Mental Retardation from current federal laws and governmental agencies and replaced it with the term Intellectual Disability. The name change reflects an alignment across agencies and disciplines, including the World Health Organization, the American Association on Intellectual and Developmental Disabilities, and the United States Department of Education.

TASH, founded in 1975, is an international leadership organization that promotes human rights, advocacy, and inclusion for individuals with significant intellectual disabilities. This organization also supports needs – those individuals who are most vulnerable to segregation, abuse, neglect, and institutionalization. TASH's definition of intellectual disabilities focuses on the following three factors:

1. The relationship of the individual with intellectual disabilities and their environment (adaptive fit), requiring the individual to learn from the demands of their environment as well as requiring these environments to accommodate the need of the individual with intellectual disabilities.
2. The need to include people with intellectual disabilities of all ages.
3. "Extensive ongoing support" needed to participate in a meaningful way in life activities.

The American Association of Intellectual and Developmental Disabilities (AAIDD, previously called the American Association of Mental Retardation [AAMR], 2002) developed the following definition:

> Intellectual disability is a disability characterized by significant limitations both in intellectual functioning and adaptive behavior, which covers many everyday social and practical skills and originates before age 18 (AAIDD, 2010).

Significant limitations in the area of adaptive behavior are identified by below average performance in at least two of the following: conceptual, social, and practical applied categories; communication; self-care; home living; social skills; community use; self-direction; health and safety; functional academics; leisure; and employment. Through time, there has been a movement to change the definition of intellectual disability from a person's limitations to the importance of identifying that person's needs. This newer way of thinking places the burden of responsibility on society to meet those needs (Falvey, 2005; Wehmeyer, 2013). Additionally, Marc Gold (1980), who developed the Try Another Way system, defined intellectual disability by noting that one should consider the following:

> The level of power needed in the training process required for the individual to learn, and not by limitations in what he or she can learn. The height of a person's level of functioning is determined by the availability of training technology and the amount of resources society is willing to allocate and not by significant limitations in biological potential (p. 5).

After Gold's (1980) work was published, the AAIDD updated their definition of intellectual disability to address the interactions between disability and the environment:

> A complete and accurate understanding of intellectual disability involves realizing that intellectual disability refers to a particular state of functioning that begins in childhood, has many dimensions, and is affected positively by individualized supports. As a model of functioning, it includes the contexts and environment within which the person functions and interacts, and requires a multidimensional and ecological approach that reflects the interaction of the individual with the environment, and the outcomes of that interaction with regards to independence, relationships, societal contributions, participation in school and community, and personal well-being (AAIDD, 2010).

The degree of developmental delay (intellectual disability) ranges from mild to moderate, from severe to profound. Researchers continue to debate the criteria for these categories; intelligence quotient (IQ) scores remain the primary decisive factor. The degree of developmental delay manifested is related to the assistance, support, and instructional opportunities available to people who have intellectual disability. These individuals possess interests and strengths that are as varied as individuals without disabilities are, and display equally diverse personalities and characteristics. In addition, an individual with intellectual disabilities is likely to have skills and abilities that vary across life functioning domains.

Prevalence of Intellectual Disability

Researchers have identified that 4.8% of the school-age population and 4.1% of post-school age populations have cognitive difficulties (United States Census Bureau, 2015). The variations of these percentages are expected and are usually related to the labeling and classifying procedures used in school programs (AAIDD, 2010; Brimer, 1990). When intellectual disability is classified within the mild to moderate range, pre-school children and adults may not be labeled or in any way classified with cognitive delays or different than the general population. Traditionally, schools have grouped and classified school-age students into distinct ability levels, resulting in the labeling of students with intellectual disability. This classification explains the higher percentage identified within the school-age population.

In the past, researchers used race and economic status to identify prevalence. Major litigation and legislation, however, has ruled that the identification of intellectual disability among minority groups based on racial factors is unjust and incorrect (Larry P. v. Riles and Diana v. State Board of Education, Public Law 94-142, 1975). Schools continue to identify a disproportionate number of school-age students with intellectual disability from certain minority groups, especially among African Americans and Hispanics or Latinos (U.S. Census Bureau, 2015). The primary method of identification has been the use of IQ tests; professionals have criticized these examinations as being culturally and linguistically biased in favor of members of the non-Hispanic White, American, middle-class. Thus, researchers consider the results of IQ tests invalid when given to children who are not members of the White middle class community (Bishop & Falvey, 1989).

Etiology of Intellectual Disability

Intellectual disability often results from an interaction between environmental and genetic factors (Chelly, Khelfaoui, Francis, & Bienvenu, 2006; Ropers, 2010). Examples of environmental factors include prenatal infections, maternal conditions (e.g., diabetes), exposure to harmful substances during pregnancy (e.g., alcohol, drugs, and environmental chemicals), complications during birth (e.g., perinatal asphyxia), preterm birth, and acquired brain injury (Peterlin & Peterlin, 2016). The impact of these factors may result in an intellectual disability before birth (prenatal), during birth (perinatal), or after the birth (postnatal). The following paragraphs describe the interplay between environmental influence and genetic factors.

Prenatal Causes

Down syndrome is the most frequently observed genetic cause. Down syndrome, identified in 1866 by Doctor Langdon Down, is commonly known as Trisomy XXI. Individuals with Trisomy 21 have an extra 21st chromosome. Factors influencing the prevalence of Down syndrome include maternal age and possible environmental contaminants. Eighty percent of children with Down syndrome are born to women under age 35. The degree of intellectual disability observed in individuals with Down syndrome ranges from mild to significant (Campbell et al., 2013).

In 1934, Dr. Asbjourn Folling, a Norwegian physician, discovered phenylketonuria (PKU) as a cause of intellectual disability. PKU is a sign of deficiency in the production of phenylalanine hydroxylase, an enzyme necessary in the metabolism of phenylalanine, an essential amino acid. Brain damage occurs with the buildup of phenylalanine in the blood. In 1959, Dr. Robert Guthrie developed a screening test for newborns that physicians routinely use today to detect PKU. When a physician identifies PKU in a newborn, a phenylalanine-restricted diet is started. The degree of intellectual disability is significantly less severe for individuals with treated versus untreated PKU; dietary restrictions during the primary years of life are essential to lessening the severity of this condition.

Other biological conditions, such as disease, can result in intellectual disability. Tay-Sachs is one such illness. This disease, a lipid metabolic disorder, is most often found in individuals of Jewish descent. Besides intellectual disability, it causes a progressive deterioration of nerve tissue and generally results in death at an early age.

There are several physical factors other than genetic ones that influence the presence and significance of an intellectual disability. Beginning with the prenatal stages of development, the mother's general eating habits and physical health are crucial. Chronic maternal illnesses, such as diabetes, may impair fetal development. Maternal use of alcohol, drugs, tobacco, and exposure to environmental pollution during pregnancy along with maternal infections and viruses such as rubella, perinatal cytomegalovirus infection (CMV), meningoencephalitis, syphilis, and toxoplasmosis increase the probability of intellectual disability and other disorders.

Perinatal Causes

During childbirth, several factors can increase the possibility of intellectual disability (Ainsworth & Baker, 2004). Cephalopelvic disproportion, for example, a condition in which the size of the birth canal is too narrow for the presenting infant's head can cause brain damage. Other factors include extreme prematurity, accidental physical trauma, asphyxia, hypoglycemia, infection, blood cell or blood type diseases, and Rh factor blood incompatibilities between mother and baby.

Postnatal Causes

Whitaker (2013) described how several other factors increase the probability of intellectual disability after birth. These factors include malnutrition, acquired traumatic brain injury, meningitis, encephalitis, other infections, and chemical substances (e.g., pesticides, drug abuse, and metal [lead] poisoning). Additional causes are demyelinating and degenerative disorders, consequences of seizure disorders, toxic-metabolic disorders, and environmental deprivation. Hyperthyroidism, whooping cough, chickenpox, measles, and Hip disease (a bacterial infection) may cause intellectual disability if not treated adequately. In children, a blow or a violent shake to the head may result in intellectual disability due to damage to the brain.

Normalization

During the nineteenth and early part of the twentieth centuries, society created institutions for individuals with intellectual disability. In the last four decades, organized coalitions of parents and advocates using the normalization principle played a significant role in the development of community-based services and supports as an alternative to institutionalization.

In the 1950s, parents of children with intellectual disability formed an advocacy organization now called the ARC for People with Intellectual and Developmental Disabilities (formerly known as the National Association for Retarded Children and National Association for Retarded Citizens). These parents rejected institutionalization for their sons and daughters. They organized alternative programs and services for children with intellectual disability. Until the 1970s, many public schools, along with state and local rehabilitation agencies, excluded individuals with intellectual disability. These parent advocates raised finances independently for their children to receive community services, until social service agencies were required to provide such community services and supports.

In 1959, the director of the Danish Mental Retardation Service, Bank-Mikkelsen, helped develop Danish law reflecting the principle of normalization. This principle states that individuals with intellectual disability must be able to ". . . obtain an existence as close to normal as possible" (Wolfensberger, 1980, p. 7). Nirje (1969) published the first systematic statement of normalization in world literature. In 1972, Wolfensberger applied this normalization principle to American society. As people with intellectual disability moved into the community and obtained employment and housing, a reconceptualization of service delivery models evolved. Instead of social service agency personnel being responsible for supporting a person with an intellectual disability, the individual takes charge, utilizing support from family, friends, neighbors, co-workers, and service providers they employ (Wolfensberger).

Deinstitutionalization

The normalization principle has been a strong driving force in establishing the deinstitutionalization movement. This movement involves integrating individuals with intellectual disability, who society previously placed in segregated institutions, into community settings. Biklen and Knoll (1987) identified the major problems with institutions and other large segregated facilities, as well as the primary reasons for deinstitutionalizing people with intellectual disability:

- Institutions are the most expensive way of providing residential or any other services to people with intellectual disability.
- Institutions disrupt family and neighborhood relationships and do not offer the warm, homelike, individualized environments necessary for full human development.
- Institutions do not provide opportunities for interaction with members of the community.
- Institutions do not allow for positive community living experiences or for development of skills needed for community life.
- Institutions perpetuate and reinforce the image that people with intellectual disability are oddities.
- People residing in institutions do not have opportunities to learn adaptive behavior from functioning non-institutionalized people.
- Institutionalized people model their behavior after other people living in the institution; these behaviors are often maladaptive.
- Institutions provide a minimum of social and recreational activities and interaction; when they do, it is often demeaning and age inappropriate.

Along with the drawbacks described above, institutional living does not offer opportunities for vocational development. Typical jobs are not performed within an institutional environment, and opportunities to learn through observation are absent. Most, if not all, people living in institutions are unemployed, as few have ever had the opportunity to become employed. Discussion of work is nonexistent; normal vocational development does not occur.

Homelike Settings

As an alternative, state and local communities and parent organizations developed group homes, board and care homes, and foster homes to create homelike settings for individuals with intellectual disability. These settings are less restrictive than institutional residences. During the later part of the 1980s, and with increasing success since the 1990s, people with intellectual disability began living in their own homes, through programs often referred to as "Supported Living." Supported Living Services typically consist of:

- Assistance and support with selecting and moving into one's home, including obtaining household furnishings
- Support for choosing personal assistants, attendants, and housemates
- Support and assistance as needed in daily living activities and emergencies
- Becoming a participating member in community life
- Managing personal financial affairs, as well as other supports

Self-Advocacy, Self-Determination, and Self-Empowerment

The fields of rehabilitation and special education have moved toward allowing and facilitating people advocating for themselves, rather than relying on service providers making all the decisions for them. This approach results in people with intellectual disabilities believing they can control their own destiny. Self-Advocacy, Self-Determination, and Self-Empowerment consist of a combination of attitudes and abilities that lead people to set goals for themselves, and take the initiative to reach those goals, even if it means they require support from others to meet those goals.

It is about being in charge of their lives, but not necessarily mean they are completely being independent. It means making their own choices, learning to solve problems effectively, and taking control and responsibility for one's life (Agran, Brown, Hughes, Quirk, & Ryndak, 2014). Shogren and colleagues (2015) additionally found that promoting self-determination during the school transitional period resulted in positive functional outcomes for youth with disabilities. Membership in independent self-advocacy groups foster a positive self-identity (Anderson & Bigby, 2015). Two self-advocacy international networks, People First and United Together, have become increasingly influential in the areas of advocacy, fair working conditions, financial compensation, and friendship development.

Legislation and Normalization

Rehabilitation Act of 1973

Professionals often refer to Section 504 of the 1973 Rehabilitation Act as the civil rights bill for individuals with disabilities. This legislation requires public and private employers, educators, and service providers to use nondiscriminatory and affirmative action practices.

Education of All Handicapped Children Act of 1975 (Public Law 94-142)

This Act and its amendments ensure a free and appropriate education in the least restrictive environment for people between the ages of 3-21. The least restrictive environment mandates education of students in the presence of their peers without disabilities and within the general education program to the maximum extent appropriate. Research has consistently supported maximum integration of students in regular education programs, per individual student educational needs, for the best outcomes for students with and without disabilities (Falvey, 2005; Steere & DiPipi-Hoy, 2013).

PL 94-192 created a system of legal checks and balances called "procedural safeguards" to ensure that students, their parents, and the school system had a clear path of due process. In 2004, Congress reauthorized PL 94-192; it is currently known as the Individuals with Disabilities Education Improvement Act (IDEA). The most recent reauthorization in 2004 aimed to align with the No Child Left Behind Act of 2001 by increasing the rigor and individualization of an educational program to meet each child's unique educational needs with goals and standards similar to their same-age non-disabled peers.

1987 Developmental Disabilities Act

The stated goals for the 1987 Developmental Disabilities Act include:
> [to] assure that individuals with developmental disabilities receive the care, treatment, and other services necessary to enable them to achieve their maximum potential through increased independence, productivity, and integration into the community,

and
> [to] establish and operate a system that coordinates, monitors, plans, and evaluates services which ensure the protection of the legal and human rights of individuals with developmental disabilities.

Social Security Act Amendments

In 1987, Congress amended the Social Security Act to provide a work incentive program within the Supplemental Security Income (SSI) program. Before these amendments, regulations encouraged dependency. Medicare coverage (medical insurance) and financial support were removed when individuals acquired jobs. The new program allows the SSI recipient to continue to receive Medicare benefits if an employer does not provide equivalent comprehensive medical coverage. Most individuals with intellectual disability qualify for SSI benefits and have been more likely to obtain employment since these changes in the Social Security Act.

Americans with Disabilities Act

Congress passed the Americans with Disabilities Act (ADA) in 1990. This act has broad implications concerning employment, transportation, housing, public accommodations, state and local government, and telecommunications. The most significant area for individuals with intellectual disability is employment. Employers and property owners may not discriminate against individuals with disabilities in hiring, promotion, renting, and selling. They need to provide reasonable accommodations, including but not limited to job modification and job restructuring. All large employers with 15 or more employees need to comply. Enactment of the ADA has helped rehabilitation counselors facilitate obtaining competitive employment for their clients.

Functional Limitations

The most salient learning characteristics of individuals with intellectual disability are slower rates of learning than their typical peers or learning in a different way, and difficulty generalizing or transferring information learned from one situation to another. Though the rate of learning is slower and/or different in individuals with intellectual disability, these individuals maintain the ability to learn and acquire new skills. However, they must be taught specific skills in environments in which they will perform these skills. For example, teaching public transportation skills needs to include using the public transportation system in the person's community; one needs to teach job-related skills in real work environments (Magnuson, 2013).

Other functional limitations include behavioral challenges, difficulty with self-management skills, and sometimes inappropriate social skills. Behavioral challenges can be expressed through short attention span, impulsivity, and difficulty making judgments. Often, individuals with intellectual disabilities need to be directly taught self-management skills. Although individuals with intellectual disabilities may be sociable, they are often unaware of social pragmatics or other rules governing social behavior (Boston, Edwards, Jr., Duncan, Edwards, & Mendez, 2014). In the workplace, individuals with intellectual disability will inevitably build interpersonal relationships with their co-workers. With limited ability to process pragmatic cues in social situations, employees with intellectual disability may inadvertently ostracize themselves.

Along with these challenges, individuals with intellectual disability face another hurdle – communication. Communication challenges, delays, and inability to use words to express themselves are often associated with intellectual disabilities. When designing a vocational rehabilitation program, an individual's reading ability, information processing rates (especially instructions given only verbally), and information output rates (vocal expression or performance) must be considered. Some individuals have limited vocal expressive skills (e.g., speech impairment, singsong rhythm of speech, and difficulty regulating volume). For the rehabilitation professional, it is important to consider using visual tools (e.g., visual schedules and instructions) and/or augmentative adaptive communication tools.

At times, individuals with intellectual disability have been characterized as no longer capable of learning or as having reached a plateau (Falvey, 1989, 1995). When an individual's learning has reached such a plateau, it may simply be an indication that different services and support are necessary. The learning possibilities and potential of individuals with intellectual disability are directly dependent upon the commitment of services and support that society is willing to provide.

Learned Helplessness

A phenomenon repeatedly observed in institutions and segregated schools, sheltered workshops, and activity centers is learned helplessness. This involves a pattern of submissiveness developing when individuals repeatedly discover that their actions are of no consequence, and that outcomes are beyond their control (Falvey, 1989). When individuals with intellectual disability have not learned or others do not believe they have learned specific skills, they often behave in such a way that they do not perform the skills needed and wait for others to perform those tasks for them. These individuals learn not to demonstrate skill proficiency, independence, or an awareness of their surroundings.

This phenomenon has a similar effect to that of the self-fulfilling prophecy, which states that those around them influence most people's opinions and expectations about themselves in significant ways. If teachers, social workers, rehabilitation counselors, and job coaches believe an individual is unable to learn, that person will be discouraged from learning. If the same group of supportive professionals expect the individual to learn and be successful, the chances for a successful outcome are greatly enhanced (Falvey, 2005).

Environmental Factors

The environment plays a significant role in influencing the success and employability of persons with intellectual disability. The traditional model provided by adult service agencies has been vocational training in a train and place model, such as that which occurs in a sheltered workshop. In such a situation, a client is trained in a simulated job setting and then employment is sought in the real world. Because clients with intellectual disability do not generalize well across different settings, this model generally does not result in successful employment in integrated community jobs. The place and train model, a reverse method of employment, has resulted in a significantly greater number of employed clients within integrated community job settings.

Societal Discrimination

Over the years, society has discriminated against people with intellectual disability primarily due to their ignorance, stereotyping, and inaccurate information. Until recently, most employers had no prior interaction with individuals with intellectual disability (Magnuson, 2013). Practitioners are working to change the attitudes and expectations of employers by allowing them to observe other employers who have hired individuals with intellectual disability. This observation often results in raised expectations of what a person is capable of performing and more positive attitudes. Negative employer attitudes are slowly changing.

Rehabilitation Potential

The Supported Employment Model

Research over the past several decades has influenced changes in the delivery of services. In 1972, Gold demonstrated that individuals with significant intellectual disabilities who were deaf and blind could assemble complex electronic circuit boards. Hunter and Bellamy (1977) taught individuals with profound intellectual disabilities to assemble harnesses. Such discoveries led to the realization that people with intellectual disabilities could successfully learn work skills for competitive, gainful employment. This form of employment, in which an employee receives support or assistance, is called supported employment. Rehabilitation counselors throughout the country are currently using the principles of supported employment. The concept and implementation of supported employment have been expanded through research and legislation (Wehman, 2013; Wehman, Revell, & Brooks, 2003).

The traditional service options available to most adults with intellectual disability before 1980 were developmental centers, work activity centers, and sheltered workshops. Professionals and advocates have criticized these settings because they generally do not provide real work (work in actual work environments). The purpose of sheltered work environments is to prepare people for employment in the real world. Yet, after a national survey was conducted by Bellamy in 1985 (cited in Bishop & Falvey, 1989), it was concluded that too much time was spent training people for competitive employment.

According to Bellamy's research, people with intellectual disability spent an average of 37 years in adult developmental centers, ten years in work activity centers, and nine years in sheltered workshops. Since most individuals with intellectual disability graduate from school at approximately age 21, a person would be, on the average, 77 years old before entering the workforce. According to Bellamy, the supported employment model has been extremely successful in placing individuals with significant intellectual disabilities in gainful work environments, as opposed to the sheltered employment model (Falvey, 2005).

Characteristics of Supported Employment

Supported employment is an alternative to sheltered workshop training. The characteristics of supported employment services are as follows:

Place and Train

This model refers to developing services that reverse the traditional method of train and place. Place and train involves placing a person on the job, regardless of job readiness and immediately training that person to perform the job. To ensure success, a job coach is available to support the person in the job (Boston et al., 2014).

Integrated Job Settings

Job settings used for training are the same as used for employees without disabilities (Wehman, 2013). Additionally, integrated job settings should not create a disproportionate number of employees with disabilities. Integrated job settings should reflect the natural proportion of individuals who do not have disabilities within the community. The rehabilitation counselor needs to make every effort to encourage healthy interactions and relationships among the trainee with an intellectual disability and co-workers.

Self-Determination and Individual Placements

Successful supported employment models foster self-determination by empowering employees with intellectual disabilities to make their own choices and to take control of their career paths (Boston et al., 2014; Wehman, 2013). Job placements should be based on accessibility along with, most important, the trainee's preferences and strengths.

Meaningful Work

This characteristic implies that counselors need to avoid providing makeshift work or otherwise made-up jobs that individuals who do not have disabilities would not perform. Wehman (2013) explained that indicators of meaningful employment occur when an employee with an intellectual disability is hired, supervised, and paid directly by the business where the job setting is located and receives wages/benefits commensurate with coworkers without disabilities.

Job Development and Marketing

This service involves systematically accessing existing jobs, modifying existing jobs, and creating new ones. Job development and marketing are essential to the delivery of supported employment, and should be provided by individuals who have knowledge of the local job market and have credibility with employers (Falvey, 2005; Magnuson, 2013).

Job Coaching

Job coaching provides instruction on the job and teaches job-related skills, including social skills. In addition, job coaches provide job-related skills instruction in the client's home and community setting. These skills include preparing for work, using public transportation, depositing and budgeting paychecks, and developing social networks and friendships within the community. The job coach provides salient yet subtle instruction to allow the individual with intellectual disability to develop skills while not discouraging the person. If they are not performing correctly, the job coach provides additional instruction. If the individual fails to arrive for work, the job coach will act as a substitute worker and perform the necessary tasks of the absentee. Also, the job coach facilitates natural supports from co-workers and supervisors.

Job coaches enhance rehabilitation potential by providing the support needed to access and maintain employment, housing, and other community services and activities (McConkey, Kelly, Mannan, & Craig, 2011). Self-determination and autonomy are positively influenced in a supported employment model while segregated vocational day programs are generally less successful. Supported employment services across the United States and within other countries (e.g., Canada and Italy) have successfully employed millions of people with intellectual disability. Nationwide, however, individuals with mild intellectual disability are more likely to be placed in competitive supported employment than individuals with more significant levels (Boston et al., 2014). Overall, many individuals have been provided with the support needed to live where they wish and with whom they want while accessing their neighborhoods and communities, while simultaneously receiving sufficient support to ensure success.

Attitudes of people in the community have changed over the years, leading to greater acceptance of their neighbors with intellectual disability (McConkey et al., 2011). Technology has influenced successful integration within the community. Simple adaptations such as calculators and other technological devices, including voice synthesizers and other electronic communication aides, have greatly enhanced the participation of individuals with intellectual disability.

Conclusion

This chapter provides rehabilitation counselors with an overview of the issues related to intellectual disability. The most critical concept is that the degree of participation and potential of individuals with intellectual disability is dependent upon society's commitment and willingness to support people who have intellectual disability in work, housing, and within the community. The supported employment model has proven to be the most effective service delivery system. The level of fidelity of the supported employment model greatly influences the success of an individual's work experience (Bond, McHugo, Becker, Rapp, & Whitley, 2008).

Case Study

Sebastian is a 28-year-old man who was diagnosed at birth with Down syndrome and an intellectual disability at age one. At age 12, his physician diagnosed him with autism. Throughout his schooling, he was fully included in general education classes, with the support of special education, accommodating and modifying his work so that it was meaningful for him and he could be successful at working at grade level with some modifications. He was successful at making friends with his classmates with and without disabilities who genuinely enjoyed his company and friendship.

After receiving his Certificate of Completion from high school, Sebastian experienced a variety of job training experiences with job coaching support while attending the transition program operated by his school district within his community. His job training experiences included working at a local bookstore, grocery store, pet shop, and fabric/craft store. He enjoyed all these experiences and it offered an opportunity for him, his teachers, vocational counselor, and others to determine which experiences were best suited for his future employment.

After completing the transition program offered by the school district at age 22, Sebastian enrolled in a community-based program for individuals with intellectual disability. Pleased to be accessing the community daily with his support staff, after two years, he indicated a desire to return to work. Sebastian secured a job at the fabric/craft store at which he had previously done job training. The employer and employees remembered him and welcomed him back to their store. He works two mornings a week, sorting and organizing the bolts of fabric and doing general janitorial work at this store.

When he turned 28, he was interested in moving out of his mother's home, but he required 24-hour supervision due to his intellectual disability and his ability to be safe in his own home. To be more independent, Sebastian moved into a house where he rented a bedroom from the homeowners, who also became part of his support team. He has access to the rest of the house; therefore, with the support of his staff, he prepares his meals, and enjoys being with his staff and his housemates. He has continued to work at the fabric/craft store two mornings a week, accessing a variety of community settings the rest of the week, including working out at the local gym and going bowling, to the park, to restaurants, and shopping. On the weekends, he attends his church and has a full life. In general, Sebastian is happy and enjoys his staff, whom he hires and fires, getting together with his family, which he does on a regular basis at least once a week. Sebastian has a wide circle of friends who are very devoted to him.

Questions

1. What are the possible causes of Sebastian's intellectual disability?
2. Identify the advantages of inclusive schooling experiences for students with intellectual disability and how it affects their lives as adults?
3. Describe the advantages of supported employment.
4. Discuss the roles and functions of the job coach in supported employment.
5. Outline the characteristics of the supported employment services model. Relate this to Sebastian's case.

References

Agran, M., Brown, F., Hughes, Quirk, C., & Ryndak, D. (Eds.). (2014). *Equity and full participation for individuals with severe disabilities.* Baltimore, MD: Brookes.

Ainsworth, P., & Baker, P. C. (2004). *Understanding mental retardation: A resource for parents, caregivers, and counselors.* Jackson, MS: University Press of Mississippi.

American Association of Intellectual and Developmental Disabilities (AAIDD). (2010). *Intellectual disability: Definition, classification, and systems of support* (11th ed.). Washington, DC: Author.

American Association of Mental Retardation (AAMR). (2002). *Mental retardation: Definition, classification, and systems of support* (10th ed.). Washington, DC: Author.

American Psychiatric Association. (2013). *Diagnostic and statistical manual of mental disorders* (DSM-V) (5th ed.). Washington, DC: Author.

Americans with Disabilities Act (ADA) of 1990, 42 U.S.C. §§12101 et seq.

Anderson, S., & Bigby, C. (2015). Self-advocacy as a means to positive identities for people with intellectual disability: 'We just help them, be them really'. *Journal of Applied Research in Intellectual Disabilities, 30,* 109–120.

Biklen, D., & Knoll, J. (1987). The disabled minority. In S. Taylor, D. Biklen, & J. Knoll (Eds.), *Community integration for people with severe disabilities* (pp. 3-24). New York, NY: Teachers' College.

Bishop, K. D., & Falvey, M. A. (1989). Employment skills. In M. A. Falvey (Ed.), *Community-based curriculum: Instructional strategies for students with severe handicaps* (pp. 165-188). Baltimore, MD: Paul H. Brookes.

Bond, G. R., McHugo, G. J., Becker, D. R., Rapp, C. A., & Whitley, R. (2008). Fidelity of supported employment: Lessons learned from the National Evidence-Based Practice Project. *Psychiatric Rehabilitation Journal, 31*(4), 300-305.

Boston, Q., Edwards, Jr., D. W., Duncan, J. C., Edwards, Y. V., & Mendez, E. (2014). Supported employment. In J. D. Andrew & C. W. Faubion (Eds.), *Rehabilitation services: An introduction for the human services professional* (3rd ed., pp. 308-325). Linn Creek, MO: Aspen.

Brimer, R. W. (1990). *Students with severe disabilities: Current perspectives and practices.* Mountain View, CA: Mayfield.

Campbell, C., Landry, O., Russo, N., Flores, H., Jacques, S., & Burack, J. A. (2013). Cognitive flexibility among individuals with Down syndrome: Addressing the influence of verbal and non verbal abilities. *American Journal on Intellectual and Developmental Disabilities, 118*(3), 193-200.

Chelly, J., Khelfaoui, M., Francis, F., Chérif, B., & Bienvenu, T. (2006). Genetics and pathophysiology of mental retardation. *European Journal of Human Genetics, 14*(6), 701-713.

Education for All Handicapped Children Act of 1975, PL 94-142m 20 U.S,C, SS 1400 et seq.

Falvey, M. A. (Ed.). (1989). *Community-based curriculum: Instructional strategies for students with severe handicaps* (2nd ed.). Baltimore, MD: Paul H. Brookes.

Falvey, M. A. (Ed.). (1995). *Inclusive and heterogeneous schooling: Assessment, curriculum, and instruction.* Baltimore, MD: Paul H. Brookes.

Falvey, M. A. (2005). *Believe in my child with special needs.* Baltimore, MD: Paul H. Brookes.

Gold, M. W. (1980). *Try another way training manual.* Champaign, IL: U.S. Department of Education (ERIC).

Hunter, J., & Bellamy, G. T. (1977). Cable harness construction for severely retarded adults: A demonstration of training techniques. *American Association for the Education of Severely and Profoundly Handicapped Review, 1*(7), 2-13.

Locke, J. (1690). *An essay concerning human understanding* (Republished in 2006 by Adamant Media Corporation, London, England).

McConkey, R., Kelly, F., Mannan, H., & Craig, S. (2011). Moving from family care to residential and supported accommodation: National, longitudinal study of people with intellectual disabilities. *American Journal on Intellectual and Developmental Disabilities, 117*(6), 305-314.

Magnuson, L. (2013). Families and uncertainty: Using problematic integration theory in transition services. *Journal of Applied Rehabilitation Counseling, 44*(1), 12-17.

Nirje, B. (1969). The normalization principle and its management implications. In R. Kugel and W. Wolfensberger (Eds.), *Changing patterns in residential services for the mentally retarded* (pp. 51-57). Washington, DC: U.S. Government Printing Office.

Peterlin, A., & Peterlin, B. (2016). Contemporary approach to diagnosis of genetic causes of intellectual disability. *Journal of Special Education and Rehabilitation, 17*(3), 62-70.

Ropers H. H. (2010). Genetics of early onset cognitive impairment. *Annual Review Genomics Human Genetics, 11*, 161-187.

Rosa's Law. Pub. L. 111-256.

Shogren, K. A., Wehmeyer, M. L., Palmer, S. B., Rifenbark, G. G., & Little, T. D. (2015). Relationships between self-determination and post school outcomes for youth with disabilities. *Journal of Special Education, 48*, 256-267.

Southward, J. D., & Kyzar, K. (2017). Predictors of competitive employment for students with intellectual and/or developmental disabilities. *Education and Training in Autism and Developmental Disabilities, 52*(1), 26-37.

Steere, D., & DiPipi-Hoy, C. (2013). Coordination in transition planning: The IEP/IPE interface. *Journal of Applied Rehabilitation Counseling, 44*(1), 4-11.

Tassé, M., J., Luckasson, R., & Nygren, M. (2013). AAIDD proposed recommendations for ICD-11 and the condition previously known as mental retardation. *Intellectual and Developmental Disabilities, 51*(2), 127-131.

United States Census Bureau. (2015). Disability Characteristics Table: 2015. *American Community Survey.* Washington, DC: U.S. Department of Commerce. Retrieved from https://factfinder.census.gov/faces/tableservices/jsf/pages/productview.xhtml?pid=ACS_15_5YR_S1810&prodType=table

Wehman, P. (2013). *Life beyond the classroom: Transition strategies for young people with disabilities* (5th ed.). Baltimore, MD: Paul H. Brookes.

Wehman, P., Chan, F., Ditchman, N., & Kang, H., (2014). Effect of supported employment on vocational rehabilitation outcomes of transition-age youth with intellectual and developmental disabilities: A case control study. *Intellectual and Developmental Disabilities, 52*, 296-310.

Wehman, P., Revell, G. W., & Brooke, V. (2003). Competitive employment: Has it become the "first choice" yet? *Journal of Disability Policy Studies, 14*(3), 163-173.

Wehmeyer, M. L., Lattimore, J., Jorgensen, J. D., Palmer, S. B., Thompson, E., & Schumaker, K. M. (2003). The self-determined career development model: A pilot study. *Journal of Vocational Rehabilitation, 19*(2), 79-87.

Wehmeyer, M. L. (2013). Disability, disorder, and identity. *Intellectual and Developmental Disabilities, 51*(2), 122-126.

Whitaker S. (2013). Causes of intellectual disability. In S. Whitaker (Ed.), *Intellectual disability* (pp. 107-121). London, England: Macmillan.

Wolfensberger, W. (1980). A brief overview of the principle of normalization. In R. J. Flynn & K. E. Kitsch (Eds.), *Normalization, social integration, and community services* (pp. 7-30). Baltimore, MD: University Park.

About the Authors

Julie Ton Fercho, PhD, BCBA-D., is an Autism and Behavior Program Specialist with Downey Unified School District in Downey, California. Dr. Fercho has worked in several capacities in the field of developmental disabilities, in particular as a behavior analyst, special education teacher, teacher trainer, and research team coordinator.

Mary A. Falvey, PhD, is Professor of Special Education and former Dean of the Charter College of Education at California State University, Los Angeles. She has authored several books on community-based intervention and inclusive education, and has consulted with school districts throughout the country.

Kathryn D. Bishop, PhD, is Professor of Special Education at the University of San Diego in San Diego, California. She has worked in the area of supported employment as a direct service provider and national trainer. Dr. Bishop provides consultation in the area of inclusive education issues.

Susann Terry Gage, PhD, is a graduate of the Joint Doctoral Program at California State University, Los Angeles and the University of California, Los Angeles. Dr. Gage is the Special Education Coordinator in Sedona, Arizona.

Chapter 26

AUTISM SPECTRUM DISORDER

Hung Jen Kuo, PhD, CRC, LPC, MCSA
Frances W. Siu, PhD, CRC
Jessica H. Franco, PhD, CCC-SLP, BCBA-D

Introduction

Autism Spectrum disorder (ASD) has received much public attention in the past few decades. Previously categorized as a subtype of Pervasive Developmental Disorder (PDD), ASD has been extracted from the group for its increasing prevalence and significant differences in symptoms (American Psychiatric Association [APA], 2013). Because of its wide range of symptoms and uncertain etiology, the myths of ASD persist and the public media has attempted to portray the ASD population. For instance, movies such as Rain Man, Adam, and The Accountant have attracted much interest. While these movies have revealed some ASD characteristics, they may not holistically and genuinely reflect reality. As such, it becomes essential for rehabilitation practitioners to be educated and be ready to educate the public.

In 2000, it was estimated that for every 150 children, one has ASD. In 2018, this number drastically increased to one in every 59 children having a diagnosis of ASD (Centers for Disease Control and Prevention [CDC], 2018). Most recently, the National Institute of Health has reported that the prevalence of ASD has risen to 1 in every 45 children in the United States (Zablotsky, Black, Maenner, Schieve, & Blumberg, 2015).

ASD is a group of neurodevelopmental disorders characterized by impairment of social reciprocity, such as limitations in social motivation and emotional recognition. Deficiencies in communication and restricted behaviors like repetitive behaviors (e.g., finger flicking, hand flapping), limited interests, and rituals or stereotypes are typically present. First identification or diagnosis usually occurs between the ages of two and four (APA, 2013), although a significant number of individuals remain undiagnosed. In 2005, the average annual medical cost for a Medicaid-enrolled child with an ASD was $10,710, six times higher than the medical costs for a child without ASD ($1,810) (Autism Speaks, 2013).

Intensive behavioral interventions for each child with ASD cost $40,000 to $60,000 per year. According to the *Diagnostic and Statistical Manual of Mental Disorders* (5th ed., DSM-5), ASD covers a group of disorders previously known as *early infantile autism, childhood autism, Kanner's autism, high-functioning autism, atypical autism, pervasive developmental disorder not otherwise specified, childhood disintegrative disorder, and Asperger's disorder*. The *spectrum* of ASD refers to the wide variation of manifestations contingent upon the severity of the autistic condition, developmental level, and chronological age (APA, 2013).

The following sections focus on (a) etiology, (b) characteristics of ASD, (c) prevalence and incidence, (d) diagnosis, (e) treatment, and (f) rehabilitation potential. This chapter concludes with a case study for further discussion.

Etiology

As Happé, Ronald and Plomin (2006) indicated in their article titled "Time to Give Up on a Single Explanation for Autism," no single answer can explain what causes this disorder. According to the DSM-5 (APA, 2013), there is strong evidence from twin concordance studies that heritability rates for ASD range from 37% to 90%. As many as 15% of the current ASD cases seem to be associated with a known genetic mutation. However, researchers have also indicated that different ASD characteristics (e.g., deficits of social communication and repetitive behavior) may be attributed to different genes.

Genes that affect the communication skills of a person with ASD is independent to that which affects his or her restricted behaviors. Consequently, two persons with ASD might have the same challenges in speaking but different behavioral symptoms. Environmental factors are also involved and interact with ASD susceptibility genes. For example, the womb is an environment for a fetus; prenatal and perinatal factors such as maternal nutrition, maternal infections, and premature birth contribute to the increase of risk factors beyond genetic mutation. A study by Grabrucker (2013) suggested that the parents' mental status (e.g., parental stress) before delivery of the baby could potentially contribute to the development of ASD.

Many suggestions have been made concerning other possible causes, including diet, environmental pollutants, antibiotics, allergies, mumps/measles/rubella (MMR) vaccines, and traces of neurotoxins, such as mercury in preservatives. None has been scientifically validated. Research scientists have concluded that vaccines do not cause autism (CDC, 2018).

Characteristics

ASD is a lifelong condition. Characteristics vary greatly and are unique to each individual. Common signs and symptoms reported are impaired social interaction skills, avoidance of eye contact, rigid adherence to daily routines, unusual or obsessive behaviors and unusual interests, and high sensitivity or under responsiveness to light, touch, and sound (CDC, 2018). The life course of individuals with ASD varies; some individuals lose skills over time, others reach a plateau in adolescence, while some display patterns of continued development into adulthood (LeBlanc, Riley, & Goldsmith, 2008).

Developmental changes during adolescence and adulthood may resemble changes in key ASD symptoms. The core symptoms of autism often diminish during adolescence and young adulthood, particularly for individuals without intellectual disabilities. As a result, children who have been diagnosed with ASD in childhood may lose this label by the time they reach adulthood. Seltzer, Shattuck, Abbeduto, and Greenberg (2004) indicated that out of a group of adults who met criteria for ASD diagnosis in childhood, only 55% meet the criteria for autism in adulthood. Researchers found that language skills were the most improved, while friendship development had the least symptom improvement in adults.

Some persons experience improvements that are limited to certain core features of ASD with variable timing of improvements across behaviors. Shattuck et al. (2007) found that adult participants had fewer maladaptive behaviors (i.e., self-injury, noncompliance, aggression) and experienced more improvement in these behaviors over time when compared to adolescents.

Social Interaction

Individuals, especially adults, with ASD may speak their minds and make insensitive remarks in social situations. Some adults on the spectrum have delayed use and understanding of speech. These individuals tend to have long-standing difficulties in non-verbal expressions, avoid mutual gaze, lack gestures, and have diminished facial expressions. They may misunderstand the reactions of others and lack empathy (Autism Speaks, 2013). People with ASD prefer solitary activities and lack spontaneous desire to share enjoyment, interests, and achievements with others.

Similarly, individuals with high functioning ASD exhibit problems with social interactions. Some isolate themselves from others, taking refuge in a world of idiosyncratic interests, routines, and private preoccupations. For those who cope in this way, close friendships and intimate relationships hold little attraction (Autism Speaks, 2013). In an attempt to better understand individuals with high functioning ASD, Vickerstaff, Heriot, Wong, Lopes and Dossetor (2007) found that intellectual quotient (IQ) of the person is negatively associated with perceived social competence. The higher the IQ the person with ASD has, the lower the social competence he or she may perceive.

Generally, even when persons with this condition develop friendships, there is often more reported loneliness compared to their typically developing counterparts. Although high-functioning individuals are more likely to report having friendships than those with less developed skills, their relationships often focus on common restricted interests rather than social interactions. Besides a low prevalence of friendships, there is minimal presence of participation in social and recreational activities (LeBlanc et al., 2008).

Work-Related Issues

According to the Bureau of Labor Statistics (2017), the employment rate for young adults with disabilities is 19.4% compared to 65.8% for those without disabilities. Whereas the employment rate may vary based on the disability type, the population of ASD is consistently one of the lowest employed among others (Newman et al., 2011). Various studies explored and confirmed this (Howlin & Moss, 2012; Strickland, Coles, & Southern, 2013). Specifically, there are two major challenges for employment: a) obtaining a job and b) job retention. Whereas individuals with ASD may have the capacity to perform essential functions of a given job, the process of obtaining employment is a challenge for them.

As Elksnin and Elksnin (2001) noted, up to 90% of job losses among individuals with disabilities may be attributed to a lack of social and communication skills. This situation is further magnified for the ASD population as impaired social communication is one of the core symptoms of this disorder (APA, 2013). They may have difficulty with work-related activities and overall employment, due to their resistance to changes in daily routines, taking prolonged periods of time to adjust after a long holiday, or refusing adaptation to a new or unfamiliar environment. Adolescents with high functioning ASD are likely to have increasing difficulties with planning and organizational skills, as well as completing assignments on time (Jordan, 2013).

Health Issues

As children progress toward adolescence, there is a high likelihood of developing various health problems that co-occur with ASD. Difficulties with social tasks can continue throughout life and be a constant source of distress. Individuals exhibit many behavioral difficulties including hyperactivity, attention problems, obsessive-compulsive phenomena, self-injury, tics, and affective symptoms. Problems with impulse control, disorganized behavior, aggression, and disruptions are prevalent (LeBlanc et al., 2008).

Generalized anxiety and depression are common in high-functioning ASD groups, and typically worsen throughout adolescence and into adulthood. Anxiety disorders are common expressions of distress; long-standing anxiety may lead to depression and substance misuse. Depression may cause increased social withdrawal and self-neglect (Kim, Szatmari, Bryson, Streiner, & Wilson, 2000).

Sexuality

Individuals with ASD have less sexual knowledge and experience than their peers. Sexual knowledge is positively correlated with cognitive functioning. Consequently, those with higher cognitive impairments display more inappropriate sexual behaviors, engage in fewer privacy-seeking behaviors, and have less sex education. Of particular concern is the likelihood that interests on the part of greater functioning individuals might be misinterpreted as threatening or predatory behavior.

As a result, only a small proportion of individuals with ASD develop intimate relationships (Mehzabin & Stokes, 2011). The centrality of social impairments in ASD may cause difficulties in initiating and maintaining relationships, making them challenging or unappealing for potential partners. Sexual relationships are more difficult to achieve, and many find their self-esteem further eroded by rejections. Sometimes, when relationships do develop, they are based on exploitation of the person with Asperger syndrome, and the effect is undermining rather than rewarding (Jordan, 2013).

Prevalence and Incidence

A study conducted by Zablotsky, Black, Maenner, Schieve, and Blumberg (2015), reported an increase of ASD prevalence to one in every 45 children in the United States. As noted, about one in 68 children in the United States has been identified with an ASD according to estimates from the CDC Autism and Developmental Disabilities Monitoring Network in 2008 (CDC, 2018); this is a significant rise from one in 150 children in 2000. ASD is five times more prevalent among males than females, and occurs in all racial/ethnic groups and socioeconomic levels.

Possible reasons for the increase in prevalence and incidence include: (a) changes in diagnostic criteria; (b) variations in methods used in research studies; (c) increased awareness among professionals, parents, and the general public of the existence of autistic spectrum disorders; (d) the growth of specialist services; (e) probable causes and relation to age of onset; (f) the association of autism conditions with intellectual disability, other developmental or physical disorders, besides psychiatric disorders of any type; and (g) a true increase in these population (APA, 2013). Nevertheless, most, if not all, of the reported rise in prevalence and incidence is because of changes in diagnostic criteria and greater awareness among parents and professionals.

Diagnosis

Diagnosis of ASD is composed of standardized behavioral diagnostic and clinical observation measures, questionnaires, caregiver interviews, and self-reports, when appropriate. A diagnosis can be made by many different professionals, including developmental pediatricians, neurologists, psychologists, and speech-language pathologists. According to the *DSM-5* (APA, 2013), ASD should be considered only when all four diagnostic criteria are met.

Criterion A: Persistent impairment in social interaction and social communication.

Criterion B: Restricted and repetitive patterns of odd behavior, interests, and activities.

Criterion C: Signs and indicators must surface during early developmental stages.

Criterion D: Symptoms must cause clinically significant impairment in daily functioning.

In clinical recording for ASD, severities are recorded as the level of support needed for each of the two psychopathological domains: (a) social communication and (b) restricted repetitive behaviors. Severity levels include Level 1: Requiring support; Level 2: Requiring substantial support; and Level 3: Requiring very substantial support (APA, 2013).

Comorbidity

It is not unusual for someone with ASD to be diagnosed with a known medical condition, a genetic condition, an environmental factor, or with another neurodevelopmental, mental, intellectual, or behavioral disorder. For example, approximately 50% of children with ASD have at least one of the three co-occurring conditions: attention-deficit/hyperactivity disorder, intellectual disability, or epilepsy. Psychiatric disorders, especially social anxiety disorder and oppositional defiant disorder, are common and frequently co-occur in these children (Jordan, 2013).

Functional Limitations

Table 1 presents a summary of functional limitations of individuals with ASD.

TABLE 1
Summary of Functional Limitations of Adolescents and Adults with ASD

Areas	Limitations
Cognitive	Difficulty with planning & organizational skills
Social/sexual	Insensitivity
	Limited nonverbal skills
	Difficulty forming friendships
	Delayed use & understanding of speech
	Conversations limited to their topics of interest
	Steer away from romantic relationships
	Changes in nature of friendship, body shape, & so forth
	Suffer victimization of different types
Behavior	Impulsive, disorganized, aggressive, & disruptive
	Hyperactivity & attention problems
	Engage in self-injury
	Low empathy
	Adherence to rituals
Health problems	Mood disorders
	Depression, generalized anxiety, obsessive compulsive, & conduct disorders
	Use of illegal substances to cope with daily challenges
Employment	Inflexibility
	Trouble completing assignments
	Interest in only a few types of activities
	May not discern the reason for rejection at job interviews
	Seldom plans for the future
	Hesitant to assume adult responsibilities

Source: Jordan, R. (2013). *Autism Spectrum Disorder: An introductory handbook for practitioners*. Oxon, England: David Fulton.

Treatment

Autism is a lifetime condition. To a vast degree, the symptoms can be managed and adapted to with proper care and attention. In general, individualized and intensive behavioral interventions are used to help individuals with ASD, especially during childhood. The goals of intervention are to (a) optimize the functional independence of the individual by minimizing the symptoms; (b) facilitate development and learning, including social skills of the individual; (c) reduce restricted interests and stereotypical behavior; and (d) eliminate maladaptive behavior. A comprehensive plan of treatment is needed for each individual (APA, 2013).

Rehabilitation Potential

Social Skills

Individuals with ASD experience countless challenges in daily living. People with high-functioning ASD often learn the social rules and skills, but do not apply them in social situations. They frequently lack the ability to recognize social cues, understand reciprocal conversation, and use humor appropriately. Social skills are a prominent part of employment success (Elksnin & Elksnin, 2001). While employers place great importance on functional aspects of a job, socialization and integration in the workplace are crucial. As a result, social impairment of individuals with ASD causes difficulties in employment and job retention. For those qualified individuals in the workplace, employment levels and occupational statuses are typically low; often, these individuals are underemployed.

The majority of adults with ASD need lifelong care such as ongoing supervision, work and self-care training, and reinforcement of skills. The public school (K-12) systems provide these services, which terminate when the person exceeds school age. In some cases, adults with ASD continue to live at home, provided that necessary support, such as constant supervision, is available. One can use a variety of residential care facilities in both the private and public sectors providing 24-hour care. Unlike many of the older institutions, facilities today view residents as people with human needs, and offer opportunities for recreation and simple but meaningful work activities.

Work Issues

People with severe or profound symptoms of ASD may work in sheltered workshops or other placements with high levels of support and structured work requirements. Individuals with mild or moderate symptoms are often successful with supported employment. People with ASD working in an environment utilizing a supported employment model were found to achieve significantly more than those in non-supported employment (Wehman et al., 2012).

Supported employment as an approach to hiring and retaining people with developmental disabilities has a mission to provide stable and predictable work environments where individuals with ASD can become contributing members of the productive workforce. A job coach or employment specialist is usually hired to provide individualized training for the *supported employe*e. The chapter on intellectual developmental disabilities provides a discussion on supported employment. With the passage of the Workforce Innovation and Opportunity Act (WIOA) in 2014, the supported employment funded by the public vocational rehabilitation program can be extended from 18 months to 24 months.

Work is a significant aspect of life. Having employment is a source of pride and accomplishment in American society. People with high-functioning ASD have many positive qualities to offer employers. Typically, they are punctual, detail-oriented, appreciate routine and repetitive work, and become loyal employees. Yet, overshadowing difficulties, such as employment issues associated with social skills, problem solving, and on-the-job bullying, may mask their positive qualities. These difficulties bring the individual with ASD to the attention of rehabilitation professionals. With the increased prevalence rate and rise of public awareness, there are more training programs aiming to promote social skills and the employment readiness for individuals with ASD. With the advancement of modern technology, technology-infused interventions can shed some light on new avenues of rehabilitation.

Job advancement is often a slow and challenging process. Job loss is more common than job advancement. Often, the reason for being terminated is poorly understood by the person with autism (Wehman et al., 2012). Reasons that individuals usually understand, such as harassing coworkers of the opposite sex, could be meaningless to someone with ASD. Finding new jobs becomes increasingly difficult with each job loss, as periods of unemployment have to be explained to prospective employers. When helping a person select training and educational programs, rehabilitation counselors need to be particularly cautious.

Basic employment and adaptive skills are often lacking among individuals with ASD. For example, handling of feedback, incorporating requested changes in performance, and adapting to new job routines are challenging. Vocational-related social skills that are crucial for an individual with ASD to learn include: organization of tasks, transitioning, task completion, asking for help, and social demeanor (Bureau of Labor Statistics, 2017).

Individuals with this condition need to be individually educated and assisted. Besides on-the-job-training, structured teaching with written expectations of job responsibilities and in-depth work procedures are vital to overall success. At the workplace, employees need to know whom to go to for help. Specific training strategies found to be effective in training these individuals include: (1) the use of cognitive aids, particularly technology, to assist with organization and planning, (2) clear differential reinforcement contingencies to provide motivation for task completion and accuracy, and (3) corrective feedback that is specific and multifaceted (Palmen, Didden, & Lang, 2012). The use of aids such as written schedules, checklists, as well as a focus on teaching self-monitoring, have been effective in supporting people with ASD (Southall & Gast, 2011).

Disclosure

Counselors must assess potential ramifications of disclosure or non-disclosure with their clients. Younger workers are more likely to disclose their disabilities. Recent support in the education system has taught young employees with ASD to maximize their strengths and ask for accommodation. They frequently have the support of career planning, and have greater access to governmental supports than their predecessors. Early intervention has resulted in higher self-esteem among those individuals who have entered the workforce in recent years. ASD in high functioning people is *usually invisible*. Many think of low functioning or nonverbal individuals when they hear of autism, and do not believe that a high functioning person can have ASD. Although only 10% of people with ASD are considered savants (a rare condition in which persons with developmental disorders have one or more areas of expertise, ability, or brilliance which are in contrast with their overall limitations), many people on the autism spectrum are extremely intelligent and excel in art, mathematics, music, and visual skills (Autism Speaks, 2013). Nonetheless, decision-making on disclosure of disability needs an individualized approach.

Conclusion

Each individual has unique strengths and limitations. Some may be of average to below-average intelligence, while others are above average. Despite the common beliefs and media portrayals of the ingenious abilities of people with ASD, only 10% of the population with ASD have been tested and are considered to be savants. Academic and training goals and objectives need to be tailored to each person's intellectual capability and level of functioning. With the proper services and supports, people with autism can live full, healthy, and meaningful lives.

Case Study

Andy Yeung is a 20-year old freshman student in college who has autism; the two of you first met when Andy was in his high school's Transitional Partnership Program (TPP). As long as he follows his routines and is well-informed of possible changes, Andy has been able to pass all his classes in high school; also, he enjoys the challenge of video games. Recently, Andy's mother called and conveyed concerns about her son because he became totally absorbed in computer games and often stayed up almost all night playing video games. Mrs. Yeung is frustrated about not being able to inquire about Andy's academic progress from his college counselor. When asked, Andy refuses to respond and frequently hides himself in his bedroom after school, refusing to come out even for meals.

Knowing the urgency of Andy's situation, you, as his rehabilitation counselor, made a home visit. While you were at the Yeung's residence, Andy did not respond to his mother's call to come to the living room. You entered his bedroom, where he was playing a video game. When he eventually looked up, his eyes were blood-shot and he seemed to have neglected personal hygiene. Andy reported failing most of his courses. When asked why, Andy said that he was lost being an adult in the new environment. He did not want to be a burden to his mother and yet, had no idea what to do. At the same time, he was fired from his part-time job at a local coffee house.

Andy's job responsibilities included cleaning tables, taking out trash, refilling condiments, and maintaining bathroom supplies and cleanliness. He had been working four times a week since he was a junior in high school. While there was a change of ownerships a few months back, Andy's supervisor who had hired him was transferred to another location. Andy commented that *people are evil* before putting himself in a rocking position. As he covered his head with his hands, you saw some old scars and bruise marks on his forearms.

Questions

1. Provide a vocational profile for Andy. Identify additional information you need to best help this client from a multidisciplinary approach and discuss how you will obtain the needed information.
2. Besides autism, do you suspect any additional disorders that Andy might have? Explain.
3. Has *abuse* crossed your mind? If yes, what are the steps to properly handle the situation?
4. Would a career in computer software design be realistic for this client? Discuss.
5. What services will help Andy get back on track? Describe these possible services and the potential benefits for Andy.

References

American Psychiatric Association (APA). (2013). *Diagnostic and statistical manual of mental disorders* (5th ed.). Washington, DC: Author.

Autism Speaks. (2013). *What is autism?* Retrieved from https://www.autismspeaks.org/what-autism.

Bureau of Labor Statistics. (2017). *Employment status of the civilian population by sex, age, and disability status, not seasonally adjusted*. Retrieved from https://www.bls.gov/news.release/empsit.t06.htm

Centers for Disease Control and Prevention (CDC). (2018). *Autism spectrum disorders (ASDs): Data and statistics*. Retrieved from http://www.cdc.gov/ncbddd/autism/data.html

Elksnin, N., & Elksnin, L. K. (2001). Adolescents with disabilities: The need for occupational social skills training. *Exceptionality, 9*(1–2), 91–105.

Grabrucker, A. M. (2013). Environmental factors in autism. *Frontiers in Psychiatry, 3*.

Happé, F., Ronald, A., & Plomin, R. (2006). Time to give up on a single explanation for autism. *Nature Neuroscience, 9*(10), 1218–1220.

Howlin, P., & Moss, P. (2012). Adults with autism spectrum disorders. *Canadian Journal of Psychiatry. Revue Canadienne De Psychiatrie, 57*(5), 275–283.

Jordan, R. (2013). *Autistic spectrum disorders: An introductory handbook for practitioners*. Oxon, England: David Fulton.

Kim, J. A., Szatmari, P., Bryson, S. E., Streiner, D. L., & Wilson, F. J. (2000). The prevalence of anxiety and mood problems among children with autism and Asperger syndrome. *Autism, 4*, 117-132.

LeBlanc, L. A., Riley, A. R., & Goldsmith, T. R. (2008). Autism spectrum disorders: A lifespan perspective. In J. Matson (Ed.), *Clinical assessment and intervention for autism spectrum disorders* (pp. 65-87). Burlington, MA: Elsevier.

Mehzabin, P., & Stokes, M. (2011). Self-assessed sexuality in young adults with high-functioning autism. *Research in Autism Spectrum Disorders, 5*(1), 614-621.

Newman, L., Wagner, M., Knokey, A. M., Marder, C., Nagle, K., Shaver, D., & Wei, X. (2011). The post-high school outcomes of young adults with disabilities up to 8 years after high school: A report from the National Longitudinal Transition Study-2 (NLTS2). NCSER 2011-3005. *National Center for Special Education Research*. Retrieved from http://eric.ed.gov/?id=ED524044

Palmen, A., Didden, R., & Russell, L. (2012). A systematic review of behavioral intervention research on adaptive skill building in high-functioning young adults with autism spectrum disorder. *Research in Autism Spectrum Disorders, 6*(2), 602-617.

Seltzer, M. M., Shattuck, P., Abbeduto, L., & Greenberg, J. S. (2004). Trajectory of development in adolescents and adults with autism. *Mental Retardation and Developmental Disabilities Research Reviews, 10*, 234-247.

Shattuck, P., Seltzer, M. M., Greenberg, J. S., Orsmond, G. I., Bolt, D., Kring, S., & Lord, C. (2007). Change in autism symptoms and maladaptive behaviors in adolescents and adults with an autism spectrum disorder. *Journal of Autism and Developmental Disorders, 37*, 1735-1747.

Southall, C. M., & Gast, D. L. (2011). Self-management procedures: A comparison across the autism spectrum. *Education and Training in Autism and Developmental Disabilities, 46*(2), 155-171.

Strickland, D. C., Coles, C. D., & Southern, L. B. (2013). JobTIPS: A transition to employment program for individuals with autism spectrum disorders. *Journal of Autism and Developmental Disorders, 43*(10), 2472–2483.

Vickerstaff, S., Heriot, S., Wong, M., Lopes, A., & Dossetor, D. (2007). Intellectual ability, self-perceived social competence, and depressive symptomatology in children with high-functioning autistic spectrum disorders. *Journal of Autism & Developmental Disorders, 37*(9), 1647-1664.

Wehman, P., Lau, S., Molinelli, A., Brookes, V., Thompson, K., Moore, C., & West, M. (2012). Supported employment for young adults with autism spectrum disorder: Preliminary data. *Research and People with Severe Disabilities, 37*(3), 160-169.

Zablotsky, B., Black, L. I., Maenner, M. J., Schieve, L. A., & Blumberg, S. J. (2015). Estimated prevalence of autism and other developmental disabilities following questionnaire changes in the 2014 National Health Interview Survey. *National Health Statistics Reports, 87*, 1-20.

About the Authors

Hung Jen Kuo, PhD, CRC, LPC, is Assistant Professor of the Rehabilitation Services Program at California State University, Los Angeles. He received his PhD in Rehabilitation Counselor Education at Michigan State University. Before coming to Cal State LA, he was a faculty member of the Rehabilitation Counseling Program at Michigan State University. Research interests of Dr. Kuo include promoting evidence-based practices and improving quality of life for people with disabilities. Currently, Dr. Kuo is involved in projects concerning educational interventions for transition-age individuals with Autism Spectrum Disorders. Also, he is involved in projects using technology to promote quality of life for individuals with neurodevelopmental disabilities.

Frances W. Siu, PhD, CRC, is Associate Professor and Coordinator of the undergraduate Rehabilitation Services Program at California State University, Los Angeles. She received her PhD in Special Education and Counseling, option in Rehabilitation Counselor Education, from the University of Texas at Austin. Research interests of Dr. Siu include medical aspects of disability, multicultural issues, and violence against people with disabilities. She has published over 35 articles and book chapters, and given over 70 professional presentations on violence against people with disabilities, rehabilitation education, and rehabilitation services.

Jessica H. Franco, PhD, CCC-SLP, BCBA-D, is Clinical Assistant Professor in the Department of Communication Sciences and Disorders at the University of Texas at Austin. Dr. Franco has focused her clinical practice and research on assessment and treatment of children with autism spectrum disorders. She has experience with a variety of evidenced-based approaches for teaching communication skills and methods for reducing severe challenging behaviors. Dr. Franco was the founding Executive Director of Autism Community Network. Within the community, she is involved with many autism-related committees, organizations, and agencies.

Chapter 27

ORTHOTICS, AMPUTATION, AND PROSTHETICS

Lance R. Clawson, BS, CPO
Martin G. Brodwin, PhD, CRC

Introduction

Orthotics and prosthetics are devices designed to support and/or replace compromised or missing parts of the body. While orthotics (orthoses), commonly referred to as braces, are designed to support, stabilize, and assist compromised segments of the body, prosthetics (prostheses), most often referred to as artificial limbs, are designed to replace the function of missing segments of the body.

This chapter is divided into five sections which describe the history of orthotics and prosthetics, different types of orthotics and limitations, amputation and complications, prosthetics, and assistive technology and work. The chapter concludes with a case study.

History of Orthotics and Prosthetics

The study of prosthetics has been closely associated with amputation surgery performed as a lifesaving measure from the aftermath of war. Injured soldiers who returned home from battle with traumatic amputations utilized primitive wooden prostheses. Each major war has been a stimulus for the improvement of amputation surgical techniques, and for the development of improved prostheses.

The most significant contributions to prosthetic/orthotic sciences occurred in the twentieth century. These contributions were stimulated by the aftermath of the first and second world wars as injured veterans increased the demand for services, as well as the polio epidemics of the late 1940s and early 1950s. To improve the quality and performance of assistive devices at the end of World War II, particularly for veterans with amputations, the United States government sponsored a series of research and development projects focused on human locomotion, biomechanics, and the development of new materials and devices (Lusardi, Jorge, & Nielsen, 2013).

By the 1980s, the introduction of new materials and methods spurred the profession of prosthetics and orthotics to rapidly evolve; by the 1990s, there were significant advances in the development of educational programs around orthotics and prosthetics (Fishman, 2001). Continued technological advancements in engineering and medicine have led to today's advanced prosthetics technology, which includes lighter, more intimately fitting, and computer-assisted brain implant controlled prostheses.

Orthotics

Each year, tens of thousands of Americans are affected by injuries and diseases that require orthotics to assist the healing process. Someone who fractures a finger may receive a splint from a physician; this splint constitutes a simple orthosis. Other types of simple braces are found at local pharmacies and sporting goods stores. When a simple support like one of these is insufficient, the physician typically prescribes an orthosis and directs the patient to an orthotist, a specialist in these devices.

Orthotic devices are divided into three categories that refer to the part of the body they are designed to support: lower extremity, upper extremity, and spinal. A fourth category includes all other assistive devices. These are further divided into the categories of acute, chronic, and assistive orthoses. Orthoses are categorized after the joint areas of the body the particular orthosis stabilizes or effects (see Table 1). A simple brace for the foot and ankle is referred to as an AFO (ankle-foot orthosis); one for the hand and wrist is called a WHO (wrist-hand orthosis). In the prescription for the orthosis, the physician indicates the type of motion to be limited, stabilized, or assisted, and the purpose of the device or goal to be achieved (e.g., greater strength, improved range of motion) (Lusardi et al., 2013).

TABLE 1
Categories of Orthoses

Ankle-Foot Orthosis	AFO
Knee-Ankle-Foot Orthosis	KAFO
Hip-Knee-Ankle-Foot Orthosis	HKAFO
Wrist-Hand Orthosis	WHO
Wrist-Driven Wrist-Hand Orthosis	WDWHO
Shoulder-Elbow Orthosis	SEO
Lumbosacral Orthosis	LSO
Thoraco-Lumbo-Sacral Orthosis	TLSO
Cervico-Thoraco-Lumbo-Sacral Orthosis	CTLSO

External Powered Orthoses

Externally powered orthoses, like their non-powered counterparts, improve and/or restore function, protect the affected part of the body, and contribute to the notion of neuroplasticization, or changes in neural pathways and synapses which result from injury. Externally powered orthoses have become a regular part of treating lower and upper extremity weakness, often in conjunction with managing tone and spasticity. They often are used to help manage a superficial electrical stimulus to cause the muscles to contract. An interface, much like the leads used for an EKG or EEG, is placed over the muscle and connected to the stimulus system. Stroke, peripheral nerve injuries, traumatic brain injury, and many other conditions have the potential for benefit from these devices. Bioness and Walk-Aid are two systems which utilize a superficial electrical stimulus to cause muscular contraction at or about the time the stimulated muscle would normally function (MIT News, 2017).

Lower Extremity Orthoses

Following an acute episode, like a stroke with resulting hemiplegia, the physician may prescribe a static or functional (dynamic) AFO or KAFO. An AFO can be designed to simply compensate for paralytic drop foot, preventing the foot from dragging during the swing phase of gait and to control the rate at which the forefoot contacts the ground. If more stability is needed, the AFO has a rigid ankle (at 90 degrees), thereby preventing the tibia and knee from collapsing forward in mid to late stance during walking. The same device can be designed with movement, such as with an articulating joint. If the knee also has significant weakness or instability, the orthosis may span another joint (the knee) proximally, becoming a KAFO.

A more recent development is a device called a high-tech orthotic leg brace. One example is a C-Brace, a customized electronic leg brace often referred to as a robotic knee. A C-Brace works with a computer microprocessor located adjacent to the mechanical knee joint, providing the individual with greater control of the affected leg. This is helpful for activities such as walking, stopping, and descending ramps and inclines. The microprocessor analyzes the joint stabilization required using accelerometers and ankle sensors, thereafter providing the appropriate resistance to knee flexion and extension. It is a fluid control unit which the microprocessor monitors to appropriate joint resistance when performing activities. When walking on declines, for example, there is joint resistance to prevent the knee from buckling. Research has shown that devices like these significantly improve some aspects of activities of daily living (ADLs). Studies also suggest that these devices improve the person's perceived mobility and safety (Probsting, Kannenberg, & Zacharias, 2017).

Upper Extremity Orthoses

The arm, hand, and fingers are significantly more complicated to design and fit with orthotic devices than the lower extremities. Sensation, dexterity, and function of the fingers and hand are crucial to ADLs and independence. Similar to the lower extremity, the hand and arm may be fit with a static or functional orthosis; a static orthosis is designed to maintain as functional a position as possible. With patients who have had stroke, there is typically less return of function in the upper extremity, and what motion does return is less than the return in the lower extremity. When muscle function begins to return, both static and functional devices are used and continually modified as the muscles slowly regain improved or normal function.

A person with quadriplegia (paralysis involving the four extremities), injured at the C-6 (sixth cervical) level, loses ability to close the hands. This loss of pinch and grasp is accommodated by use of a wrist driven wrist-hand orthosis (WDWHO) (Lusardi et al., 2013). Specialized upper extremity orthotic devices, such as the WDWHO, are used for specific levels of quadriplegia. Studies have shown that in some cases with training from an experienced physical therapist, an individual with C-6 quadriplegia is able to perform many functions otherwise thought impossible (Hamill, Carson, & Dorahy, 2010).

Spinal Orthoses

Spinal orthotic systems are used to decrease pain, provide support, and prevent or reduce unwanted motion in the spine. Simple designs are commonly found in sporting goods and hardware stores where an elastic waist belt with suspenders is used for abdominal/low back support during lifting and moving of heavy objects. While soft orthotic devices provide compression and support, rigid devices are designed to prevent or control unwanted motion; they are typically used after injury or following surgery. For example, after a spinal fusion, spinal orthoses allow the spine to heal or fuse in an optimal position (Murphy, 2014). Spinal braces are designated by the segment of the vertebral spine that needs to be stabilized and supported, such as lumbosacral orthosis (LSO) or thoracolumbosacral orthosis (TLSO).

Cervical vertebrae are more difficult to stabilize because there is little supportive structure; conversely, injuries to this part of the spine are common. The human head is heavy and rests atop the spine (the seven cervical vertebrae). The junction between the head and first vertebrae (C-1) provides the flexion and extension (up and down tilt) of the head. At the C-1 and C-2 articulation, a majority of the overall rotation is afforded with C-3 through T-1 (first thoracic vertebrae) contributing to flexion, extension, rotation, and lateral bending of the neck in smaller but proportional amounts.

One of the most common automobile crash injuries to the cervical spine that often requires an orthosis is whiplash (a snapping backward of the head). Someone who has suffered whiplash typically is helped by a soft collar that is designed to reduce the motion of the head. Depending on the injury, cervical orthoses, or collars, can be more extensive and rigid to further stabilize the head.

With severe injury, or when maximum cervical immobilization is needed, a device called a halo fixation device may be used, with or without associated surgery (See Figure 1). The halo, which holds the head in a functional position and protects the spine until sufficient strength returns to the muscles of the neck and shoulders, was developed by Dr. Jacqueline Perry at Rancho Los Amigos National Medical Center in Downey, California. Initially, it was designed to be used on polio patients whose neck muscles had been rendered so weak by the illness they could not hold their head erect. Today, halo devices are widely used to help stabilize the cervical region of the spinal cord after injury or surgery while the area heals (Lusardi et al., 2013).

FIGURE 1
Halo Fixture

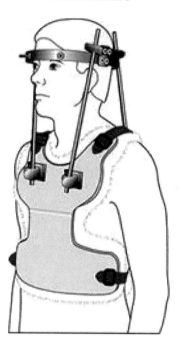

Source: University of Wisconsin Health. *Health facts for you: Using your halo orthotics at home.* (2011). University of Wisconsin Hospitals and Clinics Authority. Retrieved from http://www.uwhealth.org/healthfacts/b_extranet_health_information-flexmember-show_public_hffy_1126651619530.html

Other Assistive Devices

Beyond extensive orthotics, other assistive devices or aids help assist in movement while an injury is healing. They may be used on a permanent basis for support. These devices may be as basic as canes, crutches, and walkers or as particular as reachers, long-handled grippers, thickened writing implements, and adapted computer keyboards. Their purpose is to increase a person's daily activities, from dressing and grooming to eating, writing, and typing. Recent smart devices allow computer function to be achieved through verbal speech and commands.

Assistive devices include modifications to existing technology or equipment. Orthotists and prosthetists, being well acquainted with manufacturing and fabricating custom devices, are called upon to design and provide special assistive systems (Falvo & Holland, 2018). Automobiles, for example, can be modified to relocate the brake and gas pedals and provide hand controls, more extensive rear-view mirrors, and easy-to-open door handles. Extensive modifications and minivan conversions for almost any kind of disability can be provided (Brodwin, Siu, & Cardoso, 2018).

Unique devices may be formulated to provide specialized assistance for particular disabilities. Devices called mouth sticks, for example, are used by individuals with high-level paralysis (quadriplegia). The device has a portion made to fit into the mouth with a rod extending out to a point where a rubber tip is affixed. The person uses this device to push the buttons of a telephone, type on a keyboard, and perform other tasks. Special equipment is manufactured by certified orthotists that are only limited by the imagination and assessment skills of those involved (Cohen, Edelstein, Bayona, & Kort, 2017).

Psychological Limitations

Orthotic devices help minimize functional limitations, thus assisting people to overcome physical limitations. As a result, psychological and emotional concerns may diminish as well. Use of orthotic devices helps people obtain and maintain employment; one sees a positive impact on a person's emotional state.

Provision of orthotic devices helps with activities of daily living and independence, thus impacting self-esteem and confidence. Positive emotions can replace anxiety and depression, and help in adaptation to disability and loss.

Amputation

Amputation is the general term for loss of all or a portion of a body part. The loss can be congenital, the result of injury, or the outcome of a surgical procedure to treat disease (e.g., cancer). The loss of a limb is devastating to both the person and the family. An amputation causes changes in body image and functional capacity; much of this relates to a person's interpretation of the loss. Adaptation depends on the circumstances involving the amputation, usefulness of a prosthetic device, and the person's perception of the resulting disability (Cohen et al., 2017).

In cases of traumatic amputation, such as occurring in a vehicular accident or armed conflict, there is no time to prepare. Adjustment and adaptation become more difficult than for individuals who have had time to prepare for amputation, such as occurs with systemic illnesses (e.g., diabetes). A prosthesis can be perceived in a negative way by signifying loss, or in a more positive and productive manner as a means of restoring function, thereby diminishing limitations.

The majority of amputations within the United States are a result of poor arterial circulation caused by complications of diabetes. One long term adverse health effect caused by diabetes is a vasculopathy (poor blood circulation to peripheral tissues), occurring especially in the lower extremities, but also to nerves, retinas, heart, kidneys, bone, connective tissues, muscles, and the vascular system itself. As a result, over time, the tissues become malnourished, increasing their susceptibility to injury, infection, and necrosis. Commonly, the person who has diabetes loses sensation in a lower extremity at the most distal segment first, such as in the toes. Because of a potential unrecognized injury, the person is prone to infection (Kirkup, 2010).

Individuals in good control of their diabetes are less likely to have complications and, if they do, to a lesser degree. It is not likely that the person who has diabetes was healthy one day and requires an amputation the next. Diabetes is a chronic condition and a simple accident, such as a stubbed toe, may be all that is needed to cause an injury from which the body of a person with diabetes has difficulty healing. When infection sets in and complicates already diminished circulation, the wound becomes more extensive and lacks sufficient blood circulation and cellular metabolism to heal. Infection can become so severe that surgical amputation becomes necessary (Cohen et al., 2017; Edelstein & Moroz, 2011). If circulation continues to be impaired at a higher level, further surgery may be required.

Levels of Amputation

Lower Extremity

Amputations are classified according to their location relative to the nearest joint (see Figure 2). The lowest level is called a partial foot; as the name implies, it goes through a part of the foot. The next level up is referred to as a Syme and occurs through the ankle joint. Other levels include below the knee (BK) trans-tibial, knee disarticulation (KD), above the knee (AK) trans-femoral, and hip disarticulation (HD).

Upper Extremity

Amputations involving the upper extremities are likewise categorized relative to the nearest joint (see Figure 2). The lowest level involves removal of part of the hand or fingers and is called a partial hand amputation. If the amputation occurs at the wrist level, it is referred to as a wrist disarticulation (WD). Other levels include below the elbow (BE) trans-radial, elbow disarticulation (ED), above the elbow (AE) trans-humeral, and shoulder disarticulation (SD).

Complications of Amputation

Complications ranging from edema (swelling), ulceration, contracture, infection, vascular insufficiency, and pain at the site of a recent amputation (Murphy, 2014). Normally, a certain amount of

Figure 2
Levels of Typical Amputations

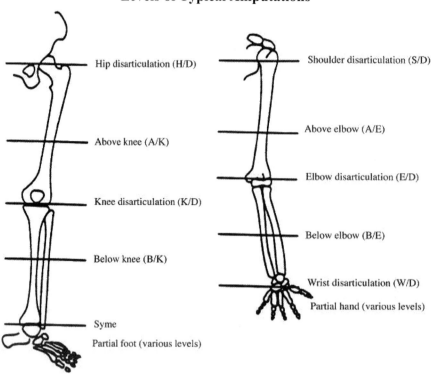

Source: Krajbich, J. I., Pinsur, M. S., Potter, B. K., & Stevens, P. M. (2018). *Atlas of amputations and limb deficiencies* (4th ed.). Philadelphia, PA: Wolters Kluer Health.

edema of the residual limb occurs following surgery; it has been found that immediate or early fitting of a prosthesis minimizes this swelling. If abnormal or excessive edema occurs the person is at risk for developing skin ulcers which require immediate medical attention and a new prosthetic socket with an appropriate fit. Hot and humid environments can exacerbate existing tissues and cause breakdown of the skin, resulting in fungal infection; dirt and lack of cleanliness in the area leads to potential infection.

Treatment for infection ranges from the use of antibiotics to possible surgical excision (Murphy, 2014). Another common complication of amputation is muscular contractures, which occur when an extremity is not used or because of blockage within a joint. This can happen either before the limb is surgically removed or after removal when the person does not use a prosthesis. Depending on severity, treatment includes exercise or surgery.

Phantom-limb sensation is a normal, painless occurrence for most people who have had amputation; people feel an awareness or kinesthetic sense of where the missing portion of the body is in space. However, a sensation of *pain* in a removed part is abnormal and known as *phantom-limb pain*. Unlike phantom-limb sensation, phantom-limb pain can be disabling and cannot always be relieved even through surgical intervention (Knotkova, Crucian, Tronnier, & Rasche, 2012). Still, researchers have noted a tendency for chronic phantom-limb pain to diminish over time (Murphy, 2014).

If severe, phantom-limb pain will interfere with a person's daily life and work. If the pain is chronic, it may warrant referral to a medical specialist, who may be able to provide surgical or non-surgical procedures to help alleviate the pain. While phantom-limb pain may seem "not real," clinicians should *never* tell patients that the pain is "in their head." In reality, all pain is in the head - the brain decodes electrochemical stimuli through nerves as tickle, itch, pressure, hot, cold, or pain. Much like "real" limb pain, patients with phantom limb pain often indicate that their phantom-limb experience is worse at night.

At nighttime, there are no distractions as life activities have paused and pain may be the only stimulus. Whether phantom limb pain or real limb pain, the patient hurts, and unaddressed pain can lead to emotional and interpersonal complications (Falvo & Holland, 2018). The following section describes lower and upper extremity prostheses.

Prosthetics

Lower Extremity Prosthesis

Physical implications of amputation are dependent not only on the loss itself, but also on how the person adapts to that loss. The more proximal the amputation, the greater the functional loss and the more challenging the fitting of a prosthesis. A lower extremity prosthesis can be transformational as it can enable a person to transfer, stand, and walk. As a result of increasing ability to ambulate, an individual may be capable of more extensive work. Still, there are challenges, including walking on uneven surfaces, rough terrain, and inclines/declines as well as pushing, pulling, and stair climbing.

Activities are easier to perform with an amputation below-the-knee (BK) as only the ankle joint is missing. An individual with a BK amputation generally expends 10% to 37% more energy for walking (Cohen et al., 2017; Murphy, 2014). With an above-the-knee (AK) amputation, both the ankle and knee joints are artificial, making standing and walking more challenging and energy consuming. Since a person with an AK amputation expends 60% more energy walking, some people choose to use wheelchairs for ambulation to save energy for work and other activities (Cohen et al.). The less standing and walking a job involves, the more energy the person retains for other functions.

Advanced prosthetics technology has led to development of lighter, more comfortably fitting, and technologically efficient lower extremity prostheses. The C-leg system is the first completely microprocessor-controlled prosthetic knee/shin system with hydraulic swing and stance phase control (MIT News, 2017). This product is so revolutionary that individuals who have been fitted with the device often state that the most obvious benefit is they do not have to think consciously about walking. This occurs because the advanced microprocessor control does the thinking for them (Murphy, 2014).

Lower extremity prosthetics with microprocessor-controlled ankle and knee joints are increasingly common. The microprocessor joint system significantly reduces the energy demands of walking and even allows users to walk down stairs, ramps, and other previously difficult terrains without the risk of knee flexion collapse. Previously, this would cause the patient to fall (Young, Stiens, O'Young, Baldwin, & Thatcher, 2017). Since 1997, several manufacturers have developed microprocessor controlled knees that address the same goals as the C-Leg (Edelstein & Moroz, 2011). More advanced microprocessor controlled systems have resulted in an ability to walk up stairs step-over-step also involving active propulsion at the knee (Ossur power knee) and at the ankle (biOM foot).

There are several varieties of microprocessor-controlled prosthetic ankles as prosthetic options. These technologies allow the patient to walk on inclines and declines with the ankle accommodating for the terrain such that the wearer perceives the same forces as though walking on level ground. An individual with two lower extremity prostheses has a more difficult time walking and standing and frequently uses a wheelchair for extended periods or distances of mobility. Many persons become proficient with two lower extremity prostheses and are able to ambulate with use of a cane or other assistive devices (Murphy, 2014). Light or sedentary work not involving significant amounts of standing and walking may be found appropriate for a worker with bilateral lower extremity limb loss.

Upper Extremity Prosthesis

An upper extremity prosthesis is designed to help increase a person's manual dexterity, bilateral dexterity, and allow for more complex tasks requiring both hands. These devices are often specially designed and fabricated to meet specific needs; specialized devices can be made and used solely for particular job functions.

Electronic hand technology has progressed significantly within the past 15 years. While more basic devices like hook terminal devices allow for grasping, gripping, lifting, and carrying, devices that allow for simultaneous function, where combinations of motions can be done at the same time, are available. Previous control systems involved skin surface sensors (electrodes) placed over the belly of the controlling muscle. Today, surgeons can implant the sensors directly into the controlling muscle. In some instances, surgeons can even implant electrode sensors into the brain so that the thought of flexing or extending an elbow, opening or closing a hand or finger, results in that very motion (MIT News, 2017; Murphy, 2014).

In some cases, devices like these enable the fingers and thumbs to be programmed to function independently. One example of an advanced prosthetic involving targeted muscle reinnervation is the i-LIMB prosthetic hand, which has motorized digits allowing the prosthetic hand to bend at the joints of each digit. It provides a grip strength, allowing a person to perform such activities as opening jars, holding and carrying a suitcase, and typing. The person "thinks" the action prompting the chest nerves to react. As of 2017, only 35 people worldwide had these particular prosthetic upper extremities; the technology is still being developed and researchers believe it is currently in its infancy stage (MIT News, 2017).

Another area of future research is muscle grafting, which is currently being studied in laboratory rats. The concept with muscle grafting involves creating an interface between the muscles and the nerves that allows the brain to send signals to a grafted muscle, which then contracts and initiates movement in the muscle with which it has been paired. The grafted muscles work together in tandem, with one contracting while the other is stretching. Current experiments on rats suggest that this technique could allow for fine-grained control of a human prosthetic, but more research is needed. Human trials are expected within two years (MIT News, 2017). The common goal is to allow prosthetic limbs to feel more natural and help people sense where the limb is in space, as well as to feel how much force is being applied.

Functional or cosmetic hands can be used instead of hook devices. The old style functional hand has a three-finger pinch, grasp, and hold action, but lacks the power and stability of a hook. Many current hand technologies have remedied that earlier deficiency. Cosmetic hands are used primarily for social purposes, as they resemble a natural hand in color, tones, and texture. A more sophisticated device is the external power myoelectric arm and hand.

The *myoelectric arm* is computerized and contains electrodes that are placed on the skin over muscles. Electrical impulses from the muscles allow the person to open and close the hand simply by tensing the particular muscles normally involved. Although the myoelectric arm has the appearance of an actual arm and hand, it is not usually prescribed due to the expense (Edelstein & Moroz, 2011).

Psychological Considerations

People with amputation almost always make a variety of permanent behavioral, social, and emotional adjustments to cope with the various problems and issues presented with loss of a limb (Falvo & Holland, 2018). The emotional impact of amputation of any body part is devastating; many experience feelings which include anger, depression, resentment, fear, and withdrawal. Helpful interventions involve the early fitting of a prosthesis, which helps hasten the adjustment period.

Prompt intervention by a rehabilitation counselor makes adjustment and adaptation less traumatic; the focus is shifted from loss to the efforts required to be able to return to work. It is important to remember that a prosthesis is a tool. It increases capabilities and helps minimize limitations, thereby making emotional adjustment easier. The prosthesis provides the person with a feeling of wholeness.

There are a plethora of emotions associated with amputation, many of which are founded on facts and involve cultural perceptions. These effects are influenced by many factors, including the timing of the amputation and the person's emotional support network (Hamill et al., 2010). There is a naturally occurring grieving process involving loss of a part of the body that is similar to the stages of death and dying identified by Dr. Elizabeth Kübler-Ross (1969). These stages include: (a) denial and isolation, (b) anger (rage, envy, and resentment), (c) bargaining, (d) depression, and finally, (e) acceptance or adaptation. Not all people go through these stages in the order listed, nor does everyone experience each stage. Some never reach the final stage. Feelings of hope often persist through all these stages and are a positive indication of emotional recovery. In most people, a gradual transition takes place from the first four negative stages to the final positive stage – acceptance or adaptation.

Family Involvement

Family counseling is usually made available to help with adaptation to a newly acquired disability and the process of rehabilitation. The family can help the person with the grieving process by assisting in adaptation to loss and changed body image. Capability of the family to provide emotional support is invaluable (Hamill et al., 2010). Yet, one must be aware that excessive attention can be dysfunctional to the person's full recovery. Psychological health improves as one adjusts and again begins to enjoy activities and social relationships.

Sexuality and Intimacy

Amputation negatively affects one's self-concept, body image, and self-perception, and as a result impacts sexuality as well. This is one of the reasons recovery - not just from the physical effects of amputation but also from its psychological effects - is crucial. Over time, people with disabilities become better able to engage in intimate relationships (Brodwin & Frederick, 2010; Connell, Coats, & Wood, 2015). When reviewing ongoing relationships, Falvo and Holland (2018) stated that "the stability of the relationship prior to amputation as well as communication and understanding are important components to adjustment and, consequently, to the quality of the relationship" (p. 437).

Employment Issues

Lower Extremity

Individuals with lower extremity amputations may find that the physical demands of work (walking, standing, lifting, and carrying) need to be modified. For an employee with a lower extremity amputation, use of a wheeled cart for transporting material, a backpack for smaller items, powered carts or scooters for greater mobility, and minimizing the need for reaching up, reaching behind, bending down, and squatting is helpful. These actions are difficult to perform with a prosthesis and also involve energy expenditure (Brodwin, Parker, & De La Garza, 2010).

Often, the overall amounts of standing and walking need to be decreased as moving around with a prosthesis requires substantially more energy. Climbing, squatting, and kneeling can also be difficult or impossible to perform (Cohen et al., 2017).

Upper Extremity

People with upper extremity amputation lose a significant amount of manual dexterity, even with the use of a prosthesis. Because of the absence of feeling and sensation in the prosthetic device, function is further limited. Hooks, prosthetic hands, and other terminal devices only partially substitute for the wide variety of movements and functions of a human hand. Still, an upper extremity prosthesis helps to increase manual dexterity, bilateral dexterity, eye-hand coordination, gripping, grasping, lifting, and carrying. Although a prosthesis does not replace a fully functional arm, wrist, and hand, it does allow a worker to perform many essential tasks. A workstation with appropriate accommodation and modification is immensely helpful.

Workplace Accommodation

Employers who understand chronic pain (i.e., phantom-limb pain) are more willing to consider possible accommodations. Accommodations for chronic pain are as variable as chronic pain itself. For this reason, people with chronic pain need individualized attention and case management services.

Through careful evaluation of needs, limitations, strengths, and an awareness of functioning and the kinds of accommodations and assistive devices available, rehabilitation counselors can enhance the employability of clients who have amputations. Counselors should always remember the emotional trauma that has occurred and its impact on the total functioning of the individual within the home environment, at the workplace, in school, as well as socially.

Activities are easier to perform with an amputation below-the-knee (BK) as only the ankle joint is missing. An individual with a BK amputation generally expends 10% to 37% more energy for walking (Cohen et al., 2017; Murphy, 2014). With an above-the-knee (AK) amputation, both the ankle and knee joints are artificial, making standing and walking more challenging and energy consuming. Since a person with an AK amputation expends 60% more energy walking, some people choose to use wheelchairs for ambulation to save energy for work and other activities (Cohen et al.). The less excess standing and walking a job involves, the more energy the person retains for other functions.

Advanced prosthetics technology has led to development of lighter, more comfortably fitting, and technologically efficient lower extremity prostheses. As stated, the C-leg system is the first completely microprocessor-controlled prosthetic knee/shin system with hydraulic swing and stance phase control (MIT News, 2017). This product is so revolutionary that individuals who have been fitted with the device often state that the most obvious benefit is that they do not have to think consciously about walking. This occurs because the advanced microprocessor control does the thinking for them (Murphy, 2014).

Medicare Functional Levels

Medicare has established definitions for functional levels of lower extremity amputation. These five levels are described below.

- Level 0 - Patient does not have the ability or potential to benefit functionally from a prosthesis.
- Level I - Person has the ability or potential to use a prosthesis functionally for transfers or ambulation on level surfaces at a fixed cadence. This level is typical of the limited and unlimited household ambulator.
- Level II - Individual has the ability or potential for functional ambulation with the ability to traverse low-level environmental barriers such as curbs, stairs, and uneven surfaces. Level II is appropriate for the limited community ambulator.
- Level III - Patient has the ability or potential for functional ambulation with variable cadence. This level is used for the community ambulator who has the capability to traverse most environmental barriers and has vocational, therapeutic, and exercise activity that demands prosthetic utilization beyond simple ambulation.
- Level IV - Person has the ability or potential for functional prosthetic ambulation that exceeds basic ambulation skills, exhibiting high impact, stress, or energy levels. Level IV is appropriate for the prosthetic demands of a child, active adult, or athlete.

According to Medicare, the reason for these levels is to set a standard for which types of component parts are appropriate, based on the individual's projected needs.

Conclusion – Assistive Technology and the Workplace

Assistive technology (AT) is defined in the Technology-Related Assistance for Individuals with Disabilities Act of 1988 (popularly referred to as *The Tech Act*) as "any item, piece of equipment, or product system, whether acquired commercially off the shelf, modified, or customized, that is used to increase, maintain, or improve the functional capabilities of individuals with disabilities." The goal of AT is to increase the functional independence for people who have disabilities. This is continuing to have a profound impact on improving the lives and employment opportunities of many people (Young et al., 2017).

AT is an effective and powerful tool to help restore someone's functioning, enhance his or her quality of life, and remove or reduce physical and attitudinal barriers. Rehabilitation counselors attempt to maximize this independence at the workplace (Brodwin et al., 2010). Through the use of modern-day orthotics and prosthetics, AT enables workers with upper or lower extremity limitations to reduce and perhaps minimize their functional limitations.

Through orthotic and prosthetic devices, rehabilitation counselors have seen their clients achieve greater productivity within education and employment, leading to enhanced self-sufficiency, independence, freedom to choose, and social reintegration. Many workers can continue working, return to work, or secure alternative employment following a disabling event. With the provision of orthotic and prosthetic devices, they are able to participate more fully and actively in all aspects of life. Technology helps equalize the capacities of employees with disabilities when compared to workers without limitations. Greater independence and satisfaction in daily life, including both work and leisure, become enhanced (Edelstein & Moroz, 2011). With daily use of orthotic and prosthetic devices, a person's emotional outlook also is improved (Brodwin et al., 2018).

Case Study

Paulette Abbott is 43 years old, born and raised in the United States. She has a law degree and, for the past 15 years, has worked in a law firm where she writes contracts for business entities. Last year, Paulette was involved in a skiing accident which resulted with a BK amputation. The accident also left her with a weakened ability to grip and grasp (50% loss) with her right dominant hand. Ms. Abbott is devastated with the loss of her leg and difficulty in performing daily tasks. As a single professional woman, she has always been independent and is having a difficult time adjusting to the new level of dependency. Paulette experiences a moderate amount of phantom-limb pain, but when she brought this up to her initial physician was told that the pain was in her head. Recently, Ms. Abbott has been on medical leave from work and is in a deep depression.

A month ago, Paulette began seeing a different treating physician who has an understanding of phantom-limb pain. With this newfound support and knowledge that the pain is real, she began attending therapy sessions to work through the depression and has gained the desire to return to work. Through therapy and at the suggestion of her physician, Ms. Abbott has decided to be fitted for a prosthesis. Her previous employer is willing to welcome Paulette back to work, but is inexperienced with the type of accommodations that may be needed.

Questions

1. Discuss Dr. Elizabeth Kübler-Ross' stages of death and dying from the standpoint of adjustment to disability. Relate this discussion to this case study and the role of the rehabilitation counselor.
2. Describe the various levels of amputation, the functional limitations at each level, and psychosocial implications. Relate these limitations to school, work, and social activities.
3. What are Ms. Abbott's functional limitations as related to future employment? Will she be able to drive an automobile? Discuss the psychosocial factors relevant to this case.
4. What types of accommodations would you suggest for her employer, and what assurances can you provide them that she will still be able to complete her work tasks?
5. Paulette is having great difficulty with adjustment to her disability and the phantom pain. As her counselor, offer recommendations in regard to these two conditions. Discuss both phantom-limb sensation and phantom-limb pain.

References

Brodwin, M. G., & Frederick, P. C. (2010). Sexuality and societal beliefs regarding persons living with disabilities. *Journal of Rehabilitation, 76*(4), 37-41.

Brodwin, M. G., Parker, R. M., & DeLaGarza, D. (2010). Disability and reasonable accommodation. In E. M. Szymanski & R. M. Parker (Eds.), *Work and disability: Contexts, issues, and strategies for enhancing employment opportunities for people with disabilities* (3rd ed., pp. 281-323). Austin, TX: Pro-ed.

Brodwin, M. G., Siu, F. W., & Cardoso, E. (2018). Users of assistive technology: The human component. In I. Marini & M. Stebnicki (Eds.), *The psychological and social impact of disability* (7th ed., pp. 345-353). New York, NY: Springer.

Cohen, J. M., Edelstein, J. E., Bayona, C. & Kort, C. J. (2017). Limb deficiency. In A. Moroz, S. R. Flanagan, & H. H. Zaretsky (Eds.), *Medical aspects of disability for the rehabilitation professional* (5th ed., pp. 383-414). New York, NY: Springer.

Connell, K. M., Coats, P. & Wood, F. M. (2015). Sexuality following traumatic injury: A literature review. *Burns and Trauma, 2*(2), 61-70.

Edelstein, J. E., & Moroz, A. (2011). *Lower-limb prosthetics and orthotics: Clinical concepts.* Thorofare, NJ: Slack.

Falvo, D. R., & Holland, B. E. (2018). *Medical and psychosocial aspects of chronic illness and disability* (6th ed.). Burlington, MD: Jones and Bartlett Learning.

Fishman, S. (2001). The professionalization of orthotics and prosthetics. *Orthotics and Prosthetics Business News, 10*, 24-30.

Hamill, R., Carson, S., & Dorahy, M. (2010). Experiences of psychosocial adjustment within 18 months of amputation: An interpretive phenomenological approach. *Disability Rehabilitation, 32*(9), 729-740.

Kirkup, J. R. (2010). *A history of limb amputation.* London, England: Springer.

Knotkova, H., Crucian, R. A., Tronnier, V. M., & Rasche, D. (2012). Current and future options for the management of phantom limb pain. *Journal of Pain Research, 5*, 39-49.

Krajbich, J. I., Pinsur, M. S., Potter, B. K., & Stevens, P. M. (2018). *Atlas of amputations and limb deficiencies* (4th ed.). Philadelphia, PA: Wolters Kluer Health.

Kübler-Ross, E. (1969). *On death and dying.* New York, NY: McMillan.

Lusardi, M. M., Jorge, M., & Nielsen, C. C. (2013). *Orthotics and prosthetics in rehabilitation* (3rd ed.). St. Louis, MO: Elsevier Saunders.

MIT (Massachusetts Institute of Technology) News. (2017). *Making prosthetic limbs feel more natural.* Retrieved from http://www.news.mit.edu/2017/making-prosthetic-limbs-feel-more-natural-0531

Murphy, D. E. (2014). *Fundamentals of amputation care and prosthetics.* New York, NY: Demos Medical.

Probsting, E., Kannenberg, & Zacharias, B. (2017). Safety and walking ability of KAFO users with the C-Brace Orthotronic Mobility System, a new microprocessor stance, and swing control orthosis. *Prosthetics and Orthotics International, 41*(1), 65-77.

Technology-Related Assistance for Individuals with Disabilities Act of 1988, 29 U. S. C. § 2201 *et seq.*

University of Wisconsin Health. (2011). *Health facts for you: Using your halo orthotics at home.* University of Wisconsin Hospitals and Clinics Authority. Retrieved from http://www.uwhealth.org/healthfacts/b_extranet_health_information-flexmember-show_public_hffy_1126651619530.html

Young, M. A., Stiens, S. A., O'Young, B., Baldwin, R., & Thatcher, B. N. (2017). Assistive technology: Adaptive tools of enablement for multiple disabilities. In A. Moroz, S. R. Flanagan, & H. H. Zaretsky (Eds.), *Medical aspects of disability and the rehabilitation professional* (5th ed., pp. 697-712). New York, NY: Springer.

About the Authors

Lance R. Clawson, BS, CPO, received his prosthetics and orthotics education at California State University, Dominguez Hills. In 1987, he completed a prosthetics residency at Rancho Los Amigos National Medical Center in Downey, California, and an orthotics residency at San Bernardino County Hospital. Mr. Clawson is an American Board Certified Prosthetist/Orthotist, and President and CEO of J & K Orthopedics, Inc., in Pomona and Covina, California.

Martin G. Brodwin, PhD, CRC, is Professor Emeritus in the Rehabilitation Education Programs at California State University, Los Angeles. He is a vocational expert for the Office of Hearings Operations, Social Security Administration, providing testimony on disability-related issues. As a rehabilitation and vocational consultant, he provides assessment for long-term disability, case management, and reasonable accommodation. Dr. Brodwin has published over 115 refereed journal articles, book chapters, and books on the subjects of counseling, disability, rehabilitation, and medical aspects of chronic illness and disability.

Chapter 28

SOCIETAL REINTEGRATION FOLLOWING A BURN INJURY

Cindy Rutter, RN, MS
Ann Malo, RN
James Bosch, LMFT

MY SKIN
Nobody sees what I see
For back of my eyes there is only me
And nobody knows how my thoughts begin
For there's only myself inside my skin
Isn't it strange how everyone owns
Just enough skin to cover their bones
The scars that I wear seem a little unfair
Because there's nobody like me anywhere
Author Unknown

Introduction

Each year, over two million Americans suffer from burn injuries (American Burn Association [ABA], 2016). Of these, 486,000 receive medical treatment, either in a hospital or emergency room. These injuries are the result of fires in homes, vehicle crash fires, and other events, such as smoke inhalation, contact with electricity, scalding liquids, or hot objects. Between 2005 and 2014, 97% of people admitted to burn centers survived. Seventy-three percent of these burns occurred in the home, 8% were occupational, 5% happened on the street/highway, 5% were the result of recreational accidents, 9% had other or unknown causes. Over 60% of the estimated United States acute hospitalizations related to burn injury were admitted to 128 burn centers. Almost two-thirds of hospital admitted burn patients were White. Another 20% were Black, while 14% were Latino (ABA).

Risk factors associated with burn injuries are gender (male), age (children), minority race/ethnicity, lower socio-economic status, tobacco smoking, drug use, and unsafe heating practices. More burn injuries occur during holidays. While some burns are accidental, others result from child abuse, self-inflicted injuries, and assault. This chapter discusses burn classifications, complications, treatment, psychological challenges, post-traumatic stress disorder (PTSD), and recovery. Also described are reintegration to life and society, loving relationships following burns, intimacy and sexuality, and information on the Phoenix Society for Burn Injury Survivors.

Caring for a patient who has suffered a burn injury requires a multidisciplinary team approach, and can require months and sometimes years of surgeries, recovery, and rehabilitation. It is a continuum of care that needs active therapy from surgery for skin grafting, pain management, nutritional care, physical therapy, occupation therapy, and psychological intervention.

Classification of Burns

Skin consists of multiple layers as seen in Figure 1.

FIGURE 1
Layers of the Skin

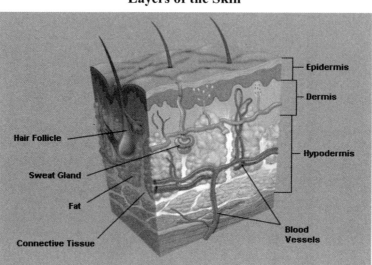

Source: WebMD. (2018). *An overview of the skin.* Retrieved from http://www.webmd.com/beauty/wrinkles/cosmetic-procedures-overview-skin

Burns are classified according to the depth of the burn within the tissue. A first degree, or superficial burn, such as sunburn, affects only the epidermis (top layer) of the skin. Second degree, or partial thickness burns, damage both the epidermis and dermis layers. Third degree, or full thickness burns, involves damage to the epidermis, dermis, hypodermis, hair follicles, sweat glands, fat, connective tissue, and blood vessels. The most severe burn is a fourth degree burn, in which a burn is so deep that internal organs are damaged as well. An inhalation burn, for example, causes damage to the lung tissue due to the inhalation of smoke or damaging chemicals. Fourth degree burns can necessitate amputations and may lead to organ failure (WebMD, 2018).

Burn injuries are not only classified by their depth; also relevant is the percentage of the body burned. This is referred to as a *total body surface area* (TBSA). Generally, for every 1% of body burned, a patient will require one day of hospitalization. While first degree burns do not require hospitalization, second degree burns may need skin grafting; third and fourth degree burns always require skin grafts (Tufaro & Houng, 2017). Physicians use a medical device, called a *dermatome*, to take skin, a procedure in which an area where the patient has not been burned (called a donor site) is placed over the burn area and sutured or stapled in place.

Complications

The skin is the largest body organ; it protects the body in multiple ways. After a severe burn, the physician determines the ultimate prognosis for the burn patient by multiple factors: the extent of the burn and loss of skin, mechanism of injury, patient's age, and presence and severity of other medical issues.

When burns heal, hypertrophic scars may form. This is characterized by raised erythematous (red) borders with significant distinctions from normal texture (Tufaro & Houng, 2018). Hypertrophic scars occur when the body overproduces collagen, causing the skin to be raised above the surrounding skin. The

FIGURE 2
Body Burn Percentage

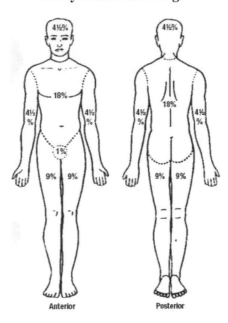

Source: Retrieved from: https://www.uwhealth.org/emergency-room/assessing-burns-and-planning-resuscitation-the-rule-of-nines/12698

occurrence of hypertrophic scars ranges between 4% and 75% of all burn scars. There is no clear medical explanation of why this occurs in some people and not in others. During scarring, the skin can become thick, dry, and discolored. In hypertrophic scarring, patients develop thick, red, raised, and sometimes ropelike scars that remain within the boundary of the injury. Keloids occur when the body continues to produce tough, fibrous protein known as collagen after a wound has healed. Keloid scarring involves thick, raised, itchy clusters of scar tissue that grow beyond the edges of the wound or incision, very often red or darker in color than the surrounding skin. Burns can also cause changes in the shape of body parts depending on the damage done to the underlying tissue or body parts.

Burns may cause other physical problems as well. These include contractures (abnormal shortening of muscle tissue), when a scar is located over a joint. Consequences of contractures include severe acute or chronic pain, nerve damage, and loss of the ability to regulate heat and cold in that area. Other problems include the inability to sweat in the affected area, and chronic itching.

Treatment

Many burn patients are required to wear pressure garments for up to a year after their injuries. These garments help control scarring by compressing the scar tissue, allowing it to heal faster with less scarring. The garment pictured below is used on the hand and part of the lower arm.

When the survival rate for burn patients was much lower, physicians focused on the physical and rehabilitative stages of care. Today, when individuals with burns covering as much as 95% of the body are able to survive, physicians and caregivers can focus not only on physical care, but also on the psychological aspects. In addition to physical pain, burn patients experience depression, anxiety, and post-traumatic stress disorder (PTSD). They may have negative body image, lower self-esteem, guilt, grief, and issues encompassing sexuality and intimacy.

Severe acute or chronic pain interfere with a patient's physical and psychological healing. Depending on the patient, pain can cause depression and feelings of hopelessness (pain is different for each individual). As

FIGURE 3
Pressure Garment

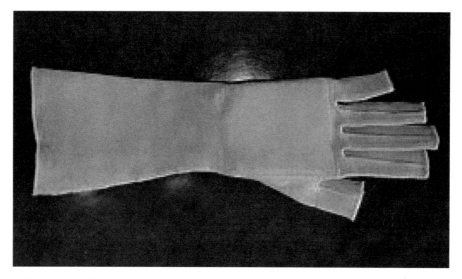

Source: Pratt, J., & West, G. (1995). *Pressure garments: A manual on their design and fabrication*. Oxford, England: Butterworth-Heinemann.

a result, it requires continuous assessment. Medication is only one treatment modality to alleviate pain. Alternative methods for pain relief include relaxation techniques, meditation, yoga, and music/art therapy. In conjunction with pain medication, the following methods can improve a patient's quality of life.

Immediately after suffering a burn, a patient may need multiple surgical procedures. Additionally, some patients require multiple reconstructive surgeries, a process which may span years. Some require years of physical and occupational therapy, and others may never return to their pre-injury functioning. In the case of amputations, still more complications arise. "A burn injury is a lifelong process" (Jill Sproul [nurse manager], personal communication, August 15, 2013).

Persons with severe burn injuries are generally cared for in hospital burn units. The ABA establishes guidelines for treatment and determines when a burn patient will be transferred depending on the field assessment by Emergency Medical Services. In providing care to burn patients, health care providers must consider the person's existing psychosocial support, insurance, and financial resources. Issues include concern over family, especially children, insurance, employment, housing, and coping with the losses that accompany burn injuries.

Once a patient is discharged from the hospital, family members may have to take on additional responsibilities to care for the family member, such as changing dressings. This is difficult as the procedure continues to be painful and personal. While healthcare providers can help teach family members how to change a patient's dressings, it does not alleviate the loved one's discomfort.

Psychological Challenges

Many burn survivors ask caregivers if they will ever be like they were before. The reality is that survivors have to adjust to a new image given all the changes they have had and will face in the future. They must reassess priorities and learn to establish new ones. Patients recovering from burns are often concerned with maintaining relationships with family and friends (Gilboa, 2001). It takes determination, perseverance, and courage for an individual to journey through and recover from a severe burn injury.

The fact that burns affect the physical, emotional, and spiritual well-being of an individual means that their psychological well-being is impacted on all levels. The physical devastation to the body creates feelings of despair and often isolation. For major burns, recovery and hospitalization is lengthy and painful.

Managing pain and the frustration of the slow process of surgeries and rehabilitation can lead to depression, hopelessness, and emotional exhaustion. The initial trauma often brings a flood of support and then as the long rehabilitation continues support becomes overwhelming or people just go back to their lives and visit less often. Many times, loved ones and friends feel awkward or afraid to confront the drastic changes that have happened to the patient's life and appearance.

Emotional distress is a normal response to a devastating trauma. If a patient does not have emotional stability before the injury or if the nature of the accident had multiple factors, such as injury or death of others, property loss, and circumstances such as an intentional or neglectful burn by a loved one for example, the natural process of emotional recovery can become blocked and arrested. The patient may develop symptoms of an anxiety disorder or a post-traumatic stress disorder.

Post-Traumatic Stress Disorder (PTSD)

Symptoms of PTSD disrupt an individual's life and make it hard to continue with daily activities. It may be difficult just to get through the day. There are four types of symptoms of PTSD:

1. Reliving the event (also called re-experiencing symptoms). Memories of the traumatic event can return at any time. The person may feel the same fear and horror as when the event occurred. An example is the repeated experience of nightmares.
2. Avoiding situations that remind one of the event. Seeing, hearing, or smelling may cause a reliving of the event. These are referred to as triggers. News reports, seeing an accident, or hearing a car backfire are examples of possible triggers.
3. Negative changes in beliefs and feelings. The way one thinks about himself or herself changes as a result of the trauma. This symptom has many aspects. These include: (a) avoiding positive or negative feelings toward others and avoiding relationships: (b) forgetting parts of the traumatic event and an inability to speak about it, and (c) thinking that the world is completely dangerous and no one can be trusted.
4. Hyperarousal. Having difficulty sleeping, trouble concentrating, having a startle response to loud noise or surprises, and always having one's back to a wall, such as in a restaurant or waiting room.

Recovery

There are an abundance of potential resources to aid in the recovery process (Acton, Mounsey, & Gilyard, 2007). One can view the stages of recovery (sometimes referred to as the journey through the burn injury) as (a) the acute in-hospital care and physical recovery, (b) rehabilitation after discharge from the hospital, and (c) reintegration to life and society.

When a loved one has been injured, family members are also affected. They too go through stages or phases of recovery or adjustment. . In the journal, *Burn Care and Rehabilitation*, Watkins, Cook, May, and Ehleben (1998) outlined what a normal psychological healing process might look like for burn survivors. The seven stages include (1) Survival Anxiety, (2) The Problem of Pain, (3) The Search for Meaning, (4) Investment in Recuperation, (5) Acceptance of Losses, (6) Investment in Rehabilitation, and (7) Reintegration into Society.

A second model, described by Herman (1997), outlined the psychological recovery and reclaiming of personal power following a burn injury. The three phases are (a) Recovering a Sense of Safety, (b) Remembering, Telling One's Story, and Mourning, and (c) Reconnecting with Life. Patients and family members may go through these stages and phases at different times and in no particular order.

Survivors Offering Assistance to Recovery (SOAR)

Survivors Offering Assistance to Recovery is a program designed by the Phoenix Society (Phoenix Society for Burn Survivors, 2018) for survivors and family members so they may offer one-on-one support to burn survivors and loved ones affected by burn injuries. This program is beneficial for the patient, as well as the family. Oftentimes, it is a family member who needs help first; the patient may be too involved with struggling to survive.

The Phoenix Society and the American Burn Association have formed a committee to help develop standards accessible for all burn survivors to have help with their reintegration into life. The Aftercare Reintegration Committee (ARC) includes burn survivors, family members, nurses, physicians, occupational and physical therapists, counselors, and social workers. Together, members of ARC help survivors and family members move forward.

Reintegration to Life and Society

Once burn survivors begin the process of reintegrating into the public sphere, they face a variety of challenges (Blakeney, Rosenberg, Rosenberg, & Faber, 2008). Many survivors experience negative feelings from the public, including staring, question asking, teasing, bullying, avoiding, name-calling, and discrimination. This can be overwhelming. Survivors may feel anxious and unsure how to react. The Behavioral & Enhancement Skills Tools (BEST) developed by Quayle (Kammerer-Quayle, 2002) helps survivors develop skills to address some of the issues noted above; the program is located on the Phoenix Society website (Phoenix Society for Burn Survivors, 2018).

Image enhancement, including the use of corrective cosmetics, is another tool for burn survivors during the reintegration process. The STEPS techniques (Kammerer-Quayle, 2002) can help a person feel more comfortable entering new social situations. Steps include Self-Talk, Tone of Voice, Eye Contact, Posture, and Smile (STEPS). The more burn survivors can create a positive image of themselves, the easier it is for those individuals to help others be more comfortable around them.

Returning to school or work after a burn injury, while challenging, is an important part of recovery because it helps an individual return to a routine (Livneh, 2018; Livneh & Antonak, 2018). Returning to work gives a burn survivor a sense of purpose and is a confidence builder. At times, a burn survivor needs to be retrained for a new occupation. This can cause confusion and anxiety and also excitement. Vocational rehabilitation is a resource for people able to return to work. There are Re-Entry to Work programs that help ease the transition back to the workplace (Phoenix Society for Burn Survivors, 2018).

Loving and Relationships Following a Burn Injury

As discussed, burn injuries change how a body looks and impacts body image and self-esteem. There are many questions regarding relationships, love, sexuality, and intimacy that need to be addressed for burn survivors. Emotional healing, though infrequently addressed, is just as important as physical healing (Kammerer-Quayle, 2002; Livneh & Antonak, 2018).

Burn survivors recognize it is important to have relationships in supporting their role in healing after their injuries (Blakeney et al., 2008). Talking about ways to be more comfortable in one's new skin is beneficial. An important part of experiencing love, partnership, and sexuality is self-acceptance. Seldom does any person fulfill today's ideal of beauty, and even less so for the person with a physical difference.

Loss of relationships, as well as change in body image and self-concept are all common following a burn injury (Livneh & Antonak, 2018). The physical appearance of the burn survivor's body has undergone change which most likely is permanent. A survivor reconnecting to others after beginning to recover is essential. He or she must learn to take risks, as well as reach out and take on challenges. Survivors have fought a battle to stay alive, and now must try to live life to the fullest in spite of what has happened (Blakeney & Meyer, 1994).

Burn survivors need a relationship with themselves and know who they are and what they want. People need to feel that they are in control of themselves and how they feel about themselves. It takes courage to accept a new image and take pride in one's new image. Our relationship with ourselves includes how we feel about who we are as people, as sexual beings, as men or women, and how we feel about our bodies and behaviors.

Sexuality is integral and inseparable from body image and self-esteem. It is a form of communication, a way of expressing part of one's personality to another. Sexuality spans the biological, psychological, emotional, spiritual, cultural, and social dimensions of our lives; it begins with us and extends to others.

Intimacy and Sexuality

An issue that burn survivors face regarding sexuality and intimacy is altered skin integrity. Skin can be overly hypersensitive or hyposensitive (less sensitive than usual). Survivors will experience changes in the texture, color, and appearance of their skin. They may experience pain, issues with mobility, and variations in energy level.

With disruption in skin sensitivity, touch may be experienced in a completely different way. The burn survivor must know how to communicate what feels good (as well as what does not) to his or her partner. Initially, survivors may feel hampered by a lack of energy. As a result, one must plan time for intimacy and sex.

Depending on where the burns have impacted the body, mobility and positioning issues may need to be addressed. New positions can be learned that are more comfortable for survivors. In the beginning, being touched may cause pain. Survivors may need their partners to go slow, take baby steps, make it as fun as possible, and try to find some humor in this trying time. Open, honest communication is essential during this period.

To appreciate one's sexuality is a lifelong process that takes courage and understanding, with or without a physical difference. Survivors begin to identify how they view themselves independent of negative interactions with others. Relationships are developed slowly between individuals sharing their experiences and learning to appreciate each other for who they are.

The following is a man's intimate letter to his girlfriend, a burn survivor.

Dear Ann:

This is a letter to you, to tell you how I feel. As you know, I had some familiarity with burns when we first met. Your scars from the burns on your face and hands were quite visible, the ones on the rest of your body were not. Burns over 2/3rds of your body "take a long time to heal." I saw the burns first, because they were there . . . just as when I meet a very tall or short person for the first time, I notice the most obvious features first . . . and then as I get to know them, I learn more about their likes, dislikes, job, intelligence, fears, loves and dreams . . . so they grow (in my mind) to be complete people . . . and so I grew to know and be attracted to you. We were attracted to each other from the first although you guarded yourself from letting me know you, for a while. I'm the same way about my feelings. Perhaps most of us are. We, I, fear rejection so we keep our distance until we are sure.... and of course, there are no guarantees . . . so we went ahead and let down the battle defenses. At the party that night, we were feeling "happy" and went home together and got to know each other . . . we woke up feeling closer. It took a couple of years to learn a lot more about each other since only intimacy really lets out a lot of feelings.

But, this letter wants to talk about burns, love, relationships and sex. Let me put it bluntly. You turned me on...the way you talked, moved and reacted to others and especially to me. One of the most attractive things about others is that they are attracted to us. I was attracted to you, physically at first and as that continued, I learned more about you. We meshed great physically. We could hold on to each other, wrestle, tickle each other and love it.

I know you. Let me tell you about scars and how I feel about yours. I love their texture. I figure I'm lucky. Most people have one or two textures to touch on their partner. I have ten or more. There is the soft smooth part below your hips, on your legs, which weren't burned. There is a soft, slightly rougher part on your thighs from whence came some of your grafts. There's the tough but smoother part under your arms, which wasn't released and so is still tight when you raise your arm. There's the checkerboard pattern on your grafted upper arms, which feels like I'm running my hand over goose bumps. There's the area on your shoulder, which didn't heal to well and is soft but has little hills and valleys. And there's the cheekbone area where the fat was left out and so the skin is closer to the bone. And, there's a dozen more. But I don't think about it quite the way I've described. I just think about each part as part of you. As the saying goes, we're the sum of our parts, good and bad.

Now, if I had known you before the burn, knowing you would be a relearning process. I'd have to change the parts of you, in my mind, but if I knew you then as I know you now, the greatest part of you would be what you are...honest, tender, sensual, caring and a great cook, etc. If I would have known you only in a physical sense and not in a close emotional sense, then yes, I would have to relearn "everything" about you.

But this isn't only for burns. All the ads, stories, movies, and television programs emphasize only the superficial: "Ooh, I'm two pounds over . . . " "Porcelana gets rid of those age spots." "Which hands are mine and which are my daughter's?" Part of what the rock generation of the 60's and 70's and the punk rockers of the 80's were trying to say is, "Know me as a person, first, last, and always." The punkers make their outward appearance so bizarre that people are forced to look at them as a person. Unfortunately, very few people can get past outward appearance. They say, "Hey there are so many normal regular looking kids, I don't think you are worth the effort." Well, that's their problem . . . . It's part of our problem too.

The next part of this letter is about questions that go through your mind—-some that you tell me about and some that you don't.

Myth #1: "*Because I have scars, you hit on me because you thought others won't want me because others have hit on me and tried to pick me up for that reason.*" Well, there are boys and men like that, but you and I were attracted to each other for the right reasons. The men and boys who "Think they are going for easy pickings," have a low opinion of themselves number one, and number two, they're not much as people.

Myth #2: "*You like me, but you are only staying with me out of pity.*" Well, that might be part of some people's makeup, but what a waste that would be of my life and yours. Relationships based on pity are doomed and full of resentment. Our relationship has none of that. I can see where it would be easy to fall in that pattern and I don't know if it's true for others who are burned or have some handicap. The problem with those relationships is that there is no value . . . no give and receive . . . no values exchanged by each partner. We exchange values, besides physical contact, which we both dearly love (as if we exchange eccentricities), but we, you in particular, listen to my dreams, ideas, and bad jokes. You can read my mind, which is helpful, and most important, you let me be myself. You are interested in my work and are willing to cheer me on in my artistic and sports endeavors, etc. On the other side, I feel I support you in your work and play (Though we should go out more) . . . I listen, though not as well as you . . . . I let you be yourself . . . . and I have developed an understanding of the thoughts and fears that go with being burned and having visible scars. There are other things I do, but that is another letter.

Myth #3: "*When we love or argue or fight or enjoy, the burn plays a large part in what you say or do.*" Well only in as much as you can't raise your arm to full extension (because of a tight band of tissue) to slug me, and because of how it makes you feel sometimes.

By and large, when we are together, I don't notice people staring unless they are obvious, and if so I just stare back at them. I know that most of their intentions are benign and not hateful, so it's only a sense of proportion and taste that I am trying to instill in them.

You know that all the things you are is what I know about you. I fell in love with your scars, your shorter nose, your skin, and your sense of life . . . . your smiles, your frowns, your ups, your downs. They are all part of you and part of who you are. And I like and love who you are. This is not to say you are perfect, but nine out of ten ain't bad!

As to being unsure of our relationship, relationships are built from scratch, and the more we share together the stronger the relationship becomes. That's true for everyone. The burn doesn't have anything to do with the survival of our relationship. That's determined by how we care for each other.

Love always,

William

Burn Traumas United Journal Fall 1983

Sexuality and Burns-Part I: Appearance, Body Image & Relationships

The Phoenix Society for Burn Survivors

For over 35 years, the Phoenix Society for Burn Survivors (2018) has been connecting burn survivors, their loved ones, and burn care professionals with valuable resources and a network of support.

A burn injury not only affects patients but also the people who love and support them. The recovery process is ongoing after one's release from the hospital. For these reasons, groups like the Phoenix Society have created resources for survivors, spouses, significant others, children, siblings, healthcare professionals, first responders, and others who are involved in the recovery process.

World Burn Congress (WBC) is an annual international conference that brings together thousands of burn survivors, their families, caregivers, burn care professionals, and firefighters. It is a forum to share stories, provide support, and increase one's knowledge of burn recovery. For many, it is the first opportunity to meet and share with others who have experienced burn traumas. The three days of the WBC are filled with inspirational stories of survival, courage, and personal growth. Many have described their experience at WBC as both a powerful and life changing experience.

The conference also serves as a productive learning experience for burn care professionals to better understand the issues that impact the lives of burn survivors. Many firefighters that attend talk about the closure it brings for them as they witness burn survivors and their families living meaningful lives. For individuals who are active in the burn support community at a local level, WBC serves as a wonderful networking opportunity.

The Phoenix Society for Burn Survivors serves as a National Resource Center for all survivors. They can direct a person to children's burn camps, adult retreats, and young adult summits throughout the nation. This is the leading national nonprofit organization dedicated to empowering any person affected by a burn injury through peer support, education, and advocacy. For over 35 years, the Phoenix Society has partnered with survivors, families, health care professionals, burn centers, and the fire industry to support recovery, improve the quality of burn care, and prevent burn injury. This organization promotes and supports a positive return to life and living. For further information, visit www.phoenix-society.org or call (800) 888-2876.

Phoenix Society Resources:

SOAR (Survivors Offering Assistance to Recovery)

World Burn Congress

Online Learning

Online Support Community (Chat)

The Journey Back (School Re-Entry)

Burn Support News

BEST Image Enhancement Program

STEPS Social Skills Training

Phoenix Educational Grants

Prevention and Advocacy

Speakers Bureau

Conclusion

The process of psychosocially adapting to a severe burn is complex (Corry, Pruzinsky, & Rumsey, 2009). Common issues faced by burn survivors include traumatic stress, depression, body image changes, social anxiety, grief, pain, itching, sleep disturbance, substance abuse, adapting to physical limitations, and coping with permanent burn scarring. In addition, burns often interfere with a person's ability to work and perform familial responsibilities (Blakeley et al., 2008). Often, the survivor's family also is traumatized, and the family's material and social resources can be greatly taxed during the course of burn recovery. Despite the sudden life-altering nature of burn injuries, studies of the psychological morbidity for burn survivors suggest that most burn survivors are resilient and adjust well over time.

References

Acton, A., Mounsey, E., & Gilyard, C. (2007). The burn survivor perspective. *Journal of Burn Care and Research, 281*(4), 1-6.

American Burn Association (ABA). (2016). *Burn incidence and treatment in the United States: Burn incidence fact sheet.* Chicago, IL: Author.

Blakeney, P., & Meyer, W. (1994). Psychological aspects of burn care. *Trauma Quarterly, 11*(2), 166-179.

Blakeney, P., Rosenberg, L., Rosenberg, M., & Faber, A. W. (2008). Psychosocial care of persons with severe burns. *Burns, 34*(4), 433-440.

Corry, N., Pruzinsky, T., & Rumsey, N. (2009). Quality of life and psychosocial adjustment to burn injury: Social functioning, body image, and health policy perspectives. *International Review of Psychiatry, 21*(6), 539-548.

Gilboa, D. (2001). Long term psychosocial adjustment after burn injury. *Burns, 27*, 335-341.

Herman, J. (1997). *Trauma and recovery.* New York, NY: Basic Books.

Kammerer-Quayle, B. (2002). Image and behavioral skills training for people with facial difference and disability. In M. G. Brodwin, F. A. Tellez, & S. K. Brodwin (Eds.), *Medical, psychosocial, and vocational aspects of disability* (2nd ed., pp. 95-106). Athens, GA: Elliott & Fitzpatrick.

Livneh, H. (2018). On the origins of negative attitudes toward people with disabilities. In I. Marini & M. A. Stebnicki (Eds.), *The psychological and social impact of illness and disability* (7th ed., pp. 13-25). New York, NY: Springer.

Livneh, H., & Antonak, R. F. (2018). Psychological adaptation to chronic illness and disability: A primer for counselors. In I. Marini & M. A. Stebnicki (Eds.), *The psychological and social impact of illness and disability* (7th ed., pp. 77-90). New York, NY: Springer.

Pratt, J., & West, G. (1995). *Pressure garments: A manual on their design and fabrication.* Oxford, England: Butterworth-Heinemann.

Phoenix Society for Burn Survivors. (2018). Retrieved from http://www.phoenix-society.org

Tufaro, P. A., & Houng, A. P. (2017). Rehabilitation in burns. In A. Moroz, S. R. Flanagan, & H. H. Zaretsky (Eds.), *Medical aspects of disability for the rehabilitation professional* (5th ed., pp. 113-131). New York, NY: Springer.

UW Health.(2018). *Emergency medicine 3. Assessing burns and planning resuscitation: The rule of nines* Madison, WI. University of Wisconsin-Madison. Retrieved from https://www.uwhealth.org/emergency -room/assessing-burns-and-planning-resuscitation-the-rule-of-nines/12698.

Watkins, P. N., Cook, E. L., May, S. R., & Ehleben, C. M. (1998). Psychological stages in adaptation following burn injury: A method for facilitating psychological recovery of burn victims. *Journal of Burn Care and Rehabilitation, 9*(4), 420-424.

WebMD. (2018). *An overview of the skin.* Cleveland, OH: Cleveland Clinic. Retrieved from http://www.webmd.com/beauty/wrinkles/cosmetic-procedures-overview-skin

About the Authors

Cindy Rutter, RN, BSN, is a registered nurse and a burn survivor since age six when she sustained 3rd degree burns over 85% of her body in a house fire. After more than 100 surgeries before her 18th birthday, she has devoted her life to help other burn survivors in all aspects of the recovery process. As a registered nurse, Ms. Rutter worked as a burn recovery nurse and a burn center nurse manager at the University of California, San Diego Regional Burn Center. She received the Alan Breslau Award for her continued commitment to the burn community, California Nurse of the Year, San Diego Chargers Community Quarterback Award, and recognition as a "Remarkable Woman" by Redbook Magazine, among others. More recently, she earned her Master's degree in Marriage and Family Therapy from San Diego State University. Her work with couples, individuals, and families has helped transform lives.

Ann Malo, RN, has 25 years of nursing experience, including 25 years in burn critical care. Her career in nursing in the area of burns began in 1994 as a nurse for the University of California, San Diego (UCSD) Regional Burn Center. She has been active in pediatric burn camp and burn survivor support. Burn prevention education and patient care are her passions. Currently, Ms. Malo is an assistant nurse manager, Department of Surgery, UCSD Regional Burn Center.

James Bosch is a licensed Marriage and Family Therapist (LMFT). He brings a distinguished background in helping individuals and families successfully navigate through the physical and emotional process of healing from severe trauma. Having been burned as an infant, he has been part of the healing experience of other burn injured children. James works with individuals, couples, and families who have survived life-changing tragedies. His philosophy is to assist clients learn to use their strengths, knowledge, and understanding to begin the next phase of healing. Drawing on a variety of influences and modalities, Mr. Bosch helps individuals find meaning in their stories, develop tools to deal with the stressors of life, as well as find love, intimacy, and lead fulfilling lives.

Chapter 29

EVALUATING UPPER EXTREMITY FUNCTION AND IMPAIRMENT

George W. Balfour, MD
Martin G. Brodwin, PhD, CRC
Ashley T. Du, MS

Introduction

Treatment of upper extremity injuries has been developing for centuries. As early as 1717, an Italian physician wrote about "the harvest of diseases reaped by certain workers" caused by "certain violent and irregular motions and unnatural postures of the body that impair the natural structure of the vital machine." In the early 20th century, maladies that were called upper extremity disabilities were seen as distinct problems. These disabilities were named individually after the specific blue-collar occupation in which they developed. *Stitcher's wrist, bricklayer's shoulder, cottontwister's hand, writer's cramp* (clerical workers), and *telegraphist's cramp*, are examples of documented upper extremity disabilities. Today, upper extremity disabilities are found in all populations of workers, including high-technology fields, such as software engineering, online brokering, and customer service. One of the most common type of injuries, upper extremity injuries can have the most devastating and long-term social and economic consequences.

According to the American Medical Association's (AMA) *Guides to the Evaluation of Permanent Impairment,* 60% percent of the function of a *whole person* is assigned to a single upper extremity, 90% of which is defined to be in the hand (American Medical Association, 2009). Hand function represents more than half (54%) of one's total body functioning.

This chapter addresses the etiology of upper extremity injuries, function of the hand, anatomy and physiology of the upper extremity, assessment of impairment, and evaluation and treatment of injuries. Additionally, the chapter covers work and physical capacity evaluation, functional limitations, assistive technology, and rehabilitation potential. Lastly, the authors conclude with a case study on a veteran who sustained an upper extremity injury during military service.

Etiology

Impairment is the loss of function in the physical sense, while disability is an inability to overcome or compensate for that impairment. Oskamp (1988) defined impairment and disability as follows: **Impairment** describes an abnormality or a loss of a physiological structure or function. From this medical definition of impairment, the rehabilitation counselor can more readily understand the impact of a hand injury on an individual's ability to function in the workplace. **Disability** refers to the consequences of impairment – a restriction or lack of ability to perform some activity that is considered appropriate.

Injuries resulting in upper extremity disabilities occur in many different ways and in a variety of settings such as in the home, highway, sports field, battlefield, and workplace. "Accidents involving machinery include use of power tools, firearms, and motor vehicle accidents" (Cohen, Edelstein, Bayona, & Kort, 2017, p. 398). In the United States, injuries to the hand and upper extremity represent 40% of all work-related injuries. Upper extremity injuries are additionally characterized by long periods of recovery.

In 2015, approximately 346,000 people working in business and industry in the United States lost time from work due to an upper extremity injury (Bureau of Labor Statistics, 2015).

Function of the Hand

A variety of functions rely on the movement of the hands, including sensory, fine manipulation, gripping, cosmetic appearances, and use in social interactions. The hand is a sensory organ; a high concentration of nerve endings in the palms and fingers provide information about one's environment. Imagine picking up an object, feeling it, and discerning its weight, hardness, surface texture, temperature, size, and shape.

The somasensory surface of the brain receives signals from touch. Figure 1 is a schematic picture of the somasensory area of the brain that depicts the proportion of brain tissue devoted to the sense of touch. Note that only the lips and face are given more sensory area than the hand. Other areas of the body, like the face or thigh, are not able to read objects with the same accuracy or detail identification as the fingers. The amount of brain surface devoted to a body part is proportional to the sensitivity of that body part. The hand's high sensitivity to touch, for example, is a result of the high concentration of nerve endings in this area, particularly the palmar skin.

Besides providing sensory input, the hands function as the primary instrument of the upper extremities for functions like grasping, lifting, and carrying. Hands also perform fine and gross manipulative tasks such as turning a key, holding a glass, crafting, writing, using tools, and operating office equipment. In social situations hands are used for shaking, holding, and gesturing, characterizing feelings, emotions, greetings, and enthusiasm. The hands also serve cosmetic purposes, such as painting fingernails, wearing rings, and

FIGURE 1
Illustration of Sensory Distribution of the Central Gyrus of the Cerebral Cortex

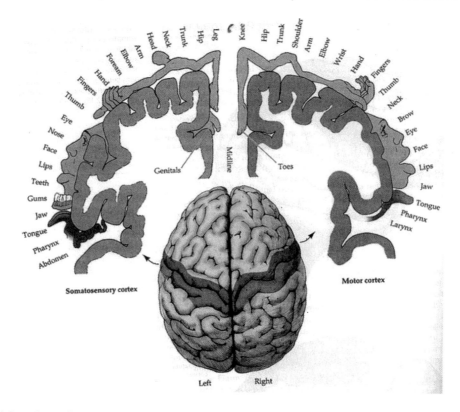

Source: Retrieved from https://qph.fs.quoracdn.net/main-qimg-cca3bfec18810f4f0201fe56cfc2d8cb

putting on gloves. The multi-faceted use of hands from work functions, social interactions, and cosmetic appearances demonstrate the many functions of the hand.

Hands function during activities requiring gross strength (i.e., in lifting, carrying, pushing, pulling, and while using large tools). When working with shovels, hammers, or saws, the function of the hand is to grip and hold the equipment; the principal force and motion occurs at the wrist, forearm, elbow, and shoulder. During the assessment of impairment and rehabilitation potential, each of these multi-faceted functions and any associated limitations need assessment (Strickland & Graham, 2005).

Anatomy and Physiology of the Upper Extremity

Neurological

Median Nerve

This nerve supplies sensation to the palm and palmar aspects of the thumb, index, long, and radial half of the ring finger. It is the most essential sensory nerve to the hand, and is the motor nerve for most of the muscles of the ventral forearm (forearm flexors), the muscles that bend and flex the wrist and flex or close the fingers and thumb. These median nerve controlled flexors provide power for gripping, lifting, and flexing the wrist (Wolfe, Peterson, Hotchkiss, & Cohen, 2016). Below the wrist, the median nerve supplies motor and muscle innervation to the small, intrinsic muscles of the thumb (the thenar muscles located at the base of the thumb) which aid in rowing the thumb out of the plane of the palm into opposition, and contribute to the power of pinch.

Median nerve injuries are classified as either *high* or *low* (Strickland & Graham, 2005). A *high* median nerve injury results in an inability to flex the wrist, fingers, and thumb. This type of injury makes gripping of objects impossible and causes numbness of the thumb, index, center fingers, and half of the ring finger. Contrastingly, a *low* median nerve injury causes numbness and weakness of the intrinsic muscles of the thumb, preventing actions relying on these muscles, such as pinching, turning a key, or touching the tip of the thumb to the tip of the little finger.

Ulnar Nerve

In the hand, the ulnar nerve provides sensation to the little finger, the ulna half of the ring finger, and muscle innervation and control to the small intrinsic muscles of the hand. Intrinsic muscles provide balance to the fingers and fine manipulative control of the hand. Injury to the ulnar nerve principally impairs dexterity and fine manipulation, including functions like pinch and manipulation of small objects, such as screws, coins, and buttons.

Radial Nerve

The radial nerve is the sensory nerve for the back (dorsum) of the hand and thumb. In the forearm, it supplies muscle innervation to the extensor muscle group. These muscles extend the wrist, fingers, and thumb. Radial palsy leads to wrist drop, a condition in which the hand drops toward the ground because the person is unable to raise the hand or fingers against gravity. A lower radial nerve injury causes numbness (Trumble, Rayan, Baratz, Budoff, & Slutsky, 2017).

Muscular

Forearm

There are two sets of extrinsic muscles (those located outside the hand itself) in the forearm, the ventral (flexion group) and the dorsal (extensor group). Ventral extrinsic forearm muscles (flexors), reach the hand through tendons and act to flex or bend the wrist and fingers. An extensor group of extrinsic muscles functions principally to extend the wrist, fingers, and thumb; they are innervated by the ulnar nerve (except those of the thumb) and balance finger motion, add strength to grip, and abduct and adduct the fingers (Wolfe et al., 2016).

Vascular

Most arterial injuries are due to direct laceration, blunt trauma, and thrombosis. Lacerations compromise the blood supply to the affected part (Trumble et al., 2017). If there is no collateral circulation to a body part, it will become ischemic (deficient in blood) and die. Collateral circulation means that two vessels supply the same part or area. If only one vessel is damaged, collateral circulation (the alternative blood pathway) may be adequate to keep the part alive and functional (Wolfe et al., 2016). Upper extremity hand injuries impacting the blood flow to the hand may result in cold intolerance, pain, numbness, tingling, and swelling.

Kinesiology

Combined function of the shoulder, elbow, and wrist allows the hand to move anywhere within a large circular area. The shoulder girdle consists of the arm, scapula, and clavicle. The elbow is a complex set of three joints that control the simple extension and flexion of the elbow and supination (palm up) or pronation (palm down). The wrist involves a complex set of joints that function in supination and pronation, the turning of the hand palm up and palm down. It functions in dorsiflexion and palmar flexion movement of the hand upward and downward (as in the hand motion of saying good-bye), and in radial and ulnar deviation (motion of the hand from side to side) (Trumble et al., 2017).

The Dermis

Palmar Skin

Skin serves as an outer covering of the body, protecting it from the external environment. Palmar skin is thicker than the rest of the skin. The early healing phase typically takes three months to resolve, an important characteristic for the rehabilitation counselor to know when providing vocational services for workers with injuries involving the palm of the hand.

Defects in palmar skin caused by injury such as tears, lacerations, or burns can be covered or replaced with grafted skin or skin flaps. Skin graft is a thin layer of healthy skin removed from one site and placed in an area needing skin coverage. Transferred skin, as compared to palmar skin, is thinner, more mobile, and less adherent to deep structures. Full thickness graft may involve skin with hair follicles. A physician utilizes a variety of flaps to provide thicker more durable skin (Trumble et al., 2017).

Nails

The nails are specialized structures that act as protective covering for the tips of the fingers. An open wound near or under the nail is a source of pain and a viable route for infection. Nail injuries can heal abnormally with ridges or splits, also known as bifid nails (Saunders, Astifidis, Burke, Higgins, & McClinton, 2016).

Assessment of Impairment

Assessment of impairment is accomplished using a scoring system which assigns specific values to various functions. Within the hand, evaluated functions include loss of parts (amputation), cosmetic defects, pain, tenderness, diminished sensation, limited range of motion, and loss of strength. An assessment describes subjective pain, including intensity and frequency, along with the appearance of the hand, together with the presence of dirt or calluses, and condition of the nails. An evaluator describes sensation using a variety of testing methods; the report measures loss of parts, presence of scars, ranges of motion, and strength of grip, pinch, lifting, and resistance.

In the first part of the evaluation of the upper extremity, the individual reports his or her functional history and present activities. The history needs to illustrate the patient's functional capabilities by describing duration and frequency of performed activities. Similarly, the report should explain activities that cannot be performed. Questions concerning lifting, carrying, pushing, pulling, gripping, pinching, manipulating, and sensing are all relevant to the physician's overall assessment of injury (Weiss & Falkerstein, 2013).

Range of Motion

The American Academy of Orthopaedic Surgeons has published standards for measuring joint motion. Each joint has a normal or typical range of motion and for any individual, the extremity on the opposite side is used as a normal standard (Wolfe et al., 2016). The range of motion after an injury will determine the level of impairment the disability will have on daily living and work activities.

Grip Loss

Atrophy can be caused by injury, disease, and disuse. Forearm circumference is measured as an estimation of atrophy; the physician compares the uninvolved extremity as a control to the involved side. Grip strength is measured with a calibrated dynamometer. The ratio between the involved and uninvolved hand determines grip loss. The loss of grip strength can impact many every day functions, such as the ability to grab, hold, twist, and squeeze.

Radiological Assessment

An examination requires radiological evaluation to define the status of the skeletal system and the degree of joint injury, disorganization, and degeneration (Weiss & Falkerstein, 2013). Bone shortening and angulation is reported in degrees. Density changes, for example, from disuse (osteopenia) are seen on x-rays as thinner, less dense, and more radiolucent bone tissue. The examiner notes joint surface changes, narrowing, sclerosis, fractures, osteophytes, arthritic changes, joint displacements (subluxations), and any additional x-ray findings (Strickland & Graham, 2005).

Medical Reporting

Medical reports begin with subjective complaints and extend to the history of the medical problem or injury in which the individual's past occupational record and social functioning are addressed, followed by the physical examination. The physical exam contains inspection, palpation, range of motion, muscle testing, neurological examination, and results of special tests including x-rays, MRIs, and CAT scans.

Pain and Sensory Deterioration

Pain

Pain is a unique and subjective experience which varies among individuals. *Nosocomi*a is defined as a physically unpleasant experience; pain is the individual's perception of that experience. If one takes a standardized needle and sticks it an equal depth at an equal rate into a dozen individuals, each person experiences an equal amount of nosocomia (unpleasant stimulation). Yet, each person describes a different degree and sensation of pain. Swanson, Goran-Hagert, and Swanson (1987) defined pain as "a disagreeable sensation that has as its basis a highly variable complex made up of afferent nerve stimuli interacting with the emotional state of the individual and modified by past experience, motivation, and state of mind" (p. 896). Readers can refer to the Chronic Pain Management chapter for more information on the impact of pain on individuals with upper extremity disabilities.

Sensory Deficits

Subjective complaints of sensory deficit are measurable and, in some patients, quantifiable. Testing for sensory deficits includes distinguishing sharp from dull, static two-point discrimination, moving two-point discrimination, Von Frey hair testing, hot versus cold discrimination, proprioception, coin discrimination, and vibration. *Proprioception* is the sense that indicates body position. It tells people if their hands are open or closed, if they are below the waist or overhead, and allows individuals to perform activities such as typing without looking at the keyboard. Proprioception can be tested by placing the hand behind a screen to hide it from visual feedback (Trumble et al., 2017).

Stereognosis is the sense that allows a person to read or see objects by feel; it is how one tells a dime from a quarter in a pocket without visual feedback, and how Braille is read. Patients with nerve lacerations and poor recovery, or following stroke or spinal cord injury often have severe sensory impairments, and may simply ignore the severely impaired hand; the hand then becomes nonfunctional solely on a sensory basis.

Nerve Compression

Individuals with nerve compression syndromes, such as herniated disks (causing pressure on nerve roots), thoracic outlet syndrome, cubital tunnel syndrome, and carpal tunnel syndrome, experience decreased sensibility (capability to feel or perceive). Those experiencing these deficits lose the sense of vibration more than the ability to perceive two-point discrimination. *Pins and needles* sensations, deep aching, a loss of the sense of position, and spontaneously dropping objects are associated with compression syndrome (Wolfe et al., 2016).

Evaluation and Treatment of Injury

Pain Evaluation

Evaluation of upper extremity injuries follows a consistent procedure and order of priorities. The first step includes obtaining a detailed history and physical. During the physical examination, any abnormalities are noted and each injury is categorized in relation to the skin, color, and overall condition of the hand. Specific examinations are administered for particular injuries. For example, palpation demonstrates losses of tendon continuity, fractures, dislocations, and torn ligaments. Loss of sensation is tested by touch or pinprick. Radiologic examination (x-rays) provides detail of bone injury and indicates the presence of metal and other foreign bodies.

Treatment

Once the surgeon understands the injury, he or she formulates a treatment plan. Individuals with vascular injuries may need arterial and occasionally venous repair. If, however, the vascular injury is categorized as vascular insufficiency, emergency care is necessary. In the case of venous insufficiency, muscle tissue not receiving an adequate blood supply dies within six hours while other tissues of the hand take longer to become necrotic. The patient must undergo repair of tendons, nerves, and skin, though these procedures can be delayed. Skin coverage is done immediately and before any deeper structures are reconstructed to avoid infection and problems due to scaring. The simplest skin replacement is performed with a skin graft in which an extremely thin layer of skin is taken from a healthy place on the body and sewn over a defect or open wound (Trumble et al., 2017; Weiss & Falkerstein, 2013).

Stabilization

When a patient has a deformity that cannot be corrected by non-operative methods, he or she undergoes a fracture stabilization procedure. The usual reason for instability is that an unopposed muscle or ligament force creates and maintains a deformity. Another indication for fracture fixation is when the fracture involves a joint surface. Joints are like machine parts; if their smooth surfaces heal unevenly, joint wear is accelerated, eventually leading to painful arthritis. Many different types of fixation devices such as splints and braces, are used to help stabilize the injury to assist proper healing (Cohen et al., 2016).

Ligaments

Many ligament injuries heal spontaneously, while others require casting or surgery. Incomplete tears heal independently with time, but complete tears need surgical repair. Torn ligaments that are not repaired become sources of chronic instability and impairment and, if neglected, lead to arthritis. Proper early medical attention and self-care reduces the risk of long term side effects.

Tendons

Tendon injuries include acute laceration, rupture, avulsion from the bony sites of attachment, erosion (such as in rheumatoid arthritis), attrition, and tendonitis. Tendonitis is a series of very small tears in the tissue or surrounding tendon (WebMD, 2010). Tendons are repaired end-to-end, replaced by tendon graft, or substituted by tendon transfer. Other conditions causing pain can be acute or result in chronic inflammation, such as those which occur in cases of tendonitis of an elbow or knee joint (Saunders et al., 2016).

Newer Developments

Like all medical specialties, the discipline of hand surgery continues to evolve (Trumble et al., 2017). In the past few decades, microsurgery has developed from a research tool into a viable technique commonly performed. Free tissue transfers have become common practice. Arthroscopic surgery, initially developed for the knee, has become an accepted approach for the shoulder, elbow, and wrist (McBeath & Osterman, 2012). Arthoscopic procedures are being performed on small joints, such as metacarpal/carpal joints and metacarpal/phalangeal joints. Similarly, fracture treatment has continued to improve with newer, smaller, and stronger implants and progressively less invasive methods.

Work and Physical Capacity Evaluation

Physical Capacity Evaluation

Work capacity evaluation measures the capability of a person to function over time. Under the direction of a physician, occupational therapists and work evaluation specialists observe the individual performing tasks over several days to provide an accurate assessment. Specific capacity testing enables the evaluator to quantify the capacity to perform work-related actions. Physical capacity evaluation documents a person's hand function, including strength and range of motion. The three components to physical capacity evaluation include administration of hand function tasks, standardized tests, and observation of the person performing the physical demands of the job. An accurate and detailed job description tailored to the specific worker's impairments helps a physician determine if the individual is capable of returning to the previous job, with or without accommodation.

Work Limitations

Injuries to the upper extremities cause limitations in eye-hand coordination, range of motion in one or both hands, manual dexterity, strength for lifting and carrying, as well as pushing and pulling activities. Accommodating such an employee at the workplace may involve dividing heavier weights or large items into lighter or smaller units. Use of mechanical lifts and movable carts decrease lifting and carrying (Mueller, 1990). The most effective way to meet the accommodation needs of the client is to complete a detailed job analysis, paying particular attention to job functions requiring use of the injured hand(s). A step-by-step analysis allows the counselor and injured employee to work with the employer in suggesting reasonable accommodation which benefits both employee and employer (Brodwin, Parker, & DeLaGarza, 2010).

Many people who have serious hand injuries are unable to return to their previous employment because of residual impairments. As a result, some employers offer lighter duty work or a different position within the company. Rehabilitation counselors can provide suggestions concerning alterations to the work environment to accommodate impairments.

In addition to possessing an enhanced awareness of their environment, persons with severe upper extremity injuries, including amputation, face attitudinal, psychosocial, and emotional adjustments. Limitations in activities which can be performed and changes in body image may require an adaptation period. Many individuals also benefit from short-term counseling or in-depth psychological intervention (Livneh & Antonek, 2018). Factors such as a person's interpretation of loss of function, circumstances involved with the injury, premorbid personality (personality before the loss), and extent of loss help the counselor analyze needed rehabilitation and psychological services.

Emotionally, everyone reacts differently to injury and impairment. Psychological counseling is an important aspect of recovery for many individuals. Some persons with disfigured hands may engage in various activities and do not feel self-conscious while in public. Others, with even minor injuries, attempt to hide their hand(s) from sight. Rehabilitation counselors need to evaluate the impairment, taking into account individual needs.

Functional Limitations in Commonly Occurring Hand Injuries

Finger Injuries

Fingertip injuries are the most common industrial accidents and the most frequent reason for amputation (Saunders et al., 2016). As a guide, the entire thumb contributes to 40% of hand function, while the long and ring fingers contribute 20% each. The border digits (the index and little fingers) account for 10% each. The loss of several digits increases impairment more than the sum of the parts lost. Multiple digit injuries require longer recovery time, more hand therapy to regain motion and strength, and result in greater residual impairment (American Medical Association, 2009). Variables involved include level of amputation, amount of soft tissue coverage on the remaining part, presence or absence of tender neuromas or bone prominence, and nail deformities. Involvement of flexor tendons influences the person's strength, active motion, and range of motion.

Hand Fractures

Fractures are another common hand injury in industry, with each kind of fracture having a different treatment and prognosis. Fractures result in both pain and immobility. Physicians can splint simple non-displaced, non-angulation, and non-articular fractures; usually, these fractures heal within three weeks. Employees can typically return to work within six to eight weeks. If the fracture is displaced, angulated, intra-articular, and therefore requires reduction or surgery, the time for healing to resolve stiffness, regain strength, and return to work is much longer.

Some of the residual effects of finger injuries are permanent. Residuals such as tendon adherence (scar between the tendon and bone) can prevent returning to customary work. For an individual with tendon adherence, the only way to regain motion may be through surgical intervention. Full range of motion is rarely regained after surgery, and manipulative tasks are often impaired as a result (American Occupational Therapy Association, 2013).

Wrist Fractures

The most frequent wrist fractures involve the waist of the scaphoid, one of the eight small bones of the wrist (Trumble et al., 2017). Median time to union in non-displaced fractures is 15 weeks, and the non-union (non-healing) rate is as high as 40%. Following injury, stiffness and weakness are common; return to heavy labor takes an extensive period of time. Wrist fracture is a leading cause of disability and loss of productivity.

Carpal Tunnel Syndrome

The carpal tunnel is the final common pathway of multiple conditions, all of which increase pressure within the wrist. Symptoms include tingling, numbness, weakness, and pain (WebMD, 2010). Carpal tunnel syndrome is the most common nerve compression syndrome. Muscle strength within the hand may be compromised. Thyroid disease, masses, extra muscles (congenital), rheumatoid arthritis, amyloidosis, repetitive trauma, vibration disease syndrome, synovial hypertrophy, and prior wrist fractures are some of the causes of carpal tunnel. Repetitive use of the hand, as in a cashier's use of an optical scanner throughout the work shift, or activities like typing, packing, and assembling, frequently are the basis of claims of an industrial etiology. Workers may develop carpal tunnel syndrome as a result of vibratory tools, such as pneumatic tools, jackhammers, and power wrenches.

Factors which increase the occurrences of carpal tunnel syndrome in women include gender, age, generalized mild synovitis, and physique. Those at or near age 40, and women with thin or fragile physiques are more prone to carpal tunnel. Initial conservative treatment consists of decreased use of the wrist, splints, non-steroidal anti-inflammatory medication, and diuretics. If the diagnosis is confirmed, steroid injections into the wrist are given; if this fails and the symptoms remain severe and prolonged, the person may need surgical decompression to relieve pressure on the nerve (Shy, 2016). Following surgery, the individual is splinted in dorsiflexion for a month; the scar can remain tender for up to six months. Return to work will take two to twelve weeks, depending on the physical demands of the job. Clerical and professional occupations take less recovery time than physically demanding occupations.

Assistive Technology

The goal of assistive technology is to increase the functional independence for people who have disabilities. The focus is not on the disability but on the remaining functional (residual) abilities that individuals use to accomplish their chosen objectives and daily tasks. Because the vast majority of jobs require use of the hands and fingers, counselors must be adept at providing accommodation for workers with upper extremity injuries. There are a variety of orthotic and prosthetic hand devices that provide improved function. Prostheses are artificial devices used to replace a missing body part, and orthoses are specialized mechanical devices used to support or supplement weak or damaged joints and limbs (Cohen et al., 2017). Individuals who use prosthetic and orthotic devices should cultivate an increased awareness of their environment to assure proper functioning of the devices.

These devices can be modified to accommodate specific job duties. For example, an adaptive device allowed a filling station attendant, who had lost two fingers from his dominant hand, to pump gasoline. The device was worn only for this job duty and, in essence, was a custom tool that was put away when the worker performed other job functions. Orthotists and prosthetists custom design a variety of devices to help workers perform job duties. The following orthoses may improve an employee's function of the upper extremities: a wrist-hand orthoses, a wrist-driven wrist-hand orthoses, and a shoulder-elbow orthoses. Upper limb orthoses can substitute for the absence of muscle power, assist or support weak areas of the upper extremity, and be used for the attachment of specialized assistive devices (Clawson, 2014).

Assistive technology can help people with dexterity limitations. An example is difficulty using a standard keyboard. "A chin mouse, an eye-gaze unit, a mouth stick, and other hands-free devices can enable an individual to operate a computer. There are on-screen computer keyboards which operate without using a mouse" (Young, Stiens, O'Young, Baldwin, & Thatcher, 2017, p. 705). Keyboard filters include typing aids such as word prediction utilities and add-on spell-checkers which reduce the number of keystrokes and enable quick access letters and avoiding incorrect key selection.

Ability to use the hand involves sensibility, dexterity, and mobility. Rehabilitation of hand injuries often requires time and effort; maximum return of function is the goal of the hand surgeon, hand therapist, work evaluator, and rehabilitation counselor. Counselors must work closely with other professionals to return the person to employment. At the workplace, use of upper extremity prostheses enhances manual dexterity, bilateral dexterity, eye-hand coordination, grabbing, grasping, lifting, and carrying. Although a prosthesis does not replace a fully functioning arm and hand, it may allow an employee to perform the necessary work tasks (Clawson, 2014). A workstation, with accommodation and job modification, helps the worker with an upper extremity limitation to efficiently perform required work functions. As noted by Jette, Spicer, and Flaubert (2017), appropriate assistive technology devices may lessen the impact of impairments enough to allow a user to work or return to work. For additional information, the reader is referred to the Orthotics, Amputation, and Prosthetics chapter within this book.

Rehabilitation Potential

Potential for rehabilitation depends on multiple factors, including whether the injury involves the dominant or non-dominant hand. When the dominant hand is severely injured, training to improve use of the opposite hand is appropriate (American Occupational Therapy Association, 2013). A plan of physical rehabilitation includes:

- Strengthening exercises
- Exercises to develop skills in activities of daily living
- Writing exercises
- Activities to improve manual dexterity

Hand injuries cause different functional limitations and thus have varying rehabilitation potential. Attitude and motivation play a significant role in the potential for rehabilitation and success in returning to work (Brodwin et al., 2010). When serious injuries result in major impairment, the motivation and attitude of a person may mean the difference between successful medical and vocational rehabilitation and failure. Highly motivated individuals with severe impairment enjoy greater success rates than those with significantly less impairment who are not as motivated, even if they have significantly less impairment.

Other factors contributing to rehabilitation potential include age, educational level, and work history. Younger, more educated persons with skilled or professional work backgrounds can more readily adjust to impairment and disability; older workers are more tolerant of residual discomfort. The role of the counselor is to go beyond the injury to include the entire person and his or her functional needs and roles. A comprehensive plan may include therapeutic activities, joint protection, energy modification, sensory re-education, scar management, pain management, work conditioning, and training in activities of daily living.

Conclusion

Approximately 4.3 million people in the United States have some form of limitation involving impairments of manual dexterity, range of motion, strength, and endurance of the hands and arms. Of this number, almost 357,000 employees are unable to fully use their upper extremities in a significant way. This figure includes people with paralysis or absence of part or all of one or both upper extremities. Many industrial injuries involve the hands and fingers, causing different degrees of impairment depending upon the extent of injury, loss of function, and the dominance of the hand. Rehabilitation counselors must possess knowledge of hand function and impairment to recommend rehabilitation plans and reasonable accommodations for workers with these disabilities (Brodwin et al., 2010).

Case Study

Christopher Ruiz is 35-year-old veteran who is married and father of a two-month old son. He served in the army since he graduated high school and has no prior work experience.

While in military service, Christopher was injured in a vehicular accident, where the truck he was in flipped; his left arm was crushed under the weight of the vehicle. His injuries included a fractured hand and wrist, and damage to the median nerve and radial nerve. Christopher was in physical therapy for a year but stopped two months ago when his son was born. His range of motion is currently 80% and grip strength 60%. Since this injury, Mr. Ruiz has a difficult time sleeping and often feels anxious when in a car. He knows that he should talk to a professional about it but feels very hesitant about talking to a stranger about his worries.

In the past year, Christopher has been taking classes at a local community college with the goal of transferring to a four-year university to obtain a Bachelor of Science degree in Kinesiology. He has been an after-school basketball coach at a high school for the past three months with the goal of teaching physical education full time. He enjoys working with teenagers and believes he can make a difference in their lives by teaching teamwork and discipline. However, Mr. Ruiz has been having a difficult time running drills with his students due to his injuries. He has always envisioned himself to be a hands-on teacher and is feeling very discouraged that his injuries will not allow him to do so. Furthermore, he is afraid that his students will not respect him if they think he is a poor coach.

Questions

1. Define *impairment* and *disability*. Distinguish between these concepts in this case.
2. How would you approach vocational rehabilitation for this client?
3. What is the nature of Christopher's functional limitations? Explain how this may impact activities of daily living (ADL) and future employment.
4. What types of intervention would you suggest for this individual?
5. What reasonable accommodations would you recommend? Describe other career paths Mr. Ruiz may want to pursue.

References

American Medical Association. (2009). *Guides to the evaluation of permanent impairment* (6th ed.). Chicago, IL: Author.

American Occupational Therapy Association. (2013). *The role of occupational therapy for rehabilitation of the upper extremity* (Fact sheet). Retrieved from http://www.aota.org/~/media/Corporate/Files/AboutOT/Professionals/WhatIsOT/RDP/Facts/Hand%20Therapy%20fact%20sheet.ashx

Brodwin, M. G., Parker, R. M., & DeLaGarza, D. (2010). Disability and reasonable accommodation. In E. M. Szymanski & R. M. Parker (Eds.), *Work and disability: Contexts, issues, and strategies in career development and job placement* (3rd ed., pp. 281-323). Austin, TX: Pro-ed.

Bureau of Labor Statistics. (2015). *Number of nonfatal occupational injuries & illnesses involving days away from work*. Retrieved from http://www.bls.gov.iif/oshwc/osh

Clawson, L. R. (2014). Orthotics, amputation, and prosthetics. In M. G. Brodwin, F. W. Siu, J. Howard, E. R. Brodwin, & A. T. Du (Eds.), *Medical, psychosocial, and vocational aspects of disability* (4th ed., pp. 353-366). Athens, GA: Elliott and Fitzpatrick.

Cohen, J. M., Edelstein, J. E., Bayona, C., & Kort, C. J. (2017). Limb deficiency. In A. Moroz, S. Flanagan, & H. H. Zaretsky (Eds.). *Medical aspects of disability for the rehabilitation professional* (5th ed., pp. 383-413). New York, NY: Springer.

Jette, A. M., Spicer, C. M., & Flaubert, J. L. (2017). *The promise of assistive technology to enhance activity and work participation*. Washington, DC: The National Academies Press.

Livneh, H., & Antonak, R. F. (2018). Psychological adaptation to chronic illness and disability: A primer for counselors. In I. Marini & M. Stebnicki (Eds.), *The psychological and social impact of illness and disability* (7th ed., pp. 77-90). New York, NY: Springer.

McBeath, R., & Osterman, A. L. (2012). Total wrist arthroplasty. *Hand Clinics, 28*(4), 595-609.

Mueller, J. (1990). *The workplace workbook: An illustrated guide to job accommodation and assistive technology*. Washington, DC: Dole Foundation.

Oskamp, S. (1988). The editor's page. *Journal of Social Issues, 44*(4), i-ii.

Saunders, R., Astifidis, R., Burke, S. L., Higgins, J., & McClinton, M. A. (2016). *Hand and upper extremity rehabilitation: A practical guide* (4th ed.). Ontario, Canada: Elsevier Canada.

Shy, M. E. (2016). Peripheral neuropathies. In L. Goldman & A. I. Schafer (Eds.), *Goldman's Cecil medicine* (25th ed., pp. 2527-2537). Philadelphia, PA: Elsevier Saunders.

Strickland, J. W., & Graham, T. (Eds.). (2005). *Master techniques in orthopedic surgery: The hand*. Philadelphia, PA: Lippincott, Williams, and Wilkins.

Swanson, A. B., Goran-Hagert, C., & Swanson, G. D. (1987). Evaluation of impairment in the upper extremity. *Journal of Hand Surgery - Part 2, 12a*(5), 896-925.

Trumble, T. E., Rayan, G. M., Baratz, M. E., Budoff, J. E., & Slutsky, D. J. (Ed.). (2017). *Principles of hand surgery and therapy* (3rd ed.). Amsterdam, Netherlands: Elsevier.

WebMD. (2010). *Finger, hand, and wrist injuries.* Retrieved from http://www.webmd.com/a-to-z-guides/finger-hand-and-wrist-injuries-topic-overview

Weiss, S., & Falkerstein, N. (Eds.) (2013). *Hand rehabilitation: A quick reference guide and review* (3rd ed.). St. Louis, MO: Mosby.

Wolfe, S. W., Peterson, W. C., Hotchkiss, R. N., & Cohen, M. (2016). *Green's operative hand surgery* (7th ed.). New York, NY: Churchill Livingstone.

Young, M., Stiens, S. A., O'Young, B., Baldwin, R., & Thatcher, B. N. (2017). Assistive technology: Adaptive tools of enablement for multiple disabilities. In A. Moroz, S. R. Flanagan, & H. H. Zaretsky (Eds.), *Medical aspects of disability for the rehabilitation professional* (5th ed., pp. 679-711). New York, NY: Springer.

About the Authors

George W. Balfour, M.D, is an orthopedic surgeon specializing in surgery of the hand. He is in private practice in Van Nuys, California, and is Assistant Professor of Surgery and Director of the Hand Clinic at the Charles R. Drew School of Medicine - Martin Luther King, Jr. Medical Center in Los Angeles. Active in the American Association for Hand Surgery and the American Society for Surgery of the Hand, Dr. Balfour has a special interest and expertise in microvascular surgery.

Martin G. Brodwin, PhD, CRC, is Professor Emeritus in the Rehabilitation Education Programs at California State University, Los Angeles. He is a vocational expert for the Office of Hearings Operations, Social Security Administration, providing testimony on disability-related issues. As a rehabilitation and vocational consultant, he provides assessment for long-term disability, case management, and reasonable accommodation. Dr. Brodwin has published over 115 refereed journal articles, book chapters, and books on the subjects of counseling, disability, rehabilitation, and medical aspects of chronic illness and disability.

Ashley T. Du, MS, received her Master of Science degree in counseling, with options in rehabilitation and school counseling leadership. Her interests are in the areas of chronic pain management, and in providing the most effective counseling and rehabilitation services for students. Ms. Du specializes in transitional counseling with an emphasis in college and career. As a counselor at Los Angeles Valley College in Valley Glen, California, she assists community college students with academic advisement, career counseling, and transition to a four-year college or university. Additionally, Ashley provides career assessment.

Chapter 30

ASSISTIVE TECHNOLOGY AND UNIVERSAL DESIGN

R. David Black, EdD, CRC
Martin G. Brodwin, PhD, CRC

Introduction

This chapter reviews assistive technology (AT) and universal design (UD). The AT section discusses definitions, the use of technology for people with disabilities, examples of technology, and the benefits of technology. The section on UD discusses the history and background of UD, definitions, principles, legislation, accessibility versus useability, and the role of the rehabilitation professional.

Assistive Technology

People with chronic illness and disability are seeing the benefits of assistive technology and are increasingly using it to join mainstream society. This development, in turn, benefits society as people who have disabilities become more independent and less reliant on public services. As the income level for people with disabilities increases, so too does their purchasing power to buy goods, services, and products. The field of AT is helping people with disabilities increase or restore functioning, enhance their quality of life, and integrate into society, both physically and emotionally.

Definitions

Assistive technology is defined in the "Technology-Related Assistance for Individuals with Disabilities Act of 1988 as "any item, piece of equipment, or product system, whether acquired commercially off the shelf, modified, or customized, that is used to increase, maintain, or improve functional capabilities of people with disabilities." Technology service is "any service that directly assists an individual with a disability in the selection, acquisition, or use of an assistive technology device" (Assistive Technology Act, 1998). More than 20 million Americans with disabilities are using assistive devices, equipment, computers, and other apparatus. People benefit from assistive technology at work, in school, at home, and in leisure time activities.

Use of Technology

The Workforce Innovation Opportunity Act (WIOA) was reauthorized in July 2014. This legislation mandates that AT devices and services be utilized along with vocational training and transition to employment in an effort to improve the public workforce by helping individuals with barriers to employment and employers seeking to hire skilled workers. Practitioners using AT are able to provide more meaningful, practical, and realistic clinical counseling and rehabilitation services for their clients. As noted by Scherer (2007), technology is radically changing the lives of individuals who have disabilities. AT has helped enhance the quality of life and extend the lifespan of persons with congenital and developmental disabilities, as well as those who have acquired disabilities and chronic medical conditions.

Devices and equipment are low-tech (mechanical) and high-tech (electromechanical or computer-related), and can help compensate for sensory and functional loss. AT provides the means to move (e.g., adaptive equipment on vehicles, wheelchairs [including power wheelchairs], scooters, lifts), speak (e.g., augmentative and alternative communication devices), read (e.g., Braille input, voice recognition devices), hear (telecommunication devices for the Deaf [TDD], hearing aids, audio loops), and manage self-care tasks (e.g., remote environmental control systems, prosthetic and orthotic devices, devices to aid a person in grooming, eating, and other activities of daily life) (Jette, Spicer, & Flaubert, 2017; Young, Stiens, O'Young, Baldwin, & Thatcher, 2017).

Examples of Technology

Computer Assisted Technology

Computer assisted technology includes software that allows individuals with disabilities to adapt to their surroundings and increase their independence. Eye-gaze technology is one example. It functions by tracking the movement of one's eye, which in turn activates a computer, provided an individual has sufficient head control and the ability to gaze directly at a camera. Derived from military eye control systems, the camera is typically attached to the head; however, the weight of the camera requires the head to be positioned and supported. Current scientific research promises enhanced eyeglass systems. Researchers are working on innovative gaze technology featuring virtual reality goggles that include an integrated camera and viewing screen to provide communication through icon choice. The user chooses targets by gazing at the icons on the computer screen; the camera, integrated within the goggles, tracks eye gaze motion and relays information for instant processing (Brodwin, Boland, Lane, & Siu, 2012; Cook & Polgar, 2017; Scherer, 2007).

People with disabilities benefit from a number of software programs, including screen reading software that helps users with no vision use computers, magnification programs for those with low vision, and voice command software that helps people with hand or arm limitations. Mobile smartphone technology has made great improvements in the field of assistive technology. Products that were once stand alone and very expensive are now more readily available via an application download. Optical character recognition (OCR) scanning programs (for people with visual impairment), for example, once required a computer, screen reading software, and a scanner to convert print documents into characters with text-to-speech output. Now, one needs only a camera-equipped smartphone and the OCR application.

GPS (Global Positioning System) applications on smartphones help people with visual impairment travel independently. Some connect via Bluetooth to shoes with vibration sensing, which tells users when to make a right or left turn. This technology also tells users about objects in their vicinity and guides them through slow moving traffic. Ability to sense fast traffic, stairs, and sharp drop-offs are now being developed. Some smartphones come with built-in assistive technology, such as screen readers, touch assist for individuals with mobility impairment, and flash alerts and TDD for Deaf and hearing impaired. Smartphone technology has made assistive technology less costly and more accessible.

Smart technology has expanded tremendously over the past few years from not just phones, but to other devices, such as televisions and speakers. Smart speakers and hubs, such as those that control household appliances, lights, thermostats, making them smart homes, have provided more independence to individuals with disabilities.

Sensory Technology

Accommodations for people with visual impairments include both optical and non-optical devices for low vision. Examples of optical devices are magnifiers, specially coated lenses, visual prosthesis, and telescopes. Non-optical visual aids include talking clocks and watches, talking calculators, closed-circuit televisions that enlarge print electronically, and personal computers and peripherals with the capacity of print magnification, speech output, voice activated interfaces, and optical scanning (Brodwin, Siu, & Cardoso, 2018). Other assistive devices that aid in navigation include white canes with laser or ultrasonic technology. These devices enhance the reach of a white cane in that it informs users when objects are approaching, if objects are at head level, and the presence of stairs and drop offs.

Hearing aids, telecommunication devices for the Deaf (TDD), electronic ears, amplified telephones, phones or alarms that use flashing lights for alerts, and audio loops are helpful technology devices for persons who are Deaf or hard-of-hearing. Also, there is real time captioning on site or remotely converted discussions into text displayed on a computer screen (Jette et al., 2017; Young et al., 2017).

Currently, a wide variety of AT is available. Technologies used by hearing people are useful to people with hearing loss, such as web-based chat, e-mail, and text messaging. Additional communication technologies have been developed for people who are Deaf or hard of hearing, including text-based telephone relay systems and video relay systems.

A more complicated system is the infrared system. This system transmits sound into light which is sent to a receiver worn by an individual; the light is decoded and converted back to a magnetic signal which is picked up by the person's telecoil. Sound is transmitted to the listener clearly and free of distracting noise in the environment. Telecoils, available for most hearing aids, enhance the performance of wired and wireless telephones (Jette et al., 2017).

Hearing assistive technology "encompasses a wide range of products with the overall goal of enabling users to hear and communicate more effectively in their homes (e.g., television), in public spaces (e.g., movies and lectures, and through phones or other communications products and systems" (NASEM, 2016, p. 149).

Robotics

Technology includes the science of robotic controls. Robotics are able to accommodate for manipulative tasks, perform functions through prosthetic (e.g., artificial extremity) applications, render movement in spinal cord injuries (e.g., paralysis), and perform task operations in fixed workstation (at the work site) technologies (Cook & Pulgar, 2015). Someone needing the assistance of a robotic arm attaches it to a powered wheelchair, from which he or she can control it using a selection and toggle interface.

Robotic devices provide assistance with such functions as drinking, retrieving items from shelves, manipulating objects, and participating in games or leisure activities. People with disabilities can use fixed workstation (desktop) robots to manipulate objects. Similarly, someone using a desktop vocational robot can use it to perform daily activities such as preparing and eating meals, writing, reading, operating a keyboard, using a telephone, and grooming.

Neuroprosthetics

Neuroprosthetic devices are used to compensate for a damaged or missing motor or sensory function. The cochlear implant is a well-known example. This technology has been further refined and become more sophisticated with the use of robotics. Based on military technology, neuroprosthetic devices are connected to an individual's nerves and controlled through nerve impulses. These devices help to restore function of a missing or injured limb, and they can also help restore one's sense of touch (Berg et al., 2013). Neuroprostheses are especially helpful for individuals with tetraplegia; by restoring control of movement of one's limbs via a direct connection to the brain, a neuroprosthetic device helps someone become more independent (Collinger et al., 2013).

Neuroprosthetic technology has been developed to improve sight in people with visual disabilities. By using retina implants or artificial retinas, people with macular degeneration can regain some elements of sight (Humayun et al., 2012). This technology promises to go beyond assistive technology and rehabilitation by actually restoring function.

New technology called brain-machine interfaces can partially restore neurological function in individuals with spinal cord injury (Donati et al., 2016). In this study, individuals wore a lower limb exoskeleton which connects to the brain; they were given training for a year. These persons regained voluntary motor control which improved their walking, and half were reclassified as having incomplete, rather than complete paraplegia.

Prosthetics and Orthotics

In the last 15 years, upper extremity prosthetic systems have become more widely available commercially. People using hand motion control systems can now execute multiple functions simultaneously. While previous control systems employed skin surface sensors (electrodes) placed over the controlling muscle, these new systems included muscle implants, avoiding the need for skin surface contact.

"A microprocessor is 'trained' to recognize various movement, making it more 'intuitive' and less mentally taxing." (Jette et al., 2017, p. 89).

Experimental surgery involves an electrode sensor being implanted into the brain so that the thought of flexing or extending an elbow, opening or closing a hand or finger results in the intended motion. The intent is to make the movement so intuitive that thought alone causes the motion (Berg et al., 2013). The hybrid arm prosthesis includes both electric and body-powered components, allowing the user to operate the elbow and hand simultaneously (Jette et al., 2017).

The field of lower extremity prosthetics has developed in recent years as well. Microprocessor controlled orthotic ankle and knee joints are now more common. The C-Leg, for example, allows the wearer to flex his or her foot and shin. This reduces the energy demands of walking, allowing a user to navigate stairs, ramps, and other previously difficult terrains without the risk of falling (Young et al., 2017).

Haptic Technology

Haptic technology incorporates tactile feedback as part of its user interface, creating a sense of touch through vibrations, motion, or other forces (American Library Association, 2017). This technology started with video game controllers that vibrate, and are now in other commercial products such as Apple watch and computer mousses. This has opened the doors to apply this technology to help individuals with disabilities. For example, touchscreen phones can apply haptic technology so that users who have visual impairment can have tactile (and audio) feedback of a photograph, or while taking a photo to know where the center of a face is located (ABC News, 2015). It has potential to apply to online libraries to allow patrons to have hands on and more interactive experiences (American Library Association, 2017).

Access and availability coverage for various devices is available from various agencies. These include the Social Security Administration, Medicare, the VA Healthcare System, and state vocational rehabilitation programs (Jette et al., 2017).

Benefits of Technology

Increased educational and employment opportunities and a greater sense of personal well-being has led to upward social mobility. Technological devices, equipment, and services allow many people with disabilities to: (a) exert greater control over their own lives; (b) participate in and contribute more fully and readily to activities in their homes, schools, employment, and communities; (c) interact to a far greater extent with people without disabilities; and (d) benefit from opportunities taken for granted by people without disabilities (Brodwin et al., 2018; Scherer, 2007).

In the early 2000s, the main reason people with disabilities stopped using computers was because of difficulties they encountered using the product. To diminish discontinuance, the user needs to be involved throughout the process (Riemer-Reiss & Wacker, 2000). AT aims to enhance functional independence for people with disabilities. The focus is on what a person can do. By exploring a person's capabilities, functional limitations, and feelings about technological devices, rehabilitation practitioners can help people with disabilities achieve their goals.

The Promise of Assistive Technology

To maximize the impact and use of technology for persons with disabilities, the Committee on the Use of Selective Assistive Products and Technologies recommended the following (Jette et al., 2017):

1. Assistive products and technologies hold promise for mitigating the impact of impairments and enhancing work participation when appropriate products and technologies are available, when they are properly prescribed and fitted, when the user receives proper training in their use and appropriate follow-up, and when societal and environmental barriers are limited.

2. When matching individuals with appropriate assistive products and technologies, it is important to understand the complexity of factors that must be optimized to enhance function. Selecting, designing, or modifying the correct device for an individual and providing training in its use, as well as appropriate follow-up, are complex but necessary elements for maximizing function (p. 4).

Universal Design

History and Background of Universal Design

Universal design is the name of a design approach that incorporates inclusive design features while minimizing the need for individual accommodations (Jette et al., 2017; Mace, 1985; Young et al., 2017). Universal design can enhance access to higher education and employment for people with disabilities and those with chronic medical conditions. In the 1960s, Ronald Mace, an architect and wheelchair user, said physical environments should be designed to meet the needs of the "broadly diverse individuals who access these areas." Mace formed the Center for Universal Design at North Carolina State University in 1989.

The National Institute on Disability and Rehabilitation Research, U.S. Department of Education supported the initiative from 1994 to 1997 (Story, Mueller, & Mace, 1998). While the principles of universal design were originally intended for architecture, they were later applied to product and environment design as well. "Everyone benefits from UD because it takes into account the full range of human diversity, including physical, cognitive, and perceptual differences, as well as differences in body shapes and sizes" (Young et al., 2017, pp. 700-701).

Many advocates of barrier-free design and architectural accessibility recognized the legal, economic, and social power of a concept that addressed the common needs of people with and without disabilities (Heylighen & Bianchin, 2013; Mackelprang & Clute, 2009; Story et al., 1998). As an example, in architecture, segregated accessible features were not only special, they were also more expensive and usually unsightly. Architects and advocates found that many of the environmental changes needed to accommodate people with disabilities actually benefited everyone, thus laying the groundwork for universal design. Examples are as simple as having wide doorways and ramp inclines rather than stairs at entrances so that people using wheelchairs or families with strollers may easily pass through.

Assistive technology can aid in universal design, where universal design strives to integrate people with disabilities into the mainstream, and assistive technology attempts to meet the specific needs of an individual (Story et al., 1998). The Blackberry, for example, was originally intended for members of the Deaf community. The QWERTY (term comes from the fact the first six letters of the top row of keys are Q, W, E, R, T, and Y.) keyboard design made texting easier, not just for individuals with disabilities but for everyone else as well. Apple Inc. designs everything from their desktop computers to their mobile devices with universal design in mind. Its products are accessible to people with disabilities 'right out of the box' without requiring the purchase of additional software or equipment.

Realizing its potential, many educators have applied the concept of universal design to education. Silver, Bourke, and Strehorn (1998) used the concept in elementary and secondary education as a new paradigm for making instruction more readily accessible. Teachers who provide electronic copies of lecture notes or handouts are using the principles of universal design.

Workplace designers have begun applying universal design to work environments (Jette et al., 2017; Young et al., 2017). Workstations with adjustable desks is an example of universal design. While these workstations benefit people who use wheelchairs most directly, they also help employees with substantial height differences, or those for whom standing is more effective for certain work functions.

What is Universal Design?

Universal design makes accessibility issues a *proactive and integral focus* of instructional planning and creates an environment that a wide range of individuals can use (Silver et al., 1998). There are many other concepts that are closely related to universal design, such as inclusive design, design for all, and accessible design (Persson, Åhman, Yngling, & Gulliksen, 2015). Ultimately, these different terms focus on having the widest range of use. Organizations such as the Center for Applied Special Technology (CAST) are leading the field in applying universal design to teaching and learning environments.

CAST (2013) defined universal design as a set of principles for curriculum development that give all individuals equal opportunities to learn. Universal design provides a blueprint for creating instructional goals, methods, materials, and assessments that can work for everyone. It also includes flexible approaches that can be customized and adjusted for individuals.

Universal design incorporates various technologies, both assistive and mainstream. In education, computer-based testing with read aloud capability has demonstrated effectiveness for students with learning disabilities to increase test question comprehension and improve test scores (Pace & Schwartz, 2008). Educators who have embraced universal design have also used it to improve reading comprehension in students with intellectual disabilities. In employment, technologies used to improve function include audio prompting devices, video-assisted training, computers, and augmentative and alternative communication for people with developmental disabilities.

Principles of Universal Design

When originally developed, universal design included seven principles (Center for Universal Design, 1997). When applied to education, designers added two additional principles that can also be used in the workplace (Burgstahler, 2012):

1. Equitable use: design where any groups of individuals can use it. For example, a website that is accessible to all users, including people who use screen readers.

2. Flexibility in use: the design accommodates a wide range of individual abilities and preferences; that is, it provides a choice in methods of use. An example of this principle is reading technology where the software allows the option of reading a textbook aloud so that students with learning disabilities can read along for improved comprehension.

3. Simple and intuitive: use of the design is straightforward eliminating unnecessary complexity, regardless of the user's knowledge, experience, language skills, and concentration level. As an example, the controls of safety equipment or telecommunication devices can have alarm signals (light/sound) clearly identified and controls which are accessible and in high contrast.

4. Perceptible information: one needs to communicate necessary information effectively to the individual regardless of ambient conditions or sensory abilities. For example, orientation videos that are online with both sound, text script of the video, and autoplay for orientation materials.

5. Tolerance for error: the design minimizes hazards and the adverse consequences of accidental or unintended actions; it anticipates variation in the individual's pace and prerequisite skill. An example is allowing students to turn in individual components of a project for feedback.

6. Low physical effort: designed to eliminate nonessential physical effort, which is a design that can be used efficiently, comfortably, and with a minimum of fatigue. Examples of this are ergonomic chairs that decrease work-related back injuries, or doors that open automatically, beneficial for people who lack strength or physical ability to open a door, someone who uses a wheelchair, or individuals who have their hands occupied with equipment.

7. Size and space for approach and use: appropriate size and space is provided for approach, reach, manipulation, and use regardless of the user's body size, posture, or mobility. An example of this principle is a workstation that accommodates persons of different sizes.

8. Community of learners: the environment promotes interaction and communication. For example, an information desk at a business or library that is open and accessible from different angles to encourage engagement of people seeking information.

9. Climate: the instructional or workplace environment is designed to be welcoming and inclusive. An example is where input or suggestions from students or employees are invited.

Legislation and Definition

Legislation that first discussed the term universal design was the Assistive Technology Act (1998). This Act provided funding for assistive technology (a device or service used to increase, maintain, or improve functional capabilities of individuals with disabilities) projects to improve quality of life of people with disabilities. Assistive technology allows people with disabilities to more fully participate in education, employment, and daily activities. Universal design was referred to as the concept for designing and delivering products and services that are usable by people with the widest possible range of functional capabilities. It included products and services that are directly accessible (without requiring assistive technologies) and products and services that are interoperable with assistive technologies. An example includes screen reading software built into the operating system of a computer.

Recognizing that universal design can be applied to and has the potential to improve practice in classrooms and provide opportunities for students to succeed, the Higher Education Opportunity Act (HEOA) was passed and reauthorized in 2008. It became the first legislation to establish a statutory definition for the term universal design for learning (principles include representation, expression, and engagement). The term means a scientifically valid framework for guiding educational practice that provides flexibility in the ways information is presented, in the ways students respond or demonstrate knowledge and skills, and in the ways students are engaged, with the intent of reducing barriers in instruction, providing appropriate accommodations, supports, and challenges, and maintaining high achievement expectations for all students (HEOA, 2008). Universal design promotes the social responsibility of all persons in creating an environment that is usable by the highest number of people.

Accessible Versus Usable

There is a significant difference between accessible and usable. Quite often, these concepts are interchanged - it being assumed that if something is accessible, it is also usable. Yet, this is not always the case. Accessible in regard to access by individuals with disabilities means that they can access items such as instructional materials or websites. Usable means that an individual can use the instructional materials or websites efficiently, effectively, and with satisfaction (W3C Web Accessibility Initiative, 2016). Usable accessibility is a term used in web design that considers individuals with disabilities while designing usable sites.

Human factors psychology aims to design effective and user-friendly tools, machines, and systems to better match the capabilities, limitations, and needs of people. Application of universal design principles along with various modalities as human factors psychology, ergonomics, technologies such as assistive technologies, and best instructional practices help create an inclusive environment.

The following is a study conducted that exemplifies accessibility versus usability. Sapp (2007) evaluated two scheduling systems, Myschooldayonline system compared to Microsoft Outlook in secondary education. Participants included 12 students who were blind (with some or no light perception) who used a screen reader to access the computer, and two students with low vision (who met the definition of legal blindness) who used screen enlargement programs to access the computer. There were eight computer dyads total. Students who were blind worked in groups of two paired by computer skill on each computer, totaling six computers, while the two students with low vision worked on one computer each, totaling two computers.

This study revealed student preference for Myschooldayonline. Students were more successful using Myschooldayonline than Microsoft Outlook which they had difficulty using and completing tasks, indicating that Outlook was accessible, but not usable. Students with low vision who accessed Outlook visually demonstrated as many problems and performed equivalently to students who were blind and used JAWS (Job Access with Speech screen reading software) to access Outlook. This study showed that technology needs to be usable to be successful.

Other examples of accessibility versus usability are programs such as Microsoft Power Point. An individual with a visual impairment who uses a screen reader may be able to access these programs with a computer. However, navigation and use of the program can be difficult and thus not meet the definition of *usable*, depending on the screen reading software. With Power Point, the screen reader can read what is on the screen when the program is opened. However, when a person who uses a screen reader tries to move to a different slide or make edits, this process becomes time consuming since the process may not be intuitive, thus lacking efficiency and effectiveness. Hence, it may be accessible but not usable.

Application of Universal Design

There are many positive aspects to implementing universal design. Often, applying the principles of universal design and supporting the student or employee with a disability or chronic illness is accomplished through assistive technology, accommodations, changing job requirements, or modifications of the work environment or classroom instruction. These approaches also benefit other students or employees without disabilities. Applying ergonomic practices is a strategy of universal design as this benefits other employees by improving the work environment and reducing work-related injuries.

Another strategy is changing the physical environment to accommodate individuals with disabilities. An example is widening of bathroom stalls to accommodate people who use wheelchairs. Sensor equipped sinks and toilets benefit individuals who are unable to reach the sink handles due to height and individuals with visual impairment making operation more convenient.

Other examples in applying the principles of universal design are technologies, such as computers and smart phones with accessibility software built into the operating systems, enhancing access for people with disabilities and decreasing the need for third party applications. Websites of schools and businesses also need to be accessible and usable. Standards and recommendations are available for making them usable and accessible using the principles of universal design. Universal design has been successfully applied to writing centers in education, computer labs, and communication (Brizee, Sousa, & Driscoll, 2012; Wandke, Sengpiel, & Sönkse, 2012).

Training of staff, faculty, administrators, and employers is necessary to apply universal design principles in educational institutions and within the workplace (Jette et al., 2017; Young et al., 2017). Universal design principles should be incorporated into policies and procedures to ensure universal access to education and employment. Access needs to be usable, flexible, and improve learning in the educational environment, as well as enhance productivity and job satisfaction within the workplace. Although the concept of universal design has been around for over five decades in architecture and product design, the concept is still relatively recent in education and the workplace.

Many in the fields of education and business are not accustomed to designing curricula or workplace environments to meet the needs of all individuals (Black, Weinberg, & Brodwin, 2014, 2015). Currently, modifications are placed after an individual with disability requests accommodations rather than during the design process. This mind set or lack of familiarity with universal design serves as a barrier to implementation. Counselors can educate and assist schools and employers in strategies to accommodate, assist, and include individuals with disabilities by using principles of universal design.

Role of the Rehabilitation Professional

In applying the principles of universal design, the rehabilitation professional must take into account the functional needs of the individual and ensure that accommodations match those needs. This includes use of assistive or adaptive technology, devices, equipment, and changes in work tasks. For example, the use of a closed circuit television (CCTV) to magnify hard copy material, such as during exams for a student with low vision or for employees while working. In many instances, the CCTV is slow as it takes time for the individual to magnify each section of the text which can cause fatigue. Extended use may cause eye strain, and may not improve understanding of the text. In some situations, use of a CCTV may be more appropriate for short periods of time for materials that may not have been converted to electronic format.

Additionally, rehabilitation professionals need to remember that usability of equipment, technologies, and software is just as significant as accessibility. It is important to keep this in mind to limit additional barriers or constraints for individuals with disabilities. Rehabilitation professionals are valuable resources to schools and employers to provide education and evaluation for accommodations and inclusion. There are resources on universal design principles and how to apply these principles to make school curricula and work environments accessible and usable for people of all abilities.

References

ABC News. (2015). *New haptic technology helps people with disabilities.* Retrieved from http://abc7chicago.com/technology/new-haptic-technology-helps-people-with-disabilities/829715

American Library Association. (2017). *Haptic technology.* Retrieved from http://www.ala.org/transforminglibraries/future/trends/haptic

Assistive Technology Act. *(1998). 29 U.S.C. § 3002 et seq.*

Berg, J. A., Dammann, J. F., 3rd, Tenore, F. V., Tabot, G. A., Boback, J. L., Manfredi, L. R., . . . Bensmaia, S. J. (2013). Behavioral demonstration of a somatosensory neuroprosthesis. *IEEE Transactions Neural Systems Rehabilitation Engineering, 21*(3), 500-507.

Black, R. D., Weinberg, L. A., & Brodwin, M. G. (2014). Universal design for learning and instruction: A pilot study of faculty instructional methods and attitudes related to students with disabilities in higher education. *Exceptionality Education International, 24*, 48-64.

Black, R. D., Weinberg, L. A., & Brodwin, M. G. (2015). Universal design for learning and instruction: Perspectives of students with disabilities in higher education. *Exceptionality Education International, 25*, 1-16.

Brizee, A., Sousa, M., & Driscoll, D. L. (2012). Writing centers and students with disabilities: The user-centered approach, participatory design, and empirical research as collaborative methodologies. *Computers & Composition, 29*(4), 341-366.

Brodwin, M. G., Boland, E. A., Lane, F. J., & Siu, F. W. (2012). Technology in rehabilitation counseling. In R. M. Parker & J. B. Patterson (Eds.), *Rehabilitation counseling: Basics and beyond* (5th ed., pp. 333-367). Austin, TX: Pro-ed.

Brodwin, M. G., Siu, F. W., & Cardoso, E. (2018). Users of assistive technology: The human component. In I. Marini & M. A. Stebnicki (Eds.), *The psychological and social impact of illness and disability* (7th ed., pp. 345-353). New York, NY: Springer.

Burgstahler, S. (2012). Universal design: Process, principles, and applications. *DO-IT (Disabilities, Opportunities, Internetworking, and Technology).* Retrieved from http://www.washington.edu/doit/Brochures/PDF/ud.pdf

CAST. (2013). *UDL guidelines version 2.0.* Retrieved from http://www.cast.org/udl/index.html

Center for Universal Design. (1997). *The principles of universal design, version 2.0.* Raleigh, NC: North Carolina State University.

Collinger, J. L., Wodlinger, B., Downey, J. E., Wang, W., Tyler-Kabara, E. C., Weber, D. J., . . . Schwartz, A. B. (2013). High-performance neuroprosthetic control by an individual with tetraplegia. *The Lancet, 381*, 557-564.

Cook, A. M., & Polgar, J. M. (2015). *Assistive technology: Principles and practice* (4th ed.). St. Louis, MO: Elsevier Mosby.

Donati, A. R., Shokur, S., Morya, E., Campos, D. S., Moioli, R. C., Gitti, C. M., . . . Nicolelis, M. A. (2016). Long-term training with a brain-machine interface-based gait protocol induces partial neurological recovery in paraplegic patients. *Scientific Reports, 6*, 30383.

Heylighen, A., & Bianchin, M. (2013). How does inclusive design relate to good design? Designing as a deliberative enterprise. *Design Studies, 34*(1), 93-110.

Higher Education Opportunity Act (HEOA). (2008). Pub. L. No. 110-314, 122 Stat. 3078.

Humayun, M. S., Dorn, J. D., da Cruz, L., Dagnelie, G., Sahel, J. A., Stanga, P. E., . . . Greenberg, R. J. (2012). Interim results from the international trial of Second Sight's visual prosthesis. *Ophthalmology, 119*(4), 779-788.

Jette, A. M., Spicer, C. M., & Flaubert, J. L. (Eds.). (2017). *The promise of assistive technology to enhance activity and work participation.* Washington, DC: The National Academies Press.

Mace, R. L. (1985). Universal design: Barrier free environments for everyone. *Designers West, 33*(1), 147–152.

Mackelprang, R. W., & Clute, M. A. (2009). Access for all: Universal design and the employment of people with disabilities. *Journal of Social Work in Disability & Rehabilitation, 8*(3/4), 205-221.

NASEM (National Academies of Sciences, Engineering, and Medicine. (2016). *Hearing health care for adult priorities for improving access*. Washington, DC: The National Academies Press.

Pace, D., & Schwartz, D. (2008). Accessibility in post secondary education: Application of UDL to college curriculum. *US-China Education Review, 5*(12), 20-26. Retrieved from http://www.davidpublishing.com/show.html?6497

Persson, H., Åhman, H., Yngling, A. A., & Gulliksen, J. (2015). Universal design, inclusive design, accessible design, design for all: different concepts - One goal? On the concept of accessibility - Historical, methodological and philosophical aspects. *Universal Access in the Information Society, 14*(4), 505-526.

Riemer-Reiss, M. L., & Wacker, R. R. (2000). Factors associated with assistive technology discontinuance among individuals with disabilities. *Journal of Rehabilitation, 66*(3), 44-50.

Sapp, W. (2007). Myschooldayonline: Applying universal design principles to the development of a fully accessible online scheduling tool for students with visual impairments. *Journal of Visual Impairment & Blindness, 101*(5), 301–307.

Scherer, M. J. (2007). *Living in the state of stuck: How assistive technology impacts the lives of people with disabilities*. Brookline, MA: Brookline Books.

Silver, P., Bourke, A., & Strehorn, K. C. (1998). Universal instruction design in higher education: An approach for inclusion. *Equity and Excellence in Education, 31*(2), 47–51.

Story, M. F., Mueller, J. L., & Mace, R. L. (1998). *The universal design file: Designing for people of all ages and abilities*. Raleigh, NC: North Carolina State University, Raleigh Center for Universal Design.

W3C Web Accessibility Initiative. (2016). *Accessibility, Usability, and Inclusion: Related aspects of a web for all*. Retrieved from https://www.w3.org/WAI/intro/usable

Wandke, H., Sengpiel, M., & Sönkse, M. (2012). Myths about older people's use of information and communication technology. *Gerontology, 58*(6), 564-570.

Young, M., Stiens, S. A., O'Young, B., Baldwin, R., & Thatcher, B. N. (2017). Assistive technology: Adaptive tools of enablement for multiple disabilities. In A. Moroz, S. R. Flanagan, & H. Zaretsky (Eds.), *Medical aspects of disability for the rehabilitation professional* (5th ed., pp. 697-711). New York, NY: Springer.

About the Authors

R. David Black, EdD, MPH, LPC, NCC, CRC, is a researcher in universal design in education and the workplace, assistive technology, and disability associated with chronic disease and public health. He provides lectures in these areas at California State University, Los Angeles (CSULA). Within the community, Dr. Black assists individuals with disabilities, survivors of trauma, adolescents, and veterans returning to higher education.

Martin G. Brodwin, PhD, CRC, is Professor Emeritus in the Rehabilitation Education Programs at CSULA. As a vocational expert for the Office of Hearings Operations, Social Security Administration, he testifies on disability-related issues. Additionally, he provides assessment for long-term disability, case management, and accommodation. Dr. Brodwin has published over 115 refereed journal articles, book chapters, and books on the subjects of counseling, disability, rehabilitation, and medical aspects of chronic illness and disability.

Chapter 31

SICKLE CELL DISEASE AND HEMOPHILIA

John J. Howard, MD, MPH

Introduction

Hematology is the study of blood, blood-forming organs like bone marrow, and diseases of blood. Blood is composed of cellular and fluid components. The cellular components are formed from stem cells in the bone marrow and are of three major types: red blood cells (RBCs), white blood cells (WBCs), and platelets. The fluid component of blood is called plasma. Plasma is composed mainly of water, but also contains proteins, which are responsible for clotting (coagulation), and antibodies that help fight infections. The plasma also serves as the main fluid transport system of the body, delivering glucose, electrolytes (such as sodium and potassium), and other nutrients throughout the body.

RBCs are the most numerous of the cellular components circulating in the blood. Each RBC contains molecules of hemoglobin, an iron-containing protein that is responsible for transporting oxygen from the lungs to the rest of the body. Diseases affecting hemoglobin are numerous but the most common is *sickle cell disease*. There is a cascade of plasma proteins responsible for blood coagulation. The coagulation cascade serves as one of the body's most important methods of self-repair after trauma (Hoffman et al., 2013). Disorders affecting coagulation are numerous, but the most common is a genetic bleeding disorder called *hemophilia*. Sickle cell disease and hemophilia are the two most common conditions that a rehabilitation counselor is likely to encounter when providing services to people with hematological disorders.

Sickle Cell Disease

Sickle cell disease (SCD) is a genetic disease caused by the production of an abnormal hemoglobin, called hemoglobin S (HbS). Presence of HbS leads to chronic anemia and acute and chronic tissue damage secondary to blockage of blood flow produced by abnormally *sickle-shaped* RBCs. SCD occurs most commonly in individuals of African ancestry, but also affects people of Mediterranean, Caribbean, South and Central American, Arab, and East Indian ancestry. It is estimated that approximately 100,000 persons have SCD in the United States (Hassell, 2010).

Genetics

SCD was the first disease for which a single molecular cause was discovered (Ingram, 1956). SCD results from a single amino acid substitution in the â globin chain of the hemoglobin molecule, valine for glutamic acid, which produces HbS. If an individual inherits the sickle cell gene from only one parent, the person carries the *sickle cell trait*. Individuals with sickle cell trait do not exhibit any symptoms of SCD, but are protected from severe malaria (Piel, Steinberg, & Rees, 2017). If an individual inherits the sickle cell gene from both parents, he or she has *sickle cell disease.*

Clinical Manifestations

HbS is a hemoglobin molecule of reduced solubility; when deoxygenated (lacking oxygen), it becomes rigidly polymerized. Polymerization of HbS inside the RBC converts the RBC from its normal biconcave shape to a crescent or sickle-shape, reducing the flexibility of the RBC. As a result, the blood containing many sickled RBCs becomes more viscous (thicker). Sickled RBCs block blood vessels, damaging them. This leads to death of the cells supplied downstream by the affected blood vessels (vaso-occlusive crisis). Sickled RBCs are responsible for producing all the clinical manifestations of disease in people who have SCD (Howard & Telfer, 2015).

Vaso-occlusive crisis causes acute complications to nearly every organ of the body (Piel et al., 2017). Acute pain is the first symptom of a vaso-occlusive crisis in most individuals. A painful vaso-occlusive crisis has a sudden onset, usually lasting five to six days, and may be localized in one area of the body or generalized. One type of vaso-occlusive crisis, acute chest syndrome, is the second most common cause of hospitalization, and the leading cause of death in persons with SCD (Hassell, 2010). Acute chest syndrome is caused by simultaneous vaso-occlusion and infection, and can progress to respiratory failure if not treated aggressively with antibiotics, transfusions, and bronchodilators to improve oxygenation (Castro, Brambilia, & Thorington, 1994).

Other organs of the body can be affected by vaso-occlusive complications (Howard & Telfer, 2015). Leg ulcers can occur due to cell death in the skin around the ankles. Vaso-occlusion involving the joints can be physically limiting. Bone infarcts (aseptic necrosis) in the lower extremities and the vertebrae of the spinal cord precipitate collapse of the involved bone, and lead to degenerative osteoarthritis in older individuals. Occlusion of the arteries supplying the brain can result in a stroke. Both intellectual and physical disabilities may result from central nervous system complications in childhood, leading to limitations in adulthood.

Treatment

Clinical outcomes for persons with SCD have improved as a result of supportive care and treatment (Piel et al., 2017). The following interventions are mainstays of current treatment: (1) avoiding dehydration; (2) providing immunizations, preventive antibiotics, and early treatment of infections; (3) administering regular blood transfusions; and (4) using the drug hydroxyurea to prevent acute pain and the acute chest syndrome (Platt, 2008). A new drug, crizanlizumab, has been shown to significantly lower the rate of sickle cell-related pain crises, and may become an important adjunct to current treatment (Ataga et al., 2017). Stem-cell transplantation is a potentially curative option, but its cost, the toxicity of the conditioning procedures necessary prior to transplantation, and the limited availability of suitable donors, makes its use of limited value (Bernaudin et al., 2007). Gene therapy to correct the underlying molecular cause of SCD is showing promise as a potentially curative treatment for SCD (Ribeil et al., 2017).

Complications and Functional Limitations

Comprehensive management of *lifespan* health conditions, like SCD, is challenging and there are no effective models of SCD care (Minniti & Vichinsky, 2017). A full range of medical, psychiatric, and social services are needed to maximize overall functioning for successful rehabilitation.

Physical Limitations

Physical limitations are primarily the result of the decreased energy level associated with the chronic anemia of SCD, and the pain associated with sickle cell crises (Raphael & Lin, 2017).

Chronic anemia. Chronic hemolytic anemia is a hallmark of SCD. Sickled RBCs are destroyed randomly throughout the body, including in the spleen and liver, resulting in an average RBC lifespan of only 17 days compared to 120 days for a RBC in a non-affected individual. Chronic anemia diminishes an individual's energy level and makes activities requiring physical exertion difficult.

Pain crisis. Although variable, painful sickle cell crises may occur several times a year. The crisis usually resolves within a week, but residual symptoms can last an additional five to ten days. Some people maintain work activity throughout a pain crisis, but others need time off work. Counselors need to consider the level of work when providing vocational rehabilitation (Brodwin, Parker, & DeLaGarza, 2010). Employees with sedentary or light jobs are able to continue working through sickle cell crises more often than persons who have physically demanding jobs.

Pulmonary complications. Shortness of breath in lung disease becomes the limiting factor for work requiring exertion (Greer et al., 2013). Job restructuring or accommodation is useful when a position even has occasional physical demands beyond the person's capacity.

Neurologic complications. Seizures (especially in childhood SCD), spinal cord compression, central nervous system infections, vestibular dysfunction, and hearing loss are neurologic complications of sickle cell disease. The most serious of the neurologic complications is the occurrence of a stroke. Approximately 11% of individuals with SCD have clinically apparent strokes before the age of 20 years. That risk increases to 24% by the age of 45 (Ohene-Frempong et al., 1998), although regular blood transfusions help prevent silent strokes (DeBraun et al., 2014). The residual effects of strokes include mild muscle weakness and sensory impairment.

Eye complications. In SCD, visual field defects and visual loss in one or both eyes can occur because the retinal artery is vulnerable to vaso-occlusion. Functional limitation is dependent on extent of visual loss; improvement in function occurs with use of visual aids.

Skin complications. Leg ulcers produce pain and limitations of motion in the affected extremity. This interferes with activities such as standing, walking, climbing, and balancing. Prolonged standing is one possible cause of these ulcers (Falvo & Holland, 2018).

Bone and joint complications. Bone and joint disease interfere with physical activity because of pain, deformity, and loss of strength. Walking, standing, bending, climbing, and balancing may be affected. Some limitations are overcome by a person learning new techniques for physical activities through physical therapy. Prosthetic implant surgery has been a successful technique in this area.

Environmental Factors

Several environmental conditions worsen symptoms. Jobs involving exposure to cold and dampness are to be avoided since these environmental factors can precipitate a pain crisis. Exposure to noxious fumes, high levels of dust, and poor ventilation are not tolerated well, especially for individuals with pulmonary problems. Hot and humid conditions add stress on the heart and precipitate dehydration. On all jobs, persons with SCD need easy availability of water and other fluids to prevent dehydration (Francis & Johnson, 1991).

Psychosocial Issues

Emotional stress exacerbates symptoms and make management of SCD difficult. An inability to predict or control symptoms leads to heightened anxiety. Recurrent painful episodes of sickle cell crises impact emotional distress. Depression is the major psychological factor associated with SCD; it affects ability to cope with the variable nature of the disease (Brodwin et al., 2010). Consequently, psychological consultation is helpful when preparing a client for vocational rehabilitation.

Rehabilitation Potential

Most individuals will not need vocational rehabilitation services, but those with recurrent sickle cell crises that interrupt their work lives, and persons with chronic complications benefit from rehabilitation services. Counselors need to explain to employers what SCD is and its symptoms.

An employee with an otherwise consistent employment record may be able to use accumulated sick leave for occasional sickle cell crises. Reasonable accommodation often facilitates a successful return to work for someone with moderate to severe symptoms (Brodwin et al., 2010). An example of reasonable accommodation for an employee with SCD is an agreement with the employer that the individual will work through minor illnesses, and save or accumulate sick days to be used for major sickle cell crises. Another accommodation is to have the worker put in non-paid overtime between crises to be used when work is missed during a crisis.

Onsite observation of the job helps the counselor modify physical aspects of the position. When a worker is having difficulty with physical exertion, the counselor can assist the client and employer in modifying the amount of lifting and carrying required (Falvo & Holland, 2018). One may be able to break down the amount lifted and carried into lighter loads; if this is not possible, the counselor may want to recommend job restructuring.

Mental stress present on the job and its effect on potential development of sickle cell crisis needs careful assessment. Modification of emotional stressors is more difficult than alteration of physical activities. At times, positive facilitation by the counselor is effective and results in decreasing emotionally stressful aspects of the job. Employer education creates a more thorough understanding of SCD, helping diminish work-related stressors.

When determining rehabilitation potential, the counselor evaluates any physical complications the individual has and whether time off from work may be necessary when sickle cell crises occur. This information, appropriate medical consultation, and an understanding supervisor enables the counselor to provide effective rehabilitation for clients with this disease.

Hemophilia

Hemophilia refers to a collection of X-linked hereditary bleeding disorders which arise as a result of deficiencies in the plasma proteins which control blood coagulation. Blood coagulation is necessary to prevent hemorrhage (severe bleeding). Severe hemophilia causes lifelong recurrent bleeding into soft tissues, muscles, and joints. There are three main types of hemophilia. A deficiency of factor VIII results in the coagulation disorder known as *hemophilia A* (classic hemophilia). Deficiency of factor IX results in *hemophilia B* (Christmas disease). Deficiency of factor XI results in *hemophilia C* (Rosenthal Syndrome).

Hemophilia occurs in 1 in 10,000 male births in the United States; 85% are deficient in factor VIII, 14% are deficient in factor IX, and only 1% are deficient in factor XI or one of the other coagulation factors (Greer et al., 2013). Timely treatment of bleeding and the preventive use of clotting factors has decreased the limitations associated with hemophilia and normalized the lifespan of persons with hemophilia (Soucie et al., 2000).

Genetics

The genetic defects accounting for deficiency of factors VIII and IX both occur on the X chromosome. Males have one X and one Y chromosome (XY), whereas females have two X chromosomes (XX). A mother carrying the genetic defect causing hemophilia (X^h) on one of her X chromosomes (X^hX) may transmit hemophilia to her son (X^hY), or pass the defect to a daughter (X^hX), who then becomes a carrier for hemophilia. The mother may transmit her normal X chromosome to her son (XY) or daughter (XX), and no genetic transmission of the mutated gene takes place. Sons of a carrier mother and a normal father have a 50% chance of having hemophilia; daughters have a 50% chance of being carriers.

Since a father with hemophilia (X^hY) contributes only his Y chromosome to his sons, none of his sons will have hemophilia, but all his daughters will receive his X^h chromosome and will be carriers (X^hX). This explains why hemophilia is almost exclusively a disease among males. Usually, a male inherits his mutant gene (X^h) from his carrier mother (X^hX), but in about 30% of cases of hemophilia, there is no family history and hemophilia is believed to arise from a spontaneous mutation (Mannucci & Tuddenham, 2001). The gene causing hemophilia C (factor XI deficiency) is not present on a sex chromosome (X or Y), but rather on chromosome number 4. Therefore, hemophilia C affects both genders equally.

Disease Severity

There is a close relationship between disease severity and the activity level of the coagulation factor. Individuals without hemophilia have from 50% to 170% activity of any coagulation factor. Individuals with less than 1% activity have severe hemophilia with frequent, life-threatening bleeding. Persons with 1% to 5% activity have moderate hemophilia, with bleeding episodes weekly or monthly. Those with greater than 5% activity have mild hemophilia with infrequent bleeding (Greer et al., 2013).

Clinical Manifestations

The major clinical manifestations of hemophilia are bleeding into a joint (hemarthrosis), a muscle, or other soft tissue (hematoma). Hemarthrosis occur primarily within the knees, but can occur in the elbows, ankles, shoulders, hips, and wrists, and cause pain, swelling, and limitation of joint motion. The frequency of hemarthrosis varies widely from patient to patient despite similar levels of coagulation factor activity.

Bleeding into the joint initiates the development of hemophilic arthropathy, a disabling chronic joint disease. During a joint bleed, various blood components cause inflammation of the lining of a joint, resulting in synovitis. The joint responds to repetitive bleeds by producing a fibrous, highly vascular tissue, replacing the normal joint lining tissue. This vicious cycle leads to progressive degeneration of cartilage, destruction of bone, and replacement of joint space with fibrous (scar) tissue. Bones may fuse (ankylosis) resulting in deformity and severely impaired range of motion in the affected joint (Rosendaal et al., 1998). The early stage of synovial proliferation and joint destruction resembles the disease process of rheumatoid arthritis, whereas end-stage hemophilic arthropathy is similar to severe osteoarthritis (Papadakis, McPhee, & Rabow, 2018).

Diagnosis

Genetic testing for hemophilia is recommended to determine carrier status when there is a known family history of hemophilia on the maternal side of a family (Greer et al., 2013). At birth, a diagnosis of hemophilia can be made by analysis of umbilical cord blood. When there is no family history of hemophilia, any episode of prolonged bleeding suggests the presence of hemophilia. The diagnosis of hemophilia is then determined by laboratory testing to establish the type of hemophilia (deficiency of factor VIII, IX, or XI), and level of factor activity.

Treatment

The mainstay of treatment for hemophilia A and B is periodic replacement of the deficient factor with human blood products (factor concentrates). Factor concentrates were first extracted from pooled or multiple donor plasma, but substantial numbers of men with hemophilia developed antibodies to the human immunodeficiency virus (HIV), and many developed the acquired immunodeficiency syndrome (AIDS) (Mannucci & Tuddenham, 2001). Now, factor concentrates are synthesized by newer and safer recombinant technology and are not contaminated with HIV (Oldenburg et al., 2017).

Self-administered factor concentrates have led to prompt control of bleeding, reduced joint and muscle damage, and a longer lifespan. Studies have shown that a home-based program for self-infusion significantly reduces bleeding complications and absences from school or work (Soucie et al., 2001). Furthermore, prophylaxis (providing concentrate in anticipation of trauma, as opposed to *on-demand* treatment when a bleed occurs) reduces medical costs and minimizes loss of productivity (Papadakis et al., 2018).

In the 1990s, the introduction of recombinant factor concentrates to replace hard-to-obtain donated plasma, led to the use of preventive factor replacement therapy as opposed to on-demand therapy (at the time of a bleed). This therapeutic change has enabled persons with hemophilia to engage in physical activities including employment, and to reduce chronic joint damage (DiMichele, 2016). Researchers are developing newer therapies aimed at extending the half-life of circulating factor concentrates and disrupting the inhibitory antibodies that occur from the repeated use of factor concentrates (Hartmann & Croteau, 2016). They are also exploring gene therapy technologies that correct the genetic defect (Davidoff & Nathwani, 2016; Nathwani et al., 2011).

Functional Limitations

The rehabilitation counselor can expect to encounter widely different degrees of functional limitations among individuals who have hemophilia (Hoots, 2003). The extent of limitations usually correlates inversely with the person's factor activity level. Those with severe disease who have not had the benefits of modern treatment have severe joint impairment. These individuals need to use wheelchairs for ambulation if they have not had surgical correction to restore joint function (Logan, 1995). Those with hemophilia who grew up during the era of modern treatment have fewer vocational limitations.

Counselors should concentrate on surmounting any erroneous notions surrounding individuals with hemophilia. These incorrect notions include beliefs that people with hemophilia: (1) necessarily require sedentary jobs; (2) must be in protected environments; (3) cannot perform manual labor jobs; (4) and frequently miss work because of the disease. Many work successfully in physically demanding jobs and also in light and sedentary white-collar and blue-collar vocations. Yet, persons with severe hemophilia, especially those who bleed more frequently despite maximal therapy, need counseling regarding jobs that require maneuvers which are potentially traumatic to joints. Since an individual with hemophilia can normalize coagulation within minutes by injection of a factor concentrate, many potentially hazardous jobs have little risk.

Intellectual Functioning

Persons with hemophilia do not display any inherent intellectual limitations. Lower scores on intelligence tests and achievement tests in the 1960s are generally attributable to disrupted school attendance. Within two decades following the advent and implementation of factor replacement and self-supervised treatment, individuals with hemophilia were attaining educational levels equivalent to age-matched, unaffected men (Hoffman et al., 2013).

Psychosocial Factors

As a group, these individuals display the same range of psychological variation present in non-affected persons. There is no general personality pattern for persons with hemophilia. However, employment remains a concern for people with hemophilia. Unemployment diminishes self-esteem and fosters passivity, pessimism, and depression (Raphael & Lin, 2017). A client's self-concept as being *unemployable* is a key reason for reluctance to seek a job and failure to present oneself in the most positive light when seeking employment. Failure to find a job often reinforces initial self-doubts. If the rehabilitation counselor can help the client surmount reticence and negativism regarding employability, the client will be able to take a significant step forward.

Specific Functional Limitations

Physical limitations vary with each person. Arthropathy of a lower extremity, weight-bearing joint is most likely to be physically limiting. For some, elbow or shoulder joint disease may pose the greatest limitation. The client can provide reliable information about which joints are disabling and in what manner. For example, a person with a knee with almost no range of motion due to severe joint disease, but who has only rare joint bleeds, is less disabled for work than is a person with severe chronic inflammation of the joint lining (synovitis) and frequent hemarthrosis.

Occupational Limitations

Occupational limitations correlate closely with severity of hemophilia. There is a close correlation between successful self-management of the disease and ability to function at work. Clients with severe hemophilia who are on self-supervised treatment are best able to manage the effects of a job injury that causes a bleed. A 15-minute break is generally sufficient for an individual to self-infuse a factor concentrate (Raphael & Lin, 2017). Most clients with mild to moderate disease have few vocational limitations. A characteristic feature of severe hemophilia is unpredictability. Therefore, those with severe hemophilia may not always optimally perform certain tasks out of their routine or familiarity.

The rehabilitation counselor evaluates the client's vocational limitations individually and provides precise assessment of functionality (Brodwin et al., 2010). Most employees with hemophilia perform equal to their peers who do not have hemophilia in a variety of jobs and professions. Inaccurately perceived limitations by prospective employers outweigh actual functional limitations of individuals who have this condition.

Rehabilitation Potential

Rehabilitation potential for people with hemophilia is excellent. Effective treatment of bleeding episodes, prevention or minimization of the disabling complications of joint bleeds, and the ability to correct deformities through surgery has greatly enhanced employability. Because of modern treatment modalities, many persons have completed high school, and increasingly pursue higher education.

Counselors need to educate employers to maximize potential employment opportunities for these clients (Brodwin et al., 2010; Falvo & Holland, 2018). Most employers are unfamiliar with self-supervised infusion that allows persons with hemophilia to live near-normal lives. Contrary to popular misconception, persons with hemophilia are not fragile individuals only suitable for very specialized jobs located in protected environments. Erroneously called *bleeders*, many people incorrectly believe individuals with hemophilia are vulnerable to rapid blood loss upon exposure to the slightest trauma. Actually, people with hemophilia bleed no more rapidly or excessively from minor cuts and superficial abrasions than do those who do not have this condition.

Appropriate medical treatment can prevent further progression of existing disabilities and help the person avoid additional complications. The rehabilitation counselor may consider the initial status upon first seeing the client as being relatively stable, and jointly work toward selecting a vocation in which the disability will not adversely affect functioning on the job. For clients who have frequent bleeds, the opportunity to self-infuse at the worksite effectively reduces morbidity and lost work time. An employee needs to be able to store concentrate and necessary accessories (needles, syringes, and gauze pads) at the workplace.

Individuals self-infuse in their offices or in restrooms. Some self-infuse at a nearby gasoline station or restaurant to conceal their hemophilia. Many employers have a first aid room where employees can self-infuse at the worksite. Persons with hemophilia frequently learn to compensate for their limitations and, therefore, often have fewer injuries than other workers in similar jobs. In many respects, people with hemophilia are optimal clients for vocational rehabilitation because the disease itself can be effectively controlled (Brodwin et al., 2010).

Case Study

Mr. Leroy Jones is a 43 year-old college-educated, self-employed machinist, with sickle cell disease. He is married and has two young children, ages 7 and 10. Mr. Jones developed bacterial septicemia (infection in the blood) and multiple complications of SCD requiring intermittent hospitalization over several months. Both his marriage and business failed. Mr. Jones' wife is Chinese and bicultural, maintaining some of the beliefs of traditional Chinese culture. Her parents always wanted her to marry within their ethnicity and maintain a traditional Chinese home. This has caused emotional issues, especially when it comes to raising their children. His wife left him and moved to another state, taking their two children with her and moving in with her elderly parents.

Marriage problems and the failed business contributed to Mr. Jones' anxiety and depression. Dr. Carla Williams, his treating physician, noted that Leroy had severe depression and referred him for psychological counseling. As a result of his condition, Mr. Jones developed a fatalistic attitude and did not complete the recommended course of counseling. Consequently, his depression deepened. In the area of physical functioning, Dr. Williams restricted Mr. Jones to light work. Additionally, there are some limitations in the areas of standing and walking.

The daily work activities of a machinist (National Center for O*Net Development [2012], #51-4041.00 Machinists. (See http://www.onetonline.org/link/summary/51-4041.00) include setting up and operating machine tools and fitting and assembling parts to make or repair metal parts, mechanisms, tools, and equipment. One reads blueprints, diagrams, and mechanical drawings, uses precision-measuring tools, and understands a variety of machining procedures. Machinists use hand tools and power tools throughout the work shift. Mr. Jones had been self-employed for 30 years in this line of work.

Due to physical limitations related to bone destruction (avascular necrosis) in both hips, Mr. Jones was unable to return to his machinist business, which often required ten-hour days, six days a week. Besides him, he had two helpers in the business who did general machining. Work in the machine shop involved occasional lifting up to 80 pounds when shipment orders arrived, and regular lifting of 45 pounds, with repetitive lifting of 20-25 pounds. Mr. Jones stood and walked 50% of the workday.

After the business failed and for the next ten years, Leroy filled his days with a variety of activities related to his church and various social clubs. By assuming a demanding schedule of responsibilities associated with these activities, he kept busy. During this period, Dr. Williams needed to hospitalize Leroy as often as six times a year for acute pain crises and recurrent bone infections (osteomyelitis).

Eventually, Mr. Jones was reunited with his children when they returned to the city to attend college. With these new family responsibilities, he gave up many of his outside activities and concentrated on assisting his children with their studies and making a home for them. Within a few months, Leroy noticed a remarkable decrease in the frequency of hospital admissions, which he related to improved self-care. Proper rest, careful attention to fluid intake, monitoring of physical activities, and regular medical appointments contributed to the improved clinical course of the disease.

Mr. Jones' depression cleared. Subsequently, he felt the need for a higher income and sought vocational rehabilitation services. A counselor from the state department of rehabilitation provided counseling, guidance, and job placement. These services were successful and Leroy was placed as a reader and driver for people with visual impairments.

Questions

1. Discuss physical, environmental, and psychosocial aspects of sickle cell disease.
2. Outline a vocational profile for Mr. Leroy Jones including age category, educational level, work history (exertion and skill levels), occupationally significant characteristics, and transferable skills.
3. If Leroy had decided to make further attempts to make his machinist business succeed, how would you as his rehabilitation counselor approach this decision? Provide supporting arguments.
4. Would you recommend use of transferable skills as a viable vocational rehabilitation option for Mr. Jones? If so, describe what skills are transferable to other skilled and semiskilled jobs.
5. Discuss the rehabilitation goal pursued in this case and explain why the counselor may have recommended it. Do you agree with this rehabilitation plan?
6. Speculate on how Mr. Jones was able to achieve his vocational goal.
7. Evaluate this case from a multicultural perspective.

References

Ataga, K. I., Kutler, A., Kantar, J., Liles, D., Cancado, R., Friedrisch, J., ... Rother, R. P. (2017). Crizanlizumab for the prevention of crises in sickle cell disease. *New England Journal of Medicine, 376*(5), 429-439.

Bernaudin, F., Socie, G., Kuentz, M., Chevret, S., Duval, M., Bertrand, Y., ... Gluckman, E. (2007). Long-term results of related myeloablative stem-cell transplantation to cure sickle cell disease. *Blood, 110*(7), 2749-2756.

Brodwin, M. G., Parker, R. M., & DeLaGarza, D. (2010). Disability and reasonable accommodation. In E. M. Szymanski & R. M. Parker (Eds.), *Work and disability: Issues, contexts, and strategies for enhancing employment outcomes for people with disabilities* (3rd ed., pp. 281-323). Austin, TX: Pro-ed.

Castro, O., Brambilia, D. J., & Thorington, B. (1994). The acute chest syndrome in sickle cell disease: Incidence and risk factors: The Cooperative Study of Sickle Cell Disease. *Blood, 84*, 643-649.

Davidoff, A. M., & Nathwani, A. C. (2016). Genetic targeting of the albumin locus to treat hemophiliacs. *New England Journal of Medicine, 374*(13), 1288-1290.

DeBraun, M. R., Gordon, M., McKinstry, R. C., Noetzel, M. J., White, D. A., Sarnaik, S. A, ... Casella, J. F. (2014). Controlled trial of transfusions for silent cerebral infarcts in sickle cell anemia. *New England Journal of Medicine, 271*(8), 699-710.

DiMichele, D. (2016). Hemophilia therapy: Navigating speed bumps on the innovation highway. *New England Journal of Medicine, 374*(21), 2087-2089.

Falvo, D. R., & Holland, B. E. (2018). *Medical and psychosocial aspects of chronic illness and disability* (6th ed.). Burlington, MA: Jones and Bartlett Learning.

Francis, R. B., & Johnson, C. S. (1991). Vaso-occlusion in sickle cell disease: Current concepts and unanswered questions. *Blood, 77*, 1405-1414.

Greer, J. P., Arber, D. A., Glader, B., List, A. F., Means, R. T., Paraskevas, F., . . . Foerster, J. (Eds.). (2013). *Wintrobe's clinical hematology* (13th ed.). Baltimore, MD: Lippincott Williams and Wilkins.

Hartmann, J., & Croteau, S. E. (2016). 2017 clinical trials update: Innovations in hemophilia therapy. *American Journal of Hematology, 91*(12), 1252-1260.

Hassell, K. L. (2010). Population estimates of sickle cell disease in the U.S. *American Journal of Preventive Medicine, 38*, Supplement S512-S521.

Hoffman, R., Benz, E. J., Silberstein, L., Heslop, H., Weitz, J., & Anastasi, J. (Eds). (2013). *Hematology: Basic principles and practice* (6th ed.). Philadelphia, PA: Elsevier Saunders.

Hoots, W. K. (2003). Comprehensive care for hemophilia and related inherited bleeding disorders: Why it matters. *Current Hematology Reports, 2*, 395-401.

Howard, J., & Telfer, P. (2015). *Sickle cell disease in clinical practice*. London, UK: Springer.

Ingram, V. M. (1956). A specific chemical difference between the globins of normal human and sickle-cell anaemia haemoglobin. *Nature, 178*, 792-794.

Logan, L. J. (1995). Hemostasis: Hemorrhagic and thrombotic disorders. In J. J. Mazza (Ed.), *Manual of clinical hematology* (2nd ed., pp. 349-379). Boston, MA: Little Brown.

Mannucci, P. M., & Tuddenham, E. G. D. (2001). The hemophilias: From royal genes to gene therapy. *New England Journal of Medicine, 344*(23), 1773-1779.

Minniti, C. P., & Vichinsky, E. (2017). Lifespan care in SCD: Whom to transition, the patients or the health care system? *American Journal of Hematology, 92*, 487-489.

Nathwani, A. C., Tuddenham, E. G. D., Rangarajan, S., Rosales, C., McIntosh, J., Linch, D. C., . . . Davidoff, A. M. (2011). Adenovirus-associated virus vector-mediated gene transfer in hemophilia B. *New England Journal of Medicine, 365*(25), 2357-2365.

National Center for O*Net Development. (2012). *Occupational Information Network (O*Net)*. Retrieved from http://www.onetonline.org/

Ohene-Frempong, K., Weiner, S. J., Sleeper, L. A., Miller, S. T., Embury, J. W., Moohr, J. W., . . . Gill, F. M. (1998). Cerebrovascular accidents in sickle cell disease: Rates and risk factors. *Blood, 91*(1), 288-294.

Oldenburg, J., Mahlangu, J. N., Kim, B., Callaghan, M. U., Young, G., Santagostino, E., . . . Shima, M. (2017). Emicizumab prophylaxis in hemophilia A with inhibitors. *New England Journal of Medicine, 377*(9), 809-818.

Papadakis, M. A., McPhee, S. J., & Rabow, M. W. (Eds.). (2018). *Current medical diagnosis and treatment* (57th ed.). New York, NY: McGraw-Hill Lange.

Piel, F. B., Steinberg, M. H., & Rees, D. C. (2017). Sickle cell disease. *New England Journal of Medicine, 376*(16), 1561-1573.

Platt, O. S. (2008). Hydroxyurea for the treatment of sickle cell anemia. *New England Journal of Medicine, 358*(13), 1362-1369.

Raphael, B. G., & Lin, R. J. (2017). Hematological disorders. In A. Moroz, S. R. Flanagan, & H. H. Zaretsky (Eds.), *Medical aspects of disability: A handbook for the rehabilitation professional* (5th ed., pp. 229-244). New York, NY: Springer.

Ribeil, J-A., Hacein-Bey-Abina, S., Payen, E., Magnani, A., Semeraro, M., Magrin, E., . . . Cavazzana, M. (2017). Gene therapy in a patient with sickle cell disease. *New England Journal of Medicine, 376*(9), 848-855.

Rosendaal, G., Vianen, M. E., Wenting, J. G., van Rinsum, A. C., van den Berg, H. M., Hafeber, F. P., & Bijlsma, W. J. (1998). Iron deposits and catabolic properties of synovial tissue from patients with haemophilia. *Journal of Bone and Joint Surgery, 80-B*(3), 540-545.

Soucie, J. M., Huss, R., Eratt, B., Abdelhak, A., Cowan, L., Hill, A., . . . Wilbur, N. (2000). Mortality among males with hemophilia: Relations with source of medical care. *Blood, 96*(2), 437-442.

Soucie, J. M., Symons, J., II, Evatt, B., Brettler, D., Haszti, M., & Linden, J. (2001). Home-based factor infusion therapy and hospitalization for bleeding complications among males with hemophilia. *Hemophilia, 7,* 198-206.

About the Author

John J. Howard, MD, MPH, is Professor Lecturer in Environmental and Occupational Health, Milken Institute School of Public Health, The George Washington University, Washington, DC. Dr. Howard is board-certified in internal medicine and occupational medicine. He is admitted to the practice of medicine in California and the District of Columbia.

Chapter 32

GENETIC TESTING, DISCRIMINATION AND COUNSELING

John J. Howard, MD, MPH

Introduction

The initial sequencing and analysis of the human genome was published in 2001 (International Human Genome Sequencing Consortium, 2001). Since then, genetic tests have been developed for more than 2,200 diseases, of which about 2,000 tests are currently available for use in clinical settings (Centers for Disease Control and Prevention [CDC], 2018). A genetic test involves "the analysis of human DNA, RNA chromosomes, proteins, and certain metabolites in order to detect heritable disease-related genotypes, mutations, phenotypes, or karyotypes for clinical purposes" (Holzman & Watson, 1999).

Genetic testing is used for many reasons, such as to screen carriers of gene mutations (Brody, 2016). These tests aim to identify unaffected individuals who carry one copy of a gene for a condition (e.g., sickle cell disease) that requires two copies to be present to develop the symptomatic form of the genetic disease. Genetic tests are used for prenatal and newborn screening, predicting the probability of developing a neurological disease or a type of cancer, predicting whether an individual will respond to particular types of chemotherapy, or for forensic identification purposes (Hartl & Jones, 2012).

Genetic testing raises concerns that results of testing may be used in discrimination in employment and health insurance. For example, individuals who test positive for a genetic test relating to a particular disease may be perceived by an employer or an insurer as actually having the disorder. In 2008, this concern led to enactment of a new federal anti-discrimination law called the Genetic Information Nondiscrimination Act of 2008 (GINA, 2008). This act serves to prevent discrimination in employment and insurance based on one's genetic makeup.

Since genetic testing may cause legal, ethical, and psychological concerns, genetic testing should be, and often is, accompanied by counseling. Genetic counseling is the process of helping people understand and adapt to the medical, psychological, and familial implications of genetic contributions to disease. This process integrates: (1) interpretation of family and medical histories to assess the chance of disease occurrence or recurrence; (2) education about inheritance, testing, management, prevention, resources, and research; and (3) counseling to promote informed choices and adaptation to the risk or condition (National Society of Genetic Counselors, 2005).

This chapter briefly reviews genetic testing, genetic discrimination, genetic counseling, and the role of the rehabilitation counselor. Three brief case studies conclude the chapter.

Genetic Testing

The three major types of genetic tests include: (1) gene tests (e.g., individual genes or relatively short lengths of DNA or RNA are tested); (2) chromosomal tests (e.g., whole chromosomes or very long lengths of DNA are tested); and (3) biochemical tests (e.g., protein levels or enzyme activities are tested) (Burke, 2002). Most genetic tests look at single genes and are used to diagnose rare genetic disorders. Yet, a growing number of tests are being developed to look at multiple genes that may increase or decrease a person's risk of common diseases, such as cancer or diabetes (CDC, 2018).

Except for genetic testing for the single-gene disorder, Huntington's disease, genetic tests are based on limited scientific information and may not yet provide valid or useful results because most illness stems from multiple factors. Furthermore, genetic testing does not establish the onset date, nature, severity, course of a disease, or ensure the efficacy of treatment for a genetic disorder. All we know definitely is that "significant scientific uncertainty surrounds much genetic testing" (Gostin, 1991).

Once used only for medical reasons to diagnose a disease, predictive genetic tests (tests used on people without symptoms) are now available online for a modest price. People need not utilize a physician to gain access to genetic testing. Direct-to-consumer marketing for genetic testing occurs through the Internet, radio, television, and other media. This has prompted concerns that such testing does not provide appropriate counseling, and will create the potential for physical or psychological harm to individuals (Wolfberg, 2006). Most members of both the general public and at-risk groups express favorable attitudes toward, and interest in, being tested (Croyle & Lerman, 1995). Likewise, persons with disabilities who seek genetic counseling are generally favorable to the service (Chen & Schiffman, 2000).

Genetic Discrimination

"Genetic discrimination has been defined as the differential treatment of asymptomatic individuals or their relatives on the basis of their real or assumed genetic characteristics" (Wauters & Hoyweghen, 2016, p. 275). The history of genetic discrimination started in the early 19th century during the eugenics movement. Eugenics advocated various practices designed to improve the genetic composition of the human population. This negative and discriminatory practice was evident during the late 19th and early 20th centuries in Germany where the term *eugenics* originated.

Eugenics was also evident in the United States. By 1937, 32 states had passed sterilization laws aimed at preventing people with disabilities, especially those with intellectual disabilities, from having offspring (Houser & Lash, 1996; Nussbaum, McInnes, & Willard, 2016). "Since the 1990s, development in the field of genetics have led to many questions on the use and possible misuse of genetic information" (Wauters & Hoyweghen, 2016, p. 275).

The current genetic testing industry, a multi-billion dollar business, is growing by 25% annually (Pollack, 2006). As genetic testing increases, so does the potential of an employer, a health or disability insurer, or other entity to discriminate against an individual based on the results of a genetic test. The potential for discrimination exists because the increasing costs of health, life, and disability-related insurance, may encourage employers and insurers to use genetic tests to exclude those with the potential to incur expensive medical or disability claims. Genetic information could become available to employers, insurers, educators, law enforcement, and others who might not have the skill to understand or correctly serve individuals with a propensity for disability (whether perceived or actual) (Hudson, 2011). In sum, genetic testing can have serious negative implications for the individual tested. It has been noted that "prejudice, alienation, and exclusion often accompany genetic disorders, even though the conditions are neither the result of willful behavior nor subject to the person's control" (Gostin, 1991).

To date, there have been very few cases of genetic discrimination in health insurance and employment, but the fear of such discrimination prompted passage of federal legislation to protect genetic information (Hudson, Holohan, & Collins, 2008). On May 21, 2008, the GINA was signed into law by President George W. Bush.

GINA (2008) defined *genetic information* as including a person's genetic tests, genetic tests of a person's family members (up to and including fourth-relatives), any manifestation of a disease or disorder in a family member, and participation of a person or family member in research that includes genetic testing, counseling, or education. Genetic services are defined as testing, counseling, and education. Examples of protected tests include: (1) tests for BRCA1/BRCA2 (breast cancer) or HNPCC (colon cancer) mutations; (2) classifications of genetic properties of an existing tumor to help determine therapy; (3) tests for

Huntington's disease mutations; and (4) carrier screening for disorders such as cystic fibrosis, sickle cell disease, spinal muscular atrophy, and fragile X syndrome.

GINA prohibits genetic discrimination in employment and health insurance (Nussbaum et al., 2016). However, GINA does not apply to life insurance, disability insurance, long-term care insurance, or other potential uses of genetic information, so it is not entirely clear that "its limited protections will be sufficient to allay the fears of individuals currently dissuaded from undergoing genetic testing" (Rothstein, 2008). Nor does GINA prohibit an employer (as provided by the Americans with Disabilities Act of 1990), after making a conditional offer of employment to an individual, to require that person sign an authorization to disclose all of his or her health records. This could result in the employer gaining access to genetic information about the individual.

Genetic Counseling

Genetic counseling is "a process of communication and education that addresses concerns relating to the development and/or transmission of a hereditary disorder" (Turnpenny & Ellard, 2017, p. 317). Physicians who specialize in genetic disorders (medical geneticists), and non-physicians who have an academic background in genetics and training in counseling, do genetic counseling. Genetic counseling is a new field that began in 1959 with the first application of educating about human genetics (Gardner, McKinley, Sutherland, & Shaffer, 2012).

Genetic counselors apply what is known about human genetics in providing advice to: (1) those concerned about the possibility of having a genetic disease themselves (genetic diagnosis); (2) those family members concerned about having the same genetic disease as an affected family member (familial risk); and (3) those concerned about passing a genetic mutation to their offspring (prenatal genetic testing) (Uhlmann et al., 2009).

Genetic counselors assist the client in understanding the medical diagnosis, its prognosis, and any available treatment. They also provide an understanding of how heredity contributes to the disorder and the risks for family members. Counselors assist the client in selecting the most appropriate course of action after considering the risks, resources, and long term family goals. Counselors also assist the client in making the best possible adjustments to a disorder in an affected family member, or in dealing with the risks of recurrence of the disorder (Shiloh, 1996a, 1996b).

Before genetic testing is performed, counselors can advise a client about what would happen if genetic test results should become available to other parties, particularly potential or current employers and insurers; whether genetic disorders would make it difficult for applicants to obtain health, life, or disability coverage; and whether insurance companies would decrease benefits for certain conditions. Genetic counseling addresses the medical, employment, insurance, and psychological problems associated with the risk of a genetic disorder, not with the medical management of the disorder itself. Goals of genetic counseling include helping clients learn, understand, choose, cope, and adjust to unexpected circumstances (Veach, Le Roy, & Bartels, 2003).

Role for Rehabilitation Counselors

Counselors, whether rehabilitation counselors or genetic counselors, share much in common. Several additional roles for rehabilitation counselors related to genetic counseling have been identified. These include education, support, advocacy, and technical assistance (Evans & Biesecker, 2006).

Education has been identified as a prerequisite for providing genetic services for both the public and professionals (Le Roy, Veach, & Bartels, 2010). Counselors need to be well versed and current in human genetics and possess sensitivity in working with clients. They can provide information concerning genetic processes and explain potential procedures and results in ways that are understandable and meaningful to clients. In the process of counseling, counselors must be sure to be nonjudgmental and not express their particular beliefs and values to their clients.

In the supportive role, rehabilitation counselors perform a variety of services. These include assisting families to identify and address underlying psychosocial and cultural issues related to genetic concerns, and provide referral to support groups when beneficial to persons and their loved ones. Counselors assist clients while making decisions and providing supportive follow-ups. They help clients understand and cope with the reactions of family members. Counselors may also mediate peer counseling.

In the role of advocate, rehabilitation counselors discuss issues concerning employment, insurance, and other types of potential social discrimination against clients (Biesecker, Schwartz, & Marteau, 2013). Potential counseling interventions include informing employers and insurers about the legal protections afforded persons with disabilities, potential accommodations for those persons in the workplace, and providing information to clients about their legal rights.

Additionally, rehabilitation counselors assist clients by providing technical information. This type of technical assistance may involve construction of a life care plan for the individual and the family (Weed & Berens, 2018; Weed & Owen, 2018). The life care plan can identify potential services and costs that may be required for the family and child, as well as resources to secure such services. The use of life care plans is a practical means by which to inform the client of future responsibilities engendered by an adult and child with a disability. It can serve as a basis for planning future life care services and avoiding lapses in the provision of services for the foreseeable future.

Case Studies

Descriptions of three case scenarios adapted from Fletcher and Evans (1994) are provided to show the complexity and interaction of issues encountered during genetic counseling. Analysis of these cases will help the counselor understand genetic counseling. The cases illustrate the need for counselors to have a firm understanding of their own beliefs. It is essential to provide meaningful information and discussions with the client and other family members without actually giving decisional advice about what choice to make.

Case 1. A 42 year-old woman is considering prenatal diagnosis for possible Down Syndrome. Down Syndrome, or trisomy 21, is a chromosomal condition caused by the presence of all or part of a third copy of chromosome 21. Down Syndrome is the most common chromosome abnormality in humans and causes moderate to severe congenital intellectual disability. She and her husband have a child with this condition. They tell the counselor that abortion is not an option and that she plans to carry the fetus to full term despite the results of genetic testing. The family's reason for seeking the diagnosis is to provide more time for preparation if this child has Down Syndrome. They ask for the counselor's advice. How should the counselor proceed? Discuss various options.

Case 2. A 25 year-old woman with no history of genetic disorders in her family is considering prenatal diagnosis. This client has a problem with alcohol but is in denial, believing she is only a social drinker. She is a client because she acquired a below elbow upper extremity amputation as a result of an automobile accident. Although she did not have any abnormal sequelae, at the time of the amputation she received several blood transfusions and is concerned she may have contracted hepatitis or AIDS. The client appears very anxious about the normalcy of the fetus, even after being told that, in her case, the potential medical risks of the genetic procedure (including possible miscarriage) are greater than the likelihood of diagnosing an abnormality. She asks for the counselor's advice. As her counselor, describe what approach you might take.

Case 3. A couple in their late twenties requests prenatal diagnosis to determine the sex of their fetus. The father is a client of yours due to a recent back injury. They already have four girls and feel desperate to have a son. They stated that if it is a girl, they plan to abort the fetus and keep trying to have a boy. If they cannot have testing, they will abort the fetus rather than face the possibility of having another girl. They have requested your advice. Discuss the ramifications of this case.

References

Americans with Disabilities Act of 1990 (ADA). 42 U.S.C. §12101 *et seq.*

Biesecker, B. B., Schwartz, M. D., & Marteau, T. M. (2013). Enhancing informed choice to undergo health screening: A systematic review. *American Journal of Health Behavior, 37*, 351-359.

Burke, W. (2002). Genetic testing. *New England Journal of Medicine, 347*(23), 1867-1875.

Centers for Disease Control and Prevention (CDC). (2018). *Genetic testing*. Retrieved from http://www.cdc.gov/genomics/gtesting/genetic_testing.htm

Chen, E. A., & Schiffman, J. F. (2000). Attitudes toward genetic counseling and prenatal diagnosis among a group of individuals with disabilities. *Journal of Genetic Counseling, 9*(2), 137-152.

Croyle, R. T., & Lerman, C. (1995). Psychological impact of genetic testing. In R. T. Croyle (Ed.), *Psychosocial effects of screening for disease prevention and detection* (pp. 11-38). New York, NY: Oxford University.

Evans, C., & Biesecker, B. B. (2006). *Genetic counseling: A psychological conversation*. New York, NY: Cambridge University.

Fletcher, J. C., & Evans, M. E. (1994). Ethics in reproductive genetics. In J. F. Monagle & D. C. Thomasma (Eds.), *Health care ethics: Critical issues* (pp. 24-42). Gaithersburg, MD: Aspen.

Gardner, R. J., McKinley, L. M., Sutherland G. R., & Shaffer, L. G. (2012). Chromosome abnormalities and genetic counseling. *Oxford monographs on medical genetics, No. 61*. New York, NY: Oxford University.

Genetic Information Nondiscrimination Act of 2008 (GINA). Public Law 110-233, 122 Stat. 881. Retrieved from http://www.eeoc.gov/laws/statutes/gina.cfm

Gostin, L. (1991). Genetic discrimination: The use of genetically based diagnostic and prognostic tests by employers and insurers. *American Journal of Law and Medicine, 17*, 109-144.

Hartl, D. L., & Jones, E. W. (2012). *Essential genetics* (6th ed.). Sudbury, MA: Jones and Bartlett.

Holzman, N. A., & Watson, M. S. (Eds.). (1999). *Promoting safe and effective genetic testing in the United States: Final report of the Task Force on Genetic Testing*. Baltimore, MD: Johns Hopkins University.

Houser, R., & Lash, M. (1996). Implications of research from the Human Genome Project for rehabilitation counselors. *Journal of Applied Rehabilitation Counseling, 27*, 3-7.

Hudson K. L. (2011). Genomics, health care, and society. *New England Journal of Medicine, 365*(11), 1033-1041.

Hudson, K. L., Holohan, M. K., & Collins, F. S. (2008). Keeping pace with the times – The Genetic Information Nondiscrimination Act of 2008. *New England Journal of Medicine, 358*(25), 2661-2663.

International Human Genome Sequencing Consortium. (2001). Initial sequencing and analysis of the human genome. *Nature, 409*, 860-921.

Le Roy, B. S., Veach, P. M., & Bartels, R. M. (2010). *Genetic counseling practice: Advanced concepts and skills*. Hoboken, NJ: John Wiley and Sons.

National Society of Genetic Counselors. (2005). *Genetic counseling as a profession*. Retrieved from http://www.nsgc.org/About/FAQsDefinitions/tabid/97/Default.aspx

Nussbaum, R. L., McInnes, R. R., & Willard, H. F. (2016). *Thompson and Thompson: Genetics in medicine* (8th ed.). Philadelphia, PA: Elsevier.

Pollack, A. (2006, April 13). A crystal ball submerged in a test tube: Genetic technology reshapes the diagnostics business. *New York Times,* Business/Financial.

Rothstein, M. A. (2008). GINA, the ADA, and genetic discrimination in employment. *Journal of Law, Medicine, and Ethics, 36*(4), 837-840.

Shiloh, S. (1996a). Decision-making in the context of genetic risk. In T. Marteau & M. Richards (Eds.), *The troubled helix: Social and psychological implications of the new human genetics* (pp. 82-103). Cambridge, Great Britain: Cambridge University.

Shiloh, S. (1996b). Genetic counseling: A developing area of interest for psychologists. *Professional Psychology: Research and Practice, 27*, 475-478.

Turnpenny, P., & Ellard, S. (2017). *Emery's elements of medical genetics* (15th ed.). London, UK: Elsevier.

Uhlmann, W. R., Schuette, J. L., & Yashar, B. M. (2009). *A guide to genetic counseling* (2nd ed.). Hoboken, New Jersey: Wiley-Blackwell.

Veach, P. M., Le Roy, B. S., & Bartels, D. M. (2003). *Facilitating the genetic counseling process: A practice manual*. New York, NY: Springer-Verlag.

Weed, R. O., & Berens, D. (Eds.). (2018). *Life care planning and case management handbook* (4th ed.). Abingdon, UK: Routledge.

Weed, R. O., & Owen, T. (2018). *Life care planning: A step-by-step guide* (2nd ed.). Athens, GA: E & F Vocational Services.

Wauters, A., & Hoyweghen, V. (2016). Global trends on fears and concerns of genetic discrimination: A systematic literature review. *Journal of Human Genetics, 61*, 275-282.

Wolfberg, A. J. (2006). Genes on the Web – Direct-to-consumer marketing of genetic testing. *New England Journal of Medicine, 355*(6), 543-544.

Acknowledgement

The author would like to acknowledge the work of Joseph Havranek, PhD, the author of the original chapter on Genetic Counseling, for his lifetime of contributions to the field of rehabilitation counseling.

About the Author

John Howard, MD, MPH, is Professorial Lecturer in Environmental and Occupational Health, Milken Institute School of Public Health and Health Services, The George Washington University, Washington, D.C. Dr. Howard is board-certified in internal medicine and occupational medicine. He is admitted to the practice of medicine in the State of California and the District of Columbia.

Chapter 33

REGENERATIVE MEDICINE AND DISABILITY

John J. Howard, MD, MPH

Introduction

Prometheus, a Greek Titan, was punished by Zeus for giving fire to mankind. Zeus had him chained to a rock and sent an eagle to eat his liver each day, but Prometheus' liver regenerated each night. Like Zeus, medical science is now creating new tissues to replace or repair organs lost to congenital defects, age, disease, or trauma. These newer scientific technologies involve growing tissues and organs in the laboratory and then implanting them into the body when the body's own healing responses fail to restore function (Atala, Lanza, Thomson, & Nerem, 2010; Brody 2016).

The term *regenerative medicine* was first used in 1992 to describe futuristic medical technologies (Kaiser, 1992), and the field has progressed since then thanks to advances in cell and developmental biology, biomaterials science, and biomedical engineering (National Institutes of Health, 2006). "Regenerative medicine holds the promise of regenerating damaged tissues and organs by stimulating previously irreparable organs to heal themselves" (Sor, Krackov, & Madormo, 2018, p. 1).

This chapter presents a brief introduction to the emerging field of regenerative medicine. Although the present practice of rehabilitation counseling has not been affected as yet, regenerative medicine is a field of therapeutics that has the potential to greatly improve the lives of people who have disabilities and significantly affect the practice of rehabilitation counseling.

The human body has the ability to replenish some cells and tissues, but that ability is limited to blood, skin, and intestinal lining cells. Humans cannot grow another limb like a newt, grow new heart muscle cells after a heart attack, or grow new nerves after a spinal cord injury. The cells of a human embryo differentiate into specialized cell types after only a few divisions following conception. After that, they go into a type of cellular *lock down* when cellular differentiation ceases and cells are committed to their genetic fate (DeWitt, 2008).

Regenerative medicine has taken medical science beyond living donor or cadaveric transplants, first introduced in the early 20th century. By 1954, the first human kidney transplant had been performed. Currently, donor organ transplant surgery involves many different organs. The most common are bone marrow, heart, kidney, and lung transplants. Organ transplantation has become so successful that there is a shortage of donor organs; people needing organs remain on waiting lists for extended periods. Regenerative medicine has the potential to alleviate this organ shortage problem by providing a laboratory-grown source for replacement organs.

There is a wide array of unmet medical needs affecting tens of millions of people which could be addressed by regenerative medicine (Brody, 2016). Among these needs are spinal cord injuries, heart disease, Parkinson's disease, Alzheimer's disease, birth defects, diabetes mellitus, severe burns, and bone and muscle diseases (Committee on the Biological and Medical Applications of Stem Cell Research, 2002). Over the past 20 years, several therapeutic applications of regenerative medicine have been introduced into everyday medical practice, or are in animal or human trials to test their safety and efficacy.

Research investments in cell-based therapies that characterize advanced regenerative medicine have come primarily from private industry. Government funding has been problematic because the source of some cells used to grow tissues and organs in the laboratory - cells harvested from human embryos - is controversial. Financial investment by the government is increasing, though, as other non-embryonic cell sources are identified. For example, the *Armed Forces Institute for Regenerative Medicine* (AFIRM) is a multi-institutional, inter-disciplinary network funded by the United States Army. AFIRM is working to develop treatment options using multiple different cell sources for severely wounded servicemen and women in five areas: (1) limb and digit salvage; (2) craniofacial reconstruction; (3) scarless wound healing; (4) burn repair; and (5) compartment injuries arising from blast explosions (AFIRM, 2016).

Basics of Regenerative Medicine

Cell-based regenerative medicine therapies involve three steps. First, a cell must be obtained that ideally possesses the twin traits of self-renewal and pluripotency. Self-renewal means that the cell can go through numerous cell divisions but still remain in a relatively undifferentiated state. Potency means that the cell has the capacity to differentiate into many different specialized cell types when stimulated in the laboratory. Stem cells are the starting point in developing many regenerative medicine applications. Second, techniques are used to produce the desired cell type from the source cell by modulating the source cell's microenvironment in the laboratory. Third, the specialized cells produced from source cells are then embedded into a tissue matrix structure or scaffold by means of *tissue engineering* and transplanted into the body to replace damaged cells (Brody, 2016; Khang, 2012).

Types of Stem Cells

Stem cells are generally divided into three categories depending on their origin: (1) embryonic stem cells; (2) fetal stem cells; and (3) adult stem cells. Embryonic stem cells - derived from inner cell mass of the blastocyst phase of an early human embryo - are capable of infinite self-renewal and are broadly *pluripotent*, meaning they can differentiate into all cell lines - ectoderm, mesoderm, and endoderm. Obtaining human embryonic stem cells requires the destruction of early human embryos which makes obtaining this type of stem cell ethically controversial. Because of the controversial nature of stem cells, the authority of the Federal government to fund and conduct embryonic stem cell research was restricted in 2007 by President George W. Bush (Bush, 2007). In 2009, President Barack Obama removed the restrictions and expanded support of human stem cell research (Obama, 2009). However, regenerative medical research involving human embryonic stem cells remains controversial.

Fetal stem cells are derived from the placenta, amniotic fluid, or from umbilical cord blood. Harvesting fetal stem cells does not require destruction of the fetus. Adult stem cells, also known as *somatic* stem cells, are found throughout the body, but in small numbers. As a source of stem cells, adult stem cells are not considered controversial as they are derived from adult tissue samples through biopsy or organ donation rather than from destroyed human embryos (Atala et al., 2010). However, fetal and adult stem cells lack the same power of self-renewal and pluripotency as do embryonic stem cells; they need more coaxing in a laboratory to express those traits. These types of stem cells are becoming an important source for regenerative medicine.

Laboratory Modulation of Stem Cells

All cells are influenced by their microenvironments. Stem-cell modulation technologies are a complex area of laboratory science that involves manipulating the stem cell into desired specialized cell types. A full description of these techniques is beyond this chapter, but suffice it to say that stem cells can now be grown and coaxed into differentiating into stable cell lines of various tissues such as heart muscle cells, nerve cells, and muscle cells, by means of advanced cell culture techniques and stem-cell technologies.

Tissue Engineering

The procedure of replacing damaged tissue with new cells is called *tissue engineering* (Berthiaume, Maguire, & Yarmush, 2011). Tissue engineering uses laboratory-grown source cells embedded in a biomaterial-derived matrix structure that has the capability of functioning in three dimensions (Liu, Hui, Bhatia, & Chen, 2009). Engineered scaffolds derived from porcine intestines are used to provide a matrix for embedding regenerated cells. The cell-matrix is incubated in the laboratory to promote cell adhesion and organ formation and then transplanted into the body (Viola, Lal, & Grad, 2003). Advanced tissue engineering envisions a technology for 3D organ printing which would dramatically accelerate and optimize tissue and organ assembly (Mironov, Boland, Trusk, Forgacs, & Markwald, 2003). Through tissue engineering techniques, regenerative medicine is moving closer to developing therapeutic applications for damaged organs that would significantly expand what rehabilitation medicine can offer people with disabilities (Khademhosseini, Langer, Borenstein, & Vacanti, 2005).

Therapeutic Applications

Although few medical therapies using stem cells are in clinical practice at this time, regenerative medicine holds great promise for people who have severe burns, are disabled by spinal cord injuries, who sustain a heart attack and lose heart muscle cells, or who undergo cartilage loss in their joints (Sor et al., 2018; Zhu, Wei, & Ding, 2011). Regenerative medicine research holds promise for developing solutions to many disabling conditions (Committee on the Biological and Medical Application of Stem Cell Research, 2002), but "much remains to be learned about how stem cells and their derivatives can be manufactured and delivered safely to integrate into existing tissue architecture and restore function" (Daley, 2017). The following four examples illustrate the potential future impact of regenerative medicine for people with disabilities (Badylak & Nerem, 2010).

Burns

Mortality from full-thickness burns is high due to the slow pace of wound healing. Approaches to the treatment of severe burns involve skin auto-grafting, but this technique is limited in extensively burned people because they have little healthy skin available for auto-transplantation. Transplanting skin from healthy donors to the burned individual is another approach, but transplant rejection often occurs (Gerlach, Wolf, Johnen, & Hartman, 2010). Researchers are investigating newer cell-based regenerative medical therapies. A very small population of the burned individual's skin cells (*keratinocytes*) are harvested and rapidly reproduced in the laboratory. The new keratinocytes are applied to the burned area, either by embedding them in a tissue scaffold or by spraying them on the burned area. Fetal skin-derived cells also serve as a source of keratinocytes in burn therapy (Hohlfeld et al., 2005).

Spinal Cord Injury

One of the first studies using a human embryonic stem cell involved individuals with neurologically complete traumatic spinal cord injuries. Currently, cell-based regenerative medical research into spinal cord regeneration is focused on determining which stem cell would best restore spinal nerve function.

An obstacle to nerve cell regeneration is the tendency of scar tissue to form at the site of the spinal cord injury. Scar formation can block the growth of any transplanted cells, rendering cell-based regenerative medicine solutions to spinal cord injury ineffective. Scarring is promoted by axon growth inhibitors (Kingwell, 2011). In animal studies where these axon growth inhibitors are blocked, some axon *sprouting* and functional recovery has been seen (Lee, McKeon, & Bellamkonda, 2010). Other studies have shown that stabilization of the axonal microtubule with paclitaxel (a cancer drug) promotes axon growth in animals (Hellal et al., 2011).

Heart Disease

Heart failure following a heart attack is a leading cause of death worldwide (World Health Organization [WHO], 2015). After cardiac muscle cells (cardiomyocytes) die from a lack of oxygen (ischemia) during a heart attack, they are replaced by fibrotic scar tissue, not by new heart muscle cells. Scar tissue does not contract like normal cardiomyocytes. The pumping function of the heart is impaired and heart failure may result. Heart failure treatment is limited, as are donor hearts for replacement. These factors have spurred the development of approaches to replace damaged cardiomyocytes through cell-based therapies (Laflamme & Murray, 2011). Studies with human adult stem cells or with human embryonic stem cells have shown promise in achieving cardiomyocyte regeneration and restoration of cardiac function (Passier, van Laake, & Mummery, 2008). Clinical trials using adult stem cells in post-heart attack therapy are among the most advanced regenerative medicine applications of stem cells to date (Ahsan, Doyle, & Nerem, 2010; Daley, 2017).

Cartilage

Adults lack the regenerative ability to repair cartilage that becomes damaged by osteoarthritis, traumatic injury, or joint disorders like rheumatoid arthritis. Currently, chrondrocytes (cells which make cartilage) can be harvested from an individual with damaged cartilage, multiplied in the laboratory, and surgically transplanted back into the individual. Although effective, this process involves a complex surgical procedure. A search for cell-based regenerative therapies is ongoing. Cell-based therapies using a type of adult stem cells, such as mesenchymal stem cells (MSCs), and a scaffold of self-assembling biofibers, have shown promise in animal models of cartilage regeneration (Shah et al., 2010). Also, a simple intra-articular injection of a chemical called kartogenin into the joint stimulates endogenous MSCs to differentiate into cartilage-producing chondrocytes (Johnson et al., 2012). Stimulating an individual's own MSCs to differentiate and populate the joint surface with mature cartilage by an injectable chemical would be more effective than what is currently available (Marini & Forlino, 2012).

Risks

No medical therapy is free of risk. Three risks associated with cell-based regenerative medicine are important to mention.

Neoplasms

Differentiation of a source cell into a particular cell type so that only cells of the desired cell type grow in the recipient is the aim of regenerative medical therapies. However, cells can differentiate into unwanted cell types after being transplanted. If this occurs, a tumor mass of unwanted cells, usually of different cell types, occurs. This is called a *teratoma*. For example, transplanted heart muscle cells could continue to differentiate after being transplanted into a person's heart, forming a neoplasm of cartilage, neural cells, teeth, bone, or other cell types. Development of a teratoma defeats the purpose of the cell therapy and can further impair the function of an already damaged heart.

Immune Rejection

A second risk is rejection of the transplanted cells by the person's immune system. Source cells obtained from the same individual into whom they will be re-implanted, called *autologous* cells, have little risk of rejection. If autologous cells cannot be obtained, cells which come from a donor of the same species, called allogeneic cells, can be used as source cells. Allogeneic cells and xenogenic cells (cells from another species) also can be used as source cells, but increase the risk of rejection.

Zoonosis

Zoonosis refers to the transmission of animal diseases to humans. Scaffolds that are used to form the structural support for source cells used as replacement tissues are produced from animals, most commonly pigs. Although the scaffold is washed clean of animal cells leaving only the connective tissue scaffold, the risk of contamination with animal viruses still exists (Khang, 2012).

A Word about Cloning

In 1962, Sir John Gurdon of Great Britain found that the specialization of adult somatic cells is reversible. Gurdon replaced the nucleus of a frog egg cell with a mature frog intestinal cell nucleus. The modified egg cell grew into a normal tadpole. He proved that the nucleus of the mature frog intestinal cell, which many thought up to that time had lost the ability to direct new life, still contained the ability needed to grow all the cells of a frog. The reprogramming of somatic nuclei to direct the differentiation of enucleated eggs is known as *somatic cell nuclear transfer* (SCNT). In 2012, Gurdon shared the Nobel Prize in Medicine with Shinya Yamanaka of Japan for the discovery that mature cells can be reprogrammed to become pluripotent. Their research showed that somatic cells that normally cannot regenerate other cell lines because they are already specialized to perform specific functions in the body, can be stimulated to do so under certain circumstances. This is the basis of reproductive and therapeutic cloning.

Reproductive Cloning

The most controversial aspect of SCNT involves cloning of an entire individual. In 1996, Dolly, a female domestic sheep, was the first mammal to be cloned by SCNT (Wilmut, Schnieke, McWhir, Kind, & Campbell, 1997). A mammary gland cell nucleus was used. The production of a healthy cloned sheep proved that a highly specialized cell like a mammary gland cell could be made to recreate a whole individual. Reproductive cloning that creates a genetically identical copy of an existing, or previously existing, human being is controversial. In fact, 15 states have passed laws prohibiting reproductive human cloning (National Conference of State Legislatures, 2008).

Therapeutic Cloning

Only slightly less controversial is therapeutic cloning. SNCT is used to implant a somatic cell nucleus into an enucleated human egg; the egg is then stimulated to divide into a blastocyst. The inner cells of the blastocyst are isolated and used to create embryonic stem cells for regenerative medical purposes. In addition to the advantages of embryonic stem cells, self-renewal and pluripotency, another advantage is that the risk of immune rejection is less because the individual who will benefit from the transplanted source cells is the source of the DNA used in SCNT. Since therapeutic cloning results in destruction of an embryo, it is as controversial as reproductive cloning.

Future

There is no doubt that regenerative medicine has the potential to improve the lives of people with disabilities (Sor et al., 2018). Many scientific and ethical hurdles remain before that potential can be fully achieved, but counseling is undergoing change as a result of the advances that regenerative medicine brings to the practice of rehabilitation. Rehabilitation specialists are now working with regenerative scientists to guide the development of clinical protocols for individuals with disabilities who are undergoing regenerative medical procedures (Ambrosio, Wolf, & Delitto, 2010). The practice of rehabilitation counseling will expand in the future to include not only traditional whole body physiological and mechanical approaches, but also cellular and molecular regenerative medicine approaches (Ambrosio & Russell, 2010).

References

Ahsan, T., Doyle, A. M., & Nerem, R. M. (2010). Stem cell research. In A. Atala, R. Lanza, J. Thomson, & R. Nerem (Eds.), *Foundations of regenerative medicine* (pp. 28-48). New York, NY: Elsevier.

Ambrosio, F., & Russell, A. (2010). Regenerative rehabilitation: A call to action. *Journal of Rehabilitation Research and Development, 47*(3), xi-xv.

Ambrosio, F., Wolf, S. L., Delitto, A., Fitzgerald, G. K., Badylak, S. F., Boninger, M. L., & Russell, A. J. (2010). The emerging relationship between regenerative medicine and physical therapeutics. *Journal of the American Physical Therapy Association, 90*(12), 1807-1814.

Armed Forces Institute for Regenerative Medicine (AFIRM). (2016). Retrieved from http://www.afirm.mil/

Atala, A., Lanza, R., Thomson, J., & Nerem, R. (Eds.) (2010). *Foundations of regenerative medicine*. New York, NY: Elsevier.

Badylak, S. F., & Nerem, R. M. (2010). Progress in tissue engineering and regenerative medicine. *Proceedings of the National Academy of Sciences, 107*(8), 3285-3286.

Berthiaume, F., Maguire T. J., & Yarmush, M. L. (2011). Tissue engineering and regenerative medicine: History, progress, and challenges. *Annual Review of Chemical and Biomolecular Engineering, 2*, 403-430.

Brody, H. (2016). Regenerative medicine. *Nature, 540*, S50-S-51.

Bush, G. W. (2007). *Expanding approved stem cell lines in ethically responsible ways*. Executive Order 13435 (June 20, 2007). Retrieved from http://georgewbushwhitehouse.archives.gov/news/releases/2007/06/20070620-6.html

Committee on the Biological and Medical Applications of Stem Cell Research. (2002). *Stem cells and the future of regenerative medicine*. Washington, DC: National Academy Press.

Daley, G. Q. (2017). Polar extremes in the clinical use of stem cells. *New England Journal of Medicine, 376*(11), 1075-1077.

DeWitt, N. (2008). Regenerative medicine. *Nature, 453*(7193), 301-302.

Gerlach, J. C., Wolf, S. E., Johnen, C., & Hartman, B. (2010). Innovative regenerative medicine approaches to skin cell-based therapy for patients with burn injuries. In A. Atala, R. Lanza, Thomson, & R. Nerem (Eds.), *Foundations of regenerative medicine* (pp. 688-712). New York, NY: Elsevier.

Hellal, F., Hurtado, A., Ruschel J., Flynn, K. C., Laskowski, C. J., Umlauf, M., . . . Bradke, F. (2011). Microtubule stabilization reduces scarring and causes axon regeneration after spinal cord injury. *Science, 331*(6019), 928-921.

Hohlfeld, J., de Buys Roessingh, A., Hirt-Burri, N., Chaubert, p., Gerper, S., Scaletta, C., . . . Applegate, L. A. (2005). Tissue engineered fetal skin constructs for pediatric burns. *Lancet, 366*, 840-842.

Johnson, K. Zhu, S., Tremblay, M. S., Payette, J. N., Wang, J., Bouchez, L. C., . . . Schultz, P. G. (2012). A stem cell-based approach to cartilage repair. *Science, 336*(6082), 717-721.

Kaiser, L. (1992). The future of multihospital systems. *Top Healthcare Financing, 18*, 32-38.

Khademhosseini, A., Langer, R., Borenstein, J., & Vacanti, J. (2005). Microscale technologies for tissue engineering and biology. *Proceedings of the National Academy of Sciences, 103*(8), 2480-2487.

Khang, G. (Ed). (2012). *Handbook of intelligent scaffold for tissue engineering and regenerative medicine*. Singapore: Pan Stanford.

Kingwell, K. (2011). Regeneration: A regenerative medicine. *Nature Reviews Neuroscience, 12*, 123.

Laflamme, M. A., & Murray, C. E. (2011). Heart regeneration. *Nature, 473*, 326-335.

Lee, H., McKeon, R. J., & Bellamkonda, R. V. (2010). Sustained delivery of thermostablized chABC enhances axonal sprouting and function recovery after spinal cord injury. *Proceedings of the National Academy of Sciences, 107*(8), 3340-3345.

Liu, W. F., Hui, E. E., Bhatia, S. N., & Chen, C. S. (2010). Engineering cellular microenvironments. In A. Atala, R. Lanza, J. Thomson, & R. Nerem (Eds.), *Foundations of regenerative medicine* (pp. 284-301). New York, NY: Elsevier.

Marini, J. C., & Forlino, A. (2012). Replenishing cartilage from endogenous stem cells. *New England Journal of Medicine, 366*(26), 2522-2524.

Mironov, V., Boland, T., Trusk, T., Forgacs, G., & Markwald, R. R. (2003). Organ printing: Computer-aided jet-based 3D tissue engineering. *Trends in Biotechnology, 21*(4), 157-161.

National Conference of State Legislatures (2008). *Human cloning laws.* Retrieved from http://www.ncsl.org/issues-research/health/human-cloning-laws.aspx

National Institutes of Health (NIH). (2006). *Regenerative medicine.* Retrieved from http://stemcells.nih.gov/staticresources/info/scireport/PDFs/Regenerative_Medicine_2006.pdf

Obama, B. (2009). *Removing barriers to responsible research involving human stem cells.* Executive Order 13505 (March 9, 2009). Retrieved from http://www.gpo.gov/fdsys/pkg/FR-2009-03-11/pdf/E9-5441.pdf

Passier, R., van Laake, L. W., & Mummery, C. L. (2008). Stem-cell-based therapy and lessons from the heart. *Nature, 453*, 322-329.

Shah, R. N., Shah, N. A., Del Rosario Lim, M. M., Hsieh, C., Nuber, G., & Strupp, S. I. (2010). Supramolecular design of self-assembling nanofibers for cartilage regeneration. *Proceedings of the National Academy of Sciences, 107*(8), 3293-3298.

Sor, M., Krackov, W. S., & Madormo, C. (2018). *Regenerative medicine: Immediate reality and long-term promise.* Retrieved from https://newsroom.fmcna.com/whitepapers/regenerative-medicine-immediate-reality-longterm-promise/

Viola, J., Lal, B., & Grad, O. (2003). *The emergence of tissue engineering as a research field.* Cambridge, MA: Abt Associates. Retrieved from http://www.abtassociates.com/reports/emergence_tissue_engineering_research.pdf

Wilmut, I., Schnieke, A. E., McWhir, J., Kind, A. J., & Campbell, K. H. S. (1997). Viable offspring derived from fetal and mammalian cells. *Nature, 385*, 810-813.

World Health Organization (WHO). (2015). *Top ten causes of death.* Retrieved from http://www.who.int/mediacentre/factsheets/fs310/en/index.html

Zhu, S., Wei, W., & Ding, S. (2011). Chemical strategies for stem cell biology and regenerative medicine. *Annual Review of Biomedical Engineering, 13,* 73-90.

About the Author

John Howard, MD, MPH, JD, is Professorial Lecturer in Environmental and Occupational Health, School of Public Health and Health Services, The George Washington University, Washington, D.C. Dr. Howard is board-certified in internal medicine and occupational medicine. He is admitted to the practice of medicine and law in the State of California and the District of Columbia.

Appendix

MASTERING MEDICAL TERMINOLOGY

Prefixes

Word roots can be modified by prefixes that denote:

1. Position in time or space
   - ab - means **away from**

   abnormal – away from normal
   abduction – drawing away from the midline of the body by the arm or leg
   - circum – means **around**

   circumcision – a cutting around of the prepuce
   circumarticular – around a joint
2. Quantitative information
   - a or an – means **without**

   anorexia – without appetite
   anoxia – without enough oxygen
   - hemi – means **half**

   hemiplegia – paralysis of one lateral half of the body
   heminephrectomy – removal of a portion of a kidney
   - diplo – means **double**

   diplopia – double vision
   diploscope – an apparatus for study of binocular vision
   - quint – means **fifth**

   quintipara – a woman who has five pregnancies continued beyond the 20th week of gestation
   quintuplet – one of five offspring produced in one gestation period
3. Qualitative information
   - mal – means **bad** or **ill**

   malfunction – defective function
   malocclusion – faulty positioning of the upper or lower teeth in relation to the other
   - eu – means **good** or **healthy**

   euphoria – sense of well-being or condition of good health
   euthanasia – easy or painless death
4. Sameness and difference
   - hetero – means **different**

   heterogeneous – differing in kinds or nature
   heterosexual – sexual orientation directed to the opposite sex
   - homo – means **same**

homogeneous – of the same kind

homosexual – sexual orientation directed to the same sex

5. Physical attributes (size, shape, color)
   - micro – means **small**

   microcephalia – abnormal smallness of the head

   micromelia – abnormal smallness or shortness of the extremities
   - brachy – means **short**

   brachycephalia – having a short head

   brachydactylia – having abnormally short fingers and toes
   - oxy – means **pointed** or **sharp**

   oxycephaly – having a high and pointed head
   - albo – means **white**

   albinism – absence of pigmentation

   albinuria – passing of white or colorless urine

Suffixes

Suffixes and significant word endings characteristically function in compound words to:

1. Form adjectives
   - -al means **pertaining to**

   periton**eal** – pertaining to the peritoneum

   arteri**al** – pertaining to an artery
   - -ible, or –able means **ability**

   diges**tible** – capable of being digested

   oper**able** – subject to being operated

2. Express diminutive size – a number of suffixes serve this purpose,
   - -cule, –icle, –ium, –ole, –ule, and variations

   arteri**ole** means a small artery

   gran**ule** means a small grain

3. Indicate a surgical procedure
   - -ectomy means **removal** of an organ or part

   append**ectomy** – removal of the appendix
   - -lysis means **loosening**, usually of adhesions

   cardio**lysis** – freeing of the heart of pericardial adhesions
   - -ostomy means an operation in which an **artificial opening** is formed between two hollow organs or between one or more such viscera and the abdominal wall for discharge of intestinal content or urine.

   col**ostomy** – the surgical creation of an opening between the colon and the exterior of the body
   - -pexy means **fixation**

   nephro**pexy** – the surgical attachment of a floating kidney
   - -plasty means **plastic surgery**

   blepharo**plasty** – plastic surgery of the eyelids
   - -rrhaphy means **suture** or **operative repair**

teno**rrhaphy** – the suturing of a tendon
- -**scopy** means **viewing** or **examining**, usually with an instrument

endo**scopy** – visual inspection of any body cavity by means of an endoscope
- -**tomy** means **cutting** or **incision**

laparo**tomy** – the surgical opening of the abdomen
- -**tripsy** means the **intentional surgical crushing** of a structure

litho**tripsy** – the disintegration of a kidney stone by a high-energy shockwave

4. Express conditions or changes related to pathological processes
   - -**mania** means **excessive excitement** or **obsessive preoccupation**

   pyro**mania** – an irrational compulsion to set fires
   - -**sis** means an **action, process,** or **condition**

   silico**sis** – a fibrotic disorder of the lungs following inhalation of dust containing silicone dioxide

   thoracente**sis** – surgical puncture of the chest wall for removal of fluid
   - -**itis** means **inflammation**

   appendic**itis** – an inflammation of the appendix

Besides these loosely formulated classes of suffixes, there are a number of miscellaneous word endings, the most significant of which is included in the basic prefix/suffix vocabulary that follows. Rehabilitation counselors need to be familiar with this vocabulary.

Basic Prefix and Suffix Terms

The following list of prefix and suffix terms aid in understanding medical terminology. This list will familiarize the reader with the flexibility of nomenclature. As new terms are encountered, the counselor can more readily recognize the components from which they are made.

Prefix/Suffix	**Definition**	**Example**
-algia	pain	neur**algia**
angio-	blood vessel	**angio**gram
ante-	before	**ante**cubital
arth-	joint	**arth**roscopy
blephar-	eyelid	**blephar**ospasm
cardi-	heart	electro**cardi**ography
cele-	1) a swelling	varico**cele**
	2) a hernia	recto**cele**
cerebr-	cerebrum	**cerebr**al
chole-	gall or bile	**chole**cystectomy
chondr-	cartilage	**chondr**ocostal
contra-	opposed to	**contra**ception
cost-	rib	inter**cost**als
cyst-	bladder	**cyst**itis
-desis	fusion	arthro**desis**
derm-	skin	**derm**atology
dys-	difficult, abnormal	**dys**pnea

Medical Terminology

ect-	outside	**ect**omorph
-ectomy	removal	spen**ectomy**
-emia	condition of the blood	polycyth**emia**
enceph-	brain	**enceph**alitis
end-	within	**end**ocrine
enter-	intestine	**enter**ostomy
epi-	upon, above	**epi**thelium
genic-	giving rise to	psycho**genic**
glyco-	sugar	**glyco**suria
hemi-	half	**hemi**plegia
hepat-	liver	**hepat**itis
hyper-	in excess	**hyper**tension
hyster-	uterus	**hyster**ectomy
-iosis	a pathologic condition	ameb**iosis**
-itis	inflammation	tonsill**itis**
leuk-	white	**leuk**ocyte
lip-	fat	hyper**lip**emia
-lith	stone	nephro**lith**iasis
-megaly	a state of largeness	hepato**megaly**
myel-	1) bone marrow	**myel**ocyte
	2) spinal cord	polio**myel**itis
myo-	muscle	**myo**cardium
neph-	kidney	**neph**rosis
-oid	resembling	thyr**oid**
-oma	tumor or swelling	carcin**oma**
-oscopy	visual examination	lapar**oscopy**
-osis	disease process or condition	necr**osis**
osteo-	bone	**osteo**arthritis
-ostomy	creation of an artificial opening in an organ	trache**ostomy**
-otomy	incision	crani**otomy**
para-	near, alongside, beyond, outside	**para**vertebral
-pathy	disease of	cardiomyo**pathy**
-penia	lack of	leuko**penia**
-plasty	reparative or reconstructive surgery	rhino**plasty**
pneumo-	air	**pneumo**thorax
pre-	before	**pre**cancerous
pro-	in front of, before	**pro**gnathism
proct-	rectum or anus	**proct**ology

-ptosis	lowering of an organ or part	nephro**ptosis**
pyel-	pelvis	**pyel**ogram
pyo-	pus	**pyo**rrhea
spondyl-	vertebra	**spondyl**olysis
sub-	under	**sub**mandibular
super-	above, excessive	**super**sensitivity
supra-	above	**supra**ventricular
syn-	together	**syn**arthrosis
trans-	across	**trans**urethral
tri-	three	**tri**ceps

Anatomical Landmarks

A rehabilitation counselor should be familiar not only with the names of anatomic structures and pathological conditions, but with the "landmark" terms that designate anatomic position and direction. These are described in relation to the patient who is standing in the erect position, looking forward, with arms to the side of the body, and hands with palms forward (see Figure 1). The most commonly used landmark terms are the following:

lateral	to the side (used in contradistinction to medial)
medial	to the center
superior	above (used in contradistinction to inferior)
inferior	below
anterior	before or in front (used in contradistinction to posterior)
posterior	behind or in back
proximal	nearest to the point of attachment or center of the body (used in contradistinction to distal)
distal	farthest from the center
prone	lying face downward (used in contradistinction to supine)
supine	lying face upward
volar	pertaining to the sole of the foot or the palm of the hand
dorsal	pertaining to the back (used in contradistinction to ventral)
ventral	pertaining to the front or abdominal surface
palmar	pertaining to the palm of the hand
plantar	pertaining to the sole of the foot

Body Areas

Specific sites of illness or injury are usually designated by terms derived from the adjacent anatomic structure. Among the commonly used terms to indicate body areas are the following:

abdominal	pertaining to the stomach and intestinal area
carpal	pertaining to the wrist
cervical	pertaining to the seven vertebrae in the neck, or the neck region
costal	pertaining to the ribs
cranial	pertaining to the skull
femoral	pertaining to the thigh

FIGURE 1
Anatomical Positon of the Human Body for Descriptive Purposes

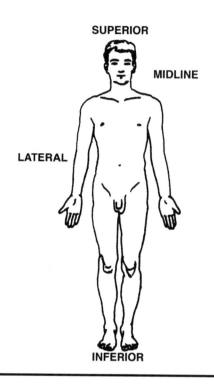

frontal	pertaining to the forehead
lumbar	pertaining to the five vertebrae in the lower portion of the back, or that region
pelvic	pertaining to the pelvic girdle
renal	pertaining to the kidney area
sacral	pertaining to the four vertebrae in the lowest portion of the back, or that region
sternal	pertaining to the sternum or breastbone
thoracic	pertaining to the twelve vertebrae in the upper portion of the back, or that region

Medical Abbreviations

Abbreviations denote instructions that are included in prescriptions for medications; some signify symptoms as reported by patients, and some refer to anatomic parts or body systems. Examples are noted:

a.c.	before meals (ante cibum)
b.i.d.	twice daily (bis in die)
B.P.	blood pressure
C-1 through C-7	cervical vertebrae by number
CBC	complete blood count
C.C.	chief complaint
C.N.	cranial nerve
C.N.S.	central nervous system
CPR	cardiopulmonary resuscitation
CT	computerized tomography

CVA	cerebrovascular accident
DB	decibel
DX	diagnosis
ESR	erythrocyte sedimentation rate
F.H.	family history
FX	fracture
GI	gastrointestinal
Hg	hemoglobin or mercury
GU	genitourinary
HBV	hepatitis B virus
HDL	high density lipoprotein
h.s.	at bedtime (hora somni)
H & P	history and physical examination
HX	history
L-1 through L-5	lumbar vertebrae by number
L.L.Q.	left lower quadrant
L.M.P.	last menstrual period
L.U.Q.	left upper quadrant
MRI	magnetic resonance imaging
OA	osteoarthritis
O.D.	right eye (oculus dexter)
O.S.	left eye (oculus sinister)
p.c.	after meals (post cibum)
P.H.	past history
P.I.	present illness
p.r.n.	as needed (pro re nata)
q.i.d.	four times daily (quater in die)
RA	rheumatoid arthritis
R.B.C.	red blood count
R.L.Q.	right lower quadrant
R/O	rule out
R.U.Q.	right upper quadrant
Rx	prescription
S-1 through S-5	sacral vertebrae by number
SOAP	subjective findings, objective findings, assessment, plan
T-1 through T-12	thoracic vertebrae by number
t.i.d.	three times daily (ter in die)
TX	treatment
W.B.C.	white blood count

The abbreviations cited are examples of the hundreds, perhaps thousands, in use. Unlike medical nomenclature, abbreviations cannot be divided logically into components, nor is it feasible to try to memorize a list of abbreviations. With experience, one becomes increasingly competent in interpreting this medical shorthand.

INDEX

A

abbreviations - see medical abbreviations
accommodation, 6-9, 245-246, 303-306, 343-344
acquired hearing loss, 107, 110
acquired immunodeficiency syndrome - HIV/AIDS, 89-101
acupuncture, 139-145
addiction, 287-297
agoraphobia, 269
alcohol abuse (see addiction)
Alcoholics Anonymous (AA), 291-292
alcoholic cardiomyopathy, 70
alcoholism, 287-291, 294
alternative medicine, 139-149
Americans with Disabilities Act, vii, 7, 47, 48, 61, 83, 292, 294, 300, 317, 393
amputation, 53-55, 57, 131, 335-345, 350, 362, 365-367
aneurysm, 55, 152, 167-168
aneurysmal subarachnoid hemorrhage, 168
angina pectoris, 72, 75
ankylosing spondylitis, 131, 250, 258-259
anoxia, 72, 121, 153, 166, 177, 216
antidepressant, 134, 266, 269-271
antiretroviral, 92-98
anxiety disorders, 45-46, 156-157, 267-271, 327
aortic stenosis, 67, 69
aphasia, 156, 169, 170, 173, 179, 194-196, 300
arterial venous malformation, 153, 168
arthritis - see rheumatic disease
Asperger syndrome, 327
assistive listening devices (ALD), 108-109
assistive technology (AT), 1, 119-120, 125, 158-159, 173, 222-225, 305, 334-335, 359, 367, 371-378
Assistive Technology Act (Technology-Related Assistance for Individuals with Disabilities Act), 344, 371, 376
asthma, 79-80, 145, 215
AT - see assistive technology
ataxic, 217
atrial septal defect, 67
auditory system, 103-104
aural rehabilitation, 109
autism spectrum disorder (ASD), 325-331
autonomic hyperreflexia, 206

B

Becker Muscular Dystrophy (BMD), 230-231
biofeedback/neurofeedback, 146-147
bipolar disorders, 270-271
blast injuries, 153
blindness, 55, 57, 115-126
blood pressure - see hypertension
brain injury, 151-161, 165-174, 177-185, 189-197, 215-224, 241-246, 311-320
bronchitis, 70-86
burn injury, 347-356
brain tumor, 152, 153, 193, 194, 195

C

CAM - see Complementary and Integrative Health
cancer, 37-48
cannabis - see marijuana
cardiac disease, 65-75
cardiac muscle, 27, 66-75
cardiac radionuclide imaging, 73
cardiac transplantation, 74
cardiomyopathy, 70
cardiovascular disease, 65-75
cardiovascular system, 27-29
carpal tunnel syndrome, 366-367
case study approach, 2-6, 13-15
cataract, 123
catheterization, 73
cellular and chemical levels, 17
central nervous system, 25
cerebellum, 25-27
cerebellar function, 25-27
cerebral cortex, 25-27
cerebral embolus, 167
cerebral hypertensive hemorrhage, 167-168
cerebral palsy, 215
cerebral thrombus, 224
cerebral vascular accident - see stroke, 167
cerebral vascular malformation, 168
cervical spine, 204-206
chemical level, 17
chemotherapy, 43
chiropractic, 144-145
chronic bronchitis - see bronchitis
chronic obstructive pulmonary disease, 79-86
chronic pain disorders, 130-131
chronic pain management, 129-136
circulatory system, 27-29
classifications of heart disease, 65-66
cloning, 401
closed head injury, 152-153
cochlear implant, 109
cognitive functioning, 154-159
color vision testing, 117
complementary and integrative health, 139-146
complex regional pain syndrome, 131

computerized tomography (CT), 191
conductive hearing loss, 106, 108
congenital heart disease, 66-67
congestive heart failure, 74-75
contracture, 207, 349
co-occurring disorders - see dual diagnosis, 289
COPD - see chronic obstructive pulmonary disease, 79-86
coronary artery disease, 71-72
corpulmonale, 80
CVA - see stroke

D

Deaf, 103-113
deafness - see hearing loss
deinstitutionalization, 274, 375
dementia, 94, 96, 152, 194-195
depression, 267, 270
dermatomyositis, 257-258
detoxification, 291
Developmental Disabilities Act, 312-313, 315
diabetes mellitus, 53-61
diabetic nephropathy, 54-55
diabetic retinopathy, 55
dialysis, 59-60
diffuse connective tissue disease, 250
digestive system, 31-32
disability - defined, 1
disclosure, 183-185
disinhibition, 154, 157, 196
drug use/drug use disorder, 287-294
DSM - see autism spectrum and psychiatric diagnosis; substance-use disorders
dual diagnosis - see co-occurring disorders
Duchenne Muscular Dystrophy (DMD), 230, 232, 233
dynamic hyperinflation, 82
dyskinetic, 216, 217

E

echocardiogram, 73
educational level, 2-3
Education of All Handicapped Children Act, 300, 316
Electroencephalogram (EEG), 191
Electromyography (EMG), 191
embolus, 167
emotional lability, 156
emphysema, 79
employability, 65, 110, 182, 305, 306, 318, 343, 386
endocrine system, 34-35
environmental factors, 7, 10, 11, 18, 39, 84, 104, 105, 132, 222, 241, 256, 263, 266, 288, 313, 318, 326, 383
epilepsy, 177-185
exertional categories of work, 3-5
external powered orthoses, 336

F

Facioscapulohumeral Muscular Dystrophy (FSHMD), 231, 232, 236
fibromyalgia, 131
focal seizure, 178-179
frontal lobes, 157, 193
functional capacity categories, 3-5, 65-55, 74-75
functional limitations, 6-7, 65-66, 252
functional MRI (fMRI), 192

G

gait and station, 190
generalized anxiety disorder, 267-269
gene transformation, 39
genetic counseling, 393
genetic discrimination, 392-393
genetic hearing loss, 106-108, 110
genetics, 391-394
genetic testing, 391-394
genitourinary system, 32-34
glaucoma, 121
gout, 249-250

H

hallucinogens, 287
hand injuries - see upper extremity injuries
hard-of-hearing - see hearing loss
hearing aids, 108-109
hearing loss, 103-111
heart disease - see cardiovascular disease
heavy work - see physical exertion requirements
hematological disorder, 383
hemiparesis, 154, 169-171, 195, 256
hemiplegia, 158, 169, 171, 195, 217, 336
hemodialysis, 59-61
hemophilia, 381-382, 384-387
HIV/AIDS, 89-97
Holter monitor, 73
holistic, 1-2, 10-12, 139-149
homeopathy, 141, 143-144
human body systems, 17-36
human brain, 24, 192-194
human heart, 26
human immunodeficiency virus - see HIV/AIDS
human skin, 28
Huntington's Disease, 194. 196, 392, 394
hypertension, 65, 70-72
hypertensive heart disease, 65, 70-72

I

ICD (International Classification of Diseases), 263, 265, 268
ICF (International Classification of Functioning, Disability and Health), 10-12

illiteracy, 3
immunomodulatory, 92
immunotherapy, 43-44
impairment defined, 1
integrative medicine, 139-147
integumentary system, 29
intellectual developmental disorders, 268, 311-320
intellectual disability, 194, 215-216, 268, 280, 300-304, 311-330
internal medicine, 12-13
interventional treatments, 1-13, 41, 291-293
intracranial hemorrhage, 167-170
involuntary (autonomic) nervous system, 25
ischemic stroke, 165-171

J

job accommodation/modification, 7-9
Job Accommodation Network (JAN), 9
job coaching, 319-320
job modification, 7-9
job restructuring., 9
joints - see muscular system

K

kidney disease, 58-61
kidney transplantation, 60

L

LD - see learning disabilities
learned helplessness, 317-318
learning disabilities (LD), 299-307
LGBTQIA, 293-284
ligaments, 23, 249-250
light work - see physical exertion requirements
limb-girdle muscular dystrophy (LGMD), 231, 232
limited education, 2-3
lower extremity orthoses, 336-337
low vision, 119-120
lungs, 30
lupus - see systemic lupus erythematosus
lymphatic system, 28-29

M

macular degeneration, 117, 119, 122, 373
magnetic resonance imaging (MRI), 41, 157, 191
major depressive disorder, 263, 269-270
manual techniques, 133
marginal education defined, 3
marijuana, 287
meaningful work, 319, 330
median nerve, 198, 361
medical abbreviations, 410-411
medical specialties, 12-13
medical terminology, 5, Appendix
Medicare functional levels, 344

medium work- see physical exertion requirements
mental disorders, 46, 129, 146, 190, 263-274
mitral valve prolapse, 65, 69
mixed hearing loss, 106-107
mononeuropathy, 191, 198
mood disorders, 130, 269-271
motor function, 182, 189-196, 202-206, 215-220
motor neuron, 25, 190-192, 194, 196, 202, 204, 206
multicultural perspective, 48, 283-284
multiple sclerosis, 118, 119, 121, 194, 241-246
muscle dysfunction, 81
muscular degeneration, 215-260
muscular dystrophy, 197, 229-237
musculoskeletal system, 18-24
multiaxial, 266, 267
multicultural, viii, 48, 234, 283-284
myocardial infarction, 13, 55, 72-73
myocardiopathy - see cardiomyopathy
myopathy, 65, 69-70, 94, 231
myositis, 94, 249, 250, 257-258
myotonic muscular dystrophy (MMD), 231, 233, 235

N

narcotic, 289, 293
nervous system, 25-27
neurologic, 94-95, 122-123, 165-169, 177, 189-199
neuromuscular disease, 189, 199, 220, 229-236, 241-246
neuropathy, 54-55, 131, 198
noise-induced hearing loss, 107
non-narcotic, 133
normalization, 311, 314-316

O

occupationally significant characteristics, 5
open head injury, 152
opiates/opioids, 289-293
optic atrophy, 119, 121
oral hypoglycemic agents, 57
organ level, 18
orthotics (orthoses), 335-339
osteoarthritis, 131, 249-251, 254-255
otosclerosis, 107-108
ototoxicity, 107

P

pain, 129-136, 252
pancreas, 12, 32, 35, 38
panic disorders, 269
paralysis, 154, 168-170, 201-208
paraplegia, 202-206, 210, 217
paresis, 154, 169
Parkinson's Disease, 118, 155, 194, 196, 397
patent ductus arteriosus, 67, 68
perinatal, 177, 216, 313-314, 326

peripheral nervous system, 25-26
peripheral neuropathy, 53-55, 91, 151, 198
peripheral vascular insufficiency, 55, 339
peritoneal dialysis, 59-60
peroneal neuropathy, 198
personality disorders, 154, 156, 266-267, 272-273
phantom limb, 129, 131, 340-343
phantom limb pain, 129, 131, 340-341, 343
physical exertion requirements, 3-5
PNS - see also peripheral nervous system
polymyositis, 257-258
positron emission tomography (PET), 41, 158, 192
postnatal, 216, 313-314
post-traumatic stress disorder (PTSD), 46, 132, 209, 288, 347, 349, 351
prenatal, 216, 313-314
presbycusis, 107
pressure sores, 207
primary progressive multiple sclerosis (PPMS), 242
progressive immunodeficiency, 90
prostheses, 335, 341-345, 367
psychiatric disabilities, 263-274
psychosocial implications, 45-47, 110, 221-222
PTSD - see post-traumatic stress disorder
pulmonary stenosis, 67, 69
pure tone audiometry, 104, 105

Q

quadriplegia, 202, 217, 337

R

RA - rheumatoid arthritis, 203, 249-256
radiation therapy, 42-43
radiculopathy, 197-198
reasonable accommodation, 7-9, 48, 294, 303-304
refraction, 116, 117
regenerative medicine, 397-401
rehabilitation intervention, 7-9
relapsing remitting multiple sclerosis (RRMS), 242
renal failure - see kidney disease; Diabetes
residual functional capacity, 3-5
respiratory system, 29-30
retinal diseases, 122
retinitis pigmentosa, 117, 119, 121-122
retinopathy of prematurity, 119, 123
rheumatic disease, 249-260
rheumatic heart disease, 68-69
rheumatoid arthritis - see RA

S

sacral, 202-205, 336
schizophrenia, 267-273
scleroderma, 249, 250, 257
secondary progressive multiple sclerosis (SPMS), 242
sedentary - see physical exertion requirements
seizures, 155, 177-185
self-regulation strategies, 135
semiskilled - see skill requirements
sensorineural hearing loss, 106
sensory system, 30-31
sexuality, 46, 279-284, 327, 343, 353
sexuality and disability, 279-284, 343
sheltered employment, 85, 318-320
sickle cell disease, 381-388, 391
skeletal structure and function, 18-23
skilled - see skill requirements
skill requirements, 3
skin - see integumentary system
SOAR, 351-352
Social Security Act, 316
somatic nervous system, 25-27
spasticity, 206-207
speech audiometry, 104-105
spinal cord, 25, 134, 194, 201-211
spirituality, 10, 283
staging classification, 41
Stargardt's disease, 119, 122
status epilepticus, 178-179
stem cell, 42, 93, 122, 140, 171, 211, 221, 382, 397-400
stigma, 273-274
stroke, 55, 165-174
substance abuse, 46, 132, 154, 157, 268, 287-294
substance use disorders, 156, 157, 267-268, 287-294
supported employment, 160, 182, 318-320
systemic lupus erythematosus, 249-250, 255-256

T

TBI - see traumatic brain injury
tinnitus, 108
tolerance - defined, 289
tonic-clonic, 178
Traditional Chinese Medicine, 141-142
transferability of skills, 5-6
transplantation, 44, 60, 74
traumatic brain injury, 122-123, 151-160
traumatic epilepsy, 155
tympanometry, 104, 105

U

undue hardship, 7, 304
universal design, 223, 371-378
unskilled - see skill requirements
upper extremity impairment, 169, 253, 359-368
upper extremity orthoses, 336, 337, 367

V

valvular heart disease, 65, 68-69
vertigo, 108

very heavy work - see physical exertion requirements
vestibular disorders, 103-110
veterans, 153, 209
vision aids, 119-125
vision enhancement, 125
vision substitution, 125
visual acuity, 116-124
visual disabilities, 115-126
visual field, 117
visual impairment, 9, 115-126
visual system, 115-119
vocational profile, 2-7
vocational skills, 1, 3, 5-6
voluntary nervous system, 18, 25-27

W

WHO (World Health Organization), vii, 10, 143, 263, 264, 268, 312
whole medical systems, 140-143
withdrawal, 289, 291
work history, 2-6

Y

younger person, 2

Z

zoonosis, 400-401